'The 5th edition of this important book, which includes 13 brand new chapters, is as relevant to the work of primary school teachers as it was when it was first published in 2006. It is a hugely useful resource for prospective and qualified primary teachers at all stages of their careers, from those going through their ITE, to Early Career Professionals and to those with many years' experience in the classroom as well as to those in leadership positions.

'It provides practical advice and support alongside an explanation of where that advice comes from, how it can be contextualised and how its impact can be evaluated. Subject knowledge and pedagogy are given equal weight. As the editors explain; "knowing how to support subject knowledge through different teaching strategies and interactions is as important as understanding the subject in its own right". This book has made a positive difference to primary school teaching and will continue to do so.'

James Noble-Rogers, *Executive Director, Universities Council for the Education of Teachers (UCET)*

'Any book reaches a fifth edition only if it is a very valuable source for its readers, and so I am delighted to see this latest edition of *Learning to Teaching in the Primary School*. For me, it remains a classic text of its kind. This edition has added a series of new chapters in addition to the updates of the whole text. The book is important because it reflects a profound knowledge of the practice and relevant research that should underpin primary education.'

Dominic Wyse, *Professor of Early Childhood and Primary Education, Institute of Education, University College London*

'There are many reasons why this outstanding, comprehensive text is the "go-to" core reader for those embarking on a primary teacher education course. This latest edition has retained the original key features of this very accessible, interactive book with wide-ranging contributions from experienced, highly respected teacher educators. The new chapters focusing on curriculum areas and professional behaviours are welcomed additions and further enhance the relevance for anyone wanting to become a fully rounded professional teacher.'

Jane Warwick, *Associate Teaching Professor, University of Cambridge*

'This updated edition is a thoughtful exploration into the heart of what it means to "Learn to Teach in the Primary School". This comprehensive text invites the reader to reflect on their personal perspective of education and how their individual characteristics, encounters and strengths have drawn them into teaching. It explores how these can be harnessed to prepare for learning and teaching. The wide range of contributors masterfully combine a comprehensive guide to a knowledge based, inquiry led, enriched curriculum with practical wisdom. The result is a fantastic resource that is both deeply reflective and immensely practical. The reader is left in no doubt that they are being prepared to support the development of the "whole child".

'The authors emphasise the all-encompassing purpose of education: making sense of life and understanding how to develop the whole child. This holistic approach to education is refreshing and much needed in today's fast-paced, results-driven educational landscape. It reminds us that teaching is not just about imparting knowledge but about nurturing well-rounded individuals who are prepared for life's challenges.'

Megan Stephenson, *Associate Professor, Leeds Trinity University*

'This is a welcome update to a classic text. The editorial team have made some excellent and timely updates responding to the current challenges facing teachers and the profession more generally. New chapters around gender, sustainability and wellbeing dovetail superbly with updated thinking around key areas such as planning, professionalism and social justice. This excellent text is ideal for a variety of audiences. On one level it will help trainee teachers build foundations from which to make evidence-based decisions about practice. On another level it makes a great "go to" text for school-based mentors and yet another for teacher educators as an evidence-base for practice.'

Adrian Copping, *Primary PGCE Programmes Lead, University of Cumbria*

'It comes as no surprise that there is now a fifth edition of *Learning to Teach in the Primary School*! Almost two decades after the publication of the first edition, it will be as invaluable to trainee and Early Career Teachers – and to those teaching and mentoring them – as ever.

'Thoughtful revisions mirror developments in research, policy and practice while retaining key perspectives and voices. New chapters dedicated to different curriculum areas, as well as to contemporary issues such as mental health and climate change, are testament to how effectively this book moves with the times, ensuring that it continues to offer the most current, relevant support to new teachers.'

Claire Williams, *Deputy Headteacher, St. Andrew's C of E Primary School, Reading, ECT Induction Lead, All Saints Academy Trust, Essex*

'This is a great one stop shop for all your teaching questions. I used previous editions religiously in my degree through placement and in assignments. I am particularly excited to use the new chapters on planning and adaptive teaching, I think these will be particularly useful for teaching students as they are the building blocks of good teaching practice. It was also nice to see the new mental health chapter, especially as this is my area of specialism but also because of its relevance with today's challenges. I am looking forward to continuing to use this updated resource as part of my daily teaching practice.'

Ellen Carson, *student teacher, Liverpool Hope University*

'*Learning to Teach in the Primary School* is the most wonderful collection of wisdom for anyone learning to teach in the primary school.

'It manages to balance being comprehensive, thoughtful, thought-provoking and, as you'd expect from the stellar set of contributors, full of carefully researched ideas and inspiration while all the time remaining readable and accessible.'

'The need to read as widely as you can means it might not be the only book you want to read as you begin your journey to becoming a primary teacher, but it should probably be the first one you reach for.'

James Clements, *Education writer and researcher*

LEARNING TO TEACH IN THE PRIMARY SCHOOL

How do you become an effective primary school teacher? What do you need to be able to do? What do you need to know?

Flexible, effective and creative primary school teachers require subject knowledge, an understanding of their pupils and how they learn, a range of strategies for managing behaviour and organising environments for learning, and the ability to respond to dynamic classroom situations.

The fifth edition of this bestselling textbook has been fully updated with the latest research and initiatives in the field, as well as the most recent curriculum and policy changes across the UK. It features two new co-editors and 13 new chapters and enhanced accessibility throughout. New or completely rewritten chapters have been included on:

- Reading curriculum
- Writing curriculum
- Maths curriculum
- Science curriculum
- Arts-enriched curriculum
- Humanities curriculum
- Adaptive teaching
- Education and wellbeing
- Education for sustainability
- Applying for jobs and preparing to be an ECT.

A selection of extra tasks have been woven throughout, with an emphasis on innovative, reflective practice, and new 'vivid examples' bring each chapter's argument to life in a classroom context.

Providing a comprehensive but accessible introduction to teaching and learning in the primary school, covering everything a trainee needs to know in order to gain QTS, this accessible and engaging textbook is essential reading for all students training to be primary school teachers.

This textbook is supported by a free companion website with additional resources for instructors and students and an accompanying series of books on Teaching Creatively across the curriculum.

Teresa Cremin is Professor of Education (Literacy) at The Open University, UK and Co-Director of the Centre for Literacy and Social Justice. She has served as President of the UKRA and UKLA, and as Board member of BookTrust, The Reading Agency and the Poetry Archive. Her research focuses on volitional reading and writing, creative pedagogies and teachers' literate identities (https://ourfp.org/).

Helen Hendry is a Senior Lecturer in Primary Education at The Open University, UK and Co-Director of the Centre for Literacy and Social Justice. Her recent research focuses on teacher professional development for reading, informal book talk in the early years, and reading and writing for pleasure.

Anna Harrison is a Senior English Lecturer in ITE at Roehampton University, UK. Her research interests are young children's engagement as readers and children's literature within education. Her current PhD research at Cambridge University is focused on a newer area within children's family literacy of siblings as independent peer to peer readers.

THE LEARNING TO TEACH IN THE PRIMARY SCHOOL SERIES
Series Editor: Teresa Cremin, The Open University, UK

Teaching is an art form. It demands not only knowledge and understanding of the core areas of learning, but also the ability to teach these creatively and foster learning in the process. *The Learning to Teach in the Primary School Series* draws upon recent research which indicates the rich potential of creative teaching and learning and explores what it means to teach creatively in the primary phase. It also responds to the evolving nature of subject teaching in a wider, more imaginatively framed 21st century primary curriculum.

Designed to complement the textbook *Learning to Teach in the Primary School*, the well informed, lively texts in this series offer support for student and practising teachers who want to develop more creative approaches to teaching and learning. Uniquely, the books highlight the importance of the teachers' own creative engagement and share a wealth of research informed ideas to enrich pedagogy and practice.

Titles in the series:

Teaching Geography Creatively, 2nd Edition
Edited by Stephen Scoffham

Teaching Science Creatively, 2nd Edition
Dan Davies and Deb McGregor

Applying Cross-Curricular Approaches Creatively the Connecting Curriculum
Jonathan Barnes

Teaching Languages Creatively
Edited by Philip Hood

Teaching Physical Education Creatively, 2nd Edition
Angela Pickard and Patricia Maude

Teaching Mathematics Creatively, 3rd Edition
Linda Pound and Trisha Lee

Teaching Art Creatively
Penny Hay

Teaching English Creatively, 3rd Edition
Teresa Cremin

Teaching Religious and Worldviews Education Creatively, 2nd Edition
Edited by Sally Elton-Chalcraft

For more information about this series, please visit: www.routledge.com/Learning-to-Teach-in-the-Primary-School-Series/book-series/LTPS

LEARNING TO TEACH IN THE PRIMARY SCHOOL

Fifth edition

**Edited by
Teresa Cremin, Helen Hendry
and Anna Harrison**

LONDON AND NEW YORK

Designed cover image: © Lisa Dynan

Fifth edition published 2025
by Routledge
4 Park Square, Milton Park, Abingdon, Oxon, OX14 4RN

and by Routledge
605 Third Avenue, New York, NY 10158

Routledge is an imprint of the Taylor & Francis Group, an informa business

© 2025 selection and editorial matter, Teresa Cremin, Helen Hendry and Anna Harrison; individual chapters, the contributors

The right of Teresa Cremin, Helen Hendry and Anna Harrison to be identified as the authors of the editorial material, and of the authors for their individual chapters, has been asserted in accordance with sections 77 and 78 of the Copyright, Designs and Patents Act 1988.

All rights reserved. No part of this book may be reprinted or reproduced or utilised in any form or by any electronic, mechanical, or other means, now known or hereafter invented, including photocopying and recording, or in any information storage or retrieval system, without permission in writing from the publishers.

Trademark notice: Product or corporate names may be trademarks or registered trademarks, and are used only for identification and explanation without intent to infringe.

First edition published by Routledge 2006
Fourth edition published by Routledge 2018

British Library Cataloguing-in-Publication Data
A catalogue record for this book is available from the British Library

Library of Congress Cataloging-in-Publication Data
Names: Cremin, Teresa, 1959- editor.
Title: Learning to teach in the primary school / Teresa Cremin, Helen Hendry, Anna Harrison.
Description: Fifth edition. | Abingdon, Oxon ; New York, NY : Routledge, 2025. | Series: Learning to teach in the primary school series | Includes bibliographical references and index. | Identifiers: LCCN 2024060300 (print) | LCCN 2024060301 (ebook) | ISBN 9781032691763 (hardback) | ISBN 9781032691756 (paperback) | ISBN 9781032691794 (ebook)
Subjects: LCSH: Elementary school teaching--Great Britain. | Elementary school teachers--Training of--Great Britain.
Classification: LCC LB1556.7.G7 L43 2025 (print) | LCC LB1556.7.G7 (ebook) | DDC 372.1102--dc23/eng/20250213
LC record available at https://lccn.loc.gov/2024060300
LC ebook record available at https://lccn.loc.gov/2024060301

ISBN: 978-1-032-69176-3 (hbk)
ISBN: 978-1-032-69175-6 (pbk)
ISBN: 978-1-032-69179-4 (ebk)

DOI: 10.4324/9781032691794

Typeset in Interstate and Helvetica
by KnowledgeWorks Global Ltd.

Access the Instructor and Student Resources: www.routledge.com/cw/Cremin

CONTENTS

List of figures — *xvi*
List of tables — *xviii*
List of tasks — *xix*
List of contributors — *xxiii*

SECTION 1
BECOMING A TEACHER — 1

1.1 Primary teaching: Personal perspectives — 3
TERESA CREMIN, HELEN HENDRY AND ANNA HARRISON

Introduction • What inspired you to train to be a primary school teacher? • What does becoming a teacher mean to you? • What helped us stay within the teaching profession? • What challenges did we overcome? • Moving onwards and making best use of this text

1.2 Becoming a professional in the current context — 12
JANET GOEPEL AND SALLY HINCHLIFF

What do theory and research tell us about professionalism? • What influences have you experienced in your journey towards becoming a teacher? • Professional bodies and professionalism in the UK • How is teacher professional identity developed? • What are the influences and complexities of developing professionalism? • Policy: The core content framework and the teachers' standards • Accountability: Ofsted • Institutional: Situational learning/different contexts

1.3 Capitalising on professional practice: Making the most of your placements — 31
JANE WARWICK, JOHN-MARK WINSTANLEY AND MARY ANNE WOLPERT

Introduction • Preparing for 'practice shock' • Establishing effective dispositions • Being a reflective practitioner • Evaluating your lessons • Working with expert colleagues • Making the most of learning conversations • Conversations with subject specialists • Structured conversations • Engaging in challenging professional conversations • Understanding that your learning is a journey

SECTION 2
EXPLORING THE NATURE OF LEARNING AND TEACHING 47

2.1 Looking at children 49
JANE PAYLER AND MARY SCANLAN

Introduction • Situated, holistic development • Key theorists of child development • Challenging norms, stages and deficit views

2.2 Building on firm foundations: Early years practice 66
JANET ROSE, REBECCA DIGBY AND VINCE MACLEOD

Introduction • Early years policy • The early years Foundation Stage • 'School readiness' and starting school • The learning environment • The role of the adult in play • Reception Baseline Assessment and Foundation Stage profile • Transition from the Foundation Stage to Key Stage 1

2.3 Revisiting ideas around learning and teaching 84
LIZ CHAMBERLAIN AND ROGER MCDONALD

Introduction • Learning theories: A historical perspective • The need for more contemporary approaches to learning and teaching • The context of learning is central to teaching • Factors influencing teaching and learning • Developing creative and inclusive learning communities • Emotional labour through teacher talk

2.4 Developing as a professional 96
SAMANTHA TWISELTON AND SALLY ELTON-CHALCRAFT

Introduction • The gift of teaching and the freedom of the pupil: Implications for teacher development • Knowledge and learning: For the pupil and the teacher • Quality versus quantity: Organisation of knowledge • Teacher as task manager, curriculum deliverer or concept/skill builder • Knowledge and creativity: Deep learning, not surface learning • Teachers' use of knowledge • Knowing the underlying principles, using knowledge efficiently

SECTION 3
PLANNING AND MANAGING LEARNING 109

3.1 Building inclusive communities of engaged learners 111
ALISON PEACOCK

Introduction • Principles of an inclusive classroom • The intellectual domain • The affective domain • The social domain

3.2 Lesson planning: Thinking beyond the template   123
PAULA AYLIFFE AND RACHEL LOFTHOUSE

Introduction • Foundations of lesson planning • Planning for knowledge, skills and understanding • Developing details • Prioritising pedagogy • Working collaboratively

3.3 Organising your classroom and using technology for learning   135
PETER KELLY

Organising learning • Classroom approaches

3.4 Managing classroom behaviour: Creating a positive classroom climate   148
ROLAND CHAPLAIN

Introduction • Building an evidence-based Classroom Management Plan (CMP) • Whole-school behaviour management • Teacher stress and pupil behaviour • Managing yourself • Classroom management strategies • Making an early impact on your class • Conveying your expectations: Rules and routines • Developing routines • Rewards and sanctions • Classroom layout • Coping with challenging behaviour

3.5 Addressing social, emotional, mental health and behaviour needs   164
JANICE WEARMOUTH AND LOUISE CUNNINGHAM

Introduction • Frameworks for understanding difficult behaviour • Understanding and addressing social, emotional and mental health (SEMH) needs in schools • Potential effects of traumatic experiences on children's behaviour • Addressing SEMH concerns in primary schools • Individual targeted approaches • Neurological and biological explanations of behaviour

3.6 Organising effective classroom talk   178
LYN DAWES

Introduction • The crucial importance of classroom talk for learning • What is talk for learning? • Dialogic teaching • Exploratory talk • When and how to move between types of talk • Direct teaching of oracy skills • Raising children's awareness of talk for learning • Planning for exploratory talk • Listening

3.7 The value of outdoor learning   191
STEPHEN PICKERING AND SOPHIE BROOKES

Introduction • How the national curriculum supports learning outdoors • How the Teachers' Standards support teaching outdoors • The benefits of learning and teaching outdoors • Preparing to teach outdoors • Case study: A vegetable garden • Planning to teach outdoors

SECTION 4
APPROACHING THE CURRICULUM 207

4.1 Critical perspectives on the curriculum 209
AYSHEA CRAIG AND DOMINIC WYSE

Introduction • Knowledge in the curriculum • What can we learn from looking at other countries? • A national curriculum? The consequences of sector diversification • The statutory curriculum in England • The journey from statutory curriculum to the classroom • Influences on the curriculum: Inspection and testing • Broadening and enriching the curriculum • Revisiting curriculum aims: Ways forward • The teacher's role

4.2 Developing a rich reading curriculum 225
HELEN HENDRY AND SONIA THOMPSON

Introduction • What makes a reader? • Reading for pleasure • Early reading • Developing reading comprehension • Working with others • Formative assessment for reading

4.3 Teaching the craft of writing 243
DEBRA MYHILL

Introduction • Different disciplinary perspectives on writing • Crafting and creating: Enabling metalinguistic understanding for writing • Creating a community of writers

4.4 Teaching mathematics: What, how and why 254
VIVIEN TOWNSEND AND MARK BOYLAN

Introduction • Preparing to teach • Teacher beliefs • Knowledge for teaching • Primary mathematics curriculum content • Primary curriculum aims • Conclusion

4.5 The science curriculum 270
NICOLA TREBY AND VANESSA MATTHEWS

Introduction • Science in the primary national curriculum for England • Finding the science within the child's world • Pedagogical approaches that are particularly appropriate to teaching science

4.6 Developing arts-enriched curricula and practice 286
JO TROWSDALE, KERRY CHAPPELL AND SARAH BRACKEN

Introduction • The role of the arts, and their distinctive contributions • The arts in the national curriculum • What do 'arts-enriched' curricula look like in schools? • The role of the teacher in developing arts-rich practices • Developing arts-rich learning with partnership support

4.7 Teaching the humanities — 300
KARIN DOULL

Introduction • Why is an understanding of the humanities important?
• What important metacognitive strategies can the humanities develop?
• The place of humanities within the curriculum • Ofsted • History • Geography
• Religious education • Sequence of planning for a sequence of humanities lessons

SECTION 5
ASSESSMENT — 317

5.1 Assessment for learning: Formative approaches — 319
ELEANORE HARGREAVES AND SHIRIN SHEIKH-BAHAI

Introduction • AfL: From theory to practice • Planning for AfL • Effective questioning: By teachers and – particularly – by children • Peer and self-assessment • Feedback • Recognising and celebrating children's work

5.2 Assessment and learning: Summative approaches — 334
PAULA LEHANE AND ALAN GORMAN

Introduction • What is assessment and why do we do it? • Producing good evidence of achievement • Summative assessment and reporting: Current policy • Summative and formative assessment: Key comment

SECTION 6
DIVERSITY AND INCLUSION — 347

6.1 Understanding and implementing adaptive teaching — 349
SARAH LEONARD

Introduction • The 'why' and 'what' of adaptive teaching • The 'how' of adaptive teaching

6.2 Special educational needs and inclusion — 362
NOEL PURDY AND ADAM BODDISON

Introduction • The development of UK policy in relation to SEN • Legal definition of SEN • The inclusion debate • The *Code of Practice* • Changing policy and support in mainstream primary schools • Teachers' Standards • SENCO • Teaching assistants • Parents and carers • Meeting the needs of children with SEN: Where do I begin? • Appendix: Additional material on regional variations

6.3 Teaching for social justice: Creating equity for pupils living in poverty and those from black and minority ethnic backgrounds 377
HANNEKE JONES AND HEATHER SMITH

Introduction • Supporting pupils living in poverty • Race, racism and education • Conclusion

6.4 Responding to cultural diversity and citizenship 389
DES BOWDEN

Introduction • Case studies in modern diversity • Entitlement to diversity education • Obstacles to entitlement to diversity • Value of diversity awareness: Beyond tokenism • Flexibility and the curriculum • Diversity and inclusion • School confidence in addressing diversity issues • Possible challenges and opportunities in the classroom • Bullying and name-calling of minority ethnic groups • Controversial issues • Teacher attitudes

6.5 Responding to linguistic diversity 406
VIRGINIA BOWER

Introduction • Historical background: How did we get to where we are now? • Knowledge of children's backgrounds: How this can support us to respond positively to linguistic diversity • Learning a second language: What does this entail? • Celebrating and capitalising upon linguistic diversity: Developing good practice and improving the learning experience for all

6.6 Gender matters: Respectful approaches to gender equity in primary school 421
JAYNE OSGOOD

Introduction • Background • Shifting ideas about gender in childhood • Primary school and the 'heterosexual matrix' • Classroom matters • In-between spaces and places matter • 'Teaching' RSE • Home matters

SECTION 7
WIDER CURRICULUM ASPECTS 433

7.1 Listening to pupils: Developing mutually respectful teacher–pupil relationships to enhance pupils' learning 435
CAROL ROBINSON

Introduction • Pupil voice, pupil participation and pupil engagement: What do these terms mean? • Legislation promoting pupil voice work in schools • How can listening to pupils be of benefit to them? • Listening to pupils: Vignette 1 • How can listening to pupils benefit teachers? • Listening to pupils: Vignette 2 • Ways to facilitate listening to pupils in school • Guiding principles for listening to pupils

7.2 Creativity and creative teaching and learning — 445
TERESA CREMIN AND JONATHAN BARNES

Introduction • Creative practice • So what is creativity? • Creative teaching and teaching for creativity • Personal characteristics of creative teachers • Features of a creative pedagogical stance • Creating environments of possibility • Planning for creativity • Creative curricula in action

7.3 Teaching thinking: Developing children's thinking skills and metacognition — 460
ROBERT FISHER

Introduction • What are thinking skills? • Why are thinking skills important? • What does research tell us about thinking? • The importance of metacognition • Key principles in teaching for thinking • How do we teach for thinking and metacognition in the classroom? • Teaching thinking across the curriculum

7.4 Mental health and wellbeing in initial teacher education — 472
JONATHAN GLAZZARD

Introduction • Mental health and wellbeing • Risk and protective factors • Education and mental health practitioners • Looking forward: Becoming an early career teacher

7.5 Sustainability and climate change education — 488
VERITY JONES AND JOANNA FARBON

Introduction • Sustainability and climate change education – on your bike! • Sustainability and climate education in the curriculum • Supporting wellbeing and education for sustainable development

7.6 Primary education in a digital age — 499
JOHN POTTER

Introduction • Artificial Intelligence (machine learning) • Screen use, datafication and children's digital rights • Digital texts and media literacy • Social media and education • A note on safety • Final thoughts and a note on the computing curriculum

SECTION 8
PARTNERSHIP IN PRACTICE — 513

8.1 Working effectively with teaching assistants — 515
CARRIE WINSTANLEY

Introduction • The (changing) roles and responsibilities of teaching assistants • Working relationships and collaboration • Overcoming challenges and setting professional boundaries • Wellbeing

8.2 Partnerships with parents — 527
STEPHEN GRIFFIN

Introduction • Professional requirements: Statutory expectations • Advantages of secure relationships with parents • First impressions: Managing the narrative • Dealing with difficult situations • Parents' evenings • Parental expertise

8.3 Understanding the teacher's pastoral role — 540
HELEN CHILDERHOUSE

Introduction • What is the teacher's pastoral role, and why is it important for effective teaching? • Transition through school • Looked-after children • The development of UK policy in relation to pastoral provision in schools • Safeguarding • E-safety • Attendance • Scenario 1 • Scenario 2 • Strategies to support the teacher's pastoral role • Whole-school strategies to support the teacher's pastoral role

SECTION 9
YOUR PROFESSIONAL DEVELOPMENT — 553

9.1 Ready, steady, teach… — 555
ANNA HARRISON AND PAULA MOSES

Introduction • Applying for your first teaching role • Creating and making a job application • Visiting schools before applying • Your first interview • Congratulations, you are now an early career teacher • Working closely with your mentor • Consolidating your professional identity • Building your professional networks • And finally

9.2 Understanding and planning your continuing professional development — 571
ALISON FOX

Introduction • What is CPD or what could it be? • The scope of CPD activities • Schools' responsibilities for professional development: The policy context • Setting agendas for professional development: Links with appraisal • How does reflective practice relate to my professional development? • The roles of enquiry and others in developing as a reflective practitioner

9.3 Research and professional learning: Using research and enquiry to develop practice through asking 'What if?', 'What else?' and 'What for?' as well as 'What might work?' 588

CATHY BURNETT

Introduction • What is research, and why is it important to professional development? • 'Evidence' and the Education Endowment Foundation • Beyond what works • Critical engagement with published research • Getting involved in research • Collaboration beyond schools • The value of professional associations

Index 604

FIGURES

1.2.1	Taking on professional identity through socialisation	16
1.2.2	Key influences in moulding emerging professional identity	19
1.3.1	The seven characteristics of reflective teaching	34
2.2.1	Creating towers with adult support	76
2.2.2	A learning journey entry	78
2.3.1	Main learning theories as a continuum	86
3.2.1	Foundations of lesson planning	125
3.2.2	An example of a linear lesson planning template	129
3.2.3	Lesson chat outline	132
3.4.1	Behaviour change cycle	158
3.7.1	Learning through independent play	196
3.7.2	How many triangles can the children make?	199
3.7.3	Mindmap demonstrating how topics from two subject areas may be delivered in an outdoor environment	199
3.7.4	Example of a risk/benefit assessment template	202
4.2.1	The double helix of reading and writing	229
4.4.1	Types of mathematics teacher knowledge with the given examples sorted	256
4.4.2	Pictorial representations of multiplication facts as arrays demonstrating the distributive law	258
4.4.3	Written and mental methods for calculating 2000-12	259
4.4.4	Expanded and compact multiplication methods	261
4.4.5	Concrete, pictorial and abstract representations of 52+37	263
4.4.6	Progression in concrete representations of two cars from most real to most abstract	263
4.4.7	Progression in concrete representations of the number 43, becoming more abstract	263
4.4.8	Bar model and the concrete-pictorial-abstract principles	264
4.4.9	Bar model examples for addition, subtraction, multiplication and division	265
4.5.1	Classroom model of the solar system, demonstrating relative sizes and distances between planets	279
4.5.2	3D paper model of a flower	280
4.5.3	Paper collage of a flower	281
4.5.4	Circuit drawing	281
4.5.5	Water pump visual to be used as an analogy for understanding the flow of electricity through a circuit	282
4.6.1	Children physicalise the walls of an eye	293
4.6.2	Children working together to create a large-scale diagram of an eye	294
4.7.1	Word cloud related to humanities teaching	302
4.7.2	Planning sequence	312
5.1.1	Assessment for learning should take account of the importance of learner motivation	321

5.1.2	Pupil assessment sheet	323
5.1.3	Structuring a lesson to support children's question generation to aid formative assessment	328
6.1.1	Core learning processes	352
6.2.1	Comparisons informing the identification of SEND	365
6.2.2	EHC needs assessment process	369
6.4.1	Ethnic diversity in England and Wales	390
6.4.2	Memorial plaque to Asquith Xavier, a railway guard who broke the colour bar on employment at Euston Station as recently as 1966	399
7.4.1	Biopsychosocial model of health	475
7.4.2	Wellbeing see-saw	476
7.4.3	Whole school approach to mental health	479
7.4.4	Model of teacher resilience	483
8.1.1	Jigsaw model: Retaining and supporting Teaching Assistants	522
9.1.1	CV template	559
9.1.2	The ECT mentoring relationship	564
9.1.3	Watch out for pigeons!	568
9.2.1	Visualising your professional identity	573
9.2.2	A beginning teacher's learning opportunities map	575
9.2.3	Coaching and mentoring as a continuum	581

TABLES

1.2.1	Table showing a comparison of the professional standards required of the four different countries of the UK	14
1.2.2	A summary of the Teachers' Standards	23
1.3.1	Five dimensions according to which the variation among the student teachers' accounts of their learning from experience were analysed	33
1.3.2	An example of appropriate comments that highlight successes of a lesson	36
1.3.3	An example of appropriate comments that relate to children's learning	36
1.3.4	An example of critical comments that relate to evaluation of the teaching	37
1.3.5	An example of the implications for future practice identified after teaching a lesson	38
3.3.1	Organising your classroom for learning	145
3.4.1	Classroom management strategies	152
3.4.2	Examples of hierarchical rewards and sanctions	153
3.6.1	Dialogic teaching: Talk between a teacher and a class of children	180
3.6.2	Exploratory talk: Talk between groups of children with no adult support	181
4.4.1	Types of mathematics teacher knowledge	255
4.4.2	The structure of the primary maths curricula in the four nations of the UK	257
4.4.3	Formal and informal written methods	260
4.4.4	Different views and beliefs about problem solving	266
4.7.1	Key concepts within geographical thinking	309
5.1.1	Classifying children's questions	326
5.2.1	Assessments in English primary schools	344
6.1.1	Adaptive teaching strategies to support attention	354
6.1.2	Adaptive teaching strategies to support memory	355
6.1.3	Adaptive teaching strategies to support processing	356
6.1.4	Adaptive teaching strategies to support social and emotional aspects of learning	357
6.4.1	Diversity in action: The class names in the seven most spoken languages at Gascoigne Primary School	394
7.3.1	Bloom's taxonomy	462
8.1.1	Promoting positive teaching assistant and teacher work relationships	519
8.3.1	Key legislation and documentation for safeguarding in schools	543
8.3.2	School strategies for supporting your pastoral role	549
9.1.1	Some questions to consider asking when visiting a primary school before interview	560
9.2.1	Schools as professional learning environments	574

TASKS

1.1.1	Reflecting on your starting points	5
1.1.2	Reflections	9
1.1.3	Values	10
1.2.1	How does this theory and research influence your own view of professionalism?	13
1.2.2	Plotting your journey to becoming a teacher to date	14
1.2.3	Developing professionalism	17
1.2.4	Building social capital through collaborative practice	17
1.2.5	Putting professional values into practice	22
1.2.6	Thinking about the 'learn that' and 'learn how to' statements	23
1.2.7	Considering the impact of Ofsted on professional decisions	24
1.2.8	Questions for Pierre	25
1.3.1	Lesson evaluations	37
1.3.2	Dimensions and their associated orientations	41
1.3.3	Reflecting on learning conversations	42
1.3.4	Reflecting on teaching experiences	43
2.1.1	Time to move?	52
2.1.2	Reflecting on speech language and communication needs	54
2.1.3	Exploring childhoods	58
2.1.4	Reviewing age-in-cohort consequences	59
2.2.1	Principles into practice	70
2.2.2	Child-initiated play	73
2.2.3	Supporting transition	79
2.3.1	Exploring learning theorists	87
2.3.2	Reflection	87
2.3.3	Considering teachers' talk	92
2.4.1	An evidence-led profession?	98
2.4.2	Lesson plans 1	99
2.4.3	Lesson plans 2: Moving from novice towards expert teacher	100
2.4.4	Creativity and knowledge	101
3.1.1	Openness	113
3.1.2	Scaffolding play	114
3.1.3	Practice	114
3.1.4	Self-limiting behaviours	115
3.1.5	Embracing difference	116
3.1.6	How well do you know your class?	116
3.1.7	Overcoming a challenge	119
3.1.8	Assessment to inform teaching	120
3.2.1	Planning with the students in mind	124
3.2.2	Create an outline planning narrative	127

Tasks

3.2.3	Lesson chat	132
3.3.1a	Looking for learning	137
3.3.1b	Looking for learning	137
3.3.2	Classroom culture	138
3.3.3	Planning for learning	143
3.3.4	Exploring approaches to group work	144
3.4.1	Understanding your school	149
3.4.2	Monitoring professional social skills	150
3.4.3	Classroom rules	155
3.4.4	Planning classroom routines	157
3.4.5	Classroom layout	159
3.5.1	Reflecting on ways to establish a calm and peaceful environment in primary classrooms	166
3.5.2	Exploring resources available to primary schools: The example of 'Targeted Mental Health in Schools' (TaMHS)	170
3.5.3	Implementing effective classroom management strategies	173
3.6.1	Children's classroom talk	183
3.6.2	New vocabulary	186
3.6.3	Children's rules for classroom talk	186
3.7.1	Reflection	193
3.7.2	Planning for learning	198
3.7.3	Taking children out of the classroom	200
3.7.4	Risk assessment	202
4.1.1	Other national curricula	214
4.1.2	Thinking about national curricula	217
4.1.3	Creating a rich curriculum	219
4.2.1	Reflect on your knowledge of children's texts	226
4.2.2	Reflecting on phonics teaching	233
4.2.3	Mapping text potential for reading	235
4.2.4	Exploring concepts for reading comprehension	235
4.3.1	Reflecting on writing lessons	246
4.3.2	Teaching language choice	247
4.3.3	Teachers as writers	250
4.4.1	Your beliefs about mathematics and your experiences	255
4.4.2	What do teachers of maths need to know?	256
4.4.3	Calculation methods in national curricula	259
4.4.4	Encouraging maths talk	261
4.4.5	Becoming familiar with the representations used in your school	264
4.4.6	Becoming familiar with non-routine problems	265
4.5.1	Reflecting on your own primary science education	270
4.5.2	Linking children's prior experiences to a programme of study	275
4.5.3	Local areas for science	276
4.5.4	Preparing to teach a science unit of work	282
4.6.1	Positive memories	289
4.6.2	Design an arts-rich activity	294
4.6.3	Observe an arts-rich learning activity	295
4.6.4	Making links to real world organisations	296
4.7.1	Reflecting on the humanities	302

4.7.2	The value of the humanities	303
4.7.3	Exploring humanities in the national curriculum	304
4.7.4	Your view on the role of the humanities	305
4.7.5	What does Ofsted say about the humanities?	305
4.7.6	Challenging stereotypes in Geography	310
5.1.1	Pupil assessment sheet	323
5.1.2	Self-assessment	329
5.1.3	Questions to ask yourself in relation to your planning for AfL	331
5.1.4	Peer reflection	331
6.1.1	Understanding differences in outcomes for some groups of pupils	350
6.1.2	Final reflection task	358
6.2.1	'Breaking down' special educational needs	364
6.2.2	What SEN knowledge do I need?	372
6.3.1	Putting yourself in the shoes of the poorest child	379
6.3.2	Class and values portrayed as 'normal' in school resources	380
6.3.3	What does BME *mean*?	381
6.4.1	Provision for diversity	396
6.4.2	Unconscious bias	397
6.4.3	Racism	398
6.4.4	Intersectionality	399
6.4.5	Watching children	400
6.4.6	Tokenistic gestures or real understanding?	401
6.4.7	Teachers' viewpoint	402
6.5.1	Examining your own context	409
6.5.2	Considering children's backgrounds	410
6.5.3	Using knowledge about language learning to ensure a positive response to linguistic diversity	411
6.5.4	Creating lexical sets and language mats	416
6.6.1	Gender equity audit	424
6.6.2	Space matters: 'Mapping the in-between'	426
6.6.3	'What Jars You?'	428
7.1.1	Why is it so important to listen to pupils?	438
7.1.2	Listening to pupils in your classroom	440
7.2.1	Ownership of learning	448
7.2.2	Teaching as a cocktail party	450
7.2.3	Creative engagement	452
7.3.1	Questions for thinking	462
7.3.2	Creating a metacognitive classroom	464
7.3.3	Creating a thinking classroom	466
7.3.4	Create a think book	467
7.3.5	What do good teachers do to stimulate thinking?	468
7.4.1	Reflecting on James' experience as a trainee teacher	476
7.4.2	Reflecting on Ned's experience as a trainee teacher	477
7.4.3	Reflecting on transitions for a child refugee	478
7.5.1	Mapping the Sustainable Development Goals in school	490
7.5.2	Reflecting on education for sustainability	493
7.5.3	Analysis of a case study	495
7.6.1	A short film describing a mood or emotion (no longer than 10 seconds)	503

7.6.2	Social media reflections	505
8.1.1	Prioritising the TA's activities	517
8.1.2	Observing TAs in action	518
8.1.3	Rewriting the script	520
8.2.1	Relationships with parents	531
8.2.2	Managing pupil absence	532
8.2.3	Parents' evenings	534
8.2.4	Using critical reflection to support positive teacher/parent relationships	535
8.3.1	How do you know if the children in your class are happy?	542
8.3.2	Safeguarding children: Your role	546
8.3.3	Identifying approaches to support specific needs in Scenario 1	546
8.3.4	Identifying approaches to support specific needs in Scenario 2	547
9.1.1	Creating a CV for teaching	558
9.1.2	Preparing for an interview	562
9.2.1	Reflecting on your expertise	573
9.2.2	Reflecting on your learning opportunities	574
9.2.3	Engaging with your professional development planning	582
9.3.1	Considering relationships between research and teaching	591
9.3.2	Reflecting on your own assumptions when analysing practice	592
9.3.3	Thinking differently about a focus area	593
9.3.4	Critical review of research	597
9.3.5	Investigating subject associations	599

CONTRIBUTORS

Paula Ayliffe has worked in edufcation for over 40 years, starting her career teaching chemistry in a comprehensive school, where she stayed for over ten years, finishing as head of department. She then moved to primary, specialising in Early Years and, until recently, was co-headteacher of Mayfield Primary School in Cambridge. She is a CollectivEd Senior Fellow and a Fellow of the Chartered College of Teaching. Paula has recently successfully completed a MRes, researching the Co-headship that she was part of.

Dr Jonathan Barnes is Visiting Senior Research Fellow at Canterbury Christ Church University. He has more than 50 years of experience in all sectors of education and was a headteacher for nine years. His current role in education involves research on curriculum well-being and inclusive values and focuses on the arts and creativity applied across all subjects. His periods of teaching in Africa and Asia have resulted in a particular interest in diversity and the creative value of difference. His charity, education4diversity, uses the lives and stories of refugees and other immigrants to celebrate diversity and the creativity that arises in bringing different mindsets together. He is author of *Cross Curricular Learning 3-14* (Sage, 2015) *Applying Cross-Curricular Approaches Creatively* (Routledge, 2018) and *Positive Pedagogy across the Primary Curriculum* (Sage, 2023).

Professor Adam Boddison is the Chief Executive for the Association for Project Management. Prior to this Adam held multiple executive leadership roles including more than a decade at the University of Warwick and six years as CEO of the National Association for Special Educational Needs. As an educationalist, he was the Academic Principal for IGGY (an educational social network for gifted teenagers) and held a range of teaching and leadership posts in both primary and secondary schools. Adam has a portfolio of consultancy and volunteering roles supporting organisations and initiatives that benefit society. He is a Visiting Professor at the University of Leicester School of Business and Stranmillis University College in Belfast. He has authored multiple books and is a qualified clinical hypnotherapist. In 2022, Adam was awarded the OBE for services to children and young people with special educational needs and disabilities.

Des Bowden was formerly Head of Geography at Newman University, Birmingham. He spent two years lecturing in Geomorphology at the University of Sierra Leone (Njala University College) and has worked in further education. Des has carried out research in Iceland, Sierra Leone, Malawi, the Gambia and India and, like most geographers, he is widely travelled. He is now co-director, with Pam Copeland, of B&C Educational Ltd (www.bandceducational.com/blog/tags/bearings-report), which is a small company specialising in three interrelated activities: developing and publishing geography and history subject resource materials for primary schools; working with primary schools to develop sequenced and progressive geography and history curricula; and running study visits to the Gambia for primary school staff (heads, teachers, LAs and governors). Since 2010, many primary schools in the West Midlands have developed sustainable partnerships with schools in the Gambia.

Dr Virginia Bower is an Associate Lecturer with The Open University, having followed a career in primary education as a teacher, senior leader and teacher educator. She has completed her doctorate based on supporting children with English as an additional language and is particularly interested in how bilingual approaches might be adopted in primary schools, to support all learners. Dr Bower is the author of seven publications: *Creative Ways to Teach Literacy*; *Games, Ideas and Activities for Primary Poetry*; *Developing Early Literacy 0–8*; *Supporting Children with English as an Additional Language*; *Debates in Primary Education*; *Language Learning and Intercultural Understanding*; and *Poetry and the 3–11 Curriculum*.

Mark Boylan is a Professor of Education at Sheffield Hallam University. Mark's background is in mathematics teaching and mathematics teacher education. He led the design of the Yorkshire Mathematics Specialist Teacher (MaST) programme for primary teachers. Much of Mark's current work involves research of policy initiatives and innovations in mathematics education. He led the longitudinal evaluation of the Mathematics Teacher Exchange: China–England, a government-funded programme of exchange visits with Shanghai teachers aimed at promoting mastery methods in English schools

Sarah Bracken is headteacher at Finham Primary School, Coventry, with over 30 years teaching experience. She has enabled arts-based teacher development across the school trust, city and in China. Her expertise spans nursery to Year 6, although nursery is her passion. She believes that early years, often overlooked and undervalued, is where we lay the foundations for children to discover their own learning, make links between different areas of learning and apply their knowledge to different situations. This is done through encouraging children to take risks using a variety of stimuli and provocations and supporting children to take responsibility for their own learning while developing their own approach to learning. Sarah believes these skills should be transferred into all year groups within school. Her ethos is that teaching should leave memories that last forever; memories can then be used and applied to different situations in life.

Sophie Brookes is an experienced primary teacher and has taught across the primary age range within a number of schools in the South West of England. Sophie works in Forest Schools and is qualified as an Outdoor Curriculum Co-ordinator. She is currently teaching a Year 1 class in a village school in North Devon where the children engage with regular learning outdoors. During her career, she has led several subjects, including maths, PE and science. Her main area of interest is Outdoor Learning and unpicking the barriers for teachers in facilitating learning in the natural environment.

Cathy Burnett is Professor of Literacy and Education at Sheffield Institute of Education, Sheffield Hallam University. She has published extensively on the relationships between new technologies, literacy and schooling. Her most recent work focuses on research and data in education. She is currently leading the ESRC-funded, *Research Mobilities in Primary Literacy Education*, and has led and contributed to projects funded by British Academy, Booktrust, Social Sciences and Humanities Research Council of Canada, Department for Education, JISC and the Education Endowment Foundation. She is an editor of *Journal of Early Childhood Literacy* and a past president of the United Kingdom Literacy Association (UKLA). She has also worked as a primary teacher and in teacher education.

Dr Liz Chamberlain is a Professor of Primary Education at The Open University and past co-director of the Children's Research Centre. Her research is predicated on her expertise of complex professional contexts exploring the knowledge intersection between educational practice, learner and practitioner, through the lens of literacy education. Liz's main expertise is as a literacy case study researcher with a focus on developing children's experiences of writing both in and out-of-school.

Dr Roland Chaplain is a Chartered Psychologist and Associate Fellow of the British Psychological Society. He is an Educational Consultant and the Behaviour Management Specialist in The Faculty of Education, University of Cambridge, where he designed and teaches the Behaviour Management

Training and Support Programme to all PGCE trainees. The quality of this programme has been highlighted in all recent Ofsted inspections at Cambridge. He has experience as a teacher, headteacher and Senior Lecturer in Psychology. As an educational consultant, Roland also provides behaviour management training to schools and ITT providers. He has produced many books, chapters and journal articles on classroom management, behaviour disorders and teacher stress. His book, *Teaching Without Disruption in the Primary School* (2nd edn; Routledge, 2016), is an extremely practical book underpinned by contemporary educational, psychological and neuroscientific research.

Dr Kerry Chappell is an Associate Professor at University of Exeter where she leads the Creativity and Emergent Educational futures Network (CEEN) and the MA Education Creative Arts Programme. She researches creativity in education in the arts, transdisciplinary settings and futures through funding from the EU, ESRC, AHRC and ACE. Recently this has included core research and facilitation roles on the SciCulture/D HE transdisciplinary intensives project, research lead for the Penryn Creativity Collaboratives project developing teaching for creativity in Cornish schools and for the Road STEAMerEU Horizon project developing a STEAM education roadmap for EU policymakers. She is the lead editor for *Creative Ruptions for Emergent Educational Futures* (2024), published by Palgrave Studies in Creativity and Culture. She is also an Adjunct Associate Professor at Western Norway University of Applied Science and a practicing dance artist with the Exeter-based Dance Lab Collective.

Dr Helen Childerhouse is Director of Professional Practice in the School of Education at the University of Lincoln. She has almost 20 years' experience of teaching in mainstream primary schools and working with children with a diverse range of needs. Helen has taught in universities since 2007 and is involved in primary teacher training, special educational needs and disability research and teaching. She has a particular interest in pupil and teacher well-being, child development and pedagogy. Helen supervises research students who are focusing on practice in the primary learning environment.

Dr Ayshea Craig is on the leadership team of the Primary PGCE Courses at UCL Institute of Education. She specialises in primary mathematics and is part of the UCL team delivering the new National Professional Qualification in Leading Primary Mathematics. She is interested in all aspects of primary teacher education and the teaching and learning of mathematics including the broader social, cultural, political and historical context of its place in education systems and value to society. Ayshea has worked on research projects on teachers' pedagogical responses to testing and on mainstream provision for primary school pupils with statements for special educational needs.

Professor Teresa Cremin is Professor of Education (Literacy) at The Open University. Her sociocultural research focuses mainly on teachers' identities as readers and writers and the potential influence of these on both their classroom practice and their students' literate identities and practices. She also researches creativity and creative pedagogical practice. An ex-teacher and teacher-educator, Teresa worked in initial teacher education for nearly 20 years and now undertakes research and consultancy for numerous organisations. Her research is frequently coparticipative, involving teachers as researchers both in schools and in children's homes. A Fellow of the Academy of Social Sciences, the Royal Society of the Arts and the English Association, Teresa is also a Reading Agency board member, Trustee of the UK Literacy Association and DfE expert on reading for pleasure. Previously she has been a board member of BookTrust and the Poetry Archive, a Director of the Cambridge Primary Review Trust, President of UKLA and UKRA and editor of the journals *Literacy* and *Thinking Skills and Creativity*. Teresa has written and edited over 30 books with colleagues and is series editor of Teaching Creatively in the primary school (13 texts, Routledge). A selection of Teresa's forthcoming and current volumes include: *International*

Perspectives on Reading for Pleasure (Routledge, 2024); *Reading Teachers: Nurturing Reading for Pleasure* (Routledge, 2022); *Teaching English Creatively* (3rd edn; Routledge, 2021); *Reading for Pleasure in the Digital Age* (Sage, 2018); *Writer Identity and the Teaching and Learning of Writing and Storytelling in Early Childhood: Enriching Language, Literacy and Culture* (Routledge, 2017).

Louise Cunningham is a highly qualified teacher with over 23 years of experience in both primary and secondary education. She served as a subject lead for PE, PSHE and Citizenship before advancing to the role of assistant headteacher and Special Educational Needs and Disabilities Coordinator (SENDCO) in 2013. Her passion for inclusive education led her to undertake a research project for her Masters degree at the University of Bedfordshire. Her thesis primarily focused on effective teaching methods for the inclusion of challenging behaviours within an alternative provision (AP). With the collaboration of a local authority, Louise established and led an AP that specifically catered for primary-aged children with social, emotional and mental health needs. Her hands-on experience in this unique educational setting provided invaluable insights into tailoring teaching methods to meet the diverse needs of her learners. Recently, Louise's personal interest in dyslexia and specific learning differences has led her to pursue further teaching and assessing post-graduate qualifications at Liverpool Hope University.

Lyn Dawes worked as a teacher in primary and middle schools before lecturing in Science and English at Bedford, Northampton and Cambridge Universities. She now provides workshops for education professionals with a focus on Talk for Learning. Lyn has authored and co-authored several books for teachers, including *Talk Box* (KS1; 2004) and *Talking Points* (KS2; 2011), both David Fulton publications, and *Teaching Primary Science* (Sage, 2009). She has a chapter in the classic *The Articulate Classroom*, edited by Prue Goodwin (Routledge, 2017). Lyn is a committee member of Oracy Cambridge.

Dr Rebecca Digby has worked in education for more than 20 years and within higher education for 12 years. Her roles have included Advanced Skills teacher, deputy headteacher, Senior Lecturer and Subject Leader across the early years, primary and post compulsory age phases. Rebecca is currently Head of Learning, Teaching and Research at Norland. Her responsibilities include leading on pedagogical innovation and curriculum development and supporting the implementation of cycles of continual improvement for student experience. Rebecca also leads the Norland Educare Research Centre (NERC). Her research has been focused on pedagogy and practice in early childhood education and is inspired by posthumanist and new materialist methodologies. Rebecca has authored and co-authored a number of publications. Most recently, these have included experiments with diffraction and transdisciplinary space to explore the materiality of young children's creative knowledge making practices in science enquiry.

Karin Doull was a primary teacher and subject lead before becoming a teacher educator at the University of Roehampton. She is an Honorary Research Fellow for the University. She is a Senior Fellow with the Higher Education Association and a professional affiliate of the Chartered College of Teaching. She is now a freelance consultant and writer in primary history. She is strongly involved with the Historical Association being an Honorary Fellow, a member of primary committee and the lead editor for *Primary History Journal*. She was also a chartered teacher of history with the Historical Association. She writes extensively for Primary History, has published text books on teaching history and edited and published two books, one on teaching climate change and the other on diversity across the primary phase. She has long advocated for women's history through her work and writing. She has two historical short stories both set in 1620s London and India with female protagonists.

Sally Elton-Chalcraft is Professor of Social Justice in Education and Director of the Learning Education and Development Research centre, University of Cumbria. She is convenor of the Religions, Values and Education special interest group for the British Education Research Association. She teaches on undergraduate, graduate, Masters and doctoral programmes and publishes in the areas of Religious Education, anti racism and professional practice. Currently she is researching different approaches in education, including art-based community focused provision, and also the relevance of 20th century Charlotte Mason's practice for contemporary pedagogy. She has given keynotes in India, Germany, Ireland and the UK.

Joanna Farbon is a Fellow of the Chartered College of Teaching and a Chartered Teacher (Leadership). She has been headteacher of Icknield Primary School, a large school based in Luton, since 2019. The school hosts the Luton Primary Deaf Provision which caters for the educational needs of nursery and primary-aged deaf pupils from across the authority. Her current work includes supporting schools as a school improvement adviser (SIA) and as a school governor. She is co-chair of Luton Primary Headteachers' Group. Prior to leading Icknield, Joanna was an SIA for Central Bedfordshire Council supporting the development of 25 schools. She was headteacher at Cranfield Church of England Academy and a Local Leader of Education for over five years. Joanna is currently studying for a Masters degree in Teaching and Learning.

Dr Robert Fisher taught in schools in the UK, Africa and Hong Kong before becoming a teacher trainer and Professor of Education at Brunel University. His PhD was awarded for research into philosophy for children and his many books include *Teaching Thinking*; *Teaching Children to Think*; *Teaching Children to Learn*; *Creative Dialogue*; the *Stories for Thinking* series and *Brain Games for Your Child*. Since retiring he continues to write on philosophy and education, and to develop his creativity through painting, sculpting and dancing Argentine tango.

Alison Fox is a Senior Lecturer at the Faculty of Wellbeing, Education and Language Studies at The Open University, and Associate Head of School for Research and Knowledge Exchange for the School of Education, Childhood, Youth and Sport. After training as a secondary school science teacher, Alison moved into initial teacher training and research about and for the support of beginning teachers. She has been involved in the Teaching and Learning Research Programme, 'Learning how to learn: In classrooms, in schools and in networks' project (2002-2006), which investigated the development of assessment for learning practices across five local authorities, the Department for Education-funded 'Schools and continuing professional development in England – State of the Nation' project (2008) and an evaluation of the National College for Teaching and Leadership's leadership curriculum provision (2012-2016). Her recent consultancy (2018-2023) has led to the development of a set of resources for trainees, tutors and school-based mentors to support a School Centred Initial Teacher Training based on a longitudinal study with training teachers into their early career of how they draw on networks for support.

Professor Jonathan Glazzard is the first Rosalind Hollis Professor of Education for Social Justice in the School of Education at the University of Hull. Jonathan's research focuses on the experiences of minoritised individuals and groups. Jonathan sits on the editorial boards of several journals including the *International Journal of Educational and Life Transitions* and *Equity in Education and Society*. He is a co-convenor of the British Educational Research Association Special Interest Group, Mental Health and Wellbeing in Education. His current research focuses on the experiences of LGBTQ+, disabled youth. Recent publications have focused on mental health, educational and life transitions and early reading development in children. Jonathan holds Visiting Professorships at BGU, Lincoln, Newman University, Birmingham and the University of Northampton.

Dr Janet Goepel is an Associate Lecturer in Primary Education at Sheffield Hallam University. She teaches Special Educational Needs and Inclusion to primary undergraduate students as well as in-service teachers on the Special Educational Needs Coordinators (SENCOs) Masters-level award. Janet's doctoral thesis concerned the professionalism of doctors and teachers in working together to support children with special educational needs. She has presented papers on this theme in the UK and in Australia to both teachers and health professionals. She has also presented at conferences on teacher professionalism and published papers on this theme. Janet has contributed chapters to several books and has co-authored a book entitled *Inclusive Primary Teaching: A Critical Approach to Equality and Special Educational Needs* (Critical Publishing, 2015) as well as a book entitled *A Critical Guide to the SEND CODE of PRACTICE 0-25 years (2015)*, published in 2020.

Dr Alan Gorman is Assistant Professor in the School of Policy and Practice at the Institute of Education, Dublin City University. He is also a Research Fellow at the National Anti-Bullying Research and Resource Centre (ABC), where he specialises in the analysis of anti-bullying policy in schools, specialising in leadership, policy enactment and impact. He previously worked as a primary teacher. Alan teaches across a number of teacher education programmes. He is the APF (Area of Professional Focus) leader for Professional Learning and Teacher Education on the Doctor of Education (EdD) programme at DCU. His research interests and publications are in the areas of policy analysis, professional learning and teacher education.

Dr Stephen Griffin is Co-Lead of the MA in Education at Birmingham City University. A former primary school deputy headteacher, Stephen has taught extensively in a range of educational settings from KS1 to KS3. In his current role, as well as teaching across the MA programme, he supervises a number of doctoral researchers within the field. His research interests focus on the implementation of neuroscientifically informed learning theory in schools, teacher agency and the impact of educational consultancy upon educational change in school.

Eleanore Hargreaves is Professor of Learning and Pedagogy at the UCL Faculty of Education and Society, Institute of Education, London University. She taught in the primary phase in England and abroad before entering the NFER's Department of Assessment and Measurement in 1992. Later, she registered with the UCL Institute of Education for a PhD exploring the roles of assessment in primary education. Since then she has led MA modules on learning, teaching and assessment and carried out research into these areas. From 2018-2023 she led the Children's Life-histories In Primary Schools longitudinal research project (CLIPS). Her first book was as co-author of *What Makes a Good Primary School Teacher?* (Routledge, 2000) and her recent, sole-authored book is *Children's Experiences of Classrooms* (Sage, 2017). Her work in formative assessment, especially feedback, has led her to carry out educational consultancies in a range of countries, including Egypt, Hong Kong, Macedonia and Pakistan.

Anna Harrison is a Senior English Lecturer at Roehampton University. She was a primary school teacher for 13 years in the London Boroughs of Richmond and Hounslow and worked as an editor in children's publishing for eight years at Dorling Kindersley, Penguin Group. Anna teaches several ITE courses at Roehampton and has a strong sense of wishing to support, encourage and mentor new students as teachers. Her doctoral research at Cambridge University focuses on siblings as readers in home settings and their responses to both print and digital versions of singular stories. She is an active member of the UKLA and the Beatrix Potter Society. Anna likes to promote student teachers' reading-for-pleasure practices involving her interest in the intersectionality between education and children's literature.

Dr Helen Hendry is a Senior Lecturer and researcher in primary education, and co-director of the Centre for Literacy and Social Justice at The Open University. An early years and primary English specialist, Helen draws on a longstanding career as class teacher, senior leader, advisory teacher and teacher trainer working with diverse schools across the UK. She currently contributes to Education Studies undergraduate modules 'Learning and Teaching in the Primary Years' and 'Comparative and International Education'. Her recent research focuses on early career teachers and reading, informal book talk in the early years, reading and writing for pleasure programmes for children, teachers and families, and continuing professional development. Helen works with English subject leaders on the OU Reading Schools programme to develop a whole school approach to reading for pleasure. She leads the OU/UKLA Student teacher reading for pleasure ambassador scheme with student teachers from initial teacher education programmes across the UK.

Sally Hinchliff is a Senior Lecturer in Primary Education at Sheffield Hallam University. For the last eight years she has led the PGCE Primary and Early Years QTS course at Hallam. She teaches across the curriculum and works closely with mentors and trainee teachers across a number of routes to QTS. She has a specialist interest in Foreign Languages, P4C and P4TE (Philosophy for Teacher Education). Sally's Masters in Education examined the emotional dimension of training to teach, and she is now working towards her Doctorate in Education with a focus on how teachers navigate their educational values in their professional work. She has presented on her emerging study at TEAN and IPDA and is fascinated by the complex relationship between the personal and the professional which underpins the teacher's lived experience. Sally has contributed a chapter in *Nurturing 'Difficult Conversations' in Education: Empowerment, Agency and Social Justice in the UK* (Bloomsbury Publishing, 2024).

Hanneke Jones is affiliated with Newcastle University. Her areas of expertise are social justice in relation to socio-economic disadvantage; enquiry-based pedagogies such as Philosophy for Children; creativity and creative thinking; and comparative education.

Verity Jones is an Associate Professor in the School of Education and Childhood at the University of the West of England, Bristol where she supports the training of primary teachers. Her research focuses on social and climate justice, drawing from her experience as a teacher and education officer with both charities and local government. Recent projects Verity has worked on include: developing integrated food systems in European schools with Food for Life; creating the online course 'Who Made My Clothes?' for international charity, Fashion Revolution; working with young people to design immersive learning experiences and exploring eco-anxiety with Global Goals Centre and Friends of the Earth; and working on an interdisciplinary project that developed creative learning tools to embed water scarcity and drought into UK classrooms.

Peter Kelly is Reader in Comparative Education at the University of Plymouth's Institute of Education, where he has worked since 2003. His research focuses on the working lives of teachers in Europe, and he has an interest in comparative pedagogy. He leads the module Policy and Professional Practice in the Education Doctorate and is Director of Studies for both professional doctorate and PhD students. He is also a tutor on the MA (Education) Programme, which provides practice-focused Masters-level study in all areas of education.

Dr Paula Lehane is an Assistant Professor in the School of Inclusive and Special Education in the Institute of Education at Dublin City University (DCU). She previously worked as a primary school teacher for a number of years and was the Special Educational Needs and Disabilities Coordinator (SENDCO) for a large urban primary school in Ireland. Her interests include educational assessment, pedagogy and inclusion.

Dr Sarah Leonard is Head of Primary Initial Teacher Education at the University of Roehampton where she also leads the professional studies programmes for undergraduate and postgraduate students. Her doctoral studies in psychology explored how context influences learning which supported cross-school work on behaviour and social and emotional aspects of learning. She has led primary and 3-to-19 through schools and has extensive experience in school improvement work, with a focus on developing learning, teaching, leadership and management to improve outcomes for pupils vulnerable to underachievement in the school system. She is involved in school-based CPD on multilingualism with the Bell Foundation and works in an advisory capacity in special schools.

Rachel Lofthouse is Professor of Teacher Education at Leeds Beckett University. She has worked in education for 30 years and has maintained a keen interest in understanding and enabling professional learning at all career stages and across education sectors. She has a specific research expertise in mentoring and coaching and has regularly published in this area for 20 years. Her current extended interests include developing practices to support a more sustainable education profession and more inclusive schools, and she is participating in EU funded projects on these areas. Rachel Lofthouse is the founder of CollectivED The Centre for Coaching, Mentoring, Supervision and Professional Learning. CollectivED is a global community of teachers and other professionals, academics and students as local, national and international friends, partners and practitioners.

Vince MacLeod is a qualified teacher who has taught in reception and Year 1. He has a Masters degree in Early Childhood Education, in which his research focussed on children's self-regulation and their engagement with sociodramatic roleplay. Before becoming a teacher Vince had a career in recruitment advertising for ten years. He has also worked for a family as a childminder, managed children's activity centres and taught canoeing to children in England and France. Vince is currently an Early Years Lecturer at Norland College. His responsibilities include teaching on the BA (Hons) Early Childhood Education and Care degree and leading modules on self-regulation and music, drama and theatre. He intends to complete a PhD in the near future and is interested in researching toddlers' nonverbal communication strategies.

Vanessa Matthews is a Senior Lecturer in the School of Education at University of Roehampton, working with undergraduate and postgraduate students in primary science education. Prior to this Vanessa transitioned into HEI by undertaking school supervision responsibilities with Canterbury Christ Church University. She has worked for more than 20 years in primary schools in South London and Spain. While teaching, Vanessa held posts of assistant headteacher and curriculum leader and has a particular interest in learning beyond the classroom, which was the focus of her Masters studies at UCL.

Roger McDonald is an Associate Professor of Primary Education (Literacy) in the School of Education at the University of Greenwich, with a passion for creating curiosity and intrigue and generating love and desire to learn from children and adults alike. His research interests include: the pedagogy of imagination, reading for pleasure, the power of picture books, drama education and the place of emotion in teaching.

Paula Moses is an experienced primary school teacher and former headteacher with a good track record of working with a wide range of schools in areas of high deprivation. Paula now runs Permanent Education CIC to enable schools to integrate a broad range of high-quality thinking skills and understanding about sustainability throughout their whole school ethos and curriculum. Paula is also approaching completion of a PhD at The University of Cumbria examining the English primary curriculum's role in enabling people to achieve 'success in life'.

Debra Myhill is Professor Emerita in Language and Literacy Education at the University of Exeter. Her research has focused particularly on young people's composing processes and their metacognitive awareness of them; the interrelationship between metalinguistic understanding and writing; the talk-writing interface; and the teaching of writing. Over the past 15 years, she has led a series of research projects in these areas, in both primary and secondary schools, and has conducted several commissioned research studies. Debra runs numerous professional education courses for teachers, examining the practical classroom implications of her research on the teaching of writing, and, in 2014, her research team was awarded the Economic and Social Research Council award for Outstanding Impact in Society.

Dr Jayne Osgood is Professor of Childhood Studies at the Centre for Education Research & Scholarship, Middlesex University. Her work addresses issues of social justice through critical engagement with policy, curriculum and pedagogical approaches in early childhood education. She is committed to extending understandings of the workforce, families, gender/sexualities and the child in early years contexts through creative, affective methodologies. She has published extensively within the post-modernist paradigm with over 100 publications in the form of books, chapters and journal papers.

Jane Payler is Professor of Education (Early Years) at The Open University. Jane has taught, examined, researched, published and practised in early years education and care for over 30 years. She has taught and developed curricula for early years students on vocational courses through to university doctoral level. Jane was closely involved in the development of Early Years Professional Status and Early Years Teacher in England. Her publications and research have focused on inter-professional practice, professional development, young children's learning experiences and children living in difficult family circumstances. She is former co-director of the Children's Research Centre at The Open University.

Professor Dame Alison Peacock is Chief Executive of the Chartered College of Teaching, a charitable professional body that seeks to empower a knowledgeable and respected teaching profession through membership and accreditation. Prior to joining the Chartered College, Dame Alison was executive headteacher of The Wroxham School in Hertfordshire. Her career to date has spanned primary, secondary and advisory roles. She is an Honorary Fellow of Queens College Cambridge, Hughes Hall Cambridge and UCL, a Visiting Professor of both the University of Hertfordshire and Glyndŵr University and a trustee for Big Change, Institute for Educational & Social Equity and the Helen Hamlyn Trust. Her research is published in a series of books about Learning without Limits offering an alternative approach to inclusive school improvement.

Stephen Pickering lectures in teaching and learning at the University of Bristol. He sits on the editorial board of Primary Geography and is a consultant for the Geographical Association. Stephen has written widely for the Geographical Association and TIDE, as well as being the editor of *Teaching Outdoors Creatively* (2017) and contributing a chapter to S. Scoffham's *Teaching Geography Creatively* (2013, 2nd edn, 2017), both for Routledge. Stephen is a qualified Forest School Leader and Earth Education Leader. His doctoral research explores a socio-material perspective of place and space in learning, using outdoor learning areas. His other research interests include learning and teaching outdoors, geographical education, the global dimension, global citizenship and literature as a vehicle for learning.

Professor John Potter is Professor of Media in Education at the IOE, UCL's Faculty of Education & Society, based at the UCL Knowledge Lab. He is the Director of the ReMAP research centre (Researching Media Arts and Play), formerly known as DARE (Digital Arts Research in Education), and Associate Director (Media) of the UCL Knowledge Lab. His research, teaching and publications are in the fields of media education, new literacies, play on- and offscreen, theories of curation and agency in social media, and the changing nature of teaching and learning in the context of digital media culture. He is particularly interested in the co-production of research with children and young people and uses a variety of participatory, ethnographic and multimodal research methods. He is the co-editor of the journal, *Learning, Media and Technology*.

Professor Noel Purdy is Director of Research and Scholarship and Director of CREU (the Centre for Research in Educational Underachievement) at Stranmillis University College, Belfast. A former Modern Languages teacher, he has worked in teacher education for 17 years. His main areas of research interest are in educational underachievement, special educational needs and pastoral care, with a particular interest in addressing on- and offline bullying in schools. He chaired the Expert Panel on Educational Underachievement in Northern Ireland (the final action plan A Fair Start was launched on 1 June 2021), and also chaired the DE Steering Committee in the Republic of Ireland which reviewed the national Action Plan on Bullying (the new action plan Cineáltas was launched on 1 December 2022). He is editor of *Pastoral Care in Education – An International Journal of Personal, Social and Emotional Development* and is a parent governor of a local special school outside Belfast.

Carol Robinson is Professor of Children's Rights at the Strathclyde Institute of Education. She is a trained teacher and has experience of teaching in secondary schools and of teaching both primary- and secondary-aged pupils in pupil referral units. Carol's research interests combine theoretical and empirical work focusing on the voices, experiences and rights of children and young people, as well as children's rights education. Carol has led several pupil voice projects in primary, secondary and special schools, helping staff to develop ways of listening to the voices of children and young people. More recently Carol's work has focused on eliciting the voices of children from birth to 7.

Dr Janet Rose is currently Principal of Norland College, a specialist, vocational early years higher education institution. She is a former Reader in Education (Associate Professor) and has led numerous undergraduate and postgraduate early childhood degrees and teacher training programmes at several universities. She initially trained as a primary teacher working in schools and a range of early years settings, and went on to work as an ITE Ofsted Inspector. She is a co-founder of Emotion Coaching UK and has worked closely with numerous local authorities and professional organisations around the country. She has also led several national research projects with a particular focus on trauma, well-being and behaviour and is frequently invited to speak at national and international conferences. She has authored a wide range of academic and professional publications, including co-authoring books on early years education. She is currently undertaking a Fellowship programme at the University of Massachusetts in America.

Mary Scanlan was a Senior Lecturer in Education at the University of Winchester where she led early years provision across undergraduate and postgraduate courses. She had a particular interest in supporting young children's development in the areas of reading, writing and oracy. Mary's PhD, undertaken at the University of Bristol, explored how home and school can work together to support children's literacy learning. Mary is a Senior Fellow of the HEA.

Shirin Sheikh-Bahai is a British-Iranian science educator. She completed her undergraduate degree in Physics and Astronomy at The Open University and further pursued a Masters degree in Science Education from UCL Institute of Education. Currently, she is engaged in her PhD research, which focuses on exploring the thought processes of students in relation to their questions at UCL Institute of Education. Prior to embarking on her academic journey, she served as a science lead practitioner across many primary schools in London. Presently, she holds the position of the

Director of Science, where she oversees curriculum and pedagogy in the primary and secondary schools. Shirin has authored numerous science projects, teaching programs and educational resources for various organisations with national and international partnerships.

Heather Smith is Professor of Race and Language Equality in Education at Newcastle University. She is a critical race theory scholar. Her teaching and research focus on developing greater understandings about and action for race and language equality, and includes critical analyses of education policy, and a focus on translanguaging as an emancipatory pedagogy for multilingual pupils. She is co-author of the anti-racism framework for ITE/T. She was principal investigator for an Erasmus+ European Project, entitled ROMtels (Roma translanguaging enquiry learning space), which improved education for Roma pupils through a translanguaging pedagogical approach (€261,317).

Sonia Thompson is the headteacher at St Matthew's C.E. Primary School and the Director of St Matthew's EEF (Education Endowment Foundation) Research School, in Nechells Birmingham. St Matthew's previously held DfE Teaching School status and is still a Support School. The school hosts visits for teachers, headteachers and Multi Academy Trusts (MATs), from across the country and internationally, who want to see evidence-informed practice. Sonia has worked as an LA English Consultant, where she was part of the original United Kingdom Literacy Association (UKLA), Building Communities of Readers research. Sonia is passionate about evidence-based reading for pleasure practices and her school won the first (2018) Egmont/UKLA Reading for Pleasure Award. She is a trustee for the Church of England National Society, Classics for All and the Education Endowment Foundation (EEF). Sonia is also a member of the DFE External Reference Group, advising on Teacher Training and Early Career Framework reforms.

Vivien Townsend has worked as a primary school teacher, a local authority adviser and as the mathematics lead at a primary School-based Initial Teacher Training (SCITT). She currently works part time as Assistant Director (Evaluation and Impact) at NCETM, and the rest of her time is spent doing freelance work including leading subject knowledge workshops for teaching assistants on behalf of her local Maths Hub. She is an accredited NCETM PD Lead and is also a member of ATM, MA, AMET, NAMA, BERA and BSRLM. Vivien's PhD research focused on how primary school teachers in England were implementing the 2014 National Curriculum for mathematics, and this has led to an interest in how teachers' histories contribute to how they engage with educational discourses.

Nicola Treby is an Associate Professor in the School of Education at the University of Roehampton, working with undergraduate, postgraduate, Masters and doctoral students; she has previously been a Senior Lecturer at Kingston University. During her employment within HEIs Nicola has been the course leader for the MA in Educational Practice, led the university component of SCITT partnerships, acted as co-investigator for Gatsby-funded research and undertaken UK and international CPD. Her expertise spans both the primary and secondary phases of science education, professional practice and professional learning. Prior to working in HEIs Nicola was an advanced skills teacher in Surrey. Collectively Nicola has 25 years of experience in education.

Jo Trowsdale is Senior Lecturer in Education at Birmingham Newman University and honorary Associate Professor in Sociology at the University of Warwick. Jo has extensive experience in teacher education in both primary and secondary phases. As a regional director of Creative Partnerships (2002-2010) she enabled school improvement, curricula and pedagogic developments between professional artists, businesses and teachers. She has a longstanding research interest in developing young people through the arts, creativity and interdisciplinary curricula. Her current research is concerned with the importance of 'art making' practices as a context for more personally meaningful, inter- and transdisciplinary learning that stimulates pupils' affective as well as cognitive dimensions. This includes the role of the arts in STEAM (science, technology, engineering, arts and mathematics) education. Jo continues to work directly with schools, teachers, pupils and artists.

Professor Samantha Twiselton, OBE is Emeritus Professor at Sheffield Hallam University and was its founding Director of Sheffield Institute of Education. She is also a Visiting Professor at University of Sunderland and an independent education consultant and advisor for the government and many other organisations. With highly regarded expertise in teacher and school leader development, recruitment and retention and curriculum, Sam has been heavily involved in shaping and advising government policy on teacher education. She sits on many government advisory groups and chaired the DfE Core Content in ITT group. Sam is a Founding Fellow and former Vice President (external) of the Chartered College of Teaching. She is trustee for Shine, Teach First, several multi-academy trusts, a teaching school hub and Now Teach. In June 2018 she was named in the Queen's Birthday honours as a recipient of an OBE for services to Higher Education.

Jane Warwick is Associate Professor at the Faculty of Education University of Cambridge where she has been the Primary PGCE Course Manager since 2006. This role involves supporting beginning teachers through their one-year initial teacher education course and having responsibility for all aspects of the course, including partnerships with schools, preparing trainees for placements and mentor training, which is a particular research interest. Prior to that she taught for 15 years in primary schools, taking on various leadership roles including induction tutor for early career teachers. She worked as a local authority science advisor and support teacher for PE. Research interests include supporting trainees' well-being and mentor training.

Janice Wearmouth has many years' experience of teaching and research work in schools and universities, in the UK and overseas. In her research work, she brings together a concern for the learner whose educational experience is problematic with a concern for professionals who have to deal with, and mitigate, the problems that are experienced and facilitate opportunities for learning. Since 2000, she has been researching and publishing on issues related to literacy difficulties, behavioural concerns in schools, teacher professional development and inclusion, and special educational needs and disability, with colleagues in New Zealand, at the University of Waikato, and in the UK.

Carrie Winstanley is a Professor of Pedagogy at Roehampton University. She has taught in schools and universities for 30 years, currently holding responsibility for learning and teaching, working with faculty and across various student programmes. She is fascinated by ideas of challenge, with an emphasis on inclusion, diversity and social justice in all phases of education. Carrie's monograph *The Ingredients of Challenge* (Trentham, 2010), explores the provision of worthwhile challenge for children in schools, following on from her 2004 publication *Too Clever by Half*, introducing the notion of 'Equality of Challenge'. She is an Executive Council member of the Philosophy of Education Society of Great Britain and has co-edited a collection considering the role of *Philosophy in Schools* (Bloomsbury, with Hand, 2008), among other publications about teacher education (2006); the contemporary relevance of Dewey's ideas on museum learning (2018); Community Philosophy (2019); and creating engaging activities for higher education faculty and students (2019).

John-Mark Winstanley is an Associate Lecturer at the Faculty of Education, University of Cambridge. After gaining a PGCE at the University of Cambridge, he spent several years teaching across EYFS, KS1 and KS2 in a number of middle and senior leadership roles. During his time working in schools, John-Mark worked as an assistant headteacher in two contrasting settings and was also seconded to support various school improvement projects across the local authority. He was a Leading Teacher of Literacy and EAL for Cambridgeshire and a Specialist Leader of Education for Primary English, EAL and Initial Teacher Education. John-Mark is currently Deputy Course Manager of the Primary PGCE. His main research interests include primary English; pedagogy surrounding the teaching of children who speak English as an additional language; primary languages and the professional identities and learning of beginning teachers.

Mary Anne Wolpert is a former Affiliated Lecturer and Deputy Course Manager of the Primary PGCE at the Faculty of Education, University of Cambridge. Prior to this, she taught for 12 years in primary schools, specialising in literacy education, and also worked as a literacy advisor for local authorities. She now lives and works in New York City where she is an Executive Committee member of The Children's Book Committee at The Bank Street College of Education.

Dominic Wyse FAcSS FRSA is Professor of Early Childhood and Primary Education at the Institute of Education (IOE), University College London (UCL). He is Founding Director of the Helen Hamlyn Centre for Pedagogy (0-11 Years) (HHCP), a research centre devoted to improving young children's education. Dominic was President of the British Educational Research Association (BERA) from 2019 to 2022. Dominic has made a leading contribution to research on curriculum at national, regional and local levels for more than 25 years. Dominic's main research is on effective teaching of reading and writing. His book, *The Balancing Act: An Evidence-Based Approach to Teaching Phonics, Reading and Writing* (co-authored with Charlotte Hacking, Routledge, 2024), presents 'The Double Helix of Reading and Writing' which theorises a new teaching approach based on analyses of hundreds of robust research studies. His book, *Teaching English, Language and Literacy* (with Helen Bradford and John-Mark Winstanley, 5th edn, Routledge, 2023), has been a leading text for teachers and teacher education for more than 20 years. Dominic's research on writing developed 'the ear of the writer' as a metaphor for effective writing across the life course, for novice and expert writers. This multidisciplinary research was published in the book, *How Writing Works: From the Invention of the Alphabet to the Rise of Social Media* (Cambridge University Press, 2017). An original feature of the work was the comparisons made between language and music. Dominic's research on grammar and writing, in the context of national curriculum, has included seminal papers and more recently a randomised controlled trial to examine a new approach to teaching grammar.

SECTION 1
BECOMING A TEACHER

UNIT 1.1

PRIMARY TEACHING

Personal perspectives

Teresa Cremin, Helen Hendry and Anna Harrison

INTRODUCTION

This chapter introduces us (the editors), what inspired us to be teachers, what helped us stay within the teaching profession and how we navigated the changes and challenges of being a professional teacher. In doing so, we suggest questions that you might ask yourself as you begin your pathway as a teacher. *Learning to Teach in the Primary School* aims to support you during your initial education as a teacher, through your early career years, and beyond, regardless of the route through which you enter the profession.

It is a huge responsibility, but also a joy and a privilege to be a primary teacher and you are uniquely positioned to support children and young people's learning and their future life chances for the better. What teachers do and say really matters to children! You will be one of the most important people in the lives of each of the children in your class whilst you work with them, and many will remember you and build on what they learned in your lessons for the rest of their school career and beyond.

You may have views of an ideal teacher, or an expectation of what sort of people become teachers, which are sometimes based on your experience, or even media portrayals of teachers and teaching. In reality, teachers can be very different, and becoming a teacher is very much a personal journey which is different for everyone. Your own interests, skills and values; previous life experiences; memories of school; the influence of a previous career and perspectives of family and friends will shape the sort of teacher that you want to be and the relationships you build in the classroom. Your individuality is valuable and getting to know your own strengths and areas for development is part of the process of learning to teach and developing as an informed, passionate and effective educator.

Learning to teach begins with your initial teacher education programme, and whilst this period of time will come to a close, you will want (and need) to continue to reflect upon your practice, engaging in professional learning and drawing on research to develop further. Consequently, learning to teach in the primary school is something teachers continue to do as students, early career teachers and as middle or senior leaders. This is why we, the editors, have dedicated our careers to working with both new and experienced teachers and carrying out research with (not on) teachers and children. We want to understand more about the ways in which teachers can make the most difference to children through their curriculum offered, their classroom practice and the relational connections that are built. In particular, we are concerned with exploring and supporting educators in working effectively with those young people who may be at risk of educational disadvantage because of socio-economic or other challenging circumstances.

> **OBJECTIVES**
>
> By the end of this unit, you should be beginning to:
>
> - realise what drew you into primary school teaching;
> - recognise your own individual strengths and how those might contribute to your development as an inspiring teacher;
> - develop an awareness of the significance of the personal in the professional.

We commence by considering our different perspectives, with the intention of encouraging you to reflect on your own experiences.

WHAT INSPIRED YOU TO TRAIN TO BE A PRIMARY SCHOOL TEACHER?

As Teresa remembers:

I never intended to become a teacher. After studying psychology at Bristol University, I wanted to become an Educational Psychologist, but had to teach for three years before I could take the relevant Masters and qualify. So, I planned to do just that – become a teacher, work in classrooms for three years and move on. I hadn't reckoned on loving teaching. The opportunity to make relationships that mattered, to support youngsters on their life journeys and become imaginatively involved with different schools, communities and local authorities reoriented my career plans and in many ways, my life.

I was the first in my family to go to university, so was delighted when I got a PGCE place at Homerton College, Cambridge and had Morag Styles as my English tutor. She inspired me. In that manic year I re-found my love of reading, devoured children's literature, joined her Saturday poetry club for local children and much more. It was an extraordinary experience – demanding, exciting and rejuvenating. It felt like a serious party; we learnt about teaching and learning, about child development and we revisited many fascinating subjects I hadn't studied for years. In those pre-National Curriculum days, we could as teachers focus on topics of interest to the children (and ourselves) and the opportunities for innovation, exploration, storytelling and creativity abounded.

After nearly 80 applications, I got a post in Medway and lived locally on the housing estate which the school served. Many children came to school without breakfast, few had books at home, there was no local library and off duty I often bumped into children from my class. That felt strange at first, but gradually I became part of the community, ran a Guide group, umpired ladies' netball and set up some small book events. I tried to make personal connections with the children I taught – I wasn't the kind to stand on ceremony or create professional distance and wanted to develop a sense of authentic engagement.

As Helen remembers:

Volunteering in a school helped me realise that I wanted to be a primary teacher. At secondary school I didn't know what I wanted to do, and I chose to study English literature at university, because it was the subject which I enjoyed the most, with the thought that I might pursue something in journalism or theatre. However, during my time at university in Birmingham I began volunteering once a week in a school for children with special educational needs, taking several buses early in the morning to get there. I remember feeling quite nervous about everything in this unfamiliar environment, especially the complex needs of children in the setting, but was soon inspired by the wonderful, supportive atmosphere and the way that teachers, teaching assistants and volunteers worked together as part of an incredible, positive team. I was particularly motivated by the ways in which the staff adapted learning opportunities creatively to engage children with profound disabilities and personalise their learning.

Observing children experiencing success through different teaching strategies really made me notice how fulfilling it could be to help children to learn. It also became clear that every day in primary teaching was unique, never boring and required teachers to respond creatively to unexpected challenges. Getting to know how best to support children's learning and finding innovative ways to keep them interested and explain new ideas really appealed to me. As I entered the final year of my degree, I realised that I wanted to feel that my career was making a difference to society, and that helping children to succeed and enjoy learning as part of a caring primary school community, whatever their starting point, was what I wanted to do.

As Anna remembers:

What drew me into teaching? For me, there are strong family connections. My Granny was an early years' teacher, and my parents met each other at a teacher's union meeting as both were primary school teachers! In many ways, deciding to be a teacher was an instinctive choice as my family were so immersed in the profession. However, I think the most important reason for knowing this was *the* profession to belong to was having a strong desire to connect with children. I felt happy when I could see children's self-esteem increase. Observing children's 'learning leaps' always felt a privilege within a continuous cycle of teaching, learning and feedback. Importantly, I feel this same excitement of observing the teaching and learning cycles in action as I help to train future teachers.

More recently, I have been inspired by Katriona O'Sullivan's autobiographical book, *Poor* (2023), where she succeeds against her own family's deprivation. Yet, despite her parents' downward spiralling addictions, Katriona charts how many inspirational teachers encouraged her own journey, from Ms Arkinson in the reception class and the practical gifts needed to alleviate extreme poverty to Mr Pickering in secondary school, her English teacher who never gave up in believing that she could succeed. In Katriona's autobiography, there is a strong sense of teachers who are the fabric of a 'good' society and whose passion for personalised learning can cut through extreme poverty to enable individuals to flourish. I hold onto that belief that good teachers are the bedrock of a 'good' society where all can flourish regardless of their background.

So, three teachers and three very different motivational points for starting: In Teresa's case she changed career direction from wanting to become an Educational Psychologist when she fell in love with the teaching role; Helen, whilst not knowing precisely, found that work experiences drew her in and for Anna it seemed a natural decision based on her family's existing experiences of teaching.

Task 1.1.1 Reflecting on your starting points

Talk to a peer student and think through your own answers to these questions:

1. What has brought you here to start your own teaching journey?
2. Do you have any close friends or family who are already teachers…what are their experiences like?
3. What work experiences with children have you had already?
4. What did you learn from being with the children about how they learn?

WHAT DOES BECOMING A TEACHER MEAN TO YOU?

As we mentioned at the beginning of this chapter, teachers are all individuals and bring different strengths and experiences to their role. Some researchers argue 'we teach who we are' (Henriksen and Mishra, 2015), is that the case for you? The personal qualities, dispositions and attitudes of teachers at all points in their career impact on pupil learning (Ripski, LoCasale-Crouch and Decker, 2011; Day and Gu, 2014). One particular quality that researchers have seen to be important is 'professional commitment', especially in the face of difficult school circumstances, external pressure and work-life tensions (Day, 2008; Hunt, 2009; Day and Gu, 2014), but of course this will depend on the support and community around you and is not simply a personal characteristic. The ability to create respect and rapport with children is also central to effective teaching, as well as reflecting upon and adapting practice (Louden *et al.*, 2005; Coe *et al.*, 2014). Alongside personal qualities are essential teacher subject knowledge and pedagogy (considered throughout the book). Knowing how to explain and support subject knowledge through different teaching strategies and interaction is as important as understanding the subject in its own right.

As well as considering what you uniquely have to offer it might be useful to think about what the role of a teacher might be in a classroom in the 2020s and beyond? What do primary children need from their teachers? Researchers have suggested possibilities including:

- curriculum deliverers;
- concept builders;
- creative practitioners;
- reflective practitioners;
- possibility thinkers;
- passionate, principled, pedagogues;
- artistically engaged professionals.

Whatever your view, a teacher's role in school is more than facilitating learning; teachers are also part of the school community, networks of schools and the local community surrounding the school, often signposting support for families and working with other organisations to address community needs, or working with other schools on professional development (Hargreaves, 2019). A combination of the values and priorities motivating your classroom teaching, and the relationships and opportunities available within your school and wider community, will help to sustain your teaching journey.

WHAT HELPED US STAY WITHIN THE TEACHING PROFESSION?

As Teresa remembers:

Once I realised how much I loved teaching, I didn't plan to leave the classroom, and knew I didn't want to go down the leadership and management route, but was invited to help organise courses at a local teachers' centre and ended up doing that as a job share. I learnt so much about how to engage adult learners (or not!) and began to be interested in teaching and supporting teachers. Later I got a job as a staff development co-ordinator in the local authority and then moved to Canterbury Christchurch University to train student teachers and eventually, years later, to lead master's courses on literacy and literature. On this journey, I found myself making new relationships and became part of many communities of learners. Perhaps it was inevitable, therefore, that my research interests began to focus on the social and relational nature of literacy and on teachers' identities as readers, writers and artistically engaged professionals. My master's dissertation explored children's informal playful conversations about poetry and my PhD investigated children's voice and verve in writing. The ways we as teachers influence children's identities as learners remains a matter of deep fascination to me, and my most recent work and reading on teacher-student relatedness affirms the significance of relational connections for all learning.

As Helen remembers:

My teaching career was varied, including schools in Cornwall, Buckinghamshire and Slough, a small village primary school with around 100 pupils on roll, and a four-form entry infant school where 93% of pupils spoke English as an additional language. In each one I learned something new, particularly enjoying thinking about how to support those who might find school more difficult, e.g., how to support children learning English as an additional language and help new refugee families to make sense of the school system, or help to include children who experienced bereavement, or family addiction. I also learned about the communities and really valued building strong relationships with parents, finding new ways to involve them in classroom activities, such as using early morning and afterschool stay and play opportunities.

As Anna remembers:

My 14 years in the classroom started with a wonderful nursery setting in Clifton, Bristol where I remember planning for hours when I was given my first group to work with. After a formal PGCE training at Cambridge, I then enjoyed two teaching roles in different parts of Southwest London – Richmond and Hounslow. In both settings, one a C of E school and the other a multicultural school, I was fortunate to work with inspirational headteachers who afforded me a lot of freedom to contribute both for individual classes and to wider whole school roles. Even in my first year of teaching, I became the music co-ordinator helping to lead choirs and assemblies. Working with children to see their delight in learning new songs and performing them for wider audiences was a privilege. A few years into teaching, I co-ordinated a *Cats* musical (Lloyd Webber) and *Joseph and his Technicolour Dreamcoat* production (Lloyd Webber) – both productions were rewarding and creative. To see children sing, perform and act together, with their parents and carers' appreciation, was an act of pure creativity that few jobs can boast!

So, three teachers and three perspectives on staying within teaching: Teresa found the relational side of the teaching role became central and she valued that and sought to understand it better; Helen expanded her own experiences by teaching in very contrasting school settings and found that deeply enriching; and Anna's enjoyment of performance helped her design school musicals, which the children loved, too, making it feel like a win-win situation. You will no doubt find your own reasons for staying within teaching, for remaining committed to the enterprise of educating young (or older) people and experience your own unique satisfactions and pleasures on the journey. These may relate, for example, to the difference educators make to children's lives and life chances, the staff teams who you are privileged to work with and learn from in school, across a Trust, or the new knowledge you develop and seek to apply and adapt in different contexts through research and professional development. However, not everything can be plain sailing or smooth. The teacher you become will be shaped by your unique journey and how you handle the difficulties you experience. Rocky headwinds will inevitably surface in any career, so in this next section we all reflect on the challenges we faced and how we overcame them.

WHAT CHALLENGES DID WE OVERCOME?

As Teresa remembers:

As to challenges … I had plenty! I lacked confidence in teaching maths and science and rapidly came to rely on the science workcards which the children were expected to complete. I was barely one step ahead of them. So, I was delighted when in one three-form entry school, the deputy head led the science teaching in Year 6, and another colleague taught the RE, while I led a drama and literature course for each of the classes across the year. Developing this as a specialism was exciting and satisfying.

Another challenge was really getting to know the children. I recall one parents' evening when three parents described their children in words that I simply didn't recognise – who were these youngsters, I wondered? I was kidding myself I knew them; I didn't have a rounded picture of each child and was far too reliant on reading ages and maths test scores. It was a well-deserved jolt and made me work much harder – to listen more, to pay more attention and to make connections by offering opportunities to meet the children and their parents on their own terms, not on mine. This remains a challenge for all of us as educators, with learners of whatever age, for without genuine relationships, shared knowledge, respect and trust, teaching and learning are not nearly as effective.

As Helen remembers:

My biggest challenge was at the beginning of my career when I first started teaching in a school next to a large RAF base, full of children who had already changed schools several times, sometimes starting school outside of the UK, and whose families were often under emotional and organisational strain as one parent worked away, sometimes in conflict zones. Often children's individual needs were not known as they joined the school, and class members changed regularly. I struggled to know how best to support the unpredictable behaviour in my class of 7-year-olds: one was silent and withdrawn, one hid under tables, another ran around the room or threw things, seemingly finding it funny to disrupt. Sadly, I received limited support from senior colleagues. I soon lost the confidence and enthusiasm I had experienced during my training. However, my earlier experiences in very different school environments gave me the determination to continue. I took advice from friends, colleagues and a friendly school improvement advisor who came to observe me, and I slowly started to get to know the children's individual personalities and find ways to make learning enjoyable for them (and me). I favoured practical investigations across different topics and learning outside which engaged some of my class new to English, new to the school system and not yet ready for a more formal classroom.

From this very challenging experience, I learnt that I needed to be in a school where the leadership team and I had the same values; after two years I was excited to gain a new role in a mainstream community primary school with a unit for pupils with disabilities. Working with this staff team was incredibly different. I had frequent opportunities for additional training, worked with a supportive team of like-minded individuals, and am still friends with my parallel class teacher from this school, now nearly 30 years later. I learned so much from the external experts who helped each teacher to include individuals with cerebral palsy, Down Syndrome and other physical and sensory needs into their class. I worked closely with speech and language therapists, learned about alternative communication and also became part of the local community, where parents made me feel welcomed and valued.

As Anna remembers:

The biggest challenge I have had over my teaching and lecturing career has been fitting everything into 12-hour days! In other words, balancing all the ideas I have had for contributing to schools or university against my own capacity levels. So, I think taking all the advice about time management and finding ways for relaxation and restoration are critical. The primary teaching job is one of service to children, parents and the community. At the heart of the teaching role, is YOU. So, looking after yourself is genuinely important.

A constant thread within my professional experience has been my own love of learning. In my third year of teaching, I embarked on a distance learning diploma course on Children's Literature and Language at Cambridge University. It is never easy to combine more work on top of an already full teaching role, but it was essential for me to keep learning, it expanded my own horizons and enriched what I could offer the children. Working with one class is an enormous privilege but it is an insular experience too, very rooted in one area, one town, one place. Researching and reading about how to develop children's literacy skills using media at that time was a broadening experience and I would encourage you to take advantage of all the opportunities that come your way for Continuous Professional Development. It is a challenge to fit it in, but it is invaluable, and part of your responsibility as a professional.

Each of us, on our journeys thus far as educators, has built on our experiences in life and tried to make use of these and our own sense of self in our teaching - whether that has been with children, young people or adults. Your own perspective on education and what you might uniquely offer will depend on your conception of teaching. Do you see it as an 'objective science' (Coe and Waring, 2017) or perhaps you view teaching as an art form, as Richards (2018: 8) does? He notes teaching is 'a complex creative enterprise concerned with the promotion of human learning and involving imagination, sensitivity and personal response'.

We view it as engaging artistic and professional enterprise, with recognisable science, craft and relational elements. We also consider it is almost impossible 'to remove the humans from the enterprise, the children from the learning, the teacher from the teaching, the personal from the professional' (Cremin, 2019: 260). For that reason, what you bring to the profession matters. You matter.

Task 1.1.2 Reflections

Reflect on these questions with a peer student:

1 What makes you unique and special, what do you feel you personally bring to the profession?
2 What challenges are you concerned about for learning to be a teacher at this time?
3 What sort of teaching opportunities, school community or wider community involvement might sustain and support your journey?

Recognising your skills, passions and interests, however minor they may seem to you, is a critical first step in appreciating that you bring something special and unique to the profession. Can you recall a teacher whose particular enthusiasm was conveyed so effectively that you became interested in their particular subject? Perhaps you can also remember a teacher who somehow connected to you, was on your wavelength and made you feel they valued and respected you? Did they influence your journey as a learner? If so, what might this suggest to you about teaching and learning?

A recent three-year study of reading and writing for pleasure underscored the marked significance of adults' responsive involvement in children as readers and writers (Cremin et al., 2023). Those adults who were particularly successful in helping children develop positive identities as readers and/

or writers were those who engaged effectively and through their behaviour showed that they were interested in and appreciated the young people's perspectives – their views on a text and their ideas for writing, for instance. These educators often had expansive understandings of reading and writing, and strong values linked to addressing disadvantage and social justice.

You will also want to consider your beliefs and values. You do not have to leave your values or sense of self at the school gate; you can and should be genuinely engaged, both personally and professionally, in the classroom.

> ### Task 1.1.3 Values
>
> Here are some values that may be underpinning your decision to be a teacher:
>
> - Making a difference;
> - Being authentic;
> - Caring for young children;
> - Enjoying challenges;
> - Promoting peace;
> - Fighting injustice;
> - Encouraging fair play.
>
> If you can only choose three values, what would they be and why?
>
> Is there another values statement you feel is missing, one that expresses your stance more effectively?
>
> Discuss these with a peer also training to be a teacher, and looking at the chapter titles in the book, see which relate most closely so you can dip into those later.

MOVING ONWARDS AND MAKING BEST USE OF THIS TEXT

In compiling this book and reviewing and updating its contents for this fifth edition of *Learning to Teach in the Primary School*, we aimed not only to offer you practical advice and support, but also a rationale for why such advice might be useful, where it comes from, on what basis it has been formulated and how you might evaluate its usefulness. Teaching is never a neutral activity; it is always informed by experiences, values, beliefs and commitments, and the recommendations and perspectives found in this handbook are no exception. A rich range of experienced and talented professionals – researchers, academics, teacher educators, headteachers and current classroom teachers – have all worked to offer you their expertise, advice and talents. Nonetheless, we hope that as you read and discuss the chapters you will reflect critically on the perspectives shared, and in the process review your own beliefs and commitments as well as find inspiration for translating these into practice. Teaching is a highly skilled, knowledgeable, professional activity.

The book will help move you on in your development as a professional by providing you with background insights into a range of issues that affect the decisions you make in the classroom, and illustrating how such insights affect your classroom practice. Our intention is that this book will work alongside the other experiences on your journey, providing a practical introduction to the complex knowledge, skills, understanding and attitudes that teachers need to acquire, and to the theories underpinning them. In this new edition, we have strengthened chapters with more case study examples, more reflective tasks to support you to link the ideas to your own practice, and the inclusion of new knowledge. We have included new chapters that respond to wider educational changes and contemporary issues in society and schools.

Do make use of the book flexibly – some chapters may be set by your tutors as pre-reading or follow up for taught sessions or work in schools, but you can also dip into others to widen your knowledge and understanding, in response to need or interest. You might even gather colleagues in reading groups to discuss particular chapters or make use of some as support for assignments. However you use it, we hope it will help inspire in you the same deep interest in and commitment to primary education that the three of us and all our generous contributors voice.

Education is an endlessly fascinating subject, and, of course, teaching children is a highly challenging and creative activity. Enjoy the experience – we hope it will be engaging and satisfying for all involved and that this book will support you on your professional learning journey as a primary teacher.

Editorial Note:

References throughout the book to the CCF and ECF frameworks (England only) from September 2025 relate to this new document. Please see https://www.gov.uk/government/publications/initial-teacher-training-and-early-career-framework

REFERENCES

Coe R. and Waring M. (2017) *Research Methods and Methodologies in Education*, London: Sage.

Coe, R., Aloisi, C., Higgins, S. and Major, L. E. (2014) *What Makes Great Teaching? Review of the Underpinning Research*, London: Sutton Trust. Retrieved from: www.suttontrust.com/researcharchive/great-teaching/

Cremin, T. (2019) 'The personal in the professional', in S. Ogier and T. Eaude (eds) *The Broad and Balanced Curriculum*, London: Sage, pp. 259-270.

Cremin, T., Hendry, H., Chamberlain, L. and Hulston, S. (2023) *Reading and Writing for Pleasure: A Framework for Practice: Executive Summary*. Funded by the Mercers' Company. Retrieved from: https://cdn.ourfp.org/wp-content/uploads/20231201185032/Reading-and-Writing-for-Pleasure_FRAMEWORK-DIGITAL-FINAL-30.11.23.pdf

Day, C. (2008) 'Committed for life? Variations in teachers' work, lives and effectiveness', *Journal of Educational Change*, 9(3): 243-260.

Day, C. and Gu, Q. (2014) 'Response to Margolis, Hodge and Alexandrou: Misrepresentations of teacher resilience and hope', *Journal of Education for Teaching*, 40(4): 409-412.

Hargreaves, A. (2019) 'Teacher collaboration: 30 years of research on its nature, forms, limitations and effects', *Teachers and Teaching, Theory and Practice*, 25(5): 603-621.

Henriksen, D. and Mishra, P. (2015) 'We teach who we are: Creativity in the lives and practices of accomplished teachers', *Teachers College Record*, 117(7): 1-46.

Hunt, B. (2009) *Teacher Effectiveness: A Review of the International Literature and its Relevance for Improving Education in Latin America*. Washington DC: PREAL. Retrieved from: https://thedialogue.org/analysis/teacher-effectiveness/

Louden, B., Rohl, E., Barratt-Pugh, C., Brown, C., Cairney, T., Elderfield, J., House, H., Meiers, M., Rivalland, J. and Rowe, K. (2005) 'In teachers' hands: Effective literacy teaching practices in the early years of schooling', *Australian Journal of Language and Literacy*, 28(3): 181-252.

O'Sullivan, K. (2023) *Poor*. Sandycove imprint within Penguin Random House.

Richards, C. (2018) 'Primary teaching: A personal perspective' in T. Cremin and C. Burnett (eds) *Learning to Teach in the Primary School*, 4th edn, London: Routledge, pp. 5-16.

Ripski, M. B., LoCasale-Crouch, J. and Decker, L. (2011) 'Pre-service teachers: Dispositional traits, emotional states, and quality of student teacher interactions', *Teacher Education Quarterly*, 38(2): 77-96.

UNIT 1.2

BECOMING A PROFESSIONAL IN THE CURRENT CONTEXT

Janet Goepel and Sally Hinchliff

There is so much more to becoming a teacher who truly *feels like* a real professional than meets the eye! While becoming a teacher requires you to meet certain standards, becoming a professional involves grappling with the behaviours, knowledge, skills and (most importantly) beliefs and values. Attitudes inform actions, therefore gaining an understanding of them will enable you to be confident in your professional decisions and actions, leading you to *feel* like you are a professional.

This unit will help you examine your journey to becoming a true professional, including knowledge and skills required, as well as the challenges and tensions you are likely to face along the way.

OBJECTIVES

By the end of this unit, you should be able to:

- understand that the term 'professionalism' has multiple definitions;
- make sense of what this means to you in your own route to teaching in a range of different professional contexts;
- begin to explore your own developing professionalism within an ever changing political and practice-based context.

WHAT DO THEORY AND RESEARCH TELL US ABOUT PROFESSIONALISM?

We all have notions as to what we mean by 'being professional'. For most of us this includes ways in which we behave and present ourselves, including, for example, how we dress. It also includes what we do and how we do it: for example, what time we arrive and how much preparation we have done beforehand. We consider someone to be professional if they carry out a required task well and if they are polite and punctual. They often require some distinct or expert knowledge or skill that guides professional practice (Hilferty, 2008: 162). The most basic definition of being professional for teachers is of being paid to teach (Tichenor and Tichenor, 2005: 90). This idea is similar to how someone who practises their sport as their means of income is viewed and is in contrast to an amateur who might be involved in their sport in their spare time but for whom this is not their source of income. However, it is also suggested that being professional involves high standards of delivery (Demirkasimoğlu, 2010: 2048), and that this means still being professional even 'when no-one is looking' (Hargreaves and Fullan, 2012: 5). Smith and Skarbek (2013) identify the dispositions they consider to be necessary for effective teacher professionalism. These are empathy, caring, love, enthusiasm, humour and optimism. Such dispositions emphasise the relational aspect of teaching but are much more difficult to quantify and assess. In the current climate of accountability, such measures of professionalism rarely feature yet could be argued as fundamental to professional practice.

Boylan et al.'s (2023) research reminds us that the concept of teacher professionalism is complex and hard to conceptualise. Their analysis of professionalism could be categorised broadly into two types: one version which encourages the teacher to think critically, to be autonomous, to work collectively with colleagues and to be an agent for change; and on the other hand, a version of professionalism which is more directed and framed by the regulation of government policy. To unravel this complexity, it is helpful for the beginning teacher seeking to grasp what professionalism 'means' for their practice to understand professional practice as both multifaceted and dynamic. This premise will help you to develop a nuanced and flexible understanding of professionalism.

Although theoretical perspectives might help to form a definition of professionalism, it is interesting to consider what teachers themselves consider professionalism to be and look like. One study found that teachers identified characteristics such as being resilient, keeping composure, being caring, nurturing, friendly, patient, well organised and open to new ideas as important expressions of being professional (Tichenor and Tichenor, 2005). Additionally, this study found that teachers thought that being professional involved being a good communicator with parents and children, being a good role model and showing respect. A study by Poet, Rudd and Kelly (2010) found that teachers felt they had a professional responsibility to improve their practice, and that they had an intrinsic desire to do the best job they could in becoming a better teacher and in meeting the needs of their pupils. The use of self-reflection as well as peer feedback was seen as an important tool for developing professional practice.

What is clear is that the definition of professionalism is subject to change over time, through different influences, such as political and social change, and from different perspectives (Demirkasimoğlu, 2010: 2050). An important element of being able to be fully professional is concerned with having the authority to decide how to carry out practice, to be autonomous. Appleby and Pilkington (2014) outline that being a professional 'can provide an individual and collective identity with agreed values, recognised responsibilities and acceptable or required behaviour' (p.11). This in turn provides a sense of belonging to the profession, as well as opportunity for individual professional identity to be developed.

Task 1.2.1 How does this theory and research influence your own view of professionalism?

Based on the definitions of professionalism given earlier, and teachers' own views of professionalism as shown in the research, write your own definition of professionalism.

How will this definition of professionalism influence your practice as a trainee teacher?

WHAT INFLUENCES HAVE YOU EXPERIENCED IN YOUR JOURNEY TOWARDS BECOMING A TEACHER?

> **Task 1.2.2 Plotting your journey to becoming a teacher to date**
>
> Draw a horizontal line across a paper. Mark the right-hand end as being TODAY – where you are right now on your journey to being a teacher.
>
> 1. The left-hand end of the line should be the first point in your life you can identify as being formative in your decision to become a teacher – even though it was probably not the point at which you decided. For example, it could be an inspirational teacher or experience you had as a pupil, a series of baby-sitting experiences when you realised you were fascinated by young children, something in your studies that made you inspired to help others learn, and so on.
> 2. On this line, add other key points in your life that you think have played a role in helping you decide what kind of teacher you would like to become.
> 3. Add other key points in your life that you think have played a role in helping you decide the kind of teacher you *don't* want to become (in both cases, try not to restrict your experiences to things that have just involved teachers and consider broader influences).
> 4. Compare with someone else on your course – what are the similarities and differences?
> 5. Looking ahead to the next bit of the line – the next steps on your journey to becoming a teacher – what kinds of experience and support do you think you need to become the kind of teacher you want to be?
> 6. Has the process of looking back and thinking forwards raised any interesting thoughts or questions? Have your ideals about the 'perfect teacher' changed over time?

PROFESSIONAL BODIES AND PROFESSIONALISM IN THE UK

TABLE 1.2.1 Table showing a comparison of the professional standards required of the four different countries of the UK

England		
Documentation	Professional aims & Expectations	Quotations to consider
The Teachers' Standards (DfE, 2011)	Teachers' Standard 8: 'Fulfil wider professional responsibilities: make a positive contribution to the wider life of the school; deploy support staff effectively; improve teaching through Professional Development; communicate effectively with parents. Part 2: 'Personal and Professional Conduct' (e.g. safeguarding)	'Teachers must uphold public trust in the profession and maintain high standards of ethics and behaviour.'

(Continued)

TABLE 1.2.1 (Continued)

England		
Documentation	Professional aims & Expectations	Quotations to consider
The Core Content Curriculum (DfE, 2019)	Domain of 'Professional Behaviours' (Mirrors Teachers' Standard 8. 'Learn how to' statements direct how these behaviours should be enacted.)	'Learn how to develop as a professional, by receiving clear, consistent, and effective mentoring in how to engage in professional development with clear intentions for impact on pupil outcomes.'
Scotland		
A Guide to the Professional Standards: General Teaching Council for Scotland (GTC; 2021)	To create a shared language for teaching professionals, as a benchmark for professional competency. The professional values of 'Social Justice', 'Trust & Respect' and 'Integrity' are referenced.	'Commitment to reflecting on the connections between values and actions and career-long professional learning is a critical part of developing teacher professionalism.'
Wales		
An Introduction to the Professional Standards for Teaching and Leadership: Welsh Government (2018)	Values & dispositions of: Welsh Language & Culture, Professional Entitlement, Rights of Learners, Literacy, Numeracy & Digital Competence	[teacher] 'knowledge, skills and understanding and can show how reflection and openness to challenge and support informs professional learning to progressively develop pedagogy.'
Northern Ireland		
GTCNI Digest of the Teachers Competencies: General Teaching Council for Northern Ireland (GTCNI; 2018)	Signposts a 'Code of Values'. These values are expressed as competencies: 'Trust', 'Honesty', 'Commitment', 'Excellence', 'Respect', 'Fairness', 'Equality', 'Dignity', 'Tolerance', 'Integrity' and 'Service'.	'A commitment to serve lies at the heart of professional behaviour.' […] 'recognising in particular the unique and privileged relationship that exists between teachers and their pupils.'

It is interesting to reflect upon the similarities and differences of these professional standards, and what this means for the professional development of a trainee teacher, depending upon where he/she is located.

HOW IS TEACHER PROFESSIONAL IDENTITY DEVELOPED?

There are many factors that influence the kind of professional you may become, and the starting point is your own identity. Each of us has multiple identities that involve our ethnicity, gender, religion, culture, position in the family and other relationships. These identities form who you are, your values and your behaviours. As you begin to take on the professional identity of a teacher, your own personal identity will transform into this new, but ever-evolving personal and professional identity. It is a process that is never completed, no matter how long you are a teacher.

Steinert *et al.* (2014) consider that the process of developing a personal, professional identity is through socialisation and is represented in the following model.

As can be seen from Figure 1.2.1, it is through this process that you will move from peripheral participation within the profession to becoming a full participant.

It is easy as a trainee teacher to be unquestioning about what you are required to do in order to become a professional. However, as shown in the socialisation model, the process of becoming a professional is not without its tensions and challenges, each of which needs to be negotiated, accepted or rejected, or a compromise must be reached. Clark states boldly that, 'student teachers must, first and foremost, be disabused of any illusions they may have that their education system is either designed or equipped to turn them into the very best teacher they can be. They must do this for themselves'

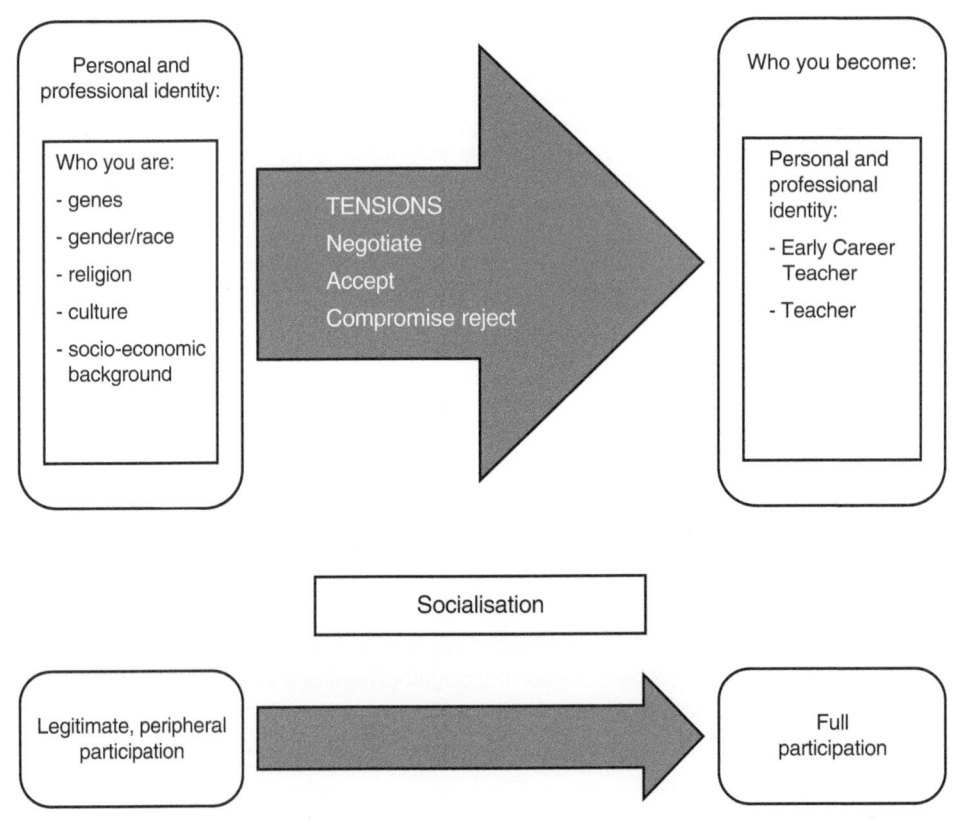

FIGURE 1.2.1 Taking on professional identity through socialisation
Source: Adapted from Steinert *et al.* (2014)

(2016: 41). However, she goes on to acknowledge that teachers must accept the expectations placed upon them, but that they should have the freedom to interpret them within the complexity of the workplace and through the uniqueness of the individual who is becoming professional.

Task 1.2.3 Developing professionalism

Consider the diagram in Figure 1.2.1.

1. What personal characteristics make up your personal identity?
2. What challenges and tensions have you faced already in developing professionalism?
3. Consider whether you accepted, rejected, negotiated or found a compromise for these challenges.
4. Why did you make the decision you did about these challenges or tensions?

A similar model of developing a professional identity as a teacher is outlined by Hargreaves and Fullen (2012). They call the personal characteristics of the socialisation model (Steinert et al., 2014) human capital. This is concerned with personal resources such as being caring, friendly, patient and resilient. The socialisation process is concerned with the importance of developing relationships with colleagues and others in the learning community, such as parents, teaching assistants and professionals from other agencies. Such relationships are seen as a resource, a way of increasing knowledge and generating trust between different groups of people. This is referred to as building social capital (Hargreaves and Fullan, 2012: 90) and is an essential element of collaborative practice.

A third element of developing a professional identity is called decisional capital. This is developed over time and relates to the ability to make 'discretionary judgements' (Hargreaves and Fullen, 2012: 92), to make wise decisions where there are no guidelines or given ways of managing a situation. Together, human capital, social capital and decisional capital make up professional capital, which is considered to be a vital concept in bringing together what is required to produce high standards for teachers. It is through the development of decisional capital that teachers also develop a sense of professional agency and autonomy.

Task 1.2.4 Building social capital through collaborative practice

1. How can you build relationships of trust with teachers, teaching assistants, parents and children?
2. What knowledge, insights and understanding have you gained through working with teachers, teaching assistants, parents and children on placement?
3. How has building social capital with others in your placement school helped you to develop your professional identity as a teacher?

As you begin to take on a professional identity as a teacher, it is likely that you will become aware of challenges and tensions that require you to respond to them. As already identified through Steinert's socialisation model, such responses could be negotiation, acceptance, compromise or rejection.

Professional identity tensions are considered to be 'internal struggles between the teacher as a person and the teacher as a professional' and as such create 'identity dissonance' (Pillen, Den Brok and Beijaard, 2013: 86-87). These dissonances may not be readily reconcilable as they are linked with a teacher's values, beliefs and perceptions and may challenge who you are. Although these tensions by their very nature may be uncomfortable or stressful, they are instrumental in developing professionalism in a way that adhering to the Core Content Framework (Department for Education [DfE], 2019) or Teachers' Standards (DfE, 2011) may not. An example of tensions that may occur for you as a trainee teacher is shown in the following story.

Esha's story

Esha was in the early days of training to teach in her first placement of her PGCE. She had previously worked as a teaching assistant for a year in an Early Years setting before starting on her course. In this pre course experience she had seen how the class teacher in reception had used 'Continuous Provision' to help the 3- and 4-year-olds to access learning, creating a well-planned learning environment which encouraged the children to follow their own interests and express their own ideas. However, now in the placement school, based in FS2 (Foundation Stage 2 – reception), Esha realised that there was barely any Continuous Provision set up for the children. Instead, the children spent extended periods of time either seated on the carpet or at tables following whole class, teacher-led input which predominantly consisted of phonics and maths, communicated via commercially produced PowerPoint resources. In her observations of these sessions, Esha noted that that many of the children lost their concentration after around 10–15 minutes of input: some became physically restless, some exhibited low level disruptive 'off task' behaviour, others were passive, appearing completely disengaged, and a few became visibly upset – for example when they were told off for 'not paying attention'. The children's responses concerned Esha and remembering back to her implementation of Continuous Provision, she decided she would suggest that her teacher might permit her to include more personalised provision for different learners, drawing on her prior knowledge and experience. However, Esha's offer was not received well. The class teacher told her she had to abide by the school policy which mandated a significant percentage of curriculum time for phonics, early writing and number. She reminded Esha that the school had to conduct the I Phonics Screening Check (www.gov.uk/government/publications/phonics-screening-check-2023-materials) in a few weeks and that it was crucial that the children had time to practice and to make progress. She emphasised too that this cohort of children had 'fallen behind' due to the Covid 19 pandemic and that the school and national priority was that they should be enabled to 'catch up'. The teacher added that the children always had 'some time to play' at the end of the day. Esha found this situation created a tension between the values she held concerning the developmental needs of 3- and 4-year-olds (for her, a need to 'learn through play') and the requirements of her current placement school. Esha felt as if she was at a crossroads: she desperately wanted to continue to train to be a teacher in the Early Years, but at the same time didn't know how she could reconcile her deeply held values around practice with the ones she would need to adopt to continue.

Esha is obviously experiencing 'identity dissonance', and research with beginning teachers (Alsup, 2006; Kelchtermans, 2005; Moore, 2018) reports that this experience is far from uncommon for those new to the profession. Esha will need to find a way of managing the

> relationships with others in the school, identify what she is willing to compromise in terms of her values and practice, negotiate differences of practice and expectation and allow this experience to shape her professional identity. Looking ahead, Esha may need to consider carefully the educational philosophy of the institution where she would hope to work as an Early Career teacher (ECT), and to research how it aligns with her own.

How you respond to identity dissonances you encounter will influence the kind of professional you will become, and in negotiating your way through these tensions, you will develop a stronger sense of belonging to the profession (Steinert et al., 2014).

WHAT ARE THE INFLUENCES AND COMPLEXITIES OF DEVELOPING PROFESSIONALISM?

As we have already seen, the process of developing one's professional identity is not straight forward. The formation of this emerging dimension within your identity will often be hard 'emotional work' (Britzman, 2003): you will face dilemma and tensions in the classroom, you will grapple with how you can reconcile your personal values with school or national educational policy which is at odds with these values and you will need to be ever open to feedback on your practice – even if sometimes you would rather not hear it! In sum, 'becoming professional' is more complicated than simply adhering to a list of professional standards, for whilst these standards provide a framework which will help you to make the concept of teacher professionalism more concrete and less abstract, you will still have to work through the complexity yourself. Indeed, research into beginning teachers' emerging identity (Alsup, 2006; Britzman, 2003; Bukor, 2015) suggests that becoming a professional is a very personal process. As Bukor (2015: 310) writes, 'The practicum [teacher training] is a unique time, not only do they test themselves as teachers, but as human beings.'

To help you negotiate this maze we have provided another framework of our own which identifies three key influences which we suggest mould emerging professional identity for the new teacher.

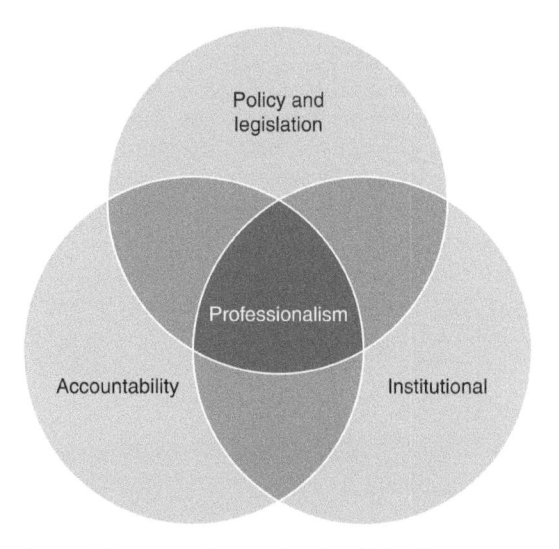

FIGURE 1.2.2 Key influences in moulding emerging professional identity

In this next section, we examine the three areas of policy and legislation, accountability and the role of the institution, all the time asking you to pause and reflect upon how these powerful forces might impact your professional journey.

POLICY: THE CORE CONTENT FRAMEWORK AND THE TEACHERS' STANDARDS

Possibly the most influential policy document for you on your professional journey to becoming a qualified teacher (an ECT) is the Initial Teacher Training Core Content Framework (CCF; DfE, 2019). As we will go on to see, this statutory framework contains a clearly defined section on *'Professional Behaviours'* and the associated expectations for you as a trainee teacher.

It is worth noting that the CCF is part of recent, deep-reaching governmental reform of English Initial Teacher Education (ITE; Ellis, 2023). With this context in mind, the new curriculum for ITE needs to be understood as a ground-breaking education policy document and one which is likely to strongly influence your journey to Qualified Teacher Status (QTS) as a trainee teacher. Whilst the CCF is now a mandatory requirement for all trainee teachers in England, at the time of writing, debates around its ideological principles and delivery are widespread and complex (Ellis, 2023; Hordern and Brooks, 2023). It is possible that future educational research will throw further critical light on the efficacy and impact of the CCF, but for the present what we can be sure of is that the CCF is now 'centre stage' in the process of training to teach, and understanding its purpose and its delivery is an essential professional expectation for the beginning teacher. Moreover, we argue that only as an informed stake holder of the CCF can you as the trainee teacher truly engage with your curriculum on a professional level; that is to say as an active and critical participant! As UCET (Universities' Council for the Education of Teachers) argues, teaching needs to be an intellectual profession, one which values teachers as thinkers and reflective practitioners, and one which develops professionals who 'make meaningful contributions to the professional knowledge base' (UCET, 2019: 1).

What do we know about the CCF?

- It is a curriculum framework, **not** an assessment tool. At the summative point of the initial training period (e.g. PGCE; Teach First Year 1; BA, year 3), Qualified Teacher Status (QTS) is assessed against the Teachers' Standards (2011).
- It is a generic document which covers a school age range of 3–16 years – thus there is no bespoke primary version of the CCF (although individual providers and schools may provide this).
- It represents the first year of a three-year training and induction package. It is followed by the Early Career Framework (ECF), which now structures the development of ECTs in their first two years of qualified teaching.
- It is a 'minimum entitlement' (DfE, 2019: 3). It does not aim to set out the full Initial Teacher Training (ITT) curriculum for trainee teachers, acknowledging that this would be an impossibility considering the complexity and nuance of training to teach. Nevertheless, the CCF clearly sets out the essential professional knowledge needed to become a qualified teacher (DfE, 2019).

How does the CCF prepare you to be a teacher?

From the outset it is important that the trainee teacher understands the twin concepts of *'learn that'* and *'learn how'*, as these two sentence starters underpin the entirety of the CCF.

- The '**Learn that**' statements identify the underpinning core knowledge necessary for the trainee teacher; that is to say, the *theoretical underpinning* of practice in the classroom. Much of this

knowledge will be embedded in the university seminars, lectures and tutorials which are part of the learning to teach process, but equally this learning could take place in school, for example through discussions with your mentor.
- The '**Learn how to**' statements relate to how this underpinning knowledge can be enacted *in practice*, in the process of training to teach, in school. This learning is achieved through observing and analysing the models provided by 'expert colleagues' in school who are central to the training process (mentors, class teachers, curriculum leads, etc.).

The curriculum is also comprised of five 'domains' of knowledge for the trainee teacher. These are:

1. Behaviour Management
2. Pedagogy (How pupils learn, Classroom practice, Adaptive teaching)
3. Curriculum
4. Assessment
5. Professional Behaviours

The 'learn that' and 'learn how to' statements are integrated into all elements of these five domains. In turn, the domains relate directly to the eight Teachers' Standards (which, as mentioned earlier, form the summative assessment for QTS). For example, the domain of 'Professional Behaviours' corresponds with both Teachers' Standard 8, and Part 2 of the Teachers' Standards. By following the CCF expectations, trainees should be working towards the expectations of the summative assessment framework of the Teachers' Standards.

What are the pedagogical principles of the CCF?

- As you start to read through the detail of the CCF you will see that 'great teaching' (DfE, 2019: 3) is defined clearly, some would argue rigidly (Ellis, 2023).
- There is a strong emphasis on prior learning, structured sequential learning, support for the acquisition of a 'core body of knowledge' through memorisation and the importance of Cognitive Load Theory (CLT).
- The goals of improving pupil outcomes and of tackling 'disadvantage' permeate the curriculum document (DfE, 2019).

How does the CCF define your professional expectations?

Having got to grips with the fundamentals of the CCF we will now move on to look at the fifth domain of the CCF, 'Professional Behaviours', exploring how this fundamental dimension of becoming a teacher is articulated for you. Next we list the seven sub-areas of 'Professional Behaviours' which trainees are expected to understand as central components of their professional knowledge (DfE, 2019: 29-31).

Learn that:

1. Effective professional development is likely to be sustained over time, involve expert support or coaching and opportunities for collaboration.
2. Reflective practice, supported by feedback from and observation of experienced colleagues, professional debate and learning from educational research, is also likely to support improvement.
3. Teachers can make valuable contributions to the wider life of the school in a broad range of ways, including by supporting and developing effective professional relationships with colleagues.

4 Building effective relationships with parents, carers and families can improve pupils' motivation, behaviour and academic success.
5 Teaching assistants (TAs) can support pupils more effectively when they are prepared for lessons by teachers, and when TAs supplement rather than replace support from teachers.
6 Special Educations Needs Coordinators (SENCOs), pastoral leaders, careers advisors and other specialist colleagues also have valuable expertise and can ensure that appropriate support is in place for pupils.
7 Engaging in high-quality professional development can help teachers improve.

What values underpin these professional behaviours?

From an analysis of these seven sub-areas, we suggest that in the CCF, a trainee teacher's professional behaviours are premised on the following four values:

- The value of **ongoing professional development**, in its many forms.
- The value of **reflective practice**.
- The value of engaging with **the wider world of the school**.
- The value of **professional relationships**: collaboration with a wide range of colleagues and with parents and carers.

Task 1.2.5 Putting professional values into practice

We believe it is important that as a developing professional you engage with and have ownership of the principles which underpin your practice and your curriculum, so we want you to reflect on how these four professional behaviours might be experienced during your training. For each value, imagine a scenario in school where you could demonstrate this particular dimension of professional behaviour

Your next step is to read the 'learn how to' statements for Professional Behaviours so that in addition to your own reflections, you have a full understanding of the CCF expectations for this domain. The following list provides some examples of how 'Professional Behaviours' can be enacted according to the CCF (DfE, 2019: 30) in the process of training to teach:

- Extending subject and pedagogical knowledge through conversations with your mentor and access to wider networks.
- Seeking feedback from expert colleagues on all dimensions of practice.
- Reflecting on practice: expressly in relation to support for pupil practice.
- Engaging critically with research to support professional learning.
- Building effective relationships with a range of colleagues: teaching assistants; SENCO; and with parents and carers.
- Understanding safeguarding responsibilities beyond your own classroom, and across the wider world of the school.
- Understanding the role of the teacher and other colleagues involved in pastoral care.
- Managing workload and wellbeing.
- Collaborating with colleagues, for example in the planning of lessons.

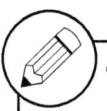

Task 1.2.6 Thinking about the 'learn that' and 'learn how to' statements

Although the CCF is a new development in the training of teachers in England, already, as is often the case with a significant educational policy change, the Framework is starting to be scrutinised, critiqued and evaluated by researchers. Here, for example, Steadman (2023) argues that the process of training to teach is much more complex than the 'learn that' and 'learn how to' CCF statements suggest: 'For teachers, discovery of their professional self will never be found solely in the individual mastery of the "learn that" and "learn how to" statements of the CCF [and the ECF]' (Steadman, 2023: 174).

Reflecting on this viewpoint, and looking carefully at the 'learn that' and 'learn how to' statements for the domain of 'Professional Behaviours', consider the following questions:

1 To what extent do you agree with the writer? Why?
2 What other influences or experiences beyond the individual mastery of the 'learn that' and 'learn how to' statements could promote the development of the professional self?
3 How might such influences or experiences be encouraged?

What is the role of the Teachers' Standards?

As stated earlier, the CCF mirrors both Part 1 and Part 2 of the Teachers' Standards. Qualified Teacher Status (QTS) is given at the end of a successful completion of training and is awarded against the Teachers' Standards (2011, revised 2021). A summary of the Teachers' Standards can be seen in Table 1.2.2.

TABLE 1.2.2 A summary of the Teachers' Standards

Part 1: TEACHING	Part 2: PERSONAL AND PROFESSIONAL CONDUCT Behaviour and attitudes
A teacher must:	Teachers uphold public trust by:
1 Set high expectations which inspire, motivate and challenge pupils	• Treating pupils with dignity, building relationships rooted in mutual respect
2 Promote good outcomes and progress by pupils	• Having regard for safeguarding pupils according to statutory provisions
3 Demonstrate good subject and curriculum knowledge	• Showing tolerance and respect for the rights of others
4 Plan and teach well-structured lessons	• Not undermining fundamental British values
5 Adapt teaching to respond to the strengths and needs of all pupils	• Ensuring personal beliefs are not expressed in ways which exploit pupils' vulnerability
6 Make accurate and productive use of assessment	
7 Manage behaviour effectively to ensure a good and safe learning environment	Teachers must have proper and professional regard for the ethos, policies and practices of the school in which they teach.
8 Fulfil wider professional responsibilities	Teachers must have an understanding of, and always act within, statutory frameworks

Source: DfE (2011)

In achieving these standards by the end of the ITE phase, you are expected to take on the values and behaviours they set out and, by doing so, to be accepted into the profession. However, it is important to recognise that fulfilling the Standards is only part of what becoming a professional teacher is about. Becoming a professional is a process that begins as you start your course to learn to become a teacher and continues throughout your professional life.

ACCOUNTABILITY: OFSTED

Throughout the UK, state education is a service which is paid for through public taxation (as is the case with the National Health Service, social care and the prison service); as such, schools are accountable for how they spend this money – that is to say, for the quality of education and the 'value for money' which they provide. The Office for Standards in Education, Children's Services and Skills (Ofsted) is a non-ministerial department of His Majesty's government, reporting to Parliament, whose role is to make sure that organisations providing education, training and childcare services in England do so to a high standard for children and students –Ofsted's role is to judge that public funds are 'well spent'. Ofsted publishes reports on the quality of education and management at a particular school and organisation on a regular basis. If you have been in a school where they are 'due Ofsted', you will know that this can be a very challenging and stressful time for the whole of the school workforce. At the time of writing, the future of Ofsted in its current form, with its significant powers which impact profoundly on the future of a school (a failed Ofsted inspection can result in the removal of the head teacher and enforced academisation), is under much scrutiny at national level (Perryman et al., 2023). At this stage we cannot predict whether Ofsted's remit will change, but what we do know is that as a public service schools will remain accountable and will be asked to demonstrate this accountability. Without doubt the weight of this accountability falls on the shoulders of the head teacher and their senior leadership team and not on those of the trainee teacher, but nevertheless, from a developing of professional practice perspective it is important for you to be aware that many of the activities which you are asked to support or lead in the classroom relate to Ofsted inspection criteria. For example, the Ofsted inspection document, 'Inspecting the Curriculum' (2019), provides details of the methodology inspectors will use to make judgements on the 'quality of education'. For example, the concept of a 'deep dive' into a curriculum area comes directly from Ofsted inspection methodology.

Task 1.2.7 Considering the impact of Ofsted on professional decisions

Read the following statement from Ofsted (2019: 6) and then respond to the questions that follow: 'In primary schools, inspectors will always carry out a deep dive in reading and deep dives in the school during the time that inspectors are on-site. In addition, inspectors will often carry out a deep dive in mathematics.'

1. In your experience as a trainee teacher, to what extent do you think that the Ofsted inspection priorities influence what is taught in school and how much time is devoted to each subject?
2. What evidence from practice do you have to support your response?
3. What do you think this will mean for your own practice as a trainee and an ECT?

INSTITUTIONAL: SITUATIONAL LEARNING/DIFFERENT CONTEXTS

As our brief exploration of professional standards in the rest of the UK (outside of England) shows, a teacher's professional expectations can look rather different depending on whether your school is in Sheffield, Cardiff, Belfast or Edinburgh! However, you do not need to leave England to encounter this contrast, and depending on where you teach, even within the same city in England, you are likely to encounter differences in professional requirements. The prolific growth of Multi-Academy Trusts (MATs) over the last ten years has had a significant impact on how many schools are governed, and on their 'freedom' to decide on policy and practice within their chain of schools (Benn, 2023, cited in Ellis, 2023). This autonomy impacts all areas of school policy and practice, including the framing of teacher professionalism. Pierre's story is a fictional scenario of a professional dilemma which could occur in an institution which expects a particular kind of professional behaviour from the teachers which it employs.

Pierre's story

Pierre has just begun his final year placement in a 3–16 through-school that is part of a large MAT. He is based in a year 4 class. He feels well supported by his mentor and is forging good relationships with the children and starting to understand their diverse needs. He is looking forward to planning his own lessons but is taken aback when his mentor informs him that he must use and not diverge from the MAT standardised lesson plan. He discovers that in addition he must adhere to clearly set out 'behaviour expectations' – for example, children must remain silent unless the teacher asks them a question. Pierre struggles to meet these expectations and feels restricted in his practice. It is very different from his previous school. However, he is afraid to raise his concerns with his mentor. He wishes he felt like the trainee teacher in the next class who values these tight parameters as she feels they 'cut down on my workload and allow me to get on with learning to teach rather than worrying about planning'.

Task 1.2.8 Questions for Pierre

- What advice would you give Pierre to empower him in developing his own professionalism?
- How could he reconcile his own professional values with the professional values of his setting?

It is, of course, not only MATs which may have a particular vision of professional practice. If you are training to teach in a Catholic, Church of England, Jewish or an Islamic school or a Montessori nursery, all will bring with them their different value bases which are likely to impact your professional experiences in school. The *situated* nature of professionalism – that is to say the influence that individual institutions play in moulding the professional identities of their trainees and teachers – has to be considered (Ball, 2021). So, how can the trainee teacher respond to the many and varied contexts they will no doubt encounter in the process of training to teach? Our advice is that it is your professional responsibility to be *informed* as to the context of the school where you will be training. You can do this by exploring the school website where without doubt you will find a mission statement. For example, what does this tell you about the values which it espouses? What does it say about expectations for behaviour management, inclusive practice, how children learn and how the school works with parents and carers and the wider community? Once you are in placement you can be proactive and talk to your mentor about the culture and values of the school – a conversation with the SENCO or even the head teacher would further expand your understanding of the specific context of the school. In our experience, the trainee teacher who approaches a new placement with an informed and open mind, with curiosity and a willingness to inquire will be well-equipped and well prepared to navigate the challenges which can arise in certain institutions.

SUMMARY

Although the CCF and the Teachers' Standards are important and necessary frameworks for you to adhere to, it is clear that being professional is more than just the meeting of standards. Baggini (2005: 7) considers that the way teachers respond to imposed standards demonstrates the extent to which they may be professional. Having to attain imposed goals and outcomes, even though they may be at odds with personal and professional beliefs and ideals, is demanding and requires teacherly wisdom. The kind of professionalism this demands is not easily attained and takes time to develop. As a trainee, it is likely that the professionalism you demonstrate will be centred on completing the CCF and meeting the Teachers' Standards, but as you continue as a teacher, the professionalism that you demonstrate is likely to extend beyond adherence to the Standards, to the development of collaborative networks, the fostering of relationships of trust and the ability to make wise decisions in 'situations of unavoidable uncertainty' (Hargreaves and Fullan, 2012: 93). In this way, you will be continuing to develop your own professional identity as a teacher.

ANNOTATED FURTHER READING

Bolton, G. (2014) *Reflective Practice. Writing and Professional Development*, 4th edn, London: SAGE Publications Ltd.

> Grounded in theory, Bolton's book captures recent developments, illuminates essential concepts, explains and clarifies major theoretical models of reflection and focuses on ethical values. At all times it is premised on the belief that reflective practice is probably the most important toll in any professional's repertoire.

Glazzard, J., Green, M. and Glazzard, J. (2022) *Learning to be a Superhero Primary Teacher: Core Knowledge & Understanding*, 2nd edn, Northwich, UK: Critical Publishing.

> This book is a comprehensive guide to becoming a primary teacher. It takes a critical approach and outlines complex issues, supported by research and current educational thinking. Chapter 11 discusses professional behaviour within the context of the Teachers' Standards as well as the Core Content Framework, while chapter 12 outlines the expectations of an ECT.

Glazzard, J. and Stones, S. (2020). *The ITT Core Content Framework: What Trainee Primary School Teachers Need to Know*. Learning Matters.
> This book outlines the ITT Core Content Framework and the need to develop a professional identity. Chapter 8 discusses professional behaviours and a very useful ITT Core Content Framework bibliography linked to the Teachers' Standards is included for further reading.

Carroll, J. (2020) *The Teachers' Standards in Primary Schools: Understanding & Evidencing Effective Practice*, 2nd edn, London: SAGE Publications.
> Chapter 9 provides a broader discussion of professionalism with the context of personal and professional conduct required to meet the Teachers' Standards. It also examines the place of values in education and how they can be evidenced in practice.

Hargreaves, A. and O'Connor, M. T. (2018) *Collaborative Professionalism: When Teaching Together Means Learning For All*. Corwin, a SAGE Company.
> This book discusses the benefits of collaboration between teachers in developing a collaborative professionalism. Chapter 8 discusses how working together can bring a sense of collective autonomy, efficiency and responsibility, as well as undertaking joint enquiries resulting in joint decisions. This, Hargreaves and O'Connor argue, is how teachers find meaning and purpose in their profession and in doing so use their influence to support their students in gaining meaning and purpose in their lives.

M — FURTHER READING TO SUPPORT M-LEVEL STUDY

Ball, S. J. (2021) *The Education Debate*, 4th edn, Bristol: Policy Press.
> Stephen Ball, a leader in the field of the sociology of policy, explores the ways in which education policy in England is constantly evolving and shines a light on an area which can seem incoherent and hard to make sense of. The book covers a range of key policy concepts including the marketisation of education, the impact of poverty and austerity and the impact of Covid 19 on school and education policy

Beijaard, D., Meijer, P. C. and Verloop, N. (2004) 'Reconsidering research on teachers' professional identity', *Teaching and Teacher Education*, 20(2): 107–128. doi:10.1016/j.tate.2003.07.001

Boylan, M., Adams, G., Perry, E. and Booth, J. (2023) 'Re-imagining transformative professional learning for critical teacher professionalism: A conceptual review', *Professional Development in Education*, 49(4), 651–669. https://doi.org/10.1080/19415257.2022.2162566
> The authors draw on a range of contemporary research around teachers' professional learning, practice and identity to set out a conceptual framework for distinct forms of professionalism. In doing so they 'trouble' taken for granted understandings of what it 'means to be professional'.

Britzman, D. (2003) *Practice Makes Practice: A Critical Study of Learning to Teach*, New York: State University of New York.
> Deborah Britzman's book is considered by many in the field to be a classic text on the discipline of teacher education. It asks the question, what does learning *do* to teachers, and mean to newcomers to the profession and to those who surround them?

Hargreaves, A. and Fullan, M. (2013) 'The power of professional capital', *Journal of Staff Development*, 34(3): 36–39.
> The authors consider two approaches of professionalism: the business model and the professional capital approach. It outlines the importance of developing decisional capital as part of professional capital and shows how different career stages provide the means for decisional capital to be developed.

Sachs, J. (2016) 'Teacher professionalism: Why are we still talking about it?', *Teachers & Teaching*, 22(4): 413–425.
> In this paper, Sachs outlines what she considers shapes teacher professionalism, arguing that the teaching profession has become controlled or compliant through the requirement to adhere to externally imposed expectations. She proposes that teachers should take control of their own professional development through engagement in teacher and classroom research, thereby defining and developing their own professional identity.

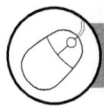

RELEVANT WEBSITES

Department for Education (DfE). (2011) *Teachers' Standards*: www.gov.uk/government/publications/teachers-standards
> This website details the Teachers' Standards, with further information and how they should be used and includes the eight Teachers Standards and Part 2 of the Professional Responsibilities.

Department for Education (DfE). (2019) *Initial Teacher Training (ITT): Core Content Framework*: www.gov.uk/government/publications/initial-teacher-training-itt-core-content-framework and www.gov.uk/government/publications/early-career-framework
> These government documents detail the curriculum for the Core Content Framework and the Early Career Framework which forms a fundamental aspect of training to become a teacher, and for the first two years of classroom practice.

The Chartered College of Teaching: https://chartered.college/
> The Chartered College of Teaching is the professional body for teachers. It works to empower a knowledgeable and respected teaching profession through membership and accreditation. It aims to bridge the gap between practice and research and equip teachers with the knowledge and confidence to make the best decisions for their pupils.

The Educational Endowment Foundation: https://educationendowmentfoundation.org.uk/
> The Education Endowment Foundation (EEF) is an independent charity dedicated to breaking the link between family income and educational achievement. It aims to support schools to improve teaching and learning through better use of evidence.

The International Professional Development Association (also has links to IPDA England, Ireland & Scotland): https://ipda.org.uk/
> The IPDA has been supporting, developing and promoting teachers' professional learning since 1968. Its membership covers all phases of education and training in a wide variety of work locations. It publishes a regular journal on international research.

British Educational Research Association (Teacher Education resources): www.bera.ac.uk/themes/teacher-education-and-development
> The British Educational Research Association (BERA) is the leading authority on educational research in the UK, supporting and representing the community of scholars, practitioners and everyone engaged in and with educational research, both nationally and internationally.

REFERENCES

Alsup, J. (2006) *Teacher Identity Discourses: Negotiating Personal and Professional Spaces*, New Jersey: National Council of Teaching of English/Lawrence Erlbaum Associates.

Appleby, Y. and Pilkington, R. (2014) *Developing Critical Professional Practice in Education*, Leicester and Cardiff: NIACE.

Baggini, J. (2005) 'What professionalism means for teachers today', *Education Review*, 18: 5–11.

Ball, S. J. (2021) *The Education Debate*, 4th edn, Bristol: Policy Press.

Boylan, M., Adams, G., Perry, E. and Booth, J. (2023) 'Re-imagining transformative professional learning for critical teacher professionalism: a conceptual review', *Professional Development in Education*, 49(4): 651–669. https://doi.org/10.1080/19415257.2022.2162566

Britzman, D. (2003) *Practice Makes Practice: A Critical Study of Learning to Teach*, New York: State University of New York.

Bukor, E. (2015) 'Exploring teacher identity from a holistic perspective: Reconstructing personal and professional selves', *Teachers & Teaching, Theory & Practice*, 21(3): 305–327.

Clark, L. (2016) *Teacher Status and Professional Learning: The Place Model*, Northwich, UK: Critical Publishing.

Demirkasimoğlu, N. (2010) 'Defining "teacher professionalism" from different perspectives', *Procedia – Social & Behavioral Sciences*, 9: 2047–2051.

Department for Education (DfE). (2011) *Teachers' Standards*. Last updated 2021. Retrieved from: www.gov.uk/government/publications/teachers-standards (accessed 12 January 2024).

Department for Education (DfE). (2019) *Initial Teacher Training (ITT): Core Content Framework*. Last updated 2024. Retrieved from: www.gov.uk/government/publications/initial-teacher-training-itt-core-content-framework

Ellis, V. (ed.) (2023) *Teacher Education in Crisis: The State, The Market, and the Universities in England*, London: Bloomsbury Academic.

General Teaching Council for Northern Ireland (GTCNI). (2018) *GTCNI Digest of the Teachers Competencies*, Belfast: GTCNI. Retrieved from: www.gtcni.org.uk/professional-space/professional-competence/code-of-values

General Teaching Council for Scotland (GTC Scotland). (2021) *A Guide to the Professional Standards*. Retrieved from: www.gtcs.org.uk/knowledge-base/articles/a-guide-to-the-professional-standards

Hargreaves, A. and Fullan, M. (2012) *Professional Capital: Transforming Teaching in Every School*, London and New York: Routledge.

Hilferty, F. (2008) 'Theorising teacher professionalism as an enacted discourse of power', *British Journal of Sociology of Education*, 29(2): 161–173.

Hordern, J. and Brooks, C. (2023) 'Towards and instrumental trainability in England: The "official pedagogy" of the Core Content Framework', *British Journal of Education Studies*, 1–18.

Kelchtermans, G. (2005) 'Teachers' emotions in educational reforms: Self-understanding, vulnerable commitment and micropolitical literacy', *Teaching and Teacher Education*, 21: 995–1006. https://doi.org/10.1016/j.tate.2005.06.009

Moore, A. (2018) *The Affected Teacher. Psychosocial Perspectives on Professional Experience and Policy Resistance*, London: Routledge.

Ofsted (2019) *Inspecting the Curriculum: Revising Inspection Methodology to Support the Education Inspection Framework*, Crown Copyright.

Perryman, J., Bradbury, A., Calvert, G. and Kilian, K. (2023) *Beyond Ofsted: An Inquiry Into the Future of School Inspection: At a Glance*. Retrieved from: https://beyondofsted.org.uk/wp-content/uploads/2023/11/Beyond-Ofsted-Executive-Summary.pdf

Pillen, M. T., Den Brok, P. J. and Beijaard, D. (2013) 'Profiles and change in beginning teachers' professional identity tensions', *Teaching & Teacher Education*, 34: 86–97.

Poet, H., Rudd, P. and Kelly, J. (2010) *How Teachers Approach Practice Improvement*, London: General Teaching Council for England.

Smith, R. L. and Skarbek, D. (2013) *Professional Teacher Dispositions: Additions to the Mainstream*, Lanham, MD: Rowman & Littlefield Publishers, Inc.

Steadman, S. (2023) '"Who is it that can tell me who I am?": What the ITE reforms in England mean for teacher identity (and why it matters)', in V. Ellis (ed.) *Teacher Education in Crisis: The State, the Market and the Universities in England*, London: Bloomsbury Academic, pp. 163–178.

Steinert, Y., Cruess, R., Cruess, S., Boudreau, D., Snell, L. and Hafferty, F. (2014, August) From Professionalism to Professional Identity Formation: A Journey not a Destiny. Symposium presented at AMEE Conference, Milan, Italy.

Tichenor, M. S. and Tichenor, J. M. (2005) 'Understanding teachers' perspectives on professionalism', *The Professional Educator*, 27: 89–95.

Universities' Council for the Education of Teachers (UCET). (2019) *Intellectual Base of Teacher Education: Values and Principles*. Retrieved from: www.ucet.ac.uk/11675/intellectual-base-of-teacher-education-report-updated-february-2020

Welsh Government. (2018) *An Introduction to the Professional Standards for Teaching and Leadership*. Retrieved from: https://hwb.gov.wales/api/storage/932d8940-56f5-4660-aa85-afb4e87560a9/an-introduction-to-the-professional-standards-for-teaching-and-leadership.pdf

UNIT 1.3

CAPITALISING ON PROFESSIONAL PRACTICE

Making the most of your placements

Jane Warwick, John-Mark Winstanley and Mary Anne Wolpert

INTRODUCTION

> The steepest learning curve for a student teacher naturally takes place in the classroom itself.
>
> (Chris, a primary PGCE trainee)

In this unit, we examine how you can capitalise on professional practice by making the most of the opportunities afforded by your school placements and how day-to-day experience of working with children in school will give you understanding of why theory and research are integral to effective teaching. We discuss the sometimes unexpected tensions that placements might raise and emphasise the importance of being a reflective practitioner, examining how the dispositions you present, the questions you ask yourself and expert practitioners and the relationships you develop on placement are key factors to becoming an effective teacher. As the quotation from Chris suggests, classroom experiences provide crucial, yet sometimes challenging, learning opportunities, and we offer vignettes from recent trainees who provide insights into significant elements of their school placements.

OBJECTIVES

This unit will help you to understand:

- what you can learn from professional placements, particularly what you can do for yourself and what you can learn from expert practitioners;
- dispositions that will maximise your learning during school placements;
- the importance of reflection and how lesson evaluations inform practice;
- the role of mentors and how learning conversations with colleagues inform professional development.

Learning how to become a teacher is a complex process that goes beyond simply acquiring the skills and knowledge to perform the functions of a teacher; it is where individuals develop a sense of a changing identity and purpose as they define themselves and are seen by others as teachers.

Developing this professional identity is the process of integrating one's personal knowledge, beliefs, attitudes, norms and values, on the one hand, with professional demands from teacher education providers and schools, including broadly accepted values and standards about teaching, on the other (Pillen, Beijaard and den Brok, 2013: 243). It is during professional placements that this professional identity emerges, is embedded and consolidated.

PREPARING FOR 'PRACTICE SHOCK'

The placement experience is often one which is approached with great excitement by beginning teachers, and so it should be! After all, school-based placements provide opportunities where you will be able to establish new skills, test out and refine different pedagogical strategies and, ultimately, discover who you are as a teacher through a process of 'personal revolution' (Caires, Almeida and Vieira, 2012). However, it should not be assumed that this will be an easy process. Evidence suggests that, whilst pivotal to beginning teachers' learning, professional placements can be a 'battleground' of emotions (Hanna et al., 2019). This is often attributed to a phenomenon referred to as 'practice shock' (Stokking et al., 2003), wherein the optimistic ideals of a beginning teacher can clash with the reality of everyday classroom teaching (Schepens, Aelterman and Vlerick, 2009). We don't share this with you in an attempt to dampen your enthusiasm, but to signpost that placements can bring many highs and lows. This isn't something you should be intimidated by, but utilise so that you can approach your placement with a sense of realism and pragmatism, knowing that research surrounding beginning teachers' learning signposts this as 'a critical source of spontaneity, creativity and growth in people's professional learning and continuing development' (Yuan, Liu and Lee, 2019: 976). In this chapter, we aim to highlight six key strategies which you can use that will enable you to manage 'practice shock' and make the most of your placement.

ESTABLISHING EFFECTIVE DISPOSITIONS

> Becoming an expert teacher ... is a transformative process rather than simply the acquisition of skills.
>
> (Wilson, 2013: 44)

In order for you to make sense of your experience across placements during your course, it will be helpful to understand dispositions towards your learning. Hagger et al. (2008), in their study of one-year PGCE trainees, defined five different dimensions to professional learning that trainee teachers take (see Table 1.3.1). Having an understanding of these dimensions and their associated orientations will equip you to navigate the effects of 'practice shock' and, ultimately, become a competent professional learner and teacher.

Hagger et al. (2008) argue that the degree of intentionality - the extent to which the learning is planned - is key. One end of the continuum is represented by a 'deliberative' approach to learning, and the other by a reactive approach to experiences. Novice teachers who take the first, proactive approach actively seek feedback on their teaching and advice from more experienced colleagues, showing an 'enthusiasm to experiment with their teaching' (p. 169). In contrast, trainees with a 'reactive approach' show 'an abdication of responsibility' (p. 168) and have difficulty identifying their personal future learning needs. We argue that those who adopt a more 'deliberative approach' are most likely to navigate the challenges brought on by 'practice shock'.

Within the second dimension (frame of reference), Hagger et al. found differences in the extent to which trainees recognised the value of looking beyond their own experience. Trainees with a proactive disposition drew on a range of sources, such as appropriate research findings and discussions

TABLE 1.3.1 Five dimensions according to which the variation among the student teachers' accounts of their learning from experience were analysed

Dimension	Orientation			
Intentionality: the extent to which learning is planned	Deliberative	←	→	Reactive
Frame of reference: the value ascribed to looking beyond their experience in order to make sense of it	Drawing on a range of sources to shape and make sense of experience	←	→	Exclusive reliance on the experience of classroom teaching
Response to feedback: disposition towards receiving feedback and the value attributed to it	Effective use of feedback to further learning	←	→	Tendency to be disabled by critical feedback
Attitude to context: attitude to the positions in which student teachers find themselves and the approaches they take to the school context	Acceptance of the context and ability to capitalise on it	←	→	Tendency to regard the context as constraining
Aspiration: the extent of their aspirations for their own and their pupils' learning	Aspirational as both learners and teachers	←	→	Satisfaction with current level of achievement

Source: Hagger *et al.* (2008: 167)

with mentors and tutors, whereas those exhibiting a 'reactive' disposition relied more exclusively on individual classroom experience. Third, dispositions towards receiving feedback ranged from those trainees who made effective use of feedback and those who were defensive and perceived the feedback as criticism. We explore this dimension more fully later. Attitude to school context was similarly characterised as a continuum ranging from trainees who accepted and capitalised on the position in which they found themselves to those who regarded the context as a constraint on their progress. Finally, Hagger *et al.* identified an aspirational orientation. At one end were trainees who constantly sought to develop professional practice and the ways in which they, and pupils, learn. At the other end were those who were complacent about their own level of performance and that of the learners.

BEING A REFLECTIVE PRACTITIONER

> Teaching is a complex and highly skilled activity which, above all, requires classroom teachers to exercise judgement in deciding how to act.
>
> (Wyse *et al.*, 2023: 68)

While on placement, you need to develop skills that will enable you to question, analyse and reflect upon your practice in order to make increasingly appropriate judgements about teaching and learning. Again, this will support you to navigate the challenges presented by 'practice shock' as you will be able to gain a deeper understanding of yourself as a teacher. Clearly, this is something considered fundamental to the work of a teacher, as evidenced through the expectation that teachers become reflective and reflexive practitioners in Standard 8 of the Core Content Framework (Department for Education [DfE], 2019) and Teachers' Standard 4 (DfE, 2011).

Reflection about an episode in the classroom starts as a series of 'questioning thoughts' (McGregor and Cartwright, 2011: 1), which will help understanding of what, when and how the event happened. These initial thoughts will become more purposeful when you start to analyse why the event happened in the way it did, especially as you become more familiar with the context and the children with whom you are working. Such questions need to be followed by consideration of how you might have behaved or done things differently, and how to improve the situation in future. This is not to suggest that reflection should only happen when things go wrong; the habit of reflection is something that needs to be developed in relation to *all* aspects of your professional work, including successful lessons.

Reflection should be a conscious activity: 'reflection at its most effective comes with growing professional knowledge based on the acquisition of theory and its critical application to practice' (Cartwright, 2011: 56). Your reading of educational research is essential to help you reflect on, and make sense of, your classroom experiences. According to Wyse *et al.* (2023), there are seven characteristics of reflective teaching (see Figure 1.3.1). Through engaging in reflective action that stems from professional thinking, rather than merely having intuitive reactions to classroom situations, teachers can raise their standards of professional competence. This process, Wyse *et al.* argue, is cyclical in nature, mediated through collaboration and dialogue with colleagues and arises through evidence-based enquiry. While you are on placements, discussions with your mentor and other colleagues will help you to gain confidence in analysing and reflecting on your teaching. Prompts to support you with these discussions will be discussed later in the chapter.

This concept of reflection in and on activity has been extended to include the notion of reflexivity, which requires 'not just the ability to reflect about what has happened and what one has done, but the ability to reflect on the way in which one has reflected' (Moore, 2004: 148). In addition, when teachers are reflexive, they take into account the impact and implications that they bring to, and have on, a particular learning situation (Sewell, 2012). This means that you should consider how your values, dispositions and possible biases might influence your teaching. You will be expected to provide evidence of your reflective and reflexive practice through discussion and recordings in more formal documentation. In the next section, we show examples of trainees' evaluations of their teaching as a tool for helping you to do this.

Reflective teaching:

1. implies an active concern with aims and consequences, as well as means and technical efficiency;
2. is applied in a cyclical or spiralling process;
3. requires competence in methods of evidence-based classroom enquiry;
4. requires attitudes of open-mindedness, responsibility and whole-heartedness;
5. is based on teacher judgement, informed by evidence-based enquiry and insights from other research;
6. along with professional learning and personal fulfilment, is enhanced through collaboration and dialogue with colleagues;
7. enables teachers creatively to mediate externally developed frameworks for teaching and learning.

FIGURE 1.3.1 The seven characteristics of reflective teaching
Source: Wyse *et al.* (2023: 76)

EVALUATING YOUR LESSONS

> The lesson does not end when the bell goes!
>
> (Hattie, 2012: 145)

Evaluating the impact of your teaching on children's learning is a fundamental part of the planning, teaching and assessment cycle; lesson evaluations are key to demonstrating reflection and will help you understand and develop your practice. These could take the form of reflective journals or diaries, annotations of individual lesson plans and sequences of lessons, or detailed, 'formal' evaluations of individual lessons. Establishing a more evidence informed approach to evaluating your teaching will ensure you avoid being hijacked by the heightened emotions associated with 'practice shock'.

Beginner teachers often have a tendency to focus their reflections on aspects of their own performance in the classroom and, most notably, how they manage behaviour. Burn *et al.* (2000) found trainees focused on four categories related to their own practice: 'their actions, their planning, the resources used (materials they had made themselves or existing resources) and their own affective state (usually judgements about their nervousness, but sometimes reflections on their sense of exhaustion)' (2000: 272). We argue that, in addition to your teaching, the focus on pupil learning is a crucial element of lesson evaluations.

To be effective and formative, lesson evaluations should focus on specific elements of learning and teaching and avoid repetition and description. They should also link to previous targets set by your mentor, other expert practitioners, course tutors or yourself. Consider the following elements in structuring your evaluations:

1. the successes of the lesson;
2. the children's learning;
3. your teaching;
4. implications for your future practice.

The successes of the lesson

Beginning teachers tend to make broad judgements about the successes of the lesson. For example, comments such as 'all the children enjoyed the lesson and understood the learning objective' or 'the lesson went well' are typical. Compare these comments with the example in Table 1.3.2 to see a more analytical approach that identifies specific evidence to support the judgements made.

The children's learning

When reflecting upon and analysing children's learning, consider the following questions:

- What did the children actually learn and do?
- Taking account of the evidence, to what extent did the children meet the learning objective?
- To what extent did children maintain interest and effort?
- Were there any misconceptions/errors for all children? If so, how will they be addressed?
- Were there any barriers to learning? If so, what were they?

In the examples in the tables, the trainees identified explicitly what the children learned, linked to the lesson learning objectives and success criteria. Judgements were made based on the learning outcomes. (Names of children have been removed.)

TABLE 1.3.2 An example of appropriate comments that highlight successes of a lesson

Question	Comment	Specific evidence
What were the successes of the lesson?	The children took pride in their work and made a lot of effort. Children were engaged and able to work in pairs, threes or independently effectively. Overall, the timings were well planned and appropriate. The lesson was accessible to all pupils, with self-differentiation taking place in the creative writing of poetry. Higher achievers were able to work on their own while less confident pupils could support each other. Children learned about important aspects of poetry such as the importance of reading it aloud and listening to it being read. The quality of work was high; they all wanted to read their poems, which demonstrated how much they had enjoyed the lesson.	Mentor was pleased with the letters and lesson had gone well. She said it was carefully planned, although she had a few points that we could adapt and improve upon. The final pieces of work were finished on time and were of a satisfactory or good standard.

It is important to get feedback from other professionals.

The quality of the children's work forms a key source of evidence.

TABLE 1.3.3 An example of appropriate comments that relate to children's learning

Question	Comment	Specific evidence
What did the children actually learn and do? Were there any unexpected outcomes?	The children learned to identify characters and their emotions and descriptions. Some learned to predict what would happen next in the story.	Work produced showed a clear understanding of the characters' emotions, and the following lesson for literacy showed that the concept of character descriptions had been learned through the application in a different context (which was commented on by the teacher). Children also showed they had learned to predict what would happen next by the discussion I had; some managed to draw what they thought would happen next.

Evidence from a range of sources supports judgements.

Your teaching

Initially, analysing your teaching tends to be easier than reflecting on children's learning. However, in order to avoid writing a descriptive narrative that focuses just on your emotional response, consider the following questions through the eyes of the children:

- How effective was the lesson/activity plan?
- How effectively did I engage/motivate pupils and ensure positive behaviour for learning?
- To what extent was my modelling and explanation clear throughout the lesson?
- Was the timing appropriate?
- Was the use of other adults efficient, and did it support the learning?

TABLE 1.3.4 An example of critical comments that relate to evaluation of the teaching

Question	Comment	Specific evidence
How effective was the lesson/activity plan? Consider: (1) timings; (2) pace	The pace of the lesson went well. Activities were 10-15 minutes to encourage the children to maintain interest while allowing them time to apply their skills. Resources were prepared before the lesson and included use of whiteboards. However, children spent a large proportion of time on the carpet, partly due to the layout and size of the class. I would have preferred the children to return to their class seats, but I would not have been able to speak to all of them effectively, and it would be more difficult to engage them. Need to keep the activities on the carpet short and snappy to maintain interest and levels of concentration.	Teacher feedback, observations *(Reflections explicitly state an issue that will have impacted on children's motivation and concentrations levels. Importantly a change of practice has been identified.)*
Question	**Comment**	**Specific evidence**
To what extent was my modelling and explanation clear throughout the lesson?	I modelled the process of creating words and then the process of joining words together to create a line of poetry. Used the words 'sneaky', 'sly' and simile 'as slow as a turtle' to show that it didn't have to be a literal description; I wanted the children to tell me what words/images evoked for them. This worked well; most children identified interesting words and used comparisons and alliteration. However, the blue group simply copied the words I wrote down. Need to be clearer about what I expect the children to do, and ask children who struggled to repeat to me what they have to do with an example.	Teacher feedback, pupil response *(Individual children who either exceeded or did not meet the learning objective are identified which will inform future planning.)*

Implications for your future practice

This is at the heart of why time should be spent writing lesson evaluations on placements; it is the 'So what?', 'What do I do next?', 'How can I overcome the barriers to learning in future lessons?'. To have an impact on your future teaching, evaluations must include an action plan that focuses both on children's learning and your own practice.

Task 1.3.1 Lesson evaluations

Using the suggested four sections of a lesson evaluation outlined earlier, reflect upon and evaluate a recent lesson you have taught. What evidence have you found to support your analysis? Discuss this with your mentor and identify an aspect of your lesson evaluation that informs your targets for development.

TABLE 1.3.5 An example of the implications for future practice identified after teaching a lesson

Children's learning	Importance of modelling both pushes and pulls before asking children to do each task. I learned how time-consuming practical investigations are and how important it is to keep the focus on science and make recording as simple as possible. In future I will allow more time and keep the written aspect to a minimum. I also learned how valuable the interactive science clips are. I will definitely use these again.
In my role as a teacher	If children aren't giving me the answers I am hoping for, I will add thinking time, talk partners and group discussions into future plans.
	To have confidence to extend the discussion if the children are still engaged.

It is important to be aware that lesson evaluations should:

- be analytical and critical, rather than descriptive;
- be informed by evidence;
- have a specific focus;
- reflect on the impact of the lesson through the learners' eyes;
- identify implications for future practice.

WORKING WITH EXPERT COLLEAGUES

> It is really important to remember that mentors … provide feedback in order for you to become a better teacher.
>
> (Becky, a primary PGCE trainee)

The process of changing identity, discussed at the beginning of the chapter, is not one which takes place in isolation; as previously discussed by Wyse et al. (2023), reflection is mediated through dialogic interactions and collaboration with colleagues. We need a range of expert colleagues to unlock the complexity of the classroom; to make sense of what we observe; to help us to interrogate and analyse our practices, using the best available evidence (DfE, 2019). They help us appreciate what makes a particular approach successful or unsuccessful; reflect upon how this approach might be integrated into one's own practice; what we are doing well, our development points and what we need support with. As such, these opportunities for coaching and collaboration should be embraced on your placements, alongside developing the skills needed to build the effective and respectful professional relationships which are a key part of becoming a teacher.

The Department of Education, in the Core Content Framework (CCF), defines 'expert colleagues' as professional colleagues, including experienced and effective teachers, subject specialists, mentors, lecturers and tutors (2019). These professional colleagues will provide you with access to a range of increasingly self-directed learning opportunities to scaffold your development and help you respond to the changing demands of your course. It is helpful to conceive of them as 'significant narrators' (Sfard and Prusak, 2005: 20) who have a major role to play in the building of your emerging professional identify as a teacher. Forming these social relationships is vital in helping you move from somewhat 'peripheral participation' (Lave and Wenger, 1991) in the school workforce to becoming a member of a community of practice. Evidence demonstrates that it is relationships with such colleagues which act as a mediating factor to the difficulties surrounding 'practice shock' (Dahl, 2020).

In this vignette, Charlotte (a primary PGCE trainee) reflects on her experiences of working with mentors during her training:

> In my first two placements, my mentors were one of the most important influences in how I learned to teach. Mentors allow you to see the role of a teacher from the inside out. I learned from observing, discussing and questioning with them about what goes on in the classroom. I realised it was essential that I took responsibility for finding out as much as possible from their wealth of knowledge and experience during the time I spent with them. This involved me asking questions and for advice, but also going to them with ideas.
>
> My mentors were there to redirect. I shared my plans with them which gave me opportunities to explain my vision and ideas. This allowed them to see how I was thinking and, moreover, how I had taken on board advice and used it to adapt my planning and teaching. At times I did not fully understand what my mentors were saying and quickly learned that I shouldn't feel embarrassed about asking what I sometimes thought were obvious questions: I realised later that some pieces of advice can remain dormant, until that 'eureka moment' when the suggestion gains its meaning.

MAKING THE MOST OF LEARNING CONVERSATIONS

> I soon came to realise that these were not tests she was setting me.
>
> (Luke, a primary PGCE trainee)

Teachers' Standard 8 (DfE, 2011) states that teachers need to 'take responsibility for improving teaching through appropriate professional development, responding to advice and feedback from colleagues'. The CCF asserts that all trainee teachers should learn how to seek 'challenge, feedback and critique from mentors and other colleagues in an open and trusting working environment' (DfE, 2019).

Whilst it is not surprising that dialogic exchanges with expert practitioners are crucial to effective professional development, how one 'receives' and responds to feedback from expert colleagues is intrinsically linked with beliefs about learning. The term feedback may seem to imply a one-way process, in which feedback discourse is characterised by the 'expert' providing a 'gift' (Askew and Lodge, 2000: 4) to support improvement. Askew and Lodge (2000) offer a second model of discourse in which feedback is a two-way process, enabling the development of understanding through the use of open questioning and shared insight. We prefer to consider their third model of feedback – a co-constructive discourse that involves a reciprocal process of learning. Here, feedback is a dialogue, formed by 'loops' connecting the trainee and the mentor that illuminate learning (Askew and Lodge, 2000). We therefore use the term 'learning conversation', as this indicates the necessary active involvement of the trainee in the dialogue as they become an active participant in their own learning.

Dweck (1986) outlines the motivational processes that affect learning and how learners vary in their beliefs about success, their 'goal orientation', about learning and their responses to difficult tasks. She defines a 'positive learning orientation', or 'growth mindset', as one that focuses on 'improving one's competence', with a belief that effort leads to success and a belief in one's ability to improve and learn. On the other hand, a more negative pattern focuses on 'performance orientation', in which one is more concerned with 'proving one's competence'. This is associated with negative effects for learners, such as greater helplessness, reduced help-seeking and reduced use of learning strategies. As we saw in the Hagger *et al.* (2008), trainees who adopt a 'defensive stance' and 'those who are disabled by critical feedback' have a tendency to blame others, including the pupils, to explain their difficulties or lack of progress.

In this vignette, Nicola reflects on learning conversations with her mentor and how these enabled her to become a more effective teacher. As you read this, consider how Nicola's positive dispositions were essential to this process.

> I was apprehensive about the initial feedback meeting and acutely aware that this very experienced teacher had not just closely observed everything I had done in my first lesson but also scrutinised my planning. 'So', he asked, 'how do you think the lesson went?' Admittedly, the whole lesson had gone by in a blur. Finding myself more self-conscious than when I had actually been standing up in front of the class, I responded with a hopeful 'Ok?' Together we reviewed and analysed several aspects of the lesson: positives were highlighted whilst areas of improvement tactfully suggested.
>
> One observation my mentor made was that I hadn't made full use of the classroom teaching assistant. This really surprised me; I had considered that my planning for the teaching assistant was good. To help clarify his point, my mentor showed me the comprehensive directions he'd written on his own lesson plans and explained how resources had been modified for her to use. Subsequently, arrangements were made for me to shadow a TA, observing how she worked and discussing what we could do to help each other in the classroom. As a result, I found myself more effectively deploying support staff for the benefit of my pupils. The mentoring feedback process prevented me from being insular, at times even a little defensive about my teaching. Instead, I understood the need to be open to advice.

CONVERSATIONS WITH SUBJECT SPECIALISTS

The joy of teaching in the early years and primary sector is that you get to teach the same group of children multiple subjects. However, as generalist age-phase specialists, this does put pressure on beginning teachers to develop 'secure knowledge of the relevant subject(s) and curriculum areas, foster and maintain pupils' interest in the subject, and address misunderstandings' thus developing your subject knowledge in all National Curriculum subjects, as specified in Teachers' Standard 3 (DfE, 2011). This is a challenge on a one-year course, so one way to address this is to ask questions of, and seek support from, expert subject leaders who have responsibility for individual subjects across the whole primary age range.

STRUCTURED CONVERSATIONS

Having the opportunity to have structured conversations with subject leaders about different approaches to teaching and learning will enable trainees to consider what is unique about each subject and develop their subject-specific pedagogical knowledge. The following questions will support these structured conversations.

What is the school's approach to teaching this subject?
How is the curriculum for this subject organised?
How much curriculum time is assigned to this subject? Is it taught weekly or blocked?
Is it taught discretely or are links make to other curriculum subjects through a topic?
What are the key skills, knowledge and experiences the school wants children to develop through this subject?
How do you ensure progression through a child's primary experience at your school?
How do you plan a unit of work in this subject?
What is the school's approach to assessment within this subject?
Which resources are available to support teaching of this subject?
Where are subject-specific resources kept in school?

> **Task 1.3.2 Dimensions and their associated orientations**
>
> Reflect on which National Curriculum subjects you feel confident in and which ones you need to prioritise for developing your subject knowledge. You could carry out a RAG rating exercise for each subject: red = priority for development; amber = secure; green = confident.
>
> For the 'red' subjects, arrange to meet with each subject lead and carry out a structured conversation using the previous questions as a prompt. Make a note of the responses and identify any further actions to further develop your subject knowledge in that subject.

The previous questions can be used for all subjects, however there are specific resources available to help beginning teachers focus on individual subjects. For example, a useful tool which enables teachers to analyse and develop their mathematical teaching and pedagogical knowledge is the Knowledge Quartet, developed by academics at the University of Cambridge (Rowland et al., 2009).

ENGAGING IN CHALLENGING PROFESSIONAL CONVERSATIONS

> Feedback thrives on error ... knowing this error is fundamental to moving towards success.
>
> (Hattie, 2012: 115)

One of the challenges in learning to become a teacher - which, at times, can be stressful - is that the classroom is a constantly changing, unique environment that requires the teacher to make decisions and judgements (Wilson, 2013). These will be influenced not only by rational thinking, but also by previous experiences and emotions (Demetriou, Wilson and Winterbottom, 2009).

In order to 'think' like a teacher, trainees need be able to make 'deliberative judgements' through understanding interrelated elements impacting on the classroom and relationships, based on responses to learning conversations, which can sometimes be challenging. It is important to reflect on the key messages of professional conversations and analyse both emotional and deliberative responses in order to move towards a constructive outcome.

Receiving and responding to feedback on a lesson you have put hours of work into can sometimes feel very difficult, as though your efforts were wasted. In the following passage, Becky describes her approach to ensure that the conversations with her mentor remained constructive:

> Initially, I found receiving feedback to be a daunting process, particularly if a lesson hadn't quite gone according to plan. I would try to focus on the positives and remind myself of the journey that I was on in developing my teaching practice. This then helped me to prepare for discussing aspects of the lesson that hadn't been as successful. I viewed receiving feedback as a tool in developing my teaching practice, rather than as a type of criticism. I found this mindset to be crucial during feedback sessions which in turn have enabled me to develop my teaching practice and become a reflective practitioner.

It is not always easy to remain as rational and positive as Becky during challenging feedback sessions; the tendency might be to have an emotional response and lose sight of the constructive nature of the feedback process. If you find yourself in this situation, working through the following questions might enable you to move towards a 'cooler action' and help you 'think like a teacher' (Wilson, 2013):

- *Summary*, description of conversation. What did you hear?
- *Initial reaction*: What's your intuitive response?
- *Emotional response*: How do you feel about what happened?
- *Evidence*: What are the facts?
- *Action*: What are you going to do to address the issue?
- *Timescale*: When will things happen?
- *Support*: What help do you need to achieve a satisfactory outcome?

Task 1.3.3 Reflecting on learning conversations

Think about a professional conversation you have found challenging (for example, with a parent or colleague) and replay it in your head. Make notes using the previous prompts in order to reflect and learn from the experience so that there is a positive outcome.

Developing these positive dispositions and skills will help you develop the professional resilience that is required to navigate the challenges of 'practice shock' and, ultimately, prepare you to deal with the many challenges that lie ahead of you throughout your future career (Day and Kington, 2008).

In summary, it is important to be:

- receptive, open-minded and active in these learning conversations;
- aware of how you learn and the strategies you find effective in order that you can talk explicitly to your mentors about the approach that suits you;
- aware of your attitude towards engaging with learning conversations; this includes how you present yourself through your body language, tone of voice and level of engagement;
- 'deliberative' during challenging professional conversations to avoid an emotional response.

UNDERSTANDING THAT YOUR LEARNING IS A JOURNEY

> Professional identity ... is negotiated through experience and the sense that is made of that experience.
>
> (Sachs, 2005: 15)

As you move through your placements, within a school or to a different school, you may find that you feel your practice has regressed – this is perfectly natural and should be expected as challenges are presented in the process of enculturation within a new setting. The learning journey of a trainee teacher is not a linear, predictable or straightforward process, so it is inevitable that some points during the year will be more challenging than others. Wilson (2103) identifies February as the low point of a specific trainee's pre-service training.

Capitalising on professional practice: Making the most of your placements

In this vignette, Luke describes his progression through a one-year PGCE course. As you read this passage, consider how Luke's role in the professional dialogue sessions changes as he becomes more experienced and develops his professional identity by becoming an active participant.

> Perhaps the most valuable moments of my teacher training attributed to my successful completion were the open, effective and professional conversations that occurred between myself and my mentors. Despite originally assuming that these feedback meetings would be wholly led by the mentors, the way in which these sessions occurred evolved throughout my practice as I became more confident in discussing myself as a practitioner – a notion that was initially rather nerve-wracking.
>
> The feedback I received during my first placement acknowledged the aspects of my teaching that I had consciously attempted to implement and also sensitively highlighted elements of my practice that I had failed to consider. I agreed with all the feedback that was provided and targets that were set, yet never really commented on or questioned the feedback. It was certainly not the case that the mentor made me feel uncomfortable in doing so, but I was just glad to have the opinion of a professional, as at the time in my training I felt merely like a teaching 'imposter' and so allowed the mentor to fully lead the evaluation.
>
> By my second placement, I was teaching sequences of lessons, which allowed me to feel more in control of the progression of the children's learning. During feedback meetings, I was praised on elements of my practice that I had not consciously intended to incorporate. Some strategies and approaches were becoming natural to me and this allowed me to stress less about constantly demonstrating 'good practice'. Instead, I could focus on the areas of my teaching that were mutually decided to be the most in need of addressing. I was certainly beginning to trust myself to contribute more to the professional discussion.
>
> My final placement mentor would frequently question my decision to implement certain strategies and ask for my opinion in regards to my teaching. Although initially my heart would skip a beat as I tried to think of the correct response, I soon came to realise that these were not tests she was setting me. Instead, she was encouraging me to truly interrogate my practice.
>
> Before I knew it, I was driving the discussions, stating the strengths and areas to adapt that I had observed during my own lessons. Finally, I had learned to not only look to my mentors for support, but also to rely on, and believe in, myself. During my placements, I began to realise the importance of instantly self-reflecting upon lessons prior to having a discussion with my mentor. It was valuable to realise that over time, my judgements and my mentors' correlated. It was empowering to discover that my judgements as a practitioner were akin to those of experienced teachers and really allowed me to believe in myself as a teacher.

Every route into teaching will have different expectations for the specific characteristics and buildup of responsibilities in school placements during the course. Training providers will take into account your prior experience of working with children, your teaching experience and your personal subject knowledge in order to individualise the training programme for you. The key to your success relies on your ability to accept that you will face many highs and lows throughout your placements; the fundamental skill is to keep pushing yourself to move forward and to treat each new day as a new opportunity to learn.

Task 1.3.4 Reflecting on teaching experiences

Reflect on a particular experience or episode from which you have gained significant insight into an aspect of your learning about teaching while on placement. Write an account that analyses the links between this experience in school and some aspect of your reading of educational research.

SUMMARY

As a beginning practitioner, it may be difficult to understand what an experienced teacher does to be effective, but gradually, as you progress through your school placements, you will develop an understanding of the craft, science and art of teaching. Becoming a reflexive practitioner is crucial to this process. Your placements will be some of the most challenging experiences of your training, but being proactive is vital, and having an aspirational disposition for both you and the children will make the process more positive, increasing the likelihood that you will successfully gain Qualified Teacher Status (QTS). Progressing through school placements may sometimes feel like a rollercoaster, as you will undoubtedly experience the highs and lows associated with 'practice shock'. During intensive, stressful periods, it is important that you take care of yourself and, as far as possible, retain a work–life balance. Make time for *all* the SPICES of life – the Spiritual, Physical, Intellectual, Creative, Emotional and Social aspects – some of which are easy to forget during school placements. First-hand experiences in schools are obviously vital in your preparation to become a teacher, and in this unit we have attempted to articulate considerations that will help you to become a successful, 'fully developed professional' who has control of their own professional development and continues learning.

ANNOTATED FURTHER READING

McGregor, D. and Cartwright, L. (2011) *Developing Reflective Practice: A Handbook for Beginning Teachers*, Maidenhead, UK: Open University Press.
> This practical guide explains some of the best-known theories on reflective practice. The very real problems faced by beginning teachers are brought to life through the use of rich case studies, as well as extracts drawn from the reflective journals of those starting their teaching career.

Hattie, J. (2012) *Visible Learning for Teachers: Maximizing Impact on Learning*, London: Routledge.
> Written with trainee teachers in mind and championing student teacher perspectives, this book links the biggest ever research project on teaching strategies to practical classroom implementation and includes step-by-step guidance on topics such as lesson preparation, interpreting learning and feedback during the lesson and post-lesson discussions.

Robinson, C., Bingle, B. and Howard, C. (2015) *Your Primary School-Based Experience: A Guide to Outstanding Placements*, Northwich, UK: Critical Publishing.
> This is an essential companion for primary trainee teachers. It focuses on the school-based experience and provides both practical strategies and opportunities for reflection, so trainees are challenged to critically evaluate their learning in order to improve attainment and succeed.

FURTHER READING TO SUPPORT M-LEVEL STUDY

Hagger, H., Burn, K., Mutton, T. and Brindley, S. (2008) 'Practice makes perfect? Learning to learn as a teacher', *Oxford Review of Education*, 34(1): 159–178.
> This article presents research conducted with 25 student teachers, following a one-year postgraduate course within two well-established, school-based partnerships. The authors' findings show that the success the trainees had in making the most of their placements was determined by their attitudes and dispositions.

Day, C. and Kington, A. (2008) 'Identity, wellbeing and effectiveness: The emotional contexts of teaching', *Pedagogy, Culture & Society*, 16(1): 7-23.
> This article links research on dispositions and developing teachers' identity. It does not directly focus on trainee teachers and their placements, but it does illustrate how these issues are relevant beyond the training year and how they impact on longer-term professional development.

Caires, S., Almeida, L. and Vieira, D. (2012) 'Becoming a teacher: Student teachers' experiences and perceptions about teaching practice', *European Journal of Teacher Education*, 35(2): 163-178.
> This study focuses on the experiences of 295 student teachers. Their feelings, cognitions and perceptions regarding teaching practice were analysed. Results emphasise some of the positive perceptions and difficulties experienced during this period.

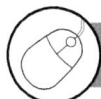

RELEVANT WEBSITES

Knowledge Quartet: www.knowledgequartet.org/
> This website provides details about the theoretical framework for the analysis and development of mathematics teaching; it is used across the globe to support beginning and experienced teachers reflect upon and enhance their teaching. The resources provide details of the Knowledge Quartet's (KQ) four dimensions with grounded exemplification scenarios to support understanding of the model and implications for future practice.

Reflective Teaching: http://reflectiveteaching.co.uk
> The resources on this website are designed to support the development of high-quality professional judgement and evidence-informed practice. It has further links to the Teaching and Learning Research Programme (TLRP).

Visible Learning: https://visible-learning.org/2014/08/john-hattie-mind-frames-teachers/
> This website contains useful information and videos about how to make learning visible as an aid for teachers to evaluate their own teaching. According to John Hattie, visible learning and teaching occur when teachers see learning through the eyes of students and help them become their own teachers.

Education Support Partnership: www.educationsupportpartnership.org.uk/about-us
> This UK charity is dedicated to improving the health and well-being of people working in education. It champions good mental health and well-being of teachers, with a wide range of tools to support and help improve professional and organisational development.

Acas (Advisory, Conciliation and Arbitration Service): www.acas.org.uk/index.aspx?articleid=3799
> This website contains free and impartial information and advice about workplace relations, including challenging conversations and how to manage them. The website contains useful information, videos and strategies to support this aspect of your professional development.

REFERENCES

Askew, S. and Lodge, C. (2000) 'Gifts, ping-pong and loops - linking feedback and learning', in S. Askew (ed.) *Feedback for Learning*, London: RoutledgeFalmer, pp. 4-18.

Burn, K., Hagger, H., Mutton, T. and Everton, T. (2000) 'Beyond concerns with self: The sophisticated thinking of beginning student teachers', *Journal of Education for Teaching*, (26)3: 259-278.

Caires, S., Almeida, L. and Vieira, D. (2012) 'Becoming a teacher: Student teachers' experiences and perceptions about teaching practice', *European Journal of Teacher Education*, 35(2): 163-178. https://doi.org/10.1080/02619768.2011.643395

Cartwright, L. (2011) 'How consciously reflective are you?', in D. McGregor and L. Cartwright, *Developing Reflective Practice: A Handbook for Beginning Teachers*, Maidenhead, UK: Open University Press, pp. 55-68.

Dahl, K. K. B. (2020) 'Mo(ve)ments in professional identification: Achieving professional identity and becoming a teacher in Danish and Kenyan teacher education', *Compare: A Journal of Comparative and International Education*, 50(1): 123-140. https://doi.org/10.1080/03057925.2018.1508333

Day, C. and Kington, A. (2008) 'Identity, wellbeing and effectiveness: The emotional contexts of teaching', *Pedagogy, Culture & Society*, 16(1): 7-23.

Demetriou, H., Wilson, E. and Winterbottom, M. (2009) 'The role of emotion in teaching: Are there differences between male and female newly qualified teachers' approaches to teaching?', *Educational Studies*, 35(4): 449-473.

Department for Education (DfE). (2011) *Teachers' Standards*. Last updated 2021. Retrieved from: www.gov.uk/government/publications/teachers-standards (accessed 8 November 2017).

Department for Education (DfE). (2019) *Initial Teacher Training (ITT): Core Content Framework*, London: Department for Education. Last updated 2024. Retrieved from: www.gov.uk/government/publications/initial-teacher-training-itt-core-content-framework (accessed 4 December 2023).

Dweck, C. (1986) 'Motivational processes affecting learning', *American Psychologist*, 41: 1040-1048.

Hagger, H., Burn, K., Mutton, T. and Brindley, S. (2008) 'Practice makes perfect? Learning to learn as a teacher', *Oxford Review of Education*, 34(1): 159-178.

Hanna, F., Oostdam, R., Severiens, S. E. and Zijlstra, B. J. H. (2019) 'Domains of teacher identity: A review of quantitative measurement instruments', *Educational Research Review*, 27: 15-27. https://doi.org/10.1016/j.edurev.2019.01.003

Hattie, J. (2012) *Visible Learning for Teachers: Maximizing Impact on Learning*, London: Routledge.

Lave, J. and Wenger, E. (1991) *Situated Learning: Legitimate Peripheral Participation*, Cambridge, UK: Cambridge University Press.

McGregor, D. and Cartwright, L. (2011) *Developing Reflective Practice: A Handbook for Beginning Teachers*, Maidenhead, UK: Open University Press.

Moore, A. (2004) *The Good Teacher: Dominant Discourses in Teaching and Teacher Education*, London: Routledge.

Pillen, M., Beijaard, D. and den Brok, P. (2013) 'Tensions in beginning teachers' professional identity development, accompanying feelings and coping strategies', *European Journal of Teacher Education*, 36(3): 240-260. https://doi.org/10.1080/02619768.2012.696192

Rowland, T., Turner, F., Thwaites, A. and Huckstep, P. (2009) *Primary Mathematics Teaching: Reflecting on Practice with the Knowledge Quartet*, London: Sage.

Sachs, J. (2005) 'Teacher education and the development of professional identity: Learning to be a teacher', in P. Denicolo and M. Kompf (eds) *Connecting Policy and Practice: Challenges for Teaching and Learning in Schools and Universities*, Oxford, UK: Routledge, pp. 5-21.

Schepens, A., Aelterman, A. and Vlerick, P. (2009) 'Student teachers' professional identity formation: Between being born as a teacher and becoming one', *Educational Studies*, 35(4): 361-378. https://doi.org/10.1080/03055690802648317

Sewell, K. (2012) *Doing Your PGCE at M-Level*, 2nd edn, London: Sage.

Sfard, A. and Prusak, A. (2005) 'Telling identities: In search of an analytical tool for investigating learning as a culturally shaped activity', *Educational Researcher*, 34(4): 14-22.

Stokking, K., Leenders, F., De Jong, J. and Van Tartwijk, J. (2003) From student to teacher: Reducing practice shock and early dropout in the teaching profession. *European Journal of Teacher Education*, 26(3): 329-350. https://doi.org/10.1080/0261976032000128175

Wilson, E. (2013) 'Building social capital in teacher education through university-school partnerships', in M. Evans (ed.) *Teacher Education and Pedagogy Theory, Policy and Practice*, Cambridge, UK: Cambridge University Press, pp. 41-59.

Wyse, D., Pollard, A., Craig, A., Daly, C. Seleznyov, S, Harmey, S. Hayward, L., Higgins, S. and McCrory, A. (2023) *Reflective Teaching in Primary Schools*, 6th edn, London: Bloomsbury.

Yuan, R., Liu, W. and Lee, I. (2019) 'Confrontation, negotiation and agency: Exploring the inner dynamics of student teacher identity transformation during teaching practicum', *Teachers and Teaching*, 25(8): 972-993. https://doi.org/10.1080/13540602.2019.1688286

# SECTION 2
EXPLORING THE NATURE OF LEARNING AND TEACHING

UNIT 2.1

LOOKING AT CHILDREN

Jane Payler and Mary Scanlan

INTRODUCTION

Why do primary teachers need to have a good understanding of child development? Every child you teach will be unique, each growing up in a family with its own culture and range of experiences. Those home and community experiences form the basis of children's developmental trajectories. Children draw upon knowledge and experience from their wider life to make sense of learning in the classroom. Teachers need to know about child development so that the classroom experiences offered acknowledge the uniqueness of each pupil, ensuring all can progress.

Although the priorities of statutory curricula are subject to continual change, what remains unchanging is the teacher's responsibility for providing the best educational experience for all children within the given constraints. In this unit, the phrase *educational experience* means the total (school) experience of every child. The role of the teacher is to cater for each child's unique needs and provide an environment in which every child can make progress across all areas of development.

The unit examines the *nature* of child development and explores three areas of development foundational to learning: physical; social and emotional; and communication and language. The unit will equip you to think critically about learning and teaching perspectives and raise questions for reflection. It will help you to understand how you can support your pupils using knowledge of child development and why this is important.

OBJECTIVES

By the end of this unit, you should:

- understand the holistic nature of child development;
- be familiar with key theorists in child development and their ideas;
- understand the importance of your role in supporting the development of *all* children you teach.

SITUATED, HOLISTIC DEVELOPMENT

Drawing on extensive research over many decades, we know that human development:

- continues throughout the life-course;
- is holistic, with interrelated rather than separate domains;
- is socioculturally-historically situated and occurs through participation.

Consider the following vignette:

> Aileen is 3 weeks old and lying in her crib. She wakes from sleep. Her tummy feels empty and hurts. She feels cold and uncomfortable. She begins to cry loudly. Her mother picks her up and holds her close. Aileen senses comforting contact and a familiar smell. She hears her mother's soothing voice and can see her face up close. She turns her head instinctively to feed, her hands tucked in close to her chest. As she feeds, she watches her mother's face and listens to her voice. She feels warm; she finds the suckling soothing and the discomfort in her tummy lessens.
>
> Aileen is now 8 months old. She sits up on the floor and reaches for the wooden hoop in the basket near to her. She grasps it, turns it around in her hands, passing it from one to the other, and puts it in her mouth. She feels the smooth wood and the rounded shape. Her brother, aged 3 years, sits nearby, searching through the basket rapidly. She watches and listens as he finds the wooden spoon, bangs it noisily in a plastic cup and pretends to eat from it while making appreciative yum-yum noises. She gurgles in response and smiles. 'Want some, Aileen?' he asks, meeting her gaze.

Child development is often researched, discussed and written about as if it occurs in separate domains, for example cognitive, social or physical, and is the same for all children. But we know that human development occurs holistically, with all domains interrelated and influencing each other. In the vignette, Aileen appears to be driven by her physical sensations. However, her experiences in having her needs met are the foundations of her social development (someone else tends to me with care), communication (voice and facial expressions are directed at me; I can return the gaze) and emotional development (I feel responded to with warmth when I am in need). These are associated with the pleasurable physical sensations of food, warmth and comfort. Later in the vignette, Aileen's physical changes – she is now able to sit, see further and handle items – enable her to reach out, grasp more accurately and explore with hands and mouth. Previous interesting experiences drive her curiosity, as do observing and interacting with her older sibling.

Although interrelatedness may seem obvious when discussing a baby's development, we can lose sight of the importance of attending to *all* domains of development once children are older in school. Yet physical changes, emotional insecurity, adapting to new social situations or learning a new language all influence cognition. For some children, their home or social circumstances make focusing on learning difficult. You will read more about this later in the unit. Essentially, all developmental domains are important to learning and are of concern to teachers.

Human development is not only holistic, but also situated. It takes place in the specific situations that make up children's life experiences. Those life experiences are woven through with culture and history, passed on from one generation to the next (Rogoff, 2003). How a child develops in a particular time in history, in a particular place and family, in a specific society with its language and cultural tools will be different to another child from a different time and place. It is the child's *changing participation over time within social situations* that constitutes development (Rogoff, 2003). Therefore, understanding something of children's home and community cultures will help you to understand what each child brings with them to school, in terms of their individual development and how that might differ to *your* individual experiences. It is important to recognise, too, that some children's experiences in school and in wider society will be affected by unconscious bias from others. This too impacts on achievement, learning and development (Peterson *et al.*, 2016).

Given that human development is holistic rather than domain-specific, there are arguably foundational aspects to development that can help our understanding of cognitive development and learning. In this unit, we indicate some of the key aspects of development that could be seen as foundational to learning.

Physical development

Recent advances in neuroscience have evidenced the interconnectedness between environment, brain and body development (Tooley et al., 2021). As seen in the vignette, Aileen's physical progress is closely connected to other areas of development. We note her rapid development in the first year, a move from dependency to growing independence as she gains control over her body. Physical development (along with communication and language development and personal social and emotional development) is one of the *prime* areas in the Early Years Foundation Stage (EYFS) curriculum (Department for Education [DfE], 2014). Achievement in later areas can be problematic without this solid foundation. For example, handwriting is a complex activity involving well-developed gross (shoulder and arm) and fine (pincer grasp) motor skills, in addition to manipulative prowess and good hand-eye coordination. Physical development is vital for the well-being and development of every child.

Hereditary factors, nutrition and lifestyle all impact on individual physical growth (Doherty and Hughes, 2014). Motor development means the child's growing ability to use their body in a variety of ways. *Gross motor skills* concern managing large muscles – pulling, pushing, bending and twisting. *Locomotor skills* are linked but involve movement – running, jumping and skipping. *Fine motor skills* involve the smaller muscles and hand-eye coordination, used in activities such as threading and turning book pages (Cooper and Doherty, 2010). Physical development usually begins in a head-to-toe (cephalocaudal) and centre-to-outwards (proximodistal) sequence. Gaining mastery over a range of physical skills similarly underpins the physical education programmes of study in the National Curriculum in KS1 and KS2, together with a focus on competition and cooperation (DfE, 2013).

Changes in lifestyle occurred during the Covid-19 pandemic and its consequent lockdowns, where families' freedom to go outside, socialise and attend educational settings were restricted. The pandemic had a significant impact on factors known to influence the physical development of children, particularly:

- less physical activity and more screentime;
- more food insecurity and increases in the consumption of unhealthy foods;
- challenges to support for breastfeeding;
- less use of oral healthcare, reduced vaccination rates and poorer sleep quality.

The impacts of these changes were greater on children from low-income families and from minority ethnic families (Stanford, Davie and Mulcahy, 2021).

The National Child Measurement Programme data for primary school children showed that in the school year 2018–2019, around 75% of 4-to-5-year-olds in Reception were a healthy weight, but only 64% of 10-to-11-year-olds in Year 6 were (National Health Service, 2019). Government guidance, *Childhood Obesity: Applying All Our Health* (Office for Health Improvement and Disparities, 2022), urged schools to register with the Public Health England's (n.d.) Change4Life School Zone to receive associate teacher packs, lesson plans and videos to support children identified as overweight and to help prevent it. Teachers have a vital role to play in promoting the physical development and well-being of their pupils.

> **Task 2.1.1 Time to move?**
>
> Consider the opportunities available for physical movement in a class you know. Over a day, record:
>
> - how much time children are required to sit still;
> - how much time children are free to move about;
> - opportunities for movement play;
> - whether those opportunities are available indoors or outside.
>
> How well do you feel that children's physical development is supported in the classroom?

Social and emotional development

Humans are social animals with powerful psychologic drives fuelling interdependency. Deci and Ryan (2002) suggest that throughout our lives we try to establish and maintain feelings of *relatedness*, *autonomy* and *competence*. For young children, relatedness begins as total dependency. But even from birth, babies seek out and contribute to their relationships with others through reciprocal facial expressions and bodily movements (Trevarthen, 2011). The need to be part of close relationships with others continues throughout our lifetimes (Morris, 2015). Our individual blueprint for how we understand and form those close relationships is developed through our earliest experiences of bonding with our primary carers, and predicated on the care, attention and responsiveness we receive. This bonding is known as *attachment*. It explains the deep-seated need for affectional bonds between a baby/child and their closest carers. Although its specific characteristics vary across cultures, it occurs internationally (Mesman, Van Ijzendoorn and Sagi-Schwartz, 2018). Early attachment experiences impact on subsequent relationships throughout childhood and adulthood. Early experiences are not entirely deterministic though; on the contrary, as humans we are highly adaptive and continue to learn from experiences throughout life. Nonetheless, early attachment influences how children subsequently try to make relationships and to make *sense* of relationships. You will refresh your knowledge of attachment theory in Unit 3.5.

Relationships with people other than their closest carers continue to be important to children's social and emotional development. Friendships play a valuable role in children's development. When playing or working with established friends, children add to each other's ideas, sustain more complex creations and experience a sense of belonging (Broadhead and Chesworth, 2015). Friendships can help children to cope with difficult situations (Adams, Bruce Santo and Bukowski, 2011), measurably reducing the level of the stress hormone cortisol. The importance of friendship in children's well-being, and in supporting social and cognitive development, is not always fully recognised by teachers or parents (Brogaard-Clausen and Robson, 2019). Papadopoulou (2016) suggested ways to create 'space' for friendships in education:

> Enabling environments would involve giving children the physical and emotional space and time they need in order to meet friends and build relationships. Rather than focusing mainly on adult-led, adult-directed and adult-controlled activities, children should be given the opportunities to exercise agency and choice, to meet peers, spend time with them and select the types of activities and resources they want to share with their friends.
>
> (Papadopoulou, 2016: 1556)

Communication and language

Returning to Aileen, we can see how her language development is promoted within her family. She knows to communicate by vocalising her needs through crying, making eye contact, gurgling and smiling. She listens carefully; her mother's voice soothes her distress, and she watches her older sibling, observing both his verbal and nonverbal behaviours. Aileen is demonstrating three key aspects of language: *expressive* (speaking), *receptive* (listening) and *understanding*.

Communication is vital. How language develops has been the subject of much investigation, as have ways of monitoring and supporting children's language development (see for example Reilly and McKean, 2023, and McKean and Reilly, 2023). A *preverbal* stage in language development refers to when babies' needs are expressed through cries and physical action. They listen and, from about 4 months, use vocal play with sounds such as 'ah' and 'oo'. From about 6 months, babies 'babble', producing strings such as 'dadada'. At about 9 months, babies use jargon, where the intonation patterns of speech are practised (Kersner, 2015). The *verbal stage* then builds on this foundation. First words are introduced from about the age of 1, and two-word phrases are used from about the age of 2. By the third year, the development of a grammatical structure becomes apparent. Helped by adult–child interaction, children gradually develop the use of tenses, plurals and word order and begin to speak in more complex sentences.

Research explored the puzzle of how infants learned to speak so well without direct focused instruction. In the 1950s, Chomsky (1957) identified what he termed the Language Acquisition Device (LAD). He theorised that young children were born with an innate ability to learn language, were sensitive to the linguistic features within their environment and learned language through imitation. However, his theories were critiqued for not acknowledging the importance of the emotional and social context in promoting language. Bruner (1975), following a Vygotskian social learning perspective, stressed the importance of opportunities for babies both to experience and to observe language interactions between others. His Language Acquisition Support System (LASS) acknowledged the way in which adults scaffold children's language development. He identified *infant-directed speech*, the way in which adult speech is modified when talking to young children, for example speaking in slower, shorter, less complex sentences. Kersner (2015) has since argued that language learning is influenced by a combination of imitation, innate ability and adult–child interaction.

Spoken language is highlighted in the English programmes of study in the National Curriculum for KS1 and KS2: 'Teachers should therefore ensure the continual development of pupils' confidence and competence in spoken language and listening skills' (DfE, 2013: 13-14). In any primary class, there can be a wide range of **speech, language and communication needs** (SLCN). Development in this area is dependent on a range of factors. Some children are adept at masking language difficulties, and others may present with alternative challenges. A child with language processing difficulties might present with apparent behavioural issues (appearing to ignore instructions), and a child who finds it difficult to make themselves understood might become socially isolated (Cross, 2015). Teachers need to be alert to possible underlying issues and their importance. Poor language skills can impact achievement:

> One child in five starts primary school in England without the language skills they need to succeed, a figure that rises to one in three of the poorest children … one in four children who struggled with language at age five did not reach the expected standard in English at the end of primary school compared with one in 25 children who had good language skills at age five.
>
> (Save the Children, 2016: 1)

The Covid-19 pandemic had a further impact on children's communication and language development, including the fact that some children's speech and language delays were not identified as early as they might have been. Ofsted (2022) found that more children were requiring speech and language support than before the pandemic. Suggested reasons include more time spent on electronic devices and missing the opportunities that early years settings provide for language enrichment, such as sharing, playing games and engaging in role play (Scanlan, 2018).

It is vital that teachers are confident to assess and support children's language development. As part of the Education Endowment Foundation (EEF) Teaching and Learning Toolkit (n.d.), EEF reviewed evidence on the effect of oral language interventions. EEF found that oral language interventions had a very high impact on children's development for very low cost. EEF also produced guidance on improving communication, language and literacy in the early years as part of preparing children for literacy (EEF, 2018). Further outputs are available online (please see the Relevant websites section).

> **Task 2.1.2 Reflecting on speech language and communication needs**
>
> - Look at the EEF Teaching and Learning Toolkit section on oral language interventions. Read about the impact of these interventions. In particular, check out 'How could you implement in your setting?'
> - Download and read the EEF (2018) guidance document, *Preparing for Literacy: Improving Communication, Language and Literacy in the Early Years*, and consider how well you accommodate activities to strengthen communication and language development in your classroom.
> - Look at the Speech Language and Communication Framework (SLCF): www.slcframework.org.uk/. The **Universal Level** outlines the basic skills and knowledge that everyone working with children should have around SLC and SLCN. Strand 5 focusses on **the communication environment**: www.slcframework.org.uk/activities/Please choose one or more of the activities, videos and a reading, to support your classroom practice.

KEY THEORISTS OF CHILD DEVELOPMENT

Jean Piaget was a Swiss biologist and psychologist, who became fascinated by how young children learn to think. Writing from the 1920s-1970s, his work included the importance of active experiential learning (Piaget, 1929) and cognitive development (Piaget, 1953).

Piaget's conceptualisation of human development was of a 'staged theory', the idea that children need to successfully complete a set of defined stages to reach their full intellectual potential. These stages moved from the physically situated *sensorimotor* stage (birth to 2 years) through the *pre-operational* stage, in which the child's social development allows them to be less egocentric (2-7 years), to the *concrete-operational* stage (7-11 years), in which, Piaget argued, logical thought was enabled. The final stage was *formal operations* (11+ years), in which children were able to think logically and hypothetically. He believed that successful negotiation through these stages was achieved through the child's active social and physical interaction with their environment. His *schema theory* of how children acquire knowledge argued that young children are born with the ability to interact with others and their environment to gain knowledge. As these experiences increase, they create mental files or *schemas* of representations and information. One of the ways in which children gain this knowledge is through their language interactions with others. When a child can understand everything in their immediate world, they are said to be in a state of balance or *equilibrium*, which is disturbed when they come across something new they cannot understand. *Disequilibrium* allows children to challenge and develop their current understanding.

Although Piaget's theories of child development were not conceived for classroom practice, they were highly influential in the 1960s. In the USA, his ideas of active learning underpinned the innovative High/Scope approach to education (Hohmann and Weikart, 1995). In the UK, his influence was seen in the Plowden Report (1967), which advocated a move from a teacher-led, formal transmission curriculum model to a more child-centred discovery approach.

Lev Vygotsky was a Russian psychologist writing primarily during the 1920s-1930s. His ideas became available in the West in the 1960s and were popularised from the early 1980s. Vygotsky's theory suggests that human development is socially formed. Although Piaget acknowledged the role of socialisation in providing experiences on which the child operates to actively construct their cognitive development, the 'social' was seen as an overlay to intrapersonal development (Piaget, 1995: 278). Vygotsky, however, understood the social not simply as setting the *parameters* for learning, but in *actively forming* higher mental functions in partnership with the child's spontaneous development, mediated by psychological 'tools' and interpersonal communication. Vygotsky saw a complex interrelationship between instruction and development, where one sometimes leads the other (Vygotsky, 1986: 184).

Although often recognised as contributing most to our understanding of the social and cultural determinants of development, Vygotsky clearly acknowledged biological aspects of development. Vygotsky noted that children's concept formation occurred along dual lines, with different forms of experience leading to different types of concept development. Although 'scientific concepts' (schooled, more abstract and logical concepts) originated in the highly structured nature of classroom activity, 'spontaneous concepts' (empirically rich and disorganised) emerged from 'a child's own reflections on everyday experiences' (Kozulin's introduction to Vygotsky, 1986: xxxiv). Scientific and spontaneous concepts are inextricably interwoven, each acting on the other.

For Vygotsky, two things are key in forming shifts in children's development. The first is the *zone of proximal development* (ZPD), of which you will learn more in Unit 2.3. The ZPD points to the fact that children can do more with the guidance of someone more competent than alone. The second key idea is that of *'crises'*. Note, though, that crises in this context do not mean something catastrophic or bad. Crises refer instead to the times at which something *changes* for the child, biologically or in terms of gaining competence, which result in a change in the child's motivations. This in turn challenges the way that the child relates to others, as relationships have been based on the child's previous biological state or level of competence (Hedegaard, 2009). Hedegaard gives the example of a 1-year-old baby whose relationships with her parents and her environment change because of her competence shifts when able to walk.

There are implications from Vygotsky's theory of child development for teachers:

- Children bring with them individual and distinctive ways of being and thinking, based on their everyday 'spontaneous' social and cultural experiences.
- Children need to draw on these, as well as on new experiences, to make sense of the world.
- Such experiences work in partnership with biological development. No matter what the experiences and the level of sensitive teaching, it is not possible to teach a 6-month-old baby to ride a bicycle. The principle remains true of older children, too. However, teaching is vital to help children to progress.
- The relationship between the teacher, pedagogy and each child evolves constantly, with shifting experiences, biology and levels of competence.

Jerome Bruner, writing and researching from the 1950s–1990s, shared Vygotsky's view that culture and context are vital to understanding learning and development. Bruner heightened our understanding of the processes involved when a more competent person guides the activity of another person in the ZPD, explaining the nature of adults *scaffolding* children's participation through graduated support (Wood, Bruner and Ross, 1976). Like Vygotsky, Bruner emphasised the importance of *language* in human development. He examined the role of story or *narrative* in helping humans to make sense of their lives and their place in it (Bruner, 1991). Bruner introduced the notion that even the most complex of subjects could be explained gradually to children of any age in appropriate terms, and revisited to develop understanding through the *spiral curriculum* (Bruner, 1991).

Urie Bronfenbrenner's seminal work, *The Ecology of Human Development*, was published in 1979. In it, he argued that every aspect of experience that impacted on the developing child, such as family structure, social circumstances, economic positioning and political factors, needed to be seen holistically rather than separately. He argued that not only was acknowledgement of the different environments in which the child grew up important, but also the relationships between them. His ecological systems theory was 'a nested arrangement of structures, each contained within the next' (Bronfenbrenner, 1977: 514). As each child was part of a different set of structures, all children's developmental experiences were unique. In his original work, Bronfenbrenner identified four structures that surrounded the child and impacted on their development. The child's immediate layer he termed the *microsystem* – for young children, largely comprising home and school. Here, children learned rules and socially acceptable behaviour. The next layer was the *mesosystem*, which was the set of relationships formed by participants within the microsystem, for example relationships between the home and the school. Bronfenbrenner argued that effective partnerships between home and school would be beneficial to the child's education, and indeed research has evidenced this positive impact. His third layer was the *exosystem*, which comprised elements such as the family's economic circumstances, local neighbourhood and influences such as the media. Bronfenbrenner's fourth layer was the *macrosystem*, which he identified as the cultural practices, laws and customs that govern society.

Bronfenbrenner later acknowledged that he had not sufficiently recognised the part played by the individual child in the process of development, for example their resilience. He also added the *chronosystem*, showing that human ecology changes over time, in response to both external and internal changes (Bronfenbrenner and Morris, 2006). Bronfenbrenner's influence can perhaps be seen most clearly in the Early Years Foundation Stage (DfE, 2014), in which three of the four themes – the Unique Child, the Enabling Environment and Positive Relations – can be viewed as being influenced by his theoretical perspectives.

Barbra Rogoff, Distinguished Professor of Psychology at the University of California, Santa Cruz, extended our knowledge of the processes involved in children developing and learning in their home and community cultures. She emphasised that human development happens through children's *participation* in the routine ways of doing things. Children learn through taking an active part in the *everyday practices* of daily life with their families and others in their homes, villages and towns (Rogoff, 2003). She explained how participation in activities acted as *apprenticeship in thinking*. Children come to *appropriate* what they learn, that is to understand and use knowledge or skills for their own purposes (Rogoff, 1990). They do so through being alongside and participating at gradually higher levels in adults' daily and cultural activities. Through her research in cultures around the world, Rogoff has demonstrated the cultural and participatory nature of human development. It reminds us to step outside our *own* experiences, to question our assumptions about human development and to view it as richly varied.

Marianne Hedegaard proposed a further extension of Vygotsky's sociocultural historical theory of children's development. Hedegaard's model of human development considers not only the societal conditions and the institutional practices that shape developmental experiences, but also the individual child's different participation through activity as they move *between* several different institutions (Hedegaard, 2009, 2012). Institutions such as home, school or preschool, after-school clubs, church, and so on, each have their own values and practices. To fully understand children's development, we need to consider how each child experiences participating in these institutions in their *individual trajectories*. Each child's perspective and trajectory are unique. Further to taking account of children's sociocultural backgrounds, growing competence and biological changes, teachers need to think about how children experience and make sense of the contexts in which they live. What is each child's cumulative story? Taking this view can help teachers to understand how seemingly small incidents can cause distress or low self-esteem when they are experienced by the child as part of a *set* of experiences, cumulative across different contexts.

Luis Moll, too, was influenced by Vygotsky, particularly the view that human thinking needs to be understood in relation to an individual's social and historical surroundings. Working with James Greenberg and focusing on low-income Hispanic students and their families in Arizona, USA, Moll carried out ethnographic research to map the cultural and social resources that families enjoyed (Moll and Greenberg, 1990). These resources were termed *funds of knowledge*: an 'operations manual of essential information and strategies households need to maintain their wellbeing' (Greenberg, 1989: 2). Moll worked with teachers in schools to explore how these funds of knowledge might support pupils' literacy development in the classroom. When they found out, for example, that many family members were employed in the building trade, a module was devised that allowed pupils to draw on this fund of knowledge to support learning in the classroom. Moll argued that this style of learning exemplified Vygotsky's ZPD where 'the child learns of things that far exceed the limits of his actual and even potential immediate experience' (Vygotsky, 1987: 180). For an exploration regarding how practices can support the child within the school curriculum, see Scanlan (2012).

CHALLENGING NORMS, STAGES AND DEFICIT VIEWS

Although some child development research, such Barbara Rogoff's, has included information about children's development in cultures across the world, the past field of child development was dominated by research based on children from Western, Educated, Industrialised, Rich and Democratic (WEIRD) societies (see, for example, Karasik *et al.*, 2010). The ensuing conceptions of how children *are* at set developmental stages have passed into popular use as developmental milestones and have been routinely used to assess children's development. Children who have experienced different sociocultural backgrounds are measured against the dominant view of child development, as if the milestones can be applied universally to all children, thus seeing some children as 'deficient' and in need of reparation. Less helpful still, it can be taken to imply a level of innate ability that is fixed and therefore indicative of future educational achievement and life outcomes.

Thinking in terms of *norms*, or averaging of levels according to the sample used, immediately places some children below or above the norm and gives rise to conceptions of 'below average' or 'above average' children. When universal developmental norms become part of routine and unquestioned practice, it is time to think critically about what they mean, the evidence on which they are based and the implications of adhering to them. There is a tendency in English schools towards a concept of natural, fixed ability. The terms low-, mid- and high-ability are stalwarts of classroom practice for grouping or categorising children (Hodgen *et al.*, 2023). Notions of universal development also leave disabled children or those with learning difficulties 'outside the box'. As Rix and Parry (2014) explain in their critique of *Development Matters* (Early Education, 2012):

> Disabled children may simply not develop in an area designated by the Framework; this then becomes identified as an individual need. Consequently, practitioners may feel encouraged to find a remedy for weakness rather than building on strengths and be more likely to design individualized solutions rather than engage with wider social learning opportunities.
>
> (Rix and Parry, 2014: 210)

When a teacher is concerned to identify and put in place interventions to support children who are 'falling behind', there are understandable dilemmas. An understanding of human development should alert us to the rich variety of diverse childhoods and thus to diverse development. Teachers need to be aware of children engaging with and building from a range of cultural, social, community, institutional, biological and home heritages, and use these as resources and contexts for learning (Payler and Georgeson, 2017).

Task 2.1.3 Exploring childhoods

Map the range of *childhoods* evident for children in a classroom you are familiar with. Using a different post-it note for each aspect, note distinctive elements of their childhoods. Mount them all on a large sheet of paper. Now reflect and make notes on the paper about:

- how much you know about each child's developmental contexts and individual childhood;
- what you need to find out;
- how the diversity is reflected in your classroom practices.

We turn now to three examples of the ways in which awareness of influences on children's development could support teachers in making sound decisions: age-in-cohort, family difficulties and disrupted childhoods.

Age-in-cohort

Are children born in the autumn cleverer than those born in the summer? This is a preposterous statement. Yet, a strong body of evidence shows that children's relative age within their school cohort is associated with different levels of academic *attainment*, rather than ability (Doebler, Shuttleworth and Gould, 2017). In England, autumn-born children consistently attain at higher levels than those born in the summer (Bell and Daniels, 1990; Campbell, 2014; TACTYC, 2015). Further, summer-born children are over-represented among children diagnosed with special educational needs (Martin et al., 2004). Exactly why this pattern of achievement should exist, we are not yet certain. Common sense tells us that autumn-born children are unlikely to be generally more academically able than summer-born children. However, it is probable that the relative immaturity of summer-born children in age-cohort classes is an important factor, including differences in absolute age at time of assessment (Crawford, Dearden and Greaves, 2013). One example of differential achievement is in the phonics check, which has been administered to all children in England at the end of Year 1 since 2012. Using data from freedom-of-information requests, Clark has shown that success in the test is closely related to age, with a clear gradient in pass rate, month on month, according to month of birth (Clark, 2016).

Teacher *perceptions* of children's ability and attainment are also associated with the child's birth month, with older children more likely to be judged 'above average' by their teachers (Campbell, 2014). Relatively younger children tend more often to be placed in the lowest ability groups, and relatively older children in the highest groups (Campbell, 2014). Daniels, Shorrocks-Taylor and Redfern (2000) found that teacher expectations of the youngest children in their classes affected the tasks that were given to children and the children's performance. They showed that summer-born children's results in standard tests at the end of KS1 were not significantly affected by spending seven or nine terms at school, because they remained the youngest in their class. Teachers need to think carefully about decisions to group children according to perceptions of ability and to be more aware of age-related factors.

Task 2.1.4 Reviewing age-in-cohort consequences

Review the ways in which age-in-cohort is reflected in the processes and structures in your classroom or one you are visiting.

- Write down the names of the six children you think of as the highest achieving and the six lowest achieving.
- Now check whether your perceptions of ability relate to children's birth dates.
- If ability grouping is used, check whether there are links between the groups and children's ages-in-cohort.

Family circumstances

Within-family factors can influence how a child develops and learns. However, these apparently 'within-family' circumstances are often linked to the resources available to the families, and to the structures and values of society. It is well evidenced, for example, that children growing up in economic disadvantage and in minority ethnic groups are more likely to be allocated to 'lower ability' groups and may not therefore be supported to achieve their full potential (Hodgen et al., 2023).

> There is a great deal of evidence highlighting how pupils are misallocated to high and low sets, and this results in the over-representation of pupils from Black and minority ethnic backgrounds in lower sets (e.g. Connolly et al., 2019) and pupils from socially disadvantaged backgrounds in lower sets (e.g. Kutnick et al., 2005).
>
> (Hodgen *et al.*, 2023: 224)

Other within-family circumstances can challenge children's development and learning. Having a close relative with a life-threatening condition can impact children's well-being, attainment and development as they struggle to cope with the emotional strain and anxiety (Payler, Cooper and Bennett, 2020). Having a parent in prison can also influence children's educational development as they experience stigma and stress alongside their families (Cooper *et al.*, 2023). Families do not always make it known to schools that a parent is in prison, meaning that behaviour can be difficult to understand.

Consider the following vignette:

> David's dad was in prison for domestic abuse. David, aged 10, found it difficult to understand and talk about. A schoolteacher became concerned about him when he was coming into school not in his uniform, electing to sit facing the back wall, with very little engagement with his teacher. Soon the relationship with his teacher deteriorated. David was distant from peers and often displayed anger and frustration. He found it challenging to talk about his dad – retreating under his hoodie – appearing to prefer silence. David was referred by the school to YSS Families First, a charity supporting children and young people with a parent in prison.
>
> Asked what would have happened to David if the support had not been made available to him, his teacher explained, 'I'd love to say that school would have swept in to help ... [but] there's only so much a school can do to help parents ... For David, I think possibly he would now be living with dad [by now out of prison]. ... Going into high school, there'd be truancy, ... I think without support, David would very soon have been known to the police'.
>
> (Adapted from Cooper *et al.*, 2023: 42–43 and 76)

As a teacher, how can you be sure to find out about and respond appropriately to family difficulties that children might be facing? How can your actions and beliefs influence their outcomes?

Disrupted childhoods

A growing body of research has examined the effects of disrupted childhoods on children's development (MacFarlane and Van Hooff, 2009; Masten and Narayan, 2012). Although natural disasters, war and terrorism might sometimes seem remote from the everyday life of the primary classroom, in recent years, our awareness of close-to-home disaster events and of migrant children's experiences has been sharpened. Exposure to such experiences inevitably affects children, but the nature and extent of the experiences, together with interventions in the aftermath, play an influential role in shaping how children's development is affected (Masten and Narayan, 2012). There are cumulative effects of repeat exposure to traumas, and the age at which exposure takes place has a differential effect on children: in some ways worse in early childhood; in other ways worse in later childhood. Stress can affect brain development; the effects of trauma can be passed on to the next generation through biological, behavioural or socioeconomic processes; effects on one part of life can have a negative effect on other parts, such as managing at school (Masten and Narayan, 2012: 233). However, there are also ways in which the effects of trauma can be made more manageable for children. *Protective factors* for the longer-term consequences of trauma include attachment relationships and continuing, consistent care from parents and close caregivers, as well as promotion of children's sense of agency and self-efficacy – in other words, being encouraged to believe that they have some control over their own lives. Further, re-establishing steady routines, including schooling, and opportunities to play and socialise with peers are all important aspects that can help protect children from longer-term damage (Masten and Narayan, 2012).

For teachers, the implications for practice are to:

- become aware of the individual circumstances of children's experiences;
- understand that each child may react differently to similar events, depending on previous and subsequent experiences and the protective factors available to them;
- encourage a sense of agency and self-esteem;
- work closely with children's parents, families and communities to support their role in being the child's 'first line of defence'.

SUMMARY

An understanding of child development is important for all primary teachers, not just those teaching the youngest children. We have illustrated how areas of learning are interconnected and highlighted that, as teachers, we need to take a holistic overview of learning and development. We have explored the work of key theorists, particularly those who take a sociocultural perspective, in which the importance of a child's world and their participation within it are acknowledged. Different conceptualisations of child development can impact on policy and practice in classrooms. Teachers need to be proactive in both finding out about, and acknowledging, the out-of-school social worlds of the children they teach, thereby creating an inclusive classroom. Our understanding regarding the links between poverty, circumstances, disruption and development means teachers can use this knowledge in the classroom, offering individualised support or sharing knowledge and resources with parents and carers to enhance home learning.

Furthermore, although an in-depth knowledge of child development is essential for every teacher, it is equally important that we can critique standardised models of progression. Young children are all unique at birth and continue to grow and develop in different ways, dependent on a wide range of factors, such as environment and experience. In the same way, we are all unique as teachers; a wide range of differing experience and knowledge supports our practice, and this understanding of, and reflection on, our own individuality should underpin the learning experiences we offer to the children we teach.

ANNOTATED FURTHER READING

Morris, K. (2015) *Promoting Positive Behaviour in the Early Years*, Maidenhead, UK: Open University Press.
> This book gives a highly readable account of research and theory relating to children's social and emotional development and their impact on behaviours. Strategies are helpful and constructive, with currency beyond the early years.

FURTHER READING TO SUPPORT M-LEVEL STUDY

Nelson, C. A., Bhutta, Z. A., Harris, N. B., Danese, A. and Samara, M. (2020) 'Adversity in childhood is linked to mental and physical health throughout life', *bmj*, 371.
> This article explains adverse childhood experiences (ACE) and how they can impact upon children's short- and long-term mental and physical health. It defines terms such as toxic stress and childhood adversity and explains the consequences of exposure. The article will help teachers to understand how cumulative difficulties with little support can have serious consequences for the children in their care.

Fleer, M. and Hedegaard, M. (2010) 'Children's development as participation in everyday practices across different institutions', *Mind, Culture, & Activity*, 17(2): 149-168.
> This article builds on the theoretical approach in Hedegaard (2009) and applies it to a study of a child across different institutions. It highlights the processes involved in development and emphasises the importance of knowing about children's participation in settings beyond school or nursery.

Hedegaard, M. (2009) 'Children's development from a cultural-historical approach: Children's activity in everyday local settings as foundation for their development', *Mind, Culture, & Activity*, 16(1): 64–82.

> This interesting article attempts to set out a theoretical approach that takes account both of individual psychology and of children operating in concrete, everyday institutions infused with societal values. It is well illustrated with extracts from research.

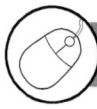

RELEVANT WEBSITES

activematters: www.activematters.org

> The activematters website is dedicated to early years physical development. It provides a range of relevant materials and ideas for practitioners.

Education Endowment Foundation: https://educationendowmentfoundation.org.uk/education-evidence/teaching-learning-toolkit/oral-language-interventions.

> The Education Endowment Foundation website provides teachers with reviews of evidence and guidance to ensure that time spent on educational interventions is well spent.

ICAN Children's Communication Charity: www.icancharity.org.uk/

> ICAN's Talking Point gives parents/carers and practitioners the information they need to help children develop their speech, language and communication skills.

Anna Freud Centre: www.annafreud.org/

> The Anna Freud Centre distils, translates and disseminates knowledge about what works for the wellbeing and mental health of children and young people. Sections of the website offer tools, resources and guidance for schools, colleges and early years.

OpenLearn, *Attachment in the Early Years*: www.open.edu/openlearn/health-sports-psychology/childhood-youth/early-years/attachment-the-early-years/content-section-0

> A free online course produced by the Open University.

REFERENCES

Adams, R. E., Bruce Santo, J. and Bukowski, W. M. (2011) 'The presence of a best friend buffers the effects of negative experiences', *Developmental Psychology*, 47(6): 1786–1791.

Bell, J. F. and Daniels, S. (1990) 'Are summer-born children disadvantaged? The birthdate effect in education', *Oxford Review of Education*, 16(1): 67–80.

Broadhead, P. and Chesworth, L. (2015) 'Friendship, culture and playful learning', in J. Moyles, *The Excellence of Play*, 4th edn, Maidenhead, UK: Open University Press, chap. 9, pp. 94–105.

Brogaard-Clausen, S. and Robson, S. (2019) 'Friendships for wellbeing? Parents' and practitioners' positioning of young children's friendships in the evaluation of wellbeing factors', *International Journal of Early Years Education*, 27(4): 345–359. Available at: https://doi.org/10.1080/09669760.2019.1629881.

Bronfenbrenner, U. (1977) 'Toward an experimental ecology of human development', *American Psychologist*, 32: 513–531.

Bronfenbrenner, U. (1979) *The Ecology of Human Development*, Cambridge, MA: Harvard University Press.

Bronfenbrenner, U. and Morris, P. A. (2006). 'The bioecological model of human development', in W. Damon and R. M. Lerner (eds) *Handbook of Child Psychology*, 6th edn, Hoboken, NJ: John Wiley & Sons, pp. 793–828.

Bruner, J. S. (1975) 'The ontogenesis of speech acts', *Journal of Child Language*, 2(1): 1–20.

Bruner, J. S. (1991) 'The narrative construction of reality', *Critical Inquiry*, 18(1): 1–21.

Campbell, T. (2014) 'Stratified at seven: In class ability grouping and the relative age effect', *British Educational Research Journal*, 40(5): 749–771.

Clark, M. M. (2016) *Learning to be Literate: Insights from Research for Policy and Practice*, revised edition, Abingdon: Routledge.

Chomsky, N. (1957) *Syntactic Structures*, The Hague/Paris: Mouton.

Cooper, L. and Doherty, J. (2010) *Physical Development*, London: Continuum.

Cooper, V., Payler, J., Bennett, S. and Taylor, L. (2023) *From Arrest to Release, Helping Families Feel Less Alone: An Evaluation of a Worcestershire Pilot Support Project for Families Affected by Parental Imprisonment*, Milton Keynes: The Open University. Retrieved from: https://oro.open.ac.uk/88511/7/Evaluation_of_the_YSS_Families_First_project%20FINAL.pdf (accessed 29 August 2023).

Crawford, C., Dearden, L. and Greaves, E. (2013) *When You Are Born Matters: Evidence for England*. Retrieved from: www.ifs.org.uk/comms/r80.pdf (accessed 27 May 2013).

Cross, M. (2015) 'Links between social, mental and emotional health difficulties, and communication needs', in M. Kersner and J. A. Wright (eds) *Supporting Young Children with Communication Problems*, London: Routledge, pp. 86–103.

Daniels, S., Shorrocks-Taylor, D. and Redfern, E. (2000) 'Can starting summer-born children earlier at infant school improve their National Curriculum results?', *Oxford Review of Education*, 26(2): 207–220.

Deci, E. L. and Ryan, R. M. (2002) *Handbook of Self-determination Research*, Rochester, NY: University of Rochester Press.

Department for Education (DfE). (2013) *The National Curriculum in England: Framework Document*, London: Crown Copyright. Last updated 2014. Retrieved from: www.gov.uk/government/publications/national-curriculum-in-england-framework-for-key-stages-1-to-4 (accessed 12 September 2023).

Department for Education (DfE). (2014) *Statutory Framework for the Early Years Foundation Stage*, London: DfE. Last updated 2024. Retrieved from: www.gov.uk/government/publications/early-years-foundation-stage-framework-2 (accessed 9 February 2025).

Doebler, S., Shuttleworth, I. and Gould, M. (2017) 'Does the month of birth affect educational and health outcomes? A population-based analysis using the Northern Ireland longitudinal study', *The Economic and Social Review*, 48(3, Autumn): 281–304.

Doherty, J. and Hughes, M. (2014) *Child Development: Theory and Practice 0–11*, Harlow, UK: Pearson.

Early Education. (2012) *Development Matters in the Early Years Foundation Stage*, London: Early Education.

Education Endowment Foundation (EEF). (n.d.) *Teaching and Learning Toolkit: Oral language interventions*. Retrieved from: https://educationendowmentfoundation.org.uk/education-evidence/teaching-learning-toolkit/oral-language-interventions (accessed 29 August 2023).

Education Endowment Foundation (EEF). (2018) *Preparing for Literacy: Improving Communication, Language and Literacy in the Early Years*, London: Education Endowment Foundation. Retrieved from: https://d2tic4wvo1iusb.cloudfront.net/production/eef-guidance-reports/literacy-early-years/Preparing_Literacy_Guidance_2018.pdf?v=1693297760 (accessed 29 August 2023).

Greenberg, J. B. (1989) *Funds of Knowledge: Historical Constitution, Social Distribution and Transmission*. Paper presented at the annual meetings of the Society of Applied Anthropology, Santa Fe, NM.

Hedegaard, M. (2009) 'Children's development from a cultural-historical approach: Children's activity in everyday local settings as foundation for their development', *Mind, Culture, & Activity*, 16(1): 64–82.

Hedegaard, M. (2012) 'Analyzing children's learning and development in everyday settings from a cultural-historical wholeness approach', *Mind, Culture, & Activity*, 19(2): 127–138.

Hodgen, J., Taylor, B., Francis, B., Craig, N., Bretscher, N., Tereshchenko, A., Connolly, P. and Mazenod, A. (2023) 'The achievement gap: The impact of between-class attainment grouping on pupil attainment and educational equity over time', *British Educational Research Journal*, 49(2): 209–230.

Hohmann, M. and Weikart, D. P. (1995) *Educating Young Children: Active Learning Practices for Preschool and Child Care Programs*, Ypsilanti, MI: High/Scope Press.

Karasik, L. B., Adolph, K. E., Tamis-LeMonda, C. S. and Bornstein, M. H. (2010) 'WEIRD walking: Cross-cultural research on motor development', *Behavioral & Brain Sciences*, 33(2-3): 95–96.

Kersner, M. (2015) 'The development of communication: Speech and language acquisition', in M. Kersner and J. A. Wright (eds) *Supporting Young Children with Communication Problems*, London: Routledge, pp. 13–25.

Kozulin, A. (1986) 'Introduction', in L. Vygotsky, *Thought and Language*, revised and edited by A. Kozulin, Cambridge, MA: MIT Press, pp. xi-lvi.

MacFarlane, A. C. and Van Hooff, M. (2009) 'Impact of child exposure to disaster on adult mental health: 20-year longitudinal follow-up study', *British Journal of Psychiatry*, 195: 142-148.

Martin, R. P., Foels, P., Clanton, G. and Moon, K. (2004) 'Season of birth is related to child retention rates, achievement, and rate of diagnosis of specific LD', *Journal of Learning Disabilities*, 37(4): 307-317.

Masten, A. S. and Narayan, A. J. (2012) 'Child development in the context of disaster, war, and terrorism: Pathways of risk and resilience', *Psychology*, 63: 227-257.

McKean, C. and Reilly, S. (2023) 'Creating the conditions for robust early language development for all: Part two: Evidence informed public health framework for child language in the early years', *International Journal of Language & Communication Disorders*, 58(6): 2242-2264.

Mesman, J., Van Ijzendoorn, M. H. and Sagi-Schwartz, A. (2018) 'Cross-cultural patterns of attachment', in J. Cassidy and P. R. Shaver (eds) *Handbook of Attachment: Theory, Research, and Clinical Applications*, 3rd edn, New York: Guilford Press, pp. 852-877.

Moll, L. and Greenberg, J. (1990) 'Creating zones of possibilities: Combining social contexts for instruction', in L. Moll (ed.) *Vygotsky and Education*, Cambridge, UK: Cambridge University Press, pp. 319-348.

Morris, K. (2015) *Promoting Positive Behaviour in the Early Years*, Maidenhead, UK: Open University Press.

National Health Service. (2019) National Child Measurement Programme, 2018/19 School Year. Retrieved from: https://digital.nhs.uk/data-and-information/publications/statistical/national-child-measurement-programme/2018-19-school-year (accessed 21 March 2025).

Office for Health Improvement and Disparities. (2022) Childhood Obesity: Applying All Our Health. Retrieved from: www.gov.uk/government/publications/childhood-obesity-applying-all-our-health/childhood-obesity-applying-all-our-health (accessed 24 August 2023).

Ofsted. (2022) *Education Recovery in Early Years Providers*. Retrieved from: www.gov.uk/government/publications/education-recovery-in-early-years-providers-summer-2022/education-recovery-in-early-years-providers-summer-2022#the-current-state-of-childrens-education (accessed 12 September 2023).

Papadopoulou, M. (2016) 'The "space" of friendship: Young children's understandings and expressions of friendship in a reception class', *Early Child Development and Care*, 186(10): 1544-1558. Available at: https://doi.org/10.1080/03004430.2015.1111879

Payler, J. and Georgeson, J. (2017) 'Social class and culture: Bridging divides through learner agency', in J. Moyles, J. Georgeson and J. Payler (eds) *Beginning Teaching, Beginning Learning*, 5th edn, Maidenhead, UK: Open University Press, chap. 16, pp. 203-214.

Payler, J., Cooper, V. and Bennett, S. (2020) 'Children and young people living through a serious family illness: Structural, interpersonal and personal perspectives', *Children & Society*, 34(1): 62-77.

Peterson, E. R., Rubie-Davies, C., Osborne, D. and Sibley, C. (2016) 'Teachers' explicit expectations and implicit prejudiced attitudes to educational achievement: Relations with student achievement and the ethnic achievement gap', *Learning and Instruction*, 42: 123-140.

Piaget, J. (1929) *The Child's Conception of the World*, London: Routledge & Kegan Paul.

Piaget, J. (1953) *The Origin of Intelligence in the Child*, London: Routledge & Kegan Paul.

Piaget, J. (1995) *Sociological Studies*, London: Routledge.

Plowden Report. (1967) *Children and Their Primary Schools: A Report of the Central Advisory Council for England*, London: HMSO.

Public Health England. (n.d.) *Change4Life School Zone*. Retrieved from: https://campaignresources.phe.gov.uk/schools (accessed 24 August 2023).

Reilly, S. and McKean, C. (2023) 'Creating the conditions for robust early language development for all–Part 1: Evidence-informed child language surveillance in the early years', *International Journal of Language & Communication Disorders*, 58(6): 2222-2241.

Rix, J. and Parry, J. (2014) 'Without foundation: The DfE Framework and its creation of need', in J. Moyles, J. Payler and J. Georgeson (eds) *Early Years Foundations: Critical Issues*, Maidenhead, UK: Open University Press, chap. 18, pp. 203-214.

Rogoff, B. (1990) *Apprenticeships in Thinking. Cognitive Development in Social Context*, Oxford, UK: Oxford University Press.

Rogoff, B. (2003) *The Cultural Nature of Human Development*, Oxford, UK: Oxford University Press.

Save the Children. (2016) *Early Language Development and Children's Primary School Attainment in English and Maths: Key Findings*, London: Save the Children.

Scanlan, M. (2012) '"Cos um it like put a picture in my mind of what I should write": An exploration of how home-school partnership might support the writing of lower achieving boys', *Support for Learning*, 27(1): 4-10.

Scanlan, M. (2018) *50 Fantastic Ideas for Early Language Development*, London: Bloomsbury.

Stanford, M., Davie, P. and Mulcahy, J. (2021) *Growing up in the Covid-19 Pandemic: An Evidence Review of the Impact of Pandemic Life on Physical Development in the Early Years*, London: Early Intervention Foundation. Retrieved from: www.eif.org.uk/report/growing-up-in-the-covid-19-pandemic-an-evidence-review-of-the-impact-of-pandemic-life-on-physical-development-in-the-early-years (accessed 24 August 2023).

TACTYC. (2015) *Written Evidence Submitted by TACTYC to the Education Select Committee Evidence Check: Starting School Enquiry*. Retrieved from: http://data.parliament.uk/writtenevidence/committeeevidence.svc/evidencedocument/education-committee/evidence-check-starting-school/written/18334.pdf (accessed 12 September 2023).

Tooley, U. A., Bassett, D. S. and Mackey, A. P. (2021) 'Environmental influences on the pace of brain development', *Nature Reviews Neuroscience*, 22(6): 372-384.

Trevarthen, C. (2011) 'What is it like to be a person who knows nothing? Defining the active intersubjective mind of a newborn human being', *Infant and Child Development*, 20(1): 119-135.

Vygotsky, L. (1986) *Thought and Language, revised* and edited by A. Kozulin, Cambridge, MA: MIT Press.

Vygotsky, L. (1987) 'Speech and thinking', in *L. S. Vygotsky, Collected Works* (Vol. 1; R. Rieber and A. Carton, eds; N. Minick, trans.), New York: Plenum, pp. 39-285.

Wood, D., Bruner, J. and Ross, G. (1976) 'The role of tutoring in problem-solving', *Journal of Child Psychology & Psychiatry*, 17: 89-100.

UNIT 2.2

BUILDING ON FIRM FOUNDATIONS
Early years practice

Janet Rose, Rebecca Digby and Vince MacLeod

INTRODUCTION

The early years sector in the UK has seen an unprecedented period of development and change from policymakers in the past 20 years. The sociopolitical agenda to ameliorate the divisive and fragmented nature of early years provision in the UK was (and, arguably, still is) closely bound up with the desire to reduce child poverty and disadvantage, and to encourage parents (and in particular mothers) back to work. These aspirations have required a major 'root and branch' approach to services for young children and their families (Anning, 2006), and central to this has been the dual aim to both increase the quantity, and improve the quality, of early education and childcare provision.

Within this context, our task in this unit is to challenge the popular conception that working with young children is easy and of less significance than formal schooling, and to convince you that, as primary school teachers, you need to understand how and in what ways children learn in the early years, and the range of diverse experiences they are likely to have had on arrival in the primary school. We offer also a cautionary note: we acknowledge that a key aim of early years education is to build firm foundations for future learning in the primary school and beyond. However, the purpose of early years education is not simply to achieve 'school readiness', as a preparation for future life or for later schooling: it is something that is important in its own right. Understanding this will enable you to build on the firm foundations established in the first five years and value the specific characteristics of young children as learners.

OBJECTIVES

This unit will help you to:

- highlight key issues you ought to know about in relation to the early years;
- eliminate any myths that may exist in your perspective of the early years;
- emphasise the importance of the early years and outline key policy initiatives;
- clarify the nature of early years practice.

EARLY YEARS POLICY

It is widely agreed that, from birth, children are powerful, creative and competent learners, and that early years provision should capitalise on this at a time when they are particularly receptive, developmentally, to exploratory, imaginative and social activity. Key questions about what an appropriate curriculum and pedagogy for young children might look like, and how, and in what ways, adults can support the learning and development of children in the early years, have been the major preoccupations of policymakers and early years educators alike. This has included developments in the training and qualifications of the early years workforce with more recent initiatives focusing on the expansion of childcare provision for the under-3s (Department for Education [DfE], 2023).***

The considerable recognition now afforded to the early years of education by policymakers is indicative also of a wider appreciation of the fundamental significance of this phase of childhood in lifelong learning, a view underpinned by a large and robust research literature base. For example, there is compelling recent evidence from the neurosciences that testifies to the profound way in which children's earliest experiences affect their developing potential, with long-lasting implications (see, for example, Gopnik, 2016; House of Commons, 2019).

The increasing complexity and demands of contemporary life mean that many children under the age of 5 will have had experiences in one or more different early years contexts, whether they have been cared for by a nanny or childminder, or have experienced group settings such as day nurseries, children's centres and/or preschool nurseries or playgroups. Each of these settings will have provided a range of diverse experiences, and, in turn, these will have affected the knowledge, skills and understanding that children bring with them to school. Coupled with the economic climate and sociopolitical trends, the likelihood of children spending time in settings other than the home is set to increase, particularly in light of the forthcoming expansion of childcare provision to 9 months of age (DfE, 2019). It is, therefore, imperative that teachers, particularly those working in Key Stage 1, are fully cognisant of the potential range of provision and that they understand the types of experience these children will have had, in order to ease the transition process and be sensitive to the potential impact of these in helping young children to adapt and settle into the school environment. Teachers will also need to accommodate the impact of the COVID-19 lockdown on children's development in a post-pandemic world and the evidence that suggests preschool children's social, emotional and physical development has been affected, including 'school readiness' (Bernard and Hobbs, 2021). There is also the digital world young children inhabit to consider and the controversies about whether digital learning helps or hinders young children's development (Harding, 2024). Indeed, the *Teachers' Standards* refer to the need for teachers to build on pupils' prior experiences and knowledge (DfE, 2011).

> **In Wales ...**
>
> The key feature of effective development, play and early learning for all babies and young children is the interplay between the quality of adult interactions, the effectiveness of indoor and outdoor environments and the authenticity of experiences offered.
>
> (Welsh Government, 2023: 7)

> **In Northern Ireland ...**
>
> Controversially, Northern Ireland is the only country that legally obliges children aged 4 years to attend primary school. Compulsory school age is governed by Article 46 of the Education and Libraries Northern Ireland Order 1986. Children who have reached the age of 4 on or before 1 July will start primary school at the beginning of the September of that year (Education Authority Northern Ireland, 2017: 3).

> **In Scotland ...**
>
> *Realising the Ambition: Being Me: National Practice Guidance for Early Years* (Education Scotland, 2020) complements the Scottish Government's Early Learning and Childcare Expansion Programme. *Realising the Ambition: Being Me* supports practitioners working across the early learning and childcare (ELC) sector and initial stages of primary school to develop high quality interactions, experiences and spaces that best support young children's well-being, learning and development.
>
> Early Years Scotland (n.d.) supports our youngest children from pre-birth to age 5. This specialist organisation engages with families through a range of 'Stay, Play and Learn' services, provides professional learning opportunities and support to ELC settings and early years professionals, and advice and advocacy on early years legislation, policy and practice at local and national level. For more information, please visit: www.playscotland.org.

THE EARLY YEARS FOUNDATION STAGE

Educational provision for children under 5 in England is offered within a wide range of diverse settings, in both the maintained and private sectors. These settings include nursery classes, day nurseries, playgroups, childminders, children's centres and Reception classes of primary schools. All of these settings now fall within the Foundation Stage, a distinctive phase for children from birth to statutory school age, currently described as 'the term after a child's fifth birthday' (DfE, 2014).

To assist childminders, staff in nurseries and practitioners in schools in meeting the requirements of the Early Years Foundation Stage (EYFS) Framework there is the government's non-statutory guidance document *Development Matters* (DfE, 2017). *Development Matters* suggests pathways of children's development in broad ages and stages. Developmental statements propose skills and behaviours that children will typically demonstrate between the ages of Birth to Three, Three- and Four-Year-Olds and Children in Reception, although it is acknowledged that 'the actual learning of young children is not so neat and orderly' (p.4). In addition to this, the non-statutory Birth to 5 Matters (Early Childhood Coalition, 2021) was created by a coalition of early years sector organisations as a reference point for all practitioners seeking to develop their practice in a pedagogically sound, principled and evidence-based way.

Two main factors need to be taken into consideration in relation to the EYFS:

1. The EYFS is intended to create a holistic and coherent approach to the care and education (sometimes referred to as 'educare') of young children – this represents a considerable and welcome development within the early years sector in recognition that the care and education of young children are inseparable and inextricably linked.
2. The EYFS is a statutory framework, but it is not intended as a curriculum to be followed, as with the National Curriculum – rather, it is viewed as principles for practice across the early years sector.

The EYFS is based on the following principles which are intended to permeate all aspects of early years provision:

- Every child is a *unique child*, who is constantly learning and can be resilient, capable, confident and self-assured.
- Children learn to be strong and independent through *positive relationships*.
- Children learn and develop well in *enabling environments*, in which their experiences respond to their individual needs and there is a strong partnership between practitioners and parents and/or carers.
- *Children develop and learn in different ways and at different rates*; the Framework covers the education and care of all children in early years provision, including children with special educational needs and disabilities.

'SCHOOL READINESS' AND STARTING SCHOOL

A key issue in relation to early years provision is encapsulated in the debates surrounding school starting age and the notion of 'school readiness'. The notion of 'school readiness' is a point of contention which, for early years pedagogy and practice, creates a tension between applying discourses of early intervention and 'child-centred' practices which are underpinned by a range of Froebelian, developmentalist, democratic stances (Chung and Walsh, 2000) and socio-cultural contexts (Georgeson et al., 2015), to support children's learning. Nonetheless, usage of the term has increased within government discourse and is explicitly stated in the revised EYFS which makes reference to the term 'school readiness' (DfE, 2018: 5).

The sociopolitical discourse, culture and policy of school improvement and school readiness has invariably led to features of a formal school curriculum percolating down to the teachers and children in both the Reception and Nursery classes. This is echoed in a wide pool of research highlighting the pressures that are put on early years practitioners to create a more formalised learning environment in Reception classes (Rose and Rogers, 2012a; Moss and Cameron, 2020; Kay, 2022), and is compounded by the prevalence of children starting school at a younger age. In England, Scotland and Wales, the statutory school starting age is the term after a child's fifth birthday, and in Northern Ireland it is the academic year following their fourth birthday. In England, changes to the School Admissions Code in 2011 meant that, in practice, most children enter school when they are just 4. The impact of this change is felt in Reception classes, where provision needs to be made for children who are likely to have different developmental demands owing to their immaturity.

Studies of Reception class pedagogy explicitly endorse a nursery-style provision for 4-year-olds and argue that there is no compelling evidence that starting school early has lasting educational benefits (Rogers and Rose, 2007). Indeed, opponents of an early school starting age and 'school readiness' discourse warn that over-formal education, introduced too soon, may be detrimental to children's social well-being and long-term attitude to learning. Issues regarding formal instruction have been explored by Aubrey and Durmaz (2012). They report how international comparison studies create pressures for higher standards and the tensions this creates between a play-based pedagogy and a standards agenda, particularly in the light of the values and understanding practitioners bring to practice. These findings correlate with those from a study by Rose and Rogers (2012b) of newly qualified early years teachers in different parts of England who faced dissonance between their play-based pedagogical principles and the reality of the 'high-stakes' performativity culture and curriculum in schools. Other literature documents how Reception class children often experience a watered-down version of Key Stage 1 (Brooker et al., 2010; Moss, 2017). This position continues, with recent studies (see, for example, Fisher 2021) outlining teachers' perspectives on play as integral to KS1 practice, and policy constraints as inhibiting play-based pedagogical approaches. However, it sits within a context of an increased focus on more formal approaches to teaching within Nursery settings, as illustrated by Boardman (2019), who found that graduate early years educators consider formally 'teaching' Systematic Synthetic Phonics to 2-year-olds to be 'best practice' to prepare young children for school.

The emphasis on skill acquisition in Reception and indeed Nursery classes can be to the detriment of children's motivation to learn, over-emphasis on formal reading skills being a classic example of this trend. This is a long-standing position with, for example, The Cambridge Primary Review, noting that any gains have been 'at the expense of [pupils'] enjoyment of reading' (Whetton, Ruddock and Twist, 2007: 19) alongside others (see, for instance, Pupala, Kascak and Tesar, 2016). In an early review of the literature on school readiness, Whitehead and Bingham make the following pertinent points in relation to the school readiness debate (2012: 6; original emphasis):

> All children, at all ages, are 'ready to learn' and have been doing so since birth. ... the significant question is not *whether* a child is ready to learn but *what* a child is ready to learn and how adults can best support the *processes of learning*.

Task 2.2.1 Principles into practice

- Read the article by Rose and Rogers (2012b), 'Principles under pressure: Student teachers' perspectives on final teaching practice in early childhood classrooms'.
- Discuss whether the findings in the article echo your own experiences in placement.
- Outline your own principles of early years practice and consider possible challenges you might encounter when applying these principles in the classroom.

THE LEARNING ENVIRONMENT

The debate about what constitutes an appropriate learning environment in the early years inevitably draws into its sphere the role of play. In all countries of the UK, the early years curricula strongly endorse a play-based approach to learning in the early years. In practice, however, implementing a play-based approach can be challenging. Teachers often feel under pressure to ensure that children are 'school ready', emphasising literacy and numeracy activities, presented in ways that may not reflect developmentally appropriate practice. We suggest here that being school ready also requires children to be socially and emotionally secure, and increasingly able to make choices, think critically and creatively, and plan ahead, skills that are well supported in play activities. Second, it is not always clear how much structure to provide in play. Do children need manufactured and elaborate resources to play, or open-ended materials and props that provoke imagination and conversation? Should play be tied to curriculum objectives, or are the outcomes of play determined by the children or in collaboration with adults? Third, what is the adult role in play? To what extent should adults intervene, and when does intervention become interference which is overly directive? We suggest that children need a balance between activities that are child-initiated and those supported by adults who listen and tune into children.

Few would dispute the fact that one of the key ways in which children up to the age of 5 make human sense of the world around them is through their play. We can see this in the earliest sensorimotor play observed in babies and toddlers, involving mainly exploratory activity through the senses and through action on objects. You might be familiar with the tendency of babies to put things in their mouths and throw things. At this stage, children are interested in the properties of things. Take, for example, Sam, who is 10 months old. He is preoccupied with dropping objects, such as balls, from the top of the stairs, repeatedly. Though this behaviour may be difficult for adults to tolerate, it is a vital part of Sam's development in his efforts to make sense of the world around him. He is learning about his impact on the world and early scientific and mathematical concepts, such as gravity, cause and effect and trajectories. This exploratory play gradually changes as children approach their second birthday, when a profound and uniquely human capacity comes to the fore of children's activity. This is the ability to pretend, seen first in the simple imitations of toddlers and later in the highly sophisticated social pretend play or role-play of 4- and 5-year-olds. It is this social pretence that lays the foundations of many important human-centred life skills, such as problem-solving, creative activity and interpersonal relations, as well as being enjoyable and life-enhancing to children as they play.

Maintaining sight of (young children's) education as relational (Biesta, 2004) requires an acknowledgement that human participation in practices of knowing occur as part of the 'larger material configuration of the world' (Barad, 2007: 379). As such, encounters with materials and consideration for creativity as a 'material knowing' are of significance when seeking to understand children's relationships with and of the world (Digby, 2023). For example, the encounter with materials described earlier makes visible ball, stairs, air, Sam's hands, Sam's being. Less visible but still influencing the moment of encounter is the context, both at a micro and macro level, the affective experience within and of the environment, as well as time, resonance and infinite other factors. Entangled within and of each other, these factors are phenomena of 'intra-actions' creating ever-in-flux moments (Barad, 2007). In their entangled intra-actions, these moments create 'spaces in-between' from which emerge assemblages such as ball-stairs and ball-child, which offer moments and the potential for new understandings of children's relationship with the world to be made known.

For pedagogy and practice, this implies that teachers' attunement should be directed towards children's emergent knowing and becoming as a material, affective experience as well as knowing which might be mediated through talk and pre-determined scientific concepts such as Sam's experience of gravity, described earlier. In order to appreciate this, there needs to be recognition in practice that children come to know in ways that lie beyond the cognitive domain. Attention needs to be focused towards emergent points of difference in the spaces 'in-between' child and material encounters. For example, differences might manifest in the space in-between ball and hands with the materiality of the ball revealing its qualities of flow and stickiness, made visible through affective, relational knowing and becoming. Understanding young children's knowledge making practices from this perspective requires teachers to 'see' children as de-centred and materials as energetic matter. Rather than solely an agentic knowledge builder, children are in a continual state of becoming, entangled with and of their worlds.

It is important, therefore, that teachers recognise their entanglement in children's material encounters and their role in determining what is valued and made visible. Teachers' participation within playful enquiries, as relational and attuned to the entangled materiality of environment and child(ren), is perhaps one way to engage with a larger configuration of the world. Slow pedagogies, underpinned by the concept of 'slow knowledge', also affords the opportunity to 'be with' others (Clarke, 2023). Indeed, the concept advocates valuing the present moment, being attentive to children's pace and rhythms, creating opportunities for deeper, immersive experience and encouraging unhurried time for wonder and care. This is an approach which values hands-on experience and a culture which sits in contrast to a more pressured focus on 'school readiness'.

In Scotland ...

'There is a balance where we need to raise the profile of play and also to deepen an understanding for practitioners in supporting play experiences with children' (Scottish Government, 2014: 28).

In Wales ...

In the early years learning environment:

> All children need engaging experiences that are rooted in real-life contexts that reflect their interests, and that ignite their curiosity and desire to learn. Engaging experiences should build on children's natural desire to play. They should be purposeful and meaningful to the child.
>
> (Welsh Government, 2023: 18)

> Our indoor and outdoor environments should therefore be welcoming, offering rich, authentic and joyful opportunities to explore and play in contexts that will be familiar to babies and young children. We should promote a strong Welsh ethos and sense of cynefin with our families and communities. Effective environments should be safe, secure and suitable for purpose. By creating spaces that respond to the voice of the child, we show respect to the unique backgrounds and interests of each child. Through exploration of their environments, all children can begin to develop a sense of belonging and an appreciation of the world around them.
>
> (Welsh Government, 2023: 21)

> Children learn through first-hand experiential activities with the serious business of 'play' providing the vehicle. Through their play, children practise and consolidate their learning, play with ideas, experiment, take risks, solve problems, and make decisions individually, in small and in large groups. First-hand experiences allow children to develop an understanding of themselves and the world in which they live.
>
> (Learning Wales, 2015: 3)

> **In Wales ...**
>
> There must be a balance between structured learning through child-initiated activities and those directed by practitioners. A well-planned curriculum gives children opportunities to be creatively involved in their own learning which must build on what they already know and can do, their interests and what they understand. Active learning enhances and extends children's development.
>
> (Learning Wales, 2015: 4)

Research is also emerging from the neurosciences about the value and impact of play on young children's developing minds and bodies (Hassinger-Das, Hirsh-Pasek and Golinkoff, 2017; Neale et al., 2018; Wheeler and Rose, 2021). Given that play is invariably multimodal and multisensory, it increases the integration of neural networks by activating multiple areas of the brain simultaneously. For example, a child playing in wet sand is stimulating the motor cortex (movement), the occipital lobes (visual processing) and the prefrontal lobe (executive functioning). The role of play in promoting executive functioning has particular significance for school given it facilitates a child in planning, reasoning, problem-solving, goal-directed tasks, decision-making, self-motivation, concentration, emotional regulation, holding and manipulating information, filtering distractions, persistence and prioritising – all essential requisites for academic learning (Best, Miller and Naglieri, 2011). Moreover, meaningful play with novel and familiar material helps to build on cognitive processes, activates the brain's reward system and strengthens the coding of memories. Physical, social, thematic and dramatic play, and rough and tumble play all aid in brain development. As Neale et al. state, 'play is a highly complex social interactive activity that activates a combination of sensorimotor, cognitive and socio-emotional neural circuits' (2018: 4).

In recognition of the importance of all types of play across the early years phase, early years settings are developed around the concept of 'free-flow', continuous play provision, both indoors and outdoors. Classrooms are organised into resource areas to which children have access throughout the day. This approach presupposes choice and autonomy on the part of children, who will have regular and sustained opportunities to engage relationally with resources. Remember that Einstein believed that 'play is research'.

Task 2.2.2 Child-initiated play

Read the following example of real-life practice and consider whether the teacher's aims fulfil her intention:

> A teacher of six year olds is planning an art activity to develop their creative skills. She decides the children will make pine-cone turkeys and collects the range of materials they will use. She sits with a group and demonstrates how they will make them and explains exactly how the materials fit together in particular places to create the turkey. She then supports them in making them, allowing each child to choose five coloured feathers, which she encourages them to count. The children then make the turkeys, but need help with the glueing, sticking and making the pipe-cleaner feet. The children mostly watch the teacher during the whole activity.
>
> (Woyke, 2001: 15)

How could you turn this adult-led activity into one that is child-initiated and allows the child to be more active, creative and relational in the process?

Of particular importance since the introduction of the EYFS is the recognition that young children need regular access to outdoor play to enhance their well-being and development in all areas: physical, emotional, social, cognitive and creative (Evangelou et al., 2009). Outdoor spaces offer a range of different learning opportunities to children, not least the freedom to be more active, noisy and exploratory than is possible in indoor spaces. In addition to the obvious physical benefits of being in the outdoors, such activity offers young children a range of relational multisensory experiences, such as encounters with the effects of the weather and related temperatures as well as coming to know the dynamic flux and qualities of textures, smells and sounds of natural materials, such as wood, grass, ice, earth and water. Research has shown that not only do young children prefer to play outside, but that in intra-active playful encounters, they 'become with' the 'lifefulness' and materiality of outdoor spaces (Somerville, 2019).

THE ROLE OF THE ADULT IN PLAY

It is not simply the material resources that make for a stimulating and effective learning environment for young children. Knowledgeable, skilled and caring adults will create an environment that creates, nurtures and sustains a positive learning ethos that matches the dispositions and characteristics of young children and acknowledges and values cultural diversity and equity. Earlier, we raised some of the dilemmas facing early years practitioners in relation to young children's play and some of the tensions that exist within different pedagogical approaches in terms of the amount or level of adult interaction or involvement in children's play activities – in other words, whether practitioners ought to 'develop a child or watch a child develop' (Alexander, 2010: 95).

> **In Northern Ireland ...**
>
> Children need help to extend their play. Adults can contribute to the development of abstract thinking, for example, by adding resources and props, by asking open-ended questions and posing exciting challenges (Council for Curriculum, Examinations and Assessment [CCEA], 2003: 9).

One possible way forward is to reconsider the terms 'adult-led', 'adult-directed', 'child-initiated' and 'child-led' and replace these terms with more relational ones – for example, adult-initiated and child-initiated. Thus:

> By viewing all activities and exchanges as a process of initiation that immediately becomes an interconnected negotiation, rather than as an act of being led or directed by either the child or the adult, we can envisage the adult-child relationship as one that involves interchangeable processes of 'give-and-take' and mutual co-construction.
>
> (Rose and Rogers, 2012b: 9)

We have suggested that this might help early years teachers to 'understand the reciprocal nature of adult-child interactions and might help to diminish uncertainties regarding adult intervention' (Rose and Rogers, 2012b: 9). Harding (2024) also emphasises that the adult role may vary depending on a range of factors when deciding whether to be 'outside or inside the flow of the play' (p. 65). Extending this is an acknowledgement that such an understanding exists within the wider materiality of the world. From this perspective, interconnected and interchangeable processes are entangled within the complexity of 'intra-acting' and entangled phenomena, and what is made visible and known in any one moment will be dependent on the tools or 'lenses' used to see. For example, if we look through the lens of a reciprocal adult-child relationship which is mutually co-constructed, then this is what will define our understanding of a playful encounter.

In Northern Ireland ...

The role of the adult in play:

> Sensitive support and timely involvement by staff in children's play is necessary to stimulate learning and deepen play experiences. ... Successful adult involvement stems from careful observation of play and sensitivity to the needs of the children. It is also important to choose the appropriate time to become involved in the play.
>
> (CCEA, 2018: 11)

In Wales ...

> As enabling adults, we are the most important part of early childhood play, learning and care. Fundamental to our role is having up-to-date knowledge and understanding of child development ... we should take the time to get to know individual children and respect their previous experiences. In so doing, we can ensure we provide engaging opportunities.
>
> (Welsh Government, 2023: 8)

> Foundation Phase practitioners should acknowledge prior learning and attainment, offer choices, challenge children with care and sensitivity, encourage them and move their learning along. The Foundation Phase curriculum should be flexible to allow practitioners working with children opportunities to plan and provide an appropriate curriculum for children who are at an early stage of their development and for those who are more able.
>
> (Learning Wales, 2015: 4)

One study by Rogers and Evans (2008) examined the role-play activity of 4- and 5-year-olds and found that there was a mismatch between how children viewed their play and the way play was organised in the classroom. Typically, classrooms were set up with structured role-play areas around a particular theme or topic, e.g. a shop, a café. Although these areas were resourced in elaborate and inviting ways, the children paid little attention to the theme, preferring instead to play games of their own choosing. In many instances, the play was difficult to contain and manage within the confines of the classroom. An alternative approach to role-play, well suited to children over the age of 4 and throughout the primary years, is open-ended play, with suggestive rather than pre-specified props.

For example, Kelvin and his friends built a 'ship' from large bricks. They 'sailed' to a 'cave' made from a sheet draped over some chairs. In the 'cave', there were some keys, which they used to lock up the baddies. This example of sustained role-play involving five children lasted for at least 20 minutes. Kelvin, a child with identified special needs, emerged as a 'master player', leading the group and utilising language rarely heard in formal teaching activities. Social relationships were explored, formed and re-formed in the course of the play, as children negotiated roles and planned the course of the play.

In this simple example of role-play, we see a wide range of important learning and potential assessment opportunities for the observant adult. McInnes *et al.* (2013) argue that children's performance is enhanced if they perceive an activity to be playful. Their research demonstrates learning is enhanced in settings that promote co-constructed play with shared adult–child interactions, open questions and more choice and control for children.

These ideas are evident in the findings from the Effective Provision of Pre-school Education (EPPE) (Siraj-Blatchford *et al.*, 2002; Sylva *et al.*, 2004) which suggested that the potential for learning through play can be extended by what the researchers have termed 'sustained shared thinking'. This essentially involves adults 'getting involved' in children's thinking, interacting in a shared (verbal or nonverbal) dialogue. In this way, as Siraj-Blatchford explains, adults can act as co-constructors to

FIGURE 2.2.1 Creating towers with adult support

'solve a problem, clarify a concept, evaluate activities or extend narratives' (2004: 18). Sustained shared thinking builds on other research that demonstrates the importance of meaningful, child-initiated and supportive interactions, such as Bruner's (1986) work on scaffolding and learning as a communal activity, inspired by Vygotsky and by Schaffer's (1996) work on 'joint involvement episodes'.

Sustained shared thinking involves the adult being aware of the children's interests and understandings, and the adult and children working together to develop an idea or skill. When engaged in sustained shared thinking, the adult shows genuine interest, offers encouragement, clarifies ideas and asks open questions. This supports and extends the children's thinking and helps children to make connections in learning (Sylva *et al.*, 2004). This aligns with a rights-based approach to education, where practitioners actively seek children's participation in decision-making (Lundy, 2007).

RECEPTION BASELINE ASSESSMENT AND FOUNDATION STAGE PROFILE

Internal baseline assessments, undertaken by early years practitioners when children begin Reception year, have traditionally been a fundamental part of gaining informed knowledge and understanding of individual children in Reception classes (Meechan *et al.*, 2022). The Reception Baseline Assessment (RBA) statutory guidance (DfE, 2019) has now established a formal process for assessing all Reception-aged children within six weeks of starting primary school in areas such as early mathematics and literacy. It should be noted that most Reception teachers will still conduct their own baseline assessments, in conjunction with the RBA, to establish starting points for their children and to inform their planning.

The EYFS Profile is a statutory assessment at the end of Reception, intended to provide a reliable and accurate picture of each child's development and support successful transitions to Year 1. In England, every government-funded setting, including schools, must complete an EYFS Profile for every child in the final term of the academic year in which they turn 5.

In essence, it requires Reception class teachers to assess each child in relation to the 17 Early Learning Goals (ELGs), across all seven areas of learning in the EYFS. The assessments need to identify whether children are meeting *expected* levels of development, or if they are not yet reaching this level and should be assessed as *emerging* (DfE, 2018). Children are considered to have reached a Good Level of Development (GLD) at the end of the EYFS if they have achieved the *expected* level for the ELGs in the prime areas of learning (which are: communication and language; personal, social and emotional development; and physical development) and the specific areas of mathematics and literacy. This indicates broadly what a child can do and informs professional dialogue about their next steps between EYFS and Year 1 teachers.

Since the revised Early Years Framework was implemented in 2021, there is less emphasis on gathering evidence in 'Learning Journeys' and more freedom afforded to teachers to spend time interacting with their students, building relationships and supporting development (DfE, 2014). Teachers' deep knowledge of each child, gained through lived experiences and expert professional judgement, is considered sufficient to make accurate summative assessments in relation to the ELGs. Despite this change, many Reception teachers still opt to record their pupils' progress in online learning journals, to help with formative assessments throughout the year and to keep parents informed of their child's development. Equally, parents can upload photos and videos from home to share weekend news, home learning and key life events.

FIGURE 2.2.2 A learning journey entry

TRANSITION FROM THE FOUNDATION STAGE TO KEY STAGE 1

Transition from one key stage to another inevitably presents children and practitioners with both challenges and opportunities. It involves unlearning and relearning, and the teacher's transition practice needs to take this into account. In conversation with Reception class children, Rogers and Evans (2008) found that, for some, moving from the Foundation Stage to Key Stage 1 was an exciting prospect, signifying progress and achievement. For others, it was a source of anxiety, perceived as 'hard work', with fewer opportunities to play with friends.

> **Task 2.2.3 Supporting transition**
>
> Undertake an audit of Reception and Year 1 in a school from a child's perspective:
>
> - What do the children see in the Year 1 classroom that is the same as the Reception classroom?
> - What is different?
> - What do the Reception children experience that is the same as the Year 1 children?
> - What is different?
>
> Now undertake an audit of transition procedures in the school:
>
> - What does the school do to reinforce the similarities?
> - What does the school do to accommodate the differences?
>
> Evaluate your findings in terms of the suggestions made in this section about how teachers can support the transition process.

Research shows that educational transitions are highly significant to pupils and can be a 'critical factor in determining children's future progress and development' (Fabian, 2006: 4).

When handled with diligence and care, the EYFS to Key Stage 1 transition can have a transformative impact on children's social, emotional and academic development (Bryce-Clegg, 2017; Palaiologou, 2021). To ensure that all children have a positive experience, some settings provide a play-based transition period at the beginning of Year 1, where the principles of effective EYFS practice underpin an active, enquiry-based pedagogy. High levels of Year 1 academic attainment are gradually promoted and children are supported to meet increased expectations (Quirk and Pettett, 2020). Fisher (2021) found that this is not ubiquitous and there is a spectrum of transitional approaches being implemented in UK schools. These range from teaching elements of the Year 1 curriculum at the end of Reception to a whole school play-based learning approach.

Key Stage 1 teachers should be aware that some children may have experienced multiple transitions before starting school, and Demkowicz *et al.* (2023) highlight the emotional impact of transition on children's well-being and resilience, as they move from their 'comfort zone' into a new environment. A final key point is the evidence that transitional programmes need to accommodate culturally appropriate practices to help minimise inequalities (Peters, 2010). With this in mind, it will be helpful to consider the following factors to ensure effective transition programmes:

- Children need ample opportunity to become familiar with the new situation through visits to the setting or class and contact with the teacher.
- Rules and rituals are significant issues in the transition process, and assumptions are often made by adults that children will automatically understand these and their complexities.
- Once the move has taken place, continuity of practice, where possible, is beneficial, with a gradual introduction to new and more formal activities (Smith, 2011).
- Teachers should critically question their implicit beliefs about cultural 'norms' and be sensitive to prior experiences to facilitate a sense of welcome and belonging (Peters, 2010).

SUMMARY

This unit has provided a brief review of government policy and statutory curricular requirements related to early years education, notably in England. The unit has looked at, and should have helped you formulate a view on, a number of issues: first, on the controversial topic of when children should start school and the notion of 'school readiness'; second, on the most effective ways for young children to learn, and why play is important in early learning; finally, on the nature of the adult role in early learning and the important part you can play in this, including easing the transition to Key Stage 1.

ANNOTATED FURTHER READING

Hedges, H. (2022) *Children's Interests, Inquiries and Identities Curriculum, Pedagogy, Learning and Outcomes in the Early Years*, Abingdon, UK: Routledge.
> This book advocates for placing children's interests at the heart of teaching and learning and challenges practitioners to leave behind long-standing, fixed ideas about early years development. Drawing on research with children aged under 5, Professor Helen Hedges presents new and original models for interest-based curriculum and new principles for understanding what really matters to children and taking their interests seriously.

Rose, J. and Rogers, S. (2012) *The Role of the Adult in Early Years Settings*, Maidenhead, UK: Open University Press.
> This book provides a helpful insight into the many different dimensions of the adult role in working with young children. It draws on a range of recent and classic theoretical perspectives and research that will help you to become an effective early years professional.

Moylett, H. (ed.) (2013) *Characteristics of Effective Early Learning: Helping Young Children Become Learners for Life*, Maidenhead, UK: Open University Press.
> This edited book provides a number of insightful chapters framed around the characteristics of effective early learning enshrined in the EYFS, including a helpful chapter on transition to Key Stage 1.

FURTHER READING TO SUPPORT M-LEVEL STUDY

Siraj-Blatchford, I. and Manni, L. (2008) '"Would you like to tidy up now?" An analysis of adult questioning in the English Foundation Stage', *Early Years*, 28(1): 5–22.
> This study focuses attention on effective forms of questioning applied by early years practitioners and makes some significant points about the value of open-ended questions and the links to sustained shared thinking.

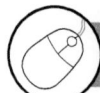

RELEVANT WEBSITES

Early Years Foundation Stage: www.gov.uk/early-years-foundation-stage
> This is the government site for the new Early Years Foundation Stage.

Early Years Foundation Stage Forum: http://eyfs.info/home
> This is a very useful support network and online community website for early years professionals.

REFERENCES

Alexander, R. J. (2010) *Children, Their World, Their Education*, London: Routledge.

Anning, A. (2006) 'Early years education: Mixed messages and conflicts', in D. Kassem, E. Mufti and J. Robinson (eds) *Education Studies: Issues and Critical Perspectives*, Maidenhead, UK: Open University Press/McGraw-Hill, pp. 5-11.

Aubrey, C. and Durmaz, D. (2012) 'Policy-to-practice contexts for early childhood mathematics in England', *International Journal of Early Years Education*, 20(1): 59-77.

Barad, K. (2007) *Meeting the Universe Halfway: Quantum Physics and the Entanglement of Matter and Meaning*, Durham: Duke University Press.

Bernard, R. and Hobbs, A. (2021) *Impact of COVID-19 on Early Childhood Education and Care. Government Rapid Response Briefing*, London: UK Parliament.

Best, J. R., Miller, P. H. and Naglieri, J. A. (2011) 'Relations between executive function and academic achievement from ages 5 to 17', *Journal of Learning and Individual Differences*, 21(4): 327-336.

Biesta, G. (2004) 'Mind the gap!: Communication and the educational relation' in C. Bingham and A. Sidorkin (eds) *No Education Without Relation*, New York: Peter Lang, pp. 11-22.

Boardman, K. (2019) 'The incongruities of "teaching phonics" with two-year olds', *International Journal of Primary, Elementary and Early Years Education*, 47(7): 842-853.

Brooker, E., Rogers, S., Robert-Holmes, G. and Hallett, E. (2010) *Practitioners Experiences of the Early Years Foundation Stage: A Research Report*, London: DCSF.

Bruner, J. (1986) *Actual Minds, Possible Worlds*, Cambridge, MA: Harvard University Press.

Bryce-Clegg, A. (2017) *Effective Transition Into Year One*, London, UK: Featherstone Education.

Chung, S. and Walsh, D. J. (2000) 'Unpacking child-centredness: A history of meanings', *Journal of Curriculum Studies*, 32(2): 215-234.

Clarke, A. (2023) *Slow Knowledge and the Unhurried Child: Time for Slow Pedagogies in Early Childhood Education*, Abingdon, Oxon: Routledge.

Council for the Curriculum, Examinations and Assessment (CCEA). (2003) *Learning Through Play in the Early Years: A Resource Book*, Early Years Inter-board Panel, Belfast: CCEA.

Council for the Curriculum, Examinations and Assessment (CCEA). (2018) *Curricular Guidance for Pre-School Education*, Belfast, CCEA. Retrieved from: www.education-ni.gov.uk/sites/default/files/publications/education/PreSchool_Guidance_30May18_Web.pdf

Demkowicz, O., Bagnall, C., Hennessey, A., Pert, K., Bray, L., Ashworth, E. and Mason, C. (2023) '"It's scary starting a new school": Children and young people's perspectives on wellbeing support during educational transitions', *British Journal of Educational Psychology*, 93(4): 1017-1033.

Department for Education (DfE). (2011) *Teachers' Standards*, London: DfE. Last updated 2021.

Department for Education (DfE). (2014) *Statutory Framework for the Early Years Foundation Stage: Setting the Standards for Learning, Development and Care for Children from Birth to Five*, London: DfE. Last updated 2024.

Department for Education (DfE). (2017) *Development Matters: Non-Statutory Curriculum Guidance for the Early Years Foundation Stage*, London: DfE. Last updated 2023.

Department for Education (DfE). (2018) *Early Years Foundation Stage Profile Handbook*, London: DfE. Last updated 2024.

Department for Education (DfE). (2019) *Reception Baseline Assessment: Collection Page. Information About the Reception Baseline Assessment (RBA) for Schools*. Last updated 2024. Retrieved from: www.gov.uk/government/collections/reception-baseline (accessed 9 February 2025).

Department for Education (DfE). (2023) *Free Childcare: How We Are Tackling the Cost of Childcare*, London: DfE.

Digby, R. (2023) 'Diffractive encounters with empirical and theoretical understandings of children's creativity in science enquiry', *Journal of Digital Culture and Education*, 14(5): 127-150.

Early Childhood Coalition. (2021) *Birth to 5 Matters: Non-statutory Guidance for the EYFS*, London: British Association for Early Childhood Education.

Early Years Scotland. (n.d.) *Early Years Scotland: Investing in Our Youngest Children. About Us*. Retrieved from: https://earlyyearsscotland.org/about-us/

Education Authority Northern Ireland. (2017) *Starting School Age: A Guide for Parents*, Belfast, Education Authority. Retrieved from: www.eani.org.uk/about-us/latest-news/school-starting-age-guidance-for-parents-is-published/ (accessed 18 October 2017).

Education Scotland. (2020) *Raising the Ambition: Being Me: National Practice Guidance for Early Years in Scotland*, Livingston: Education Scotland. Retrieved from: https://education.gov.scot/media/3bjpr3wa/realisingtheambition.pdf

Evangelou, M., Sylva, K., Kyriacou, M., Wild, M. and Glenny, G. (2009) *Early Years Learning and Development: Literature Review*, London: DCSF.

Fabian, H. (2006) 'Informing transitions', in A.-W. Dunlop and H. Fabian, *Informing Transitions in the Early Years*, Milton Keynes, UK: Open University Press, pp. 3–20.

Fisher, J. (2021) 'To play or not to play: Teachers' and headteachers' perspectives on play-based approaches in transition from the Early Years Foundation Stage to Key Stage 1 in England', *Education 3-13*, 50(3): 1–13.

Georgeson, J., Campbell-Barr, V., Bakosi, É., Nemes, M., Pálfi, S. and Sorzio, P. (2015) 'Can we have an international approach to child-centred early childhood practice?', *Early Child Development and Care*, 185: 1–18.

Gopnik, A. (2016) *The Gardener and the Carpenter: What the New Science of Child Development Tells Us about the Relationship between Parents and Children*, London: Bodley Head.

Harding, J. (2024) *The Brain that LOVES to Play*, London: Routledge.

Hassinger-Das, B., Hirsh-Pasek, K. and Golinkoff, R. M. (2017) 'The case of brain science and guided play', *Young Children*, 72(2): 45–50.

House of Commons (2019) *First 1000 Days of Life, Health and Social Care Committee Report*, London: House of Commons.

Kay, L. (2022) '"What works" and for whom? Bold Beginnings and the construction of the school ready child', *Journal of Early Childhood Research*, 20(2): 172–184.

Learning Wales. (2015) *Curriculum for Wales: Foundation Phase Framework*, Cardiff: Welsh Government (WG). Retrieved from http://learning.gov.wales/docs/learningwales/publications/150803-fp-framework-en.pdf (accessed 18 October 2017).

Lundy, L. (2007) '"Voice" is not enough: conceptualising Article 12 of the United Nations Convention on the Rights of the Child', *British Educational Research Journal*, 33(6): 927–942.

McInnes, K., Howard, J., Crowley, K. and Miles, G. (2013) 'The nature of adult-child interaction in the early years classroom: Implications for children's perceptions of play and subsequent learning behaviour', *European Early Childhood Education Research Journal*, 21(2): 268–282.

Meechan, D., Whatmore, T., Williams-Brown, Z. and Halfhead, S. (2022) 'Why are we tracking Reception-aged children? Teachers' and key stakeholders' perspectives on the reintroduction of national Reception Baseline Assessment', *Educational Futures*, 13(2): 113–139.

Moss, P. (2017) 'Power and resistance in early childhood education: From dominant discourse to democratic experimentalism', *Journal of Pedagogy*, 8(1): 11–32.

Moss, P. and Cameron, C. (2020) 'Introduction: The state we're in', In C. Cameron and P. Moss (eds) *Transforming Early Childhood Education*, London: UCL Press, pp. 1–18.

Neale, D., Clackson, K., Georgieva, S., Dedetas, H., Scarpate, M., Wass, S. and Leong, V. (2018) 'Toward a neuroscientific understanding of play: A dimensional coding framework for analyzing infant–adult play patterns', *Frontiers in Psychology*, 9(273): 1–17.

Palaiologou, I. (2021) *The Early Years Foundation Stage: Theory and Practice*, London, UK: Sage Publications Ltd.

Peters, S. (2010) *Literature Review: Transition from Early Childhood Education to School*, Wellington: Ministry of Education.

Pupala, B., Kascak, O. and Tesar, M. (2016) 'Learning how to do up buttons: Professionalism, teacher identity and bureaucratic subjectivities in early years settings', *Policy Futures in Education*, 14(6): 655–665.

Quirk, S. and Pettett, V. (2020) *Let Me Be Five Implementing a Play-Based Curriculum in Year 1 and Beyond*, Abingdon, UK/New York, NY: Routledge.

Rogers, S. and Evans, J. (2008) *Inside Role-play in Early Education: Researching Children's Perspectives*, London: Routledge.

Rogers, S. and Rose, J. (2007) 'Ready for Reception? The advantages and disadvantages of single-point entry to school', *Early Years International Research Journal*, 27(1): 47–63.

Rose, J. and Rogers S. (2012a) *The Role of the Adult in Early Years Settings*, Maidenhead, UK: Open University Press.

Rose, J. and Rogers, S. (2012b) 'Principles under pressure: Student teachers' perspectives on final teaching practice in early childhood classrooms', *International Journal of Early Years Education*, 20(1): 43–58.

Schaffer, H. R. (1996) 'Joint involvement episodes as context for development', in H. Daniels (ed.) *An Introduction to Vygotsky*, London: Routledge, pp. 251–280.

Scottish Government. (2014) *Building the Ambition. National Practice Guidance on Early Learning and Childcare Children and Young People (Scotland) Act 2014*, Edinburgh: Scottish Government. Retrieved from: www.gov.scot/Resource/0045/00458455.pdf (accessed 21 March 2016).

Siraj-Blatchford, I. (2004) 'Educational disadvantage in the early years: How do we overcome it? Some lessons from research', *European Early Childhood Education Research Journal*, 12(2): 5–20.

Siraj-Blatchford, I., Sylva, K., Muttock, S., Gilden, R. and Bell, D. (2002) *Researching Effective Pedagogy in the Early Years (REPEY)*, DfES Research Brief 356, London: DfES.

Smith, H. (2011) 'The emotional impact of transfer: What can be learned from early years practice', in A. Howe and V. Richards (eds) *Bridging the Transition from Primary to Secondary School*, London: Routledge, pp. 14–25.

Somerville, M. (2019) *Posthuman Theory and Practice in Early Years Learning, Research Handbook on Childhoodnature: Assemblages of Childhood and Nature Research*. Springer International.

Sylva, K., Melhuish, E. C., Sammons, P., Siraj-Blatchford, I. and Taggart, B. (2004) *The Effective Provision of Preschool Education (EPPE) Project: Technical Paper 12 – The Final Report: Effective Pre-school Education*, London: DfES/Institute of Education, University of London.

Welsh Government. (2023) *A Quality Framework for Early Childhood Play, Learning and Care in Wales*. Retrieved from: https://hwb.gov.wales/api/storage/031bbc2d-d2f8-429d-a944-5fc33484827d/a-quality-framework-for-early-childhood-play-learning-and-care-v1.pdf (accessed 25 April 2024).

Wheeler, L. and Rose, J. (2021) *The Neuroscience of Play, Literature Review Report*, Bath: Norland College.

Whetton, C., Ruddock, G. and Twist, L. (2007) *Standards in English Primary Education: The International Evidence (Cambridge Primary Review: Research Survey 4/2)*, Cambridge, UK: Cambridge University Press.

Whitehead, D. and Bingham, S. (2012) *School Readiness: A Critical Review of Evidence and Perspectives*, Occasional Paper 2, London: TACTYC.

Woyke, P. P. (2001) 'What does creativity look like in a developmentally appropriate preschool classroom?', *Earthworm*, 2(3): 15.

UNIT 2.3

REVISITING IDEAS AROUND LEARNING AND TEACHING

Liz Chamberlain and Roger McDonald

INTRODUCTION

Whilst it might seem obvious that anyone wanting to become a teacher understands teaching; it is not always the case that a distinct link is made between the way you teach and its impact on a learner's experiences. As a student teacher, or a new teacher, the emphasis can often appear to be focused more on your own performance; for example, how well behaved the children were in your lesson, if your classroom organisation meant that all learners were engaged and if you successfully met all the objectives set in your previous lesson observation. In this chapter, we will cover some of the historical perspectives of learning theory and development, before bringing you up-to-date with contemporary theories of learning. We discuss the complexity of teaching and learning and the decisions teachers make on a daily basis to develop creative and inclusive learning communities in their classrooms. Underpinning all of the ideas in this chapter is the unique role that you play as the teacher in the lives of the young learners in your classes. We hope this chapter gives you the opportunity to reflect on the distinctive skill set you bring into the classroom every time you teach.

OBJECTIVES

By the end of this chapter, we hope that you will be able to:

- contrast and compare the historical nature of learning theory and theorists;
- describe the ways in which contemporary thinking has led to more inclusive understandings of teaching and learning;
- recognise the role of communities of practice when designing effective learning experiences;
- identify aspects of your own approaches and practice that underpin your principles for teaching.

LEARNING THEORIES: A HISTORICAL PERSPECTIVE

Learning theory is a key tenet on your journey towards becoming a teacher; it is also likely to be one of the first assignments you'll hear about at the start of your education course. Understanding how children learn is crucial in ensuring that from the outset you understand the best way to teach the young learners in your class. However, what you may already have learned if you have a psychology or early childhood background, is that there is no single theory and no one theorist that will be appropriate for all children in all situations.

Many of the early theorists in the 17th and 18th centuries, including John Locke (1693) and Jean-Jacques Rousseau (1762), were interested in the individual in response to their societies – in that individuals needed to be taught to be virtuous and through self-improvement and development, society would also improve. Later theorists in the 19th and 20th centuries began to consider the individual child and what they needed to thrive – Friedrich Froebel (1885) in Germany and Maria Montessori (1967) in Italy both promoted the idea of creativity and play as the mainstay of positive early learning experiences. In the 1960s Jean Piaget, a developmental psychologist, posited the idea of four specific stages of children's learning: sensorimotor stage, pre-operational stage, concrete operational stage and formal operational stage (1964), with each stage occurring at a different phase in a child's life. While later criticisms of development stage theory considered it to be too fixed and too linear and some of his experiments flawed (some based on his own children's responses), much of our understanding of child-centred learning is still underpinned by his work.

Two other theories could not have been more different: B. F. Skinner's theory (1938) relied on the notion that all behaviour is determined by consequences, something you might see in the classroom through a reward system – if you follow the classroom rules you'll receive praise and this in turn is a positive reinforcement, so you are more likely to do the same thing again. Whereas, if you receive negative feedback for talking at the wrong time or coming in late from play, you'll receive a negative consequence, for example, losing some of your play time or golden time. John Dewey (1938), a philosopher and psychologist, working in the US, took a wider view and challenged traditional notions of education through his argument that children should be active learners making sense of their own worlds.

Another psychologist working in 1930s Russia also had at the heart of his work the individual; he argued that fundamental to learning was the symbiotic relationship of language and culture. Lev Vygotsky's work only became popular in the 1970s and 80s, many years after his death, when his work was published outside of Russia for the first time (1978). Like Piaget, although the two had different views on the role of language in learning, many of his ideas are mainstays in our understanding of how children learn. You will likely have heard of his concept of the Zone of Proximal Development (ZPD) and seen it in practice as teachers scaffold the gap between what children can do by themselves and what they can go on to do with the help of a more experienced other. Jerome Bruner's work (1961) also considered the role of scaffolding, through his notion of a *spiral curriculum*: this is the idea that children are introduced to and then grasp new ideas through simple concepts before revisiting them later in a more complex way. He also put forward *discovery learning*: with the view that children could explore ideas and construct their own knowledge, rather than being solely reliant on the teacher (or another adult) imparting instruction.

As well as referring to individual theorists, it is also possible to group and theme learning theories together. Depending on whose work you include, you might label the three aforementioned major theories: *Behaviourism* (Skinner), *Cognitivism* (Piaget) and *Constructivism* (Bruner). However, these theories ignore the active role of the social aspects of learning, so two further theories can be added to this group: *social constructivist* learning theory, which aligns to both Dewey and Vygotsky's interest in the role of culture and society, and a fifth theory, that of *humanism*. Humanist learning theory centres on the view that people have a natural desire to learn and that the process of learning is more important than the outcome. These ideas are based on the original ideas of Abraham Maslow (1954, cited in McLeod 2023a) and his hierarchy of needs which he later further developed into an expanded hierarchy, and further built upon by Carl Rogers (1959, cited in McLeod 2023b) and James Bugental

(1976). Central to the theory in terms of education is that the learner is in control and can exercise autonomy and agency and this puts education within the context of a holistic approach and positions the teacher as an encourager and motivator of the whole child.

There is also a third way of framing different learning theories and that's through grouping the ideas together at the individual, the interpersonal and the social or situational level. At the **individual** level, and you would include constructivism and behaviourism at this level, the focus is on the individual's experience. Within a learning situation, learners seek out connections between existing knowledge as they acquire new knowledge, and as they learn they reorganise their immediate worlds in the light of new circumstances. They also learn that actions have consequences, both positive and negative, which are then reinforced through various stimuli and responses that occur within the classroom, both in relation to the teacher and classmates. At the **interpersonal** level, the theories of social constructivism and culturalism shift the focus from the individual's acquisition of knowledge to the view that learning is a social practice and knowledge development a collective process. Meaning is acquired through experience, and learning unfolds through the various social interactions that take place based on prior knowledge where teaching is based on group work and scaffolding strategies are used to bridge the ZPD. This importance of the interpersonal is then extended into the **social** or **situational** level, where the role of the community is fundamental to the learning of all individuals as they interact together, create shared meanings and work together towards a common goal.

Essentially, understanding all these different learning theories means that you as the teacher understand how different children learn, and by appreciating how the environment or setting impacts on learning, you can be better prepared to teach the 30 or so individuals in your class.

Finally, we might even view learning theories as a continuum (Figure 2.3.1) where we have the behaviourist approach on one end and neuroscience on the other. The difficulty of this is that a continuum suggests that you move from one theory to another. Whilst it may serve to show the development of our understanding of theories of learning over time, it is not an accurate representation of the classroom context. It fails to fully acknowledge the role of the teacher and the decisions they make when planning meaningful learning activities.

Visit the SAGE 20 learning theorists every education student should know. You can access the learning cards through the QR code or by following the URL: https://us.sagepub.com/en-us/nam/20-learning-theorists-you-must-know. You may like to download them and keep a copy to refer back to.

Behaviourism → Cognitivism → Constructivism → Social constructivism → Humanism → Neuroscience

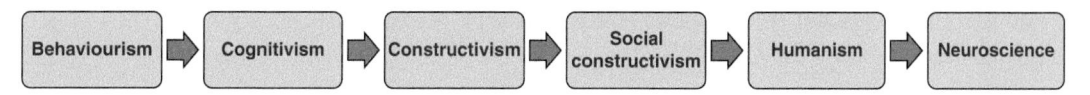

FIGURE 2.3.1 Main learning theories as a continuum

Task 2.3.1 Exploring learning theorists

Read through the learning cards. Note down which theorists you know or have heard about and then choose two different theorists, either because you like their ideas or because you disagree with them. It is helpful to use this strategy as it enables you to better articulate why your own teaching approach is aligned to particular beliefs or theories of learning. As you move through your education course, you will need to be both reflective and reflexive about the choices you make within your own teaching practice. Being aware that the decisions you make never take place within a knowledge vacuum will ensure that you develop as a research-informed practitioner.

Task 2.3.2 Reflection

Consider how the following scenario might be viewed from your chosen theorist's perspective:

On placement you are observing in a class of 7–8 year olds. All the children are on the carpet, except one. They are working at a table on what appears to be a separate activity. Every so often, the solo child calls out to the teacher. In response, the teacher tells the child they have two questions left for the rest of that lesson. The child continues with their task and calls out three more times. At the third time, the teacher replies, 'Alex, I've answered all three of your questions, and now I'm going to ask you to save any more questions until after break'. Sometime later, the child begins to call out again, but this time they stop themselves before continuing with their task.

As you read the vignette again, consider, beyond Skinner's theory of positive reinforcement, the other learning theories you could apply here. For example, could Carol Dweck's (2006) work on growth mindset be applied as maybe this child is learning to persevere with a task, or Albert Bandura's social learning theory could be at play as the child observes and then changes their behaviour.

To conclude, in this section, we have emphasised that learning is complex and the reflection task, we hope, has prompted you to think how different theories intersect and cross over depending upon the context and your knowledge of that context. You will also have noted that theories that were prevalent and groundbreaking in their day give way to new voices and new ways of thinking and, as children's lives evolve, so must our understanding of our role as educators.

THE NEED FOR MORE CONTEMPORARY APPROACHES TO LEARNING AND TEACHING

Historical perspectives of learning are, of course, important and can be used to analyse and inform your own practice. In teacher education, these theories are sometimes explored discretely, and you may be asked to identify which approach best matches your own developing practice, as we highlighted in the previous task. However, there are also voices within the field that are less visible; for example, at the turn of the 20th century, Anna Julia Cooper, a US-based educator, was stressing the importance of teachers' understanding of the diverse backgrounds of the children in their classes (Muhammad et al., 2020), and 'how their students' experiences represent their social locations, and their place in school and the broader society' (p. 423). Within your studies of learning theory, you may recognise the approach being proposed here as aligning to 'intersectionality'. The lives of two other influential Black women educators, Mary McLeod Bethune and Nannie Helen Burroughs, are brought to prominence in the same article, and we urge you to continue to seek out the less visible voices of authors and theorists.

A rapidly developing field within learning theory is that of neuroscience. Both authors of this chapter are English specialists, and, in their work, they have both drawn on the work of two psychologists, Berninger and Swanson (1994, cited in Chamberlain, 2018), who developed a visual model to capture the complexity of the writing process for beginner or developing writers. This involves the idea that writers are constantly drawing on both their long term and working memories, whilst at the same time as interacting with the affect, motivation and context of the writing underpinned by the writer's declarative (information I am aware of and can verbalise) and procedural knowledge (something I can do without necessarily knowing how) of writing. You may also connect neuroscience with our attempts to understand why and how some children find some aspects of learning more difficult, for example, those with dyslexia or dyscalculia. In short, neuroscience seeks to understand the mental processes that are involved in learning.

You may also align your understanding of neuroscience with the idea of 'learning styles' – the idea that each learner has a preferred *style* of learning, and they may be referred to as, for example, an auditory, visual or kinaesthetic learner. Whilst very popular in the 1990s, the Education Endowment Fund (n.d.) suggests there is a lack of evidence and unclear impact as to its effectiveness. Indeed, as with learning theories, there is a danger in labelling children as a particular type of learner, as it may limit both their attainment and motivation in tasks that are apparently less suited to their style. This approach may align itself to the idea of a fixed mindset, in that having a particular learning style label potentially limits my belief as to what I can achieve because I am concerned about failing.

On the other hand, adopting a growth mindset, advocated through the work and research of Dweck and Leggett (1988), suggests that by adopting a resilient attitude individuals can learn to overcome potential difficulties, and even thrive, as they understand that their personal characteristics and ability are not 'fixed' and can continue to develop. Many schools have adopted this approach and promote the idea to children that working hard at a problem and not giving up is a strength. However, as with many theories, there can be misinterpretation of what the author intended. A common misconception of growth mindset is that children should not be praised; however, as Dweck (2006: 175) explains, 'Praising children's intelligence harms their motivation and it harms their performance.' Therefore, as a teacher, your feedback should focus on the effort rather than the inherent ability – in a sense, the focus of the praise should be on the process of the learning; for example, 'I really like the way you tackled that problem; that was clever', rather than 'You are clever, well done'. Dweck argues that using the latter strategy can become problematic, as when the child runs into a more challenging problem, and if their *fixed* mindset suggests that being clever equates to being successful, then they are more likely to believe that 'failing' a task means they are no longer clever.

THE CONTEXT OF LEARNING IS CENTRAL TO TEACHING

In this next section, we illustrate that teaching and learning are complex, intertwined and active processes with a range of factors that influence the decisions taken by teachers as they teach. We argue that rather than subscribing to one theory or theorist, the decisions you make as a teacher will depend on a number of influencing factors. We also discuss the importance of understanding the pedagogical approaches taken by the teacher which underpin the choices they make when planning for learning. When we talk about pedagogical approaches, we use the following definition of the word *pedagogy*:

> that set of instructional techniques and strategies which enable learning to take place and provide opportunities for the acquisition of knowledge, skills, attitudes and dispositions within a particular social and material context. It refers to the interactive process between teacher and learner and to the learning environment.
>
> (Siraj-Blatchford *et al.*, 2002: 10)

Consider the following two examples of practice adapted from two classroom observations (McDonald, 2020). In each school there are various factors, both internal and external, which influence the approach adopted by the teachers. As you read each example, think about the different pedagogical approaches taken by the teachers and how they might facilitate a learning environment which empowers the children to be active participants in their learning.

Roundfield Primary School

In Roundfield Primary School, halfway through the academic year, the teacher, of a class of 8 and 9 year olds, has developed a learning community where children and adults learn from each other and build knowledge and experiences together. The senior leadership promotes creativity and actively encourages staff to try out new ideas as long as they are pedagogically principled.

> It is just after 9am and there is an atmosphere of curiosity and intrigue as the teacher introduces the literacy lesson for the day. The lesson is a continuation of the exploration of 'The Daughter of the Sea' by Berlie Doherty. The class are keen to get started so they can see if their predictions from the previous lesson are borne out through the next chapter. The teacher shares in the excitement as a learner and explorer of the text alongside the children. There is a clear objective for the lesson, but this is not explicitly shared with the children until later, instead the start features a hook linking to the previous predictions which captures the children's interest and sparks curiosity.

It is clear that the children feel the freedom to test their own learning without fear of failure. Through role play, they draw on their knowledge of the text, of other stories they have read as well as their own experiences to make observations and predictions about the characters and their predicament. In the midst of the role play, the teacher expertly weaves their ideas into the fabric of the lesson thereby valuing, celebrating and acknowledging the importance of the children's voices.

Lakeview Primary School

In Lakeview Primary School, halfway through the academic year, the teacher, of a class of 8 and 9 year olds, is focused on ensuring the predetermined set objectives are achieved by the pupils in their class. They have excellent tracking records, meaning the teacher is able to implement intervention groups when necessary. The school senior team believes that consistency is key, and as such carry out regular observations of teaching as well as scrutiny of children's books to ensure that all policies are being followed.

> It is just after 9am and the teacher has set the objective for the literacy lesson on the interactive white board. The first task is for the children to copy the date and objective neatly in their books and then 'show they are ready'. (This invariably means putting their pencils down and folding their arms.) The teacher enthusiastically gives out class points for children who have completed the objective and date and are waiting patiently. Once all the class members are ready, the teacher asks one child to read the objective followed by the set of success criteria. The children are told that points can be gained for successfully showing evidence of the success criteria in their written work. There is an atmosphere of expectation in the classroom as the children wait to be told what their task is. Once the learning has been explained, via a sequence of PowerPoint slides, the children start the task which is slightly adapted depending on which ability table children are sat at.

Reading the examples, it is possible to identify the different approaches taken by the two teachers. In Roundfield Primary School, the teacher appears to focus on building a community of learners, whereas in Lakeview Primary School, the teacher appears more focused on ensuring the children meet the expectations for the lesson. You may also identify the possible influence of each school's leadership team on the decisions that the teachers can make at classroom level. In both examples, the teachers are making choices. These choices are complex, some are taken by the teacher in the moment, and some are external factors based on what is expected by the school. These choices can also vary from lesson-to-lesson and even change within lessons. There is also a distinction between the types of practice which can be seen; for example, how teachers organise their classroom, how children are grouped and so on. Additionally, be aware of what Freeman (2002: 1) calls the 'hidden side of teaching' which is a teacher's cognition and associated actions; for example, the complex decision-making and thinking a teacher is constantly engaged with whilst in the moment of teaching. Understanding, being aware and actively responding to the range of factors that make you aware of your own decision-making will enable you to strengthen your pedagogical knowledge and practice.

FACTORS INFLUENCING TEACHING AND LEARNING

Studies by researchers from the UK, Finland and the US (Hall and Harding, 2003; Kennedy, 2004; Gholami and Husu, 2010) identify a range of significant factors that determine the types of decisions made by teachers. These include teachers':

- beliefs about education and teaching;
- understanding of the subject matter;
- decision-making processes;
- commitment to continuing professional development.

As a trainee teacher or early career teacher, you may have experienced being observed teaching and receiving feedback from your tutor/teacher along the lines of the previous points. Often the observation and feedback concentrate on what you did and what was visible in the lesson (your actions), but what about the unseen elements (teacher cognition)? Does the feedback always reflect on why you took a particular course of action?

Look again at Lakeview Primary School, where you might have felt that the teacher was more influenced by external factors, like the expectations of the senior leadership team and the school policy around book scrutiny. This is in contrast to Roundfield Primary School, where the teacher appears to have more freedom and is afforded professional trust, which together seems to give the teacher greater flexibility. In so doing, they have the opportunity to demonstrate their 'teacher cognition', as we see evidence of their ongoing evaluation and adjustment of their thinking and decision-making.

The work of Brian Street is useful here to understand the consequences of the teachers' practices and the impact on the children's learning. Street (2000) would argue that the choices made by the teacher in Lakeview Primary School resulted in what he would term a skill-based, quantitative or school-centric approach. In contrast, the teacher in Roundfield Primary School would be characterised as adopting what Street termed an ideological, qualitative or social approach, where the teacher was not only concerned with the children's learning but also the context within which their learning was being developed. What is important here is that you understand that teaching is directly influenced by the decisions and actions you take, all of which impact on children's learning.

DEVELOPING CREATIVE AND INCLUSIVE LEARNING COMMUNITIES

So far, we have argued that teachers need to understand how their children learn and that teachers make decisions all the time, some visible and some hidden. In this next section we consider how teachers develop creative and inclusive learning communities, where learners and teachers work together to generate a learning culture characterised by intrigue and curiosity.

Research by Jean Lave (a cognitive anthropologist) and Etienne Wenger (an educational theorist) in the early 1990s proposed the idea of communities of practice (CoP). A CoP needs three specific elements: a domain – the general area of interest; a community – evidenced through a willingness to share ideas through interactions; and a practice – developed through the interaction of its members and through different activities, for example, problem solving or developing confidence. In later work, Wenger (1998) talked specifically of learning being a social process and located within a particular community influenced by its culture and history. The published work of bell hooks (a scholar and activist) from the same decade also stresses the communal nature of learning by, 'Seeing the classroom always as a communal place enhances the likelihood of collective effort in creating and sustaining a learning community' (1994: 3). Her work builds on the idea of critical pedagogy that is a way of teaching where the classroom is viewed through the lens of social justice.

Central to a creative learning community is emotion. Depending upon your own beliefs about the purpose of primary education (and your experience in the classroom), the concept of emotion and teaching may be relatively new to you. Indeed, we sometimes separate teaching and learning from emotion (as seen in Lakeview Primary School), but in this section, we argue that emotion is a vital component of a creative learning community (Bächler, Segovia-Lagos and Porras, 2023). Fredrickson (2001) notes how emotion in teaching broadens the cognitive repertoire (which we looked at in the previous section), that can in turn enhance creativity and imagination. One of our favourite quotes on emotion comes from Hargreaves, who notes that 'emotions are at the heart of teaching' (1988: 835). This is developed in more recent research by Bächler, Segovia-Lagos and Porras (2023), who explore the role of emotions in education and note that the new generation of teachers need to know (and believe) that emotions are at the core of every teaching and learning process.

Therefore, we argue that teaching, learning and emotion are inextricably linked, and Nias (1996) helps us to understand this a little more by highlighting three main reasons:

- Teaching involves interaction with people.
- Teachers' personal and professional identities are often inseparable from the workplace.
- Teachers invest so much of themselves into teaching meaning that they are often passionate about the learning they design for the children.

We can probably all identify with these points, and indeed may have experienced various levels of emotion as we go about our planning and designing of stimulating and engaging lessons. There is emotion invested by us at every stage of being a teacher, but it is felt more intently when we are actually in the process of teaching. This is due to what O'Connor (2008) terms as 'emotional labour'. Emotional labour refers to the love, care and positive relationships that are developed within the learning community (our classroom) by both the teacher and the children to create a safe, supportive and motivating environment. This is further explored by Bächler and Pozo (2016) and later by Bächler, Segovia-Lagos and Porras (2023), who argue that emotions should not be seen as separate from learning, as that can lead to a loss in motivation for the children and teachers alike due to the fact that emotion is central to the functioning of the human brain.

EMOTIONAL LABOUR THROUGH TEACHER TALK

More visibly, we can identify emotional labour through the talk teachers use in the classroom. Let's return to the teacher from Roundfield Primary School and look at some of the language she commonly used, taken from transcripts of the classroom talk happening in her classroom (McDonald, 2020):

What an amazing, amazing thing to do.
Brilliant. I love that comment.
You've picked up another important issue.
That was a really important reason that made that piece of letter-writing so amazing.
You've really captured that because of the way you've used that emotive language and taken us through the event so clearly.
How interesting. Truly, I hadn't seen it that way before. We almost have two lots of taste when you taste something. That's brilliant.

Task 2.3.3 Considering teachers' talk

Read through the previous comments again and ask yourself the following questions:

1. How do you think the children in her class would feel about themselves and about their learning?
2. How does the teacher show that she appreciates the children's thoughts and ideas?
3. How might the language she uses reflect her relationship with the children?

Your ideas may have focused on the positive language used by the teacher – that children would know their ideas and answers were valued, that they felt known by the teacher, all of which would contribute to the learning in this classroom happening within a conducive and inclusive learning environment. In this section, we have argued the emotional labour invested by the teacher is crucial in the creation of a community of practice where children and adults learn alongside each other.

SUMMARY

Having spent time in this chapter discussing the complexity of teaching and learning, we turn our attention to some principles you might take into your practice.

Our first suggestion is that as you start your primary teaching career, you take enough time to learn about the children in your class. Not only their previous attainment, but what they like to do and what they think they are good at; for example, what they like to read, the hobbies they have and the subjects they enjoy. Our second suggestion is that you reflect on, and find ways of describing, your own pedagogy, including the factors which have the greatest influence on your teaching and the learning theories your values align to most closely. Our final suggestion is that you develop an emotional connection with your children through the language you use. Think about the impact of your words on the learners and consider which words enable a sense of community amongst all the learners in your classroom.

Across this chapter and central to our argument is that you need to understand how children learn. You need to know them as individuals and be able to respond to their differing needs through your informed approach to your teaching. As your experience grows, so will your understanding of your practice and most likely the way you teach will change over time. This reflects the very nature of teaching and learning. It is always evolving and with each new challenge brings new ways of thinking about learning theories. Over the next decade, as developments around artificial intelligence and machine-generated learning increase apace, the nature of education will change again, and with it will be implications for how we understand teaching, therefore learning will need to change too.

ANNOTATED FURTHER READING

Aubery, K. and Riley, A. (2022) *Understanding and Using Educational Theories*, 3rd edn, London, UK: Sage.
> The third edition of this book has been updated to include more contemporary theorists, each offered as one of 19 distinct chapters. Written by teacher educators, this book and its sister text, *Understanding and Using Challenging Educational Theories*, have been designed specifically for M-level study.

Hall, K., Curtin, A. and Rutherford, V. (2014) *Networks of Mind: Learning, Culture, Neuroscience*, Oxon: Routledge.
> This is an excellent source for finding out more about the development of learning within the theories of sociocultural and neuroscience. Although not often associated together, this text identifies the area where the two theories converge.

Pekrun, R. and Linnenbrink-Garcia, L. (eds) (2014) *International Handbook of Emotions in Education*, 1st edn, New York, Routledge. https://doi.org/10.4324/9780203148211
> This brings together knowledge relating to how emotions affect teaching and learning in the classroom. The handbook is an excellent starting point to explore this area.

Smith, M. K. (2003) 'Jean Lave, Etienne Wenger and communities of practice', *The encyclopaedia of pedagogy and informal education*. Retrieved from: https://infed.org/mobi/jean-lave-etienne-wenger-and-communities-of-practice/.
> This readable article by Mark Smith provides a useful overview of the work of Jean Lave and Etienne Wenger. It highlights some of the specific concepts of their work, as well as an explanation of some of the key terms and how they might apply at an organisational (school or educational setting) level.

Wolf, M. (2008) *Proust and the Squid*, London, UK: Icon Books.
> Specifically focused on reading and with a title designed to elicit curiosity, this book sets out to explore how, through the invention of reading, the human brain evolved in such a way to change both its structure and organisation. Wolf's more recent text, *Reader, Come Home*, talks about advances in neuroscience and the reading brain in a digital world.

FURTHER READING TO SUPPORT M-LEVEL STUDY

Noddings, N. (2013) *Caring: A Relational Approach to Ethics and Moral Education*, 2nd edn, Berkeley: University of California Press.

Broughton, A. (2020) Black skin, White theorists: Remembering hidden Black early childhood scholars. *Contemporary Issues in Early Childhood*, 23(1): 16-31. https://doi.org/10.1177/1463949120958101

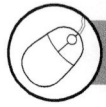

RELEVANT WEBSITES

Education Endowment Foundation: Teaching and Learning Toolkit: https://educationendowmentfoundation.org.uk/education-evidence/teaching-learning-toolkit
> Maintained by the Education Endowment Fund (EFF), the Teaching and Learning Toolkits (both primary and early years) provide real life data about particular approaches used in schools to improve learning outcomes. Whilst the site takes a neutral stance, the information provided allows teachers and senior leaders to make evidence-informed decisions about the types of approaches that may be appropriate within their own settings. Some useful explainer videos are included.

Welsh Government: Curriculum for Wales: https://hwb.gov.wales/curriculum-for-wales/designing-your-curriculum/
> As a student teacher training within a specific nation, you may wish to develop your subject knowledge around how priorities differ across the home nations. The Curriculum for Wales site provides useful guidance on key principles teachers and senior leaders should implement when designing a curriculum to match the needs of their learners.

Impact: Issue 2: The science of learning: https://my.chartered.college/impact/issue-2-science-of-learning/
> The Chartered College provides a range of resources, both research-informed content through their various hubs and their journal, *Impact*. Issue 2, *The science of learning*, includes articles, original research and a range of practical resources through their CPD packs on growth mindset and retrieval practice.

REFERENCES

Bächler, R. and Pozo, J. (2016) 'I feel, therefore I teach? Teachers' conceptions of the relationships between emotions and teaching/learning processes', *Infancia y Aprendizaje*, 39(2): 312-348. doi: 10.1080/02103702.2015.1133088

Bächler, R., Segovia-Lagos, P. and Porras, C. (2023) 'The role of emotions in educational processes: The conceptions of teacher educators', *Front. Psychol*, 14: 1145294. doi: 10.3389/fpsyg.2023.1145294

Bruner, J. S. (1961) 'The act of discovery', *Harvard Educational Review*, 31: 21-32.

Bugental, J. (1976) *Search for Existential Identity*. Retrieved from: www.bugental.com/written-works

Chamberlain, L. (2018) *Inspiring Writing in Primary Schools*, London: SAGE.

Dewey, J. (1938) *Experience and Education*, US: Kappa Delta Pi.

Dweck, C. S. (2006) *Mindset: The New Psychology of Success*, New York, NY: Random House.

Dweck, C. S. and Leggett, E. L. (1988) 'A social-cognitive approach to motivation and personality', *Psychological Review*, 95(2): 256-273. Accessed from: https://doi.org/10.1037/0033- 295X.95.2.256

Education Endowment Fund. (n.d.) *Teaching and Learning Toolkit: Learning Styles*. Retrieved from: https://educationendowmentfoundation.org.uk/education-evidence/teaching-learning-toolkit/learning-styles

Fredrickson, B. L. (2001) 'The role of positive emotions in positive psychology: The broaden-and-build theory of positive emotions', *American Psychology*, 56(3): 218-226.

Freeman, D. (2002) 'The hidden side of the work: Teacher knowledge and learning to teach. A perspective from North American educational research on teacher education in English language teaching', *Language Teaching*, 35(1): 1-13.

Froebel, F. (1885) *The Education of Ma*, translated by J. Jarvis, New York: A. Lovell & Co.

Gholami, K. and Husu, J. (2010) 'How do teachers reason about their practice? Representing the epistemic nature of teachers' practical knowledge', *Teaching and Teacher Education*, 26(8): 1520-1529.

Hall, K. and Harding, A. (2003) 'A systematic review of effective literacy teaching in the 4 to 14 age range of mainstream schooling', in *Research Evidence in Education Library*, London: EPPI-Centre, Social Science Research Unit, Institute of Education.

Hargreaves, A. (1998) 'The emotional practice of teaching', *Teaching and Teacher Education*, 14(8): 835-854.

hooks, bell (1994) *Teaching to Transgress: Education as the Practice of Freedom*, New York: Routledge.

Kennedy, M. (2004) 'Reform ideals and teachers' practical intentions', *Education Policy Analysis Archives*, 12(13).

Lave, J. and Wenger, E. (1991) *Situated Learning: Legitimate Peripheral Participation*, Cambridge: Cambridge University Press.

Locke, J. (1693) *Some Thoughts Concerning Education*, London: A and J. Churchill. Retrieved from: https://archive.org/details/somethoughtscon02lockgoog

McDonald, R. (2020) 'How do current notions of effective literacy teaching, held by three primary school teachers in South East England, encourage opportunities for imagining?' Unpublished dissertation for Doctor of Philosophy, University of Greenwich.

McLeod, S. (2023a) *Maslow's Hierarchy of Needs*. Retrieved from: www.simplypsychology.org/maslow.html

McLeod, S. (2023b) *Carl Rogers Humanistic Theory and Contribution to Psychology*. Retrieved from: www.simplypsychology.org/carl-rogers.html

Montessori, M. (1967) *The Discovery of the Child*, New York: Ballantine Books.

Muhammad, G. E., Dunmeyer, A., Starks, F. D. and Sealey-Ruiz, Y. (2020) 'Historical voices for contemporary times: Learning from Black women educational theorists to redesign teaching and teacher education', *Theory Into Practice*, 59(4): 419-428. Retrieved from: www.tandfonline.com/doi/full/10.1080/00405841.2020.1773185

Nias, J. (1996) 'Thinking about feeling: The emotions in teaching', *Cambridge Journal of Education*, 26(3): 293-306.

O'Connor, K. (2008) '"You choose to care": Teachers, emotions and professional identity', *Teaching and Teacher Education*, 24(1): 117-126.

Piaget, J. (1964) 'Cognitive development in children', *Journal of Research in Science Teaching*, (2): 176-186.

Rousseau, J-J. (1762) *Emile, or Education*. J. M. Dent.

Siraj-Blatchford, I., Muttock, S., Sylva, K., Gilden, R. and Bell, D. (2002) *Researching Effective Pedagogy in the Early Years* (Research Report 356), London: Department for Education and Skills.

Skinner, B. F. (1938) *The Behaviour of Organisms: An Experimental Analysis*, Appleton-Century.

Street, B. (2000) 'Literacy events and literacy practices', in K. Jones and M. Martin Jones (eds) *Multilingual Literacies: Comparative Perspectives on Research and Practice*, Amsterdam: John Benjamins, pp. 17-29.

Vygotsky, L. S. (1978) *Mind in Society: The Development of Higher Psychological Processes*, Cambridge, MA: Harvard University Press.

Wenger, E. (1998) *Communities of Practice: Learning, Meaning and Identity*, Cambridge: Cambridge University Press.

UNIT 2.4

DEVELOPING AS A PROFESSIONAL

Samantha Twiselton and Sally Elton-Chalcraft

INTRODUCTION

> Good teaching makes a difference. Excellent teaching can transform lives.
>
> (Alexander, 2010: 279)

This chapter will look at the skills and knowledge required for you to be able to create and support successful learning experiences that, ultimately, could transform lives. What you decide to do in the classroom can have a profound influence on the children you work with. We unpack factors you need to consider when you plan for the children's learning. But we begin by asking you to consider what kind of teacher you want to be as you develop professionally. Biesta (2019) considers the possible marginalisation of the role of the teacher in the shift from the art of teaching to the importance of learning. So in this unit the role of the teacher is scrutinised and we invite you to consider your own attitude towards teaching and how you want to develop as a professional.

OBJECTIVES

By the end of this unit, you should be beginning to:

- consider your attitude towards 'being a teacher' and your view of 'developing as a professional';
- understand that excellent teaching involves being aware of the underlying factors that underpin learning objectives (e.g., organisation of the curriculum; concepts of knowledge; a child's background, prior learning, aptitude, etc.);
- understand how knowledge is organised (connections);
- develop strategies to help your own decision-making in the classroom (creativity and knowledge, problem analysis).

THE GIFT OF TEACHING AND THE FREEDOM OF THE PUPIL: IMPLICATIONS FOR TEACHER DEVELOPMENT

What kind of a teacher do you want to become? Biesta outlines the supposed shift in focus from teacher-led, in contrast to child-focused, education, with the role of the teacher moving from 'sage on the stage' to 'guide from the side' or even 'peer at the rear' (2019: 549). So your philosophical opinion

DOI: 10.4324/9781032691794-9

about the role of the teacher can be plotted along a line – from the marginalisation of the teacher in 'learning-focused education' to the other extreme of the marginalisation of the pupil in 'teacher-led' education, or possibly somewhere in between which we unpack later.

Furthermore, your professional development as a teacher could be influenced by the current external context in which you are located, such as geographic and political context (whether you teach in one of the UK jurisdictions or elsewhere in the world). In some contexts, you may be required to follow particular professional development programmes, for example in England there is a requirement to follow the Early Career Framework (ECF) (Department for Education [DfE], 2019). Your professional development as a teacher could also be influenced by a range of philosophical views about the role of the teacher – such attitudes may have been gleaned from your teacher education course or literature you have been exposed to, from your own experience when at school or your observations of teachers. You can learn about different modes of being a teacher in various teacher education handbooks such as this one and others (e.g., Cooper and Elton-Chalcraft, 2022; Pollard and Wyse, 2023, etc.) and by theorists such as Biesta (2017, 2019, 2022).

In 2024, the DfE updated its policy paper on the roll out of the ECF, which suggested that there were 'frustrations around perceived inflexibilities of the structure of the programme and lack of tailoring the content to early career teacher (ECT) needs and school contexts, and the repetitive nature of the content' (DfE, 2019: 5). The lack of time mentors and early career teachers could spend on reflecting on practice and engaging in the scheme was also identified as a major issue. However, the report notes that the scheme has been successful in increasing ECT confidence and developing other competencies (DfE, 2019). For further insight into the ECF, see Scutt, Coleman and Madgwick (2022).

We would recommend that you consider a range of sources to support your development, bearing in mind both the requirements in your country (such as the ECF in England) but also draw on wider philosophical and worldwide ideas. Next, we highlight some theories and practice.

KNOWLEDGE AND LEARNING: FOR THE PUPIL AND THE TEACHER

According to Bruner (1996) and many others, learning involves the search for pattern, regularity and predictability. We can only make sense out of the confusion of information continuously bombarding our senses if we can *relate* the pieces of information to each other in some way.

Input from a teacher should help children in the formation and discovery of the patterns and rules that are most likely to help them (1) make sense of the experience and (2) generalise it to other experiences. Complex tasks can be broken down into manageable smaller problems, so that the learner can detect patterns and regularities that could not be discovered alone. So, a task such as building a tower with bricks can be made possible by the presence of a teacher who helps the pupil through decisions and actions in small steps, while still holding 'the bigger picture' of the ultimate goal of the tower in mind.

The opening quotation is from *Children, Their World, Their Education: Final Report and Recommendations of the Cambridge Primary Review*, a report undertaken by a range of scholars and educationalists (Alexander, 2010). We would argue that, despite being over a decade since its production, the review nevertheless has currency today, and if you encompass the review's suggested principles and aims when designing your lessons, you will thus be engaging in excellent teaching. Alexander's aims (2010: 197) of primary teaching provide a framework that is consistent with (but goes beyond) the 2012 Qualified Teacher Status (QTS) standards (DfE, 2011). The first few aims call on you to nurture the qualities and capacities of the child, namely well-being; engagement; empowerment and autonomy. The second group of aims relate to self, others and the world, namely encouraging respect and reciprocity; promoting independence and sustainability; empowering local, national and global citizenship; and celebrating culture and community (Alexander, 2010: 197–199). The third group of aims focus on what should be going on in the classroom, namely exploring; knowing; understanding and making sense; fostering skill; exciting the imagination and enacting dialogue (Alexander, 2010: 197–199). Other units in this volume consider the philosophies and values underpinning the curriculum and specific subjects; here, we restrict our discussion to development of your teaching skills and the learning opportunities you provide. We would argue that teaching ought to be a research-led profession (Elton-Chalcraft, Hansen and Twiselton, 2008), requiring you to:

1. think more deeply about *why you* have planned to do x, y and z with your pupils;
2. evaluate more rigorously what effect your teaching has on your pupils;
3. reflect more comprehensively on your practice and the progress of your pupils.

Task 2.4.1 An evidence-led profession?

Access the Cambridge Primary Review website (www.primaryreview.org.uk) and read the booklet *Introducing the Cambridge Primary Review* (http://cprtrust.org.uk/wp-content/uploads/2013/10/CPR_revised_booklet.pdf). Reflect on the notion of teaching as an 'evidence-led profession'. Does M-level study as part of your ITE course have a role to play in this? To what extent do you draw on knowledge in the public domain (research papers, journal articles and books, professional journals, etc.) to enhance your planning and teaching?

An effective teacher will have an excellent grasp of these fundamental concepts and will be able to break down tasks in ways that will make them achievable, while remaining consistent with the core ideas that underpin them. This means that core ideas are developed in nucleus as early as possible and are returned to with ever-increasing complexity and sophistication in a 'spiral curriculum', as children's experience and understanding make them ready for it.

Biesta (2022) calls for the teacher to position the pupil as a 'subject' in their own education, rather than an object. He calls for teachers to 'point out' knowledge in an active manner – 'You, look there!', thus redirecting the pupil's attention.

QUALITY VERSUS QUANTITY: ORGANISATION OF KNOWLEDGE

The answer to the problem of primary teaching's wide-ranging knowledge base may be helped by Sternberg and Horvath's (1995) attempt to define what is involved in teacher expertise. They comment that there are a number of studies (e.g., Larkin *et al.*, 1980; Chi, Feltovich and Glaser, 1981) that show that it is not so much the *amount* of knowledge that the expert possesses, but *how it is organised* in the memory. In general, experts are sensitive to the deep structures of the problems they solve – they are able to group problems together according to underlying principles. This supports Bruner's model (1996). It seems that the key to being able to teach, for example, history or mathematics is not so much your knowing endless information about the subject, but your understanding of some of the key underlying principles and concepts that underpin it.

This is very much supported by the study by one of the authors (Twiselton and Webb, 1998; Twiselton, 2000, 2003, 2004, 2006, 2007) of the types of knowledge and understanding that primary student teachers develop as they go through their initial teacher education (ITE) programme.

TEACHER AS TASK MANAGER, CURRICULUM DELIVERER OR CONCEPT/SKILL BUILDER

Twiselton found that (partly dependent on how far through the programme they were) student teachers could be placed into one of three main categories (or points on a continuum) - task manager, curriculum deliverer or concept/skill builder. The task managers (who were likely to be near the beginning of ITE) viewed their role in the classroom in terms of task completion, order and business - without any explicit reference to children's learning. The curriculum deliverers did see themselves as there to support learning, but only as dictated by an external source - a scheme, curriculum or lesson plan - and they struggled to give a rationale for *why what was being taught mattered* in any other terms. In contrast, the concept/skill builders (likely to be at or near the end of ITE) were aware of the wider and deeper areas of understanding and skill needed by pupils that underpinned their learning objectives. Of the three types, the concept/skill builders were much more likely to be able to support learning at every stage of the learning experience, effectively, consistently and responsively. The most outstanding quality that separated the concept/skill builders from the other two categories was their ability to see the 'bigger picture' and give a rationale for what they were attempting to do in terms of key principles and concepts. This would appear to be particularly important at a time when policymakers in England swing from one end of the pendulum, a child-centred curriculum, to the other, a subject-focused one. Over the last few years, there has been a somewhat erratic, but nevertheless consistent, desire to make teaching an M-level profession, thus encouraging intending teachers to think beyond the current governmental directives, for example the Prevent Strategy and promoting fundamental British values (DfE, 2015; Elton-Chalcraft *et al.*, 2017).

Task 2.4.2 Lesson plans 1

- Choose the subject you feel most confident in – for example, (1) English; (2) science; (3) religious education.
- Choose a key area within it – for example, (1) poetry reading and writing; (2) solids, liquids and gases; (3) belief.
- Write the key area in the middle of a piece of paper and write words and phrases you associate with it around the edge – for example, (1) rhyme, rhythm, verses, language play, imagery; (2) evaporation and condensation, state, materials, properties; (3) beliefs, religious and secular food laws.
- In a different colour, write keywords and phrases for all the ways in which this area is important – for example, (1) it gives a pattern and meaning to chaotic experiences, it expresses emotion, it entertains, it communicates powerful ideas; (2) the changing properties of materials allow us to manipulate our environment; we can manufacture things using these changes; life on land requires the fresh water produced by evaporation and condensation; (3) beliefs and values can often affect action.

- Look at the words and phrases in the two different colours you have used. Is it possible to connect them? For example, (1) rhyme and rhythm help to entertain and impose pattern and meaning; imagery is an effective way of communicating powerful ideas; (2) evaporation and condensation are important examples of key processes we use to manipulate the environment; (3) the way we behave is often influenced by our beliefs and values. (The 'what' and the 'why' are connected – concept/skill builders do this.)
- Consider the implications for how these aspects of the subject should be taught to pupils. How can you ensure that they are presented with the 'why' sufficiently?

The next stage is to identify what other factors will be involved, and how this translates into classroom practice.

The need for teachers to develop a broad, rich curriculum is strongly promoted. This is set alongside a notion of a very individualised, highly child-centred approach to supporting learning and a strong emphasis on multi-agency working and the sharing of expertise and information. All of this implies a notion of the teacher that goes well beyond the technician who delivers a prescribed curriculum.

This broad, more flexible, child-centred view of the teacher is welcome, but is not without its challenges, particularly for those who are learning to teach. For a student teacher, it is very easy to become so enmeshed in the practicalities of simply 'surviving' in the classroom that it is difficult to focus on underpinning concepts or how to connect these meaningfully to the needs of individual learners. Task 2.4.3 is designed to lead you through a process that will help you to begin to do this in stages, away from the hurly burly of the classroom, and make the link back to the classroom and your planning.

Task 2.4.3 Lesson plans 2: Moving from novice towards expert teacher

Take a recent lesson plan – ideally one that is your own and that you have already taught. Focus on the learning outcomes that you planned for this lesson. Attempt to answer the following questions:

- Why were these learning outcomes important for these children?
- What importance/usefulness would this learning have beyond this lesson?
- How was this communicated to the children? Were they aware of why what they were learning mattered?

If you feel able to answer these questions with some confidence, the next step is to analyse the lesson chronologically to work out how well this was communicated at each stage. If possible, identify places where this could have been improved, and how.

If you don't feel able to answer these questions with confidence, the next step is to replan the lesson, starting with the learning outcomes and rewriting them in a way that you feel can be justified in terms of their importance. You then need to go through the rest of the plan to amend it, to ensure this is clearly and meaningfully communicated to the children throughout the lesson.

This process will encourage you to move from novice towards expert teacher.

KNOWLEDGE AND CREATIVITY: DEEP LEARNING, NOT SURFACE LEARNING

Other sections later in this volume discuss the 'what' and 'how' of teaching and learning in more detail; here, we are showing the link between the structural underpinning of lesson planning 'why' and the ways in which you can achieve this 'what and how'; (Elton-Chalcraft and Mills, 2013), together with the 'where and when' (Claxton, 2007).

Boden argues that knowledge and creativity are not opposing forces (2001: 95). For example, children need to know the rules of rhyme, or the tenets of belief, before they can playfully create new poems, or work out their own responses. It is important for teachers to support children's understanding of a curriculum area, but, as we have argued earlier, the organisation of this learning (how we teach) can lead either to mundane completion of tasks (task managers) or effective learning (concept/skill builders). Research in neuroscience tells us that knowledge is contextualised, and teachers need to support the child to make connections in the brain (Claxton, 1997; Heilman, 2005). If the curriculum is seen as a blueprint for learning, Copping (2011) argues, then tasks will not be meaningful. For example, task managers would happily ask children to complete a worksheet about Muslims fasting during Ramadan, perhaps filling in missing words. Concept builders, on the other hand, would have used the Internet/books/Muslim visitors to inform their own subject knowledge, thus enabling the children to explore reasons why many Muslims fast (yet other Muslims choose not to fast for particular reasons), why the children themselves eat or do not eat certain foods at particular times, and so on. Concept builders would make the links between the religious education lesson and the Personal, Social, Health and Economic(PSHE) education topic on healthy lifestyle, to discuss what foods the children eat and why, and how this relates to religious food laws (Elton-Chalcraft, 2024). Thus, task managers merely present knowledge – a blueprint – that the children learn, and the children have no interaction with that knowledge. Knowledge is a requisite, as Boden (2001) says, for creating new ideas and concepts and embedding learning in the child's own, personalised web of belief. Kuiper, Volman and Terwel (2009) show how children can be encouraged to use resources appropriately to ensure deep learning, using a 'healthy eating' topic. Elton-Chalcraft (2024) describes how a teacher can engage learners in deep reflection on what they eat and the factors behind people's choice of foods – for example, allergies, texture, taste, appearance, moral or religious reasons, and so on. An effective teacher designs creative learning activities and provides creative learning environments that are not only fun but also challenge the children (Elton-Chalcraft and Mills, 2013). Claxton (2007) urges the teacher to engage in split-screen thinking – with a dual focus on both the content of the lesson and the learning disposition of the child. In his compelling article, Claxton (2007) suggests teachers build children's 'learning capacity' and encourage children to strengthen their 'learning muscles'. All this requires pedagogical knowledge and understanding, which we outline next.

Task 2.4.4 Creativity and knowledge

Access Denis Hayes's (2011) *Guided Reader to Teaching and Learning*, extract 7, pp. 29–31, TASC (thinking actively in a social context), from Wallace *et al.* (2009). Hayes (2011: 31) asks in what ways are pupils seen as equal partners in learning? How is such a state of working attainable?

Read Cedric Cullingford's (2007) passionate article, 'Creativity and pupils' experience of school'. Is Cullingford convincing in his argument about 'children's preferred modes of thinking' (2007: 137)? How does this relate to our discussion of knowledge and concept/skill builders?

> Read Claxton (2007), 'Expanding young people's capacity to learn'. What is your response to Claxton's argument that teachers should be concentrating on children's 'learning muscles', as well as teaching the topic? Do you think this approach is appropriate?
>
> Gordon Stobart's (2014) *The Expert Learner: Challenging the Myth of Ability* discusses surface, strategic and deep/profound learning, with ideas taken from John West-Burnham (Stobart, 2014: 70, 71). To what extent do you help children to engage in deep, profound learning? Are there some times when strategic learning is necessary? Can children be challenged to understand that surface learning is to be avoided? Strategic learning might help them achieve the highest possible grades, but deep learning enables them to develop ideas for themselves, seek underlying patterns and become actively interested in their learning.

TEACHERS' USE OF KNOWLEDGE

Any attempt to define all the different kinds of teacher knowledge required in effective practice is bound to hit the problem that the list can be infinitely extended. However, it is worth noting that most people agree that, however you describe it, the knowledge base is wide-ranging and varied, and that different kinds of knowledge are required at different times. Tochon and Munby (1993) studied expert and novice teachers and found that a key characteristic that distinguished the experts was their ability to draw on a wide range of different kinds of knowledge (e.g., the subject, the plan, the individual pupil, the context, etc.) in making one teaching decision. The novices tended to think about one thing at a time and to stick quite rigidly to their plan, regardless of whether the pupil responses, the context, and so on, supported this.

Lee Shulman (1987) has classified the knowledge base of teaching in seven categories: content knowledge (better known to us as subject knowledge), general pedagogical knowledge, curriculum knowledge, pedagogical content knowledge, knowledge of learners and their characteristics, knowledge of educational contexts and knowledge of educational ends. The important thing for student teachers to note is not so much the items on the list (though these are useful), but the fact that they are so varied. It is the *drawing together and combining* of these varied factors that is important. For example, Devine, Fahie and McGillicuddy (2013: 83) investigate teacher effectiveness in terms of 'passion, reflection, planning, love for children' and the 'social and moral dimension' of what constitutes good teaching. They argue that, when discussing quality teaching, it is vital to consider sociocultural contexts such as gender, social class and ethnicity (Devine, Fahie and McGillicuddy, 2013). Sims and Fletcher-Wood (2021) and Zhang *et al*. (2021) also discuss the impact of teacher development programmes. Medwell *et al*. (1998) found that effective literacy teachers tended to have more coherent belief systems about communication, composition and understanding, linking to Bruner's views. In a parallel study of effective numeracy teachers, Askew *et al*. (1997) characterised effective numeracy teachers as being 'connectionist-oriented', having a rich network of connections between different mathematical ideas. Beck (2013) discusses the 'knowledge of the powerful' and calls for teachers to be more politically aware. We encourage you to engage with these themes in Task 2.4.4 and the further reading to support your professional development.

KNOWING THE UNDERLYING PRINCIPLES, USING KNOWLEDGE EFFICIENTLY

In Sternberg and Horvath's (1995) study of teaching expertise, three key features are identified. The first is *knowledge*, and we have already considered their claim that the organisation of the knowledge around principles is the central factor. The second and third features are *efficiency* and *insight*. Efficiency is closely linked to experience, in that the claim is that experts are much faster at processing information and making well-informed decisions, partly because what is initially effortful and time-consuming becomes effortless and automatic with practice. This is obvious, and one of the most comforting pieces of advice that can be given to student teachers is that, as time goes on, many things that are difficult now become much easier. However, it is worth noting that Sternberg and Horvath (1995) also claim that experts typically spend a greater proportion of time trying to understand the problem, whereas novices spend more time actually trying out different solutions. Sometimes, deciding on the best response through more detailed analysis is a much more efficient way of dealing with problems than rushing in without clear judgement. *Insight*, Sternberg and Horvath's third feature of teacher expertise, involves a combination of the first two (knowledge and efficiency) whereby the teacher distinguishes information that is relevant to the problem solution, from that which is irrelevant.

SUMMARY

It does not require a unit in a book to tell you that teaching is a very complicated business, and that effective teaching requires a wide range of types of knowledge and a large number of skills. In this unit, we have tried to elaborate on some of the more important components of teaching skills and to explore the implications of these for your teaching. We have also drawn your attention to different approaches to teaching which have implications for the types of professional development you choose to undertake. It is important to close this unit with a reminder of the importance of quality over quantity. It is not the amount you know, or the number of teaching skills in which you have some competence, that is crucial. Your depth of knowledge and level of confidence in your skills are of much more importance. As you experience teaching, keep asking yourself the 'why' question and keep your eyes and ears open to children's responses, deeper knowledge and surer confidence in your actions will follow if this becomes your natural mindset. Finally we would encourage you to be selective in choosing from the wide range of teacher professional development courses, workshops, MA and PhD provision, in addition to your own academic and research-based professional development. Growing as a teacher can involve top-down but also bottom-up professional development.

ANNOTATED FURTHER READING

Alexander, R. (2010) *Children, Their World, Their Education: Final Report and Recommendations of the Cambridge Primary Review*, London: Routledge.
> An impressive body of research underpins this volume, which covers most aspects of teaching and learning, philosophy and practice.

Bergmark, U. (2023) 'Teachers' professional learning when building a research-based education: context-specific, collaborative and teacher-driven professional development', *Professional Development in Education*, 49(2): 210-224, DOI: 10.1080/19415257.2020.1827011
> This article, while located in the Swedish context, also discusses European and international contexts to highlight the need for research-based professional development. It argues that greater academic demands have been placed on teachers which may be challenging for teachers who were educated when teacher education prioritised practical teacher training rather than academic training.

The study includes reflections from 50 teachers in preschool, compulsory and upper secondary school, and shows that the teachers' professional learning included changes in the ways they think, act and relate to others in three areas: teaching, research and collaboration. The article provides insights into the importance of a professional development process being collaborative, context-specific, integrated in teachers' work and based on a bottom-up perspective.

Boyd, P., Hymer, B. and Lockney, K. (2015) *Learning Teaching: Becoming an Inspirational Teacher*, Northwich, UK: Critical Publishing.

A text for intending teachers who wish to move from novice towards expert teacher by recognising their own agency. The book includes critical exploration of metacognition and self-regulated learning, deep and surface learning and feedback.

Elton-Chalcraft, S., Hansen, A. and Twiselton, S. (2008) *Doing Classroom Research*, Milton Keynes, UK: Open University Press.

This book has been designed to support those studying at Masters-level as part of their initial teacher education programme.

Graham-Matheson, L. (2014) 'How children learn', in *Essential Theory for Primary Teachers*, London: Routledge, chap. 6, pp. 128-153.

Graham-Matheson analytically discusses theories of learning in an accessible format, with pointers to further reading.

M FURTHER READING TO SUPPORT M-LEVEL STUDY

Beck, J. (2013) 'Powerful knowledge, esoteric knowledge, curriculum knowledge', *Cambridge Journal of Education*, 43(2): 177-193.

John Beck highlights three tensions that impede teachers' efforts to extend powerful learning to disadvantaged pupils. This clearly written but conceptually challenging article draws on sociological and philosophical ideas that can challenge a novice student teacher to move towards expert teacher. Beck discusses 'knowledge of the powerful' in terms of the ruling ideas (p. 180) that can lock working-class children out of 'high culture'. Beck claims that education inflicts 'symbolic violence' on working-class children. He describes how the relatively accessible arts, as opposed to the conceptually challenging sciences, are still used as a benchmark for defining 'good taste'. The tensions that confront a teacher include, first, the problem of disciplinary knowledge being esoteric and accessible primarily for the initiated. The second tension, related to the first, is the breadth versus specialisation debate. The third tension is the cultural capital afforded to the ruling classes, which perpetuates hegemony.

Claxton, G. (2007) 'Expanding young people's capacity to learn', *British Journal of Educational Studies*, 55(2): 115-134.

In this article, particularly useful for M-level students, Claxton expands his view that hesitancy and unclear knowing are vital aspects of intelligence, and that the teacher's role is to help children to become better learners – increase their 'learning capacity' – as opposed to supporting them to become conformist pupils, which, Claxton argues, can result in learned helplessness.

Biesta, G. (2019) 'Should teaching be re(dis)covered? Introduction to a symposium', *Stud Philos Educ*, 38: 549-553. https://doi.org/10.1007/s11217-019-09667-y

In this article, Biesta unpacks many of the ideas in his book about the re discovery of teaching (Biesta, 2017). He challenges teachers to consider the underlying philosophy of teaching and thus teacher development, which emphasises the role of 'learning'and marginalises the role of teaching. He calls teachers to question the redefinition of all things educational in terms of learning – such as calling students learners, calling schools learning environments or places for learning, referring to adult education as lifelong learning and seeing teachers as facilitators of learning. This has implications for the role of the teacher in developing professionally as 'teacher' rather than facilitator of learning. So the article can be used as an antidote for the ECT to consider what type of professional development to pursue.

Cullingford, C. (2007) 'Creativity and pupil's experience of school', *Education 3-13*, 35(2): 133-142.
> Cullingford discusses children's preferred modes of thinking and how teachers can appropriately support children to learn more effectively. This journal article is ideal for M-level study concerning relevant curriculum design and appropriate teaching skills.

Devine, D., Fahie, D. and McGillicuddy, D. (2013) 'What is "good" teaching? Teacher beliefs and practices about their teaching', *Irish Educational Studies*, 32(1), Special Issue on Research in Education Related to Teacher Accountability.
> This journal article discusses the need for teachers to take into account the broader sociocultural context of the school and the needs of their learners, which will have an influence on the way they construct learning. M-level students will find this an engaging read to inform effective classroom practice.

RELEVANT WEBSITES

Chartered College of Teaching: https://chartered.college/
> The Cambridge Primary Review website is located in that of the Chartered College of Teaching, an independent organisation run by teachers for teachers.

Early Career Framework (ECR): www.gov.uk/government/publications/early-career-framework
> The Early Career Framework (ECR) for teachers in England was first introduced in 2019 with further updates in 2024.

REFERENCES

Alexander, R. (2010) *Children, Their World, Their Education: Final Report and Recommendations of the Cambridge Primary Review*, London: Routledge.

Askew, M., Brown, M., Rhodes, V., William, D. and Johnson, D. (1997) *Effective Teachers of Numeracy*, London: Teacher Training Agency.

Beck, J. (2013) 'Powerful knowledge, esoteric knowledge, curriculum knowledge', *Cambridge Journal of Education*, 43(2): 177-193.

Biesta, G. (2017) *The Rediscovery of Teaching*, New York: Routledge.

Biesta, G. (2019) 'Should teaching be re(dis)covered? Introduction to a symposium', *Stud Philos Educ*, 38: 549-553. https://doi.org/10.1007/s11217-019-09667-y

Biesta, G. (2022) *World-Centred Education: A View for the Present*, New York: Routledge.

Boden (2001) 'Creativity and knowledge', in A. Craft, B. Jeffrey and M. Leibling (eds) *Creativity in Education*, London: Continuum, chap. 6.

Bruner, J. S. (1996) *The Culture of Education*, Cambridge, MA: Harvard University Press.

Chi, M. T. H., Feltovich, J. P. and Glaser, R. (1981) 'Categorization and representation of physics problems by experts and novices', *Cognitive Science*, 5(2): 121-152.

Claxton, G. (1997) *Hare Brain, Tortoise Mind: Why Intelligence Increases When You Think Less*, London: Fourth Estate.

Claxton, G. (2007) 'Expanding young people's capacity to learn', *British Journal of Educational Studies*, 55(2): 115-134.

Cooper, H. and Elton-Chalcraft, S. (eds) (2022) *Professional Studies in Primary Education*, 4th edn, London: Sage. https://us.sagepub.com/en-us/nam/professional-studies-in-primary-education/book273439

Copping, A. (2011) 'Curriculum approaches', in A. Hansen (ed.), *Primary Professional Studies*, Exeter, UK: Learning Matters, pp. 23-43.

Cullingford, C. (2007) 'Creativity and pupils' experience of school', *Education 3-13*, 35(2): 133-142.

Department for Education (DfE). (2011) *Teachers' Standards: Guidance for School Leaders, School Staff and Governing Bodies*. Last updated 2021. Retrieved from: https://assets.publishing.service.gov.uk/media/61b73d6c8fa8f50384489c9a/Teachers_Standards_Dec_2021.pdf

Department for Education (DfE). (2015) *Promoting Fundamental British Values*. Retrieved from: www.gov.uk/government/publications/promoting-fundamental-british-values-through-smsc (accessed 1 November 2016).

Department for Education (DfE). (2019) *Early Career Framework*. Last updated 2024. Retrieved from: www.gov.uk/government/publications/early-career-framework (accessed 8 January 2025).

Devine, D., Fahie, D. and McGillicuddy, D. (2013) 'What is "good" teaching? Teacher beliefs and practices about their teaching', *Irish Educational Studies*, 32(*1*), Special Issue on Research in Education Related to Teacher Accountability.

Elton-Chalcraft, S. (2024) *Teaching Religious Education Creatively*, 2nd edn, London: Routledge

Elton-Chalcraft, S. and Mills, K. (2013) '"It was the funnest week in the whole history of funnest weeks." Measuring challenge, fun and sterility on a "Phunometre" scale: A case study evaluating creative teaching and learning with PGCE student teachers and children in a sample of primary schools', *Education 3-13: International Journal of Primary, Elementary and Early Years Education*. http://dx.doi.org/10.1080/03004279.2013.822904.

Elton-Chalcraft, S., Hansen, A. and Twiselton, S. (eds) (2008) *Doing Classroom Research: A Step-By Step Guide for Student Teachers*, Maidenhead, UK: Open University Press.

Elton-Chalcraft, S., Lander, V., Revell, R., Warner, D. and Whitworth, L. (2017) 'To promote, or not to promote fundamental British values? Teachers' standards, diversity and teacher education', *British Journal of Educational research*, 43(1): 29-48.

Hayes, D. (2011) *Guided Reader to Teaching and Learning*, London: David Fulton.

Heilman, K. (2005) *Creativity and the Brain*, Hove, UK: Psychology Press.

Kuiper, E., Volman, M. and Terwel, J. (2009) 'Developing web literacy in collaborative inquiry activities', *Computers & Education*, 52(3): 668-680.

Larkin, J., McDermott, J., Simon, D. and Simon, A. (1980) 'Expert and novice performance in solving physics problems', *Science*, 208: 1335-1342.

Medwell, J., Wray, D., Poulson, L. and Fox, R. (1998) *Effective Teachers of Literacy*, London: Teacher Training Agency.

Pollard, A and Wyse, D. (2023) *Reflective Teaching in Primary Dchools: A Handbook*, London: Bloomsbury.

Scutt, C., Coleman, R. and Madgwick, H. (2022) 'Early Career Framework' in H. Cooper and S. Elton-Chalcraft (eds) *Professional Studies in Primary Education*, 4th edn, London: Sage, Chapter 21.

Shulman, L. S. (1987) 'Knowledge and teaching: Foundations of the new reform', *Harvard Educational Review*, 57(1): 1-22.

Sims, S. and Fletcher-Wood, H. (2021) 'Identifying the characteristics of effective teacher professional development: A critical review', *School Effectiveness and School Improvement*, 32(1): 47-63. DOI: 10.1080/09243453.2020.1772841

Sternberg, R. and Horvath, J. (1995) 'A prototype view of expert learning', *Education Research*, 24(6): 9-17.

Stobart, G. (2014) *The Expert Learner: Challenging the Myth of Ability*, Maidenhead, UK: McGraw-Hill/Open University Press.

Tochon, F. and Munby, H. (1993) 'Novice and expert teachers' time epistemology: A wave function from didactics to pedagogy', *Teaching & Teacher Education*, 2: 205-218.

Twiselton, S. (2000) 'Seeing the wood for the trees: The National Literacy Strategy and initial teacher education; pedagogical content knowledge and the structure of subjects', *Cambridge Journal of Education*, 30(3): 391-403.

Twiselton, S. (2003) 'Beyond the curriculum: Learning to teach primary literacy', in E. Bearne, H. Dombey and T. Grainger (eds) *Interactions in Language and Literacy in the Classroom*, Milton Keynes, UK: Open University Press, pp. 63-74.

Twiselton, S. (2004) 'The role of teacher identities in learning to teach primary literacy', *Education Review: Special Edition: Activity Theory*, 56(2): 88-96.

Twiselton, S. (2006) 'The problem with English: The exploration and development of student teachers' English subject knowledge in primary classrooms', *Literacy*, 40(2): 88-96.

Twiselton, S. (2007) 'Seeing the wood for the trees: Learning to teach beyond the curriculum. How can student teachers be helped to see beyond the National Literacy Strategy?', *Cambridge Journal of Education*, 37(4): 489-502.

Twiselton, S. and Webb, D. (1998) 'The trouble with English: The challenge of developing subject knowledge in school', in C. Richards, N. Simco and S. Twiselton (eds) *Primary Teacher Education: High Standards? High Status?* London: Falmer, pp. 155-168.

Zhang, L., Carter Jr., R. A., Zhang, J., Hunt, T. L., Emerling, C. R., Yang, S. and Xu, F. (2021) 'Teacher perceptions of effective professional development: Insights for design', *Professional Development in Education*. DOI: 10.1080/19415257.2021.1879236

SECTION 3
PLANNING AND MANAGING LEARNING

UNIT 3.1

BUILDING INCLUSIVE COMMUNITIES OF ENGAGED LEARNERS

Alison Peacock

OBJECTIVES

This unit will help you to:

- reflect on core dispositions that will support an inclusive community;
- introduce you to the principles of *Learning without Limits*;
- understand more about the impact of pedagogy free from labeling;
- provide practical ways of ensuring your classroom is inclusive;
- celebrate cultural difference and diversity.

INTRODUCTION

I was the headteacher of a primary school with nursery for over a decade. During that time the school was transformed from being in 'special measures' to becoming an outstanding teaching school and educational research centre. Throughout my career, I have been inspired by the principles of *Learning without Limits* (Hart et al., 2004; Swann et al., 2012; Peacock, 2016). When my school was studied for the book, *Creating Learning without Limits* (Swann et al., 2012), the research team uncovered seven key dispositions for leadership and learning. These dispositions enabled a culture of opportunity for everyone, refusing to set a limit on what might be achieved. This ethos provided the background for pedagogy, curriculum and assessment in our school and enabled many children (and adults) to achieve much more than anyone could have expected. *Assessment for Learning without Limits* (Peacock, 2016) documents ways that we can assess progress in classrooms without resorting to endless tick sheets and 'data drops'. The death of George Floyd in 2020 led to an upsurge in awareness about the importance of identity and diversity. For children to feel trusted they also need to know that they are seen, that their individuality is celebrated and the cultural heritage of their family is recognised. Within this chapter I will explore ways of ensuring that your classroom is somewhere that children are trusted, included and listened to.

PRINCIPLES OF AN INCLUSIVE CLASSROOM

The ethos of *Learning without Limits* (Hart et al., 2004) is underpinned by core principles of:

1 **trust** (*every child and adult is trusted to learn*);
2 **co-agency** (*children and teachers recognise the power of working together*);
3 **inclusion** (*every individual matters*).

These principles apply equally to children and adults.

A *Learning without Limits* philosophy aligns with every child's natural intrinsic motivation to explore, to find out and to connect. Children flourish within a class community if they know that they are trusted to learn and that they are able to challenge themselves (Whitebread and Coltman, 2015). If your classroom is going to be a place where no-one feels limited or labeled then it follows that, as all children are different, there are going to be times when they will need opportunities to self-differentiate within and between tasks. From their earliest days in school, it is crucial that we actively listen to children and encourage them to talk about their learning (Grenier and Vollans, 2023). All this should take place within a classroom where the teacher is knowledgeable and confident to teach in a manner that fosters a climate of ambition amongst every child to achieve a 'personal best' effort.

Dispositions for a Learning without Limits *classroom*

The culture you create within your classroom has the capacity to transform children's perception of themselves as learners. The following dispositions illustrate the impact that we have upon others when we are able to resist notions that 'ability' is fixed. These dispositions for learning will enable flourishing of a culture of opportunity for all.

The dispositions are divided into three areas or domains: intellectual, affective and social. They apply equally to adults and children. You may wish to reflect on your own experience of being a learner and note how each domain has relevance to your own background and learner identity. Each disposition relates to an approach to learning that resists labeling, refusing to set limits on what may be achieved. The dispositions apply to all areas of the curriculum and to the breadth of day-to-day experience that learners encounter from the moment they enter the school grounds until they leave at the end of the day.

THE INTELLECTUAL DOMAIN

This domain encompasses the intellectual and academic approaches to learning and teaching within your classroom. You are most likely to enable children to engage if they are learning within a culture of:

- openness;
- questioning; *and*
- inventiveness.

Openness

Openness to the art of the possible is fundamentally about the capacity to wonder. You will want to stimulate thinking and ideas amongst the children so that they become intrigued and motivated to engage. Openness from the teacher is the opposite to closed pedagogy that seeks one or maybe two answers (usually one that the teacher has predetermined). Divergent thinkers will thrive in a learning environment where anything feels possible. A teacher with an open mind is someone who can change and adapt planning to suit the needs of the children as they emerge. This is a particularly important quality in relation to supporting the learning of children with special educational needs or disability (SEND) as the typical ways of teaching or learning may not work. At this point, being open to 'finding a way through' for the child, as opposed to seeking to identify and address a deficit condition, enables the teacher to creatively seek ways of teaching that help the learner to achieve understanding. It is important to celebrate difference amongst your class community. Stating that you treat all children equally and that you are blind to colour of skin tone is to deny that differences exist. All our children deserve to be celebrated and recognised for who they are (Choudry, 2021).

Task 3.1.1 Openness

If you spend time planning a lesson and a child tells you they already know about what you are going to cover, how do you respond?

Are you open to the possibility that you may need to adapt your planning to accommodate this?

Are you pleased by the knowledge of your pupil?

How can you ensure that no child in your class is unintentionally limited by the confines of your plans?

Questioning

A classroom that celebrates questions and generates even more questions is a space that is vibrant and interesting. The opposite to a questioning learning environment is one where knowledge is neatly packaged and fixed. Robin Alexander (2008) coined the term 'dialogic pedagogy' to describe learning where children are given regular opportunities to explain and develop their thinking in dialogue with the teacher or with other learners. Dialogue that is open and valued within the classroom establishes a culture where ideas matter, and questioning of those ideas strengthens understanding. Children who may not necessarily be able to explain their thinking on paper may nonetheless have a great deal to contribute that should be valued. It is important to create the conditions where every learner's voice is heard. You can read more about dialogue and metacognition in 'Think!' (Mughal, 2021) where examples of classroom practice that inspire language and deep thought are shared.

Inventiveness

How inventive are you? How inventive do you hope the children in your class will be? A capacity for inventiveness is at the heart of creativity and enables learners to apply knowledge to new situations and contexts through making new connections. In an inventive classroom, everyone knows that the unexpected can happen and that new ideas are celebrated and shared. This is highly motivating as it means there is space for anyone in the room to share their thinking.

> ### Task 3.1.2 Scaffolding play
>
> *Last week, Pria joined other children playing with percussion instruments in the Foundation Stage garden. She took control of the play and began to conduct her orchestra. The musicians responded and this extended to an impromptu concert at carpet time, conducted by Pria with 15 children and the teacher delightedly following her lead.*
>
> **Things to reflect upon:**
>
> What enabled Pria to extend her play?
>
> How did the teacher's response to Pria's play enable other children to become involved?

THE AFFECTIVE DOMAIN

It is necessary to create an emotionally secure experience for every child. Social development and interaction is central to enabling every child to flourish. The dispositions of persistence and stability will be needed by you and any support staff you work with. You will need to remember that we can never give up on a child and that consistently high expectations create an exciting learning environment. If children and adults build trust and listen to each other within an environment open to opportunity, amazing things happen.

Persistence

This disposition is a necessary quality to instill within young learners but also applies to teachers. Observations of people in all areas of life that have achieved success show almost without exception that they have worked with dogged determination to practice for hours and hours to improve their skills, whether they are artists, scientists, entrepreneurs, writers, athletes … the list is endless. The idea, for example, that some people are naturally 'good' at mathematics and others are not is a limiting notion that provides an excuse rather than a motivation to apply effort towards achieving understanding. Within your classroom encourage a climate that rewards effort and persistence, underpinning a learning process that is ultimately hugely rewarding as what seemed unachievable comes within reach.

> ### Task 3.1.3 Practice
>
> How much opportunity do you provide for children in your class to practise their developing skills?
>
> Opportunities to practise enable children to build confidence. If we move on too quickly we risk losing learning that is almost (but not quite) embedded.

Stability

Children need stability to build certainty that they are safe. Once children know what you and the school expect of them and the routines that form the overall structure of the school day, they can use the spaces that exist to concentrate. All humans need stability and to lose this is often to lose a sense of control. Children who feel out of control or emotionally threatened are unlikely to learn effectively and may even seek to disrupt or break out of the learning environment you are trying to create.

> **Task 3.1.4 Self-limiting behaviours**
>
> *Jason in Year 4 says he is 'rubbish' at drawing and screws up his art work throwing it in the bin.*
>
> **Things to reflect upon:**
>
> Have there been aspects of learning that you have found difficult? How have you tried to overcome these?
>
> How could you help children like Jason to experience success within art?
>
> How could you help Jason change his perception of himself as an artist?

THE SOCIAL DOMAIN

How do we help children to build relationships, to share and to understand the feelings of others? The importance of individuality, respect for every child and a good relationship between home and school is crucial. The social domain impacts on every child within your class. If you are building an inclusive culture where children know they can trust you and their peers, they will be in a place where they are safe to take risks with their learning.

Generosity

The disposition of generosity is crucial. If we believe that essentially people are good but may have difficulty in showing this, we need to offer a generous view that seeks to find positive ways forward. This quality is needed if we are to resist the temptation to label children. It can be much easier to point to deficit, than to constantly strive to see flickering sparks of hope.

Empathy

The disposition of empathy is easily aspired to and more difficult to achieve. How will you know what it feels like to be a child in your classroom? How can you find out? When we show empathy we enable others to see that we care about their perceptions and their concerns. Literature – especially picture books – can be a powerful means of building empathic skills amongst children and gives you valuable insight into children's responses to challenging ideas and situations. Ensure that the books you choose to read daily include characters, story lines and images of children from a range of diverse backgrounds. Shared experience of story is a powerful way of building a community.

> **Task 3.1.5 Embracing difference**
>
> *Mary, 9 years old, has a diagnosis of autism. She has a work station at the back of the classroom and often has a teaching assistant working with her. She calls out sometimes during your teaching but always in relation to what you are talking about. How do you react?*
>
> **Things to reflect on:**
>
> Your response to Mary will be noted by every child in the class and will impact on the way she is valued (or not) by her peers.
>
> If you are able to acknowledge her contributions gently and with good humour this is likely to set a positive tone for everyone.
>
> Are there ways you could draw her in to the lesson more before she calls out?

How can we be inclusive of every child?

Genuine inclusion is about understanding the individual needs of every child whilst enabling them to become highly valued members of the class. It is important that you get to know every child in your class really well and that no child ever becomes defined by their special educational need. If you are working alongside a member of support staff you need to remember that every child in your class is your responsibility and this cannot be delegated. Ideally you will have a good working relationship with other adults who join your classroom and allocated time when you can plan and assess together. A team approach to supporting individual children and groups is an effective way of ensuring that additional help is available for those that need it. Remember, every teacher is a teacher of special educational needs. Aubin's book, *The Lone SENDCO* (2022), is a brilliant read about inclusive practice.

> **Task 3.1.6 How well do you know your class?**
>
> Every child will have a story to share of their experience of living in the neighbourhood of the school. Where do they play? How do they spend time beyond school? Do they attend religious classes or after school activities? What do they know about the history of where they live and how their community was formed?
>
> Think about asking family members to share their experiences and memories of the local area. One school in Bolton carried out a project on migration and the experiences of families moving to join the area. Ultimately the writing and podcasts became part of a large exhibition in the local shopping area.

Finding a way through

The most important aspect of a *Learning without Limits* ethos is to take responsibility for 'finding a way through' for every child. If the child is finding any aspect of learning difficult it is the school's collective responsibility to think about how everyone might help. Often this may take time, but there is always something that will become a breakthrough. One of our children with Down Syndrome began emergent writing and drawing in Year 1, but at the beginning of Year 2 she found the transition to a new class very difficult and stopped writing. It took us a term and a half until we finally found a way to inspire Annie to begin writing again. How did we achieve this finally? One day we decided to ask Annie if she would like a visit in school from Peggy the dog, a chocolate Labrador owned by one of our staff. The prospect of a visit by Peggy was the spur that Annie needed to begin writing again. She worked with Hannah, her teaching assistant, to compose an invitation and the very next day when Annie arrived in school, there was a written reply from Peggy's owner saying she would be in Year 2 that afternoon. From that exciting moment onwards, Annie began joining in with writing in class. There is no magic wand in these situations but the learning dispositions outlined earlier clearly help us to resist giving up.

Seeking advice

If a child in your class is finding it difficult to learn, you will want to do everything possible to find out why. If the child has a specific learning difficulty or impairment it will be important to access specialist advice in order that you can provide as much help to support the child as you can. Talk to your Special Educational Needs Co-ordinator (SENCo), as they should be able to help you observe any children you are worried about and advise you of next steps.

Working with parents and carers

The starting point for talking with families should always be that their child is precious and important. Focus on all the positive aspects of their child's learning or behaviour and show them that their child matters to you. They will be experts about their child and will be able to help you understand in greater depth how you may be able to teach the child. Ensure that any language barriers are overcome and that someone can act as interpreter if necessary. Sometimes the family is under great stress and a partnership approach between home and school can be of real benefit on both sides. It is unlikely that there will be any magic solutions but providing a consistently caring inclusive environment will reap rewards.

An irresistible curriculum

What is going to take place within your classroom and the school grounds that will mean children in your class cannot wait to come to school each day? For that matter, what will you be planning that means you cannot wait to teach?

In our Year 6 class prior to Remembrance Sunday the teacher, Sally Barker, planned an English lesson where she wanted the children to write a short descriptive piece of prose. She booked the school hall, talked to them about the experiences of soldiers in the trenches during the First World War and then played them sounds of the battlefield. The children engaged in a drama session where they enacted leaving the trench and going 'over the top' into the battlefield. The session in the hall was only for 15 minutes and the children then returned immediately to their classroom where they all wrote in respectful silence about their thoughts as they imagined that experience. The quality of writing that emerged from the lesson was very moving. Several children chose to read aloud their compositions during the Remembrance Day assembly later that week. Here is an extract from 10-year-old Frankie's writing:

> His legs shake, his hands wobble, his heart pounds. He is paralysed with fear. He thinks of his family, his lovely wife … Suddenly a whistle shrieks like an eagle in agony, reverberating across the ditches. The signal to attack.

Eleven-year-old Aathira writes:

> Karl rocked himself back and forth. Ears covered, eyes closed. Knees too shaky to stand. He fumbled in his coat pocket and muttered goodbye to his framed family. 'I'm not here, I'm not here' he prayed.

The experience offered to the children enabled their imaginations to inspire their writing. English is a curriculum subject that can readily be differentiated by outcome through shared tasks across the class that have a low threshold but high ceiling. In this lesson, every child in the class was able to participate in the drama and every child felt able to communicate their feelings afterwards through the written word.

The environment as enabler

The classroom environment, along with shared areas of the school such as the library and the outdoors, all provide opportunities to extend learning and delight children. If you are fortunate to work in a school with a field or wooded area, there are huge benefits to providing 'forest school' lessons on a regular basis (Maynard, 2007). Some children behave so differently in the outdoors as if the ceiling has literally been holding them back. One child in our school was an elective mute during the Foundation Stage and Year 1. He spoke his first ever words in school whilst playing in the woodland during a forest school lesson. Some time later I heard chattering in assembly and stopped myself just in time before telling Benjamin to be quiet …!

We encourage every adult in the Foundation Stage to see themselves as leaders of learning at all times, whether they are helping to build a den or reading a story. The environment in which we learn, both indoors and outdoors, reinforces and extends a culture of ideas and opportunity. Our garden includes spaces for quiet, small world fantasy play, woodland areas, tools for investigation and enquiry, room to run, leap and so much more. A well-organised environment supports independence, providing a constant supply of irresistible resources for play. Make sure that children can see images or objects throughout the school that remind them of themselves or their family. Ensure that the curriculum is diverse and that stories from history are not just about white mono-cultural males. The Chartered College has developed a webinar series, *Diversifying and Decolonising the Curriculum*, which may be of interest (Miller, Maharasingam and Peacock, n.d.). You may also wish to read *Diverse Educators* (Wilson and Kara, 2022), which presents an array of information about the rich possibilities of teaching through celebration of diversity. Opportunities for children to make meaningful choices and decisions should be present throughout the primary phase. Too often freedom may be replaced by compliance in primary classrooms, thereby unintentionally setting limits. Give every child sufficient challenge and opportunity to extend their thinking.

Beyond 'ability' groups

Think carefully about how you organise your classroom. Children seated in 'ability' groups will always know what the group labels actually mean. You may decide to seat children with learning partners (these may change each week) or in learning groups where you judge that there will be a good balance of friendships. Choosing learning partners randomly with named lollipop sticks is a transparently fair way of organising who works with who. You may wish to ensure that any child who finds it difficult to make friends is chosen quickly from the pot!

In *Assessment for Learning without Limits* (Peacock, 2016), I describe a range of classrooms where teachers have decided not to pre-judge what children may be able to achieve and have offered choices of tasks for the children to select from. Proponents of 'mastery' learning subscribe to the view that to differentiate automatically is to set limits. Seeing the classroom from the children's perspective means ensuring that you plan learning that offers what Mary Myatt (2016) describes as 'high challenge, low threat', subsequently explaining that all children have an 'entitlement' to 'demanding, concept-rich, complex work' (2020: 52). Children do not want to be bored and you want them to achieve well. This means planning lessons with clear learning intentions in mind that will enable high quality outcomes. Children who experience lessons where they are able to choose their own challenges and work collaboratively describe their experience as being liberated and trusted to extend their thinking (Craft *et al.*, 2014). This sense of agency that occurs when one feels inspired and trusted can be very empowering for learning.

Task 3.1.7 Overcoming a challenge

Think of a time when you know that you have found something difficult to learn.

What helped you?

Have you given up?

Are you still learning about this?

What are the factors that you can recall that have helped you along the way?

Are you providing these or something similar for the children in your class?

How should I deploy my teaching assistant?

If you are fortunate enough to have a colleague within your classroom to support your teaching you will want to plan how to ensure that the children gain maximum benefit from this. It may be that your teaching assistant will be able to lead the class for some of the time, thereby enabling you to spend time with an individual or small group to further support their learning. It is very important that the children in your class who find some aspects of learning challenging know that their teacher is there to help. Rob Webster and colleagues (2016) have researched the impact of teaching assistants and offer very helpful practical advice. Essentially, the key is to ensure high quality communication between you and your team member, ideally with shared opportunities to plan and discuss lessons. You will want to ensure that your learning objectives for each lesson are fully understood by all adults working with you in your classroom. The aim should always be to build children's self-regulation and independence. It is important to recognise that a dependency on adult support can quickly build, thereby reducing a child's capacity to challenge themself.

Assessment

There will doubtless be a comprehensive tracking system in place at your school. Tracking, however, is not assessment. Assessment is what you do every time you work with an individual, group or class of children. It is an intrinsic part of teaching and provides you with the feedback you need as you work with the class to help you gauge what children already know and need to learn next. As a general rule, it is helpful to think that planning for the next day should always be influenced by what the children engaged with and achieved the day before.

There are many ways of assessing learning. Within a *Learning without Limits* classroom, the point is not to assess in order to rank children in a hierarchy, but to hold the very highest expectations of everyone. Ideally, you will want to establish a culture of competition against self where 'personal best' is the main aim, as opposed to high stakes assessment. Within a class of 30 children with one teacher, there should be 31 assessors.

Instead of setting targets for children to assess themselves against, you may wish to consider encouraging children to record their individual next steps at the back of their exercise book. They may use feedback from the teacher or their peers, and also from marking, but the crucial aspect is that they recognise where they need to improve and how to achieve the improvement. Feedback that is specific enables the learner to move forward. Feedback that is a judgement (with or without grade) may unintentionally reinforce self-limiting behaviour.

Task 3.1.8 Assessment to inform teaching

James is planning a lesson on forces for his Year 5 class. What could he do to ensure that the children's misconceptions about forces are revealed in order that he can pitch his teaching accordingly?

Things to reflect upon:

Strategies to reveal children's thinking could include:

- providing a range of 'factual' statements around the room which children can review and choose to stand next to in agreement;
- opportunities for children to move again if they change their mind in the light of new evidence;
- silent debate where up to six children add comments silently to an explanation, e.g. Why do boats float?;
- exit tickets at the end of lessons with key learning points or facts.

Allowing children to surprise us

When we welcome children to a classroom where our expectation is that they will be able to surprise and delight us with what they may achieve, we offer an opportunity that is truly ambitious for all. This means focusing on providing learning opportunities that will enable every child to succeed. Activities that offer a 'low threshold and a high ceiling' allow children to take small steps initially but do not set a limit on what may be achieved. Writing tasks are usually open ended and allow for this kind of range in response. Mathematical investigations, such as those on the www.nrich.maths.org website, provide tasks that encourage depth of thinking. The more limitations we set within tasks, the less chance children have of revealing their knowledge and understanding.

SUMMARY

In this chapter we have discussed ways of creating a classroom where every individual child has the opportunity to thrive. We have considered seven dispositions for *Learning without Limits* and explored how these can impact on every aspect of classroom life. In considering the needs of a wide range of children within the class we have recognised that the teacher has the opportunity to celebrate difference whilst maintaining an ambitious open environment where every child retains the capacity to surprise us.

ANNOTATED FURTHER READING

Peacock, A. (2016) *Assessment for Learning without Limits*, London: McGraw-Hill.
> Following on from *Creating Learning without Limits*, this book explores how assessment can be used as a tool for improvement, rather than leading to the labelling of individuals or groups of children.

Swann, M., Peacock, A., Hart, S. and Drummond, M. J. (2012) *Creating Learning without Limits*, Maidenhead, UK: McGraw-Hill.
> A compelling account of how the Learning without Limits approach was implemented and developed in one primary school.

FURTHER READING TO SUPPORT M-LEVEL STUDY

Craft, A., Cremin, T., Hay, P. and Clack, J. (2014) 'Creative primary schools: Developing and maintaining pedagogy for creativity', *Ethnography & Education*, 9(1): 16-34.
> This explores characteristics of creative teaching and learning practices based on case studies of two primary schools.

Marks, R. (2013) 'The blue table means you don't have a clue: The persistence of fixed-ability thinking and practices in primary mathematics in English schools', *Forum for Promoting 3-19 Comprehensive Education*, 55(1): 31-44.
> This article draws on interviews and observation in two Year 4 classes, to critique the ways in which 'fixed ability thinking' can inform teaching in primary schools, as well as being significant to children's views of themselves as learners of mathematics.

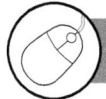

RELEVANT WEBSITES

www.myattandco.com
> A wide range of CPD content focusing on primary curriculum.

www.diverseeductors.co.uk
> A collaborative community that celebrates diversity in all its forms.

www.chartered.college
> Includes a web-based course on Inclusive Leadership.

REFERENCES

Alexander, R. J. (2008) *Towards Dialogic Teaching: Rethinking Classroom Talk*, 4th edn, York: Dialogos.

Aubin, G. (2022) *The Lone SENDCO*, Woodbridge: John Catt Educational Ltd.

Choudry, S. (2021) *Equitable Education*, St Albans: Critical Publishing Ltd.

Craft, A., Cremin, T., Hay, P. and Clack, L. (2014) 'Creative primary schools: Developing and maintaining pedagogy for creativity', *Ethnography and Education*, 9(1): 16–34.

Grenier, J. and Vollans, C. (2023) *Putting the EYFS Curriculum into Practice*, London: Sage Publications Ltd.

Hart, S., Drummond, M. J., Dixon, A. and McIntyre, D. (2004) *Learning without Limits*, Maidenhead: Open University Press.

Maynard, T. (2007) 'Forest schools in Great Britain: An initial exploration', *Contemporary Issues in Early Childhood*, 8(4): 320–331.

Miller, P. W., Maharasingam, N. and Peacock, D. A. (n.d.) *Webinair: Diversifying and Decolonising the Curriculum*, Chartered College. Retrieved from: https://my.chartered.college/research-hub/webinar-diversifying-and-decolonising-the-curriculum/(Webinar series).

Mughal, A. (2021) *Think! Metacognition-powered Primary Teaching*, London: Sage Publications Ltd.

Myatt, M. (2016) *High Challenge, Low Threat*, Woodbridge: John Catt Ltd.

Myatt, M. (2020) *Back on Track*, Woodbridge: John Catt Ltd.

Peacock, A. (2011) 'Circles of influence', in E. Sanders (ed.) *Leading a Creative School: Learning about Lasting School Change*, London: David Fulton, pp. 29–41.

Peacock, A. (2016) *Assessment for Learning without Limits*, London: McGraw-Hill International.

Swann, M., Peacock, A., Hart, S. and Drummond, M. J. (2012) *Creating Learning without Limits*, Maidenhead: McGraw-Hill International.

Webster, R., Russell, A. and Blatchford, R. (2016) *Maximising the Impact of Teaching Assistants*, Oxon: Routledge.

Whitebread, D. and Coltman, P. (eds) (2015) *Teaching and Learning in the Early Years*, 4th edn, London: Routledge.

Wilson, H. and Kara, B. (2022) *Diverse Educators: A Manifesto*, London: University of Buckingham Press.

UNIT 3.2

LESSON PLANNING

Thinking beyond the template

Paula Ayliffe and Rachel Lofthouse

INTRODUCTION

> Why plan lessons? Just give me a teaching assistant to help me deliver what I know the children need!
>
> (Teacher overheard in a staffroom, 31 October 2023)

When we think about planning lessons we enter deep into the debates regarding the role of the teacher. Given the growing pressures of teachers' workload and the need to enhance teachers' well-being, it is tempting to categorise planning as a bureaucratic burden which might wisely be avoided. Combine this with the growth in commercially available teaching schemes, online access to lesson plans and artificial intelligence, which can generate content on demand, it is easy to fall for the argument that individual teachers planning individual lessons for their individual classes is outdated and unnecessary. As authors we are an experienced headteacher and an academic working in teacher education and research with over 60 years of combined professional experience, including as classroom teachers and curriculum leaders. We appreciate that it would be easy for new teachers to regard our advice as outdated, but even in our current roles, planning for learning is fundamental, and we still believe that lesson planning is a foundation stone of professional practice for all teachers.

We are offering our perspective that lesson planning matters. It matters to individual teachers who are grappling with the relationship between curriculum and the needs of their classes and who need to fathom out what pedagogical decisions to make to navigate that dynamic. It matters whether you are new or very established in teaching. It matters to the people you work with, your teaching assistants and your colleagues, and it matters to the parents and carers of the children you teach. Most of all, it matters to your students.

OBJECTIVES

We hope that engaging with this unit will allow you to:

- understand how you can plan lessons that make a positive difference to learning;
- develop your expertise by planning lessons which draw effectively on your growing professional knowledge, including your pedagogic repertoire;
- recognise the value of collaboration to support planning.

There are three tasks embedded in the chapter to help you reflect and put ideas into practice. We have included vignettes based on two new primary teachers, Faiza and Leon, to illustrate the key ideas.

FOUNDATIONS OF LESSON PLANNING

The curriculum is taught through sequences of lessons. At the beginning of the planning process you will find yourself reflecting on fundamental questions before you can put the finer details into place. These include:

- Who am I teaching?
- What am I teaching?
- Why am I teaching this?
- When should I teach this?
- How should I teach this?

These questions then lead to further thinking about the curriculum itself. What are the broad objectives of this curriculum and why is it relevant to the students? Where has it come from? What key knowledge is contained within it? Do I understand this key subject knowledge for myself? If not, who can help me with this? How should the lessons be sequenced? What do I already know about the students who are to receive these lessons? What different elements need to be present in the lesson so that all students can access it? Does it need to include discussion, group work, direct instruction and/or self-study opportunities?

Re-reading this list of questions helps us appreciate why starting with lesson planning can seem overwhelming. It is true that you may not be able to answer all the questions all the time, but recognising that they underpin good planning is an excellent starting point. As a teacher, the privilege that you have is that you are planning for a class of individuals who you will get to know better over time. This is one of the reasons why commercially or centrally produced lesson plans sometimes fall short and why you can gradually make yours better. With this many questions underpinning planning, it also explains why you should not be reluctant to draw on the expertise and support of others.

Task 3.2.1 Planning with the students in mind

The task should act as a reminder that you are planning for a unique class. You will begin by thinking about the memorable characteristics of your class.

1. Without referring to your register, write down the names of the children in your class. Note which order you have listed them in and which names you found hard to remember. What does the order tell you about which children are more memorable than others, for what reasons?
2. Use the class list you have just written to understand how you think about the children (this was probably sub-conscious). To do this, look at each name and the name above and below it. Write down the word that describes how those children are most alike. Then write down another word that describes how they are most different.
3. When you have done this, look at the words you have chosen. What does this show to you about the ways in which you recognise the individuality of people within the community of your class? Are there qualities that you are surprised you did not use?

Now be a bit more reflective. These prompts will help you reflect on the breadth of your knowledge about your class. Don't feel pressured to write too much – your 'first thoughts' and quick responses can often be the most helpful and revealing.

What is it that I know about:

- each child in my class?
- what I have to do as a teacher to support their learning?
- how my class members work together?
- how I have organised the space of my classroom and my resources so that they work for everybody?

Now I know, I wish

>I had…
>I could…
>I hadn't…
>I'd noticed…

I am really proud that we…

To plan well for your classes, you need to start with strong foundations. This might seem overwhelming at first, but you will become more fluent at it as you build on the knowledge and expertise that you are accruing over time. Like a lot of learning to teach, there is some trial and error at work here! Figure 3.2.1 provides an outline of key planning components and questions that you will be addressing.

Foundations for planning						
Curriculum content & design	Students' existing knowledge & expertise	My teacher knowledge	My teacher expertise	My knowledge of the students	Expertise from others	Key questions guiding planning (curriculum)

⬇

What are the specific details of curriculum & assessment requirements, e.g. content, skills & cross-curricular links?	
What do I already understand about the area of the curriculum & what else do I need to find out?	Who might be a good source of subject expertise in this area?

⬇

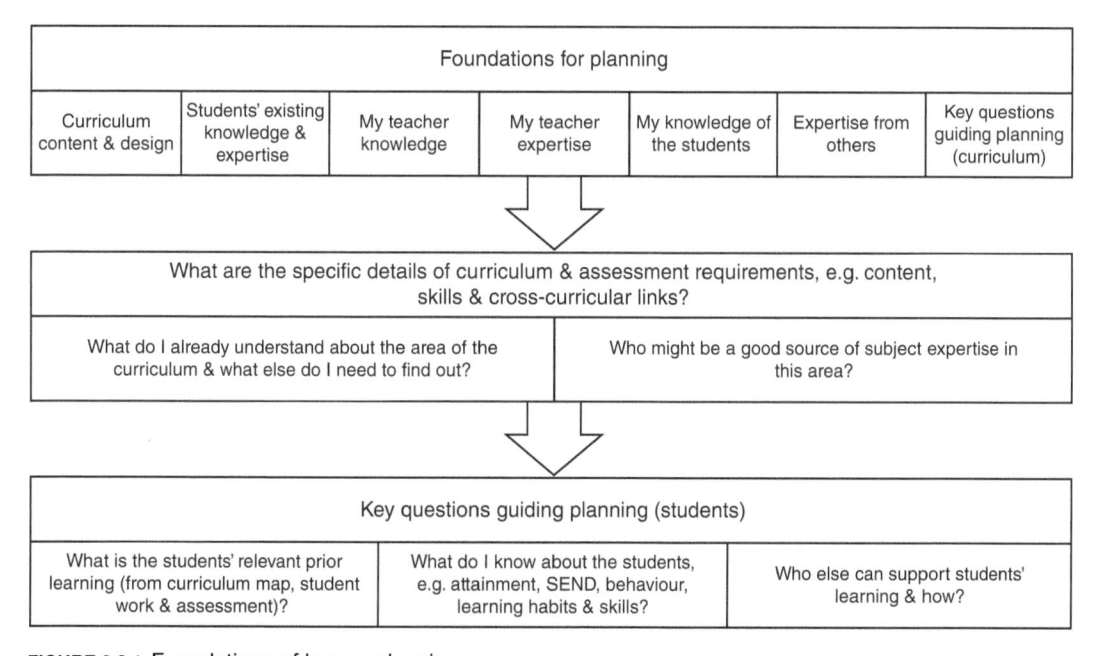

Key questions guiding planning (students)		
What is the students' relevant prior learning (from curriculum map, student work & assessment)?	What do I know about the students, e.g. attainment, SEND, behaviour, learning habits & skills?	Who else can support students' learning & how?

FIGURE 3.2.1 Foundations of lesson planning

Leon reflects on who and what he will be teaching

Leon is an Early Career Teacher (ECT) in his first year. He teaches a Year 2 class of 26 children in a two-form entry school in an economically deprived coastal town in north-east England. His class includes three children who have identified special educational needs or disabilities; one has speech and language delay, one is partially sighted and one is autistic. The school receives pupil premium funding for ten children in the class, including the autistic child, a looked-after child living in foster care and three children whose families are refugees from Syria who have lived in the town for over a year and whose home language is not English. Leon feels more confident with the class than he did at the start of the year, although if asked about his class he says that they are quite excitable. Watching them during playtimes and PE has shown him that many of them embrace being outdoors. He has also had a chance to talk to their Year 1 teacher who is part of the key stage (KS) team and who is his ECT mentor. She has helped him flesh out the progress data with more about their individual characters and life stories.

Having taught History in the first half term, Leon is now switching to Geography in the run up to Christmas. He feels more in his comfort zone. The Geography subject lead is new to the role and has taught KS2 since becoming a teacher three years ago. She has indicated that she would like to do lesson observations of KS1 Geography lessons to develop her own knowledge and support the KS1 team.

The topic Leon is teaching is 'weather and climate' and the main focus is to learn about seasons and regional weather differences in the UK, as designated in the National Curriculum. Children will learn more about the natural environment, the differences between the four seasons and how location makes a difference to weather and climate. He has decided to start with this topic directly after half term because he thinks the children will be able to relate what they are learning to their experiences of the seasons changing at this time of year. He has 90 minutes allocated to Geography per week this half term and has four weeks for this topic. Teachers in the school are encouraged to use non-core curriculum time fluidly rather than in precise timetable slots.

The lessons need to include facts about the seasons and a chance for children to understand how different features of the weather are described. There are some shared resources available, but these have not been updated recently. He wants to draw on the prior knowledge and experience that the children have, linking the topic to different memorable traditions across the year (typical weather on their birthdays, school summer holiday, Christmas and experiences of Ramadan, which was in spring this year). He will build literacy and numeracy skills into the lessons focusing on new vocabulary and how temperature, wind and rainfall are measured and vary across the year. He wants to use weather forecasts on the TV and visual information from weather apps for the children to explore differences across the UK. There will be a chance to link this topic to Forest School, and he intends to talk to the teaching assistant who leads this about what might work well. He also knows that two of the children's parents work on North Sea windfarms and he thinks that they might bring the topic to life.

Whenever you plan a lesson, you are always building on something – it is never completely from scratch – whether that is your own existing subject knowledge or new research, the lives of your students, existing resources available to integrate or adapt, the support of colleagues or the repertoire of teaching you are developing and gaining confidence in. While chipping away at one lesson at a time might seem sensible in terms of workload, having an overarching plan that can be fleshed out and adapted as you go along is usually more time efficient.

> **Task 3.2.2 Create an outline planning narrative**
>
> For the class that you identified in Task 3.2.1 and a topic you are due to teach soon, either write, or audio record in your phone, a planning outline narrative like the one previously written about Leon. You can use the key ideas and prompt questions in Figure 3.2.1 to help shape your thinking. Thinking in this way helps you to capture what you are building on as you start to plan and may help reassure you that the task is not insurmountable.

PLANNING FOR KNOWLEDGE, SKILLS AND UNDERSTANDING

When we hear the term 'knowledge-rich' applied to the curriculum and teaching, it is worth looking beyond the strapline. There are many ways that knowledge has been defined and theorised. The Department for Education (DfE) frameworks for Initial Teacher Training (ITT) and Early Careers Framework (ECF) in England, for example, infer two types of knowledge new teachers need:

- propositional knowledge 'learn that ...';
- 'knowhow' knowledge 'learn how to ...'.

When you plan lessons, start by having these in mind in terms of what types of knowledge you would like children to learn. Leon, for example, wants to ensure that students 'learn that' the four seasons in the UK have typical weather features. He also wants them to 'learn how to' interpret weather symbols on a weather app or map.

A more holistic understanding of knowledge is offered in the revised Bloom's taxonomy (Anderson *et al.*, 2001), which suggests four types of knowledge:

- factual knowledge: subject-specific information and its direct application, including terminology (vocabulary);
- conceptual knowledge: organisational frameworks, principles and characteristics of a subject;
- procedural knowledge: how to do something, including methods of subject-specific enquiry;
- metacognitive knowledge: knowledge of cognition, awareness of one's own thinking and strategic knowledge (sometimes referred to as thinking skills or learning to learn).

> **Faiza is making sense of relevant knowledge underpinning a new topic**
>
> Faiza is in her final ITT placement. Her mentor has indicated that the Year 4 class she is working with will be learning about 'living things and their habitats' and has asked Faiza to develop a sequence of lessons which incorporate a documentary on woodlands.

> Faiza thinks she should include an introduction to vocabulary (such as deciduous, coniferous, canopy, undergrowth, insects, birds, hibernation) perhaps by some pre-teaching and checking of prior knowledge before watching the documentary. This is factual knowledge.
>
> The documentary includes footage of woodland predators and prey, as well as the insects, birds and herbivores supported by an oak tree. Faiza knows that some children think predators are always large and fierce animals like lions and wolves. She wants them to understand that they include smaller animals like hedgehogs. She realises that understanding food webs is key conceptual knowledge applicable to other ecosystems and she decides to teach students how to draw a food web diagram. This is procedural knowledge.
>
> Faiza also wants to encourage some metacognition and knows from a task that the students completed last month that they are still not all fully grasping questions which ask them to 'compare and contrast'. So she plans to use photographs from the same woodland in different seasons and ask students to look for and describe the differences and go on to explain some of the changes. Faiza will be helping students become reacquainted with their prior Year 2 learning on weather, climate and seasons.

As Faiza starts to create her lesson plans she is conscious that she will be helping students learn through a range of activities which encourage them to 'zoom in' (to details, facts and skills) and 'zoom out' to concepts (Stern et al., 2021). This will help them to grasp the bigger and more connected picture, not just to acquire and memorise new content. The bigger picture creates meaning and can thus help students understanding, retrieve and apply relevant knowledge.

Being familiar with the curriculum that students have already been taught and checking on prior learning is necessary so that you are building on firm foundations. Understanding typical misconceptions also matters. An example of a science misconception is that as whales swim in the sea and have fins and tails they must be fish, when in fact they are mammals. You can see exactly how this misconception might arise, because it seems logical, and it is not just an error or misremembering. As well as reading up on common misconceptions to help you plan your lesson, you also need to include activities that allow students' actual misconceptions to be aired and worked with to ensure that correct information is learned.

DEVELOPING DETAILS

Once you have recognised the foundations and steps to learning underpinning your planning, you can get down to detail. A lesson plan might be the final document you use as a teaching guide and can be shared with an observer when needed. The precise nature of detail you need to think through and to record will depend on existing expectations of your setting (including the school and possibly your training provider if you are not yet qualified), and it is likely that you will have document templates that you are able to use to guide this. Depending on the quality of these planning templates you may find them sufficient to scaffold your more detailed thinking, or you may like to add further information that you find most useful for the stage that you are at. Try to avoid relegating this to the category of paperwork or admin task; using a template for planning can really help you feel confident that you have not overlooked anything that might make a difference. Figure 3.2.2 is an example from Mayfield Primary School. It has a typical linear structure outlining how the teacher expects the lesson to flow.

Overview			
Unit/course		Topic	
Day, date and time		Venue	
Learning outcomes			
Transferable skills			
Plan of activities			
Time N.B. Break session into bite-size chunks (examples below)	Teacher activity	Learner activity (What the students will do)	Hand-outs, resources and bookings needed
Prior to session	*Are there additional activities for those who finish early?*	*Are the students required to do any reading or activity before the session?*	*What materials and support do you need to be inclusive of all students?*
5 mins *E.g. Welcome and recap of relevant prior learning*			
5 mins *E.g. Intro topic with learning outcomes and expected development of skills*			
10 mins *E.g. Give and/or demonstrate necessary information*			
15 mins *E.g. Activity to reinforce understanding*			
10 mins *E.g. Verify understanding by all students*			
5 mins *E.g. Wrap-up learning, go over tasks and gather feedback on how the session went*			
Preparation for next lesson and gather student feedback to incorporate into future teaching	What learning took place? Which aspects of the lesson went well? Which aspects could be improved on? Actions for the future		

FIGURE 3.2.2 An example of a linear lesson planning template

Lesson planning is fundamentally a consideration of what the learning objectives are (what you want students to learn) and what learning outcomes you hope the children will achieve (how the students will recognise and demonstrate their learning). Between the two exist the active components. These may include teacher explanation and instruction, new vocabulary, teacher modelling, individual practice, paired and group activities, researching and reading, practical and skill-building tasks, scaffolded thinking, questions and answers, class discussion, recording new knowledge, showing understanding, creativity and problem solving – but not all in one lesson and not necessarily in that order.

A lesson plan is a considered choice about how to integrate appropriate components into a finite amount of time, allowing all students to engage positively in learning and make progress. Each subject you teach will lend itself to different decisions about teaching and learning – these are based on subject-specific pedagogic knowledge, which you will need to accrue over time. You will also realise that the more you learn about meeting individual needs, adaptive teaching, memory (see further reading by McGill, 2022), creative and critical thinking (see further reading by Grigg and Lewis, 2019), the more fluently you will be able to plan lessons. The same applies to learning about developing literacy, communication and mathematical skills, co-operative learning and group work, physical, emotional and cognitive development and the subjects themselves. As you expand your knowledge you will have more insights to draw on to make adaptions to your plans as you teach your lessons.

PRIORITISING PEDAGOGY

Over time you should develop a wide pedagogic repertoire. This will allow you to make good choices about which teaching methods are likely to enable students to engage with the curriculum and make progress. Pedagogy has a cultural component; it can be rooted in traditions as well as evolve through innovation. There is little substance to statements such as 'knowledge-rich curriculum' without an understanding of the pedagogical choices that bring the curriculum to life and make it both challenging and accessible for all learners.

The word 'instruction' has crept into the vocabulary of teaching in England as teachers are introduced to an international evidence base, including Rosenshine's principles of instruction (Rosenshine, 2012). It is important to note that the word instruction in this context means teaching and learning or pedagogy. Earlier work on instruction by Newmann and Wehlage (1993) provides insights into what they called 'five standards of authentic instruction':

1. 'Higher-Order Thinking', including tasks in which students synthesise, generalise, explain, hypothesise, draw conclusions or interpret meaning.
2. 'Depth of Knowledge', in which they propose that it is less valuable to gain broad, but shallow, knowledge, and more useful to work towards a greater understanding of key subject concepts or ideas, allowing students to develop explanations and arguments.
3. 'Connectedness to the World Beyond the Classroom', where planning introduces real world problems, and invites students to use their own experiences.
4. 'Substantive Conversation', where the teacher plans to guide whole class and small group discussions allowing students to talk meaningfully about the subject, proposing ideas, asking questions, using subject vocabulary in extended contributions and building on each other's responses.
5. 'Social Support for Student Achievement', in which the teacher's planning and teaching demonstrates high expectations and mutual respect for all students.

These five standards offer both guidance and a vocabulary which capture features of planning that are likely to lead to meaningful learning.

Teaching should thus involve making pedagogical decisions, not simply following a script or a formulaic plan. In his book, *Botheredness®*, Roberts (2023) offers a unique and compelling way of conceptualising pedagogy which demands some subtle shifts in planning. He explores and exemplifies the role of stories, based on people, place and problems, as ways of stimulating engagement and '"protecting" our pupils into complex thinking and learning' (Roberts, 2023: 17). All classes are unique and you are not a teacher-clone, so your planning should reflect your teacher stance. Roberts defines 'botheredness' as pedagogy which '[makes] the world of challenging content inductive, wonderful and necessary' (p. 18). His current planning components are:

- a narrative hook (people, place, problem);
- a 'let's say' scenario as an invitation to the students to engage in the story;
- stages which outline how the narrative and the scenario will unfold into learning over time;
- a consideration of the real world, the imaginative world and/or the fantastical world within the narrative;
- the purpose for each of the elements – linking to the types of knowledge outlined earlier, as well as the social constructs of learning.

Roberts stresses that these elements do not replace lesson plans, but instead offer a new way to think about how learning can be planned for, and thus reinforce the value of planning across sequences rather than piecemeal lessons.

WORKING COLLABORATIVELY

It is essential that all teachers know how to plan good lessons. It is a strong contributor to developing teacher expertise. However, planning does not need to be solitary. There are two good reasons for this. Firstly, having conversations with colleagues about lesson plans creates a genuine opportunity for sharing knowledge and testing out ideas. Secondly, taking some shared (not just allocating) responsibility for planning can help reduce some of the workload pressures. This is not the same as downloading pre-prepared lesson plans; it still involves active engagement and attuning planning to your classes.

It is important to remember that others' expertise can really improve your planning.

- Before you start to plan the details of the lesson you might need support with both subject knowledge and being better able to meet the needs of the class through better understanding them. It might help you to talk to, or observe, other teachers working with the class you are planning for.
- When you are planning you might find it helpful to work with a colleague, perhaps a teacher working in the same year group or the subject leader, to discuss the details of your planning using the 'small steps' approach or 'lesson chat' which is explained in Figure 3.2.3.
- During the lesson you can encourage support staff or an observer to help you notice how specific parts of your lesson impacted on learning. This is particularly helpful if it ties to a professional development target you are working on and can help you evaluate your planning.
- You might also video a lesson to observe yourself with or without others in the setting. This can increase your own awareness of how your planning translates into reality.

At Mayfield Primary School, an approach called 'lesson chat' has been emerging with dedicated time given to colleagues to talk about and develop lesson plans. Figure 3.2.3 outlines key questions and prompts used in their model.

Planning foundations – be focused before the lesson chat
- Class and student characteristics
- Subject and theme of lessons being planned

Lesson chat planning foundations – tackle these questions first
- What is the key knowledge the students need to know?
- What is the key vocabulary that the students need to use and understand?
- What are the key skills they need to develop in order to be successful in these lessons?
- What are the key questions you need to ask to check that they have been successful learners?

Plan 5 or 6 lessons together during the lesson chat – use these as planning prompts for each lesson
- What are the learning intentions?
- Do they ensure progression?
- How are you going to ensure that access and depth happen?
- What will this look like?
- How will the lessons start? How will they finish?
- What might the 'work' that the children produce look like? What expectations will there be?
- Remember to consider any key school initiatives in your planning (e.g. using outdoor learning, use of digital tools, involving parents, carers and the community)

FIGURE 3.2.3 Lesson chat outline
Source: Based on Ayliffe (2019)

Task 3.2.3 Lesson chat

Using your responses to Tasks 3.2.1 and 3.2.2, hold a 'lesson chat' with a colleague or mentor. Use this conversation to collaboratively refine your planning of the sequence of lessons. The questions and prompts in Figure 3.2.3 will help. As a new teacher, you might also find it useful to participate in a lesson chat with a more experienced teacher focused on their planning.

SUMMARY

As a new teacher, your response to the challenge of lesson planning may be dependent on your conceptions of learning to teach itself, which might be an adherence conception (learning to do the right thing) or more of an enquiry conception (learning to find my own way). How new teachers view the knowledge needed for teaching and how they perceive and engage in reflection underpin the dynamic between adherence and enquiry (Lofthouse et al., 2021). Some new teachers tend towards adopting or adapting existing lesson plans, while others with a greater orientation towards self-determination develop an 'awareness of different ways of teaching [...] justified by reference to theory and evidence' (Lofthouse et al., 2021: 691). The significance you attach to engaging deeply with lesson planning may be influenced by your context, your experiences and the ways that you work with other colleagues, including mentors.

This unit suggests how you can deepen your understanding of lesson planning over time and gain greater confidence and skill. As authors we acknowledge that we learned to teach in policy and practice contexts different to the current day, but as a school leader and teacher educator we remain convinced that lesson planning is a creative and developmental component of teaching, and we hope you can find time and space to engage with the challenge and see the benefits on your learners.

ANNOTATED FURTHER READING

Grigg, R. and Lewis H. (2019) *Teaching Creative and Critical Thinking in Schools*, London: SAGE.
> Grigg and Lewis explore what we mean by thinking and thinking skills in learning, and outline a range of approaches with detailed examples to support planning and teaching, which enhance cognition, communication and understanding.

McGill, R. M. (2022) *The Teacher Toolkit Guide to Memory*, London: Bloomsbury.
> McGill offers insights into how to turn cognitive science theory related to memory into practice. Each chapter includes an explainer, a worked example and a template. It is a valuable guide for both planning and teaching.

Roberts, H. (2023) *Botheredness®: Stories – Stance – Pedagogy*, Carmarthen, Wales: Independent Thinking Press.
> Roberts explains and illustrates his approach to teaching, based on stories, stance and pedagogy, with immense humour but also with real discipline, much of which starts with the planning. In the book he also offers seven extended planning examples based on his model.

FURTHER READING TO SUPPORT M-LEVEL STUDY

Newmann, F. M. and Wehlage, G. G. (1993) 'Five standards of authentic instruction', *ASCD*, 50(7).
> Although this paper is not contemporary, it offers an evidence base, including an explanation of the original research and of pedagogic principles which can be incorporated into planning to support meaningful learning. You can download it here www.ascd.org/el/articles/five-standards-of-authentic-instruction

Rosenshine, B. (2012) 'Principles of instruction: Research-based strategies that all teachers should know', *American Educator*: 12–20.
> This paper is frequently cited in contemporary education literature and policies from school to government level. You can download it here: https://files.eric.ed.gov/fulltext/EJ971753.pdf

RELEVANT WEBSITES

Twinkl: www.twinkl.co.uk
> Twinkl is an online educational publishing house founded in 2010 and headquartered in Sheffield, England, producing teaching and educational materials. It is hugely popular and seen in many classrooms. It is ever expanding and is a good resource to view, especially when starting out in the profession. Some free resources and paid plans available.

Teach Starter: www.teachstarter.com/gb/
: A series of unit and individual lesson plans and resources for primary classrooms. Some free resources and paid plans available.

nrich: Enriching mathematics for all learners: https://nrich.maths.org/
: A free-to-use collection of mathematics activities, lessons and problems designed to nurture curious, resourceful and confident learners of mathematics. Produced by the University of Cambridge.

Explorify: https://explorify.uk/
: Provides free support for science lesson planning to develop questioning, deep thinking and reasoning skills.

The Woodland and Wildlife Trust: www.woodlandtrust.org.uk/support-us/act/your-school/resources/
: The Woodland and Wildlife Trust provide a wealth of free resources to help teachers deliver engaging and memorable outdoor learning experiences.

REFERENCES

Anderson, L. W., Krathwohl, D. R., Airasian, P. W., Cruikshank, K. A., Mayer, R. E., Pintrich, P. R., Raths, J. and Wittrock, M. C. (eds) (2001) *A Taxonomy for Learning, Teaching and Assessing – A Revision of Bloom's Taxonomy of Educational Objectives*, Harlow: Addison Wesley Longman.

Ayliffe, P. (2019) 'Lesson chats' @ Mayfield. A practice insight working paper. *CollectivED*, 9, pp. 86–89. Retrieved from: www.leedsbeckett.ac.uk/-/media/files/research/collectived/collectived-issue-8-may-2019-final2.pdf

Grigg, R. and Lewis H. (2019) *Teaching Creative and Critical Thinking in Schools*, London: SAGE.

Lofthouse, R. Greenway, C., Davies, P., Davies, D. and Lundholm, C. (2021) 'Pre-service Teachers' conceptions of their own learning: Does context make a difference?' *Research Papers in Education*, 36(6): 682–703, DOI: 10.1080/02671522.2020.1767181

McGill, R. M. (2022) *The Teacher Toolkit Guide to Memory*, London: Bloomsbury.

Newmann, F. M. and Wehlage, G. G. (1993) 'Five standards of authentic instruction', *ASCD*, 50(7).

Stern, J., Ferraro, K., Duncan, K. and Aleo, T. (2021) *Learning That Transfers: Designing Curriculum for a Changing World*, Thousand Oaks, CA: Corwin Press.

Roberts, H. (2023) *Botheredness®: Stories – Stance – Pedagogy*, Carmarthen, Wales: Independent Thinking Press.

Rosenshine, B. (2012) 'Principles of instruction: Research-based strategies that all teachers should know', *American Educator*: 12–20.

UNIT 3.3

ORGANISING YOUR CLASSROOM AND USING TECHNOLOGY FOR LEARNING

Peter Kelly

OBJECTIVES

By the end of this unit you should be able to:

- recognise the link between views about how learning takes place and approaches to organising your classroom;
- know the key approaches to organising your classroom;
- recognise the scope and limitation of each of these approaches;
- understand how learning can be supported across in-person and online spaces;
- be able to identify appropriate approaches for particular learning objectives.

ORGANISING LEARNING

How you organise your classroom and utilise digital spaces and tools says a great deal about how you view your children's learning. Colleagues, parents and, perhaps most importantly, children will read much about what you value from those features of classroom and digital life for which you are responsible: the areas of the curriculum you choose to link and focus on; the lessons and activities you plan; the roles you ascribe to other adults in your classroom; how you group and seat the children; the decisions you allow children to take; the digital and other resources you provide and the ways in which you make them available; your use of display and of opportunities to learn outside the classroom and school; and so on.

Consider the range of options available to you in relation to just one of these: groupings. Children can be taught as a whole class, in groups or individually. In groups, they might work collaboratively or be provided with differentiated individual tasks. Such tasks might be differentiated in terms of the level of challenge of the task or the level of support the group receives, and so on. Such features are not simple alternatives; those you choose to use and the circumstances in which you choose to use them will say something about your beliefs as a teacher, even if these are largely tacit and the decisions you make are intuitive.

There is a lot of advice available on the organisation of learning. This has not always been the case. It was not until the 1960s that the traditional model of teaching - that is, a teacher standing at the front of the classroom, with the children sat facing, working on the same task at the same time - was challenged. Progressive approaches, first introduced by John Dewey and developed largely from the

DOI: 10.4324/9781032691794-13

ideas of Jean Piaget (Brown and Desforges, 1979), suggested children should be free to work at different speeds and in different ways, learning from first-hand experiences through active exploration and personal discovery. However, traditionalists argued that such approaches were largely ineffective: there were things that children needed to be taught, such as spelling and grammar, which could not be discovered or left to chance. Thus began an enduring and polarised educational debate.

More recently, a loose consensus has prevailed that recognises that certain approaches favour certain kinds of learning, rather than one approach being best. Nevertheless, the range of approaches suggested can appear daunting and the increased use of digital resources adds further confusion. In fact, it is relatively straightforward, if you remain mindful of one thing: how you organise learning environments depends on how you believe children will learn in them.

This unit considers the organisation of learning in relation to four views: basic skills acquisition, constructing understanding, learning together and apprenticeship approaches.

Basic skills acquisition

Once a favourite of traditionalist knowledge-transmission approaches, direct teaching now dominates approaches to basic skills teaching in schools. Originally conceived somewhat behaviouristically as teacher demonstration and student imitation, leading to a period of consolidation and practice, in the 2000s direct teaching received a Vygotskian make-over, becoming an interactive approach where the importance of high-quality dialogue and discussion between teachers and pupils is emphasised. However, this was an issue with many teachers, who were less ready to move away from a teacher demonstration and student imitation model towards a more interactive one. More recently, online platforms, like the Oak National Academy, provide resources to support direct teaching using multimedia formats that demonstrate and explain.

Learning as constructing understanding

Originating in the ideas of Jean Piaget (Brown and Desforges, 1979), constructivists see learners as theory builders, developing understandings to make sense of their observations and experiences and modifying these understandings in the light of subsequent observations and experiences, so that they become more generally useful and closer to accepted viewpoints. This perspective has had a huge impact on some curriculum areas, particularly science, where a cottage industry grew before the turn of the millenium, researching the alternative understandings and misunderstandings, termed 'alternative frameworks', that children have of the phenomena they encounter. Phil Adey, Michael Shayer and Carolyn Yates's Cognitive Acceleration approach adapted and extended the constructivist approach (Adey, Shayer and Yates, 2001), and later became the Let's Think programme. By challenging children's misunderstandings of phenomena, this aims to develop their thinking. Dynamic digital environments also help learners to explore ideas and construct understandings. Here, it is the responsiveness of environments as learners engage with them that allows learners to discover relationships and build understandings.

Social learning

Social constructivists, such as Jerome Bruner (1986), cite the ideas of the Russian theorist Lev Vygotsky (1962) in positing a central role for talking and listening in learning. Making sense and developing understanding, they assert, are essentially social processes that take place through talk. From the National Oracy Project in the 1990s to a parliamentary group responding to the challenges following cononavirus, many have understood how participation with others in activities involving discussion can improve learning: it supports learners in constructing new meanings and understandings as they explore them in words; it allows learners to test out and criticise claims and different points of view as they speak and listen to others; and, importantly, talk provides raw material for learners' own thinking, because, for Vygotsky, thought is an internal, personal dialogue. Online spaces for synchronous and asynchronous discussion became important during the pandemic, extending learning through interaction and participation from an oral to a written form.

Learning as an apprenticeship

With so much focus in schools on independent learning, it is important to remember the benefits of interdependent learning. The work of social anthropologists such as Jean Lave and Etienne Wenger (1991) remains important because it illuminated how people learn in everyday contexts. This has led them to reconsider school learning in social and cultural terms. Thus, there are many metaphors that we can adopt for our classrooms: the writer's workshop, the artist's studio, the scientist's laboratory, and so on. In each case, this view suggests, the children act as craft apprentices, engaging in the authentic activities of the community to which the metaphor pertains. So, for children to think as, for example, historians, they have to be helped to act like historians by doing what historians do. The same is, of course, true for scientists or practitioners in any other area of enquiry. Online resources and digital tools extend the possibilities for authentic work in exciting directions.

I will now turn to consider approaches relating to each of these views of learning.

Task 3.3.1a Looking for learning

Think back to one particular day during a previous school placement. Write down briefly each of the learning activities that the children engaged in during the day. Consider:

- which areas of the curriculum were addressed and linked;
- the planned lessons and activities;
- the role adopted by the teacher and other adults in the classroom;
- how the children were grouped and seated;
- the decisions that the children took;
- the resources provided;
- the use of display;
- the part played by digital platforms, environments and tools;
- opportunities for learning outside the classroom.

CLASSROOM APPROACHES

Task 3.3.1b Looking for learning

Thinking about each of the learning activities identified in Task 3.3.1a, what does each suggest about how the teacher (whether it was you or the class teacher) views learning.

> **Task 3.3.2 Classroom culture**
>
> Culture can be described most simply as 'the way we do things round here'. Critically reflect on your answers from Task 3.3.1. How does each of these things contribute to the classroom culture? To help, consider the following questions:
>
> - Is there a teacher-led culture that emphasises pupils acquiring new knowledge and skills, or a student-led culture that emphasises pupils participating in developing new knowledge and skills?
> - What metaphor best describes the classroom culture – a factory production line or perhaps a writer's study, an artist's studio or a scientist's laboratory?

Basic skills and direct interactive teaching

As a whole-class approach, direct interactive teaching allows children to benefit from involvement with their teacher for sustained periods. However, direct teaching and interaction are also important during individual, paired and group work.

The role of dialogue is emphasised: children are expected to play an active part in discussion by asking questions, contributing ideas and explaining and demonstrating their thinking to the class. However, many studies have found that teachers spend most of their time either explaining or using tightly structured questions. Such questions are mainly factual or closed in nature, and so fail to encourage and extend child contributions or to promote interaction and thinking.

In recent years, new technologies, especially interactive whiteboards that provide access to a range of media, have had a significant impact on direct interactive and whole-class teaching. However, despite the potential of interactive representations for supporting learning, it is presentational approaches such as PowerPoint that tend to dominate.

Good direct interactive teaching is achieved by balancing different approaches:

- **directing and telling:** sharing teaching objectives with the class, ensuring that children know what to do, and drawing attention to points over which they should take particular care;
- **explaining and illustrating:** giving accurate, well-paced explanations and referring to previous work or methods;
- **demonstrating:** giving clear, well-structured demonstrations using appropriate resources and visual displays;
- **questioning and discussing:** ensuring all children take part; using open and closed questions; asking for explanations; giving time for children to think before answering; allowing children to talk about their answers in pairs before contributing them to the whole class; listening carefully to children's responses and responding constructively; and challenging children's assumptions to encourage thinking;
- **exploring and investigating:** asking children to pose problems or suggest a line of enquiry;
- **consolidating and embedding:** through a variety of activities in class and well-focused homework, opportunities are provided to practise and develop new learning; making use of this learning to tackle related problems and tasks;

- **reflecting and evaluating:** identifying children's errors and using them as positive teaching points by exploring them together; discussing children's reasons for choosing particular methods or resources; giving oral feedback on written work;
- **summarising and reminding:** reviewing, during and towards the end of a lesson, what has been taught and what children have learned; identifying and correcting misunderstandings; making links to other work; and giving children an insight into the next stage of their learning.

Whilst the use of multimedia can enhance instruction, digital tools can also enhance interaction. This may be as simple as using voting facilities that aggregate children's responses to questions and display them anonymously for all to see. Online access can allow teachers to follow up and respond to children's suggestions during lessons immediately, using web resources. And, as we shall see in the next section, the use of dynamic representations of mathematical, scientific or other complex ideas can help to enhance children's understanding of them. Some, like Aaron Sams and Jon Bergmann, have proposed more dramatic changes. In flipped classrooms (Sams and Bergmann, 2013), children are introduced to subject content at home and practice working through it at school. This 'flips' the traditional approach of introducing content at school and practicing this in homework. Online environments are often used to introduce new ideas and areas of understanding through pre-recorded videos and reading material, which children can engage with at their own level and go over the things they find difficult at their own pace. Ideally, this means that they come to class ready to seek clarifications and address any misunderstandings they have, making the interactive exploration of the topic in more depth than would traditionally be the case.

Direct interactive teaching approaches focus on knowledge and skills transmission and acquisition through active learning and interaction. In this, they leave little room for learners to construct their own understandings of phenomena. This is where the following approach is useful.

Constructing understanding

Constructivists believe learners build their understandings of the world from their experiences and observations. They suggest that children bring many misconceptions and misunderstandings to the classroom from their experiences of the world, and assert that the best way to change such misunderstandings is to challenge children to change them themselves through hands-on exploration. For example, in science, children may, from their experiences at home, have formed the misconception that clothes make you warmer. An investigation where chocolate is wrapped in fabric could be used to see if this causes the chocolate to melt. Such information might challenge the children's misconception, and the children would need to restructure their thinking to accommodate the new information that the chocolate is not warmed up; rather it is prevented from cooling or warming as the outside temperature changes.

However, one of the problems here is that it is assumed children will recognise the need to change their thinking or even that they will want to do it. Cognitive Acceleration takes the constructivist approach further. This can be used to formalise the thinking and restructuring process, as it contains certain key elements that many teachers have adopted or adapted in their own classrooms:

- **Concrete preparation:** the problem is stated in terms that are understandable to the children; that is, so that they see it as a problem. For example, you might ask the children to talk to the person next to them and think about clothes they might choose to take with them on holiday to a very cold country, and why.
- **Cognitive conflict:** children are encouraged to consider a range of possible explanations for causes and effects that may interact in complex ways with each other; for example, children

investigating the effects of clothing (identifying features such as fabric type, thickness and shape) on its suitability for a cold location could consider which feature or combination of features is central.
- **Social construction:** now the children work together on the challenging activity to construct new joint understandings. In this, although the teacher asks probing questions to focus debate, the children do most of the thinking. So the children might share each others' discussions and try to come to a consensus.
- **Metacognition:** in this process, the children are helped to become conscious of their own reasoning in order to understand it. In putting pupils in charge of their own learning, it is important to enable them to articulate their own thinking and learning processes.
- **Bridging:** this is the conscious transfer of new ideas and understandings from the context in which they were generated to new, but related, contexts. So the children could apply their new, shared understanding of clothing in cold countries to hot countries.

Particularly in mathematics, dynamic software can also challenge learners by allowing them to see changes as they maniplulate numbers or geometrical figures. This helps them construct an understanding of underlying mathematical relationships. In one dynamic geometry package, GeoGebra, learners can drag elements of shapes to change angles or the lengths of sides. As they do so, the shape retains its properties and learners can see how the other elements repond to achieve this. In a very simple example, regardless of how learners change the size of one angle in a triangle, they will see that the sum of the three internal angles remains 180 degrees. They will also notice that angles must stay less than 180 degrees, and that the bigger any one angle gets, the smaller the other two will be. Although these geometric insights seem straightforward, they are often missed by learners whose only experience of geometry is fixed in pictures on paper. And, of course, things can get much more complicated with other shapes and geometric constructions.

These approaches focus largely on the learning of the individual. Social learning approaches which follow focus more on what can be achieved by a group working together, with the view that what is done together the individual will eventually become able to do alone.

Social learning

Establishing ground rules

Before engaging in social learning approaches, whether in-person or online, a number of ground rules need to be established with children. Rules to stop interruptions of all those involved in group work, adults or children, should be negotiated first. Thus, children needing help might be encouraged to take greater responsibility for their learning by seeking support elsewhere, or by doing alternative work until support is available.

Such independent and self-directed learners can be referred to as *autonomous*. The American educationalist Susan Bobbit-Nolan (cited in Boud, 2015) considers three levels of autonomy. The first is when learners have autonomy or control over the strategies that they use to carry out a task without the guidance of their teacher. Thus, in mathematics, a teacher might teach a variety of strategies for children to undertake three-digit multiplication. The children can then choose which one to use in tackling a problem. Similarly, children might choose the form of recording to use for a science exploration, and so on. At the second level, learners have control over the content of the curriculum, the things to be studied and learned, the objectives of learning. Thus, children might decide to explore something in its own right or set their own goals for their learning. They might choose an area or theme in history to research, an assignment to write, an experiment to do or a book to read. This is learning for pleasure, following tangents and satisfying curiosities. At the third level, learners are able to judge things for themselves, after taking evidence and various views into account. Thus, the children might make informed decisions about changes to school routines such as playtimes, spending money on new items for class or elections to the school council. They might tackle controversial issues in school and debate these, looking at the perspectives of different parties. This third level of autonomy goes beyond simple independence in accessing resources or completing the teachers' work, and has been called 'intellectual autonomy'. Learners who have intellectual autonomy think for themselves, link their thinking to their experiences and open their minds to new ideas.

Discussions during group work should be democratic: everyone has the right to a say, and for their contribution to be valued. This means that participants should:

- listen attentively to the contributions of others without interrupting;
- speak to each other, looking at the person to whom they are responding;
- take turns and allow everyone an equal opportunity to speak;
- be sensitive to each other's needs;
- try to see things from other people's points of view, even if they disagree with their position;
- give reasons for their views; and
- be prepared to change their viewpoint in the light of new information, and accept others doing the same.

Further, children should understand that it is disrespectful to others if they monopolise the talk or if they ridicule or are unkind about others or their views. Of course, it is often most effective when the children are allowed to come up with rules such as these themselves: with prompting, they can be encouraged to address the key areas.

Collaborative group work

Group tasks are most effective when children need to share their knowledge, skills and understandings to a common end through some form of problem-solving or open-ended task with one correct solution and many alternatives. In their activity, children's talk will centre initially on their actions, but should be moved towards their understandings.

Whilst research (Kutnick and Blatchford, 2014) suggests effective group work can take a number of forms, many believe the ideal size for groups engaging in collaborative work is four – pairs are too small to generate lots of ideas, threes tend to form a pair and exclude the third member, and groups bigger than four become harder for the children to manage, and so it is less likely that everyone will be fully included. Similarly, mixed-gender and mixed-ability groups tend to be more inclusive and focused and generate the widest range of viewpoints and ideas.

There are two basic forms of task organisation for collaborative work: 'jigsaw' and 'group investigation'. The former requires each group member to complete a sub-task, which contributes to the whole group completing the assigned task. This might be the production of a picture, diagram or piece of writing about, say, Roman villas, for a group display on that topic. In the second, all of the group members work together on the same task, with each member being assigned a different role. So the children might create a small, dramatic episode portraying life in a Roman villa. Each child would play a different character, and, in addition, one child might take on the role of director.

So, for example, a group might work together on a 'jigsaw task' to produce a leaflet welcoming newcomers and informing them about the school. Each child might survey a different group of children from across the school to find out what information newcomers would need and benefit from. Particular attention would be paid to the experiences of any newcomers to the school. Then, the group would make decisions together about which areas to address, in what format, etc. Each child could then be allocated the task of developing an aspect of the leaflet, with these being finally brought together for the finished document.

Dialogical enquiry

Dialogical enquiries are discussions in which learners, through language and sometimes supported by written notes and prompts, jointly engage in:

- working towards a common understanding for all;
- asking questions and suggesting ideas relating to the evidence on which proposals are based;
- looking at issues and problems from as many different perspectives as possible;
- challenging ideas and perspectives in the light of contradictions and evidence, so as to move the discussion forwards.

Examples include book clubs or reading circles, where children discuss their reading and produce new books together. Similarly, writing conferences are extremely valuable, in which writers discuss their writing with their peers. Of course, having such shared dialogues about texts will improve participants' ability to engage in such dialogues alone.

Other opportunities exist in developing home-school learning partnerships in children's work. Thus, in one example, parents of a particular group of young children read the same book with their children at home one evening. During the shared reading, parents wrote down the children's responses to the stories on post-it notes and fixed them to the relevant pages. Next day, these notes became the starting points for discussion between the teacher and the group.

With older children, each child in a group reading the same book together might individually write, predicting the next stage of the story. This writing might provide the starting point for a group discussion about the evidence for each prediction, the likelihood and plausibility of each prediction and the group's preferred outcome. Such a discussion could equally be based on individual group members writing initially from the perspective of one of the characters of the story and providing that character's point of view. The discussion could then consider the story from this variety of perspectives.

In terms of interpretation of data, such discursive enquiries are important, because they can link the process of enquiry to the big ideas of the subject. So, for example, in science, following an investigation of the conditions in which plants grow best, rather than children simply describing the conditions that are most favourable to healthy plant growth, the discussion can focus on ideas about why this might be the case. Perhaps the children's text of the data collected can be compared in their discussion with other writing they have done, which has attempted to explain findings.

Collaborative group work and dialogic enquiries can readily take place in online platforms and learning environments, using many of the suggestions and approaches mentioned earlier. However, unlike in-person activities, those online can be oral and immediate (or synchronous) or text based and over extended periods of time (asynchronous). Just as synchronous in-person discussions depend on oracy skills, so asynchronous written ones depend on literacy competence. But in writing, as opposed to talking, participants may adopt a more reasoned, thought-through and controlled stance because they have time to compose, reflect on and edit their contributions in their own time before posting them. There are drawbacks, though, as it is harder to backtrack and cover embarrassing contributions in environments when there is a permanent record, and this may make some children reluctant to take part.

Learning through apprenticeship

Apprenticeship models of learning require groups of children to engage in the actual or authentic activities of particular groups. So, for science, children work as scientists, engaging in an enquiry to which the answer is not already known, using the key ideas and tools of science and sometimes working in partnership with others from the local community. For example, Years 5 and 6 children might set up a weather station, or get involved in monitoring environmental changes in an environmental awareness campaign. In doing this, they might involve members of the wider community, contact experts at the Met Office for advice, and so on.

There are many other possibilities for authentic activities in schools. So, in mathematics, Years 1 and 2 children might conduct a traffic survey in order to provide evidence for a letter to the council for some form of traffic control outside school, and Years 5 and 6 children might be helped to cost and plan a residential visit, while children in Years 3 and 4 could run a school stationery shop - ordering, pricing and selling goods in order to make a small profit. Similarly, in geography, children in Key Stage 2 might survey and research the school population growth, using various indicators such as local birth rates, and could be encouraged to identify the implications of their findings. Finally, children from across the school could be involved in producing a podcast or digital download, following their composition of various items for a particular event, such as a school anniversary.

Task 3.3.3 Planning for learning

Consider how you might plan a series of lessons in one subject area, so that a variety of the previous approaches is used. For example, in science, looking at plants in Years 1 and 2:

- Constructing understanding: growing sunflowers from seed in class, exploring the conditions in which these grow best.
- Group work, discussion: separate groups investigate the effects of one factor on plant growth, making hypotheses beforehand and discussing findings after.
- Online research: exploring the plants that are both attractive, resilient and easy to grow.
- Authentic activity: set up a garden centre in school, so that the children can grow a variety of plants to sell in time for the summer fair.
- Interactive direct teaching: the children are taught how to write clear instructions so that they can provide buyers at the summer fair with instructions for caring for their plants

Try doing this for another area of learning, for example data handling in mathematics in Year 4. How could you incorporate digital tools into children's activities?

Sometimes, it is important to look at particular areas of study in many different ways. For example, in an essentially historical study of the Battle of the Somme in 1916, older children could engage, not only in a historical enquiry-based approach, be it text or computer based or involving the examination of original artefacts, but also by looking at events through the eyes of poets and novelists, or through the eyes of geographers or scientists. As such, the work of others might be explored, and the children might engage in original work themselves, not only in writing and poetry, but also through the media of music, dance, drama and painting. This would provide the children with a very full and rich learning experience.

Online resources and digital tools have increased the possibilities for authentic enquiries enormously, whether by increasing the availability of material to inform learners' own research into a topic, providing opportunities for them to engage in a dialogue with experts or allowing them to share their findings with a wider audience. However, it is important to balance these opportunities for children to participate with a clear understanding of our duty to protect. Indeed, this is a good place to teach some of the dangers of online activity and the precautions that can and often should be taken, the prevalence of misinformation and disinformation in some areas, and how untrustworthy sources can be discerned and treated with scepticism.

Task 3.3.4 Exploring approaches to group work

Try out some of the activities you have planned for Task 3.3.3 with children grouped in different ways as suggested earlier and in some of the further reading. Closely observe the children taking part in two different activities that you have planned and try to answer the following:

- How does their participation differ, depending on the nature of the groups and tasks?
- Does one form of grouping or type of task appear to engage them more than others?
- How does their participation differ if they do so in digital spaces or using digital tools?

After the activities, talk to the children involved and try to answer the following:

- What did they think they had to do?
- Why did they think they were doing these activities?
- What did they think they learnt?
- How much did they enjoy them?
- What did they remember most from the activity?

Now look at the work done by the children and critically reflect on this and the answers to the previous questions. What does all this tell you about these children's learning?

The approaches described in this unit are summarised in Table 3.3.1.

TABLE 3.3.1 Organising your classroom for learning

Approaches to organising your classroom	Learning focus	Broad learning objectives	Strengths	Challenges
Whole class, small group and individual teaching of literacy and numeracy	Basic skills acquisition	To teach fluency and confidence with reading and writing in literacy and with number and calculation in mathematics	An interactive approach where the importance of teacher modelling and high-quality dialogue between teachers and pupils is emphasised	Many teachers have had difficulty adopting fully interactive direct teaching; tendency to be used at whole-class levels rather than with individuals or groups; little emphasis on learners' own starting points
Constructive science investigations and explorations	Constructing understanding	To develop enquiry and investigative process skills; to develop children's own understandings of phenomena; to apply understandings to new contexts	Starts from children's ideas and perspectives, building on these using direct hands-on experience	Assumes children will notice experiences which don't fit their understandings, challenge their understandings and be able to restructure these to accommodate the new experiences
Group work; discussion; dialogical enquiry	Social learning	To develop collaborative and speaking and listening skills; to see things from different points of view; to develop critical and creative thinking; to develop children's own understandings of phenomena	Supports learners in constructing new meanings and understandings as they explore them together in words; allows learners to test out and criticise claims and different points of view as they speak and listen to others; and provides raw material for learners' own thinking	Requires children to have certain basic skills and obey certain ground rules; sometimes difficult to organise; works best when children show areas of autonomous learning
Authentic activity and enquiry	Apprenticeship	To encourage children to act and see the world as scientists, historians, archaeologists, poets, and so on	Outward looking, considering learning as something which takes you outside the classroom; inspiring and motivating	Requires significant time to allow it to happen; often needs access to good quality resources; teachers need to feel confident and have some expertise in the area of activity or enquiry or be able to get in someone who has

SUMMARY

Many of the suggestions in this chapter parallel those of learner centred-education (Schweisfurth, 2013), an approach rooted in the ideas of John Dewey and both Lev Vygotsky and Jerome Bruner, who we met earlier. Michele Schweisfurth identifies the main characteristics of learner-centred education as follows. By understanding that different approaches might work in different contexts, lessons engage pupils and motivate them to learn and are conducted in an atmosphere of mutual respect between teachers and pupils. Teaching should involve direct instruction, interaction and dialogue, and approaches that challenge learners and build on their existing knowledge. Further, the curriculum should be accessible and relevant to learners' lives and perceived future needs, helping them to develop skills and attitudes, understand content and think creatively and critically. And rather than a narrow focus on content, a range of outcomes should be assessed.

Learning is complex, so much so that no one view of learning can fully express this complexity. It is only by considering learning in a variety of ways that we can begin to gain a fuller understanding of its nature, and it is only by planning for such a variety of approaches to address learning as have been described in this unit that we can provide rich and inclusive classroom experiences for our children.

ANNOTATED FURTHER READING

Adey, P (2008) *Let's Think Handbook. A Guide to Cognitive Acceleration in the Primary School*, London: GL Assessment.
>The 'Let's Think' approach seeks to improve children's thinking processes. It focuses on questioning, collaborative work, problem solving, independent learning, metacognition and challenge.

Baines, E., Blatchford, P. and Kutnick, P. (2016) *Promoting Effective Group Work in the Primary Classroom: A Handbook for Teachers and Practitioners (Improving Practice (TLRP))*, London: Routledge.
>This handbook is the outcome of a four-year project funded by the Economic and Social Research Council.

Sams, A. and Bergmann, J. (2013) 'Flip your students' learning', *Educational Leadership*, 70(6): 16-20.
>This article outlines the key features of the flipped learning approach.

Schweisfurth, M (2013) 'Learner-centred education in international perspective', *Journal of International and Comparative Education*, 2(1): 1-8.
>This article outlines the key principles of learner-centred education and the ways that they have been shaped and included in educational approaches and guidance worldwide.

FURTHER READING TO SUPPORT M-LEVEL STUDY

Baines, E., Rubie-Davies, C. and Blatchford, P. (2009) 'Improving pupil group work interaction and dialogue in primary classrooms: Results from a year-long intervention study', *Cambridge Journal of Education*, 39(1): 95-117.
>This is an interesting article that reports the findings of a study into the potential of group interaction to promote learning. The authors describe how they worked with teachers to develop strategies

for enhancing pupil group work and dialogue, and to implement a pupil relational and group skills training programme.

Webb, N. M., Franke, M. L., De, T., Chan, A. G., Freund, D., Shein, P. and Melkonian, D. K. (2009) '"Explain to your partner": Teachers' instructional practices and students' dialogue in small groups', *Cambridge Journal of Education*, 39(1): 49-70.

> These researchers argue that collaborative group work has great potential to promote student learning, but that the role of the teacher in promoting effective group collaboration is often neglected.

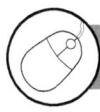

RELEVANT WEBSITES

Unicef Child Friendly Schools: www.unicef.org/documents/child-friendly-schools-manual

> From a more global perspective, Unicef has developed an approach to education development that it calls 'Child Friendly Schools' and that highlights issues of quality in classroom provision and organisation.

International Democratic Education Network: www.idenetwork.org/index.php

> As an alternative to mainstream educational approaches, Democratic Schools use organisational approaches that seek to give children a say in their own learning, and this site gives an overview.

REFERENCES

Adey, P., Shayer, M. and Yates, C. (2001) *Thinking Science*, London: Nelson.

Boud, D. (2015) *Developing Student Autonomy in Learning*, London: Routledge.

Brown, G. and Desforges, C. (1979) *Piaget's Theory: A Psychological Critique*, London: Routledge.

Bruner, J. (1986) *Actual Minds, Possible Worlds*, Cambridge, MA: Harvard University Press.

Kutnick, P. and Blatchford, P. (2014) *Effective Group Work in Primary School Classrooms: The SPRinG Approach*, London: Springer.

Lave, J. and Wenger, E. (1991) *Situated Learning: Legitimate Peripheral Participation*, Cambridge: Cambridge University Press.

Sams, A. and Bergmann, J. (2013) 'Flip your students' learning', *Educational Leadership*, 70(6): 16-20.

Schweisfurth, M (2013) 'Learner-centred education in international perspective', *Journal of International and Comparative Education*, 2(1): 1-8.

Vygotsky, L. (1962) *Thought and Language*, Cambridge MA: MIT Press.

UNIT 3.4

MANAGING CLASSROOM BEHAVIOUR

Creating a positive classroom climate

Roland Chaplain

INTRODUCTION

Effective classroom management is a complex topic which draws upon many disciplines, approaches and methods. Although the Department for Education (DfE, 2011) defined 'the minimum level of practice expected of trainees' in respect of behaviour management skills, no single behaviour management approach will work effectively for all teachers. Therefore, choose an approach based on sound theoretical principles, supported by the most compelling evidence, which best fits your teaching style and personality, your school's behaviour policy and the needs of your pupils. Pupils expect teachers to be *an authority* (know what they are talking about) and *in authority* (in control of what happens in the classroom, to create the conditions for learning and ensuring pupils feel safe). However, whilst establishing your authority is important, the ultimate target of behaviour management should be to cultivate the cognitive, socio-emotional and behavioural skills pupils need to develop their self-control, self-regulation and social competence. As with intellectual development, pupils of the same age differ in their socio-emotional development. Some pupils (and classes) will arrive highly motivated to learn, be confident and cooperate with adults and peers – others will need more teacher direction and support. This unit provides a framework for you to develop a personalised Classroom Management Plan (CMP) based on evidence-based strategies to manage and motivate pupils effectively.

OBJECTIVES

By the end of this unit, you should understand how to:

- develop a personalised Classroom Management Plan;
- manage your own behaviour;
- use a range of practical classroom management strategies effectively;
- cope with more challenging behaviour;
- use research-based evidence in your practice.

BUILDING AN EVIDENCE-BASED CLASSROOM MANAGEMENT PLAN (CMP)

A CMP represents a proactive approach to create and maintain a positive and productive classroom environment, informed by the most compelling theory and empirical evidence. It includes strategies to establish teacher authority, build professional relationships with pupils and maximise their engagement with learning.

Organise your CMP under the following three headings:

1. **Organisational factors:** School-wide behaviour policy, classroom structures (rules and routines), classroom environment (layout, seating arrangements).
2. **Personal factors:** Your expectations, criteria for satisfaction, coping skills, professional social skills, teaching style.
3. **Behaviour management strategies:** Preventative, Reorientation, Reactive (see Table 3.4.1).

WHOLE-SCHOOL BEHAVIOUR MANAGEMENT

The strongest predictor of negative behaviours in schools is perceived school ethos (MORI, 2017), that is, what a school feels like – its atmosphere. Effective schools create 'a positive atmosphere based on a sense of community and shared values' (Elton Report, 1989). The DfE (2020) produced guidance on how to create an ethos to optimise prosocial behaviour in schools. This requires attention to whole-school issues, classroom management and managing challenging individuals. Inconsistency between different levels generates ambiguity and stress for both teachers and pupils.

Schools are required to produce a behaviour policy to support staff in managing behaviour throughout the school day (DfE, 2013b). Behaviour policies *should* reflect the views, aspirations and expected behaviour of *all* stakeholders in a school, including pupils, parents and staff (Chaplain, 2016).

Task 3.4.1 Understanding your school

Read your school's behaviour policy.

What are the school's values/rules/expectations?

How is desirable behaviour rewarded?

What sanctions are used to discourage unacceptable behaviour?

Observe how the policy is translated into practice throughout the school day.

TEACHER STRESS AND PUPIL BEHAVIOUR

According to the Health and Safety Executive (2018), teachers report the highest rates of work-related stress, depression and anxiety in Britain. Disruptive pupil behaviour is consistently rated by teachers as a primary source of their stress (Chaplain, 1995, 2008) and a principal contributor to low occupational well-being (Ofsted, 2019). Despite this, many teachers still report being very satisfied with their work (Klassen and Chiu, 2010) because of features inherent to the job, e.g. pupils' achievements and positive relationships with pupils (Chaplain, 1995; Veldman et al., 2016).

Although teachers usually rate extreme behaviour (physical and verbal assault) as their biggest concern, it is not common in regular classrooms. In contrast, persistent low-level disruption (e.g. talking out of turn, defiance) is what teachers find most stressful (Elton Report, 1989; Williams, 2018). These 'daily hassles' (Admiraal, 2021) are usually offset by 'daily uplifts' (e.g. positive feedback from pupils and developing your behaviour management skills).

MANAGING YOURSELF

Effective classroom management requires attention to: what you say and how you say it; checking you are being understood; looking and feeling confident; and communicating your authority through verbal and nonverbal behaviour (NVB). Although NVBs are central to managing behaviour, they are harder to control than verbal behaviour (VB), which can result in pupils receiving contradictory messages from teachers. As Babad pointed out, '*pupils* are experts in deciphering and understanding the finest nuances of teacher behavior. ... Many teachers are oblivious of their transparency to *pupils*' (2009: 100). You may plan to communicate something, but, under pressure, fail to do so because of emotions undermining your NVB (Chaplain, 2016).

You will have observed people's habits when anxious (e.g. blushing, avoiding eye contact). Overcoming such behaviours requires first becoming aware of them (e.g. by videoing yourself), then identifying and over-learning alternative effective behaviours when *not* under pressure (Chaplain, 2016, Chapter 4).

Task 3.4.2 Monitoring professional social skills

Video yourself (not your pupils) teaching one or more of your lessons. This can be done subtly using a laptop with an integral camera.

- Were your VB and NVB (e.g. gestures and posture) as you believed them to be?
- Were your responses to behaviour consistent with all pupils?
- Did you make your expectations explicit?
- Did you reinforce required behaviour?
- Did you interact with all pupils equally?
- Were your instructions clear?
- Did you check for understanding?
- How did you respond to any disruption?

Now plan what changes to make, then practise and overlearn them at home. Use a mirror to practise posture and gestures. Then video yourself in class again to determine the effectiveness of your changed behaviour.

Several psychological characteristics distinguish teachers who manage pupil behaviour effectively from those who do not. These include personality, emotional regulation and self-presentation, locus of control and self-efficacy. It is on these final two salient constructs we will now focus.

Believing you can influence important events in your life (locus of control) is central to effective coping (Rotter, 1966). People who believe they *can* influence important events (internal locus) tend to cope far better than those who believe other people control important decisions for them (external locus). For teachers, an internal locus of control is the degree to which they attribute pupil behaviour to factors within their control (e.g. classroom) as opposed to a pupil's homelife (external locus of control). When making your CMP, you should focus on factors over which you have control and not those over which you have no control. However, sometimes we miscalculate our ability to control situations. Trainee teachers are often reluctant to modify their classroom environment – e.g. changing the seating layout – despite being aware that existing arrangements are creating management difficulties for them. Their reason for not making changes is usually because it is 'someone else's' classroom. However, most mentors (if asked) would not object to trainees changing the room settings to teach more effectively, provided the changes have a sound pedagogic rationale.

Teacher self-efficacy is 'a teacher's belief in his or her skills and abilities to be an effective teacher' (Swars, 2005: 139). It is concerned with the question, 'Can I do this?' and can be general or domain specific. Classroom management self-efficacy is a teacher's beliefs about their capability to organise and execute the actions necessary to maintain classroom order. It is a key predictor of teachers' well-being, professional competence and use of effective classroom management strategies (Zee and Koomen, 2016).

Teachers with high classroom management self-efficacy use positive classroom management strategies and encourage pupil engagement with learning, even with regularly disruptive pupils (Chaplain, 2016), and they show increased persistence when working with challenging pupils (Klassen and Tze, 2014).

Trainee teachers, unsure of their untested capabilities in managing behaviour, can experience self-doubt and anxiety (e.g. Ng, Nicholas and Alan, 2010), and 'it is difficult to achieve much while fighting self-doubt' (Bandura, 1993: 118).

However, being overly confident can lead to complacency. Weinstein (1988) found that trainee teachers had unrealistic optimism in thinking that the problems others experienced managing pupil behaviour would not happen to them. Furthermore, Emmer and Aussiker (1990) found that trainee teachers who had difficulty managing classes still had unrealistic beliefs about their ability to control behaviour, which McLaughlin (1991) attributed to the conflict between wanting to care for pupils and the need to control the class.

Having realistic, challenging and achievable expectations of yourself and your pupils, accumulating knowledge from research, mastering challenging tasks and regulating emotions provide concrete evidence of your abilities and skills and will improve your teacher self-efficacy. This can be enhanced through vicarious experiences and verbal persuasion from a knowledgeable mentor who is sufficiently experienced in training new teachers (Chaplain, 2008).

Self-monitoring is useful for determining how *all* your behaviours contribute to how you manage your class. Changing how you think, feel and behave is not easy and may feel uncomfortable; the benefits make it worthwhile, but it requires practice to replace established ineffective habits with effective alternatives (Chaplain, 2016).

CLASSROOM MANAGEMENT STRATEGIES

In your CMP, begin with *preventative* strategies to deter disruption. Some pupils will inevitably slip off-task so require *reorientation* strategies and finally more persistent disrupters require *reactive* strategies including sanctions (see Table 3.4.1).

TABLE 3.4.1 Classroom management strategies

Preventative tactics

- Make sure your lessons are interesting.
- Teach and reinforce rules and routines.
- Teach explicitly the behaviour you expect from your pupils – reinforce and check for understanding.
- Be alert to changes in pupils' VB and NVB (e.g. noise levels, restlessness).
- Scanning – make sure you can always easily see the whole class to detect potential disruption.
- Prepare for possible disruption, e.g. new pupils, time of day.
- Be enthusiastic even when you're not!
- Manipulate classroom layout, e.g. matching seating arrangements to task.
- Use appropriate reward systems for on-task behaviour.
- Be aware of pupils' goals.
- Get lesson timings right.

Reorientation tactics

- Gaze – sustain eye contact to make pupils aware that you know what they are doing.
- Posture and gesture – use to complement gaze, e.g. raised eyebrow, raised first finger, hands on hips.
- Space invasion – the closer you are to pupils, the more control you will have – the classroom is your domain to move around as you wish.
- Restate rules – remind pupils about what is expected.
- Use individual encouragement to get pupils back on task – 'You have been doing really well so far …'.
- Name-dropping – mentioning a non-attentive pupil's name while you are talking will usually get their attention.
- Reinforce peers near someone off task to 'model' the required behaviour.
- Humour – pupils like teachers with an appropriate sense of humour.
- Maintain the flow of the lesson by carrying on teaching while moving around the room, using NVB and removing anything being played with (e.g. pens).

Reactive tactics

- Caution – inform what will happen should the unwanted behaviour persist.
- Remove privileges, e.g. ban from use of the computer or miss a trip.
- Require pupil to complete extra work during break times.
- Time out as arranged with colleague in advance – avoid having disruptive pupils wandering around the school.
- Contract – agree with pupil specific expectations and record successes – review and adjust as necessary.
- Temporary removal from class – working elsewhere in school or with another class.
- Suspension from school.
- Exclusion.

Note: These are *some* examples of effective tactics, but you should modify them to suit your teaching styles and context.

MAKING AN EARLY IMPACT ON YOUR CLASS

Everyone forms impressions of other people in a few seconds, and these impressions often remain unchanged for long periods of time (Chaplain, 2016). Hence, the first part of your CMP should consider what impression you wish to make. In your early visits to the classroom, you will be observing, which can feel uncomfortable, as pupils are inquisitive and will want to know all about you, weighing you up. You will want to settle in and learn the ropes, but do not be too friendly with the pupils, as you will eventually have to establish your authority with the whole class. This is not to suggest you should be standoffish or hostile - just convey your status and authority as a teacher. Your early lessons may be relaxed, with pupils being quite passive, but at some point your behavioural limits will be tested, so make sure you are clear about your expectations and convey them explicitly to your pupils. It is essential to pay attention to detail.

Your CMP should detail how you will:

- establish your behavioural expectations;
- teach classroom routines;
- use VB and NVB to control the class - especially at critical points in the lesson (see Table 3.4.1);
- reinforce required behaviour (see Table 3.4.2);
- respond to disruptive behaviour (see Table 3.4.2);
- organise the physical layout of the classroom.

TABLE 3.4.2 Examples of hierarchical rewards and sanctions

Rewards	Example
Verbal support, private	Quiet word, 'Jamie that's excellent work'
NVB/VB support, public	Thumbs up. Teacher comment and class applaud individual
Tangible individual rewards	Stamps, stickers, certificates, pencils
Contact home (either for meeting points criteria or exceptionally prosocial behaviour)	Notes/postcards/phone calls
Public display	Happy emoticons against name ☺
Special privileges	Helping around school, attending an event
Tangible rewards for continued prosocial behaviour	Book token
School award	Small group trip to Alton Towers

Sanctions	Example
Gesture	Raised first finger, thumbs down
Prolonged gaze	Hold eye contact (with frown)
Rule reminder	'What do we do when we want to ask a question?'
Physical proximity	Move closer to pupil – perhaps stand behind them – say nothing
Verbal reprimand	'Jack, your behaviour is not acceptable'
Separate from group in class or keep back at playtime	Adjust length of time to suit needs/age of pupil
Record name	Write name in report book
Removal from classroom	Teach outside normal teaching area

(Continued)

TABLE 3.4.2 (Continued)

Sanctions	Example
Refer to SMT	Send to head/deputy (as per school policy)
Contact parents	Letter/phone home
Invite parents to school	For informal/formal discussion
Behavioural contract	Short, focused on specific expectations
Suspension	For an agreed period
Review contract	As a basis for return
Exclusion	Fixed/permanent

Note: Focus on the *effect* of a reward – what it does, NOT what it is. Does it strengthen the desired behaviour? If not, change it – the reverse being the case. If a sanction does not stop misbehaviour, then change it.

CONVEYING YOUR EXPECTATIONS: RULES AND ROUTINES

All lessons have similar patterns, e.g. entering the classroom, getting the attention of the class, transitions. Whether your teaching is enhanced or undermined by any or all of the examples in Table 3.4.2 depends on establishing appropriate, enforceable and effective rules and routines. Rules set the limits to pupils' behaviour (Charles, 1999). Whereas whole-school (core) rules are designed primarily to produce harmonious relationships among pupils throughout the day, classroom rules have the added responsibility of maximising pupil engagement with learning. Effective rules provide pupils with a physically and psychologically safe, predictable environment and work in a preventative way to establish and keep order and maintain momentum through the lesson. To gain maximum effect, rules should be:

- *positively worded* – tell pupils what they *can do* rather than what they *cannot do*, for example, 'be polite', as opposed to 'don't be rude'; negatively framed rules are not effective long term (Sen, 2022);
- *few in number* – long lists of rules will not be remembered: focus on key concerns; for example, follow directions; keep hands, feet and objects to yourself; have no more than five;
- *realistic* – have rules that are age-appropriate, enforceable and achievable by your pupils;
- *focused on key issues* – personal safety, safety of others, cooperation and facilitating learning;
- *applied consistently* – selective reinforcement of rules will undermine their effectiveness, e.g. if putting hands up to answer questions is a rule, and you respond positively to those pupils who shout out a *very* competent answer, then reprimand someone else for shouting out an unsophisticated answer, you are sending out mixed and unhelpful messages to pupils.

When taking over a class from another teacher, it is important to consider their expectations relative to your own, and whether this will affect the way in which you establish your rules. If you adopt the rules of the existing teacher, do not assume pupils will respond in the same way to you – they will not inevitably associate you with a particular rule. So teach the behaviour you require explicitly, even if it means repeating what they already should know.

Display your rules prominently, and initially keep reminding pupils about them subtly until they are established. Be creative, perhaps using cartoons or pictures to liven up your display.

> **Task 3.4.3 Classroom rules**
>
> - Think of four or five rules that embody your behavioural expectations.
> - Check the school behaviour policy – are your expectations similar?
> - Discuss with your mentors how they established rules with the class.
> - Do you feel confident applying them?
> - What, if any, changes would you make?
> - Justify your changes.

DEVELOPING ROUTINES

Although a small number of rules provide the framework for the conduct of lessons, they frame many routines, linking expectations to action. Classroom routines are well-rehearsed responses to teachers' signals organised around times, places and contexts, to provide pupils with structure, predictability and a sense of safety. Effective teachers spend considerable time in their early encounters with their classes teaching them routines (Emmer and Worsham, 2005) and when practised and reinforced become automatic, leaving more time for teaching. Jones and Jones (2020) found that up to half of some lessons were lost to inefficient non-teaching routines. The following paragraphs consider pivotal routines in more detail.

Entering the classroom

How pupils enter your classroom sets the scene for the lesson – charging noisily into a room is not the best way to start a lesson, so consider how you might control this initial movement. Greet your pupils at the door, look pleased to see them, be positive and remind them what they are expected to do when they go into class. Have an engaging activity waiting for them that has a time limit and is, preferably, linked to a reward. Physically standing by the door reduces the likelihood of pupils charging in, but, if they do, call them back and make them repeat the procedure correctly.

Getting the attention of the class

This can be done by using verbal or other noises, silence or puppets.

- *Using noise*: which method you choose (e.g. ringing bells, clapping) depends on your personal preference and its effectiveness. Make sure that you explain beforehand what the signal is and what you want pupils to do when they hear it. I witnessed one teacher, working with a 'lively' class, bang a tambourine to gain attention part way through the lesson, but the teacher had omitted to let pupils know beforehand. Although it made everyone jump (including me!), it was not associated with any required behaviour. A more effective method would have been to tell the class in advance, 'Whenever I bang the tambourine, I want you all to stop what you are doing and look at me'.
- *Using silence*: some teachers gain attention using NVB, e.g. raising their hand. These signals can be very powerful. Indeed, the more you use NVB to manage behaviour the better, as it is less disruptive to the flow of your lesson. However, to be effective it requires you to feel confident about

your presence, and to explicitly *teach* pupils to associate a specific behaviour with a particular stimulus and *immediately* reinforce those who respond the quickest.
- *Using puppets*: (e.g. puppetsbypost.com) can be very effective in behaviour management. Introduce the puppet and say that it will only come out if everyone is quiet – because it is nervous. If the noise level gets too high, put the puppet away. 'Snail puppets' that only emerge if pupils are behaving as required are excellent. They can also be used as a reward – the best-behaved group could have the puppet sitting at their table. Pupils are usually very attentive and empathetic towards puppets, and so they can be used to aid the pupils' socio-emotional development. We have had excellent results using them with pupils from Early Years to Year 6.

Briefing

Ensure that pupils understand exactly what is required from them at each stage of the lesson – unless you want those pupils who find it hard to pay attention wasting time asking other pupils what they should be doing. Taking time to do this when being observed can be difficult if you are anxious about being in the spotlight – so, use prompts to remind yourself to speak slowly and carefully (writing 'SLOW' on your lesson plan). Before the lesson, write instructions, keywords and questions on the board to support your verbal inputs, so that you can scan the whole class while briefing them. Differentiate instructions, keywords and questions, using consistent colour-coding so that pupils recognise more easily what is expected of them.

Distributing equipment

Issuing equipment in advance can create a distraction, as pupils may fiddle with it while you are talking, whereas issuing it after you have finished talking can disrupt a settled group. Choosing when is best depends on how the class responds to you, and each other. If you issue equipment in advance, make sure you tell pupils beforehand not to touch the equipment, rather than having to correct afterwards. Always check all your equipment before the lesson – do not assume that people will have returned the electrical experiment kit complete with wires untangled, otherwise you may find yourself spending 20 minutes sorting it out, giving pupils the opportunity to misbehave.

Transitions

Keeping control of pupils on the move, both in and out of the classroom, requires careful planning if it is to be efficient and safe. Always specify in advance exactly what you require people to do (including supporting adults). Reinforce those individuals who complete the transition the quickest to encourage others to copy them, e.g. by rewarding the first table to collect equipment and are back at their table ready to learn. If moving a class to a different location, think before the lesson about the group dynamics in the same way you would plan a learning activity. Plan where to position yourself in relation to the group to maintain your view of everyone you are responsible for.

Checking for understanding

Throughout your lesson, check that pupils are clear about your expectations. Where appropriate, support your verbal instructions with written versions – especially when working with pupils who have attention difficulties. Avoid repeatedly asking the same child or group; encourage all pupils to ask relevant questions if in doubt.

> **Task 3.4.4 Planning classroom routines**
>
> List the routines you consider important in your classroom.
>
> For each routine:
>
> - describe the behaviour you require;
> - how long the routine should take (can it be done quicker?);
> - are pupils allowed to speak during the routine; if so, what noise level is appropriate?
> - are pupils allowed to move around the room during the routine; if so, for what purpose?
> - what behaviour indicates successful completion?

REWARDS AND SANCTIONS

Announcing rules and routines does not guarantee they will be followed. Establishing and maintaining them requires reinforcement. From a psychological perspective, a reinforcer is *any* consequence that strengthens the behaviour it follows. In contrast, a punishment is any consequence that reduces or stops a behaviour, e.g. sanctions. Behaviour may be reinforced by a reward (e.g. praise or stickers) but may also be reinforced by what a *teacher* thinks is punishment. For example, telling a pupil off for persistent calling out in class provides the pupil with individual attention. Hence, it can be reinforcing and result in repetition of the behaviour to gain more attention. School behaviour policies are required to specify what rewards and sanctions are acceptable (DfE, 2013b). To be effective requires attention to detail – that is, following the principles of the behavioural approach (for details, see Chaplain, 2016).

Rewards and sanctions need to be fit for purpose – the reward(s) must be something the pupils like, and the sanction(s) must be something they do not like. It is unwise to assume that *you* know what pupils like or do not like. One way of discovering what pupils value is to ask them to complete a simple 'All about me' questionnaire, in which they indicate their favourite subjects, lessons, hobbies, music sports, etc. (Chaplain, 2016).

Reinforcing behaviour to establish routines, at the individual or whole-class level, does not mean issuing rewards haphazardly; rather, they should be managed through a reinforcement schedule (Chaplain, 2016). Initially, a tangible reward, (e.g. a sticker) could be given for every occurrence of the desired behaviour (e.g. being the quickest to respond to the instruction to stop what they are doing and look at you). If it brings about the desired behaviour, then you should move to intermittent reinforcement to maintain effectiveness (see Figure 3.4.1 for an outline of the process). Whenever you give out a tangible reward, simultaneously reinforce the pupil's specific behaviour verbally. Directly acknowledge the desired behaviour in a warm and natural manner appropriate to the pupil's level of development. In that way, they will learn to associate the verbal comment with completion of the task and a rewarding experience. Reinforcement should occur immediately after the behaviour to build this association, a process known as contiguity. When selecting your tangible rewards, you should ensure that they are easy to use, inexpensive and quick to administer.

Always refer to the specific behaviour and *not* the pupil when issuing rewards or sanctions – e.g. 'I am pleased to see everyone on this table has put all their equipment back in the correct place'.

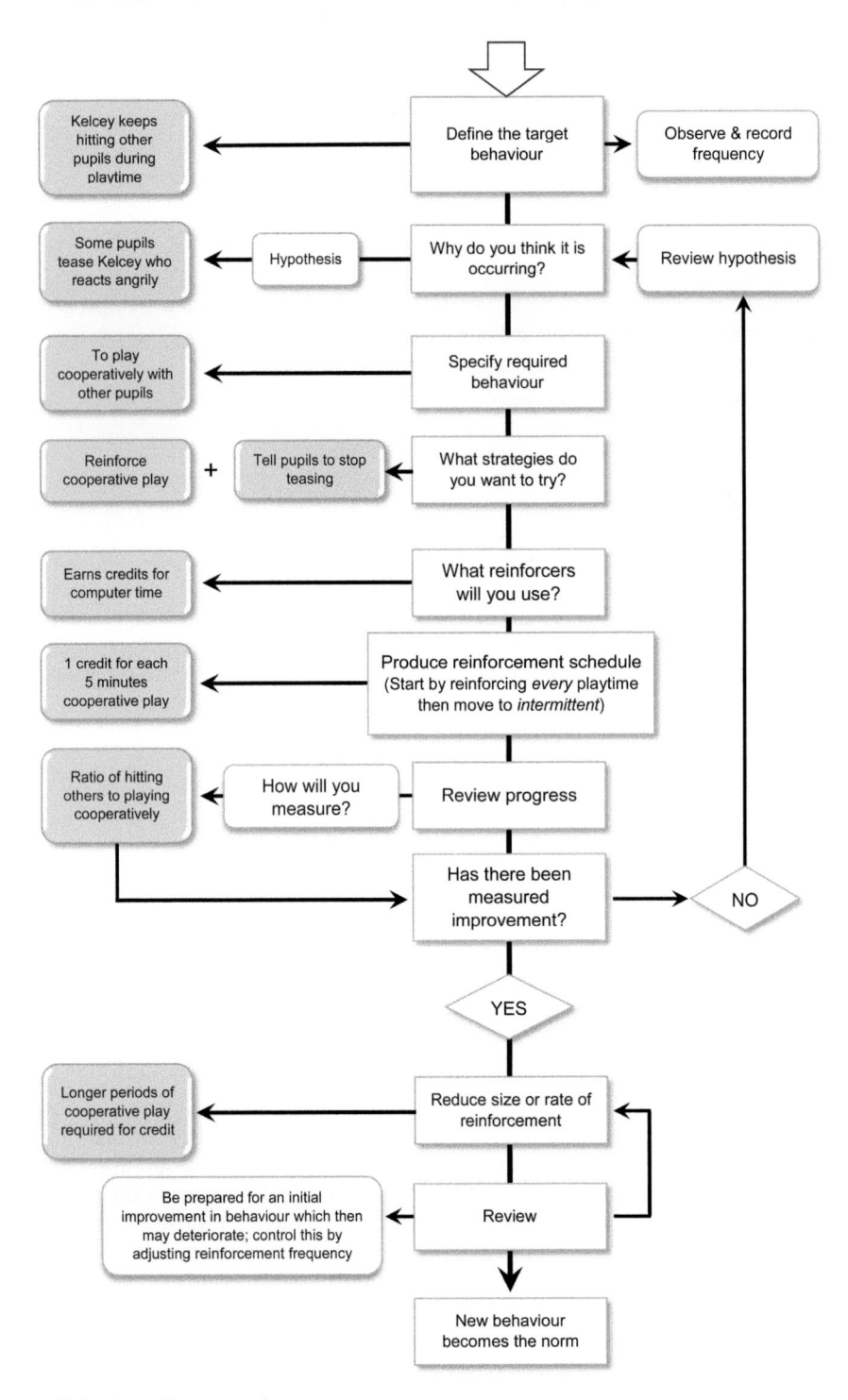

FIGURE 3.4.1 Behaviour change cycle

With difficult pupils, focus on catching them behaving as required, however rare that might be initially. When punishing unacceptable behaviour, do so in a way that suggests disappointment at having to do so, be emotionally objective. Encourage withdrawn pupils to contribute by building waiting time into your questions: 'I am going to be asking about X in five minutes, so start thinking about it now'. Teach more enthusiastic pupils to wait their turn, without disengaging them from learning: 'Thanks for putting your hand up all the time, Freya, but I am going to ask someone else to answer this one'.

List your planned sanctions and familiarise yourself with them; keep the list to hand as reference to avoid using higher-order sanctions prematurely, especially when you feel under pressure. Furthermore, when threatening sanctions, always offer the opportunity to respond positively. For example, 'Caden, you have left your seat again, despite being reminded of the rule. Now you can either sit down and stay there or stay in at break for two minutes'. Should Caden continue to ignore the rule say, 'Caden, you are already staying in for two minutes, now either sit down or you will be staying a further two minutes'. Then model appropriate behaviour by reinforcing those nearby who are behaving as required. Whatever sanction you threaten, be sure to carry it through, otherwise a future repetition of the unwanted behaviour is more likely.

Start each new day on a positive note, whatever happened the day before – feeling negative in advance will focus your attention on negative behaviour, producing a negative cycle.

CLASSROOM LAYOUT

Seating arrangements have differential effects on pupil behaviour (Steer, 2005). For example, sitting boys with girls tends to reduce disruption (Merrett, 1993), and pupils organised in rows tend to be less disruptive than when organised in groups (Wannarka and Ruhl, 2008). However, these findings need to be considered in relation to the requirements of the learning task (Hastings and Chantrey, 2002) and the pupils' level of social functioning (Kutnick et al., 2005).

Movement around the classroom should be free flowing. Where this is not the case, there is potential for disruption. Some individuals will use every opportunity to push past, nudge or dislodge the chairs or whiteboards of other pupils (Chaplain, 2016).

Task 3.4.5 Classroom layout

Have you checked whether:

- you can see all pupils' faces?
- all pupils can see you?
- all pupils can hear you?
- all pupils can see the board/screen/demonstration?

COPING WITH CHALLENGING BEHAVIOUR

Some pupils will persistently challenge your authority, with behaviour ranging from defiance and refusal to work to physical and verbal aggression, which may require specialist interventions.

When dealing with challenges to your authority, never take it personally or get angry – pupils seldom behave this way because they hate you, but some will feed on your emotional reaction. Do not become preoccupied with diagnostic labels (e.g. ADHD) – focus on the behaviour itself and record what the pupil does, and when and where they do it, *including positive behaviour*, however infrequent. Recording positive behaviours not only provides an uplift when times are tense, but also provides insight into what motivates them to behave appropriately. A useful tool for observing challenging behaviour is the strengths and difficulties questionnaire available free from www.sdqinfo.com.

Management of challenging pupils can require considerable effort and can be frustrating, which inhibits problem-solving and creativity. Challenging pupils can lead teachers to question their own ability and lower their teacher self-efficacy, which reflects in their behaviour, especially NVB – a change that pupils recognise and respond to negatively – making the situation worse. Focus on controlling your emotions and on believing that the situation can be coped with, if not completely controlled. Even situations that are so awful that you have to 'grin and bear it' won't last forever. If dealing with a pupil known to be physically aggressive, arrange for a supportive colleague to be briefed and on hand.

The DfE (2013a) published guidelines on restraining aggressive pupils. Fortunately, such occurrences are rare, and most common behaviours can be dealt with by developing your knowledge of established effective interventions (see Mennuti, Christner and Freeman, 2012).

Dealing with challenging behaviour requires attention to several issues, including the following:

- *Be consistent*. Many challenging pupils come from chaotic homes but having a predictable classroom can help them feel safe and secure. This does not mean that they will not repeatedly challenge you until they realise you mean business. They act like people playing slot machines and will keep pressing your buttons until they hit the jackpot (e.g. make you angry). Do not react. That is what they expect. Keep calm and focused.
- *Classroom organisation*. Position challenging pupils near the front, so that there are no pupils between them and you to provide an audience. This makes monitoring and controlling their behaviour easier than doing so at a distance.
- *Learning*. Carefully organise their time and the sequencing/size of their learning tasks. If concentration is an issue, break down their learning into smaller, achievable, progressive units; use coloured folders to help them organise their work and change their tasks frequently. Have a clock visible and indicate how long they are required to stay on task. Specify exactly what you want them to do and provide visual reminders of important instructions.
- *Support*. Where you have a teaching assistant, plan in advance who will deal with any outbursts and who will take responsibility for the rest of the class.
- *Changing behaviour*. Focus on observable behaviour and avoid describing a pupil as 'always badly behaved'. List the behaviours causing concern, then gather detailed observations of what triggers the unwanted behaviour, i.e. antecedent (e.g. carpet time), the behaviour itself (e.g. rolling around) and what happens afterwards, i.e. consequence (e.g. other pupils laughing), along with when, and how frequently, it occurs.

Use this information to decide what to change (antecedent or consequence) to modify the behaviour. (For practical methods to help pupils control their own behaviour, see Mennuti, Christner and Freeman, 2012; Chaplain, 2016).

SUMMARY

Developing excellence in classroom management requires attention to many different aspects of behaviour, at different levels of organisation, to prepare for the various challenges that you will encounter. Whilst establishing and maintaining your authority is important, it is only the first step, as emphasis should then shift to developing self-regulation and social competence of all your pupils. In deciding how to do this, you should follow the most compelling evidence. Cognitive-behavioural approaches introduced in this unit have consistently proved to be effective for teachers managing classes using reinforcement, as well as helping pupils learn to control their own behaviour.

This unit has emphasised the importance of classroom management planning to prepare the conditions for learning, by paying careful attention to understanding your school, yourself, your classroom and your pupils.

ANNOTATED FURTHER READING

Aas, H., Uthus, M. and Løhre, A. (2023) 'Inclusive education for students with challenging behaviour: development of teachers' beliefs and ideas for adaptations through Lesson Study', *European Journal of Special Needs Education*, 39(1): 64-78. https://doi.org/10.1080/08856257.2023.2191107

> The behaviour of challenging pupils is troublesome to classmates, undermines teacher self-efficacy and is a major contributor to teacher stress. This paper describes an intervention where teams of teachers work together to formulate goals for pupils' learning and development of the school culture to support difficult pupils.

Chaplain, R. (2016) *Teaching Without Disruption in the Primary School: A Practical Approach to Managing Pupil Behaviour*, 2nd edn, London: Routledge Falmer.

> A comprehensive account of the theory, research and praxis of behaviour management, including whole-school issues, teacher development, classroom management, coping with challenging behaviour, behaviour management theory and a roadmap of how to develop a Classroom Management Plan.

FURTHER READING TO SUPPORT M-LEVEL STUDY

Lazarides, R., Watt, H. and Richardson, P. (2020). 'Teachers' classroom management self-efficacy, perceived classroom management and teaching contexts from beginning until mid-career', *Learning and Instruction*, 69.

> Classroom management self-efficacy is a teacher's belief in their ability to effectively manage pupil behaviour. This paper examines levels of classroom management self-efficacy, as teachers progress through their careers, and how it links to other aspects of their professional behaviour.

Silk, J., Redcay, E. and Fox, N. (2014) 'Contributions of social and affective neuroscience to our understanding of typical and atypical development', *Developmental Cognitive Neuroscience*, 8: 1-6.

> Including neurodiverse pupils into mainstream classrooms has brought additional challenges for teachers in managing behaviour, hence the need to understand differences between typical and atypical brain development and social behaviour. This paper draws attention to research into four areas of social and affective neuroscience which have informed our understanding of these factors.

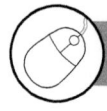

RELEVANT WEBSITES

Department for Education – Behaviour and Discipline in Schools: www.gov.uk/government/publications/behaviour-and-discipline-in-schools
    This site contains advice and information for teachers on behaviour and discipline in schools.

REFERENCES

Admiraal, W. (2021) 'Student-teachers' emotionally challenging classroom events: A typology of their responses', *Educational Studies*, 47(6): 765–769.

Babad, E. (2009) *The social psychology of the classroom*, Abingdon: Routledge/Taylor & Francis Group.

Bandura, A. (1993) 'Perceived self-efficacy in cognitive development and functioning'. *Educational Psychologist*, 28: 117–148.

Chaplain, R. (1995) 'Stress and job satisfaction: A study of English primary school teachers', *Educational Psychology: An International Journal of Experimental Educational Psychology*, 15(4): 473–491.

Chaplain, R. (2008) 'Stress and psychological distress among secondary trainee teachers', *Educational Psychology: An International Journal of Experimental Educational Psychology*, 28(2): 195–209.

Chaplain, R. (2016) *Teaching without Disruption in the Primary School: A Practical Approach to Managing Pupil Behaviour*, 2nd edn, London: Routledge Falmer.

Charles, C. M. (1999) *Building Classroom Discipline: From Models to Practice*, 6th edn, New York: Longman.

Department for Education (DfE). (2011) *Teachers' Standards*, London: The Stationery Office. Last updated 2021.

Department for Education (DfE). (2013a) *Use of Reasonable Force in Schools*. Last updated 2025. Retrieved from: www.gov.uk/government/publications/use-of-reasonable-force-in-schools

Department for Education (DfE). (2013b) *Behaviour in Schools*, London: The Stationery Office. Last updated 2024.

Department for Education (DfE). (2020) *Creating a Culture: How School Leaders Can Optimise Behaviour*, London: The Stationery Office.

Elton Report. (1989) *Discipline in Schools: Report of the Committee Chaired by Lord Elton*, London: HMSO.

Emmer, E. and Aussiker, A. (1990) 'School and classroom discipline programs: How well do they work?', in O. Moles (ed.) *Student Discipline Strategies: Research and Practice*, Albany, NY: SUNY Press, pp. 129–166.

Emmer, E. T. and Worsham, M. E. (2005) *Classroom Management for Middle and High School Teachers*, 7th edn, Boston, MA: Allyn & Bacon, Prentice Hall.

Hastings, N. and Chantrey, K. (2002) *Reorganizing Primary Classroom Learning*, Buckingham: Open University Press.

Health and Safety Executive. (2018) *Work Related Stress, Depression or Anxiety Statistics in Great Britain*, London: The Stationery Office.

Jones, V. F. and Jones, L. S. (2020) *Comprehensive Classroom Management*, 12th edn, NJ: Pearson.

Klassen, R. and Chiu, M. (2010) 'Effects on teachers' self-efficacy and job satisfaction: Teacher gender, years of experience, and job stress', *Journal of Educational Psychology*, 102(3): 741–756.

Klassen, R. and Tze, V. (2014) 'Teachers' self-efficacy, personality, and teaching effectiveness: A meta-analysis', *Educational Research Review*, 12: 59–76.

Kutnick, P., Sebba, J., Blatchford, P., Galton, M., Thorp, J., MacIntyre, H. and Berdondini, L. (2005) *The Effects of Pupil Grouping: Literature Review*, London: DfES.

McLaughlin, H. (1991) 'The reflection on the blackboard: Student teacher self-evaluation', *Alberta Journal of Educational Research*, 37: 141–159.

Merrett, F. (1993) *Encouragement Works Best*, London: David Fulton.

Mennuti, B., Christner, R. and Freeman, A. (2012) *Cognitive-Behavioral Interventions in Educational Settings: A Handbook for Practice*, 2nd edn, New York: Routledge.

MORI. (2017) *Behaviour in Scottish Schools*, Scotland: Ipsos MORI.

Ng, W., Nicholas, H. and Alan, W. (2010) 'School experience influences on pre-service teachers' evolving beliefs about effective teaching', *Teaching & Teacher Education*, 26: 278–289.

Ofsted. (2019) *Teacher Well-being Research Report*. Retrieved from: https://assets.publishing.service.gov.uk/media/5fb41122e90e07208d0d5df1/Teacher_well-being_report_110719F.pdf (accessed 28 November 2023).

Rotter, J. B. (1966) 'Generalised expectancies for internal versus external control of reinforcement', *Psychological Monographs*, 91: 482–497.

Sen, B. G. (2022) 'Teachers' views on classroom rules in basic education', *International Journal of Curriculum and Instruction*, 14(3): 1696–1715.

Steer, A. (2005) *Learning Behaviour: Lessons Learned (Steer Report)*, London: DCSF/Institute of Education, University of London.

Swars, S. L. (2005) 'Examining perceptions of mathematics teaching effectiveness among elementary preservice teachers with differing levels of mathematics teacher efficacy', *Journal of Instructional Psychology*, 32(2): 139–147.

Veldman, I., Admiraal, W., van Tartwijk, J., Mainhard, T. and Wubbels, T. (2016) 'Veteran teachers' job satisfaction as a function of personal demands and resources in the relationships with their students', *Teachers & Teaching*, 22(8): 913–926.

Wannarka, R. and Ruhl, K. (2008). 'Seating arrangements that promote positive academic and behavioural outcomes: A review of empirical research', *Support for Learning*, 23(2), 89–93.

Weinstein, C. S. (1988) 'Preservice teachers' expectations about the first year of teaching', *Teaching & Teacher Education*, 4(1): 31–40.

Williams, J. (2018) *It Just Grinds You Down*, London: Policy Exchange.

Zee, M. and Koomen, H. (2016) 'Teacher self-efficacy and its effects on classroom processes, student academic adjustment, and teacher well-being: A synthesis of 40 years of research', *Review of Educational Research*, 86(4): 981–1015.

UNIT 3.5

ADDRESSING SOCIAL, EMOTIONAL, MENTAL HEALTH AND BEHAVIOUR NEEDS

Janice Wearmouth and Louise Cunningham

INTRODUCTION

The *Teachers' Standards* (Department for Education [DfE], 2011), introduced from September 2012 and recently updated (2021), require teachers to take responsibility for promoting good behaviour in classrooms and elsewhere, have high expectations and maintain good relationships with pupils. This unit focuses on ways to understand and address a range of social, emotional and mental health (SEMH) needs that may be experienced by children, and barriers to their learning and progress in primary schools.

OBJECTIVES

By the end of this unit, you should:

- be familiar with frames of reference commonly used in primary schools to research and understand social, emotional, mental health and behavioural difficulties, and form the basis for effective responses;
- be familiar with a range of effective responses in relation to these frames of reference;
- understand that inclusive learning environments and teaching approaches that are designed to support children to engage with their learning will reduce the possibility of unsociable, withdrawn or concerning behaviour in the first place.

We begin first by discussing frames of reference that we might apply in general terms to understand and address issues relating to children's behaviour in primary schools, and then turn to more specific concerns that relate to individual and SEMH needs and ways to respond proactively and positively to these.

FRAMEWORKS FOR UNDERSTANDING DIFFICULT BEHAVIOUR

The frameworks for understanding problematic behaviour in schools really matter. Pupil behaviour does not occur in a vacuum (Watkins and Wagner, 2000). We begin the discussion here with an outline of the principles of behavioural psychology, which is probably the most common theoretical framework underpinning behaviour management in schools. We continue by looking at a range of social and emotional issues in childhood. These include the effect of trauma, undeveloped and/or broken attachments, biological and neurological explanations for difficult behaviour exemplified by Attention Deficit/Hyperactivity Disorder (AD/HD), and difficulties associated with autism.

Behavioural methodologies

Behavioural methodologies hold that all (mis)behaviour is learned (Skinner, 1938). There are two different ways of looking at this.

- First, research (Glynn, 2004) suggests that elements of a setting may exert powerful control over behaviour. It may be that something about a particular learning environment, for example the physical properties or behaviour of an adult, has provoked good, or alternatively poor, behaviour, and that the young people have come to associate good, or poor, behaviour with that setting. In behaviourist terms, we would consider that the setting has created 'antecedent conditions' for that behaviour to occur. It is very important that you think about this, because, as a teacher, you are in a good position to make changes in the learning environment and/or in your own pedagogy that can improve behaviour where required.
- Second, behaviour can be learned if it is rewarded and thus reinforced, especially if this is done consistently. Many behaviourist principles were derived from work with laboratory animals. In a famous sequence of trial-and-error learning tasks related to the use of rewards, rats learned to press levers to find food (Skinner, 1938). Learning involved the formation of an action-response association in the rats' memory. If the reward was removed, the rats' behaviour gradually ceased through 'extinction'. Translating this interpretation into human terms, pupils can learn how to behave appropriately in response to positive reinforcement (rewards). Where children behave badly you might work out whatever it is that seems to be reinforcing (rewarding) this behaviour and remove the reward(s). Whenever they behave more appropriately, you might reward them in a way that recognises the greater acceptability of the new behaviour. From this view, you can reinforce compliance in classrooms by making rules and the consequences of unacceptable behaviour clear. The way in which you, as a teacher, reward behaviour, sometimes inadvertently, by your own actions can be a very strong reinforcer of good, or poor, behaviour (Sproson, 2004).

Establishing conditions that support positive behaviour in classrooms

Many primary schools start their day with some 'early morning work'. In the experience of Cunningham, one of the current authors, it is more constructive to start by greeting everyone, walking around the room praising on-task behaviours, causing a 'ripple effect', rather than beginning the morning on a negative note. This can also be achieved by drawing a 'smiley face' on the whiteboard and adding names as you praise children responding to instructions. It is imperative to acknowledge children when they respond positively to aid the development of teacher-pupil relationships and promote self-worth (Cosgrove, 2021). This can be especially important for those who find it difficult to manage school expectations and have low self-esteem.

Establishing the right to feel safe, learn without disruption and be respected and treated fairly is essential as the basis for instituting rules and routines (Rogers, 2013). Pupils will look to you as the teacher for a sense of security and order in the learning context, an opportunity to participate actively in the class and for it to be an interesting place (Department for Education and Skills [DfES], 2006) where expectations of progress, both academic and social, are high. You should provide a limited number of rules, with predictable, positive consequences. If children disrupt the lesson, they should take ownership of this, and you should remind them what the rules are. You can give younger children a nonverbal or visual cue to appropriate behaviour and show them clearly what is expected.

> **Task 3.5.1 Reflecting on ways to establish a calm and peaceful environment in primary classrooms**
>
> Cunningham offers some practical and effective strategies for establishing a calm learning environment in your classroom at the beginning of the day. Read the following suggestions and note down which you might find useful in your own classroom:
>
> Utilising a daily emotion register in the classroom can prove advantageous for both adults and children alike. It enables adults to recognise when children may be encountering emotional challenges and encourages emotional growth and comprehension. Children can engage with the register by moving their names between a range of feelings they have learned in class, including, for example, happy, sad, angry, proud and worried, and allows adults to provide timely support. Moreover, weekly stories focused on emotions and the presence of a cuddly toy pet in class can provide additional support and comfort to children when needed.
>
> For children who require a calm space in the classroom, creating a peaceful environment with comfortable cushions, soft blankets, cuddly teddy bears and fidget toys can be highly beneficial. Additionally, displaying visually calming aids like breathing or grounding exercises can provide extra assistance. A sensory calming box can also be a useful tool, offering a range of activities and tools that allow the child to choose what works for them and provide a sense of control. The calming box may include simple and varied items such as spinners and poppers, playdough, bubbles, scented bottles, colouring books, building blocks, favourite stories, ear defenders and emotion cards.

Ways to reinforce positive behaviour

Collectively working towards a whole-class treat can be a very powerful reinforcer in a primary classroom. This could be in the form of merits, house points, stickers or pebbles in a jar, but it is important to remember that points that have been earned cannot be taken away by less desired behaviours, as this can cause resentment between class members. A favourite strategy used by Cunningham is that of the 'secret student' (Gedge, 2016: 85). The teacher picks a name secretly in the morning and if the selected child has exhibited the desired behaviour(s), they are awarded a certificate and a set number of points towards the class reward at the end of the day. They also get to wear a class 'secret student' badge the next day in school. The teacher refers to the fact that they are watching the secret student throughout the day; as this is a secret it encourages all pupils to comply with the behaviour request. If the selected child has not made standard, their name is kept a secret, but everyone should eventually have a chance to wear the badge.

Students may imitate negative behaviour, and so, for example, the use of abusive or sarcastic language should be avoided at all costs. You should model ways of resolving conflict that respect the rights of students to learn and feel safe and:

- meet the needs of both parties, that is, provide win-win outcomes wherever possible;
- bring an end to the conflict, or at least reduce it;
- do not leave either party 'wounded'.

(Sproson, 2004: 319)

Addressing social, emotional, mental health and behaviour needs

In your role as a teacher, it is important not to allow yourself to be drawn into a power struggle, which some pupils find rewarding. There are a number of techniques that can enable you to avoid power struggles:

- Some young people may take pleasure in not doing what they are asked immediately, especially if there is an audience of peers. In this situation, Rogers (2013: 240), among others, advocates that you build in a brief 'take-up' period for pupils to respond: 'Craig … Deon … you're chatting – it's whole-class teaching time'. Make the request, walk away so as to imply compliance, and acknowledge compliance when it happens.
- Pupils engaging in inappropriate activities might be given what Rogers (2013: 242) calls 'directed choices'. Wearmouth's sister, a new teacher at the time, tells of a situation where a group of girls brought long sticks into her lesson – to test her out, as they later admitted. She responded by directing their choices: 'Shall I put them in this cupboard or that one? I'll keep them safe for you till the end of the day'. They never asked for them back.
- Finally, you may be able to address inappropriate and/or disruptive behaviour by defining behaviour that is incompatible with this, and modelling and reinforcing it with positive consequences. For example, as a new teacher, Wearmouth was once in a position where all the pupils had been told not to bring 'clacker balls' into school, because one child had broken her wrist playing with these. When she walked into her classroom the next day, every single pupil pulled out their clackers and began to play, 'clack', 'clack', 'clack'. For a moment she felt sheer panic, but then she turned round and, without saying anything, wrote on the whiteboard very clearly, 'Copy this into your books', and began to write the first few sentences of a story. Very soon, all the clacker balls had disappeared into bags, and there was quiet in the room while the children began to engage in their own storytelling. Clacking the balls together and writing could not be done simultaneously.

UNDERSTANDING AND ADDRESSING SOCIAL, EMOTIONAL AND MENTAL HEALTH (SEMH) NEEDS IN SCHOOLS

Sometimes behaviour that you may experience as challenging may relate to particular social, emotional and/or mental health (SEMH) difficulties. Such difficulties are defined in the *SEND Code of Practice* (DfE/DoH, 2014: §6.32) as:

> a wide range of social and emotional difficulties which manifest themselves in many ways. These may include becoming withdrawn or isolated, as well as displaying challenging, disruptive or disturbing behaviour. These behaviours may reflect underlying mental health difficulties such as anxiety or depression, self-harming, substance misuse, eating disorders or physical symptoms that are medically unexplained.

It is essential to remember that behaviours related to SEMH are a form of communication about unmet needs, an indication of how a child is coping with difficult emotions or expressing distress. Children may encounter challenges in a variety of areas including focus, socialisation, participation, stress and anxiety management, self-confidence, anger and resistance to change.

It is essential to separate out the behaviour the child uses from the child themselves (Cosgrove, 2021). This is not always easy, however. As Greenhalgh (1994: 53) notes:

> When working with disturbed children, one might find oneself feeling hurt, abused, angry, frustrated, intolerant, anxious, de-skilled and even frightened. One of the reasons that working with children experiencing emotional and behavioural difficulties is so disturbing is that such intense and painful feelings are somehow pushed into the staff (as well as other children). Sometimes it might feel as if it is difficult to know where the feelings are coming from, and the intensity of them might lead one to question one's own competence and professional worth.

We should not ignore the fundamental need for support for key adults working with children whose behaviour is of serious concern.

Sometimes such emotional and social challenges and/or mental health problems may relate to traumatic experiences, to problems of broken, or undeveloped attachment to caregivers early in life, or to underlying factors such as attention-deficit/hyperactivity disorder (AD/HD) and/or autism.

POTENTIAL EFFECTS OF TRAUMATIC EXPERIENCES ON CHILDREN'S BEHAVIOUR

Trauma might be defined as an intense, negatively charged or distressing event that overwhelms a person's ability to cope. Loss or separation, for example parents' separation or divorce, relationships' breakdown between family members, being adopted or placed in care, life changes such as the arrival of siblings, moving schools or houses, neglect, maltreatment, domestic abuse, violence, bullying, accidents or injuries, natural catastrophes or war can be experienced as overwhelmingly stressful (DfE, 2014: §3.17). When they do not feel safe, and as a result are anxious, fearful and focused on suppressing the traumatic memories, children 'may present with behaviours such as passivity, inability to concentrate, verbal and physical blow-ups, frequent absences, and "spacing out"'(Sitler, 2009: 120).

Importance of attachment for young children

As Bowlby (1988: 26-27) notes, attachment behaviour is 'any form of behaviour that results in a person attaining or maintaining proximity to some other clearly identified individual who is conceived as better able to cope with the world'. Successful development depends on needs being adequately met at an earlier stage. If they are not, then children will persist in inappropriate attachment behaviour, being over-anxious, avoidant, aggressive or incapable of positive human relationships (Bowlby, 1988). Many young children may develop 'attachment difficulties' when early relationships are characterised by neglect, abuse and/or loss. Learning, personality and behaviour difficulties can result from inadequate early care and support from parents who struggle with poverty, damaged relationships and harsh, stressful living conditions (Boxall, 2002).

ADDRESSING SEMH CONCERNS IN PRIMARY SCHOOLS

Two different, but linked, approaches to maintaining learners' well-being and reducing incidence of behaviours associated with SEMH problems are:

- whole-school/whole-class approaches to well-being of learners and staff;
- individualised targeted approaches.

School and classroom approaches

Some educators, for example Greenhalgh (2004), highlight the importance of an environment that fosters children's sense of safety, trust and acceptance of themselves as individuals and positive responsive relationship with adults so that they can develop and learn. 'Through relationships we can help these children to learn adaptive, healthy responses, supporting them to think differently and to take control over their physical states, feelings and behaviours' (Bombèr, 2007: 9).

Pedagogy to foster positive relationships

Hughes (2006) identified key principles that are crucial in fostering strong relationships, positive self-esteem in children and inculcating a sense of safety and security among children who have been traumatised. These principles are known collectively as PACE: Playful, Accepting, Curious and Empathetic.

> Children need to feel that you have connected with the emotional part of their brain before they can engage the thoughtful, articulate, problem solving areas.
>
> (Riviere and Evered, n.d.: 5)

Playful

Playfulness can also help ease any embarrassment a child may feel in the face of a mistake, making it easier to have serious conversations or convey important messages. It is important to note that a playful tone does not mean that emotions or incidents are not taken seriously. A playful approach can be a very effective way to deliver a brief reminder about behaviour in a classroom setting.

Accepting

Hughes (2006) explains that a child's sense of safety is deeply rooted in unconditional acceptance, acknowledging their emotions without judgement or attempting to dismiss them. Using language like 'I can see you are feeling really sad, it is ok to be sad, if my friend said that to me I would feel sad too.'

To accept a child, it is essential to see them beyond their behaviour. Cunningham reflects on an occasion where a 6-year-old child in her class could not bear the embarrassment he felt when he noticed he had made a mistake in his own work. He went from initially screwing up his paper to ripping other children's work on a display board in the corridor. Using a calm tone, Cunningham acknowledged and validated the child's feelings of embarrassment. Taking some scrap paper, she started ripping and tearing, verbalising how this action was making her feel better: 'Can you rip this paper with me?'. The child joined in. 'Gosh, it looks like we have made a snowstorm,' playfully blowing some small pieces of paper towards the child, who was now smiling and blowing some back. Eventually, the child said, 'I'm sorry, I ripped my work and the display.' Working together, Cunningham and the child cleared up the paper and fixed the display. It is important to keep in mind that accepting emotions is not synonymous with accepting unwanted behaviour or agreeing. Later in the day, when the child was calm, Cunningham discussed the incident and together they identified strategies to use if he felt these emotions again.

Curious

When engaging with a child, it is vital to express interest in their thoughts, feelings, wishes and goals. You can demonstrate your inquisitiveness by posing open-ended questions such as 'I wonder if...' or 'I'm guessing you feel...'. It is critical to maintain a composed and receptive manner, conveying your willingness to understand the child's viewpoint, even if it does not align with yours.

Empathetic

When you display empathy, you are communicating to the child that their emotions are important to you and that you are there to support them through difficult times. Reflecting on her own practice as a primary teacher, Cunningham comments:

> A child who feels safe to learn and knows it is acceptable to make mistakes will thrive. A teacher who builds positive relationships with pupils and with the subject can make all the difference to engage a distraught or upset pupil within the lesson. Your response to pupil behaviour or disengagement makes a difference in fostering motivation and willingness to learn.

> **Task 3.5.2 Exploring resources available to primary schools: The example of 'Targeted Mental Health in Schools' (TaMHS)**
>
> Northamptonshire Targeted Mental Health in Schools (TaMHS) is a programme referenced by Weare (2015) as effective in encouraging early intervention for children's SEMH needs. TaMHS is focused on building capacity within schools through training, support and introducing new programmes and approaches to better meet the mental health needs of all children. It uses a 'building blocks' model to support schools in implementing approaches, programmes and interventions, which have a positive impact on children's mental health. We would like you to explore what the resources associated with this programme offer. This programme is available at www.northnorthants.gov.uk/schools-and-education/targeted-mental-health-schools-tamhs/tamhs-building-blocks.
>
> **Please note: there are ethical issues here in working with individual children. If you try out for yourself some of the suggested activities for children, please make sure that you have consulted with colleagues, your mentor or appropriate others before doing so.**

Circle Time

In primary schools, you may well see the initiative 'Circle Time' (Mosley, 1996), which was designed to resolve disputes between pupils and provide opportunities for a class to build a shared team spirit and a sense of belonging (Gedge, 2016). Both teachers and students are bound by rules that stipulate no one may put anyone down, no one may use any name negatively and, when individuals speak, everyone must listen. Everyone has a turn and a chance to speak. Members of the class team suggest ways of solving problems, and individuals can accept or politely refuse help (Wearmouth, Glynn and Berryman, 2005: 184). If a child breaks the protocol, a visual warning is given. If this persists, time away from the circle follows.

'Mindfulness' in primary schools

In many primary schools 'mindfulness' has emerged as a popular set of mainstream practices that can be integrated into all classroom levels from nursery onwards (Lyons and DeLange, 2016). It is a technique that can be a useful tool for decreasing anxiety and promoting happiness. There is evidence that mindfulness-induced emotional and behavioural changes are related to functional and structural changes in the brain (Gotink et al., 2016). Mindfulness can promote skills that are controlled in the prefrontal cortex, for example, focus and cognitive control, and can therefore have a particular impact on the development of skills including self-regulation, judgement and patience during childhood.

Nurture groups

'Nurture groups' have been established in a number of primary schools in response to concerns about broken or undeveloped attachment. The nurture group attempts to create the features of adequate parenting, with opportunities to develop trust, security and positive identity through attachment to an attentive, caring adult. Features include: easy physical contact between adult and child; warmth and a family atmosphere; good-humoured acceptance of children and their behaviour; familiar, regular routines; a focus on tidying up; provision of food in structured contexts; opportunities to play and appropriate adult participation; adults encouraging children's reflection on troublesome situations and their own feelings; and opportunities for children to develop increasing autonomy (Wearmouth, 2009).

INDIVIDUAL TARGETED APPROACHES

Therapy

Difficulties experienced by some children may be serious enough to warrant an individual referral to the local Child and Mental Health Service (CAMHS). We cannot stress enough how important it is to refer to specialists when severe emotional and mental health concerns become apparent. CAMHS professionals deal with a wide range of mental health problems. In any one team they may well include:

- child and adolescent psychiatrists who are medically qualified doctors specialising in working with young people and their families;
- clinical psychologists qualified in assessing and assisting with young people's psychological functioning, and emotional well-being;
- child psychotherapists trained in therapies intended to support young people to deal with problems related to the emotions and mental health problems;
- family therapists and trained therapists who work with children and their families together to help them understand and manage the difficulties that are happening in their lives, by focusing on the 'systems' of interaction between family members and emphasising family relationships as an important factor in psychological health;
- social workers trained to help children and families affected by social disadvantages and needing extra support through social welfare, or needing to be kept safe;
- other professionals, for example, educational psychologists, art therapists and speech and language therapists.

The example of play therapy

As Pigeon *et al.* (2015) note, primarily Play Therapy adopts a nonverbal approach, in which children aged 2 to 12 can explore their difficulties, hurts and feelings through play with, for example, toys, sand, puppets, clay, art, dance and music. A stable, secure and predictable relationship between child and trained therapist (and here we stress the importance of training) is crucial, so that the child can feel safe, accepted and free to explore and grow.

NEUROLOGICAL AND BIOLOGICAL EXPLANATIONS OF BEHAVIOUR

Sometimes behaviour that you may experience as challenging to yourself may relate to an underlying condition or dysfunction.

Attention Deficit/Hyperactivity Disorder

One such condition is Attention Deficit/Hyperactivity Disorder (AD/HD), 'characterised by chronic and pervasive (at home and school) problems of inattention, impulsiveness, and/or excessive motor activity which have seriously debilitating effects on individuals' social, emotional and educational development, and are sometimes disruptive to the home and/or school environment' (Norwich, Cooper and Maras, 2002: 182).

A diagnosis of AD/HD may result in a prescription for psychostimulants, of which the most widely used is Methylphenidate (Ritalin):

> The medication stimulates areas of the brain regulating arousal and alertness and can result in immediate short-term improvements in concentration and impulse control. The precise mechanism is poorly understood and the specific locus of action within the central nervous system remains speculative.
>
> (British Psychological Society [BPS], 1996: 50-51)

There are particular concerns about the use of such psychostimulants, including the effects and side effects of these drugs and ethical considerations about the lack of adequate monitoring of the day-to-day classroom learning and behavioural outcomes of medication (BPS, 1996: 51-52).

Responding to AD/HD

The use of drugs is not a complete answer to controlling the behaviour of children identified as having AD/HD. Children can also sometimes be taught alternative behaviours that offer a sense of belonging and increase self-control (Rogers, 2013). The BPS (1996: 47-48) identified a number of approaches that focus on the effects of consequences through positive reinforcement, training in the reduction of behaviour viewed as problematic and response cost, that is mild punishment designed to make the undesirable behaviour more difficult and more of an effort to perform, in other words an approach built on the principles of behaviourism, as outlined earlier.

Behavioural methodology is a scientifically based technology, and so the first requirement is a clear definition of the target behaviour. For instance, if a child is thought to be 'hyperactive', an operational definition of behaviours, such as 'out of seat', will be required. Once the behaviour has been operationally defined, there should be systematic observational sampling across times of day, situations, nature of activity, person in charge and so on. Once the baseline can be clearly seen, an analysis detailing the following three stages should be carried out: (1) the antecedent event(s), that is, whatever starts off or prompts the undesirable behaviour; (2) the observable behaviour; (3) the consequence(s), often referred to in schools as an 'ABC chart'. Individualised behaviour management strategies should also provide opportunities for modelling, rehearsing and reinforcing behaviours that are acceptable (Rogers, 2013).

Potentially unsafe or abusive behaviour should be addressed very assertively: '[That language] is not a joke to me – it stops now', 'Kyle ... put the scissors down, on the table – now' (Rogers, 2013: 243-244). If it is necessary to remove a student from a group of peers, this can be achieved 'by asking the other students to leave' (Dunckley, 1999: 10).

Physical restraint is a last resort that should only be used to manage a dangerous situation. In a non-statutory advisory document on the use of 'reasonable' force in schools in England (DfE, 2013b: 4; DfE, 2013a), school staff are advised that reasonable in this context means 'using no more force than is needed' to control or restrain young people.

Whatever you do, you should familiarise yourself with school policies that should indicate when restraint can be used.

Task 3.5.3 Implementing effective classroom management strategies

Cunningham asked her colleagues: If you could give a primary trainee teacher or ECT just one top tip or strategy for great classroom behaviour management, what would it be? Please read their responses next. Note down which strategies you already use, and which you might implement in your practice.

- Using PBM – Positive Behaviour Management: Now I can see B and C are ready too … and now this whole group here – well done. Keep going until you have the whole group. And as soon as they are ready get on with the lesson at a decent pace. If you hang about too much and don't engage them you could lose them again.
- Clear and consistent boundaries
- Think very carefully about your seating plan!
- My top tip would be to use the hand signals one, two and three. You use this while transitioning from the carpet to tables or to outside. Holding up one finger means stand up, two means move and three means sit down. The whole thing is done in silence. This provides for quiet, simple transitions and everyone knows the expectations.
- Smelly stickers – having the novelty of a smelly sticker has helped a lot. My class are quite fizzy this year but are responding really well to the incentive of a smelly sticker! Sometimes strategically giving a sticker to someone who is sitting well or making a good choice is enough to get the others to behave.
- 'Consistency is key'. Decide what you want/how you want it to go and implement the strategies to enable the class to achieve the goal whilst reinforcing expectations consistently.
- Always praise the positive as it encourages not just that child but others to copy them.
- Say what you mean and mean what you say. Positive affirmations all the way.
- Check the physical environment. Do I need to open a window, is the chair too small, the board too dark, etc…? Being physically uncomfortable makes learning harder.
- Consistency in whatever rule/expectation you want to achieve/enforce. Remember not to expect instant results – it takes time to see results.
- Rapport – know the children not only on paper but in themselves.
- Only talk to the whole class if they are listening to you. Wait for everyone to stop talking before you speak.
- Every day is a fresh start – make sure any problems are resolved wherever possible before a child goes home and that relationships are intact. Otherwise anxiety can feed the child's behaviour the next day.
- Be fair at all times – no child likes a teacher who is seen to have favourites.

Autism

It is highly likely that you will meet children in schools who have been diagnosed as having an autistic spectrum disorder (ASD). In recent years, Frederickson and Cline (2015: 283) have summarised the areas often associated with autism as:

- social communication and social interaction;
- restricted, repetitive patterns of behaviour, interests or activities, including sensory difficulties.

In addition, as Asperger (1994/1991) noted, children may be extremely sensitive to particular stimuli: auditory, visual olfactory (smell), taste and touch, and find their senses overwhelmed by them. Children experiencing autistic difficulties are unlikely to understand unwritten social rules, recognise others' feelings, seek comfort from others or understand and interpret other people's feelings and actions. They may appear to behave 'strangely' or inappropriately. Difficulties in social communication mean that children often find it hard to understand the meaning of gestures, facial expressions or tone of voice. They may also find it hard to plan for the future and cope in new or unfamiliar situations. This may result in restricted, obsessional or repetitive activities, and difficulties in developing the skills of playing with others.

Responding to barriers related to autism

Commonly, approaches to addressing difficulties associated with autism are based on behavioural principles. In a classroom, you might address the learning and behavioural needs by, for example, paying close attention to antecedent conditions: clarity and order, reducing extraneous and unnecessary material in order that children know where their attention needs to be directed, and maintaining a predictable physical environment with very predictable and regular routines, ensuring that everything is kept in the same place. You might teach children agreed signals to be quiet or to call for attention. You might provide specific low-arousal work areas free from visual distractions and make headphones available to reduce sound. You might also provide a visual timetable, with clear symbols to represent the various activities for the day, and a simple visual timer with, for example, an arrow that is moved across a simple timeline to show how much time has passed or is left.

To develop greater understanding of personal emotions, you might teach children in a very deliberate way to name their feelings and relate these to their own experiences, predict how they are likely to feel at particular times and in particular circumstances, and recognise the signs of extreme emotions such as anger. A visual gauge showing graduated degrees of anger in different shades of colour might be helpful here. You might also teach pupils, in small steps, to identify and name others' feelings, link these to possible causes and identify appropriate responses to others' emotions. They might keep a feelings diary in which they record times when they feel happy, sad or frightened, and what they can do about this. You might use art, drama and social stories to identify the different kinds of emotion and/or explore their physical aspects and/or talk through situations that need to be resolved. Above all, it is really important for you to get to know the pupil really well and to understand his/her individuality, strengths, weaknesses, sensory sensitivities, likes and dislikes, and that this information is shared and used consistently among adults working with the child.

SUMMARY

As a teacher, you can minimise the possibility of poor behaviour in your classroom if you recognise that appropriate behaviour can generally be taught (Rogers, 2013). Having said this, however, and as the *SEND Code of Practice* (DfE/DoH, 2014) acknowledged, a small minority of children may experience social, emotional and mental health (SEMH) needs that may negatively influence their behaviour. We take the view in this unit that, given appropriate support, children can often learn to make conscious choices about behaviour, even where it is associated with a genetic or neurological condition (Wearmouth, Glynn and Berryman, 2005). Such behaviour may be addressed in primary schools through inclusive and effective classroom pedagogy, and/or through individual interventions.

ANNOTATED FURTHER READING

Rogers, B. (2015) *Classroom Behaviour: A Practical Guide to Effective Teaching, Behaviour Management and Colleague Support*, 4th edn, London: Sage.

> Bill Rogers, an Australian educator, has written a number of books and articles on addressing challenging behaviour in schools that may be interpreted as using the principles of behavioural psychology. This publication provides strategies to meet the challenges of controlling behaviour, as well as building positive relationships with both students and colleagues to enable productive learning environments.

FURTHER READING TO SUPPORT M-LEVEL STUDY

Axline, V (2022) *Dibs in Search of Self*, London: Penguin.

> A seminal figure in the development of non-directive Play Therapy is the American clinical psychologist Virginia Axline who, in 1964, published *Dibs in Search of Self*. In it she describes a series of Play Therapy sessions, over a period of one year, with a young boy named Dibs. He was viewed by his parents and teachers as having an extreme emotional disorder, abnormal social behaviour and a learning difficulty. When Axline first met him he continuously self-isolated, rarely spoke and physically lashed out at those around him. She held weekly sessions of Play Therapy with him where he was able to do and say whatever he wanted. During these sessions he slowly opened up and began to explore his feelings as Axline showed him that she was listening without judging him. At the end of the year's sessions, Dibs had made a lot of progress in his ability to express himself, identify and cope with his feelings and interact socially with his peers and family. When he was tested on an intelligence test at the end of his therapy he scored in the extremely gifted range, with an IQ of 168.

Weare, K (2015) *What Works in Promoting Social and Emotional Well-being and Responding to Mental Health Problems in Schools?* London: National Children's Bureau.

> This is an advice and guidance document that covers two overlapping areas of school practice: promoting positive social and emotional well-being for all in schools, and tackling the mental health problems of pupils in more serious difficulty. It is designed to support schools, in particular, school leaders, in the delivery of their work on these two areas.

Bombèr, L. (2007) *Inside I'm Hurting: Practical Strategies for Supporting Children with Attachment Difficulties in Schools*, Duffield: Worth Publishing.

> This book provides educational professionals with a theoretical and practical handbook of strategies, practical tools and the confidence for supporting children with attachment difficulties.

Further reading at M-level is also to be found in the following websites.

RELEVANT WEBSITES

Evaluating the Effectiveness of Mindfulness in Schools: https://mindfulnessinschools.org/wp-content/uploads/2013/02/MiSP-Research-Summary-2012.pdf

> The 'Mindfulness in Schools Project' (MISP) is a charity established by teachers aiming to use mindfulness to support children's mental health and well-being.

Exploring How to Introduce Circle Time Activities: www.circle-time.co.uk/wp-content/uploads/2020/05/Step-by-Step-Guide-to-Circle-Time-by-Jenny-Mosley.pdf

> Mosley (undated) has published a *Step by Step Guide to Circle Time* that has been made available to schools interested in introducing Circle Time activities.

Responsibility for administering medication: www.medicalconditionsatschool.org.uk/documents/Legal-Situation-In-Schools.pdf

> Statutory guidance in relation to responsibility for administering medication such as Ritalin to children in schools and colleges across the UK.

Guidance on the use of visual supports for autistic children: www.autism.org.uk/about/strategies/visual-supports.aspx

> The National Autistic Society has made this information sheet available on the use of visual supports for autistic young people.

REFERENCES

Asperger, H. (1944/1991) '*Autism and Asperger Syndrome* [translation]', ed. U. Frith, Cambridge, UK: Cambridge University Press.

Bombèr, L (2007) *Inside I'm Hurting: Practical Strategies for Supporting Children with Attachment Difficulties in Schools*, Duffield: Worth Publishing.

Bowlby, J. (1988) *A Secure Base: Parent–Child Attachment and Healthy Human Development*, New York: Basic Books.

Boxall, M. (2002) *Nurture Groups in School: Principles & Practice: Principles and Practice*, London: Sage.

British Psychological Society (BPS). (1996) *Attention Deficit Hyperactivity Disorder (ADHD): A Psychological Response to an Evolving Concept*, Leicester, UK: BPS.

Cosgrove, R. (2021) *Inclusive Teaching in a Nutshell: A Visual Guide for Busy Teachers*, London: Routledge

Department for Education (DfE). (2011) *Teachers' Standards*, London: DfE. Last updated 2021.

Department for Education (DfE). (2013a) *Behaviour in Schools: Advice for Headteachers and School Staff*, London: DfE. Last updated 2024.

Department for Education (DfE). (2013b) *Use of Reasonable Force in Schools*. Last updated 2025. Retrieved from: www.gov.uk/government/publications/use-of-reasonable-force-in-schools (accessed 9 February 2025).

Department for Education (DfE). (2014) *Mental Health and Behaviour in Schools*. Last updated 2018. Retrieved from: https://assets.publishing.service.gov.uk/media/625ee6148fa8f54a8bb65ba9/Mental_health_and_behaviour_in_schools.pdf (accessed 21 October 2023).

Department for Education (DfE)/Department for Health (DoH). (2014) *SEND Code of Practice: 0 to 25 Years*, London: DfE. Last updated 2024.

Department for Education and Skills (DfES). (2006) *Learning Behaviour. Principles and Practice – What Works in Schools (Steer Report)*, London: DfES.

Dunckley, I. (1999) *Managing Extreme Behaviour in Schools*, Wellington, New Zealand: Specialist Education Services.

Frederickson, N. and Cline, T. (2015) *Special Educational Needs, Inclusion and Diversity*, Maidenhead, UK: Open University Press.

Gedge, N. (2016) *Inclusion for Primary School Teachers*, London: Bloomsbury.

Glynn, T. (2004) 'Antecedent control of behaviour in educational contexts', in J. Wearmouth, R. C. Richmond and T. Glynn (eds) *Understanding Pupil Behaviour in Schools: A Diversity of Approaches*, London: Fulton, pp. 239–254.

Gotink, R. A., Meijboom, R., Vernooij, M. W., Smits, M. and Hunink, M. G. (2016) '8-week mindfulness-based stress reduction induces brain changes similar to traditional long-term meditation practice – a systematic review', *Brain and Cognition*, 108(October): 32–41.

Greenhalgh, P. (1994) *Emotional Growth and Learning*, 1st edn, London: Routledge. Retrieved from: https://doi.org/10.4324/9780203424681

Greenhalgh, P. (2004) 'Emotional growth and learning', in J. Wearmouth, R. C. Richmond, T. Glynn and M. Berryman, *Understanding Pupil Behaviour in Schools*, London: David Fulton, chap. 10, pp. 151–161.

Hughes, D. (2006). *Building the Bonds of Attachment: Awakening Love in Deeply Troubled Children*, United States: Jason Aronson.

Lyons K. E. and DeLange, J. (2016) 'Mindfulness matters in the classroom: The effects of mindfulness training on brain development and behavior in children and adolescents', in K. Schonert-Reichl and R. Roeser (eds), *Handbook of Mindfulness in Education. Mindfulness in Behavioral Health*, New York: Springer, pp. 271–283.

Mosley, J. (1996) *Quality Circle Time in the Primary Classroom: Your Essential Guide to Enhancing Self-esteem, Self-discipline and Positive Relationships*, Cambridge, UK: LDA.

Norwich, B., Cooper, P. and Maras, P. (2002) 'Attentional and activity difficulties: Findings from a national study', *Support for Learning*, 17(4): 182–186.

Pigeon, K., Parson, J., Mora, L., Anderson, J., Stagnitti, K. and Mountain, V. (2015) 'Play therapy', in C. Noble and E. Day (eds) *Psychotherapy and Counselling: Reflections on Practice*, Oxford: Oxford University Press, pp. 155–172.

Riviere, H. and Evered, R. (n.d.) *Using PACE in School: Through PACE, and as they Begin to Feel Safer, Children Discover They Can Now Do Better*. The attach team. Retrieved from: www.oxfordshire.gov.uk/sites/default/files/file/children-and-families/PACEforteachers.pdf

Rogers, B. (2013) 'Communicating with children in the classroom', in T. Cole, H. Daniels and J. Visser, *The Routledge International Companion to Emotional and Behavioural Difficulties*, London: Routledge, chap. 26, pp. 237–245.

Sitler, H. C. (2009) 'Teaching with awareness: The hidden effects of trauma on learning', *Clearing House: A Journal of Education Strategies, Issues, and Ideas*, 82(3): 119–124.

Skinner, B. F. (1938) *The Behaviour of Organisms*, New York: Appleton Century Crofts.

Sproson, B. (2004) 'Some do and some don't: Teacher effectiveness in managing behaviour', in J. Wearmouth, T. Glynn, R. C. Richmond and M. Berryman (eds) *Inclusion and Behaviour Management in Schools*, London: Fulton, chap. 18, pp. 311–321.

Watkins, C. and Wagner, P. (2000) *Improving School Behaviour*, London: Paul Chapman.

Weare, K. (2015). *What Works in Promoting Social and Emotional Well-being and Responding to Mental Health Problems in Schools?* London: National Children's Bureau.

Wearmouth, J. (2009) *A Beginning Teacher's Guide to Special Educational Needs*, Buckingham, UK: Open University Press.

Wearmouth, J., Glynn, T. and Berryman, M. (2005) *Perspectives on Student Behaviour in Schools: Exploring Theory and Developing Practice*, London: Routledge.

UNIT 3.6

ORGANISING EFFECTIVE CLASSROOM TALK

Lyn Dawes

> Teachers must value the relationship between the talk they use for teaching, and the talk they hope to inspire their pupils to use for learning.
>
> (Smith and Higgins, 2006: 500)

INTRODUCTION

Most children arrive at school able to talk. Their everyday talk skills are invaluable, but may not include ways to use speaking and listening to support their own education. Children are rarely taught how to use essential oracy skills in the same way that they are taught key aspects of literacy and numeracy. By 'oracy' skills here I mean the capable and confident use of spoken language. Children who are not taught to understand and practice the important skills of listening, discussion and presentation may fail to discuss ideas, collaborate and may be unable to share what they think or know. They may instead use strategies such as talking over others, ignoring what is said, withdrawing and refusing to talk. Children need to know how to talk if they are to develop their thinking. An inability to communicate with others through talk is a true deprivation, and it is unnecessary, because in classrooms we can readily teach children the oracy skills they need, for example how to engage one another in discussion. Such extension of their talk repertoire is not simply an added social skill, but fosters a crucial capacity to think and learn in class, enabling access to educational opportunity. Effective talk – talk for learning – does not just happen along in classrooms, but is a product of professional planning, teaching and organisation. A focus on oracy skills and talk for learning is essential if every child is to benefit from classroom activities.

OBJECTIVES

By the end of this unit, you should be able to:

- consider the crucial importance of classroom talk for learning;
- identify ways that teachers use talk for learning;
- understand when and how to move between different sorts of talk within lessons;
- know that direct teaching of oracy skills is essential.

THE CRUCIAL IMPORTANCE OF CLASSROOM TALK FOR LEARNING

Children learn not just through experience, but by talking about what they are doing. Talk precipitates thought, as children share ideas and comment on what they observe. In this way, children help one another to generate new understanding while stimulating curiosity, imagination and interest. Children talking may articulate tentative or more firmly entrenched ideas, make suggestions or offer information; children can hear and consider a range of alternative points of view. Classroom talk has the social function of helping the child to learn how effective communication gets things done. The 2014 Primary National Curriculum emphasises both the importance of children's talk, and the importance of direct teaching of the relevant skills:

Spoken language

6.2 Pupils should be taught to speak clearly and convey ideas confidently using Standard English. They should learn to justify ideas with reasons; ask questions to check understanding; develop vocabulary and build knowledge; negotiate; evaluate and build on the ideas of others; and select the appropriate register for effective communication. They should be taught to give well-structured descriptions and explanations and develop their understanding through speculating, hypothesising and exploring ideas. This will enable them to clarify their thinking as well as organise their ideas for writing.

(Department for Education [DfE], 2014)

We must teach children essential oracy skills; we can't assume they will learn them indirectly. Within the classroom, we need to teach and organise the sort of educationally effective talk that we know will help everyone to develop, think and learn. We need to be able to say what *talk for learning* is, and be able to describe what it sounds like and achieves. We need to identify and teach *oracy skills*.

WHAT IS TALK FOR LEARNING?

We can start by saying what it is not. Every teacher is aware that children's talk is not so easily focused on learning. Children are marvellous beings: imaginative, funny, charming and inconsequential, but also anarchic and self-centred. Classrooms put children in a social setting in which much is expected of them in terms of behaviour and concentration. They can, and do, use language in ways we find difficult. They contradict one another, are unkind, insensitive or rude; they come up with irrelevant or oblique comments; they shout, laugh or don't speak at all; they make jokes and distract others; they talk but do not listen; their concentration wavers, and their thoughts drift off to their homes, games or friends. This is all fine – we want our children to be natural, chatty and confident. But we also want them to focus their minds on the educational task in hand. So we comment on talk in terms of behaviour: 'Everyone's being lovely and quiet'; 'Stop talking now please'; 'You need to listen, and no-one can listen if you're talking'.

Children do need to learn how to be quietly attentive. They also need to learn how and why to talk and listen to one another in ways that support everyone's learning.

Whole-class talk

Children's everyday experiences and their willingness to talk about them are invaluable resources. Children may rely on the teacher to tap into the minds of others on their behalf. Teachers can establish an ethos of mutual respect for ideas and opinions. Developing an environment in which every child has the confidence to be open is a slow process, which can be aided by the direct teaching of the knowledge, skills and understanding needed to contribute to whole-class talk.

Group talk

Children's expectations of their contribution to group talk differ enormously from what we may optimistically imagine. The moment adult attention is withdrawn, a group left to work together may find it very hard to focus on the artificial, complex and sometimes less than fascinating learning intentions that the curriculum demands. Again, direct tuition of talk skills and an understanding of why talk is so important for learning can help children to take part in effective discussions with one another in a small-group setting. The chance to hear a range of ideas or points of view can be truly motivating; children taught how to discuss things enjoy the experience and are better able to stay on task.

So what is talk for learning? Talk for learning is educationally effective talk; it is talk that is focused on the task in hand, is inclusive and equitable, and helps everyone to gain new understanding, or to articulate their inability to understand. Like everything else good that goes on in classrooms, it is unlikely to happen unless we teachers organise it; we cannot leave this to chance. We can consider ways of organising talk for learning in two common classroom contexts:

- whole-class talk between teacher and class: *dialogic teaching*;
- children working in groups with their classmates: *exploratory talk*.

Much (though by no means all) talk for learning falls into these two contexts. A brief description of each follows, with references to further information and a summary of key points in Tables 3.6.1 and 3.6.2.

DIALOGIC TEACHING

Dialogic teaching can be described as teaching in which the teacher is aware of the power of dialogue and creates everyday opportunities to engage children in dialogue (Alexander, 2006; Scott and Asoko, 2006). During whole-class dialogue, children are expected to contribute not just brief 'right' answers, but more lengthy explanations in which they go into detail about what they do, or do not, know or understand. They listen attentively and are prepared to contribute. In this way, children

TABLE 3.6.1 Dialogic teaching: Talk between a teacher and a class of children

Purpose	Children summarise and share their thinking, express hypothetical ideas, admit to lack of understanding, listen to and reflect on other points of view, follow a line of reasoning
Organisation	Everyone can see and hear one another
During dialogic teaching …	Children pay attention to each other's words, take extended turns, ask one another questions or challenge ideas
	The teacher chains responses into a coherent whole, orchestrates the talk, may speak very little themselves
Talk tools	What is your opinion/idea …? Could you say more? Have you considered …?
Ground rules	Children explain their thinking, ask questions, admit lack of understanding, reason, listen attentively and follow the discussion
	Teacher elicits contributions and maintains a focus on a line of thinking or reasoning
Outcomes	Shared understanding and developing knowledge; respect for ideas; awareness of the limits of understanding; productive questioning and learning

TABLE 3.6.2 Exploratory talk: Talk between groups of children with no adult support

Purpose	Joint problem-solving; sharing of ideas, opinions and reasons; negotiation
Organisation	Three children seated near one another, around a table
During exploratory talk …	All are invited to contribute; ideas and opinions are offered with reasons; information is shared; the group seeks to reach agreement; everyone listens; the group is on task
Talk tools	What do you think? Why do you think that? I agree because … I disagree because …
Ground rules	Everyone is invited to speak; contributions are treated with respect; reasons are asked for, and given; ideas are considered fully before agreement is reached
Outcomes	Group agreement on a joint solution, idea or course of action. Group responsibility for decisions

and teachers reflect on and modify ideas. The teacher orchestrates the discussion to lead children through a line of thinking. Crucially, there is time to deliberate, elaborate and listen to tentative ideas.

The value of teachers using a dialogic approach has been demonstrated by two large scale classroom-based studies. Researchers recorded talk of 72 Year 6 classes (children aged 11). Some classes gained significantly better results in national tests (SATs) of Maths and English (Howe et al., 2019). These were children who regularly took part in whole-class discussions. Teachers encouraged children to question ideas through talk and elaborate their thoughts, and to talk and work well together in groups.

And a research project involving 76 English primary schools found similar benefits for Year 5 children's attainment in Maths, Science and English. Teachers were trained to be more dialogic and regularly discussed ideas with their class (Alexander, 2020).

There is substantial evidence to show that the ways teachers use spoken language has a significant impact on the quality of classroom education and its outcomes for curriculum learning. Gains in understanding taught subjects and confidence in oracy skills feed into a spiral of raised achievement for the child.

An effective lesson mixes dialogic episodes with more authoritative episodes, in which the teacher sums up or clarifies the discussion and offers clear explanations; sometimes, we just need to tell children things, and they just need to listen and think. They are much more likely to do so before or after relevant dialogue.

What does dialogic teaching look and sound like?

Dialogic teaching is characterised by purposeful listening, a willingness to offer ideas or to make problems with learning explicit, and teacher contributions that keep the children talking. This might mean that one child is encouraged to hold the floor, or another to talk about problems with their work in a way that helps their classmates to identify solutions or strategies. Contributions are linked to generate an overall 'bigger picture' through which children can make connections with previous learning. A feature of dialogue is that questions are raised that, instead of leading to immediate, brief answers, lead to further questions, a discussion of detail or recognition that more information is required. Such talk fosters children's natural curiosity.

EXPLORATORY TALK

During exploratory talk children engage one another in a good discussion. Children are aware of the importance of their contributions and take responsibility for their own learning and that of the others in their group. Each child is encouraged to speak. All information is shared. Opinions are backed up with reasons and discussed with respect. The talk may be hesitant or speculative, as half-formed ideas are tentatively suggested, or particular points may be taken up and elaborated in some detail. Children may not be aware that this is what we require when we ask them to work in a group; they need direct teaching of the essential oracy skills and understanding (Mercer and Littleton, 2007).

Exploratory talk requires shared motivation and purpose; when it happens, it enables children in a group to achieve more than each child would alone, whatever their ability. Crucially, their talk with classmates enables the child to learn a powerful way to think clearly as an individual.

What does exploratory talk look and sound like?

Children are able to use questions as talk tools – 'What do you think?', 'Why do you think that?' – and as prompts – ''What happened ...', 'Please explain ...'. They offer hypothetical ideas – 'What if ...?', 'But ...' – and elaborate on ideas – 'Yes, but remember when we did this before, we ...'. They listen attentively to one another and their talk is courteous and purposeful, characterised by challenge and explicit reasoning. Every child in the group can give an account or summary of the discussion, having been fully engaged in it.

WHEN AND HOW TO MOVE BETWEEN TYPES OF TALK

Planning talk times is essential. We have to rely on our professional expertise to decide when and how to switch between types of talk.

- *Whole-class introductory dialogue* requires authoritative input; clear instruction, explanation or information. We can check for knowledge: 'What did we do last week?', 'Remind us of the difference between an isosceles and equilateral triangle?' Some questions might be targeted at individuals: the question 'Maia, what is your answer to this?' is a way of ensuring Maia's involvement without actually saying, 'Are you listening, Maia?' After a series of such closed questions, children are not usually learning much. Some children always involve themselves with such 'teacher's question'; some opt out. It is not motivating to know that the questioner already knows the answer.

  Introductions benefit from more complex dialogue with genuine questions: 'What do you already know about ...?', 'Has anyone heard of anything about this that might help us ...?', 'What is your experience of this ...?'.

- *Group work* requires children to take part in exploratory talk. The teacher's role is to ensure that the children have been taught relevant oracy skills, and to support the children's talk. We can model exploratory talk as we move around groups: 'Could you give a reason please?', 'Does anyone have any more information we can think about?', 'Has everyone been asked for their ideas?'

  A problem with exploratory talk is that a persuasive argument can sway a whole group into believing things that are not necessarily true. However, as the talk is part of an ongoing classroom dialogue, the group is subsequently able to hear other ideas from their classmates and can reconsider. Ideas considered during discussion may not be firmly held until the child has had a chance to check them against practical experience and the ideas of others. Thinking about new ideas – 'weighing things up', reflecting on how new ideas fit with one's own current thinking – is a learning process and an invaluable experience for a child.

- *Whole-class closing plenary sessions* require dialogue that brings together the children's ideas from group work. The teacher's role is to orchestrate the dialogue and ultimately provide some summary authoritative information. Dialogic teaching can be thought of as including episodes of exploratory talk and episodes of authoritative teacher input, which will later contribute to further dialogue. Plenary discussion should bring out children's thinking about new concepts and also about the quality of the talk that took place in their group. You can ask children to suggest who offered ideas, listened carefully, asked an important question, and so on.

Task 3.6.1 Children's classroom talk

Listen carefully to children's classroom talk in two contexts – a whole class in discussion with a teacher, and a small-group discussion with no adult support. Ask yourself questions about the purpose, organisation and outcomes of the talk:

- *Purpose*: What is the purpose of the talk? Is everyone aware of this purpose? Is the talk fulfilling its purpose?
- *Organisation*: Who is organising the talk? How do people bid for turns? Who gets a turn and why? What happens to people who do not get a turn? Is any of the talk to do with behaviour management? Does the talk always stay on task?
- *Outcomes*: What are the outcomes of the talk? What have different individuals learned about the topic under discussion, and how to communicate effectively with others?

DIRECT TEACHING OF ORACY SKILLS

The Cambridge Oracy Skills Framework sets out a structure for teaching oracy skills. For example, children may seem unable to explain their ideas aloud. Breaking this skill of 'explanation' down into small steps can provide oracy learning intentions; these can be paired up with curriculum learning intentions.

For example, 'Explain':

1. Describe something very familiar to a trusted partner.
2. Describe the same thing to a larger group with prompts from a partner.
3. Share a resource (picture, poem, piece of music, science puzzle) with a partner and decide what to say about it. Share ideas and questions. Explain ideas to and with one another.
4. Explain ideas about the resource to a larger group.

Oracy skills for listening, discussion, dialogue and presentation can be taught this way, in parallel with curriculum content, enhancing the child's curriculum experience whilst developing their spoken language skills.

RAISING CHILDREN'S AWARENESS OF TALK FOR LEARNING

Organising effective talk involves raising children's awareness of the power of spoken language. Children need to know that they contribute to the learning of others through sharing their thoughts.

The teacher is a powerful model for educationally effective talk. The phrases we use, such as 'What do you think?', 'Can you explain your reason please?', 'Can you say a bit more about ...?', are exactly what we want children to say to one another. You can point that out to them. Encouraging someone to keep talking, making links between contributions, rephrasing and summing up are all skills children learn from experience, especially if they happen often and are explicitly discussed as talk strategies.

We all know that group work can go wrong. The classroom becomes too noisy, or little learning seems to be happening. Children in a group may bicker or deliberately ignore one another; they may feel that talk is not helping their own learning, or that others are 'cheating' if they want to talk about their answers. Ask children what they think of group work. Groups may dip in and out of exploratory talk, just as adults working together do.

We know that talk is essential for learning. This is a real paradox and a problem for every teacher. We want to ensure effective group talk; the alternative is, we must insist on quiet. The command 'Please be quiet!' immediately confines each child to their own thoughts – sometimes, an uneasy silence reigns. Are we sure they are thinking about their work? Silence is a behaviour management strategy and not always conducive to developing minds. No doubt quiet has some value, but not if it is overused, and not when a child is trying to puzzle something out, explain something, use a recently heard word, ask a question or find out a missing piece of information. Silence cannot guarantee that children are thinking and learning about the topic in hand.

So, 'talk lessons' are necessary – that is, before you expect them to conduct a good discussion, children need direct teaching about exploratory talk. We need to make explicit the usually hidden 'ground rules' that keep a discussion on track (Dawes, 2008, 2011).

What oracy skills are needed? In essence, the ground rules that children need are to:

- listen;
- stay on task;
- include everyone;
- know how to ask what others think and why;
- respect contributions;
- ask questions;
- elaborate and explain.

Learning intentions for oracy teaching can focus on these skills. There are innumerable contexts for talk throughout the curriculum and an oracy focus can run through everyday lessons. After an activity in which groups have talked about their thinking, plenary discussion about the effectiveness of talk can help children to build up an awareness of their ability to contribute to one another's learning, and can help groups to establish an ethos of exploratory talk. Importantly, the child's own world of talk, that is their accent, bilingualism, vocabulary, dialect and indeed personality, is valued rather than diminished by learning exploratory talk as an extension to their talk repertoire.

So, we can discuss and model relevant oracy skills during introductory sessions, identify them as learning intentions and review them during plenary sessions, and thus help children to experience and evaluate the difference that effective talk makes. Children need constant chances to reflect on what they have said and heard, in order to examine what they have learned, and how, and who from. They need opportunities to identify particular talk episodes that helped them to understand something, or caught their imagination, or made them feel puzzled. It has to be made clear to children that knowledge and understanding are not simply contained in the teacher, computers or books, but in the class as a whole, and that, by talking and thinking together, such understandings can be profitably shared. They can usefully learn the term 'interthinking' – thinking aloud together – as a description of the spoken mechanism for creating joint understanding (Littleton and Mercer, 2013). Children given a direct insight into the idea of interthinking, and taught oracy skills to take part in interthinking, can see how to find out what others think, and why. They can articulate their own ideas. They can include themselves in the everyday educational conversations of their classroom. For some children, this makes a huge difference to their engagement. For others, it overcomes barriers caused by wider social issues or their personal inhibitions. For all children, interthinking is a life skill.

A Year 6 example of a teacher both modelling and eliciting the ground rules for exploratory talk

Teacher: How are your Thinking Together skills going to help you with that? Why do you need to do that in your Thinking Together group? Kelly?
Kelly: We need to talk about it.
Teacher: Why do you think we need to talk about it?
Kelly: To get more ideas.
Teacher: Excellent. If we talk about it we might have more ideas than just working on our own.
A sif: And because you can't just think that it's the answer when somebody else has got another idea – you have to check with the group – see what they think.
Teacher: So if I walk around the classroom while everybody is talking together in their groups I wonder what kind of things might I hear people saying?
Asif: 'What do you think?'
Teacher: That's a good one. Why is that an important question Carl?
Carl: Because you ask someone else their opinion.
Sarah: 'I think this – because.'
Teacher: Why did you add 'because' to the end of that sentence?
Sarah: Because then they know why you made that remark.
Teacher: Well done. Brilliant. You need to explain so that everybody understands what you think.

(Mercer and Sams, 2006)

A Year 4 example of Talk for Writing

Yasmin found it hard to put ideas on paper; Alfie refused to write words he could not spell accurately. The teacher paired friends for a new writing activity and asked, 'Why do you like your friend?' The children talked about this in groups of four, while the teacher modelled exploratory talk and jotted down key phrases and sentences. She then provided each pair with a copy of what she had written and asked them to read this together and to decide on any changes. Once this was done – with all children contributing some of the ideas in writing – she combined their ideas to create poems, such as:

Friends

I like my friend because he's funny and he's strong.
My friend is really pretty and she helps me all the time.
She helps me carry things.
My friend passes the ball to me,
He is on my side in football.
If he's not playing I'm not playing.
I can ask my friend anything. And she asks me.
My friend has time to give me.

This piece of writing was then available for handwriting, display, to take home, illustrate, read and re-read and act as a model for other pairs of friends writing in the class. There was also a chance to concentrate on spelling specific words such as 'friend', 'football', 'passes'; and to look at punctuation to convey meaning.

> **Task 3.6.2 New vocabulary**
>
> Discuss with colleagues how they tackle teaching new vocabulary. How frequently does this happen? How do they ensure new words are put to use? Can we link oracy, reading and writing?

Children learn vocabulary by hearing new words using them – the more the better! The written symbols of the English language represent sounds, and reading is what happens when sounds are put back into texts. So, reading and speaking are inextricably linked, and a child's capacity to read is profoundly dependent on their oracy skills. New vocabulary accumulates through listening and speaking.

> **Task 3.6.3 Children's rules for classroom talk**
>
> Discuss with a group of three or four children:
>
> - When they are working in a group with classmates, who do they like to work with and why? What do they like or dislike about working in a group with other children? Why do they think that teachers ask them to work in groups?
> - Ask them to suggest a list of five or six positive 'rules', which, if applied, would help a group to work well together.
> - Have the same discussion with the whole class. Collate ideas to establish a class set of ground rules for exploratory talk. Devise an activity that requires group discussion and ask the children to apply their rules. Did the rules help everyone to join in and share ideas? If not, can the class alter them?

PLANNING FOR EXPLORATORY TALK

During planning, pair up an oracy learning objective for talk with your curriculum learning objective. In this way, you can teach skills that are tailored to class or individual needs, practise their use, and reflect on their effectiveness in closing plenary discussions, within curriculum contexts. Plan time for discussion. Talk invariably takes longer than you would imagine; unless you plan for discussion time, children will lose the chance to articulate, develop and reflect on their ideas, use new vocabulary and generally thinking things through.

Example 3.6.1 is a brief lesson outline with a science context for talk.

> **Example 3.6.1 Science and talk lesson**
>
> Learning intentions:
>
> - offer reasons and evidence for ideas, considering alternative opinions;
> - identify some starting ideas about the topic of friction.
>
> *Introduction*
>
> Ask children to explain to one another what the words *reasons*, *evidence* and *alternative* opinions mean; share with the class and clarify definitions. Then ask groups to use this understanding to talk about *friction*; what does everyone already know?
>
> *Group work*
>
> Ask groups to discuss the following *Talking Points* (Dawes, 2012).
>
> *Talking points: Friction*
>
> True or false, or is your group unsure? Make sure you give reasons for what you say.
>
> 1. Grip is another word for friction.
> 2. Friction always happens when surfaces are moving against each other.
> 3. Friction is usually a nuisance.
> 4. Trainers have friction built into the soles.
>
> Focus the children on active listening and ask them to try to remember something that they think is particularly interesting from their group talk.
>
> *Plenary*
>
> 1. *Science*: Choose a talking point to discuss. Ask groups to contribute ideas about friction; what were contradictory opinions? Ask groups to explain their ideas and reasons. Sum up, or ask a child to sum up, the outcome of the discussion.
> 2. *Talk for learning*: Ask the class to suggest classmates who offered ideas, listened well, gave good reasons, summed up discussions and helped negotiation.
>
> Finish by asking children to reflect, recall and share examples of productive talk; who gave an *opinion* and what was their *reason*? Follow up with practical activity in which children have a chance to learn about friction through experience.

LISTENING

It can be useful to track a child during their school day. Who listens to them? Do they have a voice in the classroom? Some do; they are heard. They contribute. Others may not have the skills to be in this position. Every child should have a voice if the class is to learn well and as a whole. This is a key point; the class must be aware that they are not in competition for learning. We are not teaching to leave some behind and to give others advantage, but for general development. Listening to classmates is essential if all voices are to be heard. The oracy skills of listening – attending, considering words and ideas, reflecting and responding – can be developed once they are made explicit. Listening for learning is a very active process and quite demanding, but ultimately truly satisfying and rewarding. Children need to experience such listening so that they can appreciate its rewards and take pride in their own listening skills. Whole books and websites are devoted to describing and explaining listening. Briefly, listening for learning is not innate and not something that just happens. A week at the start of every term might be usefully dedicated to taking part in listening activities, with the aim of ensuring that every child understands how to hear and process spoken language, how to reflect and respond appropriately and thus how to enjoy their own learning.

SUMMARY

We can plan to teach oracy skills; children should be taught as much about talk as they are about reading and writing.

Dialogic teaching is a means to move whole classes through steps of reasoning, speculation and insight, by valuing contributions and encouraging reflection. Dialogic teaching allows children to learn by changing their minds, literally; to understand that there is another point of view than their own. By employing a dialogic approach and simultaneously teaching children how to engage one another in exploratory talk, we offer them opportunities to work on their own thinking and that of others. Exploratory talk is educationally effective talk – talk for learning – and children need an awareness of what it is and why it's important. It does not happen naturally but depends on direct tuition of key oracy skills such as listening, reasoning, questioning, explaining and elaborating.

Talk for learning can only happen if we teach oracy skills throughout the curriculum, planning time for talk and using resources and activities that necessitate discussion. Every child needs to know how and why to listen actively if they are to develop their thinking and make the most of learning opportunities.

Effective teachers move between different types of talk as a lesson proceeds. Engaging children in talk for learning helps teachers to develop effective classroom relationships. Talking about what they are doing with their group motivates children and focuses their interest. The busy hum of a classroom in which children are discussing their work – a sure sign of a well-organised teacher – is a happy feature of effective primary schools. Teachers want to hear children talking as it is an indication of learning and a sign that children are practising the talk skills that will develop their minds throughout their education.

ANNOTATED FURTHER READING

Dawes, L. and Sams, C. (2017) *Talk Box: Activities for Teaching Oracy with Children aged 4-8*, 2nd edn, London: Routledge.

Talk Box contains comprehensive activities to teach talk skills, encourage interthinking and ensure that every child starts by learning to understand the repertoire of talk that will enable them to make the best progress in school.

FURTHER READING TO SUPPORT M-LEVEL STUDY

Mannion, J. and McAllister, K. (2020) *Fear Is The Mind Killer: Why Learning to Learn Deserves Lesson Time – and How to Make it Work for Your Pupils*, London: John Catt Publishing.
> The Learning Skills curriculum offers a systematic approach to helping students become more confident, practice, self-regulated learners.

Vermunt, J., Vrikki, M., Dudley, P. and Warwick, P. (2003) 'Relations between teacher learning patterns, personal and contextual factors, and learning outcomes in the context of Lesson Study', *Journal of Teaching and Teacher Education*, 133, October, 104295.
> An understanding of how teachers develop professional expertise, such as in the teaching of oracy skills, by evaluating their own teaching and that of colleagues.

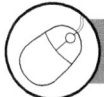

RELEVANT WEBSITES

Voice 21: https://voice21.org/wp-content/uploads/2023/01/Voice21-Impact-Report-2023-v21-web-1.pdf
> Voice 21's well-researched report into oracy teaching and learning and its impact for teachers and children in schools.

Thinking Together project: thinkingtogether.educ.cam.ac.uk
> A dialogue-based approach to thinking and learning in classrooms. This site offers links to classroom-based research and downloadable materials for classroom use.

Speech and Language UK: https://speechandlanguage.org.uk/talking-point/for-professionals/the-communication-trust/
> Providing resources to support everyone who works with children and young people, to develop children's capacity to understand and be understood through spoken language.

Oracy Skills Framework: https://oracycambridge.org/wp-content/uploads/2020/06/The-Oracy-Skills-Framework-and-Glossary.pdf
> The Oracy Skills Framework (OSF) specifies the various skills young people need to develop to deal with a range of different talk situations. This structure enables both direct teaching of oracy skills and assessment of needs.

Oracy Cambridge: https://oracycambridge.org/
> Promoting oracy in schools and society. Providing papers for governments and other organisations, training and consultancy for schools, research reports and a range of oracy information. Includes links to research mentioned in this chapter.

Voice 21: https://voice21.org/
> Supporting learning and life chances of young people through talk so that all children can use their voice for success in school and in life.

University of Cambridge: Faculty of Education: https://content.educ.cam.ac.uk/23-oracy-maths-attainment
> Recent research showing how oracy education has a positive impact on learning in maths.

REFERENCES

Alexander, R. J. (2020) *A Dialogic Teaching Companion*, Abingdon: Routledge.

Alexander, R. J. (2006) *Towards Dialogic Teaching*, York, UK: Dialogos.

Dawes, L. (2008) *The Essential Speaking and Listening: Talk for Learning at Key Stage 2*, London: Routledge.

Dawes, L. (2011) *Creating a Speaking and Listening Classroom: Integrating Talk for Learning at Key Stage 2*, London: Routledge.

Dawes, L. (2012) *Talking Points: Discussion Activities in the Primary Classroom*, London: Routledge.

Department for Education (DfE). (2014) *The National Curriculum*, DfE. Retrieved from: www.gov.uk/national-curriculum

Howe, C., Hennessy, S., Mercer, N. Vrikki, M. and Wheatley, L. (2019) 'Teacher-student dialogue during classroom teaching: Does it really impact upon student outcomes?' *Journal of the Learning Sciences*, 28(4-5): 462-512.

Littleton, K. and Mercer, N. (2013) *Interthinking: Putting Talk to Work*, London: Routledge.

Mercer, N. and Littleton, K. (2007) *Dialogue and the Development of Children's Thinking: A Sociocultural Approach*, London: Routledge.

Mercer, N. and Sams, C. (2006) 'Teaching children how to use language to solve maths problems', *Language and Education*, 20(6): 507-528.

Scott, P. H. and Asoko, H. (2006) 'Talk in science classrooms', in V. Wood-Robinson (ed.) *Association of Science Education Guide to Secondary Science Education*, Hatfield, UK: Association for Science Education (ASE), pp. 55-73.

Smith, H. and Higgins, S. (2006) 'Opening classroom interaction: The importance of feedback', *Cambridge Journal of Education*, 36(4): 485-502.

UNIT 3.7

THE VALUE OF OUTDOOR LEARNING

Stephen Pickering and Sophie Brookes

INTRODUCTION

For learning beyond the classroom's four walls to be truly valued, it needs to be considered by management, teachers, pupils and parents to be a fundamental element of every child's formal education. It should be seen to be as normal a part of school life as teaching indoors. Teaching outdoors can be fun, stimulating, exciting and rewarding, and it can be all of these things without being seen as a treat or reward. We all appreciate the importance of creating a vibrant environment within the school to aid the holistic development and progress of the children in our care. Working outside the classroom expands and enriches this learning environment across all curriculum areas.

HOW THE NATIONAL CURRICULUM SUPPORTS LEARNING OUTDOORS

Learning beyond the classroom is fully endorsed by the Early Years Foundation Stage (EYFS), where a strong emphasis is placed on the value of daily outdoor learning experiences for children's health, well-being and intellectual development (Department for Education [DfE], 2014: section 3.68, p. 26). It is also fully supported by the National Curriculum in England (DfE, 2013a) across a range of subject areas and is included within the Ofsted inspection framework (Prince and Diggory, 2023). Beyond emphasising the need for a broad, balanced curriculum in a holistic sense, the National Curriculum in England (DfE, 2013a) also states (in several areas), 'The national curriculum forms one part of the school curriculum' (DfE, 2013b: Section 2.2, p. 5). Simply put, this means that as well as teaching the National Curriculum through broad, balanced, safe environments, including the outdoor as well as the indoor environments, any school should develop its own school curriculum, of which the National Curriculum is a part. Every school has licence to develop a curriculum that reflects and develops understanding of local communities and beyond. So, if your school is in an urban environment, then explore that urban environment. If your school is very rural, then embrace the natural or farmed landscape as part of your curriculum.

DOI: 10.4324/9781032691794-17

192 Learning to Teach in the Primary School

In Northern Ireland ...

The Northern Ireland Council for Curriculum, Examination and Assessment describes the outdoors as 'one of the best possible learning environments. It provides children with an abundance of learning opportunities to develop negotiation skills, problem-solving, self-regulation strategies, social skills, and healthy relationships with their peers and adults, while creating a sense of adventure' (Council for the Curriculum Examinations and Assessment [CCEA], 2022: 4).

Regular learning outdoors is encouraged throughout the curriculum and the CCEA provides guidance through a series of online pdfs that can easily be accessed and will provide ideas for schools throughout the UK.

In Wales ...

Outdoor learning is essential to achieve the four purposes of Curriculum for Wales. Outdoor learning provides authentic contexts for many of the statements of what matters to be achieved. Outdoor learning provides a rich environment to develop and deliver the twelve pedagogical principles.

(Welsh Government, 2023a: 42)

In Scotland ...

Outdoor learning is seen as an essential element of social, emotional, intellectual and physical learning. The sites of learning may range from urban to rural spaces across Scotland to 'the rest of the world'.

Sources: Education Scotland (2020); The Scottish Government (2017)

OBJECTIVES

By the end of this unit, you should be able to:

- appreciate the value and benefits of children experiencing outdoor environments and of developing learning beyond the classroom;
- identify and plan opportunities to make effective and enjoyable use of outdoor spaces;
- plan to support the holistic development of children in your class through learning outdoors;
- help to develop your knowledge so that you have an increased awareness and confidence to teach outside.

HOW THE TEACHERS' STANDARDS SUPPORT TEACHING OUTDOORS

Taking children outside to learn can help to demonstrate excellence in a range of the Teachers' Standards (DfE, 2011), including: 'setting high expectations which inspire, motivate and challenge pupils' (Standard 1), planning and teaching 'well-structured lessons' (Standard 4) and 'managing behaviour effectively to ensure a good and safe learning environment' (Standard 7), to name just three. Indeed, the Teachers' Standards can be used as a helpful guide for all when planning teaching outside.

Task 3.7.1 Reflection

It is valuable to reflect upon your own understanding and experiences of learning and taking part in outdoor activities, not just as part of your schooling, but also through other outdoor activities such as Scouts and Guides, camps or adventurous pursuits and travel that you may have engaged in.

- For each of a range of outdoor experiences that you may have had, reflect on and note down how you felt and what you learned. Remember that learning is not just about knowledge gained, but also about challenges managed and experiences learned from.
- Could the learning, or the style of learning, you experienced in outdoor activities not associated with school be replicated through taking a class of children outdoors to learn?
- Discuss whether children should always be aware of the learning outcomes. And, if so, whether this is always possible. Should learning outcomes focus on the acquisition of knowledge alone?

THE BENEFITS OF LEARNING AND TEACHING OUTDOORS

There is clear evidence to support the benefits of regular school-based learning activities outdoors (Waite, Roberts and Lambert, 2020; Mann et al., 2022; Prince and Diggory, 2023). These benefits include improvements in academic and social skills, health and well-being. Additionally, there is evidence that teaching outdoors has a positive impact on teachers' teaching skills, professional development and job satisfaction (Waite, Roberts and Lambert, 2020). A small-scale global survey found that the trend for outdoor learning within the UK is positive: 'In the UK, 64% of primary schools take lessons outdoors once a week or more; 12% go out every day; 12% go out less than once a month' (Project Dirt, 2018: 4). This is super news, with the cautionary note that the survey was on a small-scale, and additionally the same survey found that 99% of primary teachers in the UK believe that learning outdoors is 'critical for children to reach their full potential' (p. 3). This should be set against the findings of Cutler (2016), that fewer children spend time outdoors on a regular basis outside the school environment. A report on learning outdoors in Scottish primary schools found that since the Covid-19 pandemic, the amount of time spent learning outdoors has increased from 36% of early years children to 39%, but has decreased with primary aged children to an average of just 'seven minutes per week' (Mannion et al., 2023). A lack of teacher confidence is cited as the primary reason for the recent decrease (Mannion et al., 2023). The value of learning and teaching outdoors is clearly evidenced and it is even more important when set against the trend for children to spend less time outdoors when not in school. So how can we break down the value of learning and teaching outdoors to a practical, school-based situation.

The benefits of learning and teaching outdoors operate on many levels:

1 *Cognition*: Outdoor environments tend to be messy places, and, by messy, I do not necessarily mean that they are muddy, wet and dirty (although sometimes they are), but that they are disordered (Pickering, 2017b). Forests, woodlands, playgrounds, beaches and urban areas are complex places and as such provide many opportunities for problem-solving, planning and enquiry-based work. Take, for example, den building. Children have a complex set of issues to manage and resolve when constructing and creating a den that is large, safe and secure enough to house a group of children, with irregular materials and a short timescale (Hallam, Gallagher and Harvey, 2021). There are clear links to design and technology, mathematics, and science, and the questions that may well arise can also include history and geography as part of the learning curricula. More important for the learner, though, than the teacher's ability to monitor rich cross-curricular learning, is the fact that the children will be engaging in a wide range of thinking skills and a variety of learning processes. The outdoors can become an intellectually playful classroom where children are encouraged to reflect deeply, monitor progress and modify their approach until they achieve success. Even failure can be fun and is also a valid learning experience. Children will develop their own questioning skills as they learn to collaborate on the task. Children tend to work very happily and independently with the freedom that learning outside provides, but the learning skills and processes used by the children can be brought back into the classroom with some judicious plenary work by the teacher. Metacognition simply means becoming aware of your own thinking. If, as a teacher, you can help children to reflect on and understand the thinking skills that they used to build the den, then later, perhaps back in the classroom, you can help children to re-engage with such skills gained for other problem-solving exercises. So, for example, the child stuck on a maths problem in the classroom can be reminded that she achieved success with the den by sorting and categorising the sticks before using them and then planning how best to apply them. 'Can you do the same type of thing to solve this maths problem?'

2 *Health and well-being*: Every one of us, I think, has experienced the restorative effect of being outside to a certain extent. Just think about how our breathing often relaxes when we step outside, or about the feeling of having done something good, when we step back inside after a walk. We all have a sense that being outside is good. But just how good can it be, and can time spent outside with children during a school day be justified as an important part of their learning and development? Teachers, after all, face constant time pressure with a bulging curriculum. There has been a wealth of research on the health and well-being impact of outdoor experiences in childhood over many years. The 'biophilia hypothesis' (Wilson, 1984) focuses on emotional, cognitive and aesthetic development. Attention Restoration Theory (Kaplan and Kaplan, 1989) emphasises how the restorative effect of being outside helps children learn to become better focused. Nature Deficit Disorder (Louv, 2005) is thought to occur where a lack of time spent outdoors can lead to heightened stress, anxiety and behaviour issues. More recent work by Mann *et al*. (2022) has collated research literature that examines the health and learning benefits of outdoor learning. As a teacher, I always found enormous – although not always immediately apparent – benefits in chatting to individual children while walking along the path that led to the school's Forest School site. There is an undeniable freedom that children enjoy when outside walking to something they love, and this is a super opportunity to let children open up about events and thoughts in their life – both positive and negative. This is precious time for teachers and children, and the space afforded by time outside helps children to relax into their lives, focus on something different and recharge their batteries during busy school weeks.

3. *Motivation and aspiration*: Children love creating things, experimenting and trying things out. They love to learn by doing. Experiential learning is motivational. There is neurological evidence (Goswami, 2008), but this can perhaps be described more simply as learning through a process of hand to heart to head. Children engage actively with a subject by touching and feeling, moving, building and working with tools and resources. The very texture of wood, or mud, or soft grass, or even bricks, promotes some form of emotional response, and this is coupled with the satisfaction of achieving a task independently, or problem-solving, or working as a group. Learning fixes in the brain for longer if it passes through the brain's emotional receptors, and so this emotional response is crucial for developing learning and learning skills. And then, during the activity, and afterwards too, children will think and reflect. They will engage in reasoning skills, justifying why they completed the activity in a certain way or synthesising a range of suggested ideas to complete the task. In other words, learning outdoors provides the opportunity for learning to pass through the hands to the heart to the head and, in so doing, become better fixed in the learning memory and more satisfying to complete. Success motivates children to achieve more, but failure can do so, too, if failure is seen as part of learning and is used as a platform from which to develop new skills, ideas and practices. This way of thinking is not new. Vygotsky's theories of learning and child development run deeper than a simplistic understanding of constructivism. Vygotsky described how social interaction is the cornerstone of learning, based within a cultural construct. Learners collaborate and learn as they participate. Barfod and Mygind (2022) attest to advantages of this holistic style of learning outside with their work on *Udeskole*, the Danish system for learning outdoors. Beyond the classroom walls, pupils tend to be free of the behaviourist – reward and sanction – classroom management practices that Vygotsky railed against in early twentieth-century Russia and that are still apparent in many classrooms today. Deep learning can develop through enjoyable, motivational activities in accord with constructivist processes of development.

4. *Responsibility and independence*: Forest School philosophy advocates pedagogies based on allowing children to experience and learn over a long period of time (www.forestschoolassociation.org). I have known teachers to become frustrated with the repetitive nature of some children's activities while out on Forest School. Given the choice, for example, some children will head straight into den building every week. There is an argument that, although such practice may well be repetitive and thus limit new learning, it may serve a very important part of a child's development. In permitting children to develop their own learning experiences while offering a range of opportunities, responsibility and independent incremental learning are nurtured. Outdoor activities are very experience-based, and not just through the joy of exploring outdoor environments, but also through the social learning that can develop. Consider the montage of photos in Figure 3.7.1.

Robin was determined to set up a swing with some rope he had, but he couldn't reach the branch. When Robin wanted help in a classroom situation, he tended to put his hand up and wait for help to arrive. If it didn't arrive, then he would either just sit there, or go and confront the teacher or teaching assistant. On seeing that there was no help readily available, and being determined to succeed, he looked around, spied a log used for sitting on, rolled it until it was under the branch and then, through a process of trial and error, finally managed to stand on it and reach the branch. By this time, he had attracted a small audience and so he then proudly demonstrated how he could reach the branch and he helped his friends to do the same. This is a very simple example of the type of practice that occurs in Forest Schools and other similar outdoor provisions every day, up and down the country, but within such simple steps taken there is a great deal of learning. The slow or 'eco pedagogical approach' (Payne and Wattchow, 2009; Carlsen and Clark, 2022) provides time for children to work things out for themselves. This is a clear demonstration of constructive, incremental learning: pausing to think about the resources

FIGURE 3.7.1 Learning through independent play
Source: Stephen Pickering

to hand, reviewing and problem-solving. And there are the additional aspects of multisensory learning: the thrill of finally reaching up to grab the branch will remain with Robin and help to cement the thinking skills needed to achieve success again, coupled with the additional personal satisfaction of then helping others – learning is social!

5 *Collaboration and communication*: Froebel advocated the importance of play as a learning tool in the early nineteenth century, describing it as 'the serious business of childhood' (Froebel, in Carroll and McCullogh, 2014: 31). Play promotes the effective use of imagination and creativity, self-expression and the development of many skills, such as language acquisition, emotional intelligence, social skills and, importantly, the constructivist process of 'the capacity to act and to recognise that actions have consequences' (James and James, 2004: 24). There is an important element of playing outdoors that adds scope to the development of imagination. Within the classroom, children's play makes use of purpose-made resources: a toy car is a car, a plastic dinosaur is a plastic dinosaur. In a woodland, children have little more than twigs and leaves, mud and stones. But this fosters creativity and imagination. A stick can be a car, or a plane, a fairy home or a magic wand. The unconstructed and messy nature of natural resources provides greater freedom to develop imagination and imaginative play. And, because one child's entrance to a secret medieval kingdom may look like just a hole in a bush to another child, there is a natural development of communication skills: of talking and listening, describing and contributing, taking part and acceptance.

In Northern Ireland ...

The outdoor play area is one of the best possible learning environments. It provides children with an abundance of learning opportunities to develop negotiation skills, problem-solving, self-regulation strategies, social skills, and healthy relationships with their peers and adults, while creating a sense of adventure.

[…]

Outdoors, children can experience freedom through risk–benefit assessed play, where they can play and socialise freely and use their own imagination and initiative. Progress in all the Areas of Learning can be achieved outside while the children's long-term social, emotional and mental health are being enhanced. Being physically active, spending time outdoors and connecting with nature can affect emotions and allow for relaxation, calmness and a heightened sense of wellbeing.

(CCEA, 2022: 4)

In Wales ...

Outdoor learning promotes lifelong learning and develops critical thinking.

The natural world is the best resource to stimulate children's curiosity and desire, so that learning comes from doing, seeing, hearing, touching and smelling.

Outdoor experiences promote independence and can build a child's confidence.

Outdoor learning can develop attitudes which contribute towards a greener Wales.

> Emotional health and wellbeing can be improved through opportunities in the natural environment.
>
> Outdoor activities provide children with the opportunity to challenge themselves and take appropriate risks.
>
> (Welsh Government, 2023a: 30)

In Scotland …

> The core values of *Curriculum for Excellence* (LTS, 2010) resonate with long-standing key concepts of outdoor learning. Challenge, enjoyment, relevance, depth, development of the whole person and an adventurous approach to learning are at the core of outdoor pedagogy. The outdoor environment encourages staff and students to see each other in a different light, building positive relationships and improving self-awareness and understanding of others.
>
> (Learning and Teaching Scotland, 2010: 7)
>
> The Scottish Government has set up a range of resources to help schools develop outdoor learning through their curricula. These can be easily accessed for all on https://education.gov.scot/resources/support-for-professional-development-in-outdoor-learning/(Published 01/01/2017. Last updated 11/04/2023). There is an emphasis on support for creative and sustainable approaches and there is a range of resources to support outdoor learning across all subject areas.
>
> (Learning and Teaching Scotland, 2010)

PREPARING TO TEACH OUTDOORS

First, you must consider how the learning outcomes, and by this, I mean all that you wish the children to gain academically, socially and in terms of developing further skills for learning, can best be served by activities outside or inside. When you are planning a lesson, remember that the whole lesson does not have to be in one set environment, so consider how the needs of the children are best met at each stage of the lesson. Part of these lesson-planning decisions involve looking at the bigger picture of children's learning, too. How would a lesson outside contribute to more than just the lesson itself, but as part of a whole programme of holistic education?

Task 3.7.2 Planning for learning

When completing a planning sequence, ask yourself: Am I able to take this outside? What adaptations are needed to make this possible?

The first step is to consider the learning outcome for the teaching sequence. Next draw out a simple mindmap including all subjects that are included within this planning sequence. The final stage is to map out the learning objectives with possible outdoor learning opportunities. Figures 3.7.2 and 3.7.3 show an example of a mindmap linking with Year 1 National Curriculum for England objectives.

Complete your own mindmap for outdoor learning. Choose three subjects from your next teaching sequence. For each subject identify one or more activities that you could do in the outdoor environment to support learning.

FIGURE 3.7.2 How many triangles can the children make?
Source: Sophie Brookes

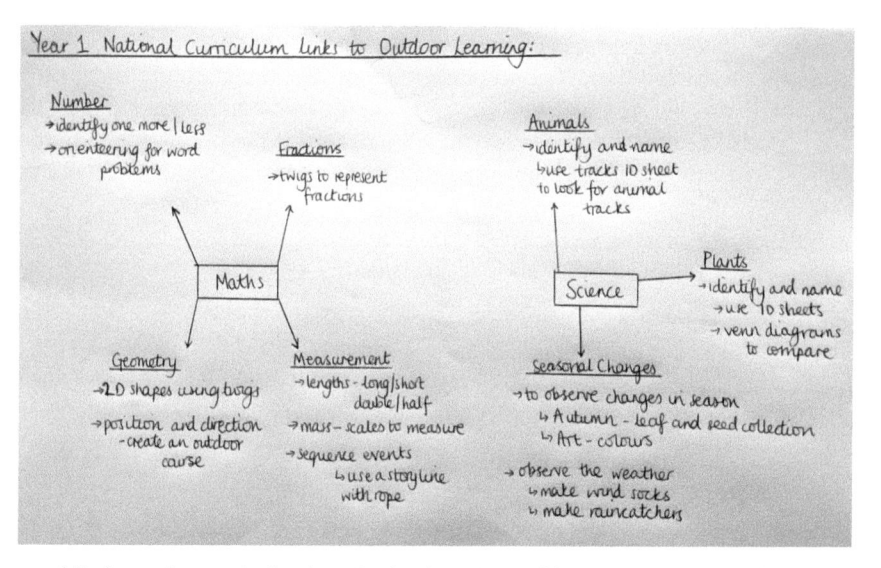

FIGURE 3.7.3 Mindmap demonstrating how topics from two subject areas may be delivered in an outdoor environment
Source: Sophie Brookes

> **In Wales ...**
>
> Being outdoors is particularly important for learners in this period of learning. Learning outdoors can lead to high levels of well-being, confidence and engagement. In an outdoor environment, learners can explore, practise and enhance their skills. To maximise the potential of being outdoors, learners need enabling adults who understand the importance and value of it. Being outdoors supports social, emotional, spiritual and physical development, as well as providing authentic opportunities for learners to develop and consolidate cross-curricular skills.
>
> The outdoors provides opportunities to inspire awe and wonder, and allows learners to be themselves in open, relaxed and stimulating spaces. The use of natural and open-ended resources enhances the development of imagination, creativity and curiosity. Rich and authentic opportunities outdoors stimulate learners' senses through what they hear, touch, see and smell, and encourage them to express themselves.
>
> Learners who are able to engage and connect with the natural world can build an empathy for the environment, showing an awareness of their potential impact on the living world. They can begin to explore the concept of sustainability in a practical way. Exploring the outdoors provides opportunities for learners to develop a sense of place within their immediate surroundings, their locality, Wales and the wider world.
>
> (Welsh Government, 2023b)

Task 3.7.3 Taking children out of the classroom

Use the Ofsted evaluation, *Learning Outside the Classroom* (2008), supplemented by recent case studies, to review the benefits and challenges of taking children to work outside the classroom. Go to the Ofsted website (www.gov.uk/government/organisations/ofsted) to review recent subject reports, too. Once you have reviewed the benefits and barriers, you can apply the same processes to reviewing the potential for your school to develop outdoor learning.

CASE STUDY: A VEGETABLE GARDEN

As part of a class topic on food from around the world, the class teacher decided to engage the help of parents and children to create a vegetable garden. The children had to research, design and present their gardens in groups, and the best garden design – based on a range of criteria – was chosen. Local community help was enlisted, with parents wielding spades and a grandfather giving a talk about how to grow vegetables, to help the children design and create their vegetable garden. The topic area was food from around the world, and so children were given the task – after conducting favourite-food surveys in class – of finding out just where and how various fruit and vegetables grow best. The start of a school partnership with a school in Gambia heralded a slight change of direction. The teacher realised that the children's knowledge of everyday Gambian life was scant, and that misconceptions were based on more general stories about Africa derived mainly from charity campaigns. So, he arranged for the children from the partnership schools to find out what was grown locally and to try growing each other's fruit and vegetables. An initial, striking, positive outcome was that, when the English and Gambian children discovered that they grew many of the same crops – such as onions and greens – there was a shift from considering the children as different to seeing each other as sharing similar ways of being. A connection was made between the children, after which they learned all about science and design technology and geography and sustainability by trying to grow, for example, bananas in England and apples in the Gambia.

Planning a lesson using the outdoors requires the same degree of thought and care that a lesson indoors requires, but it is not simply the learning space that may change. Teaching outdoors requires a different management approach, a holistic set of learning objectives and, simply because it is a different environment, a different set of safety measures to have in place. Some teachers may be put off by a perception of additional safety and risk assessment that is required for outdoor teaching. In fact, the focus on risk assessment and safety is no different from inside a classroom. In both situations, the safety and well-being of the children in your care are paramount. The difference does not occur in the *focus* on safety, only in the types of risk you need to assess and plan to manage.

> **In Northern Ireland ...**
>
> Learning outside can encourage better problem solving, critical thinking, inquiry skills and self-management in pupils. ... It is important to frame your activity with the pupils before you leave the classroom. Giving the activity context and sharing the learning expectations with the pupils will help keep them more focused on the task outside.
>
> (Eco-schools, n.d.: 9)

PLANNING TO TEACH OUTDOORS

You would probably never consider walking straight into a classroom to teach without knowing how the tables were set out, what resources were available and how any technology worked, and so it is with an outdoor learning environment. It is vital to visit the place first and complete an assessment of resources and space and possible hazards or risks. Risk/benefit assessments can be quite daunting, as they appear to carry a burden of responsibility, but then you are always responsible for the children in your care, whether you are in or out, and the aim is simply to identify any risk so that it can be managed safely. You should complete your first risk/benefit assessments with a colleague who has experience of risk assessments and then get this checked and signed by the head teacher or designated safety officer for your school. Each school will have policies for teaching off-site and for health and safety. Additionally, every local authority will have a set of regulations. Many institutions, such as the Council for Learning Outside the Classroom (www.lotc.org.uk) and the Forest School Association (www.forestschoolassociation.org), offer support and advice. *Nothing Ventured* (Gill, 2010) is an excellent starting point. Figure 3.7.4 is an example of a risk/benefit assessment template provided by Bishops Wood Centre in Worcestershire (www.field-studies-council.org/centres/bishopswood.aspx) – a centre that specialises in providing excellent quality outdoor learning opportunities for local schools and community groups. The Forest School Association provides a list of local accredited providers (www.forestschoolassociation.org). It is worth looking to see who provides such support in your local area. A second consideration when assessing the risks associated with a different learning environment concerns any risks associated with the activities. Managing children in an outdoor environment, where there is clearly greater freedom of movement requires many eyes! Make sure you follow the school and local authority guidelines for adult-to-pupil ratio. These vary according to the age of the children and the nature of the tasks. You will also need to consider the type of clothing needed and plan for any change in the weather. Planning what to do in the event of a sudden downpour of rain is not too dissimilar to knowing how to cope with a breakdown in technology in the classroom! Be prepared.

> ### Task 3.7.4 Risk assessment
>
> Use the school's risk assessment pro forma, or the one provided in Figure 3.7.4, to assess the risk of a lesson you normally teach indoors but could possibly teach outdoors. Complete the assessment for both indoor and outdoor learning, including an assessment of the site and also of the activities. In what ways do these two assessments vary?
>
> Choose one of your proposed activities from the planning mindmap and complete a risk/benefit assessment for it. Work from the school's policies and risk assessment already in place to support you.

FIGURE 3.7.4 Example of a risk/benefit assessment template
Source: Bishops Wood Centre

Bishops Wood Centre
OCN accredited training for Forest School

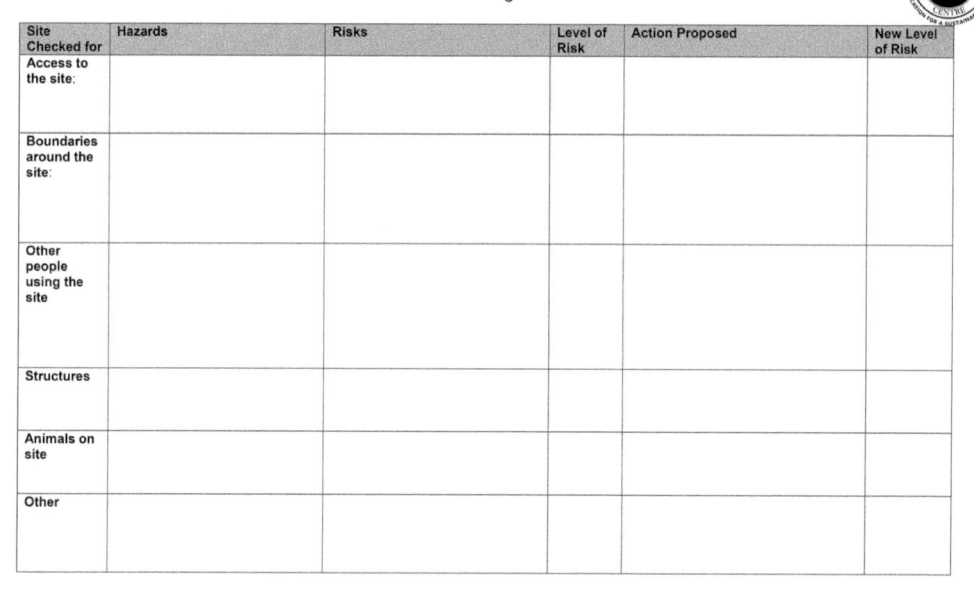

Site Checked for	Hazards	Risks	Level of Risk	Action Proposed	New Level of Risk
Canopy layer					
Shrub layer					
Field layer					
Ground layer					

Bishops Wood Centre
OCN accredited training for Forest School

Site Checked for	Hazards	Risks	Level of Risk	Action Proposed	New Level of Risk
Access to the site:					
Boundaries around the site:					
Other people using the site					
Structures					
Animals on site					
Other					

FIGURE 3.7.4 continued

SUMMARY

There are strong educational benefits to learning outside the classroom, and recent research has highlighted the value of learning and teaching outside. Indeed, it is an essential part of the curriculum with both the EYFS and the National Curriculum, and all subjects can benefit from making use of the outdoors as part of the learning environment. Learning outside can help with a child's holistic development, aiding cognitive development, health and well-being, their learning skills such as problem-solving and teamwork, and their personal development, through providing the means to work with motivating lesson activities.

Learning outdoors can take on many forms, from a quick trip out into the school grounds, to regular sessions in the outdoors, visits, residential visits and adventurous pursuits. Each has its own learning value and requires careful planning to ensure the learning is safe, effective and enjoyable. Learning outside the classroom enables key learning skills and processes to develop through practical, cognitive and affective experiences. Learning outdoors is memorable, and its impact goes far beyond the nature of the planned activities.

ANNOTATED FURTHER READING

Waite, S. Roberts, M. and Lambert, D. (2020) *The National Curriculum Outdoors*, London: Bloomsbury Education.
    This is not just one book, but a series of five award winning (LOtC resource provider award) books that make a complete primary curriculum for teaching outdoors, supported by the https://national-curriculumoutdoors.com/ website.

Pickering, S. (ed.) (2017) *Teaching Outdoors Creatively*, London: Routledge.
    The author explores the full range of opportunities for teaching outdoors, including teaching in urban and rural environments and from the calm to the adventurous. This book has a great range of practical activities and ideas grounded in current theory and research. It covers learning and teaching in early years settings as well as primary schools.

Waite, S. (ed.) (2017) *Children Learning Outside the Classroom*, 2nd edn, London: Sage.
    There are a super range of chapters that consider various aspects of learning outside the classroom, through subject areas as well as cross-curricular routes such as Forest Schools, residential centres and national parks. This book is grounded with theory and provides a strong argument for the benefits of learning and teaching outdoors.

FURTHER READING TO SUPPORT M-LEVEL STUDY

Mann, J., Gray, T., Truong, S., Brymer, E., Passy, R., Ho, S., Sahlberg, P., Ward, K., Bentsen, P., Curry, C. and Cowper, R. (2022) 'Getting out of the classroom and into nature: A systematic review of nature-specific outdoor learning on school children's learning and development', *Front. Public Health*, 10:877058. Doi 10.3389/fpubh.2022.877058
    This article reviews current literature and research on benefits for academic progress, health and well-being. It is also useful for the comprehensive range of literature that you can access through the reference list.

Prince, H. E. (2020) 'The sustained value teachers place on outdoor learning', *Education 3-13*, 48(5): 597-610. https://doi.org/10.1080/03004279.2019.1633376
>This paper focuses on the teachers and the reasons why teachers value the outdoors as places for learning. There is a strong theoretical framework that helps analyse teachers' perceptions and views.

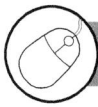

RELEVANT WEBSITES

Council for Learning Outside the Classroom: www.lotc.org.uk
>This is a site that opens up a huge range of resources and opportunities for members and it also contains a lot of useful resources and guidance for non-members.

Forest School Association: www.forestschoolassociation.org
>Again, this site has more resources for its members, but nevertheless has support and guidance for non-members. Of particular interest are the principles of Forest Schools.

Ofsted: www.gov.uk/government/organisations/ofsted
>Many people think of Ofsted as the body that only completes reports on individual schools, and, although you can find some examples of excellent practice by looking at some of these school reports, it is also worth knowing that Ofsted completes significant research in different areas of learning.

The Geographical Association: www.geography.org.uk

Learning through Landscapes: www.ltl.org.uk

REFERENCES

Barfod, K. and Mygind, E. (2022) '*Udeskole*–Regular teaching outside the classroom', in R. Jucker and J. von Au (eds) *High-Quality Outdoor Learning*, Cham: Springer, pp. 287-297. https://doi.org/10.1007/978-3-031-04108-2_16

Carroll, M. and McCullogh, M. (eds) (2014) *Understanding Teaching and Learning in Primary Education*, London: Sage.

Carlsen, K. and Clark, A. (2022) 'Potentialities of pedagogical documentation as an intertwined research process with children and teachers in slow pedagogies', *European Early Childhood Education Research Journal*, 30(2): 200-212. DOI: 10.1080/1350293X.2022.2046838

Council for the Curriculum Examinations and Assessment (CCEA). (2022) *Learning Outdoors in Pre-school and Foundation Stage*. Retrieved from: https://ccea.org.uk/downloads/docs/ccea-asset/Resource/Learning%20Outdoors%20in%20Pre-school%20and%20Foundation%20Stage.pdf (accessed 17 November 2023).

Cutler, M. (2016) *The Call of the Wild*, Cambridge Primary Review Trust blog, 30 September 2016. https://cprtrust.org.uk/cprt-blog/the-call-of-the-wild/ (accessed 20 November 2023).

Department for Education (DfE). (2011) *Teachers' Standards*, London: DfE. Last updated 2021. Retrieved from: https://assets.publishing.service.gov.uk/media/61b73d6c8fa8f50384489c9a/Teachers__Standards_Dec_2021.pdf (accessed 17 November 2023).

Department for Education (DfE). (2013a) *The National Curriculum in England Key Stages 1 and 2 Framework Document*, London: DfE.

Department for Education (DfE). (2013b) *The National Curriculum in England: Framework Document*, London: DfE. Last updated 2014.

Department for Education (DfE). (2014) *Statutory Framework for the Early Years Foundation Stage. Setting the Standards for Learning, Development and Care for Children from Birth to Five*, London: DfE. Last updated 2024. Retrieved from: www.gov.uk/government/publications/early-years-foundation-stage-framework-2

Eco-schools (n.d.) *Outdoor Learning*. Retrieved from: http://eco-schoolsni.org/eco-schoolsni/documents/007123.pdf (accessed 14 November 2023).

Education Scotland. (2020) *Outdoor Learning Resources*. Last updated 2024. Retrieved from: https://education.gov.scot/resources/outdoor-learning-resources/

Gill, T. (2010) *Nothing Ventured ... Balancing Risks and Benefits in the Outdoors*, English Outdoor Council. Retrieved from: www.englishoutdoorcouncil.org/wp-content/uploads/Nothing-Ventured.pdf (accessed 20 November 2023).

Goswami, U. (2008) 'Principles of learning, implications for teaching: A cognitive neuroscience perspective', *Journal of Philosophy of Education*, 42(3–4): 381–399.

Hallam, J., Gallagher, L. and Harvey, C. (2021) '"I don't wanna go. I'm staying. This is my home now." Analysis of an intervention for connecting young people to urban nature', *Urban Forestry & Urban Greening*, 65, p.127341.

James, A. and James, A. (2004) *Constructing Childhood. Theory, Policy and Social Practice*, London: Palgrave.

Kaplan, R. and Kaplan, S. (1989) *The Experience of Nature: A Psychological Perspective*, Cambridge, UK: Cambridge University Press.

Learning and Teaching Scotland (2010) *Curriculum for Excellence Through Outdoor Learning*. Retrieved from: https://education.gov.scot/media/gnufmnmq/hwb24-cfe-through-outdoor-learning.pdf (accessed 20 November 2023).

Louv, R. (2005) *Last Child in the Woods*, London: Atlantic Books.

Mann, J., Gray, T., Truong, S., Brymer, E., Passy, R., Ho, S., Sahlberg, P., Ward, K., Bentsen, P., Curry, C. and Cowper, R. (2022) 'Getting out of the classroom and into nature: A systematic review of nature-specific outdoor learning on school children's learning and development', *Front. Public Health*, 10. doi: 10.3389/fpubh.2022.877058

Mannion, G., Ramjan, C., McNicol, S., Sowerby, M. and Lambert, P. (2023) *Teaching, Learning and Play in the Outdoors: A Survey of Provision in 2022*, NatureScot Research Report 1313.

Ofsted. (2008) *Learning Outside the Classroom: How Far Should You Go?* Retrieved from: https://dera.ioe.ac.uk/id/eprint/9253/1/Learning%20outside%20the%20classroom.pdf

Payne, P. G. and Wattchow, B. (2009) 'Phenomenological deconstruction, slow pedagogy, and the corporeal turn in wild environmental/outdoor education', *Canadian Journal of Environmental Education*, 14: 15–32.

Pickering, S. (ed.) (2017a) *Teaching Outdoors Creatively*, London: Routledge.

Pickering, S. (2017b) 'Keeping geography messy', in S. Scoffham (ed.) *Teaching Geography Creatively*, Abingdon: Routledge, pp. 192–204.

Prince, H. E. and Diggory, O. (2023) Recognition and reporting of outdoor learning in primary schools in England. *Journal of Adventure Education and Outdoor Learning*, 1–13, https://doi.org/10.1080/14729679.2023.2166544

Project Dirt (2018) *The Impact of Outdoor Learning and Playtime at School – and Beyond: A Summary of Findings Conducted for Outdoor Classroom Day*. Retrieved from: tps://outdoorclassroomday.com/wp-content/uploads/2018/05/FINAL-Project-Dirt-Survey-Outdoor-Play-and-Learning-at-School-2018-15.05.18.pdf (accessed 17 November 2023).

The Scottish Government (2017) *Space to Grow: Design Guidance for Early Learning and Childcare and Out of School Care Settings*. Retrieved from: www.gov.scot/binaries/content/documents/govscot/publications/advice-and-guidance/2017/06/space-grow-design-guidance-early-learning-childcare-out-school-care-documents/space-grow-design-guidance-early-learning-childcare-out-school-care-settings/space-grow-design-guidance-early-learning-childcare-out-school-care-settings/govscot%3Adocument/00522564.pdf

Waite, S., Roberts, M. and Lambert, D. (2020) *The National Curriculum Outdoors*, London: Bloomsbury Education.

Welsh Government (2023a) *Professional Learning: Outdoor Learning*. Retrieved from: https://hwb.gov.wales/playlists/view/8749bee8-0243-4c7e-aedc-415806e723ac/en/1?options=SHpdkEUzhea8Hwyu%252F7E7y9NMqXBmk26eClDIszVcK4N5p8GxNedO7Kzm%252Fpu3Fx23mFQa985Iv6fpvfCtP9h7GA%253D%253D (accessed 26 April 2024).

Welsh Government (2023b) *Designing Your Curriculum: Pedagogy*. Retrieved from: https://hwb.gov.wales/curriculum-for-wales/designing-your-curriculum/enabling-learning/ (accessed 26 April 2024).

Wilson, E. O. (1984) *Biophilia*, Cambridge, MA: Harvard University Press.

SECTION 4
APPROACHING THE CURRICULUM

UNIT 4.1

CRITICAL PERSPECTIVES ON THE CURRICULUM

Ayshea Craig and Dominic Wyse

INTRODUCTION

The attention paid by governments to national curricula has continued to increase, not least because of the comparison of jurisdictions made in international testing and surveys such as PIRLS (Progress in International Reading Literacy Study), PISA (the Programme for International Student Assessment) and TIMSS (Trends in International Mathematics and Science Study). Responding to these international developments, the countries of the UK and Ireland have paid increased attention to their national curricula. As a result of political devolution in the UK, the national curricula of Northern Ireland, Scotland, England and Wales have developed important differences in their aims, structure and scope. Wales has relatively recently undergone significant curriculum reform, as has the Republic of Ireland. In England, the rise of high-stakes national testing has had a significant impact on the curriculum children have access to in schools. And the diversification of primary schools, not all of which are required to follow the 'National' Curriculum, has led to more variety, as some schools take up the opportunity to choose or design their own curriculum.

In this unit, you will explore national curricula and reflect on differences between a curriculum document and the curriculum as enacted in the classroom. You will also be introduced to some of the broader pressures and influences on what is taught in primary schools, such as statutory testing, school inspections and school type. Finally, you will consider your role in curriculum design and the skills and knowledge you will need to take an informed approach to interpreting and applying curriculum documents in order to achieve a rich, relevant, ambitious and inspiring curriculum experience for the children in your class.

OBJECTIVES

By the end of this unit, you should:

- be aware of debates about the aims of the primary curriculum;
- appreciate that the history of the curriculum is an important aspect of continuing debates;
- be starting to think about how teachers make professional decisions about the curriculum in the best interests of the children that they teach;
- be aware of the range of curricula in place in countries across the UK and Ireland and in different types of school across England;
- have considered the influence of statutory testing and inspection on the taught curriculum.

When a national curriculum was first proposed by the British government, there was strong resistance to its introduction (Haviland, 1988). Previously, teachers, schools and school boards had a great deal of freedom to decide what would be taught in their classrooms. Resistance to the idea of a national curriculum was based in part on the perception that it threatened teachers' professionalism, by introducing political involvement into an area that had previously been under the control of the profession (Haviland, 1988). However, one of the arguments mounted in favour of a national curriculum was that pupils across England and Wales were receiving an uneven education, which could include considerable repetition of subject matter, a situation that was exacerbated if children moved areas to different schools. There were also claims that some groups of children, particularly minority ethnic ones, were subject to low expectations, enacted in the curricula that were delivered to them. A national curriculum was seen as a solution to these problems, because it would ensure that all children had an *entitlement* to a continuous and coherent curriculum (one of four *purposes* of the original National Curriculum). But, exposing children to the *same* curriculum does not necessarily lead to the fulfilment of their entitlement. The purpose of a national curriculum could be seen from an equity perspective as setting out a minimum, shared entitlement. It should not, in theory, put a limit on what schools and teachers might aim for when designing local curricula. In practice, a national curriculum that suffers from 'curriculum overload' (Organisation for Economic Co-operation and Development [OECD], 2020a) and is thus challenging to teach in the time schools have with children, is likely to become the only curriculum children have access to. This puts pressure on teachers, schools and children and leaves little space for local innovation and for schools to create a curriculum that is rich, relevant and meets the needs of their community.

Despite the resistance to the National Curriculum evident in the public consultation, it was introduced in England, Northern Ireland and Wales in 1988. Following complaints that the 1988 National Curriculum was overburdening schools, it was revised in 1993, but the revisions did little to reduce the load.

Since then, control of education and of the curriculum has been devolved to the Northern Irish and Welsh assemblies, which now, along with Scotland, have their own national curricula. These curricula differ in significant ways. In spite of three significant reviews of the primary curriculum in 2009 (the government-commissioned report, Rose and Department for Children, Schools and Families [DCSF], 2009; House of Commons Children, Schools and Families Committee, 2009; and the Cambridge Primary Review, e.g. Wyse, McCreery and Torrance, 2010), the National Curriculum in England remained very similar to the previous versions until 2014, when a National Curriculum with an explicit move towards a greater focus on knowledge was introduced.

We will now consider two themes that are particularly prominent in the study of curricula: knowledge in the curriculum, and international comparison of national curricula.

KNOWLEDGE IN THE CURRICULUM

The place of theories of knowledge at the heart of thinking about curricula goes back many decades, for example to work by Hirst (1974) and Tyler (1949). In more recent theory the idea that knowledge in the curriculum had been neglected was aligned with a perceived need to 'bring knowledge back in' (Young, 2008). However, the nature of knowledge represented in England's 2014 National Curriculum for primary schools was a rather crude, 'knowledge-based' curriculum that did not reasonably reflect Young's complex ideas – for example, Young's proposition that curriculum *theory* had lost sight of its object of study, teaching and learning, and its distinctive role in education sciences (Young, 2013).

The differences between types of curricula – for example, what are called 'process' curricula (Kelly, 2009) or 'aims-based curricula' (Reiss and White, 2013) and knowledge-based curricula – have been a long-standing point of contention. Our view of England's 2014 National Curriculum for primary education, in comparison with other curricula internationally, is that it has a lack of emphasis on processes and aims in comparison with its focus on knowledge (see also Reiss and White, 2013; Manyukhina and Wyse, 2019; Greany, 2021). For example, the over-specification of the transcription elements of writing (such as grammar and spelling, including their emphasis in national testing) risks minimising the important processes of composition of writing. And the lack of attention to cross-curricular aims, such as the development of creativity or children's agency, is a problem when the emphasis of the curriculum is so heavily subject-based and knowledge-based, particularly in the modern era when cross-curricular topics such as creativity are so highly valued (Wyse and Ferrari, 2014). Finally, we might ask about the place of values and attitudes in the curriculum and whether a curriculum that focuses mainly on knowledge and skills may be in danger of failing to address vital aspects of primary education.

WHAT CAN WE LEARN FROM LOOKING AT OTHER COUNTRIES?

Another way to look at how knowledge is manifest in curricula is to compare the ways in which different countries structure their national curricula. International comparison has two quite different traditions. The first kind is exemplified in the tradition of in-depth understandings of small groups of different countries, taking due account of their different social and cultural contexts (e.g. Alexander, 2000). The second kind is exemplified by the pupil testing and surveys of teachers and head teachers that is typical of international comparative work, such as PISA, PIRLS and TIMSS (see www.oecd.org/pisa/ and https://timssandpirls.bc.edu/). In recent years, the political attention to these international surveys, including league tables of countries' performance published in the media, has grown, along with academic concern at what is called 'performativity' (Wyse, Hayward and Pandya, 2015). The idea of performativity draws attention to the consequences that arise when 'high-stakes' testing is used as an accountability measure (for schools and/or teachers), at national or international level.

With regard to curriculum policy development in England, a curious feature of its history has been governments' targeting of single countries around the world as exemplars, typically based on the kinds of international league table outlined earlier, rather than looking much closer to home at the four nations of the UK or Ireland, an approach that has been called 'home-international comparison'.

Comparing curricula within the British Isles

In 2013, Wyse *et al.* published the first book-length home-international analysis comparing the national curricula in England, Northern Ireland, Scotland and Wales. The book explored the idea of national educational policy being influenced by transnational policy trends, and it included historical perspectives on the development of a national curriculum, paying particular attention to the national curriculum texts and research evidence on the implementation of national policies. One of the findings of the work was to identify the increasingly stark differences between national curricula in England and national curricula in the other three nations as a result of political devolution. The policy in Scotland was particularly noteworthy. In Scotland, the Education (Scotland) Act 1980 very clearly gave power over the curriculum to local authorities: '(2) In any such school the education authority shall have *the sole power* of regulating the curriculum and of appointing teachers' (The Education (Scotland) Act 1980, Section 21, p. 13; emphasis added). This early legislation was an important feature of the greater democratic involvement of educators in their system. In spite of the roots in democratic involvement, the place of teacher agency was still uncertain (Priestly and Biesta, 2013).

In England, the Education Reform Act 1988 (HMSO, 1988) put the power to develop a national curriculum in the hands of the government through the Secretary of State for Education:

> Duty to establish the National Curriculum
>
> 4.-(1) It shall be the duty of the Secretary of State so to exercise the powers conferred by subsection (2) below as-
>
> to establish a complete National Curriculum as soon as is reasonably practicable (taking first the core subjects and then the other foundation subjects); and to revise that Curriculum whenever he considers it necessary or expedient to do so.
>
> (Chapter 40, section 4: 3)

In Northern Ireland ...

The revisions to the curriculum aim to retain the best of current practice while seeking to give greater emphasis to important elements, such as children's Personal Development and Mutual Understanding and the explicit development of Thinking Skills and Personal Capabilities. The Northern Ireland Curriculum sets out the minimum requirement that should be taught at each key stage. Within these requirements, schools have a responsibility to provide a broad and balanced curriculum for all children and schools should aim to give every child the opportunity to experience success in learning and to achieve as high a standard as possible.

Teachers, however, have considerable flexibility to make decisions about how best to interpret and combine the requirements to prepare young people for a rapidly changing world.

(Council for Curriculum Examinations and Assessment [CCEA], 2007: 2)

In Scotland ...

A recent OECD review of Curriculum for Excellence (CfE) highlighted that schools have been quite successful in implementing CfE and are willing to make changes where challenges remain. Key findings and recommendations from the review suggest that Scotland should continue to build on the system's existing strengths with a particular focus on how students experience CfE and progress in their learning.

Source: OECD (2021)

In Wales...

The Curriculum for Wales Framework (Framework) is a clear statement of what we see as important in a broad and balanced education. At its heart is our aspiration for every child and young person in Wales, as defined by the four purposes of curriculum

> (ambitious, capable learners, enterprising, creative contributors, ethical, informed citizens, healthy, confident individuals)... The Framework gives every school in Wales the opportunity to design their own curriculum within a national approach that ensures a level of consistency. It encourages schools to build their own vision for their learners within the context of the four purposes and the learning defined at a national level. It provides the space for practitioners to be creative and to develop meaningful learning through a range of experiences and contexts that meet the needs of their learners.
>
> (Welsh Government, 2020)

In 2020 Ireland started a process of review of its primary national curriculum which had not been changed as a whole since 1999. The process of review was led by the National Council for Curriculum and Assessment (NCCA). One of the unique aspects of Ireland's approach was that the revised curriculum framework (NCCA, 2023) would not be published until 2023, and then an additional two years would be used to develop and consult on more detailed specifications. Research was built in from the start in at least three ways:

1. the commissioning of new research projects at the beginning of the process to inform the curriculum developments;
2. the commissioning of a cohort study of children's views of their education;
3. the appointment of an advisory panel of four academics.

In contrast to curriculum development in Ireland, Scotland and Wales, in designing the 2014 National Curriculum, ministers in England opted for an expert group to make recommendations to a dedicated group of civil servants in the Department for Education, and hence rejected the opportunity for a longer-term, considered and democratic process to build a national curriculum fit for the twenty-first century. However, even accepting many of the recommendations of the national curriculum expert group proved impossible, and hence several members of the expert group resigned (see BERA, 2012).

The 2014 English National Curriculum has been described as suffering from 'curriculum overload' (reported in OECD, 2020a) with new areas added without removing others and as suffering from 'content overload' while also moving through curriculum areas more quickly than previous versions of the curriculum. This raises concerns about the depth of engagement with concepts and about what is developmentally appropriate for children, particularly in the first years of compulsory schooling (5-7 in England).

There are strong arguments to suggest that primary-phase national curriculum development in England has suffered from a lack of rigour, understanding and coherence as a result of poor government interventions. The most serious of these are:

- insufficient attention to the range of relevant scholarship and research evidence;
- curriculum acceleration and content overload;
- an undue emphasis on comparison with other countries in international league tables, as opposed to greater democratic involvement in curriculum development, including in development of curriculum aims;
- insufficiently rigorous attention to views expressed in public consultations.

(Wyse, 2013)

> **Task 4.1.1 Other national curricula**
>
> Examine a national curriculum from your own and one other country in the UK or Ireland. Try to identify some similarities and differences and then identify two or three changes that you think would be of benefit to the national curriculum you will be expected to work with.

A NATIONAL CURRICULUM? THE CONSEQUENCES OF SECTOR DIVERSIFICATION

In England, the period from 2000 to the present has seen the development of an increasingly diversified school sector where not all school types are required to follow the National Curriculum. Academies are state-funded schools that do not fall within the control of local authorities. Significantly, academies, free schools and private schools do not need to follow the National Curriculum. Instead, they are required to ensure that their curriculum is 'balanced and broadly based, and includes English, mathematics and science', but can make many of their own decisions about curriculum design. State-maintained primary schools, in contrast, fall within the control of local authorities and are required to follow the National Curriculum. In January 2023, Department for Education (DfE) figures showed that 42.1% of primary school children were being educated in academies or free schools. Having accounted for the relatively small number in independent or home schooling, the 'National' Curriculum in England applies as a statutory requirement to the education of slightly more than half of primary-age children. This is in contrast with Wales, Scotland and Northern Ireland, where the vast majority of primary-age children are educated in schools that are required to teach the same national curriculum, although there are also a number of different school types and systems in place.

Despite the potential for curriculum innovation in these schools, this has not always been realised and it may be that the opportunity to deviate from the National Curriculum has led instead to a narrowed curriculum with few academies taking up the opportunity for significant curriculum innovation (Greany and Higham, 2018). The existence of large multi-academy trusts (MATs) can restrict the potential for individual schools within these to innovate as curriculum decisions are not made at school level (Greany, 2021). It is in the provision of non-core subjects that English primary school head teachers have indicated they are most likely to deviate from the National Curriculum (Cirin, 2014), an area of entitlement once protected for all children by a statutory National Curriculum.

THE STATUTORY CURRICULUM IN ENGLAND

Although academies and free schools have a great deal of freedom, in theory, to set their own curriculum, we have seen that the government has made some elements of the curriculum statutory, and these are specified in the funding agreements for these schools. Independent schools are subject to the Education (Independent School Standards) Regulations (2014), which set out some minimum requirements for the 'quality' of education provided. Through these different mechanisms, all schools in England are required to provide teaching in English, mathematics and sciences, and all have some commitment to providing a broader curriculum.

Despite the wider influences on what is taught in school, discussed in the previous section, changes in the statutory curriculum still matter. For example, the move to make modern foreign languages compulsory in KS2 in 2014 had a big impact on provision, with an immediate increase in the number of schools teaching a language, although concerns remain about the quality of provision including a lack of time given in some primary schools (Collen, 2022) and concerns about poor curriculum planning without sufficient thought given to progression (Ofsted, 2021).

We saw in the previous section that high-stakes testing can result in a narrowing of the curriculum to focus on the areas being tested (Greany, 2021). Schools have responded in a variety of often imaginative ways to resist or mitigate these potential effects. One example of this is a move to a more topic-based curriculum as one way to find more space for subjects such as the humanities and expressive arts in a squeezed timetable. The current challenge for schools and teachers is to create time for a rich curriculum with proper engagement with a wide range of subjects, whether they approach this through high-quality cross-curricular teaching or by maintaining separate subjects.

There is no national curriculum for religious education (RE) or personal, social and health education (PSHE) in England, but both areas are currently part of the 'basic curriculum' in maintained schools, meaning that they must be taught. In these schools, they are subject to some statutory requirements and non-statutory guidelines, which set out requirements such as promoting respect for others.

Since 2020, state-funded primary-phase schools have been required to provide relationships (and health) education, considered to be an aspect of PSHE. Secondary schools are required to provide relationships and sex education (RSE) and health education. Where primary schools choose to teach sex education, parents have the right to withdraw their children (DfE, 2019).

In some countries, the national curriculum is completely secular, and state schools are not seen as an appropriate setting for religious education or instruction. In the UK, the Church of England and the Catholic Church have a long history of involvement in the education system. A key distinction here is between RE – that is, learning about religions and religious practice in general – and religious instruction in one particular religion. RE remains a requirement in most schools, whereas religious instruction is permitted in some and regulated against in others.

The guidance for RE is non-statutory and applies to local-authority maintained schools (which excludes independent schools, academies and free schools). Requirements for the nature of RE teaching provided in academies and free schools vary depending on their funding agreements and tend to reflect the history of the school and its religious character. One of the arguments for the value of RE is that, in a religiously diverse society, even where the majority of people do not actively practise any religion, knowledge of other religions is valuable for promoting mutual respect and understanding.

'Respect for others' is one of the few ideas that is required teaching across all schools in England (not least as a result of the Equality Act 2010; see Wyse et al., 2016). Independent schools are subject to the least detailed requirements but must still ensure that PSHE encourages 'respect for other people' (Education (Independent School Standards) Regulations, 2014). Academies and free schools, although not required to provide PSHE, are required to actively promote what are described as 'fundamental British values of democracy, the rule of law, individual liberty, and mutual respect and tolerance of those with different faiths and beliefs' and 'principles that support equality of opportunity for all' (DfE, 2020). Maintained schools are subject to the same requirements (DfE, 2014). These state school curriculum requirements have arisen in part as a government response to concerns about extremism and terrorism.

All state schools are subject to requirements to teach children about evolution, and academies and free schools must not 'allow any view or theory to be taught as evidence-based if it is contrary to established scientific or historical evidence and explanations' (DfE, 2020). This is another example of a relatively isolated curriculum requirement created in response to concerns about how some schools have used the freedom to set their own curriculum.

The diversity of primary school types in England means that there are very few requirements that apply to all schools and, hence, to all children, apart from the teaching of English, maths and science. As we have seen earlier, the government has made exceptions for a small number of issues, such as evolution, 'British values' and respect for others. The issues that are selected tell us something interesting about the histories of these school types, as well as current government concerns and priorities.

THE JOURNEY FROM STATUTORY CURRICULUM TO THE CLASSROOM

In spite of the importance of statutory curricula, you may find that in your school the statutory requirements are rarely referred to. One reason for this is that schools' long-term and medium-term planning has often been discussed, agreed and written down over a considerable period of time. Once this thinking has been translated from a National Curriculum document into a commercial scheme or teaching plans, the official documents are not really needed so much, although schools can benefit from revisiting the precise wording of national curricula to know what kinds of innovations in their curricula are possible. This can make it difficult for beginning teachers to appreciate the links between the National Curriculum documentation and school planning. Another area in which it is sometimes difficult to see the links with the statutory documents is the extent to which some of the important opening statements of national curricula are genuinely reflected in classroom practice. These opening statements, such as aims, principles and values, should be very important because, in theory, it is these that guide everything else in the documents. In practice, curricula vary in their internal coherence, and the values and aims implicit in the detailed curriculum can be very different from those espoused in the opening statements.

There is further room for variation in the move from planning, or the locally planned curriculum in a school, to the teaching that goes on in the classroom. This teaching can be thought of as the *enacted curriculum*, and there are many reasons why the curriculum enacted in the classroom may differ from statutory curricula and from locally planned curricula. An experienced teacher will adjust and adapt planning in response to the needs and attainment of their pupils, often as a lesson unfolds. There is a further leap to be made to consider the children and what they each learn through the experiences they have in the classroom (sometimes referred to as the *received curriculum*). Learning does not necessarily follow just because something has been taught, and it is important to recognise that 'covering the curriculum' does not in any way guarantee children's learning.

INFLUENCES ON THE CURRICULUM: INSPECTION AND TESTING

National testing and school inspection frameworks also affect the curriculum in primary schools. In England in 2024 statutory testing in mathematics and English was taking place at age 4 (baseline assessment), age 6 and for some children age 7 (the phonics screening check), age 9 (the times tables check), and age 11 (reading; spelling, punctuation and grammar; and mathematics), and in secondary education only at age 16 (examinations and other qualifications). It had been argued that the high-stakes nature of this statutory testing has narrowed and distorted the curriculum (Select Committee on Children, Schools and Families, 2008; Boyle and Bragg, 2006). This sort of high-stakes testing system is designed to hold schools and teachers to account in what is seen as one of their core purposes at primary level – to ensure that all pupils are supported to become literate and numerate. It has also been argued that lower attaining pupils may be likely to experience an even narrower curriculum as a result of high-stakes testing of 'core' subjects than their higher-attaining peers, with negative impacts on pupils' wellbeing and participation (Hargreaves, Quick and Buchanan, 2023).

The Office for Standards in Education, Children's Services and Skills (Ofsted) inspects schools and makes judgements about how well schools and school leadership perform against published criteria (Ofsted, 2023a). The inspection framework (Ofsted, 2023b), and schools' interpretations of this, is another important factor influencing the local curricula found in English schools.

In England, the quality of education provided in schools is judged through inspections which examine the 'intent, implementation and impact of the curriculum' (Ofsted, 2019) reflecting a similar awareness to the one outlined earlier of the journey of the curriculum from documents to the teaching and then the children. This emphasis on curriculum in inspections, since 2019, has influenced schools' thinking and the publication of a range of subject reports and curriculum research reviews has increased this influence further. However, questions remain about the selection of research sources to inform Ofsted subject reports, and indeed to the role of Ofsted more generally (https://beyond-ofsted.org.uk/).

Any high-stakes assessment or accountability system poses a danger that playing the game through shortcuts and quick fixes may be inadvertently rewarded over genuine improvements; thus the intended goal of raising standards can be lost, and the curriculum and pedagogy narrowed or distorted. The pressures on organisations and individuals within these systems can be immense. In English primary schools, there has been resistance to the predictable but unintended effects of SATs, both from teaching unions and from parents. The negative effects of ranking and frequent testing on the emotional wellbeing of children have also been highlighted (Hutchings, 2015) and alternative systems proposed (Moss *et al.*, 2021).

In 2022, the Independent Commission on Assessment in Primary Education (ICAPE) published its report (Wyse, Bradbury and Trollope, 2022). On the basis of surveys of teachers and parents, a review of relevant research, and a comparison of assessment in comparable nations, the report concluded that statutory assessment in England required significant changes.

Task 4.1.2 Thinking about national curricula

- Do you think that the strong emphasis on English and maths in England since 1997 has been a reasonable one? What are the advantages and potential disadvantages?
- If you were setting the regulations, what elements of the curriculum would you make statutory for all?
- What values and attitudes (if any) do you think schools should aim to teach?

BROADENING AND ENRICHING THE CURRICULUM

Despite some of the pressures on curricula outlined earlier, there are opportunities for schools and teachers to develop locally planned curricula which reflect schools', teachers' and communities' values and needs. Curricula might also reflect responses to local, national and global priorities that arise from current events: for example, a focus on sustainability; decolonising the curriculum; understanding war and conflict, human rights and the rights of the child; supporting children's wellbeing and mental health; cultural enrichment and access, breadth and local relevance. The Rethinking Curriculum project by the Chartered College of Teaching and the Helen Hamlyn Centre for Pedagogy at the Institute of Education focused on supporting curriculum innovation in schools (see https://chartered.college/rethinkingcurriculum/).

Individual schools and groups of schools are developing innovative curricula with particular areas of focus, as can be seen from networks such as the Tower Hamlets Oracy project or the nominees for School of the Year in pan-London Sustainable City Awards. These can provide powerful examples of curricula that respond to the needs of communities, empower children and exploit cross-curricular themes to engage children in relevant and meaningful learning experiences. Schools within the Tower Hamlets Oracy project have responded to local needs by putting oracy skills of speaking, listening and communication at the centre of the curriculum. International comparison, such as those outlined earlier, can also suggest ways in which to enrich the curriculum, for example through developing children's and families' agency in curriculum decisions.

Schools might also consider broadening and enriching children's experiences and cultural capital as part of their curriculum aims: for example, ensuring that children have the opportunity to experience the countryside, the coast and our cities; that they have been to the theatre, to museums, to live music or sporting events. Financial considerations can affect schools' decisions here, with senior leaders reporting trips likely to be cut when schools are experiencing funding pressures (Sutton Trust, 2023).

As we have seen, there are a range of factors at play affecting the curricula actually enacted in schools and classrooms, and these can represent both constraints and opportunities for the class teacher in planning. The National Curriculum is the starting point for understanding the curriculum in schools, but awareness of other factors, such as funding, diversification of school types and, in England, the effects of high-stakes testing, is key to making sense of what you see in classrooms. The need for a broad and balanced curriculum and the desire to address pressing societal issues may lead to curriculum overload. To avoid this, care must be taken to consider first the broader aims of the curriculum and the hoped-for outcomes for children, thought of widely in terms of knowledge, skills, experiences, values and attitudes.

REVISITING CURRICULUM AIMS: WAYS FORWARD

The OECD's Future of Education and Skills 2030 Project (OECD, 2019) aimed to examine research evidence and what can be learnt from existing practice in curriculum reform and goals for teaching and learning across a wide range of member countries and beyond. They identify the idea of a time lag in curriculum reform following significant shifts in society with a particular focus on technology, noting how curricula and our understanding of the purpose of schooling have had to adjust during the industrial revolution and the 'digital revolution' as to how people's lives and work have changed (OECD, 2020b).

Their goal is to envision the sort of curriculum likely to be required as technology continues to develop, changing society and the purpose of education within societies in ways which it is, as yet, hard to predict.

The OECD Future of Education and Skills 2030 Project

The [OECD Future of Education and Skills 2030 learning] framework offers a broad vision of the types of competencies students will need to thrive in 2030 and beyond. It also develops a common language and understanding that is globally relevant and informed, while providing space to adapt the framework to local contexts. The components of the compass include core foundations, knowledge, skills, attitudes and values, transformative competencies and a cycle of anticipation, action and reflection (see concept notes on each of these components).

> The concept of student agency [...] is central to the Learning Compass 2030, as the compass is a tool students can use to orient themselves as they exercise their sense of purpose and responsibility while learning to influence the people, events and circumstances around them for the better.
>
> (OECD, 2019)

A challenge in broadening the curriculum and responding to different needs and agendas is that the curriculum becomes overloaded with a negative effect on pupils' wellbeing as well as the danger of content being engaged with only superficially (OECD, 2020a). The OECD Learning Framework is designed to avoid this by providing a broad learning framework rather than a detailed curriculum. The Curriculum for Wales has a similar aim in reducing the detail of curriculum aim statements in favour of broader aims (six areas of learning and 27 mandatory 'statements of what matters').

THE TEACHER'S ROLE

Since 2014, there has been increased attention to the importance of curriculum planning as part of teachers' professional knowledge base/skill set. Concerns have been raised that the existence of national curricula and, more recently, the use of detailed schemes, based on off-the-shelf curricula, have left teachers deskilled in the important area of curriculum design and adaptation (Spielman, 2017).

A first step to addressing this is engaging with questions of purpose and the aims of education. This can help us to navigate the potential feeling of being overwhelmed with too many curriculum outcomes and the danger of racing to 'cover' the curriculum. Primary education must always aim to get the fundamentals of literacy and numeracy skills for all children right, but alongside this, having broad shared aims in mind which are designed to support children's ability to fulfil their potential and to contribute to society can provide an underpinning for decision making about the curriculum enacted in the classroom. Ideally this would happen at a national level, as we've seen from some of the curricula considered earlier, and at a school level, where there is space for schools to design their own curricula. The Rethinking Curriculum project by the Chartered College of Teaching (CCT) and the Helen Hamlyn Centre for Pedagogy supports schools in working on curriculum development (https://chartered.college/rethinkingcurriculum/).

Regardless of the national and school curriculum choices, all teachers can benefit from considering our aims and values. An awareness of the process of transition from written curriculum to the enacted curriculum in the classroom can raise our awareness of the teacher's role and allow for professional conversations about how and why decisions are made about the curriculum on the ground.

Task 4.1.3 Creating a rich curriculum

What small steps could you as a class teacher take to enrich and broaden the experiences of the children in your class? You might think about:

- experiences (in or out of school);
- access to powerful and exciting ideas;
- access to a wide range of cultural artefacts (e.g. music, theatre, writing, dance, sports, art, design).

How might you involve the children in deciding how to enrich the curriculum?

SUMMARY

In this unit, we have discussed the nature of national curricula and have explored how teachers make professional decisions about the curriculum for their pupils. We have also looked at the range of influences on the curriculum as it is enacted in classrooms and in variations between national curricula in different countries in the UK and beyond. The key issue that faces pupils, teachers and policymakers is the nature of autonomy over the curriculum. In England, in spite of greater school diversification, the autonomy of teachers and pupils has been increasingly challenged by high-stakes testing and by the government's particular interpretation of knowledge in the curriculum. Despite this, teachers and schools continue to find spaces to innovate. One of the most important things about curricula in the future is that they need to be relevant from the early years up to the end of schooling, and should genuinely prepare pupils for lifelong learning.

A curriculum model that reflects learning and teaching from birth to adulthood needs to put the individual person's motivation to learn and their interests foremost. The curriculum needs to encourage teaching that explicitly encourages pupils to find areas of thinking that motivate them, and to pursue these in depth, even at the very earliest stages of education. Children's rights to participate in all matters that affect them should not be an abstract item in the programmes of study for citizenship, but a daily reality in their lives.

The key elements addressed in this unit are most likely to be realised by a curriculum organised not by traditional subjects but by areas of learning. Is this suggestion that we abandon the current subject-dominated curriculum in England particularly radical? Not really. Well-tried examples include the Royal Society for the encouragement of Arts, Manufactures and Commerce (RSA)'s 'Opening Minds' curriculum, or the Helen Hamlyn Trust's *Open Futures* approach. Internationally, the primary curriculum developed by the International Baccalaureate Organization (IBO) organises its curriculum around six themes and the OECD's Future of Education and Skills 2030 Project recommends a focus on 'big ideas' to address concerns about curriculum overload (OECD, 2019, 2020a). A truly forward-looking curriculum that meets the learning needs of all children in a changing world requires our political leaders to have the knowledge, understanding and courage to change legislation and revolutionise the primary education system in order to bring it into the twenty-first century.

ANNOTATED FURTHER READING

Department for Education (DfE). (2011) *The Framework for the National Curriculum, A Report by the Expert Panel for the National Curriculum Review*, London: DfE.
    Thorough research-based review with recommendations based on a selection of evidence. Interesting to compare this with the National Curriculum produced.

Kelly, A.V. (2009) *The Curriculum: Theory and Practice*, 6th edn, London: Sage.
    An excellent overview of issues that combines comprehensive definitions with necessary political analysis. The comments about the increase in political interference with the curriculum, revealed through the author's reflections about the six editions of this book, are fascinating.

Sehgal Cuthbert, A. and Standish, A. (2021) *What Should Schools Teach? Disciplines, Subjects and the Pursuit of Truth*, London: UCL Press. Retrieved from: www.uclpress.co.uk/collections/series-knowledge-and-the-curriculum/products/165025
> This open access book explores questions of the nature of knowledge, of what knowledge schools should seek to teach and why. It considers the relevance of subject disciplines and includes chapters on different curriculum subjects exploring the nature of knowledge in each.

OECD Learning Framework. Retrieved from: www.oecd.org/en/data/tools/oecd-learning-compass-2030.html
> The OECD's evidence-based Learning Framework is based around a compass metaphor and sets out their vision for the competencies they argue we should be supporting children to develop. Generated as part of their Future of Education and Skills 2030 Project it: 'defines the knowledge, skills, attitudes and values that learners need to fulfil their potential and contribute to the well-being of their communities and the planet.'

FURTHER READING TO SUPPORT M-LEVEL STUDY

Wyse, D., Hayward, L. and Pandya, J. (2015) 'Introduction: Curriculum and its message systems: from crisis to rapprochement', in D. Wyse, L. Hayward and J. Pandya (eds) *The SAGE Handbook of Curriculum, Pedagogy and Assessment*, London: Sage, pp. 1–25.

Wyse, D. and Manyukhina, Y. (2025) *Children's Agency and the Curriculum*, London: Routledge.

Hargreaves, E., Quick, L. and Buchanan, D. (2023) 'National Curriculum and assessment in England and the continuing narrowed experiences of lower-attainers in primary schools', *Journal of Curriculum Studies*, 55(5): 545–561. DOI: 10.1080/00220272.2023.2253455.

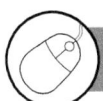

RELEVANT WEBSITES

Cambridge Primary Review Trust: http://cprtrust.org.uk/
> This website contains links to the evidence for the Cambridge Primary Review, a large-scale, wide-ranging independent review of primary education headed by Robin Alexander and originally based at the University of Cambridge's Faculty of Education.

National Curriculum England: www.gov.uk/government/publications/national-curriculum-in-england-primary-curriculum
> This is the home of the Primary National Curriculum for England.

National Curriculum Ireland: https://curriculumonline.ie/getmedia/84747851-0581-431b-b4d7-dc6ee850883e/2023-Primary-Framework-ENG-screen.pdf
> This is the national curriculum for Ireland: Primary Curriculum Framework.

National Curriculum Wales: https://hwb.gov.wales/curriculum-for-wales/
> This is the national curriculum for Wales: Curriculum for Wales

The Tower Hamlets Oracy Project: www.the-partnership.org.uk/school-improvement/oracy-primary

The Sustainable City Awards: www.globalactionplan.org.uk/events/sustainable-city-awards/school-of-the-year
> These websites provide links to schools that have developed innovative curricula based around a particular theme. This video from Cubitt Town Primary School in London is a powerful example of the effects a locally relevant curriculum with strong cross-curricular aims can have: www.youtube.com/watch?v=pxPkp9OJX6Y

REFERENCES

Alexander, R. J. (2000) *Culture and Pedagogy: International Comparisons in Primary Education*, Oxford, UK: Blackwell.

BERA (2012) *Background to Michael Gove's Response to the Report of the Expert Panel for the National Curriculum Review in England*. Retrieved from: www.bera.ac.uk/promoting-educational-research/issues/background-to-michael-goves-response-to-the-report-of-the-expert-panel-for-the-national-curriculum-review-in-england (accessed 27 November 2023).

Boyle, B. and Bragg, J. (2006) 'A curriculum without foundation', *British Education Research Journal*, 32(4): 569–582.

Cirin, R. (2014) *Do Academies Make Use of Their Autonomy? Research Report*, London: DfE.

Collen, I. (2022) *Language Trends England 2022*. British Council. Retrieved from: www.britishcouncil.org/research-insight/language-trends-2022

Council for Curriculum Examinations and Assessment (CCEA). (2007) *The Northern Ireland Curriculum Primary*, Belfast. Retrieved from: https://ccea.org.uk/learning-resources/northern-ireland-curriculum-primary

Department for Education (DfE). (2014) *Promoting Fundamental British Values as Part of SMSC in Schools*. Retrieved from: www.gov.uk/government/publications/promoting-fundamental-british-values-through-smsc (accessed 27 October 2017).

Department for Education (DfE). (2019) *Relationships Education, Relationships and Sex Education (RSE) and Health Education*. Retrieved from: https://assets.publishing.service.gov.uk/government/uploads/system/uploads/attachment_data/file/1090195/Relationships_Education_RSE_and_Health_Education.pdf (accessed 30 November 2023).

Department for Education (DfE). (2020) *Academy and Free School: Master Funding Agreement I*. Retrieved from: www.gov.uk/government/publications/academy-and-free-school-funding-agreements (accessed 30 November 2020).

Department for Education (DfE). (2023) *Schools, Pupils and Their Characteristics: January 2023*. Retrieved from: www.gov.uk/government/statistics/schools-pupils-and-their-characteristics-january-2023 (accessed 14 January 2025).

Education (Independent School Standards) Regulations. (2014) No. 3283. Retrieved from: www.legislation.gov.uk/uksi/2014/3283/contents/2024-08-19 (accessed 3 February 2025).

Education (Scotland) Act. (1980). Retrieved from: www.legislation.gov.uk/ukpga/1980/44

Greany, T. (2021) 'Leading curriculum development', in T. Greany and P. Earley (eds), *School Leadership and Education System Reform*, 2nd edn, London: Bloomsbury Publishing.

Greany, T. and Higham, R. (2018) *Hierarchy, Markets and Networks: Analysing the 'Self-improving School-led System' Agenda in England and the Implications for Schools*, London: UCL Institute of Education Press.

Hargreaves, E., Quick, L. and Buchanan, D. (2023) 'National Curriculum and assessment in England and the continuing narrowed experiences of lower-attainers in primary schools', *Journal of Curriculum Studies*, 55(5): 545–561. DOI: 10.1080/00220272.2023.2253455.

Haviland, J. (1988) *Take Care, Mr Baker!*, London: Fourth Estate.

Her Majesty's Stationary Office (HMSO). (1988) *Education Reform Act*, London: HMSO.

Hirst, P. (1974) *Knowledge and the Curriculum: A Collection of Philosophical Papers*, London: Routledge & K. Paul.

House of Commons Children, Schools and Families Committee. (2009) *National Curriculum. Fourth Report of Session 2008-09. Volume 1*, London: House of Commons.

Hutchings, M. (2015). *Exam Factories? The Impact of Accountability Measures on Children and Young People*, London: NUT.

Kelly, A. V. (2009) *The Curriculum: Theory and Practice*, 6th edn, London: Sage.

Manyukhina, Y. and Wyse, D. (2019) 'Learner agency and the curriculum: A critical realist perspective', *The Curriculum Journal*, 30: 223–243. https://doi.org/10.1080/09585176.2019.1599973

Moss, G., Goldstein, H., Hayes, S., Chereau, B. M., Sammons, P., Sinnott, G. and Stobart, G. (2021) *High Standards, Not High Stakes: An Alternative to SATs That Will Transform England's Testing & School Accountability System in Primary Education & Beyond*. BERA Expert Panel on Assessment Report, London: BERA. Retrieved from: www.bera.ac.uk/publication/high-standards-not-high-stakes-an-alternative-to-sats (accessed 30 November 2023).

National Council for Curriculum and Assessment (NCCA). (2023) *Primary Curriculum Framework For Primary and Special Schools*, Ireland: NCCA. Retrieved from: https://curriculumonline.ie/getmedia/84747851-0581-431b-b4d7-dc6ee850883e/2023-Primary-Framework-ENG-screen.pdf (accessed 27 November 2023).

Ofsted (2019) *Inspecting the Curriculum*. Retrieved from: https://assets.publishing.service.gov.uk/media/5d1dfeba40f0b609dde41855/Inspecting_the_curriculum.pdf (accessed 27 November 2023).

Ofsted (2021) *Research Review Series: Languages*. Retrieved from: www.gov.uk/government/publications/curriculum-research-review-series-languages/curriculum-research-review-series-languages (accessed 3 February, 2025).

Ofsted (2023a) *School Inspection Handbook*. Retrieved from: www.gov.uk/government/publications/school-inspection-handbook-eif (accessed 27 November 2023).

Ofsted (2023b) *Education Inspection Framework*. Retrieved from: www.gov.uk/government/publications/education-inspection-framework (accessed 27 November 2023).

Organisation for Economic Co-operation and Development (OECD). (2019) *Future of Education and Skills 2030 Project: Learning Compass Concept Note*. Retrieved from: www.oecd.org/education/2030-project/teaching-and-learning/learning/learning-compass-2030/OECD_Learning_Compass_2030_concept_note.pdf (accessed 27 November 2023).

Organisation for Economic Co-operation and Development (OECD). (2020a) *Curriculum Overload: A Way Forward*. Retrieved from: www.oecd-ilibrary.org/education/curriculum-overload_3081ceca-en (accessed 27 November 2023).

Organisation for Economic Co-operation and Development (OECD). (2020b), *What Students Learn Matters: Towards a 21st Century Curriculum*, Paris: OECD Publishing. Retrieved from: www.oecd-ilibrary.org/education/what-students-learn-matters_d86d4d9a-en (accessed 30 November 2023).

Organisation for Economic Co-operation and Development (OECD). (2021) *Scotland's Curriculum for Excellence: Into the Future*. Retrieved from: www.oecd.org/en/publications/scotland-s-curriculum-for-excellence_bf624417-en/full-report.html

Priestly, M. and Biesta, G. (eds) (2013) *Reinventing the Curriculum: New Trends in Curriculum Policy and Practice*, London: Bloomsbury.

Reiss, M. and White, J. (2013) *An Aims-Based Curriculum: The Significance of Human Flourishing for Schools*, London: IOE Press.

Rose, J. and Department for Children, Schools and Families (DCSF). (2009) *The Independent Review of the Primary Curriculum: Final Report*, London: DCSF.

Select Committee on Children, Schools and Families. (2008) *Third Report*. Retrieved from: www.publications.parliament.uk/pa/cm200708/cmselect/cmchilsch/169/16902.htm (accessed 27 October 2017).

Spielman, A. (2017) *HCMI's Commentary: Recent Primary and Secondary Curriculum Research*. Ofsted. Retrieved from www.gov.uk/government/speeches/hmcis-commentary-october-2017 (accessed 30 November 2023).

Sutton Trust. (2023) *School Funding and Pupil Premium 2023*. Retrieved from: www.suttontrust.com/our-research/school-funding-and-pupil-premium-2023/ (accessed 4 December 2023).

Tyler, R. (1949) *Basic Principles of Curriculum and Instruction*, Chicago, IL: University of Chicago Press.

Welsh Government (2020) *Designing Your Curriculum*. Retrieved from: https://hwb.gov.wales/curriculum-for-wales/designing-your-curriculum/introduction/ (accessed 26 April 2024).

Wyse, D. (2013) *What Are Consultations For?* [IOE London Blog]. Retrieved from: https://ioelondonblog.wordpress.com/2013/09/20/what-are-consultations-for/ (accessed 9 February 2017).

Wyse, D., Bradbury, A. and Trollope, R. (2022) *Assessment for Children's Learning: A New Future for Primary Education*. Independent Commission on Assessment in Primary Education (ICAPE). Final report. Retrieved from: www.icape.org.uk/reports/NEU2762_ICAPE_final_report_A4_web_version.pdf

Wyse, D., Baumfield, V., Egan, D. Gallagher, C., Hayward, L., Hulme, M., Leitch, R., Livingston, K., Menter, I. and Lingard, B. (2013) *Creating the Curriculum*, London: Routledge.

Wyse, D. and Ferrari, A. (2014) 'Creativity and education: Comparing the national curricula of the states of the European Union with the United Kingdom', *British Educational Research Journal*, 41(1): 30–47.

Wyse, D., Ford, S., Hale, C. and Parker, C. (2016) 'Legal issues', in D. Wyse and S. Rogers (eds) *A Guide to Early Years and Primary Teaching*, London: Sage, pp. 301-320.

Wyse, D., Hayward, L. and Pandya, J. (2015) 'Introduction: Curriculum and its message systems: From crisis to rapprochement', in D. Wyse, L. Hayward and J. Pandya (eds) *The SAGE Handbook of Curriculum, Pedagogy and Assessment*, London: Sage, pp. 1-26.

Wyse, D., McCreery, E. and Torrance, H. (2010) 'The trajectory and impact of national reform: Curriculum and assessment in English primary schools', in R. Alexander, C. Doddington, J. Gray, L. Hargreaves and R. Kershner (eds) *The Cambridge Primary Review Research Surveys*, London: Routledge, pp. 792-817.

Young, M. (2008) *Bringing Knowledge Back In: From Social Constructivism to Social Realism in the Sociology of Education*, London: Routledge.

Young, M. (2013) 'Overcoming the crisis in curriculum theory: A knowledge-based approach', *Journal of Curriculum Studies*, 45(2): 101-118.

UNIT 4.2

DEVELOPING A RICH READING CURRICULUM

Helen Hendry and Sonia Thompson

INTRODUCTION

Reading is a key driver of children's cognitive development and academic success at primary school and a foundation for their future learning in any subject (OECD, 2021; Sullivan and Brown, 2015). Although learning to read requires specific skills, increasingly research and government guidance highlight the importance of both the skill and the will to read (Cremin et al., 2023a; Department for Education [DfE], 2021; OECD, 2021). At the time of writing, children in England were ranked fourth in an international comparative study of reading skill (Mullis et al., 2023) and yet National Literacy Trust (NLT) research shows a decline in children's interest in reading to the lowest level since 2005, only '(43.4%) children and young people aged 8 to 18 said they enjoyed reading' (Clark, Picton and Galway, 2023).

The decline in interest is both worrying and important because other studies show that children who choose to read frequently appear to experience many benefits from doing so, including greater general knowledge, enhanced vocabulary and comprehension, improved narrative writing and better outcomes in Mathematics in comparison with peers who do not choose to read regularly (Sénéchal, Hill and Malette, 2018; Sullivan and Brown, 2015). Some studies also indicate the positive impact of reading for enjoyment on children's wellbeing (Sun et al., 2023). Whether teaching 3-year-olds or 11-year-olds, you have an important role to play as a teacher of reading, supporting the skills and motivation to read for those at early stages of reading, and nurturing progression in text choices, enjoyment and a regular reading habit for those who can read independently.

Children's attitudes towards reading and their motivation to read are influenced by adult role models (Cole et al., 2022; Cremin et al., 2023b). So, your engagement with reading, and the reading curriculum that you provide, will ultimately impact on whether they become readers for life. You can ensure that any children you work with have the skills and the will to read through developing a rich reading curriculum that includes a balance of planned learning opportunities within English teaching, and at other times in the school day.

A rich reading curriculum will provide chances to practice, apply and combine reading skills, e.g.:
- phonics;
- guided reading;
- English lessons that involve sharing, reflecting on, discussing and responding to texts in different ways;
- reading and discussing texts together in other curriculum subjects.

DOI: 10.4324/9781032691794-20

It will also include social reading experiences that are not taught lessons, e.g.:

- independent reading time;
- reading aloud;
- library visits;
- author visits;
- story time;
- book clubs;
- informal talk about texts and being a reader.

The impact of any of these reading opportunities is supported by how they are planned, monitored and resourced, as well as the classroom culture for reading. The environment, in particular the quality of texts and links to children's interests, is key to successfully engaging readers. Primary teachers need to be authentic reading role models (Commeyras, Bisplinghoff and Olson 2003; Cremin et al., 2014) – selecting, sharing, and recommending texts and authors; and getting to know children's reading habits and preferences. They must plan for progression and assess reading skills, working in partnership with parents and carers. This unit will explore key elements of a rich reading curriculum and offer strategies to develop a supportive classroom culture for reading.

OBJECTIVES

By the end of this unit you will:

- understand your role in supporting reading across the primary phase;
- be aware of some key components of a rich reading curriculum and how these link to the skills and dispositions needed to become a reader;
- recognise the importance of reading for pleasure;
- identify ways that you can select texts for different purposes;
- know some ways in which the reading curriculum can support reading comprehension, and decoding;
- be aware of possible ways to work with parents and teaching assistants (TAs) to support reading.

The next task asks you to reflect on some possible starting points and how you might develop a wider repertoire of texts to support your English teaching, reading aloud and discussions with children.

Task 4.2.1 Reflect on your knowledge of children's texts

- Do you currently read any contemporary children's books?
- Could you recommend a recent author to a child you are working with?
- Have you ever talked to primary aged children about your own reading preferences – whether a novel, a blog, a magazine or a comic?

- Visit one of these pages recommending contemporary texts and prize-winning authors:
  https://ourfp.org/awards/
  https://justimagine.co.uk/childrens-books-reviews/
  Choosing from one of these websites, which recent children's text or author might you start off by reading (even if you don't normally choose to read)?
- What could you say in a chat with a child about your reading choices as a child or an adult, that is honest, but still encourages them to read?

In Northern Ireland ...

Children should be encouraged to develop a love of books and the disposition to read. As stories are read to them by adults and older children, they should see the reader as a role model. Children should have opportunities to listen to a range of interesting and exciting fiction, non-fiction, poetry and rhymes, retell familiar stories and share a wide range of books with adults and other children. Opportunities should be given to browse in the book corner and use books to find information. As children begin to realise that print has meaning and that reading can make sense of print, they should be encouraged to develop a curiosity about words, how they sound, the patterns within words and how they are composed. Through sharing and using books, children should become familiar with letters and their shape and sound. Reading experiences should be informal and enjoyable, with children learning in an environment where print is all around them, for example, in captions, labels and instructions. Children should have access to a wide range of reading materials throughout the day, for example, menus, catalogues, fiction, non-fiction, comics, magazines, on-screen text, personalised books, class books, and books related to areas of play. They should have regular opportunities as a whole class, in small groups and individually to see modelled reading and to participate in shared reading. As they move through the Foundation Stage they should have opportunities to read individually or in small groups with teacher guidance.

They should be given opportunities to read for different purposes, developing strategies for researching, understanding, managing and refining information from traditional and digital sources. They should be encouraged, through stimulating and fun activities, to read widely for enjoyment and information. Over time, with praise and encouragement, they should have opportunities to engage independently with more challenging and lengthy texts including those in digital format, whilst reflecting, analysing and discussing the meaning of the text.
(Council for Curriculum Examinations and Assessment [CCEA], 2007: 20, 51)

WHAT MAKES A READER?

Children's identities as readers are shaped by their experiences at home and school, their access to texts, conversations about reading with peers and adults, and reading role models who they encounter. Children need the technical skills and knowledge to decode words on the page and make meaning, but **as importantly**, they need to be motivated to read and practice these skills through choosing to read regularly for pleasure, to gain the maximum cognitive, academic, personal and social benefits of being a reader.

> ### In Scotland …
>
> Every child in Scotland receives four free 'Bookbug' bags between birth and age 8. These include books, games and resources to support families to adopt a playful approach to reading interactions and experiences. The Scottish Book Trust, in conjunction with the Scottish Government, positions family engagement in reading as the foundation for building a rich reading curriculum.
>
> From the earliest years, national practice guidance positions reading as a playful act. Educators are encouraged to 'tap into' what they know about the child's interests and family life to build an authentic reading curriculum.
>
> Education Scotland offers a range of case studies from practice to support the development of pedagogy and practice when developing a rich reading curriculum. Case studies such as the Primary Literacy Programme in Renfrewshire consider whole school approaches to supporting an inclusive reading environment.
>
> Sources: Scottish Book Trust (n.d.); Education Scotland (2017, 2020).

Skills and knowledge

At the heart of a rich reading curriculum is your understanding of the different processes that are involved in reading. A common model used in teacher education and underpinning Government guidance in England is the Simple View of Reading (SVR) (Gough and Tunmer, 1986) which outlines that reading comprehension requires both word recognition and language comprehension. Word recognition involves sight recognition or decoding written words on a page, whereas language comprehension involves the understanding of spoken language (Westerveld, Armstrong and Barton, 2020). Scarborough's (2001) reading rope, and a more recent revisiting of the SVR (Tunmer and Hoover, 2019), highlight the complex range of skills, knowledge and dispositions which enable children to become effective engaged readers. These include knowledge of phonemes, the meaning of words and phrases, vocabulary, sentence structure, grammar and punctuation, background knowledge of topics and word connections, and conventions and purposes of different types of texts, all of which are influenced by children's life experiences and opportunities to listen to and share reading with adults at home and school (Scarborough, 2001; Westerveld, Armstrong and Barton, 2020).

To support the development of these skills and knowledge, a rich reading curriculum will include explicit teaching of word recognition, decoding and vocabulary, before children can read independently. Wyse and Hacking's Helix model (2024) (Figure 4.2.1) illustrates that reading, writing and talk are mutually supportive and develop concurrently. Children need frequent in-depth opportunities for reading, hearing and discussing high quality texts of different genres which will help with language comprehension, further vocabulary, knowledge of texts, sentence structure, grammar and punctuation. You can plan for these opportunities as part of English lessons, read alouds, independent reading time and book clubs (a timetabled slot in the school week, designated for social reading for pleasure and recommendations) (DfE, 2021).

Motivation and enjoyment

In addition to the knowledge and skills development underpinning the rich reading curriculum, dispositions are key to children becoming readers for life. A good reader has high levels of affective processes

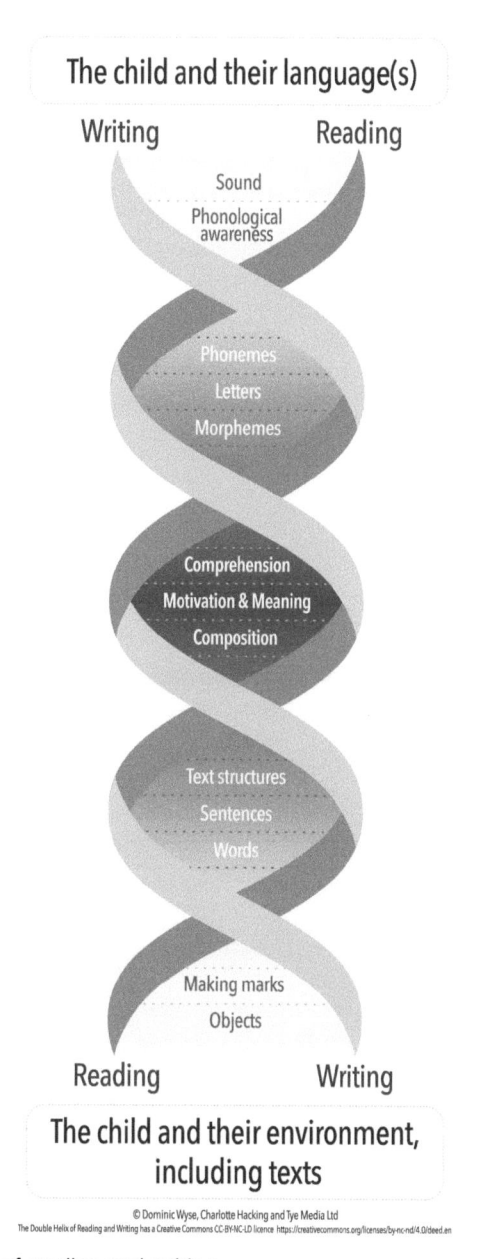

FIGURE 4.2.1 The double helix of reading and writing

For the full original account of *The Double Helix of Reading and Writing* see Dominic Wyse and Charlotte Hacking: *The Balancing Act: An evidence informed approach to teaching phonics, reading and writing*. Published by Routledge, 2024.

(including high levels of reading enjoyment) and reading behaviours (including reading outside school daily) (Clark and Teravainen, 2017). Motivation to read can be encouraged by text choice, involvement in peer interactions, relationships around reading, and family and teacher reading role models (Cremin et al., 2023b; McGeown et al., 2012; McGeown et al., 2020). Opportunities for reading for pleasure (RfP) outside of English lessons are therefore key to children's motivation to read.

READING FOR PLEASURE

The aims of the English national curriculum include developing love of literature through widespread reading for enjoyment (DfE, 2014) referred to as RfP. Key strands of RfP pedagogy include regular reading aloud and independent reading times outside of English lessons, involving informal book talk, inside text talk and reader recommendations, within a highly social reading environment (Cremin et al., 2014). These are based on children's choices and interests, and are informal and relaxed, with children and adults interacting socially, reading together and chatting. They are underpinned by the teacher's knowledge of children's texts and the interests and reading preferences of children in the class. You should be able to chat about books you have read and recommend books to individuals, thinking carefully about how you 'hook' the less motivated readers with texts beyond normal reading scheme or curriculum materials such as comics, magazines, graphic novels, football stories, etc. You can also reflect on and discuss your own reading choices, using your experiences as readers to inform your classroom practice (Cremin et al., 2023c).

> **In Wales...**
>
> They should be encouraged to experience and respond to a variety of diverse literature that gives them insight into the culture, people and history of Wales as well as the wider world. Through this, as their understanding of their own and other people's experiences, beliefs and cultures is enhanced, learners can develop their ability to demonstrate empathy.
>
> (Welsh Government, 2021)

Texts and the environment

Research highlights that teachers' knowledge of children's text focuses on those which they read as children, authors whose work has been made into films and television programmes and 'celebrity authors' (Cremin et al., 2024a; Centre for Literacy in Primary Education [CLPE], 2023). Reliance on a popular childhood canon is a problem for teachers as they need to engage children by drawing on a diverse range of contemporary authors, whose lives and works reflect those of children in the 21st century. There is a danger that teachers' over-reliance on a limited range of texts limits children's experience of more recent possibilities (Cremin et al. 2014; Farrar, 2021). Many older texts do not positively reflect children and families from a range of ethnic and cultural backgrounds, same sex parents, children or family members who are disabled; they cannot link to common current issues and concerns such as climate change, refugee families or living in poverty. Over the last seven years, UK publishers have begun to focus on increasing the ethnic diversity of characters, authors and illustrators represented in the children's book market, first concentrating on picture books and non-fiction (CLPE, 2024). There are still significant gaps in these and fiction texts for older readers, making it imperative that you are familiar with new texts that do provide greater diversity.

As Sims Bishop (1990) argued, texts that include a range of families, locations and cultures can provide mirrors, windows and sliding glass doors so that children can see themselves in texts, use texts to experience lives beyond their own and learn to empathise with others in different circumstances. It's also important for you to know about different types of texts that children might enjoy reading such as non-fiction texts, poetry or newspapers aimed at children. This variety of texts can be drawn upon in English and linked to subject specific language learning in other curriculum lessons (DfE, 2019: 14); they can be used to engage children in reading for pleasure at home and school. Researching new publications and reading alongside your class will help you to build a rich repertoire of texts to draw upon in your teaching. You also need to select texts to read with, and to, children for different purposes in curriculum lessons, as models for writing and to provide opportunities to develop comprehension.

How children engage in reading is strongly determined by their access to appealing texts, time to read and social relationships that support reading (Cremin *et al.*, 2023a, 2023b). The reading environment includes the whole school, all classrooms, the outside area, the school library or book corner, but the quality and accessibility of texts and the talk environment is much more important than spending time on 'performing' reading for pleasure, so that the environment looks attractive but is not engaging pupils to read (McDonald, Hamilton and Hesmondhalgh, 2023). Involving children in choosing books for a class book corner and designing the layout or systems for borrowing can also give children ownership and interest in participation (Reedy and De Carvalho, 2021). The DfE Reading Framework for the primary years recommends:

> Every book in a book corner should be worth reading aloud. The focus should always be on what would make the biggest difference to children's reading habits, including:
> - not displaying too many books at once
> - refreshing the display
> - making the books attractive and easy for children to find.
>
> (DfE, 2021: 37)

Reading aloud

Reading aloud in the early years offers benefits for children's early literacy and spoken language (Stahl, 2003) with longer term positive impacts on reading, maths and cognitive skills as children progress through primary school (Kalb and van Ours, 2013). Even when children can read independently, listening to texts being read aloud and discussing them provides a model for reading fluency, develops comprehension and vocabulary and allows them to experience texts and language beyond their own reading abilities. In research, reading aloud engaged less able readers and gave them confidence and motivation to participate in discussion and read more independently (Westbrook *et al.*, 2019) as well as supporting children's wellbeing through making connections with others (Batini, Bartolucci and Timpone, 2018). Parental engagement in reading aloud at home can have a significant positive impact on children's reading outcomes and engagement (Gilleece and Eivers, 2018; OECD, 2021). However, UK studies show a decline in parents reading aloud at home (Farshore, 2023). Arguably, this makes setting aside time in the school day to read aloud to primary children in any age group even more important, especially offering time where this is relaxed and engaging and not only as part of English lessons.

Key features of effective interactive read alouds that engage children and encourage them to read for pleasure include:

- regular time slots that are not interrupted by other tasks – at the end of the day may not be the best time for children to relax and pay attention;
- building up the length of read aloud sessions;
- ensuring that any longer texts are covered rapidly enough to maintain the interest of the children;
- involving children in choosing the text for reading aloud;
- varying the types of texts shared;

- ensuring that there are social opportunities for children and teacher to chat about the text and make links to their own experiences and other reading;
- using open ended prompts for talk (e.g. What other texts does this remind you of?) rather than assessing understanding through comprehension questions (unless the read aloud is part of an English lesson with this intention).

(Cremin, Harris and Courtney, 2023; Batini, 2022)

Talking about reading and why we do it also helps to motivate and include children in a class reading community (Cremin, Harris and Courtney, 2023). The outcome of regular interactive reading aloud sessions is that children may make re-readings, alone and with friends, and even 'play' the text with puppets or on the playground. When preparing for reading aloud, encourage the children to vote on the text they would like to hear, consider possible discussion points and practice reading aloud to develop your own confidence as a role model for young readers. You also need to offer a choice of books that will 'motivate pupils to read gradually more demanding texts' (DfE, 2021: 63).

EARLY READING

Early reading skills are routinely taught in the first years of the primary phase but are often still being developed by children new to English, or with additional learning needs, throughout the primary phase. Alongside teaching, decoding and word recognition, a rich early reading curriculum includes opportunities to listen to different types of texts read aloud; memorise and recite poems, stories and songs; look at texts with peers and adults; and remember and recreate stories through playing with language (DfE, 2021; Verhoeven and Perfetti, 2021). You should build time in the curriculum for sharing stories, rhymes, poems and songs, where you model playing with language and talking about texts.

Re-reading familiar texts aloud holds particular value in the early stages of reading development, for children to revisit and deepen understanding, to make connections with their life experiences and to increase participation and enjoyment (Rodriguez-Leon and Payler, 2021). It also offers opportunities outside of decodable or reading scheme texts for adults to model high quality oral language, and for children to encounter high frequency vocabulary, as required by the DfE (2019). Informal book talk about familiar texts which children have heard allows children to further consolidate new vocabulary and apply this in their conversations. This may include discussion about favourite parts or memorable events in which children can expand on language and concepts with confidence based on text familiarity. You can ensure children have access to texts which have been read aloud in class, to discuss and share in pairs in order to support this talk (Cremin et al., 2024b).

Teaching children to decode words using phonics is a key strategy, mandated as part of teaching and assessment in English schools. Schools must teach reading using specific schemes for systematic synthetic phonics and initial teacher education (ITE) providers are required to ensure that student teachers have the relevant subject knowledge for phonics teaching (DfE, 2019). Whilst international research highlights that phonic strategies for early reading support children to decode (e.g. de Graaff et al., 2009), there is still debate about the most effective method for teaching phonics, and concern that a curriculum focus on teaching and testing phonic skills has led to teachers neglecting other important parts of a rich reading curriculum (Wyse and Bradbury, 2022). Current practice in English schools involves daily small group phonics sessions with children aged 5–7 until they have learned to recognise and apply the phoneme/grapheme (sound/letter) correspondences in the English language to segment and blend unfamiliar words for reading. They are also taught to memorise and recognise words which are used frequently but are not easily decodable (DfE, 2021: 51).

In later primary years, children who have not yet developed phonic knowledge may need additional support through intervention groups or one-to-ones until they are able to decode words independently. Your underlying knowledge of phonics, ability to model using phonic knowledge with children and to notice and support them when they make mistakes will form the basis of effective practice with any scheme or age group. It is important to take any opportunities to practice your phonic knowledge and skills of segmenting and blending. In school, make sure you arrange to participate in phonics sessions, observe teachers using the scheme and ask to be involved in any training, or access teachers' handbooks to support you (DfE, 2019). Be honest with your mentor and English subject leader when you are unsure, so they can help you. As phonics teaching follows a prescribed structure, it is important to keep sessions fun and varied. A phonics session plan from St. Matthew's Primary school in Birmingham offers an example (see Task 4.2.2).

Task 4.2.2 Reflecting on phonics teaching

At St Matthew's, phonics sessions form one part of a rich reading curriculum.

- Consider how the teacher incorporates the following to make the session memorable and fun: movement and touch; listening and looking; different media/materials; individual and group activities; encouragement and praise.
- Select the activities that focus on hearing the phoneme (sound) and identifying the grapheme (letters).

Lesson: Digraph "ch" – Charming Sounds Extravaganza	

Review
5 mins
	Review previously learned sounds and concepts.
	
	1 **Engagement Warm-up: Charades Challenge (3 minutes):**
	  • "Charades Challenge" – students act out words that contain sounds they've learned so far. Incorporate the "ch" sound in some of the words.
	
	2 **Quick Recall Game: Sound Speed Round (2 minutes):**
	  • Use flashcards/whiteboard for a quick sound speed round – look for children responding with the corresponding graphemes and share a word that starts with each sound.

Teach	Introduce the digraph "ch" and its sound.
	
	1 **Introduction: Cheerful "Ch" Chant (5 minutes):**
	  • Start with a 'Silly Soup' chant for the digraph "ch." – children to repeat after you, incorporating hand movements/claps
	
	2 **Interactive Teaching (3 minutes):**
	  • Explain that "ch" makes the sound /ch/ like in "cheese." Use visuals/gestures to reinforce the sound. Invite students to imitate the /ch/ sound.

Practice	Reinforce the "ch" sound through guided practice.
	
	1 **Crafty "Ch" Collages (5 minutes):**
	  • Put out pre-cut pictures from magazines/newspapers on tables – children to find pictures of objects with the "ch" sound and create collages.
	
	2 **Phonics Relay Race (5 minutes):**
	  • Children pass a baton and say a word containing the "ch" sound before passing it to the next team member (ask another child to help those that struggle).

Apply	Children to independently apply their knowledge of the "ch" sound.
	1 **Identify words with the "ch" sound (4 minutes):**
	• Use Phonics Play (online game) to identify and interact with words containing the "ch" sound.
	2 **Charming Story Writing (3 minutes):**
	• Write a sentence using words with the "ch" sound (provide colourful markers and paper for an engaging writing experience in free flow).
	Objective: Review the "ch" digraph and assess understanding.
	1 **Review Game: Charming Bingo (3 minutes):**
	• Play a game of "Charming Bingo" using words with the "ch" sound. Students mark their bingo cards when they hear a word with the target sound.
	2 **Assessment: Ch Sound Showcase (2 minutes):**
	• Ask students to showcase an object or drawing that represents the "ch" sound. Each student explains how their item relates to the sound.
	3 **Celebration and Certificates (2 minutes):**
	• Conclude the lesson with a celebration. Each student receives a "Charming Sounds Explorer" certificate for their enthusiastic participation and effort.

DEVELOPING READING COMPREHENSION

As outlined earlier in this unit, reading comprehension draws on children's vocabulary, understanding of text types, previous life experience and text experience (Tennent, 2014). Reading comprehension is different from comprehension of spoken language. It is an active process where readers 'build' understanding as they read successive words, phrases, sentences and paragraphs in the text and create a mental picture of what is happening (Tennent, 2014: Perkins, 2015). Reading comprehension occurs at different levels, such as being able to describe an event or character in a text, understanding things that have been implied but not directly stated, considering what might happen next, why characters have behaved in a certain way or what we can learn about our own lives from a text. To make meanings from texts, skilled readers will use strategies unconsciously and simultaneously such as:

- activating and using background knowledge
- generating and asking questions
- making predictions
- visualising
- monitoring comprehension
- summarising.

(DfE, 2019: 116)

Because these different ways of understanding a text are interrelated and often co-occurring, it is not useful to try to focus on teaching one element of comprehension at a time (Tennent, 2014, DfE, 2021): 'It is better to spend time developing comprehension by increasing and activating pupils' knowledge than by teaching reading comprehension strategies' (DfE, 2021: 108).

You should plan for discussing texts and unfamiliar vocabulary, using why questions, and asking children to explain how they reached an understanding from their reading, to support children to develop comprehension skills (Tennent, 2014; DfE, 2021). Helping children to share and check their understanding of texts through drama, drawing and informal writing can also be part of a rich reading curriculum. As children become independent readers, the frequency of reading for pleasure outside of school has a strong positive influence on their reading comprehension (Malanchini et al., 2017). Furthermore, you can support the processes underpinning comprehension, such as relating reading to background knowledge and keeping track of understanding through discussion of animations, films and images, sometimes referred to as visual literacy.

It is crucial for teachers to think through the potential of any text they use. Tennent et al. (2016) recommend mapping the opportunities the text can provide, for both teaching and rich discussion, considering: vocabulary, theme, visual language, links to background knowledge, narrative features, writing opportunities, wider learning opportunities, language features, literary features and inference opportunities.

Task 4.2.3 Mapping text potential for reading

Choose a poem from the children's poet Joshua Seigel's website: www.joshuaseigal.co.uk/my-poems

Make a mind map or table of the potential opportunities in the text that you notice, under the following headings: vocabulary, theme, visual language, links to background knowledge, narrative features, writing opportunities, wider learning opportunities, language features, literary features and inference opportunities.

What would this poem work well for? E.g. Reading aloud and encouraging children to visualise to support comprehension, discussing new vocabulary? Linking to other familiar stories or poems?

Myatt (2020: 90) writes that 'concepts have a powerful effect on learning. Identifying the big ideas helps pupils to make sense of what they are being taught … The identification and explicit teaching of concepts support pupils to make rich connections.' It is these connections that the DfE (2021) espouses as an alternative to teaching comprehension strategies. Cox et al. (2023) write about how the right text provides a wealth of possibilities for teaching. They state that concepts provide 'a rich panorama of literary meaning to be explored and loved, rather than a limited curriculum of single unrelated tasks, starkly out of context' (Cox et al., 2023: 34). The next example from St. Matthew's primary school in Birmingham showcases how this might be approached in practice.

Task 4.2.4 Exploring concepts for reading comprehension

A concept/device or a theme is a technique that writers use to express ideas, convey meaning and highlight important subjects in a piece of text. The idea of literary meaning drives many of our reading sessions at St Matthew's. In Y6, *Paddington at the Palace* (Bond, 2019) provides opportunities to explore the concept of anthropomorphism (a literary device that assigns human characteristics to nonhuman entities like animals or objects). In exposing children to the concept, there are opportunities for rich discussions about:

- how the author creates a connection with a young audience, through the use of a cuddly animal;
- why anthropomorphism appeals to children – it is easily relatable to and adheres to the imaginative mind of a young child;
- how animal characters are ambiguous due to the lack of gender, race, age, etc., which allows a wider range of children to identify with them.

Can you think of other texts that also have animal characters with human characteristics and how this could be an interesting point to discuss with children? Can you think of other books that use concept/device or a theme to express ideas, convey meaning and highlight important subjects in a piece of text? See the following table for some recommendations.

Concept/Device or Theme	Things to consider	Books
Imagery	– Appeals to readers' senses through highly descriptive language – Follow the rule of 'show, not tell' – Strong imagery truly paints a picture of the scene at hand.	• *Charlotte's Web* – E.B. White • *We're Going on a Bear Hunt* – Michael Rosen • *The Snowman* – Raymond Briggs • *We're Going to Find the Monster* – Dapo Adeola and Malorie Blackman • *Where the Wild Things Are* – Maurice Sendak
Personification	– Uses human traits to describe nonhuman things. Anthropomorphism actually *applies* but personification means the behaviour of the thing does not actually change.	• *The Day the Crayons Quit* – Drew Daywalk • *Click, Clack Moo: Cows That Type* – Doreen Cronin • *The True Story of the 3 Little Pigs* – Jon Scieszka • *Winnie-The-Pooh* – A.A. Milne
Character change	– When a character changes from the story's beginning to the end, it's called a character arc. – They help to teach children about a character's growth and change – their arc.	• *The Very Hungry Caterpillar* – Eric Carle • *After the Fall: How Humpty Dumpty Got Back Up Again* – Dan Santat • *Tuesday* – David Wiesner • *Little Red* – Bethan Woolvin
Environment/Sustainability	– Caring for our planet and protecting the environment are important – Books about the environment can be a great tool for empowering children – These books can help children to understand their choices and to find hope, in making a positive impact on our planet.	• *Clean Up* – Nathan Byron and Dapo Adeola • *The Great Paper Caper* – Oliver Jeffers • *Dear Greenpeace* – Simon James • *Belonging* – Jeanie Baker • *Paperbag Prince* – Colin Thompson

WORKING WITH OTHERS

In your role as a primary teacher, you are likely to work with teaching assistants and volunteers and you may have a school librarian who can support your rich reading curriculum. You can also make links with public libraries, authors, illustrators or external programmes that support reading and literacy in the primary phase. You will want to find ways to engage parents and families in home reading activities because of the benefits for young readers in terms of the motivation and enjoyment offered by shared reading at home (Cremin et al., 2023a; DfE, 2019; Scholes, Spina and Comber, 2021; OECD, 2021). You can work with other school staff to role model reading for pleasure and provide informal opportunities to chat about and share reading across the whole school such as in reading assemblies, taking books onto the playground or through older children reading to and with younger ones in reading time.

Schools may also be able to reach out to families through reading events and opportunities planned within the school calendar, whether at weekends, before or after school. A key part of your role is to build relationships with parents, carers and families to support children's motivation to read. Finding ways to share books with families and encouraging them to read with children at home is vital, they may also need support to understand that reading of all kinds can be valuable, and that their role is more than listening to the reading scheme book at home. Key features that may make such activities successful include:

- consulting with families about what reading activities they would like to happen and timings that are convenient for them;
- arranging informal events, such as book swaps, where teacher involvement is low key, and families do not feel judged;
- providing opportunities for families (parents and children together) to experience different books and genres in a relaxed environment such as a book café.

(Levy, Doyle and Cairns Vollans, 2023)

Working with national and community-based organisations can also enrich your reading curriculum, especially when these offer opportunities to link to children's interests, encourage collaboration with peers and creative experts and provide positive feedback and encouragement that breaks down any fear of 'getting it wrong' (Cremin et al., 2023b; Mukherjee, McGreevy and Williams, 2023). This is often led by your school co-ordinator for reading or English, but making suggestions to be used across the school, or setting something small scale up for your class, may be possible for student teachers. For example, Empathy Lab (empathylab.uk) offers book guides, strategies for teaching and an annual celebration event, 'Empathy Day', around high quality picture books that support children to develop empathy for others through exploring stories. Arranging an empathy day in your own class could involve parents, children and other adults in reading and talking about texts with a different focus to the usual school expectations of reading (Mukherjee, McGreevy and Williams, 2023).

TAs and volunteers are routinely used to support groups and individuals with reading activities based on skills such as phonic groups, guided group reading of the same text or one-to-one practice for children reading out loud to the adult. You should take time to include any additional adults in your reading curriculum by ensuring you all have a shared understanding of the principles in this unit, and that they are not relying on their own memories of learning to read in school.

FORMATIVE ASSESSMENT FOR READING

Ongoing 'noticing' of children's reading behaviours, attitudes and interests is a vital part of supporting children's motivation to read, as well as tracking the development of their skills. This will involve you, and any additional adults you may be working with, observing children informally during different reading opportunities (Wilson and Scanlon, 2004). This could be every few weeks to help identify the next steps for children in terms of recommending books that could interest them or involving them in more informal book talk to help with their engagement and comprehension. You can focus extra attention on children whose reading you are concerned about, or who seem to be disengaged (one to three children in any session might be manageable). The CLPE reading scales (2016) offer descriptions of children's reading skills and behaviours at different stages, including children's ability to decode and recognise words, their knowledge of different texts and the type of talk they might engage in around reading. These scales can be useful to compare with your classroom observations of children and reflect on strategies for next steps to support them. For example, perhaps you want to set up a small group 'book tasting' activity for the children who have been observed as beginning to extend their reading choices. They would be given a small selection of books to browse and discuss what interests them and why – therefore helping them to choose and consider different types of texts. In such an activity, you could note down what they are drawn to and make sure that the texts they showed an interest in are offered to them to take home or enjoy in reading time. During one-to-one and group work, or reading for pleasure time, you or additional adults could ask children planned questions, or lead activities that capture information about their reading at home and their current interests (Wilson and Scanlon, 2004), all with the aim of adapting reading teaching to meet their needs.

SUMMARY

This unit outlines the complex balance of skills, knowledge and reading experiences that make up a rich reading curriculum in the primary phase. These include systematic teaching of phonics and word recognition, with frequent planned exposure to high quality texts and talk about them through English lessons, in other curriculum subjects, and in reading for pleasure sessions. It is essential to set aside daily, informal and social opportunities for reading for pleasure, as well as English lessons, and skills focused work on phonics (for children at the early stages of reading competency). The teachers' role as a reading role model, and in building a culture in which all kinds of reading is valued and discussed, is key to motivating children to want to read, so teacher knowledge of recent, diverse texts, from a range of genres, is vital. Children need access to a tailored selection of texts that engage them at school and home, including listening to texts beyond their own reading level. At all stages, the goal of the rich reading curriculum is to create motivated readers (and talkers and writers) who actively make meaning from their reading and want to read more. Involving parents, creatives and community groups can ensure that motivation to read is further embedded, that children develop a positive reader identity and that reading becomes a habit for life.

ANNOTATED FURTHER READING

Cremin, T., Hendry, H., Rodriguez-Leon, L. and Kucirkova, N. (2023) *Reading Teachers: Nurturing Reading for Pleasure*, London: Routledge.
    This book focuses on research-informed practical case studies for supporting reading for pleasure.

Centre for Literacy in Primary Education (CLPE). (2016) *The Reading Scale*, London: CLPE. Retrieved from: https://clpe.org.uk/system/files/CLPE%20READING%20SCALE%20REBRAND.pdf
    The reading scale offers a starting point for observing progress in reading.

Department for Education (DfE). (2021) *The Reading Framework*. Last updated 2023. Retrieved from: www.gov.uk/government/publications/the-reading-framework-teaching-the-foundations-of-literacy

    This DfE guidance offers a comprehensive, research informed view of teaching practices for reading in primary and KS3.

Tennent, W., Reedy, D., Hobsbaum, A. and Gamble, N. (2016) *Guiding Readers – Layers of Meaning. A Handbook for Teaching Reading Comprehension to 7-11-Year-Olds*. London: UCL, IoE Press.

    This book offers strategies, underpinned with clear explanations about how children can be supported to comprehend their reading.

FURTHER READING TO SUPPORT M-LEVEL STUDY

Cremin, T., Hendry, H., Chamberlain, L. and Hulston, S. (2023) *Approaches to Reading and Writing for Pleasure and Executive Summary of the Research*, London: The Mercers' Company. Retrieved from: https://cdn.ourfp.org/wp-content/uploads/20231201185032/Reading-and-Writing-for-Pleasure_FRAMEWORK-DIGITAL-FINAL-30.11.23.pdf?_ga=2.120594440.1840792751.1702661056-924204056.1683819856

    This document synthesises reading and writing for pleasure research from the last 30 years.

Rodriguez-Leon, L. and Payler, J. (2021) 'Surfacing complexity in shared book reading: The role of affordance, repetition and modal appropriation in children's participation', *Learning, Culture and Social Interaction*, 28(100496).

    This article offers an in-depth insight into the valuable processes in shared book reading.

Wyse, D. and Hacking, C. (2024) *The Balancing Act: An Evidence Informed Approach to Teaching Phonics, Reading and Writing*, London: Routledge.

    This book draws on large scale research evidence to explore how to balance the different components of an English curriculum.

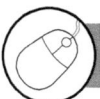

RELEVANT WEBSITES

Centre for Literacy in Primary Education (CLPE): https://clpe.org.uk/

    Charity offering training, free resources and research, including the 'Reflecting Realities' research into diversity in children's texts.

The Open University Reading for Pleasure website: https://ourfp.org/

    Offers research and examples of practice for supporting reading for pleasure in schools as well as author and text recommendations.

The Teachers Reading Challenge: https://teachersreadingchallenge.org.uk/

    This website, created by the Reading Agency and The Open University, offers recommendations to support teachers' knowledge of children's texts

The National Literacy Trust charity: https://literacytrust.org.uk/

    Offers resources, training and research.

REFERENCES

Batini F. (2022) 'Reading aloud as a stimulus and facilitation of children's narratives', *Debates em Educação*, 14(34): 113-126. DOI: 10.28998/2175-6600.2022v14n34p113-126.

Batini, F., Bartolucci, M. and Timpone, A. (2018) 'The effects of reading aloud in the primary school', *Psychology of Education: An Interdisciplinary Journal*, 55(1 and 2): 111-141.

Bond, M. (2019) *Paddington at the Palace*, London: Harper Collins.

Clark, C., Picton, I., and Galway, M. (2023) *Children and Young People's Reading in 2023*, London: NLT. Retrieved from: https://nlt.cdn.ngo/media/documents/Reading_trends_2023.pdf

Clark, C. and Teravainen, A. (2017) *What it Means to Be a Reader at Age 11: Valuing Skills, Affective Components and Behavioural Processes. An Outline of the Evidence*, London: National Literacy Trust. Retrieved from https://nlt.cdn.ngo/media/documents/ROGO_model_evidence_base_December_2017_-_final.pdf

Centre for Literacy in Primary Education (CLPE). (2016) *The Reading Scale*, London: CLPE. Retrieved from: https://clpe.org.uk/system/files/CLPE%20READING%20SCALE%20REBRAND.pdf

Centre for Literacy in Primary Education (CLPE). (2022) *Reflecting Realities, Survey of Ethnic Representation Within UK Children's Literature* November 2024, London: CLPE. Retrieved from: https://clpe.org.uk/research/clpe-reflecting-realities-survey-ethnic-representation-within-uk-childrens-literature-2

Centre for Literacy in Primary Education (CLPE). (2023) *Reading for Pleasure in 2021-22. Learning About the Teaching of Reading in Primary Schools in January 2022*, London: CLPE. Retrieved from: https://clpe.org.uk/system/files/2022-03/CLPE%20Reading%20for%20Pleasure%202021%20v3.pdf

Cole, A., Brown, A., Clark, C. and Picton, I. (2022) *Role Models and Their Influence on Children and Young People's Reading*, London: National Literacy Trust. Retrieved from: https://nlt.cdn.ngo/media/documents/Young_childrens_reading_in_2022_-_Final.pdf

Commeyras, M., Bisplinghoff, B. and Olson, J. (2003) *Teachers as Readers: Perspectives on the Importance of Reading in Teachers' Classrooms and Lives*, Newark, D.E.: International Literacy Association.

Council for Curriculum Examinations and Assessment (CCEA). (2007) *The Northern Ireland Curriculum – Primary*. Belfast: CCEA. Retrieved from: https://ccea.org.uk/downloads/docs/ccea-asset/Curriculum/The%20Northern%20Ireland%20Curriculum%20-%20Primary.pdf

Cox, B. Crawford, L. Jenkins, A and Sargent, J. (2023) *Opening Doors to Ambitious Primary English: Pitching High and Including All*, Carmarthen: Crown House Publishing.

Cremin, T., Mottram, M., Collins, F. M., Powell, S. and Safford, K. (2014) *Building Communities of Engaged Readers: Reading for Pleasure*, Oxon: Routledge.

Cremin, T., Hendry, H., Chamberlain, L. and Hulston, S. (2023a) *Approaches to Reading and Writing for Pleasure: An Executive Summary of the Research*, London: The Mercers' Company. Retrieved from: https://cdn.ourfp.org/wp-content/uploads/20231212163945/Reading-and-Writing-for-Pleasure-REVIEW_04Dec-FINAL.pdf

Cremin, T., Hendry, H., Chamberlain, L. and Hulston, S. (2023b) *Reading and Writing for Pleasure: A Framework for Practice. Executive Summary*, London: The Mercers' Company. Retrieved from: https://cdn.ourfp.org/wp-content/uploads/20231201185032/Reading-and-Writing-for-Pleasure_FRAMEWORK-DIGITAL-FINAL-30.11.23.pdf

Cremin, T., Hendry, H., Rodriguez Leon, L. and Kucirkova, N. (eds) (2023c) *Reading Teachers: Nurturing Reading for Pleasure*, London: Routledge.

Cremin, T., Mukherjee, S. J., Aerial, J. A. and Kauppinen, M. (2024a) 'Recognizing the existence of a popular childhood canon: Towards enriching teachers' reading repertoires', *The Reading Teacher*: 1–9.

Cremin. T., Rodriguez Leon, L., Hendry, H. and Hulston, S. (2024b) 'Informal book talk: Digging beneath the surface', *Education 3-13*.

Cremin, T., Harris, B. and Courtney, M. (2023) 'Reading aloud', in T. Cremin, H. Hendry, L. Rodriguez Leon and N. Kucirkova (eds) *Reading Teachers: Nurturing Reading for Pleasure*, London: Routledge, pp. 73–87.

de Graaff, S., Bosman, A. M. T., Hasselman, F. and Verhoeven, L. (2009) 'Benefits of systematic phonics instruction', *Scientific Studies of Reading*, 13(4): 318-333. DOI: 10.1080/10888430903001308

Department for Education (DfE). (2014) *Statutory Guidance: National Curriculum in England: English Programmes of Study*. Retrieved from www.gov.uk/government/publications/national-curriculum-in-england-english-programmes-of-study/national-curriculum-in-england-english-programmes-of-study

Department for Education (DfE). (2019) *Initial Teacher Training (ITT): Core Content Framework*. Last updated 2024. Retrieved from: www.gov.uk/government/publications/initial-teacher-training-itt-core-content-framework

Department for Education (DfE). (2021) *The Reading Framework*. Last updated 2023. Retrieved from: www.gov.uk/government/publications/the-reading-framework-teaching-the-foundations-of-literacy

Education Scotland. (2017) *Primary Literacy Coaching Programme in Renfrewshire*. Last updated 2023. Retrieved from: https://education.gov.scot/resources/primary-literacy-coaching-programme-in-renfrewshire/

Education Scotland. (2020) *Realising the Ambition: Being Me: National Practice Guidance for Early Years in Scotland*. Retrieved from: https://education.gov.scot/media/3bjpr3wa/realisingtheambition.pdf

Farrar, J. (2021) '"I don't really have a reason to read children's literature": Enquiring into primary student teachers' knowledge of children's literature', *Journal of Literary Education*, 4: 217-236.

Farshore (2023) *Storytime in School. Farshore, Storytime Trial Research Report*. Retrieved from: www.farshore.co.uk/wp-content/uploads/sites/46/2023/09/Farshore_Storytime-in-Schools_Whitepaper_FINAL.pdf

Gilleece, L. and Eivers, E. (2018) 'Characteristics associated with paper-based and online reading in Ireland: Findings from PIRLS and ePIRLS 2016', *International Journal of Educational Research*, 91: 16-27. doi: 10.1016/J.IJER.2018.07.004

Gough, P. B. and Tunmer, W. E. (1986) 'Decoding, reading, and reading disability', *Remedial and Special Education*, 7: 6-10.

Kalb, G. and van Ours, J. (2013) 'Reading to children: A head-start in life', *Economics of Education Review*, 40: 1-24. doi: 10.1016/j.econedurev.2014.01.002

Levy, R., Doyle, J. and Cairns Vollans, E. (2023) 'Parental and community involvement', in T. Cremin, H. Hendry, L. Rodriguez Leon and N. Kucirkova (eds) *Reading Teachers: Nurturing Reading for Pleasure*, London: Routledge, pp. 162-176.

Malanchini, M., Wang, Z., Voronin, I., Schenker, V. J., Plomin, R., Petrill, S. and Kovas, Y. (2017) 'Reading self-perceived ability, enjoyment and achievement: A genetically informative study of their reciprocal links over time', *Developmental Psychology*, 53(4): 698-712. http://doi.org/10.1037/dev0000209

McDonald, R., Hamilton, E. and Hesmondhalgh, L. (2023) 'Social reading environments', in T. Cremin, H. Hendry, L. Rodriguez Leon and N. Kucirkova (eds) *Reading Teachers: Nurturing Reading for Pleasure*, London: Routledge, pp. 114-127.

McGeown, S., Goodwin, H., Henderson, N. and Wright, P. (2012). 'Gender differences in reading motivation: Does sex or gender identity provide a better account?', *Journal of Research in Reading*, 35(3): 328-336. doi: 10.1111/j.1467-9817.2010.01481.

McGeown, S., Bonsall, J., Andries, V., Howarth, D. and Wilkinson, K. (2020). 'Understanding reading motivation across different text types: Qualitative insights from children', *Journal of Research in Reading*, 43(4): 597-608. doi: 10.1111/1467-9817.12320.

Mukherjee, S. McGreevy, C. and Williams, C. (2023) 'Celebrating reading', in in T. Cremin, H. Hendry, L. Rodriguez Leon and N. Kucirkova (eds) *Reading Teachers: Nurturing Reading for Pleasure*, London: Routledge, pp. 176-188.

Mullis, I. V. S., von Davier, M., Foy, P., Fishbein, B., Reynolds, K. A. and Wry, E. (2023) *PIRLS 2021 International Results in Reading*, Boston College, TIMSS and PIRLS International Study Center. https://doi.org/10.6017/lse.tpisc.tr2103.kb5342

Myatt, M. (2020) *Back on Track: Fewer Things, Greater Depth*, Melton: John Catt Educational Ltd.

OECD (2021) *21st-Century Readers: Developing Literacy Skills in a Digital World*, Paris: OECD Publishing. Retrieved from: https://doi.org/10.1787/a83d84cb-en

Perkins, M. (2015) *Becoming a Teacher of Reading*, London: Sage.

Reedy, A. and De Carvalho, R. (2021) 'Children's perspectives on reading, agency and their environment: What can we learn about reading for pleasure from an East London primary school?' *Education 3-13*, 49(2): 134-147. DOI: 10.1080/03004279.2019.1701514

Rodriguez-Leon, L. and Payler, J. (2021) 'Surfacing complexity in shared book reading: The role of affordance, repetition and modal appropriation in children's participation', *Learning, Culture and Social Interaction*, 28(100496): 1-12.

Scarborough, H. S. (2001) 'Connecting early language and literacy to later reading (dis)abilities: Evidence, theory, and practice' in S. Neuman and D. Dickinson (eds) *Handbook for Research in Early Literacy* (Vol. 1), New York: Guilford Press, Chapter 8, pp. 97-110.

Scholes, L., Spina, N. and Comber, B. (2021) 'Disrupting the "boys don't read" discourse: Primary school boys who love reading fiction', *British Educational Research Journal*, 47(1): 163-180. doi: 10.1002/berj.3685

Scottish Book Trust. (n.d.) *Bookbug*. Retrieved from: www.scottishbooktrust.com/topics/bookbug

Sénéchal, M., Hill, S. and Malette, M. (2018) 'Individual differences in grade 4 children's written compositions: The role of online planning and revising, oral storytelling, and reading for pleasure', *Cognitive Development*, 45: 92-104. https://doi.org/10.1016/j.cogdev.2017.12.004

Sims Bishop, R. (1990) 'Mirrors, windows and sliding-glass doors. Choosing and using books for the classroom', *Perspectives*, 6: x-xi.

Stahl, S. A. (2003) 'What do we expect storybook reading to do? How storybook reading impacts word recognition', in A. van Kleeck, S. A. Stahl and E. B. Bauer (eds) *On Reading Books to Children: Parents and Teachers*, New Jersey: Lawrence Erlbaum Associate, pp. 363-383.

Sullivan, A. and Brown, M. (2015) 'Reading for pleasure and progress in vocabulary and mathematics', *British Educational Research Journal*, 41(1): 971-991. doi: 10.1002/berj.3180

Sun, Y-J., Sahakian, B. J., Langley, C., Yang, A., Jiang, Y., Jujiao K., Zhao, X., Li, C., Cheng, W. and Fen, J. (2023) 'Early initiated childhood reading for pleasure: Associations with better cognitive performance, mental well-being and brain structure in young adolescence', *Psychological Medicine*: 1-15. https://doi.org/10.1017/S0033291723001381

Tennent, W. (2014) *Understanding Reading Comprehension*, UK: SAGE Publications, Ltd. https://bookshelf.vitalsource.com/books/9781473909557

Tennent, W., Reedy, D., Hobsbaum, A., and Gamble, N. (ed.) (2016) *Guiding Readers - Layers of Meaning: A Handbook for Teaching Reading Comprehension to 7-11 year-olds*, UCL IOE Press.

Tunmer, W. E. and Hoover, W. A. (2019) 'The cognitive foundations of learning to read: A framework for preventing and remediating reading difficulties', *Australian Journal of Learning Difficulties*, 24(1): 75-93. DOI: 10.1080/19404158.2019.1614081

Verhoeven, L. and Perfetti, C. (2021) 'Universals in learning to read across languages and writing systems', *Scientific Studies of Reading*, 26(2): 150-164. DOI: 10.1080/10888438.2021.1938575

Welsh Government. (2021) *AREA OF LEARNING AND EXPERIENCE: Languages, Literacy and Communication*. Retrieved from https://hwb.gov.wales/curriculum-for-wales/languages-literacy-and-communication/ (accessed 26 April 2024).

Westbrook, J., Sutherland, J., Oakhill, J. and Sullivan, S. (2019) '"Just reading": The impact of a faster pace of reading narratives on the comprehension of poorer adolescent readers in English classrooms', *Literacy*, 53(2): 60-68. doi: 10.1111/lit.12141

Westerveld, M. F., Armstrong, R. M. and Barton, G. M. (2020) 'Reading success', in *Reading Success in the Primary Years*, Singapore: Springer, pp. 1-17. https://doi.org/10.1007/978-981-15-3492-8_1

Wilson, A. and Scanlon, J. (2004) *Supporting Reading*, 1st edn, United Kingdom: David Fulton Publishers. Retrieved from: https://doi.org/10.4324/9781315506532

Wyse, D. and Bradbury, A. (2022) 'Reading wars or reading reconciliation? A critical examination of robust research evidence, curriculum policy and teachers' practices for teaching phonics and reading', *Review of Education*, 10: 1-53.

Wyse, D. and Hacking, C. (2024) *The Balancing Act: An Evidence Informed Approach to Teaching Phonics, Reading and Writing*, London: Routledge.

UNIT 4.3

TEACHING THE CRAFT OF WRITING

Debra Myhill

INTRODUCTION

Writing is everywhere! One significant facet of twenty-first century life has been a rapid and ever-increasing use of writing for communication, largely triggered by advances in technology. This is evident in the burgeoning of social media platforms, and the influence they can exert (for good or bad); the adoption of email for most workplace communication; and the dominant use of digital tools, rather than pen and paper, for producing text. You might also argue that there has been an increase in the demand for written texts in contemporary society, particularly in the workplace: in education, for example, this would include self-evaluation reports for Ofsted; appraisal records; strategic plans; digital newsletters for parents and so on. Technology has also enabled greater access to writing for a public audience, through, for example, blogs, personal websites and other self-publishing fora. These allow for writing for personal reasons, including writing poetry, short stories and novels. Specific software, such as speech-to-text software, is also enabling access to communication through writing to those who find this challenging, such as those with physical difficulties, with visual impairment or those who find it easier to compose orally direct onto screen. Writing is powerful: we write to record history, to complain and to campaign, to fulfil workplace demand, and to express our most personal thoughts and feelings. It is hard to deny the importance for all children of becoming confident, critical and creative writers.

Yet the one thing that research most commonly says about writing is that it is *complex*. Learning to write is one of the most challenging things that children have to do, involving cognitive skills as demanding as the planning skills involved in playing chess, or the combined creative and technical skills involved in playing a musical instrument (Kellogg, 2008). Indeed, Kellogg argues that becoming a writer requires 'more than two decades of maturation, instruction, and training' (p. 2), a timeframe which exceeds the period of compulsory education! At its heart, writing is a craft which is achieved through the shaping and sculpting of language for different communicative purposes, and as with all crafts, it can be taught (Myhill, Cremin and Oliver, 2021).

In this unit I explore the craft of writing in more depth, making connections between theoretical perspectives on writing and classroom practice in the teaching of writing.

OBJECTIVES

By the end of this unit, you should be able to understand:

- that writing research draws on different disciplinary perspectives;
- the role of metalinguistic understanding in empowering authorial choice;
- the importance of creating a vibrant classroom community of writers.

DIFFERENT DISCIPLINARY PERSPECTIVES ON WRITING

When considering research evidence on the teaching of writing, it is important to recognise that the topic has been investigated from very different disciplinary perspectives – particularly cognitive psychology, sociology/socio-cultural theory and linguistics – and the research across these disciplinary dividing-lines is rare. One exception is the more recent work of Graham, which has adopted the idea of writing within communities to integrate cognitive and socio-cultural thinking about writing. Graham (2018: 258) argues the cognitive models 'mostly ignore cultural, social, political, and historical influences on writing and devote little attention to specifying the mechanisms that advance writing development', whilst socio-cultural researchers do not address well how children become writers and 'generally ignore the cognitive and motivational resources writers bring to bear when writing'. This still omits the linguistic perspective, which, of course, is central to writing which is fundamentally about language.

In a nutshell, cognitive theories of writing are concerned with the *mental processes* that come into play during the act of writing; sociological theories explore how *culture and context* shape learning about writing; and linguistic theories focus on the *use of language* in writing (for more detail, see Chapter 1 in Chen, Myhill and Lewis, 2020). It is worth exploring each of these in a little more detail.

Cognitive perspectives on writing tend to be more interested in the individual and how they manage the writing process. Writing is seen as a problem-solving activity where writers are juggling with demands of *what* to say and *how* to say it (Bereiter and Scardamalia, 1987; Kellogg, 2008). The first, and still influential, model of the mental processes used to accomplish a writing task was that of Hayes and Flower (1980): this identifies three key processes involved in writing, planning, translating (generating text) and reviewing. The *planning process* is not simply writing an outline for a text to be written but includes researching, mulling, freewriting and thinking about the goals for writing. *Generating text* refers to the process of moving from thoughts to words on the page, including the writing of multiple drafts, if appropriate. The process of *reviewing* encompasses both evaluating ideas and written text, and revising the text. What is critical to note is that planning, generating text and reviewing are mental processes, not stages in writing: Hayes and Flower emphasise that 'the model is recursive and allows for a complex intermixing of stages' (1980: 29). In other words, we do not plan first, then generate the text, then review it; writing is much more messy than this, and we are reviewing our ideas for writing when we are planning; and after re-reading and reviewing the text partway through, we may change our plans.

Another important contribution of cognitive psychology is its recognition of the demands made by writing on working-memory (McCutchen, 2000; De Vita et al., 2021). The concept of working-memory refers to our mental capacity to hold and process information 'in the moment' (Baddeley, 1986), and it has limited capacity. You will almost certainly have experienced working-memory problems in your everyday life: for example, if you stop someone to ask for directions, and there are too many steps in the response, you may well be unable to remember them all (or any!) because it was too much for your working-memory to hold and process. Because proficient writing involves co-ordinating multiple tasks simultaneously (for example, formulating ideas, correct spelling, finding the right words, remembering what you want to write next), it makes high demands on working-memory. This is why teachers often break writing down into smaller tasks, or use scaffolding strategies, as this reduces working-memory demand.

In contrast, **socio-cultural perspectives** are concerned with writing as a *social practice* (Kostouli, 2009; Dyson, 2009), shifting the focus from the individual writer to the writer within a community of writers. This research illustrates how social contexts shape how children become writers, including how home and out-of-school experiences of writing influence both writer identity and writing performance, and how school contexts communicate to young learners what it means to be a writer and what is valued in writing. It is worth reflecting on your own classroom experiences of learning to write and what messages you now convey when you teach writing. I remember conscious awareness that what my grammar school teachers in the 70s really loved was purple prose, full of imagery: so much so that when I sat my O-level English and found none of the questions seemed to lend themselves to purple prose, I chose the option to 'write about a person whose occupation you admire' and wrote about an alpine goatherd! It was a piece of writing embarrassingly full of nodding gentians, tinkling bells and snow blushed rose by the setting sun. But it achieved a high mark. Ironically, the very year I sat this O-level, Bullock's seminal report on English teaching criticised this kind of writing as 'false, artificially stimulated and pumped up by the teacher' (Department for Education and Skills [DfES], 1975: 163).

This personal vignette is a reminder that what is valued as 'good' writing is not an internationally accepted standard, but varies over time, culture and jurisdiction, and is socio-culturally determined. Socio-cultural theory recognises that all written texts are socially and culturally constructed: for example, our western expectations of written argument are different from the expectations of written argument in Arabic. When we teach children to write, we are inducting them into the social practices of writing valued in our school community (which may be at odds with what is valued in their out-of-school writing communities). The notion of a community of writers links to another important aspect of socio-cultural perspectives, namely, the emphasis on collaboration and learning with others, drawing heavily on Vygotsky (1978).

It goes without saying that language is the principal resource for writing, and the **linguistic perspective** is fundamentally about *texts*. It addresses language at every level – whole text, paragraphs, sentences, clauses and words; and multiple dimensions of language use, for example, punctuation, figurative language, rhetorical language and spelling. It also considers development as a writer from the early stages of scribble writing and mark-making through to the composition of more extended texts, written for different readers and different purposes. The concept of genres (or text types) bridges across to socio-cultural perspectives, because as noted earlier, genres are socially determined. But they also have particular linguistic characteristics which make visible how these texts are constructed, understanding which can be shared with children. Linguist James Martin argues that this is particularly important in inclusive classrooms because:

> Bright middle-class children learn by osmosis what has to be learned [while] working class, migrant, or Aboriginal children, whose homes do not provide them with models of writing, and who do not have the coding orientation to read between the lines and see what is implicitly demanded, do not learn to write effectively.
>
> (Martin, 1989: 61)

A risk of this, however, is that writing can be reduced to a recipe or checklist of language features which should be included in a particular text (Hardman and Bell, 2019). This is a normative view of writing and does not equip children to understand language choice for themselves as authors with intentionality. What is needed is metalinguistic understanding which enables young writers to make increasingly informed decisions about the language choices they make in writing (Myhill, Watson and Newman 2020).

Although these represent three distinctly different theoretical perspectives on writing, in practice it is critically important that all three are integrated into the teaching of writing. Together, they establish a holistic view of writing, acknowledging that the writer is an *individual*, managing the cognitive processes of writing, but at the same time is learning with others about the *social practices* and expectations of writing, and is mastering the *language* used to create and craft texts.

> **Task 4.3.1 Reflecting on writing lessons**
>
> Find a sequence of three writing lessons that you have planned and annotate the plans to indicate whether the focus of teaching is cognitive, linguistic or socio-cultural.
>
> Reflect on what this tells you about your teaching of writing, and whether any of the three perspectives need less, or more, emphasis.

CRAFTING AND CREATING: ENABLING METALINGUISTIC UNDERSTANDING FOR WRITING

One key element of crafting and creating a written text requires understanding of the repertoire of language choices that can be used and how those choices subtly alter the way meaning is communicated. This is where the grammar knowledge required by the curriculum can be meaningfully embedded within the teaching of writing. Knowledge of what a noun is will not make a child a better writer, but understanding different choices and possibilities that nouns and noun phrases offer is fundamentally about the craft of writing. This understanding concerns the inter-relationship between what we say and how we say it, or as Maya Angelou expressed it, 'As a writer I know that I must select studiously the nouns, pronouns, verbs, adverbs, etcetera, and by a careful syntactical arrangement make readers laugh, reflect or riot' (Angelou, 1989: 149). Consider, for example, this sentence from *Mr Gumpy's Outing*:

> Then Mr Gumpy and the goat and the calf and the chickens and the sheep and the pig and the dog and the cat and the rabbit and the children all swam to the bank and climbed out to dry in the hot sun.
>
> (Burningham, 1970)

John Burningham has chosen to use 'and' repeatedly throughout this sentence, rather than a comma – a tiny but significant choice. The 'and' joins the noun phrases, whereas a comma would separate them; both choices create a rhythm to this sentence but not the same rhythm; and the repetition of 'and' is further intensified by the final 'and' which joins clauses. Why do you think Burningham made this choice? What effect does it have on how we read or interpret this sentence as readers? The point here is not that one choice is better than the other, but that writers need to develop understanding of the choices they can make to craft their texts to express their intentions as authors.

This kind of understanding is **metalinguistic understanding**: the 'ability to place ourselves outside of language with the goal of looking at it, examining it and manipulating the elements comprising it' (Camps, 2014: 27). In other words, metalinguistic understanding represents the capacity to shift from simply being a user of language to looking at language and how meaning is made. This foregrounds the linguistic perspective on writing because of the focus on language, but understanding is a cognitive process, a thinking process, and the exploration of language used in writing is always conducted within the context of social practice, both the social context of the classroom and curriculum, and the social expectations for the text being written.

Metalinguistic understanding is critically important because it empowers young writers to make decisions about their language choices with increasing independence, rather than treating writing like a recipe which should contain certain ingredients. The fronted adverbial is a good example of this, and has been repeatedly raised in the media as a controversial issue. There has been a tendency in school to teach that writing needs to contain some fronted adverbials: this, compounded by the fact that it is often only -ly adverbials which are referred to, leads to some children inserting -ly adverbials at the start of almost every sentence in a very artificial way. Simply putting in a fronted adverbial (or indeed any grammatical construction) does not generate good writing, and often does the opposite (Hardman and Bell, 2019). What is needed is *metalinguistic understanding* about the many different ways that adverbials work in different texts, and what the effect is of moving an adverbial to the front. The grammar then becomes a resource for exploring how language choices craft meaning. Read the following example, taken from the moment in Roald Dahl's *The BFG* when the Queen first sees the Big Friendly Giant before reading on; reflect on what you think is the effect of beginning this sentence with the sequence of three adverbial phrases:

> Twenty-four feet tall, wearing his black cloak with the grace of a nobleman, still carrying his long trumpet in one hand, he strode magnificently across the Palace lawn toward the window.

There is no single correct answer to the question, but you might have noticed, for example, that the three fronted adverbials delay the main clause so it is the appearance of the giant which is foregrounded not his action. If your intention as an author is to emphasise the BFG's magnificent striding then the fronted adverbials would not help you; if you want to spotlight the Queen's first visual impression of the BFG, then the adverbials do help.

The difference between superficial, or incorrect, knowledge about writing and meaningful metalinguistic understanding for writing lies in whether teaching tells children what they should do, or actively fosters thinking about how language works and the range of possibilities available. Developing writerly *thinking* is crucial, and in our own research, we have found that dialogic metalinguistic talk is fundamentally important (Myhill and Newman, 2019). This talk, carefully orchestrated by the teacher, opens up teacher-whole class and peer-to-peer collaborative discussion, which explores and reflects on language choices in writing. It also encourages children to verbalise their metalinguistic understanding, allowing the teacher to determine individual levels of understanding, and appropriate next steps in learning.

Task 4.3.2 Teaching language choice

Use the teaching resources on the University of Exeter website listed at the end of this unit, plan a lesson, or adapt an existing lesson, where you teach explicitly about language choice in writing, paying careful attention to how you develop metalinguistic understanding, rather than superficial knowledge about writing.

CREATING A COMMUNITY OF WRITERS

In order to learn a craft, in any sphere, it is usually necessary to work with and alongside others, to hone and refine craft knowledge. Learning occurs within a community, and the writing community of the classroom is the place where most children learn the craft of writing (although it is important not to forget the other writing communities they may belong to outside of school). So, it is critical to consider the nature of the writing community that you are creating in your classroom. Although what happens in classrooms is inevitably influenced by school and national policies relating to curriculum and assessment, each classroom and each class is unique, because of the dynamics caused by the different personalities and experiences of individuals in that class. Graham (2018) argues that writing is 'shaped and bound by the characteristics, capacity, and variability of the communities in which it takes place and by the cognitive characteristics, capacity, and individual differences of those who produce it' (p.258). In this way he emphasises the complexity of the interactions between individual and community. The idea of a community of writers is the point where the different disciplinary perspectives on writing coalesce, bringing together *individuals* within the *social context* of the classroom crafting language into written *texts*.

A supportive community of writers should be an environment where children can learn and thrive as writers. It is not simply about having fun, or attractive classroom decoration, it is about establishing a learning environment which is motivating, focused and purposeful (Myhill, Cremin and Oliver, 2023). There is a tendency, both in professional practice and policy, to divorce creativity in writing from the rigours of learning to write – this can lead to a pedagogy where sequences of lessons addressing, for example, transcription, narrative structure or the use of adverbials are punctuated (occasionally) by a 'fun' lesson, perhaps writing in an outdoor setting, or similar. But these are not binary opposites: they need to be integrated meaningfully to support growth as a writer. Discussing creativity in general, the National Advisory Committee on Creative and Cultural Education highlighted that creativity 'relies on knowledge, control of materials and command of ideas' and is not 'simply a matter of letting go' (National Advisory Committee on Creative and Cultural Education [NACCCE], 1999: 6). So an effective community of writers brings together freedom and constraint, explicitness and exploration, the creative and the critical to ensure that developing writers are both engaged and learning about being a writer. How might this be achieved? One facet has already been discussed in the previous section, namely, enabling metalinguistic understanding. In the following section I will consider two further facets of a supportive writing community: ensuring time and space for writing; and giving children autonomy and choice.

In Northern Ireland ...

To help children experience and understand the purposes of writing, they should have opportunities to talk about why people write and be given opportunities to experiment with their own written communication (emergent/experimental writing). They should have opportunities throughout the day to write for their own purposes.

Council for Curriculum Examinations and Assessment (CCEA), 2007: 20, 21

In Scotland ...

The Scottish Book Trust encourages schools to access live literature funding to understand how writers write as a creative and intellectual act. The nuances of writing different genres for different purposes starts with teachers understanding their own knowledge and identity as a writer.

Education Scotland has refreshed Scotland's Creative Learning Plan to embed creativity at the centre of Scottish education.

Sources: Scottish Book Trust (n.d.a, n.d.b); Education Scotland (n.d.)

Although the National Curriculum does give emphasis to writing, and writing does receive curriculum time in schools, it can be driven too much by statutory writing assessment rather than learning about writing and being a writer. Ensuring **time and space for writing** supports motivation and engagement, and establishes a classroom climate where children are more willing to write. One aspect of this is the physical environment. Many primary classrooms have well-thought through, attractive space for reading, such as reading corners, comfy seating and plenty of books to choose from. But far fewer have visible writing space: think about how you could use your classroom space creatively to create space for writing to signal that it is valued. This could link with the reading space, or be separate from it, depending on the affordances and constraints of the classroom itself. As well as books being visible and accessible in the classroom, think of ways that children's writing can be visible, not just as displays, but as work-in-progress. One Key Stage 1 classroom I observed had a writing area where some soft toy animals were placed on the floor surrounded by pots of pencils and pieces of coloured paper. The class were working on a cross-curricular environmental theme, and children were encouraged to use the writing area voluntarily to write letters from the animals to the class, explaining how their lives were affected by climate change. These letters were regularly shared and discussed as part of the unit of work, and fed into the final writing task. A salient point here is that a writing area does not need to be permanent and static: this one was created just for this unit of work, and a different one (in a different part of the classroom) created for the next unit. Space for writing is also mental, as well as physical, and ensuring that time is given for writing allows mental space for generating ideas, thinking and reflection.

Research in motivation to write signals strongly the importance of giving writers **autonomy and choice** (Pajares and Valiante, 2006), that too much emphasis on mastering norms of writing can decrease motivation for writing (Boscolo and Gelati, 2013) and that opportunities for autonomy as writers tend to decrease as children progress through schooling (Wright, Hodges and McTigue, 2019). The Covid lockdown experience has provided further unexpected evidence of the benefit of autonomy. Clark, Picton and Lant (2020) surveyed over 4000 students in 2020 and found that writing enjoyment had increased during the lockdown period, with students reporting enjoying having the time to write when they wanted to, and choosing what to write about. It may also be that writing helped some cope with the emotional aspects of lockdown, a reminder that writing for self is valuable, alongside writing for others. Our own research (Cremin et al., 2020; Myhill, Cremin and Oliver, 2023), drawing on children's classroom experiences of writing, also show how these young people found that greater freedom and choice empowered them as writers, and gave them enjoyment. Some typical comments included:

- ☐ 'I don't like the fact that most of the time you just have…to do stuff that the teacher says'
- ☐ 'I don't like people telling me "you have to write this"'
- ☐ 'Because we've had the chance to write what we want…it makes you more proud of what you've done because it's more yours'
- ☐ 'Before…she'd have like specific tasks, whereas now she just gives us an idea and we have to use our brains more'
- ☐ '(Before), she just gave us something to write down and we just wrote it. And now it's kind of thinking of our own ideas'

Of course, in practice, it is not possible to give students autonomy and choice all of the time as there is often a need to focus together on the same task or text. But as evidenced in the previous section on metalinguistic understanding, it is perfectly possible to combine explicit teaching with the opening up of choice. By giving time and space for writing, you create opportunities for children to write about whatever topic they choose, using whatever form they like. Students can have writing notebooks, or messy books, where they capture their own thoughts and ideas, or magpie ideas from other texts. These notebooks can later act as the seeds of ideas for development into complete texts which form part of the formal writing curriculum.

> **Task 4.3.3 Teachers as writers**
>
> This section has focused on the classroom as a community of writers, but a key person in that community is you as a teacher and your attitudes and experiences as a writer. Look at the Arvon website listed at the end of this unit and explore its work with 'Teachers as Writers'.
>
> Reflect on yourself as a writer: Your confidence; what you like writing; what you find challenging. How might this effect, positively or negatively, the writing community that you establish?

In Wales…

'Clear and effective communication through language is an important life skill. It calls for the ability to use and adapt languages in a range of roles, genres, forms, media and styles' (Welsh Government, 2021)

SUMMARY

The topic of writing and how to teach writing is huge and it is impossible to do full justice to it in a short unit. Nonetheless, this unit has addressed the different theoretical perspectives on writing from cognitive psychology, socio-cultural research and linguistics. It has discussed the role of metalinguistic understanding in empowering children as authors, and explored what it means to establish a purposeful community of writers. By framing this with the idea of writing as a craft, the unit emphasises the importance of both explicit teaching of writing which focuses on understanding of writerly decision-making, and the writing environment in which children learn.

When working on the research projects referenced earlier (Cremin *et al.*, 2020; Myhill, Cremin and Oliver, 2021; Myhill, Cremin and Oliver, 2023), Teresa Cremin and I shared the following pedagogic principles with teachers, drawing on our research findings: We believe they represent good principles for the teaching of writing:

- ☐ Create **inclusive classrooms** where children are given time and space to write, opportunities to write without being assessed and to take risks and be experimental.
- ☐ Offer inspiring opportunities and starting points for writing, including writing from the heart and writing from experience so that children experience **being an author**.
- ☐ Support young writers in understanding and managing **the writing process** and being aware of the **reader–writer relationship**.
- ☐ Explicitly teach the **language and textual choices** students can make in their writing.
- ☐ Create **a community of writers** where writing is shared, critiqued and celebrated, where feedback is purposeful.

ANNOTATED FURTHER READING

Amass, H. (2023) 'Inside the primary writing wars', *Times Educational Supplement*. 8 November. Retrieved from: www.tes.com/magazine/teaching-learning/primary/how-to-teach-writing-in-schools-research
   A thoughtful article exploring different views about how to teach writing.

Clements, J. (2023) *On the Write Track: A Practical Guide to Teaching Writing in Primary*, Oxon: Routledge.
   A well-informed, well-evidenced and practical book about teaching writing.

Graham, S., Kim, Y-S. G., Cao, Y., Lee, J., Tate, T., Collins, P., Cho, M., Moon, Y., Chung, H. Q. and Olson, C. B. (2023) 'A meta-analysis of writing treatments for students in grades 6 to 12', *Journal of Educational Psychology*, 115(7): 1004–1027. (M Level)
   This is a very detailed and critical review of evidence about effective practice in the teaching of writing.

Myhill, D., Cremin, T. and Oliver, L. (2021) 'Writing as a craft', *Research Papers in Education*, 38(3): 403–425. (M Level)
   This paper identifies features of the craft of writing through the eyes of professional writers and explores consequences for supporting young writers.

FURTHER READING TO SUPPORT M-LEVEL STUDY

Myhill, D., Cremin, T. and Oliver, L. (2023) The Impact of a Changed Writing Environment on Students' Motivation to Write. *Frontiers in Psychology*, 14. https://doi.org/10.3389/fpsyg.2023.1212940

Hogue, B. (2025) Teacher authorship as critical self-reflection and engagement in authentic student writing. *Literacy*, https://doi.org/10.1111/lit.70000

Graham, S. (2018) 'A revised writer(s) – Within-community model of writing', *Educational Psychologist*, 53: 258–279. https://doi.org/10.1080/00461520.2018.1481406

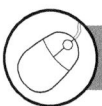

RELEVANT WEBSITES

University of Exeter: Writing Resources for Teachers: https://education.exeter.ac.uk/research/centres/languageandliteracy/grammar-teacher-resources/
   This site draws on a cumulative body of research and offers lots of practical resources to support teaching grammar as part of the craft of writing.

Arvon Foundation: www.arvon.org/
   This is the site for the Arvon Foundation, a creative writing charity, which runs writing courses for teachers and for students. Look especially at the About Arvon page and their approach to writing; and the sections on Learning resources.

Centre for Literacy in Primary Education: https://clpe.org.uk/books/power-of-pictures/about
   This section of the Centre for Literacy in Primary Education website explains the Power of Pictures programme, which brings together reading and writing, and offers free resources for teachers to use.

REFERENCES

Angelou, M. (1989) *Conversations with Maya Angelou*, Jackson: University Press of Mississippi.

Baddeley, A. D. (1986) *Working-Memory*, Oxford: Oxford University Press.

Bereiter, C. and Scardamalia, M. (1987) *The Psychology of Written Composition*, New Jersey: Lawrence Erlbaum Associates

Burningham, J. (1970) *Mr Gumpy's Outing*, London: Jonathon Cape.

Boscolo, P. and Gelati, C. (2013) 'Best practices in promoting motivation for writing', in S. Graham, C. A. MacArthur and J. Fitzgerald (eds) *Best Practices in Writing Instruction*, 2nd edn, New York: Guilford, pp. 284–308.

Camps, A. (2014) 'Metalinguistic activity in language learning', in T. Ribas, X. Fontich and O. Guasch (eds), *Grammar at School*, Brussels: Peter Lang, pp. 25–42.

Chen, H., Myhill, D. A. and Lewis, H. (2020) *Developing Writers Across Primary and Secondary Years: Growing into Writing*, London: Routledge.

Clark, C., Picton, I. and Lant, F. (2020) *"More Time on My Hands": Children and Young People's Writing During the COVID-19 Lockdown in 2020*, London: National Literacy Trust.

Council for Curriculum Examinations and Assessment (CCEA). (2007) *The Northern Ireland Curriculum – Primary*, Belfast: CCEA. Retrieved from: https://ccea.org.uk/downloads/docs/ccea-asset/Curriculum/The%20Northern%20Ireland%20Curriculum%20-%20Primary.pdf

Cremin, T., Myhill, D., Eyres, I., Nash, T., Oliver, L. and Wilson, A. (2020) 'Teachers as writers: Learning together with others', *Literacy*, 54(2): 49–59. https://doi.org/10.1111/lit.12201

Department for Education and Skills (DfES). (1975) *The Bullock Report: A Language for Life*, Report of the Committee of Enquiry, London: DfES.

De Vita, F., Schmidt, S., Carla, T. and Re, A-M. (2021) 'The role of working memory on writing processes', *Frontiers in Psychology*, 12. https://doi.org/10.3389/fpsyg.2021.738395

Dyson, A. (2009) 'Writing in childhood worlds', in R. Beard, D. Myhill, J. Riley and M. Nystrand (eds) *The Sage Handbook of Writing Development*, London: Sage, pp. 232–245.

Education Scotland (n.d.) *A Fresh Look at Scotland's Creative Learning Plan*. Retrieved from: https://education.gov.scot/media/4m4gi40x/nih319-refreshed-creative-learning-plan.pdf

Graham, S. (2018) 'A revised writer(s) – Within-community model of writing', *Educational Psychologist*, 53: 258–279. https://doi.org/10.1080/00461520.2018.1481406

Hardman, W. and Bell, H. (2019) '"More fronted adverbials than ever before". Writing feedback practices and grammatical metalanguage in an English primary school', *Language and Education*, 33(1): 35–50. https://doi.org/10.1080/09500782.2018.1488864

Hayes, J. and Flower, L. (1980) 'Identifying the organisation of writing processes', in L. W. Gregg and E. R. Steinberg (eds) *Cognitive Processes in Writing*, Jackson: Lawrence Erlbaum Associates, pp. 3–30.

Kellogg, R. T. (2008) 'Training writing skills: A cognitive developmental perspective', *Journal of Writing Research*, 1(1): 1–26. https://doi.org/10.17239/jowr-2008.01.01.1

Kostouli, T. (2009) 'A sociocultural framework: Writing as social practice', in R. Beard, D. Myhill, J. Riley and M. Nystrand (eds) *The Sage Handbook of Writing Development*, London: Sage, pp. 98–116.

Martin, J. (1989) *Factual Writing: Exploring and Challenging Social Reality*, Oxford: Oxford University Press.

McCutchen, D. (2000) 'Knowledge, processing, and working memory: Implications for a theory of writing', *Educational Psychology*, 35: 13–23. https://doi.org/10.1207/s15326985ep3501_3

Myhill, D. and Newman, R. (2019) 'Writing talk – Developing metalinguistic understanding through dialogic teaching', in N. Mercer, R. Wegerif and L. Major (eds) *International Handbook of Research on Dialogic Education*, Abingdon: Routledge, pp. 360–372.

Myhill, D., Cremin, T. and Oliver, L. (2021) 'Writing as a craft', *Research Papers in Education*, 38(3): 403–425. https://doi.org/10.1080/02671522.2021.1977376

Myhill, D., Cremin, M. and Oliver, L. (2023) 'The impact of a changed writing environment on students' motivation to write', *Frontiers in Psychology*, 14. https://doi.org/10.3389/fpsyg.2023.1212940

Myhill, D., Watson, A. and Newman, R. (2020) 'Thinking differently about grammar and metalinguistic understanding in writing', *Bellaterra Journal of Teaching & Learning Language & Literature*, 13(2): e870. https://doi.org/10.5565/rev/jtl3.870

National Advisory Committee on Creative and Cultural Education (NACCCE). (1999) *All Our Futures: Creativity, Culture and Education*, London: Department for Education and Employment.

Pajares, F. and Valiante, G. (2006) 'Self-efficacy beliefs and motivation in writing development', in C. A. MacArthur, S. Graham and J. Fitzgerald (eds) *Handbook of Writing Research*, New York: Guilford Press, pp. 158–170.

Scottish Book Trust. (n.d.a) *Live Literature*. Retrieved from: www.scottishbooktrust.com/writing-and-authors/live-literature

Scottish Book Trust. (n.d.b) *Creative Writing for Schools*. Retrieved from: www.scottishbooktrust.com/learning-and-resources/creative-writing-for-schools

Vygotsky, L. S. (1978) *Mind in Society: The Development of Higher Psychological Processes*, Cambridge: Harvard University Press.

Welsh Government (2021) *AREA OF LEARNING AND EXPERIENCE Languages, Literacy and Communication*. Retrieved from: https://hwb.gov.wales/curriculum-for-wales/languages-literacy-and-communication/ (accessed 26 April 2024).

Wright, K. L, Hodges, T. S. and McTigue, E. M. (2019) 'A validation program for the self-beliefs, writing beliefs, and attitude survey: A measure of adolescents' motivation toward writing', *Assessing Writing*, 39: 64–78. https://doi.org/10.1016/j.asw.2018.12.004

UNIT 4.4

TEACHING MATHEMATICS
What, how and why

Vivien Townsend and Mark Boylan

INTRODUCTION

Mathematics is often thought of as a subject where answers are right or wrong. Pupils and adults often discuss primary mathematics in that way, but that is not the whole story. Similarly, when it comes to teaching primary mathematics, there is no right or wrong way.

In this unit, we will explain some of the key terms used in teaching primary mathematics and describe some of the different teaching approaches and ideas. We look at two key issues in preparing to teach mathematics: teachers' views about maths and knowledge for teaching maths. We consider common curriculum content and three important aims of mathematics teaching: developing fluency and conceptual understanding; reasoning and mathematical thinking; and problem solving. We look at how to realise these aims in the classroom by focusing on some key ideas. To further develop your teaching, we point to important sources of guidance and evidence that can support you to draw these ideas together to develop your teaching approach as a primary mathematics teacher.

OBJECTIVES

By the end of this unit, you should:

- have reflected on your relationship with maths and how to develop your subject knowledge for teaching;
- know about how primary mathematics curriculum content is commonly structured;
- understand some key ideas in teaching primary mathematics.

PREPARING TO TEACH

Two important issues in preparing to teach mathematics are: first, reflecting on your beliefs about mathematics and your previous experiences, and how this might influence you as a teacher; and second, the importance of mathematics subject knowledge.

TEACHER BELIEFS

Our experiences of maths at home and school influence how we view maths, and as teachers, these experiences may have an impact on how we approach the challenge of teaching the subject to primary-age pupils.

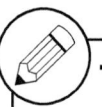

> **Task 4.4.1 Your beliefs about mathematics and your experiences**
>
> In this task you will reflect on your beliefs about maths and experience of learning maths.
>
> **REFLECT:** What is your view of mathematics? Why do <u>you</u> think maths is important? If you asked a friend or neighbour, or a family member, what do you think <u>they</u> would say?
>
> Is mathematics a subject you like, dislike or are more neutral about? What has influenced your view? Did any teachers have a significant influence on you?

Teachers influenced us as learners of maths. And now, as teachers, we are in a position to influence the learners in our classes. This is a great responsibility: the experience we provide for learners, and the messages we give about maths' importance and whether everyone can be successful, have lasting impacts on individuals' beliefs and confidence.

It is important that teachers communicate a positive view of the subject, even if our experience of learning maths was not a happy one. Teachers who enjoyed maths, or found it relatively easy at school, sometimes need to check their expectations that pupils should learn as readily as they did.

KNOWLEDGE FOR TEACHING

There are different types of knowledge needed by teachers of maths. A long standing and useful view of types of teaching knowledge is Shulman's (1986). As well as generic teaching knowledge (pedagogical knowledge), Shulman also thought that teachers needed subject-specific teaching knowledge to be most successful. He termed these: subject matter knowledge, curriculum knowledge and pedagogical content knowledge. In Table 4.4.1, we describe what each type means in primary mathematics and point to sources of that knowledge (links are found at the end of the unit).

TABLE 4.4.1 Types of mathematics teacher knowledge

Shulman's category	Meaning in mathematics	Examples of sources
Subject Matter Knowledge (SMK)	Knowledge of the maths content itself. For example, knowing how to calculate a percentage	The National Centre for Excellence in the Teaching Mathematics (NCETM) in England provides useful subject knowledge audits
Curriculum Knowledge (CK)	How the subject knowledge is organised in the curriculum. For example, how fractions, decimals and percentages are sequenced	The National Curriculum for the country in which you work
Pedagogical Content Knowledge (PCK)	How to teach the mathematics curriculum. For example, using a bar model to represent percentages	Guidance materials Initial teacher training and professional development materials

> **Task 4.4.2 What do teachers of maths need to know?**
>
> In this task, you will explore the subject-specific knowledge for teaching maths.
>
> You will need sticky notes or about 20 scraps of paper that you can write on and sort.
>
> **DO:** Before reading on, spend a few minutes thinking about what you need to know to be a teacher of maths. Try to just think about the things that are related to maths (rather than more general things like knowledge of how to manage behaviour). Write a different form of knowledge on each bit of paper. For example, you might write:
>
> - Teachers need to know the appropriate vocabulary to use with that year group.
> - Teachers need to know how to add fractions.
> - Teachers need to know how to demonstrate using a number line.
>
> **DO:** Now take your bits of paper and sort them into these the three headings shown in Figure 4.4.1.
>
> **REFLECT:** Have you missed anything out? Add other ideas as you think of them.
>
> As you get ready to teach different topics, you will find it useful to reflect on these three forms of knowledge.
>
> | Subject Matter Knowledge (SMK) | Curriculum Knowledge (CK) | Pedagogical Content Knowledge (PCK) |
> |---|---|---|
> | Teachers need to know how to add fractions | Teachers need to know the appropriate vocabulary to use with that year group | Teachers need to know how to demonstrate using a number line |
>
> **FIGURE 4.4.1** Types of mathematics teacher knowledge with the given examples sorted

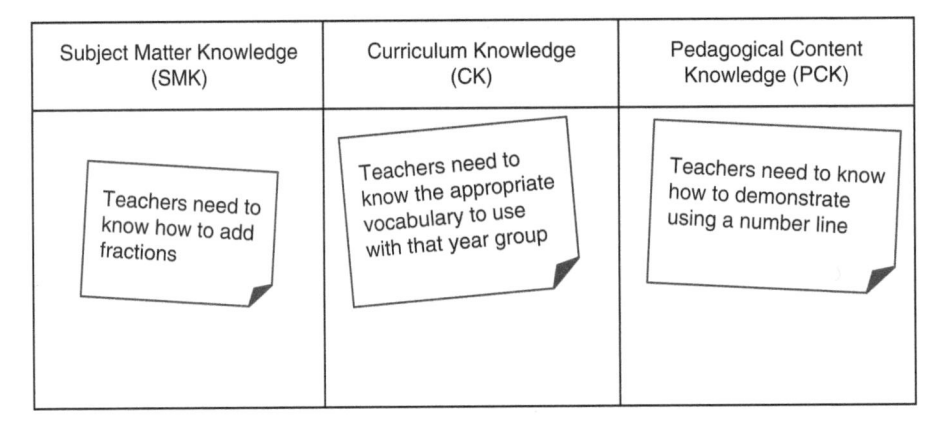

PRIMARY MATHEMATICS CURRICULUM CONTENT

In this section, we provide a brief overview of the primary maths curricula of England, Northern Ireland, Scotland and Wales. The unit then focuses on three underpinning aims of all maths curricula, namely that – across all curriculum content – pupils: gain fluency and conceptual understanding; reason mathematically; and solve problems.

In each UK nation, statutory documents set out the content that must be taught. All UK nations recognise that it is important to develop mathematical understanding in the early years of childhood before formal education begins in primary schools. However, the ages referred to as 'early years'

TABLE 4.4.2 The structure of the primary maths curricula in the four nations of the UK

England	Northern Ireland	Scotland	Wales
Number	Processes in mathematics	Number, money and measure	Developing numerical reasoning
Measurement	Number		
Geometry	Measures	Shape, position and movement	Using number skills
Statistics	Shape and space		Using measuring skills
Ratio and proportion *(age 10–11 only)*	Handling data	Information handling	Using geometry skills
			Using algebra skills
Algebra *(age 10–11 only)*			Using data skills

varies across nations and the relationship between the early years and primary curricula similarly varies. If you are teaching in an early years setting then there may be specific documentation for you to refer to, and the focus of your work as a maths teacher might be organised differently from primary.

PRIMARY CURRICULUM AIMS

While statutory frameworks set out the content that must be taught, they usually stop short of prescribing how teachers should teach. That said, they often do outline some principles, skills and behaviours that should be taught and developed alongside the curriculum content. We refer to these as curriculum aims. In this section, we focus on three of these: fluency and conceptual understanding; reasoning mathematically; and solving problems.

We will look at each of these in turn in the sections that follow. For each aim we include suggestions for teaching practices that can help realise the aim in the classroom.

Fluency and conceptual understanding

'Fluency' is most often used when talking about speaking different languages. Mathematical fluency is similar to being fluent in a language in that both require knowledge of facts. To speak a language, you need to know vocabulary and what words mean. Mathematical fluency requires knowing mathematical facts and relationships. Number facts are central, and during primary school, this progresses from knowing about addition and subtraction number bonds through multiplication and division facts to knowledge of decimals, fractions and percentages. Sometimes the word 'automaticity' is used to describe the goal of being able to recall number facts straight away.

However, learning vocabulary is not enough to speak a language; you also need to know about the relationship between words, their meaning and how to use them in different situations. Similarly, it is not enough to simply memorise maths facts. As well as learning different procedures, such as calculation methods, pupils need to understand the methods and mathematical ideas so they can choose between methods. This is called conceptual understanding.

Fluency and conceptual understanding are interlinked and develop together. Of course, sometimes you might want to focus on fluency more than understanding, or the other way round. We look at two approaches to linking them together – when learning facts and doing calculations.

Fluency and conceptual understanding with facts

In the primary phase, pupils learn number bonds to 10 and other amounts, and later learn multiplication facts. The introduction of the Y4 Multiplication Tables Check in England has renewed the focus on learning times tables in English schools.

Foster (2022) suggests that through making connections between facts and multiplication tables, the task of learning all times tables facts can be made manageable. For example, using knowledge of commutativity immediately reduces the number to learn by almost half. Commutativity is used in maths to refer to operations where the answer is the same even if the order is different (e.g. 3x4 = 4x3). Addition and multiplication are commutative; subtraction and division are not. Assuming that 1x, 2x, 5x, 10x and most of 11x are already known or easily learned, the number of facts needing to be taught is reduced again. The important thing is that the facts are learned and taught with understanding, not just by rote.

You will know that some multiplication tables are easier to learn than others. In times tables tests completed by pupils in England in 2013, 8x and 12x tables were the weakest (Cambridge Mathematics, 2016). Making connections between already-known facts can help pupils learn these tables, and the sequence in which facts are introduced should support this. In particular, splitting up one of the factors can help us to generate new facts from known facts (for example, 3x14 = 3x(10+4) = 3x10 + 3x4. This is the distributive law of multiplication which can be effectively represented using an array, as shown in Figure 4.4.2 for 8x3 and 12x3.

Timed tests and practising against the clock can lead to maths anxiety in some learners, as well as a sense that maths is about performing quickly rather than learning deeply (Boaler, 2014). Playing matching games (matching the product with the factors or with a pictorial representation) and adopting other low-stakes activities that involve recalling facts can be a less stressful approach for students. Encourage pupils to identify which facts they find challenging, and use their errors constructively.

North (2020) describes how some students find it hard to remember multiplication facts and recommends some strategies for working with students. In particular, he suggests that it can be useful to have the facts readily available for those that have not yet committed them to memory as this both

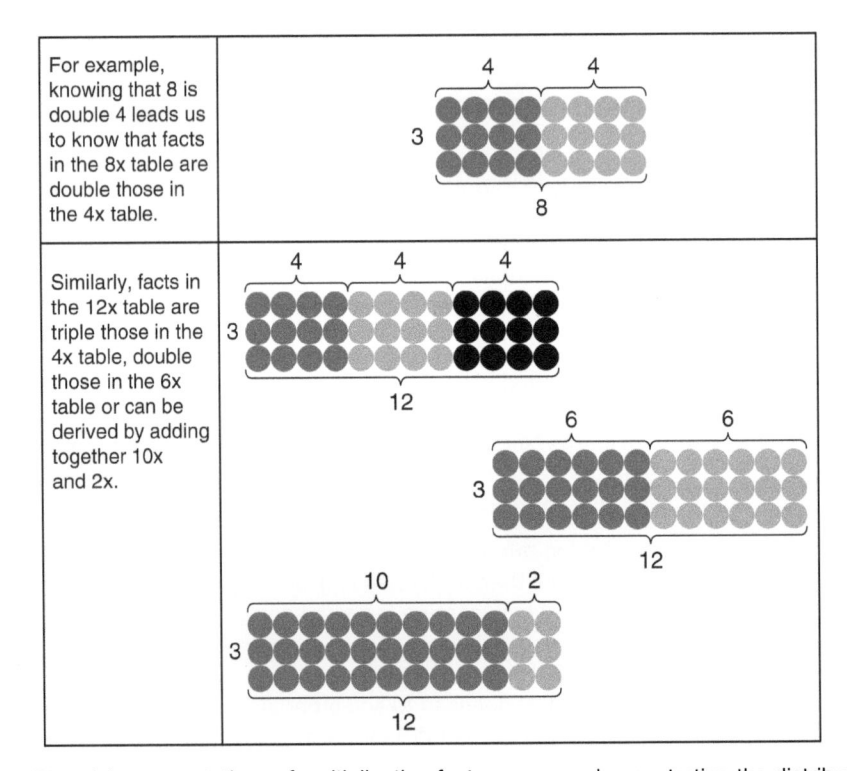

FIGURE 4.4.2 Pictorial representations of multiplication facts as arrays demonstrating the distributive law

reduces cognitive overload and ensures that the student can focus on the new learning. Having a multiplication grid on each table and encouraging pupils to access this – if needed – leads to greater familiarity and eventually to memorisation.

Linking fluency and understanding by teaching different calculation methods

One way of developing an understanding of underlying mathematical structures is through knowing different calculation methods for adding, subtracting, multiplying and dividing. Different methods can be more or less efficient depending on the question. So, knowing a variety of methods is a good idea.

It might be that over time you have arrived at a preferred failsafe method (or maybe preferred methods) with which you are fluent. However, as a teacher you will almost certainly be required to teach other methods to your pupils. Gaining confidence with new methods – and comparing them with your failsafe approach(es) – is a good way of developing your own conceptual understanding.

Key distinctions when looking at calculation methods are between mental methods and written methods, between formal and informal methods, and between compact and expanded methods.

Task 4.4.3 Calculation methods in national curricula

The curricula for each nation in the UK sets out expectations of calculation approaches per key stage or year group.

DO: Track the methods for addition and subtraction across the curriculum for one of the nations. Note the expectations for formal and informal, mental and written, compact and expanded methods.

REFLECT: Are you familiar with these methods?

When selecting a method, it is important to consider whether it is efficient. Sometimes written methods are not at all efficient and actually make the maths more complicated. Figure 4.4.3 gives an example for calculating 2000-12.

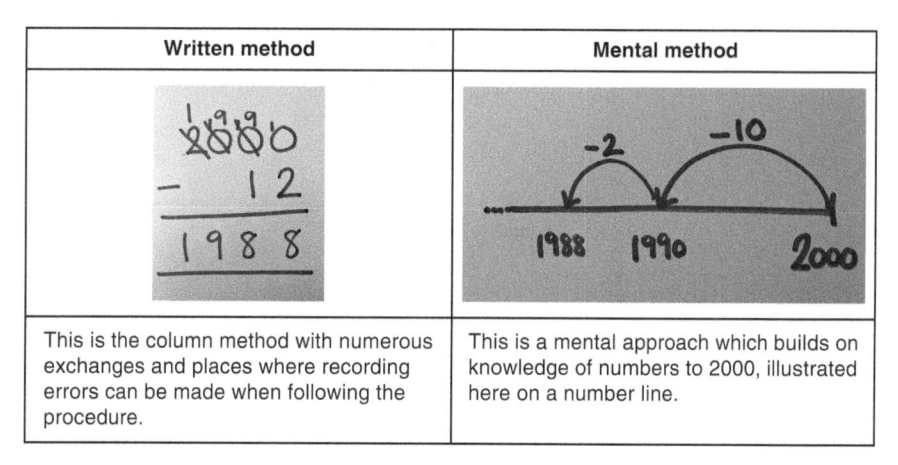

Written method	Mental method
$\overset{1}{2}\overset{9}{0}\overset{9}{0}\overset{}{0}$ − 12 = 1988	Number line with jumps −2 (from 2000 to 1990... shown as 1988, 1990, 2000 with −2 and −10)
This is the column method with numerous exchanges and places where recording errors can be made when following the procedure.	This is a mental approach which builds on knowledge of numbers to 2000, illustrated here on a number line.

FIGURE 4.4.3 Written and mental methods for calculating 2000–12

TABLE 4.4.3 Formal and informal written methods

Type of method	Example	Considerations
Formal	In the example in Figure 4.4.3, the column subtraction is a formal method following certain rules.	If the steps are followed accurately, a pupil is guaranteed to get the right answer.
		It's possible to follow the steps of a formal method without really thinking about the numbers involved, and so if the steps are misremembered (or computational errors made) then a ridiculous answer can be arrived at.
		If a pupil is encouraged to estimate first, then this can be a good way to encourage mathematical thinking alongside procedural fluency.
Informal	The jottings for the number line approach (see Figure 4.4.3) can be described as an informal method because it is recording a mental process. It is a jotting to support thinking rather than the actual calculation procedure itself.	Informal methods rely on pupils' mental methods.
		Informal jottings should support pupils' own thinking.
		As the teacher, it is not always easy to make sense of pupils' jottings.
		It can be useful to model and encourage some informal approaches, including using (and later visualising) concrete apparatus.

Mental methods are ways to do mathematics without writing anything down. Mental methods and written methods are not mutually exclusive. For example, in the column subtraction in Figure 4.4.3, the ability to mentally compute – or just know – bonds to 10 was necessary to complete each small step within the overall calculation. It is useful for teachers to draw pupils' attention to when they can use and are using known facts and mental methods across the maths curriculum.

Written methods can be formal or informal as described in Table 4.4.3.

Written methods can also be described as compact or expanded. These methods are related, as demonstrated in Figure 4.4.4, for 634x12 from most expanded through to most compact methods.

The expanded methods build understanding of the small elements making up the calculation, leading to a more compact method where these elements are 'hidden'. Experience of expanded methods – and explicit exposure to how the methods are connected – can support pupils to use compact methods with deeper conceptual understanding. For example, it is useful for pupils to see the methods side by side and notice what is the same and different about them.

School calculation approaches will include progression through different calculation methods for addition, subtraction, multiplication and division.

Reasoning mathematically

Here, we focus on two ways to promote mathematical reasoning. The first is the role of high-quality classroom talk, the second is the use of models and representations.

Promoting reasoning through high-quality mathematical talk

There is a lot that teachers can do to encourage pupils to engage and also to discuss mathematically.

The 'grid method'	Expanded 'long multiplication'	Compact 'long multiplication'
$634 \times 12 =$ 	634×12 8 (2×4) 60 (2×30) 1200 (2×600) 40 (10×4) 300 (10×30) 6000 (10×600) 7608	634×12 1268 6340 7608
This is the most expanded of the methods here. Each of the six parts of the calculation are completed, the rows are summed and then these totals are added. This method connects to using multiplication to find the area of a rectangle.	This is a more expanded version of the compact long multiplication method. It builds on the grid method by doing each of the six small calculations in turn, and labelling these reinforces what is being multiplied each time.	This is the most compact version. Knowledge of the previous methods can lead pupils to approach this with conceptual understanding. For example, rather than saying '2 times 6 is 12', with knowledge of the more expanded method, pupils will say '2 times 6 hundreds is 12 hundreds' and this contributes to their conceptual understanding of the calculation.

FIGURE 4.4.4 Expanded and compact multiplication methods

Task 4.4.4 Encouraging maths talk

There are lots of ways teachers can encourage mathematical talk in the classroom. Here are some examples:

- using open questions like 'What do you notice?';
- asking pupils to think alone and then tell a partner their answer;
- asking pairs of students to discuss and agree a joint answer to a question;
- encouraging whole class discussions where students question each other, explain their thinking and build on what someone else has said;
- asking students to come to the board or visualiser and explain their thinking to the whole class;
- scaffolding student talk using sentence starters such as 'I agree because…';
- using stem sentences such as 'there are ten hundreds in one thousand';
- celebrating when students use appropriate maths vocabulary.

When you are in school, create an observation tool using the previous list to record:

1. when you see a teacher using these techniques;
2. other ways mathematics talk is encouraged.

What are the benefits of different techniques and what are potential issues or disadvantages of the practices you observe?

We have been working with teachers from different schools to develop children's reasoning through oracy. When we tried to measure this, we all found that the higher attaining children in our schools were not reasoning at the depth we assumed they were. The children were really only describing and explaining, rather than justifying, convincing or proving. We introduced a range of strategies such as using sentence stems, concept cartoons and sentence openers, and all found that the pupils improved very quickly once we insisted on them using these.

TRISHA HENLEY and JO MAKIN ISHERWOOD,
Work Group Leads at Origin Maths Hub.

As well as encouraging talk in maths lessons, there are lots of other opportunities to generate maths talk during the school day. These include using storybooks, songs, rhymes and games. There are lots of opportunities to bring maths talk into other curriculum areas – such as when measuring in science – and other times of day such as when taking the register, tidying the classroom and moving through the timetable.

Promoting reasoning through the use of models and representations

One way to promote reasoning is through the use of the concrete-pictorial-abstract sequence used in Singapore (Hoong, Kin and Pien, 2015) which is based on the work of Bruner (1966). For example, to add two 2-digit numbers, lessons might be planned to give pupils experience of concrete (enactive), pictorial (iconic) and finally abstract (symbolic) representations as shown in Figure 4.4.5.

Griffiths, Back and Gifford (2016) remind us that not all concrete representations are equal. Some are more realistic and others are more abstract. Especially when working with younger children, it can be important to help them to understand that an abstract object like a counter can represent something as interesting as a car one moment and a cake the next.

Examples of progression in concrete representations are demonstrated in Figures 4.4.6 and 4.4.7.

When planning a lesson, it can be useful to consider whether the concrete representation is in any way hindering pupils' learning, and whether a less abstract representation may be helpful.

The bar model is a key pictorial representation

In Singaporean mathematics, a key pictorial representation is the bar model. The bar model can be used to represent a wide variety of mathematical problems: addition and subtraction, multiplication and division, and fraction and proportional reasoning problems. Bar models are very flexible, so for example, both simple addition relationships of numbers less than 10 can be represented, as can problems with larger quantities.

Concrete (enactive)	Pictorial (iconic)	Abstract (symbolic)
Pupils use Dienes base-ten equipment to complete the calculation. 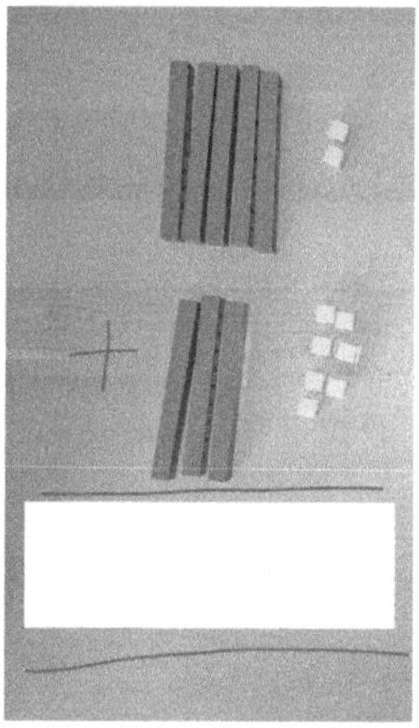	Pupils draw pictures to represent the equipment. 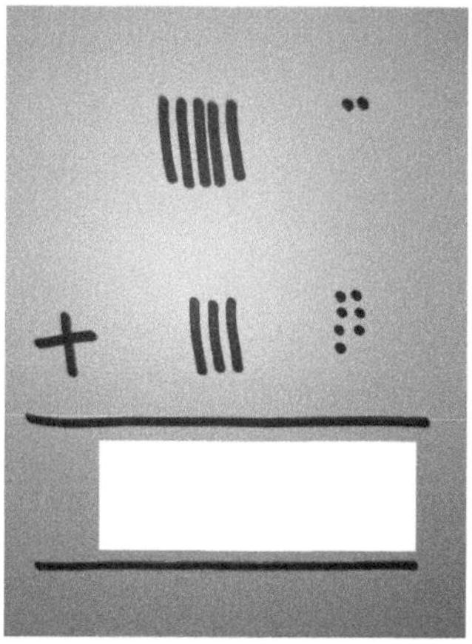	Pupils use a formal written method. 

FIGURE 4.4.5 Concrete, pictorial and abstract representations of 52+37

Two actual cars 	Two toy cars 	Two cubes *representing* two cars 

FIGURE 4.4.6 Progression in concrete representations of two cars from most real to most abstract

Straws 	Straws, bundled in 10s 	Dienes apparatus 	Place value counters 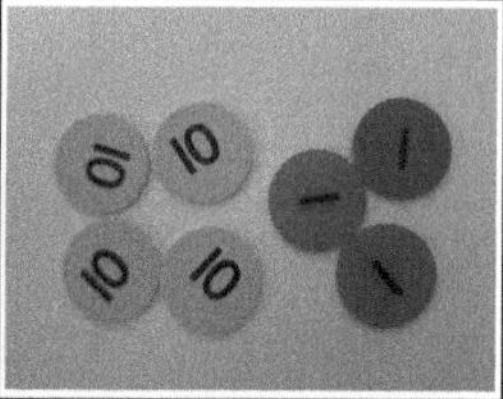

FIGURE 4.4.7 Progression in concrete representations of the number 43, becoming more abstract

> **Task 4.4.5 Becoming familiar with the representations used in your school**
>
> Whilst some representations are widely used and recommended in non-statutory guidance, schools are free to adopt these or not as they see fit. This task requires you to examine the representations used in your school across different year groups.
>
> **DO:** Ask the maths subject leader at your school about the concrete and pictorial representations adopted in your year group, and ask to see any school-wide guidance on the use of representations.
>
> **REFLECT:** As you look through the school guidance, focus on what is expected in one of the youngest and oldest year groups, and another in middle. How does the use of representations vary between these year groups? Can you see consistency? Can you see progression?

The bar model is not a calculation method; rather, it is a representation of the question that can reveal the calculations that are required.

Bar models can be introduced using the concrete-pictorial-abstract principles described earlier. Figure 4.4.8 has an example.

Figure 4.4.9 shows some examples of how bar models can be used in different year groups and different areas of maths. In each case, the '?' indicates the number that pupils are required to find. Each of these examples is shown in the abstract version only.

Problem solving

In everyday classroom language, lots of types of mathematics questions might be referred to as problems. An important distinction is between routine and non-routine problems. We look at these in turn and then consider how problem solving might be incorporated into the curriculum.

Routine problems

In class, we might refer to addition problems or division problems, and these could be described as being routine because they are essentially just calculations for pupils to complete.

For example, 66 = 45+__ or 873÷9 = __.

Concrete	Pictorial	Abstract
●●● ●●	ooo oo	3 2

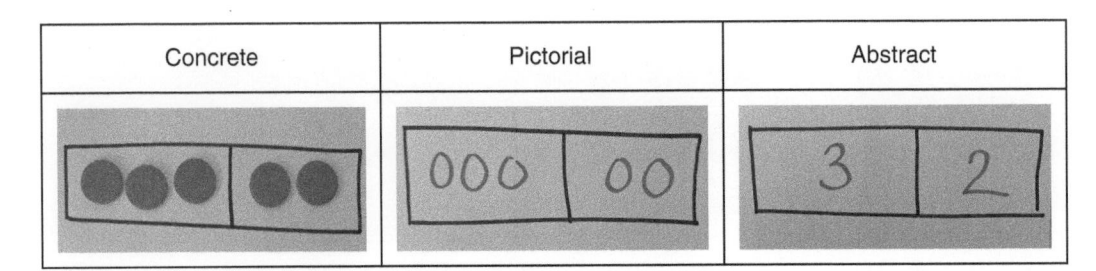

FIGURE 4.4.8 Bar model and the concrete-pictorial-abstract principles

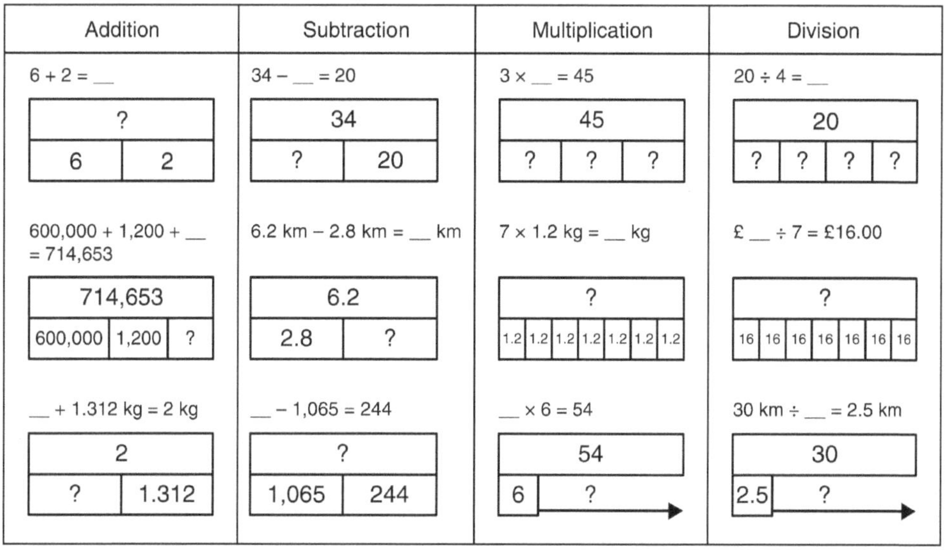

Addition	Subtraction	Multiplication	Division
6 + 2 = __	34 − __ = 20	3 × __ = 45	20 ÷ 4 = __
? / 6 | 2	34 / ? | 20	45 / ? | ? | ?	20 / ? | ? | ? | ?
600,000 + 1,200 + __ = 714,653	6.2 km − 2.8 km = __ km	7 × 1.2 kg = __ kg	£ __ ÷ 7 = £16.00
714,653 / 600,000 | 1,200 | ?	6.2 / 2.8 | ?	? / 1.2 | 1.2 | 1.2 | 1.2 | 1.2 | 1.2 | 1.2	? / 16 | 16 | 16 | 16 | 16 | 16 | 16
__ + 1.312 kg = 2 kg	__ − 1,065 = 244	__ × 6 = 54	30 km ÷ __ = 2.5 km
2 / ? | 1.312	? / 1,065 | 244	54 / 6 | ?	30 / 2.5 | ?

FIGURE 4.4.9 Bar model examples for addition, subtraction, multiplication and division

Word problems are a particular type of routine problem that uses words rather than symbols to present the question. Here are two examples of a word problem and the relevant calculation:

> The baker has two trays of biscuits. The first tray has 45 biscuits on it. There are 66 biscuits in total. How many biscuits are on the second tray?
>
> 66 = 45+__
>
> Over 9 months, Jamie saves £873. How much does he save on average each month?
>
> 873÷9 = __

The 'problem' part of the question in words is how to interpret the meaning and translate it into a mathematical operation or series of operations to solve it.

Non-routine problems

A non-routine problem is one that has some or all of the following characteristics:

- The problem may involve more than one maths concept, and sometimes these are not directly related.
- The problems may be open ended and/or have multiple solutions.
- The problem may involve maths in familiar or unfamiliar contexts.
- Pupils may need to analyse the problem and decide on strategies.
- Pupils cannot use a single memorised standard procedure.

Task 4.4.6 Becoming familiar with non-routine problems

This task will give you the experience of completing a non-routine problem and will also introduce you to ways of supporting pupils to work with these problems. If you want to develop your confidence and ability to engage your pupils with problems, then the best way is to work on non-routine problems yourself.

DO: Find the 'Neighbourly Addition' task on the NRICH website and have a go at the problem (https://nrich.maths.org/housenumbers).

You might like to look at the 'getting started' tab for some ideas.

REFLECT: What did you enjoy about working on the task? What did you find challenging?

For each problem on the NRICH website, the NRICH team provides some teachers' resources and also publishes some student solutions, both of which can help teachers to prepare for using a problem with their class. For the 'Neighbourly Addition' problem, there is also a webinar that teachers can watch.

DO: Look at the 'student solutions' and 'teachers' resources' tabs.

REFLECT: How can these resources support you to plan for leading this task with your class?

There are different views about the role of problem solving and how routine and non-routine problems can be incorporated into the curriculum. These are summarised in Table 4.4.4.

TABLE 4.4.4 Different views and beliefs about problem solving

View	Beliefs and teaching
Problem solving is in addition to the core mathematics content	Problem solving should mostly involve routine problems and word problems, particularly for younger children
	Problem solving can be broken down into classes of problems and techniques to teach problems can be taught
	Problem solving should be taught at the end of topics as a way of applying maths procedures and processes
	Problem solving is hard and hardest for low attaining pupils, so it is important that they are secure in basics first
Problem solving is an essential part of mathematics	Problem solving should be central to teaching mathematics
	All pupils should regularly be taught and engage with non-routine problems that are appropriate to their age and mathematical knowledge; this helps develop conceptual understanding
	There are general problem solving approaches that can be taught in mathematics such as looking for similarities, differences and patterns, or representing problems in different ways
	Pupils enjoy puzzles, so problem solving can build positive attitudes to maths
Problem solving is a way of teaching mathematics	Problems can be a good way to introduce new maths topics
	Careful selection of problems can help build conceptual understanding from the start of topics
	Starting with a problem encourages pupils to think about the maths they already know and supports mathematical thinking and communication
	Starting with problems can engage pupils' curiosity – this is motivating, and helps them see the value of maths

These sets of beliefs and views on problem solving are not necessarily mutually exclusive. Teachers may combine these different approaches over the course of a year. It is fair to say that often, the first view dominates.

CONCLUSION

In this unit, we have introduced some key aims and principles in teaching primary mathematics which are applicable across different ages of pupils.

Meeting the needs of all students is an important concern for primary teachers. A gap in mathematics attainment between advantaged and disadvantaged pupils at the end of primary school is an ongoing issue. In recent years, many schools have stopped grouping students by ability in maths lessons, and now adopt a 'mastery' approach where the class is taught together and the teacher has high expectations that all learners will gain a deep understanding of mathematical concepts (NCETM, 2016; Boylan, 2019).

> **Extract from a teacher:**
>
> We found that when all of the children are working on the same objective, even if it is at different depths, mixed-prior-attainment groupings work surprisingly well. Interestingly, it is the previously higher attaining children who have found the change in approach most challenging as they are now expected to explain, prove and justify rather than just produce a correct answer. It has shown us that their depth of learning was not as we believed it was.
> CLAIRE CRADDOCK, World's End Junior School, Birmingham

No matter which country you teach in, the ideas in this unit can support your thinking about teaching maths and your development as a mathematics teacher. Be reassured that these ideas can support you to meet the needs of all students.

We recommend reading Unit 6.1: Understanding and implementing adaptive teaching soon after this one, in order to consider how the strategies suggested by the authors can be applied to a maths classroom.

ANNOTATED FURTHER READING

As well as the national curricula, there are other sources for developing your knowledge for teaching maths.

EEF guidance documents
: The Education Endowment Foundation (EEF) commissioned researchers to review research and evidence into teaching mathematics, and then collated this into two useful guidance documents. There is one for EYFS and KS1 Mathematics (EEF, 2017), and one for KS2 and KS3 Mathematics (EEF, 2020). They can be accessed via https://educationendowmentfoundation.org.uk/education-evidence/guidance-reports

Espresso research summaries
: The 'Espressos' produced by Cambridge Mathematics are short documents summarising useful research and information across a range of maths education topics. All of the research summaries can be found at www.cambridgemaths.org/for-teachers-and-practitioners/espresso/.

Haylock, D. and Manning, R. (2019) *Mathematics Explained for Primary Teachers*, 6th edn, London: SAGE.
> Teacher subject knowledge is important. This book explains key concepts in primary mathematics and so is an excellent resource for any primary teacher. If you feel that you learnt how to get maths right without really understanding what you were doing, this book will support you to develop the necessary conceptual understanding to teach primary-age learners.

M FURTHER READING TO SUPPORT M-LEVEL STUDY

Here is a selection of other texts that are accessible when starting to teach primary mathematics and which could also support further study at M-level.

Askew, M. (2015) *Transforming Primary Mathematics: Understanding Classroom Tasks, Tools and Talk*, London: Routledge.
> A number of chapters in this book are very relevant to the ideas described here. In particular, in the chapter 'Mathematical activity: mindful or fluent' the author explores the difference between mindful learning and fluency, which builds on the discussion earlier about fluency and conceptual understanding. The chapter on 'Variation theory' is also highly recommended.

Drury H. (2014) *Mastering Mathematics: Teaching to Transform Achievement*, Oxford: Oxford University Press.
> This is written by the founder of the Mathematics Mastery programme. It outlines many of the principles that underpin that programme both for the classroom teacher and also includes advice for whole school implementation.

Gu, L., Huang, R. and Marton, F. (2004) 'Teaching with variation: A Chinese way of promoting effective mathematics learning', in L. Fan et al. (eds) *How Chinese Learn Mathematics: Perspectives from Insiders* (Vol. 1), NJ: World Scientific, pp. 309-347.
> This is an in depth look at variation theory which is a way of developing conceptual understanding and fluency through the careful selection of tasks.

Marks, R. (2013) '"The blue table means you don't have a clue": The persistence of fixed-ability thinking and practices in primary mathematics in English schools', *FORUM*, 55(1): 31-44.
> In this article, Marks challenges the reader to reflect on how learners are grouped for maths lessons, and the impact of labelling children as being of a particular ability.

Merttens, R. (2012) 'The concrete-pictorial-abstract heuristic', *MT*, May 2012, pp. 33-38.
> This short article challenges how Bruner's theory of representation is sometimes applied including in Singapore's concrete-pictorial-abstract formulation. Reading this article should encourage you to reflect that much in mathematics education is open to debate.

Skemp, R. R. (1976) 'Relational understanding and instrumental understanding', *Mathematics Teaching*, (77): 20-26.
> In this seminal text, Skemp explores what it means to understand mathematics. His 'relational understanding' is very much what we've had in mind when writing about conceptual understanding.

RELEVANT WEBSITES

The National Centre for Excellence in the Teaching of Mathematics: www.ncetm.org.uk

- Subject Knowledge audits: www.ncetm.org.uk/classroom-resources/pska-primary-subject-knowledge-audit/
- Teaching for Mastery: www.ncetm.org.uk/teaching-for-mastery/
- Maths Hubs: a site of regional networks promoting mastery in England. Find your hub and register with them to be kept in touch with activities in your local area: www.mathshubs.org.uk/

Support for teaching young children from Early Maths: https://earlymaths.org/

- Focus on pedagogical approaches: https://earlymaths.org/early-years-mathematics-pedagogy-exploration-apprenticeship-making-sense/

The NRICH website is a great source of non-routine problems and support for teachers: https://nrich.maths.org

Maths Through Stories is an organisation that supports the use of story books in teaching maths: www.mathsthroughstories.org/

There are two subject associations for mathematics teachers based in England (but membership is open to teachers from across the UK) – the Mathematics Association and The Association of Teachers of Mathematics. Both have discounts for beginning teachers and they have a joint working group where members of the two associations come together to focus on primary mathematics:

- Association of Teachers of Mathematics: www.atm.org.uk/
- Mathematical Association: www.m-a.org.uk/

Additionally, the Scottish Mathematics Council hosts an annual conference for Scottish mathematics teachers: https://scottishmathematicalcouncil.org/

REFERENCES

Boaler, J. (2014) 'Research suggests timed tests cause math anxiety', *Teaching Children Mathematics*, 20(8): 469-474.

Boylan, M. (2019) 'Remastering mathematics: Mastery, 14 remixes and mash-ups', *MT 266*. Retrieved from: https://atm.org.uk/write/MediaUploads/Journals/MT266/MT266_FULL_JOURNAL_NEW.pdf

Bruner, J. S. (1966) *Toward a Theory of Instruction*, Cambridge, Massachusetts: Belknap Press of Harvard University Press.

Cambridge Mathematics. (2016) *What Are the Issues in Learning and Assessing Times Tables*. Retrieved from: www.cambridgemaths.org/Images/espresso_1_learning_and_assessing_times_tables.pdf

Foster, C. (2022) *Learning Times Tables Efficiently*. Retrieved from: https://blog.foster77.co.uk/2022/05/learning-times-tables-efficiently.html

Griffiths, R., Back, J. and Gifford, S. (2016) *Making Numbers*. Oxford: Oxford University Press.

Hoong, L. Y., Kin, H. W. and Pien, C. L. (2015) 'Concrete-pictorial-abstract: Surveying its origins and charting its future', *The Mathematics Educator*, 16(1): 1-19.

National Centre for Excellence in the Teaching Mathematics (NCETM). (2016) *The Essence of Mathematics Teaching for Mastery URL*. Retrieved from: www.ncetm.org.uk/files/37086535/The+Essence+of+Maths+Teaching+for+Mastery+june+2016.pdf

North, M. (2020) 'Strategies for supporting working memory and cognitive overload in mathematics', *Mathematics Teaching*, (274), December, pp. 9-13.

Shulman, L. S. (1986) 'Those who understand: Knowledge growth in teaching', *Educational Researcher*, 15(2): 4-14.

UNIT 4.5

THE SCIENCE CURRICULUM

Nicola Treby and Vanessa Matthews

INTRODUCTION

When you think about science as a subject, the image in your mind may be of mysterious chemicals bubbling in glass flasks, a naturalist in a far-flung location discovering a new species or astronauts exploring previously unknown environments. Our minds are often drawn to the aspects of science that appear far more exciting than our everyday lives. Equally, young children are often fascinated by the world around them; the young child lying on the grass engrossed in watching a snail move across the earth, the joy of discovering the ability to build complex structures with magnetic construction toys, the beauty of a frozen spider web on a frosty morning. As teachers, we need to harness this sense of wonder and discovery.

The English National Curriculum for science explains the reason for including science in the primary phase of education as follows:

> Science has changed our lives and is vital to the world's future prosperity, and all pupils should be taught essential aspects of the knowledge, methods, processes and uses of science. Through building up a body of key foundational knowledge and concepts, pupils should be encouraged to recognise the power of rational explanation and develop a sense of excitement and curiosity about natural phenomena. They should be encouraged to understand how science can be used to explain what is occurring, predict how things will behave, and analyse causes.
>
> (Department for Education [DfE], 2013)

OBJECTIVES

By the end of this unit, you will:

- have a good understanding of science as a primary school subject;
- be able to make links between the science curriculum and the interests and experiences of the child;
- gain an understanding of science specific pedagogical approaches.

Task 4.5.1 Reflecting on your own primary science education

Reflect on your own early childhood; were there aspects of the world around you that fascinated or inspired you? Were you interested in fossils, or obsessed with spiders? Did your own experience of the primary science curriculum foster and develop this interest? Can you remember science lessons at primary school that sparked an interest and made you want to find out more?

SCIENCE IN THE PRIMARY NATIONAL CURRICULUM FOR ENGLAND

Since the inception of the National Curriculum in 1988, science has always been a core subject along with maths and English. There are several arguments as to why science should be a compulsory and core subject for *all* children and not just those who wish to pursue a career in science. Harlen and Qualter (2018: 7) highlight this as follows:

> If education is a preparation for life, it must prepare pupils for life in a world in which science and its application to technology have key roles. It follows that children need to develop a range of skills and knowledge that enable them to understand scientific and technological aspects of the world around them.

Whilst Harlen and Qualter emphasise the societal importance of having a science literate population, Sharp *et al*. (2021) draw attention to the anatomy of science as a subject and consider the relationship between the theoretical and practical aspects of school science:

> The national curriculum identifies the importance of integrating 'working scientifically' with the substantive conceptual content of science, an approach which acknowledges the importance of the relationship between knowing about science (conceptual understanding) and knowing how to do science (procedural knowledge).
>
> (p. 17)

In Wales...

> Through robust and consistent evaluation of scientific and technological evidence, learners can become ethical, informed citizens of Wales and the world, who will be able to make informed decisions about future actions. Healthy, confident individuals, ready to lead fulfilling lives as valued members of society are informed by knowledge of their bodies and the ecosystems around them, and of how technological innovations can support improvements in health and lifestyle.
>
> Ambitious, capable learners, ready to learn throughout their lives should engage with scientific and technological change. The knowledge and deep understanding gained through experiencing what matters in science and technology can help learners live independent and fulfilling lives that sees them contributing to society and culture in a variety of ways. Learners who are enterprising, creative contributors, ready to play a full part in life and work embrace such challenges, as they are encouraged to take risks, to innovate and evaluate, and learn to develop solutions. Thus, they can become more resilient and purposeful learners across all areas of learning and experience.
>
> (Welsh Government, 2021)

Within any science lesson, there is likely to be a combination of subject content and practical work. How they should be integrated is much debated. The national curriculum for England advocates for content knowledge to be taught through practical work; however, concerns have been raised about whether integrating the teaching of scientific concepts through practical activity reliably leads to optimal learning (Peacock et al., 2021). Furthermore, Ofsted's (2023) science subject report states that, 'Effective practical work has a clear purpose in relation to the curriculum. It forms part of a wider sequence of lessons and only takes place when pupils have enough prior knowledge to learn from the activity.' We adopt the view that there is not one preferred way to integrate content and process but rather we advocate for explicit intentional planning.

> **In Northern Ireland …**
>
> At Key Stages 1 and 2, The World Around Us is presented as four inter-related strands that connect learning across geography, history and science and technology. When planning topics, teachers should ensure that opportunities are provided for children to develop their skills in Communication, Using Mathematics, Using ICT and their Thinking Skills and Personal Capabilities. At all stages children should be encouraged to become active participants in the learning process. Teachers should involve children in the choice of topics that interest them and, where possible, learning should be connected to current events in the world around them. Teachers should ensure that, where appropriate, aspects of the other Areas of Learning should be integrated.
>
> (Council for Curriculum Examinations and Assessment CCEA, 2007: 84)

Are you clear about which aspects of conceptual knowledge and working scientifically are being addressed within your lesson? Are you trying to include too much? Just as you would consider the sequencing of conceptual knowledge within and across lessons, it is important to do the same when planning scientific enquiry. Ofsted (2023) highlighted the importance of this in its science subject report, 'in one school, pupils were planning an investigation, but did not have sufficient knowledge of controlling variables to do this well'.

Within one lesson, you may choose to focus on deepening children's understanding of one aspect of the enquiry, e.g. sometimes you may ask children to devise a method, at other times you may give children a method and deepen their understanding on how to present data.

Some aspects of science enquiry need to be taught directly, e.g. how to use a data logger to measure light levels whereas at other times children can be given choice and autonomy, e.g. choosing how to collect and present their data. Also, remember, skills need to be practised over time. Therefore, children need ample opportunity to engage in practical work.

Scientific process and enquiry skills, and types of scientific enquiry are specified within the curriculum. As children move through the age phases, what is required of them becomes increasingly complex, in relation to both subject content and working scientifically. Scientific process and enquiry skills are illustrated in the following table adapted from the English National Curriculum (DfE, 2013). These are likely to be familiar to you from your own science education.

Stages of a scientific enquiry	Key stage 1 (Age range 5–7)	Lower key stage 2 (Age range 7–9)	Upper key stage 2 (Age range 9–11)
Asking questions	• asking simple questions and recognising that they can be answered in different ways	• asking relevant questions and using different types of scientific enquiry to answer them	
Conducting scientific enquiries	• performing simple tests using simple equipment and observing closely	• setting up simple practical enquiries, comparative and fair tests • making systematic and careful observations and, where appropriate, taking accurate measurements using standard units, using a range of equipment, including thermometers and data loggers	• planning different types of scientific enquiries to answer questions, including recognising and controlling variables where necessary
Collecting and presenting data	• gathering and recording data • using observations and ideas to suggest answers to questions	• gathering, recording, classifying and presenting data in a variety of ways to help in answering questions • recording findings using simple scientific language, drawings, labelled diagrams, keys, bar charts, and tables	• taking measurements, using a range of scientific equipment, with increasing accuracy and precision, taking repeat readings when appropriate • recording data and results of increasing complexity using scientific diagrams and labels, classification keys, tables, scatter graphs, bar and line graphs
Evaluating and communicating findings		• using straightforward scientific evidence to answer questions or to support their findings • reporting on findings from enquiries, including oral and written explanations, displays or presentations of results and conclusions • using results to draw simple conclusions, make predictions for new values, suggest improvements and raise further questions	• reporting and presenting findings from enquiries, including conclusions, causal relationships and explanations of and a degree of trust in results, in oral and written forms such as displays and other presentations • using test results to make predictions to set up further comparative and fair tests • identifying scientific evidence that has been used to support or refute ideas or arguments

The types of scientific enquiry listed in the National Curriculum (DfE, 2013) are: observing over time; pattern seeking; identifying, classifying and grouping; comparative and fair testing (controlled investigations); and researching using secondary sources.

Observing over time enquiries can take place over minutes, hours, days or even months. Children might observe seeds germinating on the windowsill, a puddle evaporating on the playground or the apparent change in the shape of the moon. These enquiries can also offer opportunities for children to decide on the manner of their observation (how often, when) and what to record (measurements, drawings, observation notes).

Pattern seeking enquiries are used when it is difficult to control variables. They are ideal for answering questions such as, 'Do the tallest children also have the largest feet?', 'Do bees prefer yellow flowers or pink ones?'

Identifying, classifying and grouping enquiries require children to observe closely. For example, when learning about minibeasts; they may see that insects have six legs and spiders eight, which means these animals fall into two distinct groups or use statement keys to identify a specific animal. Children are often intuitively identifying and grouping from birth, as they learn about the world around them.

Comparative and fair testing or controlled investigations allow children to investigate causal relationships between one variable and another. A fair test is often planned in response to a question, for example, what happens to the distance a car travels when we change the height of the ramp it is travelling down?

Research using secondary sources is used in primary science to learn about scientific concepts which would not be possible or safe to investigate in the classroom. Children may use the secondary sources of non-fiction books and websites to answer questions such as, what is the difference between Indian elephants and African elephants, or how is electricity generated? Researching secondary sources requires children to consider how we identify a trustworthy source, how to research efficiently by asking the right questions, how to extract the information we want and present this in our own words.

Historically, the fair test was the most common type of enquiry practiced in primary science. The 2013 National Curriculum sought to address this over emphasis on the fair test by making explicit reference to the different enquiry types. The enquiry types were an outcome of the ASE-Kings College London Science Investigations in Schools research project (AKSIS, 2004). From a primary specific perspective, you may wish to read Turner *et al.* (2014), *It's not fair – or is it? A guide to developing children's ideas through primary science enquiry*. The book suggests activities and contexts for all the different enquiry types.

FINDING THE SCIENCE WITHIN THE CHILD'S WORLD

When children learn about science, they learn how the world around them works in all its interlinked complexity. It is important to note that children are exposed to science from a very young age, well before formal education begins. Consider how many scientific concepts a child could be exposed to on a simple walk in the park. They may be able to observe animals, habitats and forces to name but a few. Within the home, scientific concepts are frequently represented within story books which are often instrumental in igniting an early interest in science.

To teach children effectively, it is important to make links between children's early experiences and the formal school curriculum. Your curriculum can help to identify substantive conceptual knowledge that has been formally taught previously; however, a teacher needs to think beyond the taught curriculum and become familiar with the rich array of opportunities to link school science to the child's everyday life.

This can be achieved through becoming familiar with children's books, toys, games, songs, television programmes, websites, etc. In doing so the teacher can help the child to make meaningful links between the concepts they are learning in the classroom and their personal lived experiences. For example, the topic of magnets could include children investigating a range of toys which utilise magnets, e.g. trains which connect with magnets or travel board games which use magnets to ensure all the pieces remain on the board. Furthermore, children's own experiences can be used as a starting point to investigate potential solutions for real world problems. For example, using a light meter to investigate which material is best for bedroom curtains if the light from a streetlamp prevents you from sleeping.

In addition to the class teacher, parents and carers can help to make links to the child's world through carefully crafted homework activities. When teaching the topic of materials and their uses, children could be asked to name as many different items made from wood, metal, plastic and glass that can be found within the home. Apps which are free to download can also be used at home; for example, when teaching the topic of sound parents can be directed towards decibel meter apps, when teaching about habitats parents can be directed to plant/animal identification apps. Such activities can help to prevent children from compartmentalising school science and seeing it as distinct from the real world.

Task 4.5.2 Linking children's prior experiences to a programme of study

Take the topic of Earth and Space. Children are likely to have had a vast exposure to books, films, cartoons, toys and games about space before they even begin to learn about it in the classroom. The following table shows what they might have encountered.

Books	Film/Television
Fiction books such as	Maddie, Space and You (CBeebies)
Whatever next! by Jill Murphy	Storybots: A Space Adventure (Netflix)
Meg on the Moon by Helen Nicholl and Jan Pieńkowski	Star Wars Episode IV: A New Hope (Film)
	Wall-ee (Film)
	Lightyear (Film)
Non-fiction books such as	
Am I Made of Stardust? by Maggie Aderin-Pocock	
The Cosmic Diary of our Incredible Universe by Tim Peake	
Hidden Figures by Margot Shetterly	
Toys	**Other**
Spaceships and rockets	News reports about space missions and robots in space
Alien soft toys	
Astronaut figures	Online images of space
Solar system models	Observing the sky at night
	Noticing the changes in the shape of the moon
	Observing changes in the size and shape of our shadows

Select a different topic from your curriculum for science. Aim to identify the previous experiences children may have had in relation to the scientific concepts.

Books	Film/television
Toys	Other

As teachers of science, we would advocate for the inclusion of teaching opportunities beyond the classroom which are meaningfully integrated into a sequence of lessons. Most school sites offer some options for minibeast hunts or the close observation of different types of plants and every location has an outdoor space where children can study shadows and trace the changes in shape and size throughout the day. Botanical gardens, wetland centres, space centres and museums offer children high-quality, first-hand experiences of scientists at work. These support the development of science capital which Wong (2016) refers to as, 'the knowledge and resources that can support science learning, engagement, or participation' (p.108).

Task 4.5.3 Local areas for science

Consider a school site and local area you are familiar with. Think about the subject content for one year group. What opportunities does the school site and local area offer for learning about science?

The National Education Nature Park website www.educationnaturepark.org.uk has some suggestions for learning about plants and animals. Their Hidden Nature project might be a good starting point; this allows teachers and children to engage in 'citizen science' by submitting photographs of nature within their school grounds https://storymaps.arcgis.com/stories/8557212491554e0fb518705925f1a37e.

PEDAGOGICAL APPROACHES THAT ARE PARTICULARLY APPROPRIATE TO TEACHING SCIENCE

For many children, the prospect of carrying out science investigations in school is exciting, offering children a different type of lesson to look forward to. This enthusiasm for practical work and a high level of engagement in lessons may imply that learning is also taking place, which cannot be assumed. A classroom full of children building electrical circuits, dissecting flowers or creating a model of the digestive system can provide a rich learning environment where children can investigate, discover and deepen scientific knowledge; however, levels of engagement do not necessarily indicate high levels of cognitive activity and Ofsted's research review notes that 'understanding and retention can be limited if teachers prioritise "wow" moments without clear reference to any curricular goal' (Ofsted, 2021). Consequently, it is vitally important that teachers have a good understanding of how to teach science in a way that helps all children learn. Shulman (1986) refers to this as pedagogic content knowledge (PCK), a concept that suggests teachers need more than just (science) subject knowledge but also need skills and strategies which inform effective pedagogical choices. Whilst there are some aspects of PCK that can be said to be equally relevant to the teaching of all subjects, we believe that there are some pedagogical approaches which are particularly appropriate to the teaching of science. We have outlined our thoughts on these next.

In Scotland ...

There is a commitment to raising aspirations in science education. The science curriculum is integral to an interdisciplinary approach to Science, Technology, Engineering and Mathematics education (STEM). This aims to build capacity, interest, and equal opportunities for all learners.

Source: Education Scotland (2018a, 2018b)

Misconceptions

Children observe the world around them all the time; in doing so they construct their ideas about how the world works (Allen, 2025). Often children's constructions align with accepted science theory; however, this is not always the case. If their constructions do not align with accepted science theory, we would identify them as misconceptions. An example of children incorrectly assimilating prior and new experiences to form a misconception is shown in the following practice-based example.

> On a sunny day, a group of reception children are outside playing. One child points to the sky and draws his friend's attention to a phenomenon he has never seen before – a white rainbow. Very quickly he encourages other children to come and look at what he has seen. All express the same wonder and excitement at this new sight. Children can be heard saying, "I've never seen a white rainbow before!" and "Why is it white?"

At this stage no one is questioning whether what they can see is a rainbow. The white rainbow was in fact a condensation trail from a passing plane. Why do you think the children thought that this was a white rainbow?

It is likely that the children came to this conclusion as they do not know or understand why rainbows occur. Their knowledge and understanding of rainbows extend to the fact that rainbows appear in the sky and are curved in shape. Previously, they have only seen multi-coloured rainbows; however, due to the location and shape, they are convinced this is a white rainbow. The logical schemata the children constructed was scientifically incorrect; this is how a misconception can form. This is an example of both constructivism (Piaget, 1954), as the first child to see the 'white rainbow' constructed his knowledge from his own observations, and social constructivism (Vygotsky, 1978), as he then acted as a more knowledgeable other and through conversation and the confirmation of each other's ideas the children built new knowledge together.

This example highlights the need for teachers to have a good understanding of misconceptions and how easily they form. A good working knowledge of common misconceptions enables teachers to anticipate them when planning but also to avoid teaching in a way that may result in new misconceptions forming. *Misconceptions in Primary Science*, by Michael Allen (2025), includes examples of common misconceptions, strategies to identify them and practical suggestions to reconstruct children's ideas.

If you wish to find out more about early research on misconceptions (undertaken in the late 1980s) we'd encourage you to read the Primary Science Processes and Concept Exploration (SPACE) project research reports (see the Relevant websites section).

Vocabulary

Without secure knowledge of scientific vocabulary, children are unlikely to be able to understand the content of the lesson or articulate their conceptual scientific understanding. They must first be exposed to scientific terminology and have a secure understanding of its meaning. Although it may seem easy to expand a child's vocabulary by giving them a list of key words, when you take a closer look at the complexity of language you realise that many words have nuances and different meanings, for example, the word *light*.

Vocabulary used in science often has a different everyday meaning (polysemous words), for example, the word *force* is used in an everyday sense by children to refer to the behaviour of someone, e.g. '*My sister forced me to do it!*', however when teaching the subject of forces in science this term refers to concepts such as gravity, air resistance and friction. Other words such as *oesophagus* and *inheritance* may be new to children and will need to be taught explicitly. Often children have been using a non-scientific word, such as *backbone*, for some time and now need to use the scientific term. For children to use scientific vocabulary correctly, they first need to be taught the words and their meanings explicitly. This may be accompanied by labelled diagrams, pictures or an explanation of the etymology (word origin) and morphology (word structure). For example, the word *carnivore* is made up of *carni*, referring to meat, and *vore*, to devour or eat. New vocabulary also needs to be repeatedly modelled by the teacher so children gain an understanding of the word in context. Only then will children be equipped to use scientific vocabulary accurately to express their scientific understanding. The process of language acquisition need not be tedious, as Harlen and Qualter (2018) note, 'children pick up and use scientific words quite readily; they often enjoy collecting them and trying them out as if they were new possessions' (p.100).

Models and analogies

Whilst practical work can be used as a vehicle to test children's scientific ideas, some aspects of science cannot be examined first-hand within a primary school classroom; currently, it is not possible to arrange school trips to visit the moon. This is where models and analogies can be used to help children develop conceptual understanding. Loxley *et al*. (2018) highlight that:

> our ability to talk about and explain an event or phenomenon depends on the model of it we hold in our minds. If the model is powerful and reliable, it can be used in a wide range of contexts and may even help us explain events we may not have previously experienced.
>
> (p. 84)

The challenge for teachers is being attuned to the child's interests and experiences in order to identify which models may act as powerful models for the child. There are many types of models that can be used in the classroom:

Physical models

It is possible to purchase life-size models of the human body. Most of us will have seen a life-size model of the skeleton at some point. Schools can also readily purchase models of most organs in the human body. This allows children to disassemble, handle and reassemble model organs to see how the major organs of the human body are arranged. Models of the planets within the solar system can be purchased and are often displayed within schools to help children visualise aspects of the curriculum that they cannot physically see. There is equal benefit in children making their own models as this provides a memorable first-hand opportunity to consider, in detail, the intricacies of the object represented by the model. Figure 4.5.1 demonstrates how children can model the relative sizes and distances in our solar system using accessible classroom resources. Children are often amazed by how far away from the sun Neptune is compared to Earth.

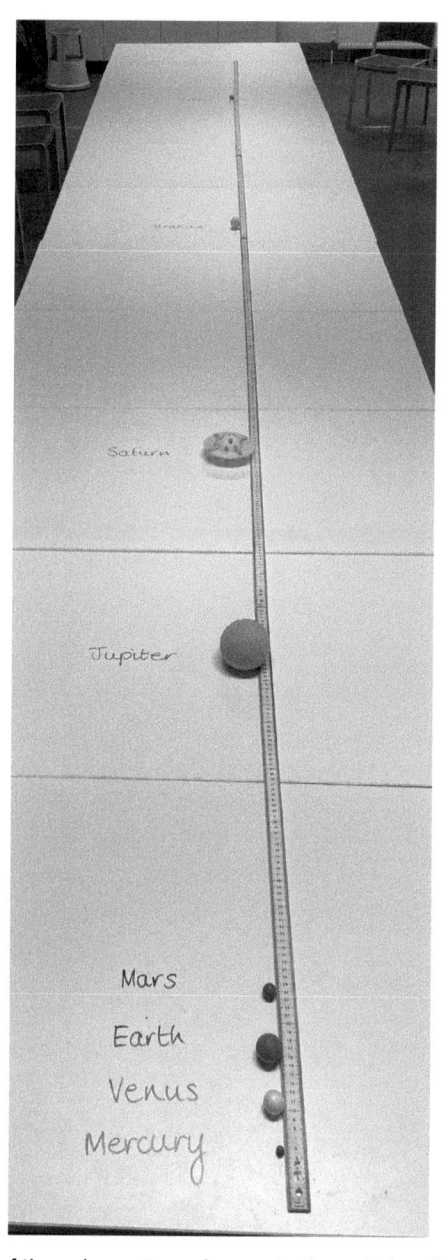

FIGURE 4.5.1 Classroom model of the solar system, demonstrating relative sizes and distances between planets

FIGURE 4.5.2 3D paper model of a flower

The model in Figure 4.5.1 is likely to be something children create and discuss as a group. At other times, it may be more beneficial for children to work individually. For example, children have created detailed models of a flower which enable children to identify and label parts which can be difficult to see and label on a real flower, see Figures 4.5.2 and 4.5.3.

Virtual models

Advances in technology have enabled children to view the world in a very different way. For example, real time 3D visualisation models of the solar system, such as NASA's 'Eyes on the Solar System' (see the Relevant websites section), can help children appreciate the relative size and movement of the planets. Augmented reality enables children to 'see inside' the human body and learn more about the organs that they are viewing. Virtual reality enables children to 'walk through' habitats that they may never be able to visit.

Analogies

Analogies differ from models in that they compare the scientific concept being taught to a process which is familiar to children. For example, the circulatory system can be compared with the road network. Arteries can be compared with motorways; arterioles can be compared with A roads and

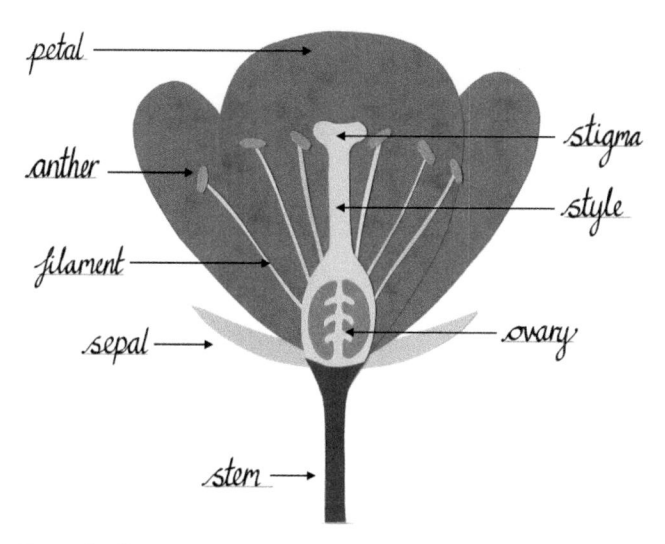

FIGURE 4.5.3 Paper collage of a flower

capillaries can be compared with B roads. A further analogy, illustrated in Figures 4.5.4 and 4.5.5, compares the flow of electricity through wires to pumped water flowing through pipes.

Whilst models and analogies can help children understand scientific concepts, it is also important to acknowledge their limitations. Models will only ever be a useful representation; they are not usually sufficient to model the concept in all its complexity. Teachers should be mindful of this and acknowledge these challenges. Furthermore, not all children find analogies helpful as they may naturally think in literal ways and find analogies confusing. Within the primary age phase, children may not have

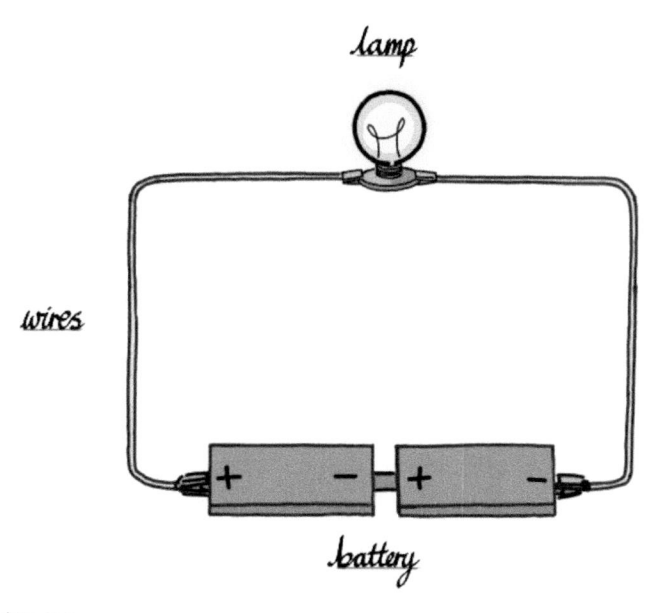

FIGURE 4.5.4 Circuit drawing

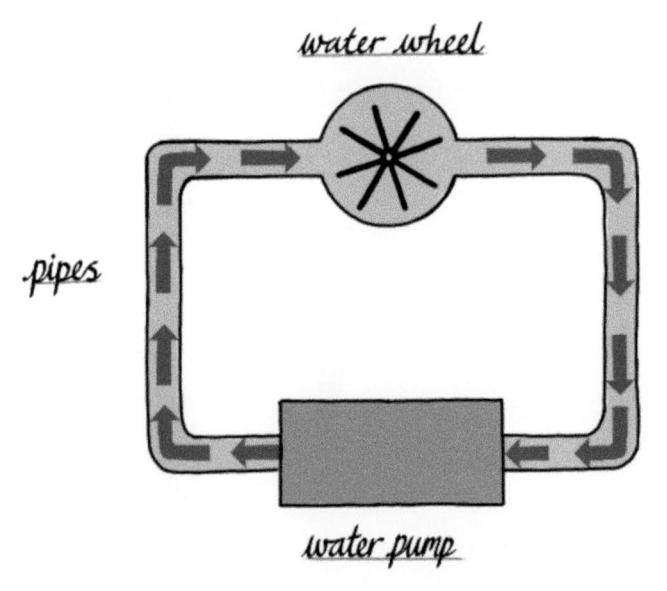

FIGURE 4.5.5 Water pump visual to be used as an analogy for understanding the flow of electricity through a circuit

developed the ability to draw comparisons, or the example chosen may be familiar to the teacher, e.g. road networks, but not the child. Therefore, careful consideration is required when using models and analogies, and their limitations need to be shared with the children (Asoko and de Boo 2001).

Task 4.5.4 Preparing to teach a science unit of work

Think about a science unit of work on your curriculum, e.g. the human body. Familiarise yourself with the scientific conceptual knowledge.

- Can you identify any likely misconceptions?
- Can you think about how you could address them?
- Can you consider which vocabulary children would need to know and identify polysemous words and terms that children are unlikely to have encountered before?
- Are there any models or analogies that you could use to help teach the digestive system?

SUMMARY

In this unit we have sought to inspire you to approach primary science teaching in a way that recognises the children's own experiences and interests while meeting the requirements of the curriculum. We have emphasised that this involves making informed choices around when and how to incorporate different approaches to practical science enquiry alongside the teaching of science content knowledge. We have broken down what the National Curriculum refers to as 'working scientifically' into scientific processes and skills and the different enquiry approaches.

Within this chapter, we encouraged you to recognise the potential of science to help children understand the world around them and appreciate its complexity. Moreover, we hope you are inspired to help children to recognise the wonder of the world that surrounds them.

ANNOTATED FURTHER READING

Brunton, P. and Thornton, L. (2010) *Science in the Early Years: Building Firm Foundations from Birth to Five*, London: Sage
> This early years' specific book breaks down different aspects of subject content, explains the science subject knowledge for the teacher before moving into highly practical and detailed suggestions for how to plan and teach science in the early years.

Harlen, W. and Qualter, A. (2018) *The Teaching of Science in Primary Schools*, 7th edn, Oxon: Routledge.
> This seventh edition provides comprehensive discussion of all matters related to teaching primary science.

McCrory, A. and Worthington, K. (2018) *Mastering Primary Science*, London: Bloomsbury.
> *Mastering Primary Science* skilfully brings together rich fundamental knowledge about the nature of science, the importance of science and how to implement principles in an innovative way. Images of children's work helpfully exemplify the key messages.

Roden, J. and Archer, J. (2014) *Primary Science for Trainee Teachers*, London: Sage.
> As well as providing subject knowledge support and activity suggestions, this book uses relevant research to highlight the importance of the curriculum content to children's wider real-world experience. Self-assessment questions (and answers) are provided for each chapter.

Turner, J. Keogh, B. Naylor, S. and Lawrence, L. (2014) *It's Not Fair – Or Is It? A Guide to Developing Children's Ideas Through Primary Science Enquiry*, Sandbach: Millgate House Publishers and Hatfield: Association for Science Education.
> This book takes five enquiry approaches and explains how teachers might get children started, how to encourage talk and questioning, possible outcomes for assessment and vivid examples of practical investigations.

FURTHER READING TO SUPPORT M-LEVEL STUDY

Dunlop, L., Compton, K., Clarke, L. and McKelvey-Martin, V. (2015) 'Child-led enquiry in primary science', *Education 3-13*, 43(5): 462-481.
> This article considers the application of a child-led approach to scientific enquiry. The authors review the outcomes of their research which indicates that increased levels of science learning, confidence and oracy. They also highlight the importance of developing teachers' facilitation skills.

Mercer, N., Dawes, L., Wegerif, R. and Sams, C. (2004) 'Reasoning as a scientist: Ways of helping children to use language to learn science', *British Educational Research Journal*, 30(3): 359-377.
> This article considers the role of language and discussion when learning science. The authors review the outcomes of their research which indicate that children can be supported to use talk more effectively to support their reasoning and understanding of scientific concepts.

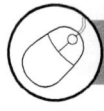

RELEVANT WEBSITES

Explorify: https://explorify.uk
> The Explorify website provides teachers with subject knowledge support, activities, planning advice and high-quality images and videos to support the teaching of primary science. At present, Explorify also collates recent research in the teaching of primary science on the pages titled '*Latest evidence on what works in primary science*'. At the time of writing, we are aware that Explorify materials will migrate to the STEM website; therefore, if the link provided does not take you to Explorify materials you should be able to locate the materials easily by typing Explorify into a search engine.

TAPS: https://taps.pstt.org.uk/
> The TAPS (Teacher Assessment in Primary Science) pyramid tool enables teachers to develop their assessment processes in science. This website offers practical guidance for assessment of a child's attainment, as well as providing a framework for assessment across the school.

PLAN: www.planassessment.com/
> This website hosts a wealth of resources to support planning and assessment. There are multiple exemplars of annotated children's work.

Primary Science Teaching Trust: https://pstt.org.uk/resources/
> The Primary Science Teaching Trust is a charitable trust which aims to 'see excellent teaching of science in every primary classroom in the UK'. They provide a range of resources; we highly recommend 'A scientist just like me', 'Enquiry Skills' and 'Enquiry Approaches'.

Primary Science Processes and Concept Exploration (SPACE) project research reports: www.stem.org.uk/resources/collection/3324/space-research-reports

NASA's Eyes on the Solar System: https://eyes.nasa.gov/apps/solar-system/#/home

REFERENCES

AKSIS. (2004) *ASE-King's Science Investigations in Schools (AKSIS) Project Second Interim Report to the QCA November 1998*. Retrieved from: www.kcl.ac.uk/archive/website-resources/education/web-files2/aksis.pdf

Allen, M. (2025) *Misconceptions in Primary Science*, 4th edn, London: Open University Press.

Asoko, H., and de Boo, M. (2001) *Analogies and Illustrations: Representing Ideas in Primary Science*, Hatfield: Association for Science Education.

Council for Curriculum Examinations and Assessment (CCEA). (2007) *The Northern Ireland Curriculum – Primary*, Belfast: CCEA.

Department for Education (DfE). (2013) *National Curriculum in England: Key Stages 1 and 2 Framework Document*, London: DfE.

Education Scotland. (2018a) *A Summary of STEM Resources*. Last updated 2024. Retrieved from: https://education.gov.scot/resources/a-summary-of-stem-resources/

Education Scotland. (2018b) *RAiSE – Raising Aspirations in Science Education*. Last updated 2024. Retrieved from: https://education.gov.scot/resources/raise-raising-aspirations-in-science-education/

Harlen, W. and Qualter, A. (2018) *The Teaching of Science in Primary Schools*, 7th edn, Oxon: Routledge.

Loxley, P., Dawes, L., Nicholls, L. and Dore, B. (2018) *Teaching Primary Science*, 3rd edn, Oxon: Routledge.

Ofsted. (2021) *Research Review Series: Science*. Retrieved from: www.gov.uk/government/publications/subject-report-series-science

Ofsted. (2023) *Subject Report Series: Science*. Retrieved from: www.gov.uk/government/publications/subject-report-series-science

Peacock, G. A., Sharp, J., Johnsey, R., Wright, D. and Sewell, K. (2021) *Primary Science: Knowledge and Understanding*, 9th edn, London: Sage.

Piaget, J. (1954) *The Construction of Reality in the Child*, New York: Basic Books.

Sharp, J., Peacock, G. A., Johnsey, R., Simon, S., Smith, R. J., Cross, A. and Harris, D. (2021) *Primary Science: Teaching Theory and Practice*, 9th edn, London: Sage.

Shulman, L. S. (1986) 'Those who understand: Knowledge growth in teaching', *Educational Researcher*, 15(2): 4-14.

Turner, J., Keogh, B., Naylor, S. and Lawrence, L. (2014) *It's Not Fair – Or Is It? A Guide to Developing Children's Ideas Through Primary Science Enquiry*, Sandbach: Millgate House Publishers and Hatfield: Association for Science.

Vygotsky, L. S. (1978) *Mind and Society: The Development of Higher Mental Processes*, Cambridge, MA: Harvard University Press.

Welsh Government (2021) *AREA OF LEARNING AND EXPERIENCE Science and Technology*. Retrieved from: https://hwb.gov.wales/curriculum-for-wales/science-and-technology/ (accessed 26 April 2024).

Wong, B. (2016) *Science Education, Career Aspirations, and Minority Ethnic Students*, Hampshire: Palgrave Macmillan.

UNIT 4.6

DEVELOPING ARTS-ENRICHED CURRICULA AND PRACTICE

Jo Trowsdale, Kerry Chappell and Sarah Bracken

INTRODUCTION

In this unit we are looking at why and how teachers might enrich their curricula and teaching through the arts. By 'the arts' we mean all art forms, which extend beyond those noted in the National Curriculum (art, music, drama and dance). Broader accounts suggest further categories, such as literature (poetry, drama), visual (painting, drawing, sculpture), graphic (design, drawing, sculpture), plastic (modelling, sculpture), decorative (mosaic, furniture design, enamelwork crafts), performing (theatre, dance, music) and architecture (often including interior design) plus digital arts (www.britannica.com/topic/the-arts). We are focusing here upon the value of the common, 'family-like' dimensions of the arts for learning, whilst not discounting the diversity and range of forms, practices and educative benefits that learning 'in' and 'through' each individual art form can offer, within and beyond school (Fleming, 2013). This unit is about enriching the whole curriculum through the arts; and finding their value in surprising places.

There is a wealth of research evidence for the educative value of the arts (Comerford-Boyes and Reid, 2005; Bamford, 2006; Jindal-Snape et al., 2018; Bowen and Kisida, 2023). The Cultural Learning Alliance (CLA) evidences how children's cognitive abilities, attainment, skills and behaviour are significantly improved through engagement in arts activity. For example, they show that

> participation in structured arts activities can increase cognitive abilities by 17% ... students from low-income families who take part in arts activities at school are three times more likely to get a degree ... and the employability of students who study arts subjects is higher and they are more likely to stay in employment.
>
> (CLA, 2017: 2)

Case studies collated by the CLA also evidence how individual art forms and transdisciplinary arts-rich practices boost children's self-esteem; critical thinking skills; responsiveness; emotional sensitivity; ability to synthesise auditory, cognitive and motor information; and enhance agency and imagination (e.g. Teasdale, 2023).

We argue here for the significant and multiple roles that the arts can play in developing children's learning. Following Maxine Greene (1995: 382), '[t]he arts, it has been said, cannot change the world, but they may change human beings who might change the world'.

Developing arts-enriched curricula and practice

> ## OBJECTIVES
>
> By the end of this unit you will be confident about:
>
> - the importance and value of the arts in promoting learning;
> - ways to develop arts-enriched approaches in your teaching and school;
> - how to enhance children's learning through arts-rich approaches.

THE ROLE OF THE ARTS, AND THEIR DISTINCTIVE CONTRIBUTIONS

The arts make multiple, important and often distinctive contributions to children's learning, these include:

Involving the whole child

Making in the arts involves the whole of a child's being (Steiner, 1923/2004; Dewey, 1934; Eisner 2002). Art-making practices attune, value and develop children's sensibilities, feelings and physicalities, as well as their logical thinking. The dynamic of making in the arts affirms children's belief in themselves as whole beings, capable of learning, because it draws on the affective, embodied and cognitive, and recognises individual interests and contexts. The highly embodied nature of making in many art forms is also a significant factor in promoting well-being (Damasio, 2000).

Different ways of expressing ideas

The varied forms of the arts are often described as languages which enable us to express ideas, feelings and experiences in ways other than words. Meaning is made using the unique characteristics of the forms (Eisner, 2004; Chapman, 2015). For children to be able to express and develop their ideas, they must have opportunities to experience and practise these languages (Robinson, 1989). This can have particular resonances for children with special educational needs and disabilities (SEND).

Exploring ideas differently

The processes of making in the arts involves engaging with the materiality, spaces and cultural contexts of art-makers. This offers children diverse materials and spaces to explore ideas which provide different insights and different ways of representing them (Eisner, 2002). This might be sketching an idea, or physicalising a structure and feeling how forces work through the body. Working in the arts can stimulate a mix of imaginative and critical processing, building on children's innate curiosity and capacity for sense-making that they have been developing since they were babies (Gopnik, Metfzoff and Kuhl, 2001).

Relating, empathising, dealing with uncertainty

Art-making and engaging in the arts in schools is a collaborative endeavour whereby children are required to listen to, hear and respond to each other's ideas and points of view. Children practise relating to others, to materials and to their environment, and thereby practise empathising with others' experiences and situations (Lähdesmäki et al., 2022). This leads to them better understanding how to negotiate and develop thinking and acting in relation to others. Art-making contexts, as relational and exploratory spaces, also provide safe environments to explore the uncertainties of the wider world which may concern and negatively impact children's education (Eisner, 2002). Such relationality therefore also supports their well-being (CLA, 2018).

Developing confidence; growing capabilities

Attuning through the arts feeds children's confidence as learners. Making in the arts encourages attentive observation and focus which are vital habits for successful learning (Ingold, 2014, 2017). Making to an open brief provides a constructive experience of bounded freedom which is vital to children's sense of autonomy, a precondition for their belief in themselves as confident and capable learners (Trowsdale, McKenna and Francis, 2019).

Embracing diversity and cultural awareness

It is important for children to be exposed to and have first-hand experience of a diversity of arts because they may have a preference or talent in a particular art form. Art works and forms also reflect a diversity of cultural beliefs and practices. Providing experiences of and through the arts is therefore an important signal to children that their individual, and others', interests and needs matter, thereby enhancing a wider cultural understanding and appreciation of their own and others' cultures (Lähdesmäki *et al.*, 2022).

Readiness for learning; self-management and discipline

Making in the arts provides safe experiences of 'failure', where adaptation or a new idea following a 'mistake' can be a fertile source of learning, something Dewey called 'flexible purposing' (Eisner, 2002: 8). It can therefore develop a positive readiness to have a go, the habit of following and safely testing rules, and it can develop a sense of pleasure in committing to and persisting with a task (Ingold, 2014, 2017). Making in all art forms requires observance of conventions and rules, as well as appropriately challenging these, alongside negotiating with others: people, materials and environments. These are all important core dispositions for children's learning and development.

Cross-curricular learning

Perhaps most significantly for the primary classroom, the arts can provide a context and media for **both** developing any or all of the previous, **and** situating curriculum content from other subjects and disciplines. Making connections across the curriculum and ensuring local and individual relevance is essential to the success of learners (Barnes, 2015) and achieving a 'balanced and broadly based' curriculum (Department for Education [DfE], 2013). As a social activity, art-making offers unstructured and structured opportunities for developing children's literacy through negotiation of roles, explaining ideas, arguing, and justifying views and decisions. Research shows the significance of gesture, drawing and physicalising in developing numeracy, mathematical and scientific processing and understanding suggesting that engaging arts-based approaches are vital to a teacher's repertoire (Alibali and Nathan, 2012; Kontra *et al.*, 2015).

Foundations for future success

Research increasingly evidences the important foundations laid by learning in and through the arts for children's future success in education and the wider world. In Catterall, Dumais and Hampden-Thompson's (2012) study, students who had intensive arts experiences in high school were three times more likely to earn a bachelor's degree than students who lacked those experiences. Catterall's earlier (2009) study argued that children who experienced arts-rich education achieved better results and were positively contributing to society a decade later.

> **Task 4.6.1 Positive memories**
>
> Discuss the following with a colleague/friend:
>
> - An experience in the arts that was positive for you (or someone you know). Tell each other as much as you can about the context of the experience. Where did it happen? Describe the space. What materials could you see and use? Who was involved? What did you do? How old were you?
> - What did you learn about yourself (do you think the person you know learnt about themselves), and about anything else?

THE ARTS IN THE NATIONAL CURRICULUM

The arts feature in England's National Curriculum (DfE, 2013) documentation and guidance in varied ways. Music, Art and Design, and Design Technology are identified as discrete subjects. Drama in Literacy and Dance in PE are both noted as elements of subjects. Schools may choose for cultural, local or other reasons to broaden their art-making practices beyond those required by the National Curriculum.

The Curriculum requirements for arts subjects focus upon three key areas:

1. exploring ideas and forms through making, and reflecting in process (sometimes described generically as 'composing' or 'making');
2. developing proficiency in the skills and techniques of the form (sometimes described as kinds of 'performing');
3. evaluating and knowing artworks and artists using the language of the forms (sometimes described as 'appreciating').

Schools may choose to employ an expert or deploy a teacher with expertise across the school to address these needs, but to maximise the value of the arts towards pupil learning, all teachers need some art-making experience, skills and knowledge (Ogier and Tutchell, 2021).

Arts-rich curricula and pedagogy support teachers in meeting aspects of all the Teachers' Standards that define the minimum level of practice expected of teachers (TS1-8) and in delivering the Core Content (DfE, 2019). For example, using an art form to demonstrate or visualise a concept in maths or science encourages memory retention, ensuring children learn and know more. Teaching through the arts helps develop children's values, motivates them and cements their learning behaviours (TS1, 2 & 7). Teachers who have good arts subject knowledge can adapt the way they teach to support and develop schemas to aid children's understanding and memory retention (TS3, 4 & 5). The arts can be used not only to teach, but also to assess children's knowledge and skills in a variety of curriculum areas. This provides opportunities for them to create, perform and showcase their work, demonstrating that they understand the subject being assessed (TS6), as well as honing their art form skills.

Becoming proficient in art-making practices in order to maximise their potential for children's education will require support to develop and maintain teachers' skills in the arts, a point which we pick up later.

Reflecting some of the arts' characteristics noted earlier, the arts are advocated as media for ways to engage learners and communicate concepts in other subjects, increasingly for the STEM subjects – Science, Maths and Technology through STEAM education approaches (e.g. https://sciartsedu.co.uk). They are also strongly associated with the development of children's creativity, confidence, collaboration, curiosity, investigating, problem solving, discipline and resilience that children need for their well-being now and for success in the future (Winner, Goldstein and Vincent-Lancrin, 2013). The best teachers not only offer arts-rich and creative pedagogies, but structure the arts into their curriculum planning, which develops children's skills in and attunement to the arts.

Art-making practices provide countless opportunities for listening and engaging in dialogue, in verbal or embodied ways. This could, for example, involve experimenting bodily with how to link motifs together in a dance, improvising together to create a piece of music, devising or acting out a scenario, describing a piece of music or poetry and how it makes children feel, which also develops children's emotional intelligence. Being involved in an art-making project allows children to mediate between their inner imagination and their outer voice, providing opportunities for authentic dialogue and talk. In contexts where schools and teachers are under pressure to achieve results, arts-rich approaches enable the teacher to address curriculum content in ways that also develop broader core behaviour for learning. Lessons in or involving the arts are often conducted in different ways and different spaces, with a more fluid, responsive and 'workshop' feel where children are engrossed in making, talking and collaborating with their peers and adults. Through contemplative, open-ended and active tasks, children have the opportunity to practice and refine particular skills dialogically, trouble shooting for themselves through talk. This increases their sense of mastery of techniques, both artistic and oral, and is an approach which can easily be applied to other subjects (Chappell *et al.*, 2019). Listening to music can generate both a particular mood and provide another stimulus for reflective talk (see DfE, 2021, Appendices for resource ideas). Extending these approaches to other subjects allows for more quality dialogue and creativity across all subjects which can only lead to better results in the arts and core curriculum areas.

In Wales …

The dynamic nature of the expressive arts can engage, motivate and encourage learners to develop their creative, artistic and performance skills to the full… Importantly, Wales wants to make the expressive arts accessible to all learners and, through this inclusive approach, expand the horizons of every learner. Experiencing the expressive arts can engage learners physically, socially and emotionally, nurturing their well-being, self-esteem and resilience. This can help them become healthy, confident individuals, ready to lead fulfilling lives as valued members of society… through the enjoyment and personal satisfaction they gain from creative expression, learners can become more confident, which can contribute directly to enriching the quality of their lives.

(Welsh Government, 2021)

> **In Northern Ireland ...**
>
> The programme for The Arts at Key Stages 1 and 2 is set out in three strands, Art and Design, Drama and Music. Children should experience a range of enjoyable and challenging arts activities. They should have opportunities to think and respond creatively in a variety of contexts. Activities offered should be relevant to children's interest and experiences. Knowledge, skills and understanding should be developed through a broad and balanced range of experiences and, where possible, connections should be made across the strands and to other Areas of Learning.
> (Council for Curriculum Examinations and Assessment [CCEA], 2007: 71)

WHAT DO 'ARTS-ENRICHED' CURRICULA LOOK LIKE IN SCHOOLS?

Schools have significant freedom to approach the design and realisation of their curriculum in ways that reflect the intentions they have for learners in their schools. By only specifying the essential knowledge that all children should acquire, the National Curriculum for England invites schools to design a curriculum that best meets the needs of their pupils and decide how to teach this most effectively. Consequently, an arts-rich approach might begin at root level, underpinning the whole school ethos, informing the school development plan, and daily practices of a school – its intent, implementation and impact (Ofsted, 2019). It might appear in the way the curriculum is designed, and how it relates to the wider school community, to the arts and cultural practices and traditions of the locality and beyond. It might be apparent in the pedagogic practices and assessment modes evident in classrooms, or in all of these ways.

The Researching Arts in Primary school project's studies of 40 schools (https://artsprimary.com) demonstrate the multiple ways that curricula can be arts enriched and the benefits for children of being in an arts-rich school. The researchers suggest that an 'arts-rich' school is one which:

- offers a broad and balanced curriculum where students experience the full range of arts subjects taught by qualified and well-resourced teachers;
- sees the arts as integral to their organisational identity and thus offer a range of extra-curricular arts opportunities and an ongoing programme of performances and exhibitions: they also support community arts;
- builds and sustain a wide range of partnerships with artists and cultural organisations.
(Researching the Arts in Primary Schools – see the Relevant websites section)

They also emphasise that there is 'no <u>one</u> way' but many different ways to arts enrichment. Being arts-rich appears to strengthen a school's distinctive identity (Thomson and Hall, 2023a and see www.culturallearningalliance.org.uk/how-to-make-primary-schools-arts-rich/ 28/11/2023 for a quick summary). The Royal Society for the Arts study of arts-enriched schools comes to similar conclusions (Cairns et al., 2020). The Paul Hamlyn Foundation is a charitable trust which promotes arts-based learning through funding projects for young people and teacher development. Its newsletters and some publications profile the approaches that many schools have taken in enriching curriculum and pedagogy through arts practice. Their case studies provide examples that can be drawn upon or adapted (www.phf.org.uk/funds/tdf/).

Reflecting Dewey (1934, 1938), an arts-enriched curriculum often designs learning to be experiential, related to but extending beyond children's home and community contexts. Many educators argue for project-based and inquiry-based learning, related to real-world practices and contexts, where children are situated and empowered as the actors in their learning (Leat, 2017). Such models ensure teachers recognise children's current knowledge and interests and thus how to adapt planning towards progress in learning (TS2, 4 & 5).

One such example is the Trowsdale Art-Making Model for Education, the TAME approach (Trowsdale and Davies, 2024). The approach foregrounds the *culture for learning* that art-making can generate. Here possibility thinking, inquiry, knowledge and skill acquisition, teamwork, responsibility and trust are coached and practised. The TAME has two key structuring principles, both characterised by art-making: a community of practice and a commission. The approach invites teachers to consider the desired learning behaviours of their scheme of work and to identify a relevant real-world community of practice that exhibits such behaviours. The commission directs the work of the community focussing the children's activity on developing the desired skills and situating the knowledge to be developed. For one scheme of work, teachers contacted a local environmental organisation that was happy to support the teacher in commissioning children as young environmental activists to create ecologically sound, aesthetically pleasing, robust structures for wildlife to improve the biodiversity and interest of their school grounds. They provided expertise and a connection with a real-world global issue, thereby naturally fostering inter- and trans-disciplinary learning. The commission may be an obviously art-making one, or require children to engage in art-making practices. It will prioritise active, whole bodied learning and careful consideration of how spaces and pedagogies affirm and signal the behaviours of the community of practice. In this example, physical storytelling enabled children to find out about the issue, and practice behaving collaboratively, empathetically and thoughtfully. The model, developed from analysis of how art-making structures and practices educate, was further developed through working with teachers on the *Teach-Make* project. Here teachers saw that this arts-rich approach motivated children, increased their enjoyment, self-esteem and self-management skills and enabled children to achieve the learning goals the teachers had designed. The TAME model itself emerged from the findings of research into a five-year project, *The Imagineerium*, led by an arts organisation working with schools to develop STEAM learning in primary schools (Trowsdale, McKenna and Francis, 2019, 2024).

Related to this, planning for learning as a physically active experience, recognises that 'we think not just with our minds but with our brains and the rest of our bodies' (Claxton, Lucas and Webster, 2010: 13). Research indicates a strong correlation between movement and thinking, that gesturing and moving, even when it appears to be unconnected to the task in hand, helps the thinking process (Goldin-Meadow, 2014). Art-making practices, such as representing an idea with their bodies, sketching it or building a model of it, offer children regular opportunities to develop and practice fine and gross motor skills so that manual dexterity informs mental agility, whilst also acknowledging that through embodied tasks the body has an intrinsic, dialogic role to play in learning (Anttila, 2007).

Dance and drama strategies are excellent media for learning across the curriculum. Drama enables children to imagine themselves in someone else's situation or circumstance and stimulate empathy and understanding for others' beliefs, perspectives, experiences or feelings. Strategies such as 'hot-seating' or 'voices in the head' enable children to imagine, rehearse and understand another person's experience: how they might think, speak and feel. Practising dance and drama can attune children to the significance of non-verbal communication to understand the complexity of experience (Damasio, 2000) and develop their understanding of social and cultural expectations, to safely practice and develop skills of negotiation and persuasion. (e.g. Baldwin, 2012; Woolland, 2009; Hammond, 2015).

FIGURE 4.6.1 Children physicalise the walls of an eye

Heathcote's educational drama approach of 'mantle of the expert' (Heathcote and Bolton, 1995; Taylor, 2016) frames children 'as if' experts within an imagined, 'as if' real-world context where they work to explore and address a problem. For the duration of the drama, in their role-play, they symbolically 'wear' the mantle of expertise and the teacher adopts a lower status role, seeking the help of the children. As a result, children experience being viewed as competent, capable of investigating the problem and thereby learning about the subject area/s chosen by the teacher (Taylor, 2016). Children typically choose to enter this imagined world and observe the rules of the drama in order to be part of the activity's imaginative world.

Sketching and journaling can feed meta-learning; for example, children in one year 4 class in a Coventry school were invited to draw large-scale diagrams of an eye. Figure 4.6.2 shows one such drawing, where children worked in groups cooperating and discussing using scientific vocabulary to ensure their work was accurate. The thoughtful use of colour, shape and intensity reflects a deepening understanding of the knowledge they had learnt in a science class. When asked later, the children were able to recall the facts accurately by thinking about the drawing they had produced. Such visual attunement is important given the visual acuity required for effective online study and future careers.

In another English class, children drew on an artificial intelligence (AI) programme in writing descriptions of characters and scenes from Beowulf. They read their descriptions into the programme and, in pairs, asked each other whether the picture the AI programme generated looked as they had intended. By asking themselves, 'How can my writing be developed to make the description how I imagined it to be?', children were able to develop their use of adjectives and descriptive language to enhance their story writing.

FIGURE 4.6.2 Children working together to create a large-scale diagram of an eye

> ### Task 4.6.2 Design an arts-rich activity
>
> Think about a concept from the core content framework that you are going to teach. Design an arts-rich activity that allows the children to explore their own ideas in relation to this concept, and to experiment with how different art-making techniques can express these ideas. For example, in a topic on toys, children could 'become' a toy as an exhibit in a museum, Children could ask the 'toy' questions and watch it move to find out more about it. Questions could be historical or scientific, about materials and movement.
>
> How did you as the adult feel about this activity?
>
> How did the children feel?
>
> How did the pupils behave?
>
> How much knowledge did the children retain/understand after the lesson?

THE ROLE OF THE TEACHER IN DEVELOPING ARTS-RICH PRACTICES

Teachers are vital in communicating belief in children as capable learners and in role-modelling the value of arts-enriched approaches. Seeing and showing yourself as a learner and maker in the arts, as one who does not know everything and who is therefore always modelling inquiry, practising and developing new learning behaviours is important. By guiding and working alongside children you are fostering behaviours vital to develop exploratory art-makers and learners. You may well need the support of senior colleagues to access continuing professional development and learning opportunities to develop skills and knowledge in and around arts education. Often partnerships with other organisations are helpful, which we discuss in the next section.

Views of the teacher as either 'sage on the stage' or 'guide on the side' are considered outdated and research emphasises the importance of working alongside learners to 'meddle in the middle' (McWilliam, 2009). Dweck (2012) argues for the importance of teachers resisting telling and instead designing learning for children to have the agency and control to make decisions, learn from mistakes and see learning as a growth process, with their intelligence as 'growable'. Art-making provides multiple opportunities for teachers to design learning opportunities where children can explore, try things out and feel able to take risks. The teacher's role in normalising exploration, risk-taking and learning from experience and mistakes is vital for children to feel secure that this is an approved way of behaving and thriving in the classroom.

Task 4.6.3 Observe an arts-rich learning activity

Observe an arts-rich learning activity in the school where you are working.

Focus on the learning that happens when the adults intervene and when they appear to resist intervening. When would you resist intervening? Why?

Reflect with the adults whose teaching you observed about the role of the teacher in the design of the session, when they intervened and when they resisted intervention and why.

DEVELOPING ARTS-RICH LEARNING WITH PARTNERSHIP SUPPORT

Working in partnership is a tried and tested way to bring the arts into schools, to embed schools into the arts communities that surround them and to develop the confidence and skills of teachers to make effective use of the potential of art-making practices and cultures (Parker, 2013; Hall and Thomson, 2021). Working with arts education academics can support activities like action research to strengthen and deepen arts practice and its benefits in schools (Childs, Crickmay and Chappell, 2024; Trowsdale and Davies, 2024). It has also been shown that the support of school leadership is critical in the success of arts partnership working (Thomson and Hall, 2023b).

Many art galleries; dance, theatre and performance companies; and music organisations initiate educational projects as a strand of their work. There are also organisations that are primarily committed to young people's development in and through art-making within and beyond schools, such as Grimm & Co. (https://grimmandco.co.uk) and Highly Sprung Performance (https://highlysprungperformance.co.uk/learning-2/schools/). Some more substantially publicly funded organisations also have ongoing programmes (see for example TATE [www.tate.org.uk/about-us/learning-programmes]; Royal Opera House, Create & programmes [www.roh.org.uk/schools]).

Such programmes are characterised by a mix of professional development for staff, and live and online lesson ideas. These give teachers confidence in enabling children to link ideas to and through the arts. Many organisations will also provide an inspirational professional venue related event. As one school noted, when discussing such a partnership project with the Royal Opera House, '[w]orking in partnership allowed artists and teachers to develop their own skills and complement each other. The children were in awe of the project and the benefits of working with "real" dancers' (Bracken, 2023).

Where a school's engagement with such partners is strategically aligned to school development plans, the potential for sustained benefit is at its strongest. ArtsMark and Arts Award programmes provide a structured way to develop teachers' approaches to more arts-rich learning.

Task 4.6.4 Making links to real world organisations

Identify three different topics you have witnessed in your school's curriculum.

What organisations local to you might have expertise, time or opportunities to connect these topics to the real world, or which might enrich children's learning by enabling children to encounter cultural practices or beliefs that they are not yet familiar with?

Share your ideas with a colleague or staff in your school to see if some might be realised.

SUMMARY

In this unit we have identified a wealth of benefits of arts-rich approaches for children's education. We have noted the distinctive and rich contributions that art-making practices and perspectives can offer for children's learning and development. Defining 'the arts' as all art forms, we have considered what 'arts-enriched' means: how schools, whole curricula and pedagogies might characterise and develop such benefits through the making practices and cultures of the arts.

We have identified the important role that the teacher has in modelling the centrality of arts-rich practices and approaches in the classroom, in seeking professional development and in forging the kinds of partnership support available, particularly in the locality of the school, but potentially also nationally and/or virtually.

ANNOTATED FURTHER READING

Ogier, S. and Tutchell, S. (2021) *Teaching the Arts in Primary Schools*, Sage.
    Ideas for both particular arts subject teaching and arts-rich approaches to the curriculum.

Sci-Arts Creative Teaching resource: https://sciartsedu.co.uk
   Teaching resource for combined science and arts teaching approaches.

Trowsdale, J. and Davies, R. (2024) How a particular STEAM model is developing primary education: lessons from the Teach-Make project (England). *Journal of Research in Innovative Teaching & Learning*. DOI: 10.1108/JRIT-10-2022-0066
   Article outlining a tested approach to planning arts-rich schemes of work.

FURTHER READING TO SUPPORT M-LEVEL STUDY

Eisner, E. W. (2004) 'What can education learn from the arts about the practice of education?' *International Journal of Education & the Arts*, 5(4). Available from: www.ijea.org/v5n4/.en

Hall, C. and Thomson, P. (2021) 'Making the most of School Arts Education Partnerships', *Curriculum Perspectives*, 41: 101-106. https://doi.org/10.1007/s41297-020-00126-0

RELEVANT WEBSITES

Cultural Learning Alliance: www.culturallearningalliance.org.uk
   A hub for policy, research and resources related to arts and cultural learning.

Researching the Arts in Primary Schools: https://artsprimary.com/raps-project/
   Studies of arts-rich primary schools and related publications.

MoE: www.mantleoftheexpert.com
   Guidance and resources for teachers interested in the MoE.

Artsmark: www.artsmark.org.uk

Arts Awards: www.artsaward.org.uk/site/?id=64

REFERENCES

Alibali, M. and Nathan, M. (2012) 'Embodiment in mathematics teaching and learning: Evidence from learners' and teachers' gestures', *Journal of the Learning Sciences*, 21(2): 247-286. DOI: 10.1080/10508406.2011.611446

Anttila, E. (2007) 'Searching for dialogue in dance education: A teacher's story', *Dance Research Journal*, 39(2): 43-57.

Baldwin, P. (2012) *With Drama in Mind*, 2nd edn., London and New York: Continuum.

Bamford, A. (2006) *The Wow Factor: Global Research Compendium on the Impact of the Arts in Education*, Munster: Waxmann Verlag.

Barnes, J. (2015) *Cross-curricular learning 3-14*, London: Sage.

Bowen, D. and Kisida, B. (2023) 'Improving arts access through multisector collaborations', *Arts Education Policy Review*. Retrieved from: DOI: 10.1080/10632913.2023.2212187

Bracken, S. (2023) Personal conversation between authors.

Cairns, S., Landreth Strong, F., Lobley, E., Devlin, C. and Partridge, L. (2020) *Arts-Rich Schools*. RSA. Retrieved from: www.thersa.org/globalassets/pdfs/reports/rsa-arts-rich-schools.pdf

Catterall, J. S. (2009) *Doing Well and Doing Good by Doing Art: The Effects of Education in the Visual and Performing Arts on the Achievements and Values of Young Adults*, Los Angeles/London: The Imagination Group.

Catterall, J. S., Dumais, S. A. and Hampden-Thompson, G. (2012) *The Arts and Achievements in At-Risk Youth: Findings from Longitudinal Studies*, Washington: National Endowment for the Arts.

Chapman, S. N. (2015) 'Arts immersion: Using the arts as a language across the primary school curriculum', *Australian Journal of Teacher Education*, 40(9): 86-101. https://search.informit.org/doi/10.3316/informit.490647529586653

Chappell, K., Hetherington, L., Alexopoulous, A., Ben-Horin, O., Nikolopoulos, K., Ruck-Keene, H., Wren, H., Robberstad, J., Bogner, F. and Sotiriou, S. (2019) 'Dialogue and materiality/embodiment in science/arts creative pedagogy: Their role and manifestation', *Thinking Skills and Creativity Special Issue: Exploring Pedagogies of Dialogic Space*, 31: 296-322. Retrieved from: https://doi.org/10.1016/j.tsc.2018.12.008

Childs, S., Crickmay, U. and Chappell, K. (2024) *Penryn Creativity Collaboratives Toolkit*, Penryn Creativity Collaborative. Open Access.

Claxton, G., Lucas, B. and Webster, R. (2010) *Bodies of Knowledge: How the Learning Sciences Could Transform Practical and Vocational Education*, London: The Edge Foundation.

Comerford-Boyes, L. and Reid, I. (2005) 'What are the benefits for pupils participating in arts activities: The view from the research literature', *Research in Education*, 73(1): 1-14.

Council for Curriculum Examinations and Assessment (CCEA). (2007) *The Northern Ireland Curriculum - Primary*, Belfast: CCEA. Retrieved from: https://ccea.org.uk/downloads/docs/ccea-asset/Curriculum/The%20Northern%20Ireland%20Curriculum%20-%20Primary.pdf

Cultural Learning Alliance (CLA). (2017) *Imagine Nation: the Value of Cultural Learning*. Open Access. Retrieved from: https://culturallearningalliance.org.uk/wp-content/uploads/2017/08/ImagineNation_The_Case_for_Cultural_Learning.pdf

Cultural Learning Alliance (CLA). (2018) *The Arts, Health and Well-being*. Open Access: Retrieved from: https://culturallearningalliance.org.uk/wp-content/uploads/2018/04/Arts-Health-and-Wellbeing-Briefing.pdf

Damasio, A. (2000) *The Feeling of What Happens*, London: Vintage.

Dewey, J. (1934) *Art as Experience*, New York: Perigee, Penguin.

Dewey, J. (1938) *Education and Experience*, New York: Macmillan.

Department for Education (DfE). (2013) *The National Curriculum in England: Key Stages 1 and 2 Framework Document*, London: DfE.

Department for Education (DfE). (2019) *Initial Teacher Training (ITT): Core Content Framework*, London: DfE. Last updated 2024.

Department for Education (DfE). (2021) *Model Music Curriculum. Key Stages 1-3*, London: DfE.

Dweck, S. (2012) *Growth Mindset*, London: Constable & Robinson.

Eisner, E. (2002) *The Arts and the Creation of Mind*, New Haven/London: Yale University Press.

Eisner, E. W. (2004) 'What can education learn from the arts about the practice of education?' *International Journal of Education & the Arts*, 5(4). Retrieved from: www.ijea.org/v5n4/ (accessed 20 November 2023).

Fleming, M. (2013) *The Arts in Education: An Introduction to Aesthetics, Theory and Pedagogy*, London and New York: Routledge.

Goldin-Meadow, S. (2014) 'How gesture works to change our minds', *Trends in Neuroscience and Education*, 3(1): 4-6.

Gopnik, A., Metfzoff, A. and Kuhl, P. (2001) *How Babies Think*, London: Phoenix.

Greene, M. (1995) *Releasing the Imagination*, Hoboken, NJ: Jossey-Bass.

Hall, C. and Thomson, P. (2021) 'Making the most of School Arts Education Partnerships', *Curriculum Perspectives*, 41: 101-106. https://doi.org/10.1007/s41297-020-00126-0

Hammond, N. (2015) *Forum Theatre for Children - Enhancing Social, Emotional and Creative Development*, Staffordshire: Trentham.

Heathcote, D. and Bolton, G. (1995) *Drama for Learning: Dorothy Heathcote's Mantle of the Expert Approach to Education*, London: Heinemann.

Ingold, T. (2014) *Making*, Abingdon: Routledge.

Ingold, T. (2017) *Anthropology and/as Education*, London and New York: Routledge.

Jindal-Snape, D., Davies, D., Scott, R. Murray C. and Harkins, C. (2018) 'Impact of arts participation on children's achievement: A systematic literature review', *Thinking Skills and Creativity*, 29: 59–70.

Kontra, C., Lyons, D., Fischer, S. and Beilock, S. (2015) 'Physical experience enhances science learning', *Psychological Science*, 1–13. DOI: 10.1177/0956797615569355

Lähdesmäki, T. *et al.* (2022) 'Tolerance, empathy, and inclusion' in *Learning Cultural Literacy through Creative Practices in Schools*. Cham: Palgrave Macmillan, pp. 45–61. https://doi.org/10.1007/978-3-030-89236-4_4.

Leat, D. (2017) *Enquiry and Project Based Learning*, London: Taylor & Francis.

McWilliam, E. (2009) 'Teaching for creativity: From sage to guide to meddler', *Asia Pacific Journal of Education*, 29(3): 281–293. DOI: 10.1080/02188790903092787

Ofsted. (2019) The Education Inspection Framework. Retrieved from: www.gov.uk/government/publications/education-inspection-framework

Parker, D. (2013) *Creative Partnerships in Practice: Developing Creative Learners*, London: Bloomsbury. https://doi.org/10.5040/9781472926722

Robinson, K. ed. (1989) *The Arts in Schools: Principles, Practice and Provision*, London: Calouste Gulbenkian.

Steiner, R. (1923/2004) *A Modern Art of Education*, New York: Anthroposophic Press.

Taylor. P. (2016) *A Beginners Guide to Mantle of the Expert: A Transformative Approach to Education*, Brighton: Singular.

Teasdale, B. (2023) *How Can Teaching Writing Through Embodied Immersion Impact Innovation, Imagination and Playfulness?* Penryn Creativity Collaboratives. Retrieved from: https://penryn-college.cornwall.sch.uk/wp-content/uploads/2023/11/PCC-AR-REPORT-Teasdale-2023.pdf

Thomson, P. and Hall, C. (2023a) *How to Make Primary Schools Arts-Rich*. Retrieved from: www.culturallearningalliance.org.uk/how-to-make-primary-schools-arts-rich/

Thomson, P. and Hall, C. (2023b) *Schools and Cultural Citizenship. Arts Education for Life*, London and New York: Routledge.

Trowsdale, J., McKenna, U. and Francis, L. (2024) 'Quantitative evaluation of *The Imagineerium* education project by students: Introducing the trowsdale index of confidence in experiential learning', *Research in Education*. 118(1): 108–118. DOI: 0.1177/00345237231216992

Trowsdale, J., McKenna, U. and Francis, L. (2019) Evaluating *The Imagineerium*: The Trowsdale Indices of Confidence in Competence, Creativity and Learning (TICCCL), *Thinking Skills and Creativity*, https://doi.org/10.1016/j.tsc.2019.04.001

Welsh Government (2021) *AREA OF LEARNING AND EXPERIENCE Expressive Arts*. Retrieved from: https://hwb.gov.wales/curriculum-for-wales/expressive-arts/ (accessed 26 April 2024).

Winner, E., Goldstein, T. and Vincent-Lancrin, S. (2013) *Art for Arts Sake: The Impact of Arts Education*. OECD. Retrieved from: https://read.oecd-ilibrary.org/education/art-for-art-s-sake_9789264180789-en#page3

Wolland, B. (2009) *Teaching Primary Drama*, London: Longman.

UNIT 4.7

TEACHING THE HUMANITIES

Karin Doull

INTRODUCTION

Today it seems as if we live in a fractured and divisive world. Conflicts have erupted round the world linked to religion, land or historic identity. It is vital that we help children understand how powerful ideas shape our lives. This is why the humanities subjects are so important. They provide children with the understanding and skill to challenge the 'fake news' culture.

The humanities form part of the suite of foundation subjects within the national curriculum. History, geography and RE (Religious Education) are what is normally meant by 'humanities subjects'. Citizenship, PSED (personal, social and emotional development), philosophy and classics also have overlap and are sometimes included within the term. The basis of this unit, however, will apply the term to history, geography and RE.

The unit will explore some of the key ideas that shape the subjects, considering initially what characteristics they have in common. It will then go on to examine each of the subjects, investigating their intrinsic and individual aspects. It will also consider how to shape learning that merges content while still retaining the integrity of the specific domains.

OBJECTIVES

By the end of this unit you should be able to:

- know what is meant by the term 'humanities' and understand the role they play within the primary curriculum;
- understand the relationship between different humanities subjects;
- know key aspects of learning in each of the three subjects;
- have some understanding of how to engender learning within humanities subjects;
- know how to engage and inspire children's learning within the humanities.

WHY IS AN UNDERSTANDING OF THE HUMANITIES IMPORTANT?

'Learning in the primary humanities begins with a deepening of children's understanding of themselves, the people around them, their communities and the wider world' (Hoodless *et al.*, 2009: 1).

The humanities subjects explore the human condition. The arts may consider how we represent and record emotions and reactions, but the humanities allow us to explore human experiences through a variety of lenses (Doull, 2021; Pickford, Garner and Jackson, 2013; Swift, 2017). They allow us to investigate different worlds: the world of past times; the world of different environments; the world of spiritual exploration and belief. We use them to consider what we want children to understand about humanity and our relationship with each other. They promote a sense of identity (Doull, 2021; Eaude et al., 2017; Swift, 2017), both individual and cultural, which are important aspects for, 'as human beings we ought to have an interest in our culture and ideas' (Holm, Jerrick and Scott, 2015: 16).

Swift describes these subjects as having powerful, sense making knowledge (Swift, 2017). They speak to children about their lives and the world they live in and allow them to investigate real world applications in exploring local and global communities. The humanities also present diverse heritages, cultures and philosophies, expanding their world view. These subjects offer children the opportunity to engage in investigative and enquiry-based learning. Common values are threaded across the subjects, such as using past, place and spirituality to explore human experiences and children's understanding of and relationship with their world. There is a strong connectivity that links both the subject matter and the methods used in its investigation. This is not to say, however, that these subjects are homogenous, as each has its own pedagogy and focus. While the subjects may be considered under the banner of humanities or social studies/sciences, each domain is individual. We need to be aware of the boundaries and essences of each to avoid creating learning that is neither one thing nor the other. Each has a unique contribution to add to the whole (Pickford, Garner and Jackson, 2013). We need to recognise the different ways in which the learning of individual disciplines are structured (Swift, 2017).

This will be discussed further in the unit.

In Scotland ...

Teaching humanities includes the teaching of social studies:

- people, past events and societies;
- people, place and environment;
- people in society, economy and business.

Learning in the social studies aims to develop children's understanding of the world to support informed and agentic contributions within their own and other people's lives. Children develop their understanding of their environment and learn about other people and their values, in different contexts.

Religious and moral education is a separate curricular area. This curricular area explores beliefs, values, issues, practices and traditions through the lens of different world religions, supporting children in the development of their own values and beliefs.

Source: Education Scotland (2017a, 2017b)

FIGURE 4.7.1 Word cloud related to humanities teaching

> ### Task 4.7.1 Reflecting on the humanities
> Look at the word cloud in Figure 4.7.1. What does this tell you about what may be perceived as important within the humanities? How would you describe these subjects from ideas in the cloud?

> ### In Wales...
>
> The Humanities Area of Learning and Experience seeks to awaken a sense of wonder, fire the imagination and inspire learners to grow in knowledge, understanding and wisdom. This Area encourages learners to engage with the most important issues facing humanity, including sustainability and social change, and helps to develop the skills necessary to interpret and articulate the past and the present.
>
> The Area encompasses geography; history; religion, values and ethics; business studies and social studies. These disciplines share many common themes, concepts and transferable skills, while having their own discrete body of knowledge and skills. Learners may also be introduced to other complementary disciplines, such as classics, economics, law, philosophy, politics, psychology and sociology, if and where appropriate.
>
> What matters in this Area has been expressed in five statements which support and complement one another, and should not be viewed in isolation. Together they contribute to realising the four purposes of the curriculum.
>
> (Welsh Government, 2021)

WHAT IMPORTANT METACOGNITIVE STRATEGIES CAN THE HUMANITIES DEVELOP?

'Humanities teach us to argue cogently and responsibly and intelligently and with integrity about a series of questions to which there are no right answers' (Beard, 2023).

When considering what might be argued as the intrinsic worth of the humanities, we tend to focus on the fundamental thinking skills that are developed across these subjects. Chief amongst these is the idea of critical thinking (Brown and Plumley, 2022: Grigg and Hughes, 2018). Ruggeri (2019) highlights the importance of questioning, rather than just accepting information. Eaude et al. (2017) would agree, suggesting that the widespread availability of possibly uncurated material, on the internet and social media, requires teachers to provide children with skills to navigate sources of information. Furthermore, he describes this as a 'post truth era' (Eaude et al., 2017: 390) where material is sometimes problematic or disputed and conversely truth can be rejected.

Central also to these subjects is the ability to debate and analyse and then present conclusions convincingly. Brown and Plumley (2022) suggest that through the justification of their reasoning, children can come to develop cognitive maturity. This is where children come to realise the subjective and possibly contested nature of the evidence that they work with (Holm, Jerrick and Scott, 2015). Here we are looking for gradations of understanding or knowledge rather than absolutes. Findings must be supported with evidence. Unlike some other subjects, history, geography and RE require children to raise questions that may have debateable answers.

Task 4.7.2 The value of the humanities

Humanities 2020 is a group dedicated to promoting the teaching of humanities. Read the Manifesto of Humanities 2020 (www.humanities2020.org.uk/). What are the aims of this group?

Listen to Stephan Scoffham's podcast on "Why the humanities matter" (Scoffham, 2023). What key points does he discuss?

THE PLACE OF HUMANITIES WITHIN THE CURRICULUM

'But the consequence of this narrowing is that pupils from disadvantaged backgrounds do lose out on building that body of knowledge that should be every child's entitlement' (Spielman, 2019).

The place of the humanities may appear self-evident, representing as it does essential elements of a 'broad and balanced curriculum' (Department for Education [DfE], 2013). But while these subjects have been part of school curricula since the 1870s (Grigg and Hughes, 2018), the importance of their contribution (and share of teaching time) has waxed and waned. In the Victorian period it was felt that all poorer children needed was to be able to read, write and cipher (the three Rs). This was linked to the economic needs of that society. Jay (2010) questions whether we still see the liberal arts (literature, humanities, philosophy, social sciences) as something more appropriate for the elite. Spielman, as former head of Ofsted, rejects that view. Although the place of the foundation subjects is enshrined in law (DfE, 2013), nevertheless there is clear curriculum hierarchy. A quick look at national curriculum documentation will show where the emphasis lies.

> **In Northern Ireland ...**
>
> The word 'humanities' does not appear in the current Northern Ireland Curriculum (NIC). Geography and history are taught within an Area of Learning called 'The World Around Us' which also contains science and technology. The curriculum has a strong emphasis on an integrated, 'connected learning' way of teaching and learning. Religious Education is a separate subject that stands alongside, rather than within, the NIC, and the curriculum also includes a new Area of Learning – 'Personal Development and Mutual Understanding'. The distinctive content and modes of teaching which the humanities subjects tend to encourage ought to be seen as particularly important in Northern Ireland – a part of the UK which has endured a complicated past and remains to a large extent segregated, both socially and educationally. This complicated past means that there is often wariness and reluctance on the part of teachers towards tackling controversial personal and social issues in the primary school.
>
> (Greenwood, Richardson and Gracie, 2019: 309)

Task 4.7.3 Exploring humanities in the national curriculum

Look at national curriculum documentation for a core subject and either history or geography.

What is different about the information provided for the subject in terms of specific curriculum material to be covered, detail across age phases and progression?

Now compare these further with one of the arts subjects.

What impression does this give you of the relevant worth of the subjects?

What implication might this have for you as new teachers trying to understand about curriculum coverage?

Gilead (2017) suggests that the education system is dominated by economic policy and modes of thought. Subjects must be seen to have economic worth. Biesta (2015) and Malik (2022) debate this concept suggesting that education should be about expanding ways of learning rather than just gaining a 'better' job (Daly, 2020). Arguing for the value of the humanities is complicated when there is a difficulty in evaluating or demonstrating benefits (Gilead, 2017). If we wish to preserve the status of humanities we must also have measurable indices to calibrate their economic worth.

While Ofsted observations in 2023 suggested that teachers ensured 'enough time was allocated to history' (Ofsted, 2023a), the suggested 45-60 minutes per week represents around 4% of teaching time (Barnes and Scoffham, 2017). The geography report highlighted the lack of teaching time as a major concern (Ofsted, 2023b). Recent changes to the Ofsted inspection framework (Ofsted, 2021) have increased attention on foundation subject teaching, however, this does not appear to have resulted in increased teaching time. History and geography are also often taught in rotation so you could expect to have around six to nine hours of each across a term (18-27 per year). There are clear implications here for planning and careful selection of content. There remains an imbalance, where literacy and numeracy teaching continue to dominate. Future government direction suggests an increased focus on maths teaching, possibly with a corresponding return to curriculum imbalance. While the humanities can provide opportunities for the development and application of language and mathematics, they have intrinsic worth as subjects.

> ### Task 4.7.4 Your view on the role of the humanities
> Thinking about what you know about the humanities (history, geography and RE), explain why they should or should not be included within the national curriculum.
>
> What issues or benefits might teachers encounter when teaching these subjects?

OFSTED

> As children move through primary school, we will expect to see that focus on the fundamentals maintained, but that should be alongside broader learning across all the foundation subjects. These are subjects which we know, from our inspections and curriculum research, are too often being squeezed in many primary schools.
>
> (Spielman, 2019)

The 2019 Education Inspection Framework (EIF) set out to ensure that the focus on broader learning was being adequately delivered within primary schools. To help schools develop greater understanding and expertise, subject lead inspectors were reinstated and research reviews for the different subjects produced. These provide new teachers with clear guidance to what government and Ofsted consider central to learning in each of these subjects. In addition, subject reports have been provided for history and geography based on subject specific inspections. These provide a good view of how Ofsted feels the subjects are being covered in schools and indicate where there may be areas of strength or for development.

You will find the different research reviews and subject reports on the government website: www.gov.uk/government/collections/curriculum-research-reviews#subject-reports.

> ### Task 4.7.5 What does Ofsted say about the humanities?
> Read and make notes of the primary section of one of the humanities subject reports.
>
> What key issues are being brought up? How might that provide a focus for your teaching? Share ideas with a colleague who has looked at the other subject and discuss implications. Are there any shared concerns? What is different or the same?

The next three sections will consider each individual subject, providing brief ideas about key elements that shape those subjects and allowing new teachers to begin to understand how these subjects work and where they can find further support.

HISTORY

'Most of us practise history not just because we love doing so but because we believe that it matters to *everyone* precisely what accounts are given of the past' (Jordanova, 2010: 10).

History is exciting and should promote active engagement from children. If we have not created an environment that stimulates questioning and involvement, then we have not been doing our job. While history is necessarily based on facts, it also relies on children's ability to select and combine information to draw conclusions about the lives of others in the past (Cooper, 2018; Doull, Russell and Hales, 2019).

To do this effectively, children need to manipulate certain conceptual aspects that are intertwined and integral to each other:

- *Substantive knowledge* relates to the basic building blocks of history: information about 'the who', 'the where' and 'the what' (Doull, Russell and Hales, 2019; Percival 2020).

    It also includes *First Order Concepts* or *Substantive Concepts*. Of these, *chronology* focuses on the 'when', creating timelines and historical contexts in which to situate people and events. There are also a series of big ideas that we encounter over and over again, such as settlement, society, trade and power. Ofsted describes these as generative or sticky learning as they allow children to use these to develop increasingly complex schemata by accumulating different aspects of the concept (Ofsted, 2021):
    - Ofsted identifies knowledge that relates to a specific focus within a unit of study as *fingertip* or core knowledge.
    - Knowledge that relates to a wider understanding, perhaps linked to historical fiction, image or film, is described as *hinterland* knowledge (Ofsted, 2021). You might read *Eagle of the North* (Rosemary Sutcliffe) to your class while studying about Roman Britain. While the children will be thrilled to hear the story, they will also take in information about life in the legions and attitudes to native Britons.
- *Disciplinary or procedural knowledge* refers to how we use the information, selecting and combining to draw conclusions about causality or significance (Cooper, 2018; Doull, Russell and Hales, 2019). It is also about understanding the constructed nature of history that relies on historians' choice of information and how it is used to draw conclusions (Ofsted, 2021). Ofsted has identified this element of history teaching as needing development in schools (Ofsted, 2023a). The following are the main concepts that we can use to make sense of the substantive knowledge, 'the why' and 'the how'.
    - *Characteristic features* – How do I know this belongs to this time? What ideas are key to this period?
    - *Causality* – Why did people act this way and what were the results?
    - *Historical interpretation* – Is there another version of this story? How has this account been created?
    - *Significance* – What is the most important theme to take from this time or why is this person or event significant?
    - *Change and continuity* – What has changed and what has stayed the same? How are these changes linked across periods?
- *Methods of enquiry* looks at how we find information using a range of evidence both primary or contemporary (created at the time) and secondary. We want children to begin to use these to ask and answer valid questions. In creating responses to those questions, they will need to observe, make deductions, evaluate and analyse (Cooper, 2018; Doull, Russell and Hales, 2019; Percival, 2020). They also need to be able to present their conclusions clearly and coherently. It is not necessary that responses need to be in written form. Children can show their understanding through art, drama, digital media and graphicacy. Examples of summative assessment tasks might include mind maps, templates, portfolio of samples of work, knowledge organisers, quizzes.

Planning for history

1. Your key question for the session should help you focus on the disciplinary concept that you want to develop, such as 'Why was Walter Tull significant?' (significance), 'What do the contents of Tutankhamun's tomb tell us about life for a pharaoh?' (characteristic features) or 'Why did the Vikings raid Lindisfarne Abbey?' (causality).
2. Think next about what resources you would need to present the story and engage the children in investigation. Make sure you use rich contemporary sources of evidence, not just cartoon type images.
3. Plan how you might use these and consider what you want the children to do. Will you use group or pairs activities or will this be an individual task? Where will the discussion and debate come?
4. Think about what evidence you need to see from the children to know that they have taken onboard these ideas, i.e.:
   a. Can the children give two reasons why Walter Tull was significant?
   b. Select images of five items from Tutankhamun's tomb and explain what they tell us of his life.
   c. As a group, put statements about the Lindisfarne raid into order of importance.

History is powerful in its ability to create or negate identity in terms of the personal, local and national. Tensions and conflicts around the world base their validity on historical perspectives, sometimes using the same evidence to support opposing views. It is essential that children learn how to navigate their way around this important aspect of the subject. In order to do this we need to ensure that the history presented to children is diverse, reflecting a wide range of experience. Examples of diversity can be found, but new teachers need to develop relevant subject knowledge. The Historical Association provides excellent support and resources and is an important tool for new teachers (see the Relevant websites section).

History is both enquiry-based and evidence-based. Questions are central here, those posed by teachers or asked by children. The answers need to be justified with reference to sources of evidence. A history classroom should be filled with debate and discussion. Children need to talk about their ideas and what they have found out. To make an activity more challenging, groups of children could be given information presenting contrasting viewpoints and asked to resolve them.

The scope of the history covered within the primary curriculum is potentially huge. Early years history is encapsulated within understanding the world in the Early Years Foundation Stage (EYFS) framework. It should start with the children's own experiences exploring the local, using simple concrete sources of information. Key Stage 1 is thematic with four broad categories. It is possible to use these to make the curriculum diverse and suitable to the needs and interest of the children within the school. Key Stage 2 has nine obligatory units of British History and ancient non-European civilisations. Schools can choose what order to teach the units but must ensure they are covered. These requirements place quite a burden of subject knowledge on teachers.

As new teachers it is important to be able to build up your subject knowledge:

- Try reading historical fiction, watch documentaries and tv series that have been carefully researched. This will develop your *hinterland knowledge*.
- It would also be useful to buy a simple British history textbook to help understand the chronology and key events from British history.
- Always research your own knowledge at adult level before beginning planning. This is important for identifying *fingertip knowledge*.
- Selection is important. You do not have to teach everything, but you do need to be able to make valid justifications for what you have chosen. To do this successfully you need to have extensive subject knowledge about the chosen focus or period. Superficial knowledge will be replicated in the activities you plan.

Remember that what is important here is to use this stimulating and exciting subject matter to engage and inspire children. Foster their curiosity and challenge them to discover the past. Provide them with tools and knowledge to make sense of this exhilarating discipline.

GEOGRAPHY

'Geography studies the world as our home, from the local to the whole planet, and people's lives, activities and events across it.' (Catling and Willy, 2018: 4)

Central to geography is a 'sense of place', an understanding of the world as an environment that constitutes the home for all life on the planet (Barlow and Whitehouse, 2019; Catling and Willy, 2018). As with history education, geography should promote a sense of fascination with this wonderful place. It has all the necessary requirements to enthuse and engage children with the unique and varied nature of our world (Barlow and Whitehouse, 2019; Roberts, 2023). Travel documentaries have opened our eyes to myriad exciting locations. We have a duty to help children engage their imagination when exploring this world (Scoffham and Owens, 2017).

Within a broad understanding of our world, geography strives to investigate and make sense of the systems and processes that shape the Earth from both a human and physical perspective. As such the subject has a foot in both the humanities and science realms. While it explores humans' relationship with their planet through narrative and image, it also deploys graphicacy and makes use of hard data. Geography explores key aspects of life on Earth, the human shaped world and the more elemental natural and physical characteristics.

This duality is represented within the national curriculum: 'Teaching should equip pupils with knowledge about diverse places, people, resources and natural and human environments, together with a deep understanding of the Earth's key physical and human processes' (DfE 2023b: 1). Children are expected to be both deductive and interpretive; they should reach conclusions through the process of reasoning as well as through developing ideas based on individual judgements. Much of the national curriculum for geography for primary is related to factual understanding, however, using terms such as 'locate', 'name', 'identify' and 'use'. These terms do not require children to actively investigate but to identify received knowledge. However, geography is 'more than factual recall' (Scoffham, 2019: 2). In line with history education, geographical knowledge should be created collaboratively (Scoffham, 2019), seeking to empower children with the ability to interact with and explore key concepts that shape the subject. These key geographical concepts are outlined in Table 4.7.1.

You should use these concepts to shape your planning; for example, in comparing your local area with a village in South America. You will need to find where it is on a map (location), compare its size with that of your place (scale) and consider how it is the same or different in relation to climate, resources and settlement (place).

As with history, geography is essentially an enquiry-based subject and as such should involve children in exploring real world problems using an extensive range of resources (Dolan, 2016). While there are commercial packs available, the internet provides a wealth of images and information (including data sets and maps). You do need to verify these carefully, but they can provide a different perspective. You can create your own information packs for children. This will allow you to tailor your enquiry to a specific focus and the needs of your children. Look for a range of data including maps, images, diagrams, aerial photographs and Geographical Information Systems (GIS). The Geographical Association also provides a wealth of support and resources (see Relevant websites section).

TABLE 4.7.1 Key concepts within geographical thinking

Concepts	Definition	Practice
Space	Spatial awareness Interconnectedness of places	How we locate ourselves in relation to distance and location
Place	Human Settlement Conditions that contribute to settlement Narratives of human land use	What characterises a particular place (climate, resources, location) and how that has contributed to people's lives
Scale	Local > national > global Recognising the links and connections between different features related to position, size and complexity	Compare different types of settlement, small/large, near/far Compare relationships between different places More than just a 'single story'
Location	Factual information linked to a particular place and ability to situate this on a map or globe	Locate different places using specific vocabulary such as continent, ocean, hemisphere, tropics, regions, etc.
Environment	Environmental processes and phenomena such as weather, climate, physical characteristics Impact created by these phenomena	Explore different aspects of climate zones, physical features such as rivers, natural phenomena such as earthquakes, weather
Sustainability	Recognise the need for sustainable practices that do not further delete the Earth's resources	Investigate situations where resources are being overused Consider how to promote sustainable living Explore effects of climate change

You should also make use of your local area; fieldwork is central to geography (Barlow and Whitehouse, 2019; Catling and Willy, 2018). You should identify a relevant issue to investigate and then explore and gather data. Sample questions might be 'How do people use our park?' or 'How is traffic affecting our school at the beginning or end of the day?' We need to help children explore outside (Dolan, 2016). Carefully managed, this can provide immersive and memorable experiences for the children and so we should be prepared to take the risk of learning outside the classroom (Learning through Landscapes, 2022).

Geography is also about identity, about helping children to relate to and understand *their place*. We should build on the knowledge that children already have of where they live. From an early age they have used their locality to become familiar with trade (local shops), transport (bus to the shop or granny) and facilities (school, library). These are known as personal geographies (Roberts, 2023). They are the foundation for exploring other places, providing a basis for comparison. Knowledge of their place can be transformed into wider world pictures. When you move into a school as a new teacher, take a walk around the area of the school to get to know the neighbourhood and see what is available.

Critical thinking (the ability to draw conclusions about people and processes) is also a key skill within geography. We might want to present children with conflicting data about an issue to encourage them to interrogate and then use it to justify a conclusion. It is also important to help children understand how geographical information is produced and used. There is a Global North bias that means that the views of the poorer communities within the southern hemisphere may be ignored. Before you start teaching, examine your own knowledge. What do you know about other places in the world, especially those that might be described as 'third world'? Try also to think about moving beyond telling a single story.

> **Task 4.7.6 Challenging stereotypes in Geography**
>
> Watch the TED talk, 'The danger of a single story', by Chimamanda Ngozi Adiche (2009).
>
> How does she define the term single story? Think about how the stories you have read might have shaped your perceptions? How can you extend your own understanding? Do you think that her description of stereotypes as incomplete impressions is accurate?

We also use geography to consider impact, the impact created by natural processes such as volcanic eruptions and, perhaps more importantly, the impact of human action on the Earth. This, as much as science, is a key subject for teaching about climate change and sustainability. As we focus on the world, its resources and people, we need to help children to understand about these big questions and provide them with tools to make sense of these complicated subjects.

RELIGIOUS EDUCATION

'To teach religious education well you must do it with conviction. Really effective RE teachers have to believe it is an important aspect of their children's education.' (Erricker, Lowndes and Bellchambers, 2010: 6)

Religious education allows children to explore the concepts of belief and spirituality, to find out how different groups of people have sought to answer some of life's 'big questions' and how these ideas have created moral codes. Like the other humanities subjects, it allows children to investigate themselves, their communities and the wider world. Religious education deals with complex and controversial issues (James and Stern, 2019). The subject is further complicated as it tries to understand how belief, faith or non-belief can shape human lives and action. It encompasses principal world religions as well as recognising alternative world views. It touches on religious tradition, community identity and individual understanding (Whitworth, 2020). It can challenge both teachers' and pupils' self-views and, as such, can cause disquiet or anxiety. And yet, in our multi-facetted, multi-diverse environments, it provides us with valuable tools to understand who we are and what is happening in our world.

Although the requirement to teach about religion has been part of the curriculum since 1944, there remain questions about its purpose and validity. There are also increasing concerns that the subject is not being taught at all in some schools (Commission on Religious Education [CORE], 2018; Whitworth, 2020). This ambivalence can perhaps be explained by the focus of the subject and the range of responses that can be generated by the word 'religion'. This can be linked to a misconception of the subject as doctrinal, instructional or proselytising in some way. From the onset it was not the case. The aims were:

- to develop pupils' knowledge, understanding and awareness of Christianity, as the predominant religion in Great Britain, and other principal countries represented in the country;
- to encourage respect for those holding different beliefs; and
- to help promote pupils' spiritual, moral, cultural and mental development.

(DfE, 1994: 12)

The Education Reform Act (1988) recognised the need to realign the focus of the subject, making it 'religious education' (RE) rather than the previous 'religious instruction' (RI). In a further response to changing societal perceptions, CORE (2018) now suggests 'religion and worldviews' (RW) when exploring understanding in this area. This widens the subject to include non-faith-based affiliations such as Humanism and Atheism.

Like other humanities subjects, RE has both substantive subject knowledge and conceptual elements that shape what and how it is taught.

- Subject knowledge relates to the beliefs, practices and expressions (art, text, architecture) of Christianity and other principal religions.
    - These are the Abrahamic religions (Christianity, Judaism and Islam) and the Dharmic religions (Hinduism, Sikhism and Buddhist).
    - Non-faith worldviews, such as Atheism, Secularism and Humanism, may also be included (James and Stern, 2019).
- Research has shown that this is the area that new teachers feel is most accessible (Whitworth, 2020) although they still worry that offence to parents and children's beliefs could be created.
- When teaching this area, it is important to teach through the lens of a believer by bringing out the nature of their ideas and feelings about those beliefs. Ideally it would be helpful to have a visitor in to provide discussion or to visit a place of worship.
- It is also important to be aware that all religions have factions and sects within them, e.g. Catholicism and Anglicanism in Christianity, Shia and Suni in Islam, Orthodox and Liberal Jews (Erricker, Lowndes and Bellchambers, 2010). Beliefs are broadly the same but with differing interpretations.

    This aspect of knowledge is often described as 'Learning about Religion'.

- Alongside this exploration of religions and world views lies the idea that children should be able to apply or translate this understanding into personal responses. Here we might look at moral behaviour or ethics. What we try to do with this element is to help children recognise parallels with their own experiences, either directly or indirectly. We are working here with identity and values education through shared human experiences. We need to acknowledge that this could cause negative responses as we work with complex ideas that are difficult to explain (Webster, 2014).

    This is 'Learning through Religion'.

Community is also an important element within RE. Many children, who do not live in multicultural urban centres, will have little knowledge of or opportunity to interact with those of different faiths. Sometimes communities with different cultures may also live next to each other with little acknowledgement of 'the other'. Education is used to develop understanding and recognise the need for respect of different beliefs. Until recently, UK societal and cultural heritage and norms have been shaped by Christianity. It is therefore important that children can recognise and understand these links.

RE requires time and space to debate, discuss and share ideas. Safe space is needed to discuss contentious issues (James and Stern, 2019; McCreery, Palmer and Voiels, 2008). Children need to be able to organise and make sense of complex ideas and vocabulary. Critical but non-judgemental thinking helps children analyse the ideas of differing world views. Immersive and enquiry-based learning with visits and exploration of lived experiences makes the subject memorable. As with all the humanities it is the human element that draws children in.

RE is not like other subjects in the curriculum. It is mandatory for community schools (those funded by the government through local authorities). You will not find a statutory programme of study within the national curriculum document, however. The content of the curriculum has been created by local

Standing Advisory Councils for Religious Education (SACREs) made up of teachers, local officials and religious representatives. The curriculums should be revised every five years. The government has provided guidance for SACREs when revising curricula (Religious Education Council for England and Wales [REC], 2013). The recent *Cumbrian Agreed Syllabus for RE 2023* (Cooper, 2018) provides a useful case study to explore how such a syllabus might be organised.

There were other legal requirements specific to this subject:

- Parents had the right to withdraw children from RE lessons or acts of collective worship.
- Head teachers must provide written notice of the RE curriculum (prospectus/website) and parental right to withdrawal.
- Head teachers and class teachers have the right to withdraw from teaching RE.

As a new teacher, get to know what faiths are represented in your area. Visit different places of worship and talk to those using those spaces if you can. Choose a focus religion to research. Don't assume that because you might know about Easter or Christmas that you can teach about Christianity, that too needs research. The National Association of Teachers of Religious Education is a useful starting point and support (see Relevant websites section).

SEQUENCE OF PLANNING FOR A SEQUENCE OF HUMANITIES LESSONS

Considerations linked to planning include:

- be creative;
- use material that allows children to see the real people at the heart of the story;
- use real documents, images and artefacts;
- go on field work or museum visits;
- interview people about past, place or belief;
- make it interesting so that children want to know more.

These subjects are exciting, challenging and infinitely fascinating. Try to pass this on to children and fire their curiosity and imagination.

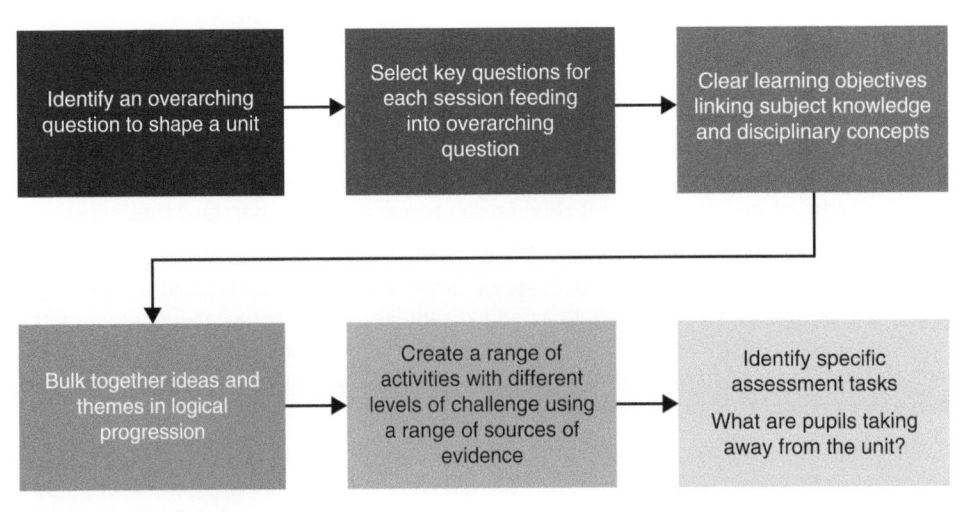

FIGURE 4.7.2 Planning sequence

SUMMARY

This unit has explored the role of the humanities subjects with the primary curriculum. It has looked at how the subjects are similar in pedagogical approaches and substantive content, while also maintaining separate identities. It has considered the basic elements that shape the subject, focussing on both substantive and disciplinary concepts. It has suggested elements that should be considered as you come to teach these important subjects. It has introduced three vibrant enquiry-based subjects that would benefit from further study.

ANNOTATED FURTHER READING

Humanities: Doull, K. (2021) 'An eye to the past: Curious explorations into the other' in S. Ogier and S. Tutchell (eds) *Teaching the Arts in the Primary Curriculum*, London: Sage, pp. 47-57.
   This chapter looks at some practical ideas for linking history, RE and geography through art and music.

History: Doull, K., Russell, C. and Hales, A. (2019) *Mastering Primary History*, London: Bloomsbury, Chapter 1.
   This chapter introduces the attributes of the subject and considers why the subject is important for children's understanding.

Geography: Barlow, A. and Whitehouse, S. (2019) *Mastering Primary Geography*, London: Bloomsbury, Chapter 1.
   This chapter considers the concept of mastery and how this might relate to the specific attributes of geography.

RE: James, M. and Stern J. (2019) *Mastering Primary Religious Education*, London: Bloomsbury, Chapter 1.
   This chapter explores the key ideas within religious education and introduces specific elements of the subject.

FURTHER READING TO SUPPORT M-LEVEL STUDY

Humanities: Swift, D. (2017) 'The challenge of developing disciplinary knowledge and making links across the disciplines in early years and primary humanities', *Education 3-13*, 45(3): 365-374.
   Swift explores the relationship between the subjects through propositional content and conceptual understanding before considering subject specific examples.

History: Doull, K. and Townsend, S. (2018) 'Investigating the issues of "Big Picture" history: Deconstructing the "long arc of development"', *Education 3-13*, 46(6): 685-699.
   Doull and Townsend explore the concept of chronology and how this can be used to shape children's understanding.

Geography: Roberts, M. (2023) 'Powerful pedagogies for school geography', *International Research in Geographic and Environmental Education*, 32(1): 69-84.
   Roberts takes Young's concept of 'powerful knowledge' and considers what this might mean in relation to teaching geography.

RE: Whitworth, L. (2020) 'Do I know enough to teach RE? Responding to the commission on religious education's recommendation for primary initial teacher education', *Journal of Religious Education* [online], 68(3): 345-357.
   Whitworth explores the concepts and substantive understanding identified within RE teaching and considers these in the light of a national plan for improving teaching and learning in RE.

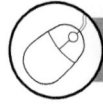

RELEVANT WEBSITES

Humanities 2020: www.humanities2020.org.uk/
   This free website offers case studies of good practice in the humanities and links to resources such as podcasts.
Historical Association: www.history.org.uk/primary
   The Historical Association website offers a wealth of resources for planning and teaching; some elements require membership to access.
Geographical Association: https://geography.org.uk/
   The Geographical Association website has more secondary, but some primary, articles, resources and research; again some elements require paid access
National Association of Teachers of Religious Education: www.natre.org.uk
   The National Association of Teachers of Religious Education offers a well-developed primary focused section and links to free resources as well as membership only.

REFERENCES

Adichie, C. (2009) 'The danger of a single story', *TEDGlobal*. Retrieved from: www.ted.com/talks/chimamanda_ngozi_adichie_the_danger_of_a_single_story

Barlow, A. and Whitehouse S. (2019) *Mastering Primary Geography*, London: Bloomsbury.

Barnes, J. and Scoffham, S. (2017) 'The humanities in English primary schools: Struggling to survive', *Education 3-13*, 45(3): 298-308.

Beard, M. (2023) 'Sidelining the humanities will harm democracy', *The Times*, 2 October.

Biesta, G. (2015) 'Teaching, teacher education and the humanities: Reconsidering education as a "Geisteswissenschaft"', *Educational Theory*, 65(6): 665-679.

Brown, R. and Plumley J. (2022) *Recognising the Importance of the Humanities* (Endoxa Learning). Retrieved from: https://endoxalearning.com/wp-content/uploads/2022/02/Valuing-the-humanities.pdf

Catling, S. and Willy, T. (2018) *Understanding and Teaching Primary Geography*, London: Sage.

Commission on Religious Education (CORE). (2018) *Religion and Worldviews: The Way Forward, a National Plan for RE*. Retrieved from: www.commissiononre.org.uk/wp-content/uploads/2018/09/Final-Report-of-the-Commission-on-RE.pdf

Cooper, H. (2018) *Cumbrian Agreed Syllabus for RE 2023*. Retrieved from: www.cumbria.gov.uk/elibrary/Content/Internet/537/6381/6528/4290215573.pdf

Daly, J. (2020) 'The elusive siloed subjects: Sacrificing humanities to techno-tehan', *Australian Universities' Review*, 62(2): 90-97.

Department for Education (DfE). (1994) *Religious Education and Collective Worship* (1/94). Retrieved from: https://assets.publishing.service.gov.uk/media/5a7cd8f740f0b6629523c2b7/Collective_worship_in_schools.pdf

Department for Education (DfE). (2013). *National Curriculum in England: Primary Curriculum*. Last updated 2015. Retrieved from: www.gov.uk/government/publications/national-curriculum-in-england-primary-curriculum

Dolan, A. (2016) 'Place-based curriculum making: Devising a synthesis between geography and outdoor learning', *Journal of Adventure Education and Outdoor Learning*, 16(1): 49-66.

Doull, K., Russell, C. and Hales, A. (2019) *Mastering Primary History*, London: Bloomsbury.

Doull, K. (2021) 'An eye on the past: curious explorations into "the other"', in S. Ogier and S. Tutchell (eds) *Teaching the Arts in the Primary Curriculum*, London: Sage, pp. 47-57.

Eaude, T., Butt, G., Catling, S. and Vass, P. (2017) 'The future of humanities in primary schools – reflections in troubled times', *Education 3-13*, 45(3): 386-395.

Education Act Reform Act. (1988) London: The Stationery Office. Retrieved from: www.legislation.gov.uk/ukpga/1988/40/contents

Education Scotland. (2017a) *Social Studies*. Last updated 2023. Retrieved from: https://education.gov.scot/parentzone/curriculum-in-scotland/curriculum-areas/social-studies/

Education Scotland. (2017b) *Religious and Moral Education*. Last updated 2023. Retrieved from: https://education.gov.scot/curriculum-for-excellence/curriculum-areas/religious-and-moral-education/

Erricker, C., Lowndes, J. and Bellchambers, E. (2010) *Primary Religious Education: A New Approach: Conceptual Enquiry in Primary RE*, Abingdon: Routledge.

Gilead, T. (2017) 'Justifying the teaching of humanities: A new economic approach', *Policy Futures in Education*, 15(3): 346-359.

Greenwood, R., Richardson, N. and Gracie, A. (2019) 'Primary humanities – a perspective from Northern Ireland', *Education 3-13*, 45(3): 309-319. Retrieved from: www.stran.ac.uk/research-paper/greenwood-r-richardson-n-and-gracie-a-2017-primary-humanities-a-perspective-from-northern-ireland/#:~:text=The%20word%20'humanities'%20does%20not,also%20contains%20science%20and%20technology

Grigg, R. and Hughes, S. (eds) (2018) *Teaching Primary Humanities*, 2nd edn, Abingdon: Routledge.

Holm, P., Jerrick, A. and Scott, D. (2015) *Humanities World Report*, London: Palgrave MacMillan.

Hoodless, P., McCreery, E., Bowen, P. and Bermingham, S. (2009) *Teaching Humanities in Primary Schools*, 2nd edn, Exeter: Learning Matters.

James, M. and Stearn, L. J. (2019) *Mastering Primary Religious Education*, London: Bloomsbury.

Jay, G. (2010) 'The engaged humanities: Principles and practices of public scholarship and teaching', *Journal of Community Engagement and Scholarship*, 3(1): 51-63.

Jordanova, L. (2010) *History in Practice*, 2nd edn, London: Bloomsbury.

Learning through Landscapes. (2022) *Teaching the Primary Curriculum Outdoors*, London Corwin.

Malik, K. (2022) 'If education is all about a job then the humanities are left to just the rich', *Observer Education*, 31 July.

McCreery, E., Palmer. S. and Voiels, V. (2008) *Teaching Religious and Early Education: Primary and Early Years*, Exeter: Learning Matters.

Ofsted (2021) *Research Review Series: History*. Retrieved from: www.gov.uk/government/publications/research-review-series-history

Ofsted (2023a) *Rich Encounters with the Past: History Subject Report*. Retrieved from: www.gov.uk/government/publications/subject-report-series-history

Ofsted (2023b) *Getting Our Bearings: Geography Subject Report*. Retrieved from: www.gov.uk/government/publications/subject-report-series-geography

Percival, J. (2020) *Understanding and Teaching History*, London: Sage.

Pickford, T., Garner, W. and Jackson, E. (2013) *Primary History: Learning Through Enquiry*, London: Sage.

Roberts, M. (2023) 'Powerful pedagogies for school geography', *International Research in Geographic and Environmental Education*, 32(1): 69-84.

Religious Education Council for England and Wales (REC). (2013) *A Curriculum Framework for Religious Education in England*. Retrieved from: www.natre.org.uk/uploads/RE_Review_Summary.pdf

Ruggeri, A. (2019) 'Why "worthless" humanities degrees may set you up for life', *BBC Worklife*. Retrieved from: www.bbc.com/worklife/article/20190401-why-worthless-humanities-degrees-may-set-you-up-for-life

Scoffham, S. (2019) 'The world in their heads: Children's ideas about other nations, peoples and cultures', *International Research in Geographical and Environmental Education*, 28(4): 1-14.

Scoffham, S. (2023) Humanities 2020: Stephen Scoffham [Podcast]. 21 June 2023. Available at: https://shows.acast.com/humanities-2020-podcast/episodes/humanities-2020-stephen-scoffham

Scoffham, S. and Owens, P. (2017) *Teaching Primary Geography*, London: Bloomsbury.

Spielman, A. (2019) *Speech at the 'Wonder Years' Curriculum Conference*. Retrieved from: www.gov.uk/government/speeches/amanda-spielman-at-the-wonder-years-curriculum-conference

Swift, D. (2017) 'The challenge of developing disciplinary knowledge and making links across the disciplines in early years and primary humanities', *Education 3-13*, 45(3): 365-374.

Webster, M. (2014) *Creative Approaches to Teaching Primary RE*, Abingdon: Routledge.

Welsh Government. (2021) *AREA OF LEARNING AND EXPERIENCE Humanities*. Retrieved from: https://hwb.gov.wales/curriculum-for-wales/expressive-arts/ (accessed 26 April 2024).

Whitworth, L. (2020) 'Do I know enough to teach RE? Responding to the commission on religious education's recommendation for primary initial teacher education', *Journal of Religious Education* [online], 68(3): 345-357.

SECTION 5
ASSESSMENT

UNIT 5.1

ASSESSMENT FOR LEARNING

Formative approaches

Eleanore Hargreaves and Shirin Sheikh-Bahai

INTRODUCTION

Assessment for learning (AfL) is a particular approach to assessment used by teachers in classrooms. It is not the same as the standardised tests or exams that you may give, but rather is a way of using informal assessment during ordinary classroom activities to improve learning. Here, assessment is seen as an integral part of the learning and teaching process, rather than being 'added on' for summative purposes. This approach brings with it a rather different relationship between teacher and learner than in traditional models of assessment, as the pupil needs to become involved in discussions about learning and assessment tasks, including learning objectives, the assessment criteria (success criteria), their performance and what they need to do to progress: the relationship is more of a partnership, with both pupil and teacher playing a role. We know that, with appropriate guidance, children as young as 5 can exercise considerable self-direction and benefit from doing so (Pramling, 1988).

Although there are many different interpretations of how AfL would ideally work, early defining sources were those of the Assessment Reform Group (ARG, 2002) and of Black and Wiliam (1998), who showed that improving children's learning through assessment depended on five, deceptively simple, key factors:

- the provision of effective feedback to pupils;
- the active involvement of pupils in their own learning;
- adjusting teaching to take account of the results of assessment;
- recognition of the profound influence assessment has on the motivation and self-esteem of pupils, both of which are crucial influences on learning;
- the need for pupils to be able to assess themselves and understand how to improve.

This unit will attempt to unpack two key issues: first, the nature of the feedback given to learners to help them understand the quality of their work and inspire them to consider how to progress in their learning; and second, the active engagement of the learner, including in asking questions, which is essential for promoting the learner's self-direction; as well as for supporting them to assess themselves.

> **OBJECTIVES**
>
> By the end of the unit, you should be able to:
>
> - understand the key factors associated with AfL;
> - develop a range of strategies that will facilitate improved learning/teaching;
> - recognise that pupils' self-direction in assessment, including their question-asking, is a powerful tool in improving learning and raising attainment in the classroom.

AFL: FROM THEORY TO PRACTICE

The ten principles of AfL

AfL should be part of the effective planning of teaching and learning

A teacher's planning should provide opportunities for both learner and teacher to obtain, explore and use information about progress towards learning goals. These opportunities must be flexible to respond to initial and emerging ideas and skills. Planning should include strategies to ensure that learners understand the goals they are pursuing, why they are pursuing them and the criteria that could be applied in assessing their work against these. How learners will receive feedback, how they will take part in assessing their learning and how they will be helped to make further progress should also be planned, ideally in negotiation with the pupils themselves.

AfL should focus on how pupils learn

The process of learning has to be in the minds of both learner and teacher when assessment is planned and when the evidence is interpreted. Learners should become as aware of the 'how' of their learning as they are of the 'what'. Up-to-date research into how the learning process works needs to be recognised (see, for example, Watkins, 2015).

AfL should be recognised as central to classroom practice

Much of what teachers and learners do in classrooms can be described as assessment. That is, tasks and questions prompt learners to demonstrate their knowledge, understanding and skills; what learners say and do is then observed and interpreted; and judgements are made about how learning can progress. These assessment processes are an essential part of everyday classroom practice and involve both teachers and learners in reflection, dialogue and decision-making. These definitions of assessment expand its meaning beyond tests to include all forms of enquiry into the learner's progress.

AfL should be regarded as a key professional skill for teachers

Teachers require the professional knowledge and skills to: plan for assessment, observe learning, analyse and interpret evidence of learning, give feedback to learners and support learners in self-assessment. Teachers should be supported in developing these skills through initial and continuing professional development. Today, there is research to indicate that continuing professional development can be most effective when it is continuous, inspired by teachers' own needs and aspirations, integrated into the school's agenda, collaborative and supported by sources beyond the school too (see, for example, Darling-Hammond and Hyler, 2020). One effective means of developing the skills of AfL has been the teacher learning community within the individual school, whereby a group of

FIGURE 5.1.1 Assessment for learning should take account of the importance of learner motivation

teachers meet together every six weeks and report back on AfL strategies with which they have experimented in the classroom (see Wiliam, 2008).

AfL should be sensitive and constructive because any assessment has an emotional impact

Teachers should be aware of the impact that comments, marks and grades can have on learners' confidence and enthusiasm and should be as constructive as possible in the feedback that they give. Comments that focus on the work rather than the person are more constructive for both learning and motivation. A student who is distracted by negative – or even positive – personal comments is less likely to be focusing on learning (see Hargreaves, Quick and Buchanan, 2023).

AfL should take account of the importance of learner motivation

Assessment that encourages learning fosters motivation by emphasising progress and achievement rather than failure. Comparison with others who have been more successful is unlikely to motivate learners. It can also lead to their withdrawing from the learning process in areas where they have been made to feel they are 'no good'. This negativity can spread to other areas of schooling too (see Francis, Taylor and Tereshchenko, 2019). Motivation can be preserved and enhanced by assessment methods that protect the learner's autonomy, provide some choice and constructive feedback and create opportunity for both success and self-direction.

AfL should promote commitment to learning goals and a shared understanding of the criteria by which they are assessed

For effective learning to take place, learners need to understand what it is they are trying to achieve and why they are trying to achieve it – and they must also want to achieve it. Understanding and commitment follow when learners have some part in deciding goals and identifying criteria for assessing progress. Communicating assessment criteria involves discussing their importance and meaning with learners, using terms that they can understand, providing examples of how the criteria can be met in practice and engaging learners in peer and self-assessment.

Learners should receive constructive guidance about how to progress

Learners need support in order to plan the next phases of their learning. Teachers should:

- pinpoint the learner's strengths and advise on how to develop them;
- be clear and constructive about any weaknesses and how they might be addressed;
- avoid comparison with other learners;
- provide opportunities for learners to improve upon their work.

AfL develops learners' capacity for self-assessment so that they can become reflective and self-managing

Reflective and self-managing (or self-directed) learners seek out and cultivate new skills, new knowledge and new understandings. They are able to engage in self-reflection and identify how to progress in their learning. Teachers should support learners to take charge of their learning through developing the skills of reflection and self-assessment and allow pupils to take their own initiatives for progressing learning at times. Pupils thrive on directing their own learning and having some choice.

AfL should recognise the full range of achievements of all learners

AfL should be used to enhance all learners' opportunities to learn in all areas of educational activity. It should enable all learners to achieve their best and to have their efforts recognised (adapted from ARG, 2002).

PLANNING FOR AFL

Effective planning enables you to provide learning opportunities that match the needs of all the children. It should include the following:

- objectives that focus on learning; the task then becomes the vehicle for the learning;
- strategies for finding out what the children already know, so that you can pitch the learning/teaching at the appropriate level;
- an element of pupil choice;
- ways in which you can share the 'bigger picture' with the children, so that they know what they are aiming for and why;
- mini plenaries, so that the children can regularly reflect back on the bigger picture;
- opportunities for peer and self-assessment, with and without teacher support.

Sharing the bigger picture

From the start, discuss the success criteria with your pupils. Articulate exactly what it is you will be assessing. In writing, for example, a success criterion might be 'a descriptive piece of writing using a range of adjectives'. Teachers and pupils can create the success criteria together. Figure 5.1.2 shows a

> **What was it like to live here in the past?**
>
> Pupils must:
> - understand that St Paul's School was different in the past;
> - make comparisons between the school in the past and as it is today.
>
> Pupils should:
> - recognise features of the school building and know how it has changed over time;
> - enquire about some of the people who have worked at the school (both pupils and staff) and understand differences in working conditions at different times;
> - be able to use a range of historical sources in a variety of ways.
>
> Pupils could:
> - describe and compare features of the school and identify changes on a time line;
> - select and combine information from different sources.

FIGURE 5.1.2 Pupil assessment sheet

pupil self-assessment sheet for a history topic. You can display a large version on the wall and have an individual copy for each child. There are three levels of attainment here, which can be used for either pupil self-assessment or peer assessment.

> **Task 5.1.1 Pupil assessment sheet**
>
> Referring to Figure 5.1.2, choose another area of the curriculum and construct a similar sheet.

Discussion during the sessions and mini plenaries

The factors involved in thinking processes have been viewed differently throughout the history of cognitive research. In addition, genetic variation, the physical structure, the condition of the brain and our social life all contribute to determining who we are and how we think (Burnett, 2016). Therefore, classroom discussion among children and with teachers are essential, not optional extras. Discussions take place before, during and after each lesson, as well as outside the classroom, so that the teacher can check the children's understanding and judge their progress. Discussion also provides a vehicle for learning itself as well as for a continued sharing of the learning objectives. Here are some strategies for guiding discussion in the primary classroom:

- Before the lesson, have discussions with the children to ascertain what they already know about the subject, in order that you can plan the work effectively to include different levels and dynamics of understanding. Identify in your planning the children you wish to support in that lesson and why.
- Once you have identified children's unexpected responses, you can follow up your individual discussion during the session to clarify these.
- Monitor the children's progress throughout the lesson by asking them questions about the task and then inviting them to ask their own questions.

- At intervals during the session, remind the children of the lesson objectives, then ask children to feed back to the class what they have found out so far, and what they still have to do to complete the task.
- Ask the children to evaluate their own progress against the success criteria given.

EFFECTIVE QUESTIONING: BY TEACHERS AND – PARTICULARLY – BY CHILDREN

Effective questioning is the key to good teacher assessment, but teachers need to make sure they know which questions to use and when. Teachers are always asking questions, but, in order to develop higher-order thinking skills, it is important for the teacher to ask open-ended, provocative and child-centred questions. Harris and Williams have suggested that open-ended questions 'provoke speculation and extend the imagination' (2012: 375). The use of open questioning is critical in encouraging children to develop and then offer their own opinions – and their own questions. This occurs when the teacher acknowledges that these opinions or questions are a valid response, rather than assessing whether they are along the 'right' or 'wrong' lines. This open-ended approach to questioning is much more productive than a closed questioning technique, where only one response is deemed appropriate by the teacher, leaving the children guessing what the teacher wants to hear, rather than basing their response on their own ideas and genuine curiosity.

A less prevalent approach to formative assessment in the classroom involves utilising children's own questioning in which they clearly reveal their own thoughts and understanding. Children's questions in this way serve as indicators of their cognitive processes, in which they draw upon their existing knowledge and attempt to bridge gaps in understanding by seeking additional information. The teacher, on receiving the question, may learn a lot about the child's thought processes and also their knowledge gaps.

The literature on the importance of children's questioning is much smaller than that on teachers' questioning, but recently it seems to be growing as more studies have identified the effect of children's questioning on thinking processes involved in learning and how insight into these can feed into teachers' assessments. Recent studies also indicate that the act of children posing questions plays a vital role in fostering critical thinking skills and enhancing learning outcomes. Teachers not only gain valuable assessment insights, but at the same time they are effectively boosting children's comprehension and engagement in the subject matter by actively encouraging them to ask questions (Chin and Osborne, 2008). By posing questions, children are empowered to engage in a more profound understanding of the content and actively participate in their own learning journey. However, it is important to cultivate a classroom environment that truly values and promotes student-generated questions in order for their value as teacher insights to be effective.

Facilitating student questioning for formative assessment

Children's questioning highlights various factors involved in the learning and understanding processes. Some studies, including Chin and Osborne (2008), focus on the questions' structures and the types of thinking required to construct a question. Other research emphasises the stages involved in the journey of asking a question – from generating an idea to revealing the thought process by verbalising it as a question. The outcome of many studies, including Chin and Osborne (2008), suggests that children ask questions either to fill a gap in their knowledge or to solve a puzzle. In other words, children use their prior knowledge in articulating their understanding when learning something new, and missing pieces in their knowledge can be formed as questions (Mercer, 2016). Other studies imply that the children ask questions to evaluate their own understanding when they try to make sense of new learning. In all these cases, these questions throw unique light onto children's progress in understanding, and thereby enlighten teachers' assessments.

Next we provide some examples of such child-generated questions in the domain of science. In each case, we preface these with the learning objective of the particular lesson within which the questions were constructed (by children aged 9-11).

EXAMPLE ONE. Learning Objectives: To plan an investigation about the micro-organism's habitats and make a prediction

Children's questions:
- Why does bacteria spread?
- Why are there different types of micro-organisms?
- How were the micro-organisms made?
- Can micro-organisms grow in our body?

EXAMPLE TWO. Learning Objectives: To describe the sexual and asexual reproduction methods in plants

Children's questions:
- What happens if there is no more pollen or nectar for bees?
- Can animals reproduce like flowers?
- How do plants get their shapes?
- Why do potatoes grow in the ground?

EXAMPLE THREE. Learning Objectives: To explain how we experience day and night and complete a scientific diagram

Children's questions:
- What would happen if the Earth orbited the moon?
- Why doesn't the sun move?
- Why can't we see if the Earth is moving? Why don't our objects move as well?
- How many moons are there all together?

In terms of their process of conceptual change, children's questions can be sorted using three main categories: consolidation, exploration and elaboration. Consolidation questions indicate children trying to understand an idea. Exploration questions indicate that they are striving to expand their knowledge. Elaboration questions tend to show a child trying to examine claims or resolve a conflict which requires a deeper thinking level (Watts et al., 1997). Classifying children's questions is a helpful aid to teachers' formative assessments. All three types of questioning can be either text-based or knowledge-based. Table 5.1.1 shows the previous questions, sorted into the three categories.

All categories essentially require knowledge and information to be processed in order to form a question; this procedure is completed through the process of thinking. A child's prior history of domain-specific thinking impacts on the richness of the questions, as they draw on different types of memories.

How to encourage rich questioning

To encourage this process, children must be given time to think deeply before responding by asking a question. If you have asked them to write a question, allow the children thinking time before listening to (or reading) their questions. Teacher expectation is important here, expecting a response (i.e.

TABLE 5.1.1 Classifying children's questions

Questioning category	Consolidation	Exploration	Elaboration
Text-based	Why are there different types of micro-organisms?	How many moons are there all together?	Can animals reproduce like flowers?
	Why do potatoes grow in the ground?	How were the micro-organisms made?	Can micro-organisms grow in our body?
Knowledge-based	Why does bacteria spread?	How do plants get their shapes?	What would happen if the Earth orbited the moon?
	Why doesn't the sun move?		What happens if there is no more pollen or nectar for bees?
	Why can't we see if the Earth is moving? Why don't our objects move as well?		

a question) from every child. A useful technique for encouraging this is the use of discussion or talk partners. The child first shares their question with a partner, before some children are selected to share theirs with the teacher and the class. This does require careful planning of partnerships to be effective, and frequent changes of partners can offer children exposure to a wider range of ideas, so long as they feel at ease with each partner. In this way, the children can test their ideas with their peers and perhaps adjust their thinking before offering a response (i.e. a question), which in turn helps them feel more confident about voicing a question. During these peer discussions, in addition, the teacher has an opportunity to listen out for any misconceptions that the children may hold, or indeed areas of the topic that excite them. They may use a randomising method to choose who responds in front of the class each time - for example, using raffle tickets or lolly sticks with names on (sometimes known by pupils as the 'unlucky draw'). The questions gained from every child can be fed into the teacher's planning, supporting them to understand what help each child needs.

Research-based example of pupil questioning as AfL

In a teaching approach which we developed during a research project in primary science classrooms, teachers were aiming to assess their children's thinking processes in order to carry out formative assessment more thoroughly. The lessons began with the teacher posing a simple question that had an obvious answer based on the learners' basic knowledge. This question served to activate children's prior knowledge related to the lesson objective and generate thinking towards the specific learning point. For instance, in a lesson about animal classification, the lesson started with the question: 'Do all animals have the same characteristics?' Regardless of the children's overall response of Yes or No, children recalled different animals, compared them with each other and identified the physical differences and similarities in order to classify the animals. This process created certain steps of thinking that were required for the children's responses in the form of questions, such as recalling, comparing and then classifying.

The following examples suggest what triggered these steps in the classroom.

> **Topic: Living things and their habitats**
> Learning Objective: To identify and group animals using the Classification Key
> Teacher's Question 1: *Do all animals have the same physical features?*

Although this question is not directly pointing to animal classification, it helps the children to recall prior knowledge about animal differences and similarities, using their own comparison. Children share their thoughts and knowledge with each other, and the teacher's questions steer the children's thinking towards further comparison, which naturally leads them to categorise the animals into different groups according to their physical features. Some examples of further supportive **teacher questions** as prompts are as follows:

What do peacocks and eagles have in common? What about bears and tigers?

Do they reproduce in the same way? How about sharks and whales?

In certain cases, children utilised questioning techniques to *think more creatively and surpass the intended objectives of the lesson*, thereby fostering motivation for further independent learning beyond the school environment. For example, the following questions were asked by the children in the same science lesson:

- How does the octopus camouflage itself?
- Why do some animals not have a backbone?
- What would happen if you put a jellyfish with a polar bear?
- Why do humans have hair and not fur?
- Why do lizards change colour?
- Why do peacocks have different coloured feathers?

It is crucial for teachers to acknowledge children's curiosity, appreciate their questions from diverse perspectives and use these questions to evaluate the children's thinking journey, to establish connections with their perceptions of the world. It is important that children understand their freedom to ask what is in their mind regardless of the relevance of the question to the learning objective.

Intriguingly, this study uncovered profound connections between children's underlying knowledge and their questions, despite the apparent divergence in focus between the questions and the lesson content. These underlying connections demonstrated a strong relationship with the new knowledge being acquired. As an illustration, within a lesson addressing the particle arrangements in various states of matter, a student's question, such as 'What is glass composed of?', exposed the thought process behind the transparency of glass and the attempt to comprehend the atomic arrangement of a transparent object in a solid state. It is crucial for teachers to be mindful of their own misconceptions when interpreting children's questions and attempting to understand their thought processes.

Children can be instructed to express their thoughts by writing their questions in their books after or during completion of their activities. In comparison to the daily interactions in their other lessons, this personalised communication of questions between teachers and children is believed to be an encouraging factor in generating ideas without children being worried about peer pressure, and, as a result, thinking can move beyond classroom boundaries. In this way, the children's freedom in expressing their thoughts seems to be somewhat protected and their confidence in thinking may be raised as the evident judgement level is lowered (Smith, 2020). However, as has been argued earlier, much assessment information and insight will have been exposed during the process, which the teacher can respond to.

The lessons are designed to maintain the balance in activities between knowledge and skills, as well as theory and practical activities.

Accordingly, each lesson contains a set of activities which aim to promote thinking by using a range of teaching methods. In every lesson, one or more activities from each of the following categories are included to approach a concept from various angles:

- verbal interactions, including classroom dialogue through group discussion;
- questioning and narrative;

FIGURE 5.1.3 Structuring a lesson to support children's question generation to aid formative assessment

- practical work, including experiments, observations, investigations, outdoor activities and games;
- using visual resources, by watching videos, pictures and models; creating models using drawing, labelling diagrams and making 3D models; and
- writing in different forms, including information text, explanation text, investigation plan, instructions and report.

In addition, the teaching aims to provide opportunities to observe the students' thought processes at various times during the journey of their learning. With this perspective, the lessons consist of several stages which are carefully selected to support and facilitate the development of the students' thinking in each lesson:

1 The lessons start with a question from the teacher and resulting talk in pupil groups.
2 The teaching points are constructed sequentially using visual resources and the teacher's questioning.
3 The associated activities are completed during the lessons in groups, and the feedback from groups is shared as a class discussion led by the teacher's questioning.
4 Students complete a literacy-based task (based on a piece of text/diagram/graph) independently and reflect on their learning and express their thoughts after summarising their new learning.
5 Students write the questions that they have in mind in their exercise books as the end point to the lesson.
6 Students assess themselves using self-assessment tasks and respond to the teacher's assessment during the lesson in their books.

PEER AND SELF-ASSESSMENT

An increased awareness of the role of the learner in the assessment process has led to changes in approaches to teaching, involving more dialogue between pupils and teachers in the setting and adaptation of the assessment process. Learners are more aware, not only of what they learn, but how they learn and what helps them learn. Pupils can assess themselves and can learn from their own and others' assessments. This, in turn, leads them to reflect on how they learn. Children should be involved, not only in their own assessment, but also in peer assessment. This gives children a central role in learning and is a really important shift from the teacher having all the responsibility for assessment to a position of sharing goals, self-evaluation and setting their own targets (see Read and Hurford, 2010). This approach can be highly motivating, but must be endorsed by a supportive classroom ethos, which should include clear guidelines for the children in terms of supporting and guiding each other's learning. Some research has highlighted that peer assessment can be anxiety-provoking unless carefully guided (e.g. Hargreaves, Buchanan and Quick, 2025). There must, for example, be a clear focus and structure for the lesson. Children need a set of success criteria and assessment criteria (see 'Planning for AfL' section earlier) by which to judge the success of their own and peers' learning, and avoiding marks or grades is essential. These criteria can be negotiated with the children. Consider some of the following methods of engaging your children in their own assessment. Notice that the final example is a class's assessment of its own learning strategies, not just focused on a particular curriculum domain.

(a) In Mr Zak's class, before starting any new topic of learning, the pupils describe what they already know about that topic and what they would like to know about that topic. Mr Zak then teaches the topic in accordance with what the pupils have told him. Sometimes he invites pupils to teach some parts if they have good knowledge about it.

(b) In Miss Sophie's class, each month pupils are asked to do 'self-assessments'. They look back at the work they have done over the past month, noticing progress made since the previous month, and write down in a Learning Log specific tasks they need to do in order to achieve the targets they have been set. Sometimes they work in collaboration with a peer assessor.

(c) Before the class does any work or project, teacher Mrs Han asks the class to suggest what features a good end product would include. For example, when writing a creative story, the children suggest that the story would be interesting to read. When all the criteria are agreed, they are written for everyone to see. At the end of the work or project, the pupils assess each other against these agreed criteria.

(d) Mr Nat's Year 5 class uses a system of peer assessment. When an assignment is finished, two peers read the assignment. The author of the assignment then assesses it against agreed criteria (making judgements about its value). The two peers then give *provocative* feedback, asking the author questions that will make the author think more deeply about the topic. No judgements are made by the peers, only by the author him/herself. The author may then rework the assignment.

(e) In Mrs Yasmina's class, there are two big noticeboards pinned up at the front of class. One is titled 'What helps our learning', and the other is titled 'What hinders our learning'. At the end of each day, the children reflect on their day's learning and contribute factors for each noticeboard. They then discuss how they can decrease the hindrances and increase the helping factors.

Task 5.1.2 Self-assessment

Support your pupils to assess themselves or their peers using one of the methods described earlier.

FEEDBACK

Effective feedback to children provides information to support self-assessment and suggests steps that will lead to progress. Feedback through written comments (if written text is easily accessible by your children) should refer back to the learning goals agreed at the beginning of the session and should be constructive. We know that many teachers focus on spelling, punctuation, grammar or the structure of the piece of work, often omitting to comment on children's learning of the specific lesson objective. It can help to keep the presentational factors as *separate but constantly important* criteria, but on *each individual occasion to emphasise comments that relate directly to the specific learning and assessment objectives* for that lesson.

A useful way of thinking about/describing feedback is whether it is evaluative, descriptive or provocative (Hargreaves, 2017). All too often, teachers provide evaluative feedback in the form of grades and short (usually non-specific) comments, praise or censure. This kind of feedback tells pupils whether they are doing well or not, but it offers little direction for moving their learning forward. Regular critical, evaluative feedback, without guidance for how to improve, can dramatically lower motivation and self-esteem (Hargreaves, Quick and Buchanan, 2023). Descriptive feedback, however, relates to the task at hand, the learner's performance and what they might do to improve in relation to specified learning objectives. Provocative feedback, finally, is less directive and inspires the learner to think more deeply and engage further, or to extend their imagination in relation to learning goals.

The ideal situation is when the teacher can discuss and annotate work with the child present, so that progress can be negotiated together. Difficulties in accessing written text can this way be decreased. However, this is not always possible, and so the teacher writes comments for the child to read and then gives them time to consider the comments. Here, a Year 5 pupil, Esther, describes the teacher's feedback during a lesson on using adjectives. The feedback led Esther to reflect further about adjectives and additionally encouraged her to draw on her own resources for progress:

> [The teacher has told Esther not to use 'silly' as her adjective]
> *Interviewer: Do you remember why [the teacher] said not to use 'silly'?*
> Esther: Well, normally she says, because we're not 5, we're Year 5, and we can actually think of much better words than just 'silly' or 'stupid' or something like that. You can think of much better words, because you've got a big thesaurus in your brain.
> *Interviewer: Indeed ... All right, then [teacher] gave you some advice, not just about what you were doing today, but always – she said the word 'always'. She said, 'It always helps to read your work out loud.'*

RECOGNISING AND CELEBRATING CHILDREN'S WORK

You need to consider how a child's successful learning is recognised. Build in time for reflection at the end of the day or the week. In an early years setting, good learning may be celebrated in a discussion at the end of each session, taking the opportunity to point out what makes it worthy of comment. Another method of highlighting good learning is by taking photographs, which can be displayed as a slide show on a computer screen, providing a permanent reminder for both child and teacher. Some teachers simply display a chosen piece of work on the wall or on a bookstand, so that everyone can share that pupil's success. In this case, a specific time needs to be allocated to focusing on the displayed work and why it has been chosen. All children need to have a turn to have their work displayed.

It is important to involve the class sometimes in pointing out the learning processes that are particularly appropriate and not to focus only on their products. Praise in the form of 'excellent' or a reward/high grade for completed work does little to direct learning processes and can encourage children to avoid risk-taking or asking questions in the future.

Task 5.1.3 Questions to ask yourself in relation to your planning for AfL

- Does the assessment allow children multiple ways to demonstrate their learning across the range of curriculum activities?
- Does it assess the ways in which learning has taken place?
- How do you ensure that feedback from assessments allows the children opportunities to develop and progress in their learning by linking your comments to agreed success criteria and indicating the next phase to encourage further learning?
- How do assessment outcomes influence session planning and modifications to future curriculum planning?
- How will you/should you keep track of this?

Task 5.1.4 Peer reflection

You have had an opportunity to evaluate your practice in relation to pupil self-assessment and questioning. Now ask one of your peers to observe another lesson and comment on another two of the principles of AfL identified by the ARG. You can then observe your peer's class and share your comments to help each other learn. Remember that your comments should focus only on the aspects requested by the colleague you observe; you are not assessing their competence, but rather helping them to learn.

SUMMARY

Assessment for learning, as opposed to *assessment of learning*, is part of ongoing learning and teaching, and is not an optional 'bolt-on'. Its aim is to assess all areas of the curriculum, and, in order to achieve this, it uses a wide range of strategies to secure a spectrum of opportunities to find out about each child. It leads to a recognition of what a child can already do and the identification of progress they might now make in their learning, so that they can proceed at a pace, and in ways appropriate for them. Even when teachers apply the same teaching approach in all lessons, children's own questions reveal that it can lead them to very different questions which indicate the different paths in their thinking journey. Children's questions are a rich source of assessment data, done by a mixture of teacher-led assessment and pupils participating in the assessment process, so that they can eventually assess their own work and set appropriate targets. When AfL works at its best, it seems to involve the teacher and pupils in a whole new approach to learning and teaching in which the teacher–learner relationship is freshly negotiated, and pupils take a greater lead over directing their own learning.

ANNOTATED FURTHER READING

Dann, R. (2018) *Developing Feedback for Pupil Learning*, London: Routledge.

Developing Feedback for Pupil Learning seeks to synthesise what we know about feedback and learning into more in-depth understandings of what influences both the structure of and changes to the learning gap. This research-informed, but accessibly written, enquiry is at the very heart of teaching, learning and assessment. It helps to support our understanding of what works (and what doesn't) for whom, and why. Split into three main parts, it covers:

- feedback for learning in theory, policy and practice;
- conceptualising the 'learning gap';
- new futures for feedback.

Hargreaves, E. (2017) *Children's Experiences of Classrooms*, London: Sage.

This book emphasises pupils' own experiences of learning, teaching and feedback in the classroom. Chapter 4 focuses exclusively on feedback, comparing traditional definitions of feedback as 'knowledge of results' with 'divergent', 'process-focused' and 'provocative' examples of teachers' feedback. It explores the dangers of feedback emphasising the pupil's character. It then provides extensive examples of pupils' responses to teachers' classroom feedback in a selection of primary classrooms.

FURTHER READING TO SUPPORT M-LEVEL STUDY

Stobart, G. (2008) 'Reasons to be cheerful: Assessment for learning', in G. Stobart, *Testing Times: The Uses and Abuses of Assessment*, London: RoutlegeFalmer, pp. 144–170.

In this amusingly written chapter on AfL, Gordon Stobart provides a thorough survey of what AfL has been defined as, how this concept has developed in relation to learning theories and what its implications are for classrooms. It is certainly useful as M-level reading and provides an insight into the ARG's thinking, as Stobart was a founder member of this. Stobart flags up the issue of teachers implementing the strategies of AfL without engaging with the 'spirit' of the strategies, that is, understanding how they might support learning most effectively. He gives considerable attention to classroom feedback, given its close relationship to enhanced learning.

Torrance, H. (2012) 'Formative assessment at the crossroads: Conformative, deformative and transformative assessment', *Oxford Review of Education*, 38(3): 323–342.

This article is suitable for M-level reading, although more demanding than the three readings suggested already. In the article, Harry Torrance suggests that the theory and practice of formative assessment (AfL) seems to be at a crossroads, even an impasse. Different theoretical justifications for the development of formative assessment have been apparent for many years. However, practice, although quite widespread, is often limited in terms of its scope and its utilisation of the full range of possible approaches associated with formative assessment. The paper reviews the issue that the aim of AfL is, ostensibly, to develop independent and critical learners, whereas, in practice, highly conformative assessment procedures are being designed and developed. The paper argues that educators need to attend to the divergent possibilities inherent in formative assessment, if the full potential of AfL is to be realised as a transformative practice.

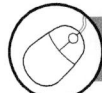

RELEVANT WEBSITES

Collaborative Group Learning: www.collaborativegrouplearning.com

This website of Rob Gratton's is mainly about how to support children in working together in productive groups and will therefore help you with the difficult task of making peer assessment successful.

Chris Watkins: http://chriswatkins.net/
> Chris Watkins's website is mainly about learning and it should help teachers to clarify the difference between performance – that is, outcomes – and learning – that is, processes.

REFERENCES

Assessment Reform Group (ARG). (2002) *Assessment for Learning: 10 Research-based Principles to Guide Classroom Practice*. Retrieved from: www.aaia.org.uk (accessed 27 October 2017).

Black, P. and Wiliam, D. (1998) 'Assessment and classroom learning', *Assessment in Education: Principles, Policy & Practice*, 5(1): 7-74.

Burnett, C. (2016) *The Digital Age and its Implications for Learning and Teaching in the Primary School*, York: Cambridge Primary Review Trust.

Chin, C. and Osborne, J. (2010) 'Students' questions and discursive interaction: Their impact on argumentation during collaborative group discussions in science', *Journal of Research in Science Teaching*, 47(7): 883-908.

Darling-Hammond, L. and Hyler, M. E. (2020) 'Preparing educators for the time of COVID … and beyond, *European Journal of Teacher Education*, 43:4, 457-465, DOI: 10.1080/02619768.2020.1816961

Francis, B., Taylor, B. and Tereshchenko, A. (2019) *Assessming 'Ability' Grouping*, Oxford: Routledge.

Hargreaves, E. (2015) '"I think it helps you better when you're not scared": Fear and learning in the primary classroom', *Curriculum, Pedagogy & Society*, 23(4): 617-638.

Hargreaves, E. (2017) *Children's Experiences of Classrooms: Talking about Being Pupils in the Classroom*, London: Sage.

Hargreaves, E., Buchanan, D. and Quick, L. (2025) *Children's Life-histories In Primary Schools: Imagining Schooling as a Positive Experience*. London: Palgrave.

Hargreaves, E., Quick, L. and Buchanan, D. (2023) 'National Curriculum and assessment in England and the continuing narrowed experiences of lower-attainers in primary schools', *Journal of Curriculum Studies*, 55(5): 545-561.

Harris, D. and Williams, J. (2012) 'The association of classroom interactions, year group and social class', *British Educational Research Journal*, 38(3): 373-397.

Mercer, N. (2016) 'Education and the social brain: Linking language, thinking, teaching and learning', *Éducation et didactique* [En ligne], 10(2). http://journals.openedition.org/educationdidactique/2523

Pramling, I. (1988) 'Developing children's thinking about their own learning', *British Journal of Educational Psychology*, 58(3): 266-278.

Read, A. and Hurford, D. (2010) '"I know how to read longer novels" – developing pupils' success criteria in the classroom', *Education 3-13*, 38(1): 87-100.

Smith, J. (2020) 'The impact of private communication on children's freedom of expression and confidence in thinking', *Journal of Education and Psychology*, 45(2): 123-140.

Watkins, C. (2015) 'Meta-learning in classrooms', in D. Scott and E. Hargreaves (eds) *The Sage Handbook of Learning*, London: Sage, pp. 321-330.

Watts, M., Alsop, S., Gould, G. and Walsh, A. (1997) 'Prompting teachers' constructive reflection: pupils' questions as critical incidents', *International journal of science education*, 19(9), pp. 1025-1037. Available at: https://doi.org/10.1080/0950069970190903.

Wiliam, D. (2008) 'Developing classroom practice: Meeting regularly in teacher learning communities is one of the best ways for teachers to develop their skill in using formative assessment', *Educational Leadership*, 65(4): 36-42.

UNIT 5.2

ASSESSMENT AND LEARNING

Summative approaches

Paula Lehane and Alan Gorman

INTRODUCTION

In this unit, you will reflect on the concept of summative assessment, its uses, and its potential impact on learners. You will also explore aspects of current assessment policy. We will begin by addressing fundamental questions about summative assessment before identifying its common purposes. We will also examine sources of summative assessment evidence and what is necessary to have good evidence of learning. The unit will cover current assessment and reporting policies, as well as the relationship between summative and formative assessment. Finally, you'll have the opportunity to share your views on current assessment policy and practice.

OBJECTIVES

By the end of this unit, you should be able to:

- define and explain the potential purposes of summative assessment;
- understand the relationship between validity, reliability and fairness;
- know the kinds of assessment tasks that are effective in generating good evidence of learning;
- describe some aspects of policy on assessment and offer an informed opinion about the current emphasis on different assessment purposes and approaches.

WHAT IS ASSESSMENT AND WHY DO WE DO IT?

Assessment refers to the process of gathering, interpreting and using information about a child's learning. It helps teachers to identify what their learners know, understand and can do. Without assessment, a teacher would be unable to identify what prior learning has occurred, leading to a unit of work that could be full of repetition or inappropriate content. Assessment is therefore a crucial part of teaching and learning. It is not something that should ever be seen as 'separate' from teaching. However, assessing learning is not a neutral or value-free activity - it is always bound up with attitudes, values, beliefs and sometimes prejudices on the part of those carrying out the assessment and those being assessed. When we make assessments of children's learning, we are always influenced by what we bring with us in terms of our previous experiences, personal views and histories. Children's responses to assessment are influenced by what they bring with them – their previous experiences and their personal views.

Summative assessment 'sums up' learning

Discussions on assessment approaches tend to refer to two important types: formative and summative assessment. Sometimes, these are also called Assessment for Learning (AfL) and Assessment of Learning (AoL). The previous unit explores formative assessment or AfL in more detail. We will focus on summative assessment or AoL approaches. Assessments that claim to serve a summative purpose generally focus on grading or ranking students. Summative assessment is retrospective: it evaluates the knowledge or skills that have been achieved by a certain point in time, e.g. at the end of Key Stage 2. Gathering the evidence necessary for such evaluations and judgements can involve a range of assessment tools such as tests, portfolios or presentations.

Purposes of summative assessment

Summative assessment is carried out for several purposes. When designed by you, the teacher, it can provide you with a summary of learners' achievements that will inform your future teaching and, of course, your planning for future learning. (This is close to the notion of formative assessment described in the previous unit.) Second, it provides information that can be shared with others about a learner's progress, e.g. parents. Third, summatively assessing learning can provide a numerical measurement that can be used in league tables. In England, these allow comparisons of achievement across schools within an education system. These usually involve formal exams or standardised tests that are not set by the classroom teacher. Finally, summative assessments are often used for certification or selection purposes, particularly in post-primary education. For example, A-Levels in the UK are used to certify a student's skills and understanding at the end of second-level education.

As you can see from these examples, the tools and methods used in summative assessments can sometimes be very far removed from the day-to-day work of teachers. How isolated the method for summative assessment is from the daily running of the classroom changes the 'stakes' of that assessment. Indeed, summative assessment is often discussed using the terms 'high-stakes' or 'low-stakes'. For example, A-Levels examinations are considered 'high-stakes' as they can be used to select students for further and higher education. The outcomes on these examinations can have a significant impact on a learner's future. End-of-term tests and examinations set by schools or teachers are relatively low-stakes in comparison, as the consequences for the learner are relatively short-term. Murchan and Shiel (2017) note that international assessments like the Programme for International Student Assessments (PISA) can be considered both low-stakes and high-stakes. As these assessments do not report results for individual schools and learners, they are quite low-stakes for them. Yet, they are very high-stakes for each country's or government's department of education, as they can be used to rank how 'successful' a country's education system is.

> ### Think about it ... PISA shock
>
> The Programme for International Student Assessments (PISA) is an international large-scale assessment that is administered every three years to representative national samples of 15-year-olds. It aims to assess students' 'preparedness' for their future lives based on their performance in tests of reading literacy, mathematics and science. In 2022, 81 countries took part in PISA.

Many countries (rightly or wrongly) use PISA to help evaluate their education system's effectiveness. Pizmony-Levy and Bjorklund (2018: 251) drew on survey data from 30 countries and found 'evidence that national performance on PISA has a significant positive relationship to public confidence in education'. Therefore, it's not surprising that a country's performance in PISA and what 'ranking' they receive can often cause significant debate and discussion in the media. The poor performance of a country in PISA can lead to something called 'PISA shock'. This refers to the *reaction* of policy-makers and the public to student performance in PISA (Niemann, Martens and Teltemann, 2017). For example, when the first PISA results were released in 2000, the perceived poor performance of German children led to significant changes in education policy. Ireland also experienced something akin to 'PISA shock' when a decline in performance in literacy and mathematics in 2009 'shocked' policy-makers into launching a new 'National Strategy for Literacy and Numeracy'.

Think... Do you think that using PISA performance to evaluate a country's education system is a good idea? What are the potential advantages or disadvantages of such an approach?

PRODUCING GOOD EVIDENCE OF ACHIEVEMENT

Characteristics of assessment

It is important to appreciate that summative assessment can take a variety of forms – it need not just be a written test. This is only one tool that we have at our disposal. Before we investigate these tools, three key characteristics of assessment should first be considered: validity, reliability and fairness. While these can be relatively abstract ideas, we will consider them in the context of Mr. Murphy's Year 1 class of 25 students.

Validity refers to whether the information being gathered can support the judgement a teacher needs to make about the learner's progress. When designing a summative assessment, teachers should ask themselves if they are collecting the 'right' information for what they want to know about their learners. Imagine if Mr. Murphy wants to understand how much his students know about subtraction so that he can plan his next week of work in maths. He gives his students a short ten-question test. However, unbeknownst to him, he picks up the wrong test sheet. All of the questions he gives his learners are about subtraction *but* they involve renaming – Mr. Murphy has not yet taught his class how to do subtraction with renaming. Mr. Murphy has asked the wrong questions for what he wants to know. He might be able to glean some information about his students' understanding of subtraction generally but not much beyond that. If he finds that his students perform poorly on the test (because they have yet to be taught how to do sums that involve renaming) and groans to his friend, 'they know nothing about subtraction!', we might have to stop Mr. Murphy and remind him that he's not drawing an appropriate inference about his learners from this assessment source.

We should try to remember three key things about validity from this example:

- Validity takes into account how appropriate the information being gathered is for a teacher's particular *purpose*.
- Validity has to do with *inferences*, i.e. the conclusions you draw from the information you gather.
- Validity is not an 'all or nothing' thing – it's a matter of *degree*. The inferences we draw from an assessment can be more or less valid depending on the situation.

A second important characteristic of summative assessments is reliability. Reliability is broadly concerned with accuracy and consistency. When we think about this characteristic of assessment, we are trying to determine whether or not the same results would have been obtained if the assessment had been given at a different time or in a different context. Let us go back into Mr. Murphy's classroom again. Mr. Murphy has a student called Fred. Based on the written work he has reviewed from Fred's history, geography and English essays for that month, Mr. Murphy has noted Fred's written work has a number of errors in it; mainly in relation to punctuation and sentence length. By gathering multiple examples of Fred's written work, Mr. Murphy can have some confidence in the reliability of his observations from his summative assessment tasks. This is because no single assessment can provide a 'perfect' overview of a learner's knowledge, skills or abilities.

A fair assessment is one that allows all learners an opportunity to demonstrate their achievement. If an assessment is discriminatory or biased towards a learner, then an inappropriate inference may be drawn about their knowledge, skills or abilities. Common sources of assessment bias include racial/ethnic bias, gender bias and socio-economic bias. Fairness is also seen in assessments that provide learners with an adequate opportunity to learn the content being assessed (unlike what happened with Mr. Murphy's earlier maths test). Let us consider another example of this in relation to computer-based exams. If Mr. Murphy's students are required to complete a computer-based test for English writing, then all of his students should be familiar with the technology required. If they must type a response when they would normally handwrite their work in class, their lack of experience or proficiency in using a word processor could unfairly influence or bias their performance.

Think about it ... Differentiating assessments

To support valid, fair and reliable inferences about the diverse range of learners you will be working with in your future classrooms, some adaptations may be necessary to your summative assessment approaches.

Accommodations are those adaptations to an assessment that do not fundamentally change what you are assessing. These changes focus mainly on the *how* of the assessment. This may involve using a larger text size in tests of reading comprehension to support those with a visual impairment. Accommodations often involve changes to the presentation or running of an assessment, e.g. allowing extra time or how learners can respond. However, if there are changes to *what* is being assessed, then it is more appropriate to call it a modification. Modifications often change the content of the assessment, e.g. asking a learner less questions on a maths test. It is important to ensure that *what* you are assessing does not fundamentally change because of your adaptations or modifications. For example, when assessing *reading* comprehension, teachers may decide to read out a text to a learner who cannot independently read long passages. This change by the teacher has altered the assessment – the teacher is no longer assessing reading comprehension. They are now assessing listening comprehension.

Think... A teacher is assessing her students' spelling skills in Year 4. For most of her students, she uses the same spelling list. However, for other students she uses a different spelling list. Is this an example of an accommodation or a modification?

Summative assessment approaches

Based on what has been discussed, we recommend that you think about three key questions that will help to guide your approach to any assessment, including summative assessment:

1. What do I want to know from the information I will gather?
2. How will I gather enough information to have an accurate and fair overview of the specific knowledge, skill or understanding of interest?
3. How well does the information gathered justify my inferences or future actions?

(adapted from Burke and Lehane, 2023: 76)

Summative assessments can include a broad range of approaches. We provide a brief overview of the following: Classroom Tests (Teacher-Designed), Performance-Based Assessments/Portfolios, Rubrics, Standardised Assessments and Examinations. It is important to note that there should be a close match between the learning being assessed and the methods used to assess it. This should guide which of the approaches you use. Furthermore, no one assessment approach is 'perfect'. In a modern primary classroom, a mix of summative assessment approaches should be used to understand learners' achievements.

Classroom tests (teacher-designed)

The word 'test' can be used to describe any written (or oral) assignment that consists of a series of questions/problems that must be answered by individual learners within a limited time frame in a classroom context (Brookhart, 2015). Teachers should always remember that tests can only assess a *sample* of what students have learned. It would be impossible to create an assessment that can address every learning target/objective/outcome. A range of item (question) types are available to teachers – constructed response (e.g. short answers, essays, completing maths problems), selected response (e.g. multiple choice, matching, binary choice (true/false, yes/no) and cloze procedures. See the next box for some examples of each.

Think about ... Question types

Imagine that you have just completed a unit of work about the Amazon rainforest. Here are some sample questions that you could include in your classroom test.

Multiple Choice Questions (MCQs)

What is the top layer of a tropical rainforest called?

A. Canopy
B. Understory
C. Emergent
D. Forest Floor

Fill in the Blanks (Cloze)

The _____ layer sits below the emergent layer. Trees have _____ to this environment by having glossy leaves and needing less sunlight.

Constructed Response

Rainforests are found in countries near the equator. What impact does this have on the climate there?

Think ... Could images or illustrations be used in any of these questions?

When trying to decide what questions to include in your classroom test, it is good to consider how your test will be administered (e.g. paper, digital, oral), what can be done to minimise learner anxiety (e.g. teach test-taking skills) and how many questions you need to ask to ensure your inferences are appropriate.

Performance-based assessments/portfolios

Performance-based assessments involve students applying their newly acquired knowledge and skills to a set task leading to a 'performance' or product that represents their learning (Brookhart, 2015). Many people argue that performance-based assessments are more 'authentic' than classroom tests but that really depends how much of the task is bounded by real-world contexts and constraints. Some examples of a performance-based assessment used in primary classrooms could include:

- designing a house for a family of field mice;
- hopping, skipping, running or jumping;
- blending sounds to read a word;
- planning a trip to another country with a sample budget and itinerary;
- representing a character from a nursery rhyme in a drama;
- constructing a bar graph from the data provided;
- working in a group to create a multi-media presentation on an historical event.

As you can see from this short list, performance-based tasks can be quite restricted (e.g. have only one correct response) or relatively open-ended (e.g. have multiple correct responses). Which one a teacher chooses is very dependent on the learning they wish to assess. Sometimes, performance-based assessments can be organised into a portfolio – a collection of 'artefacts' that can showcase the learner's work and development over time. It is very common in subjects like visual arts, physical education, science and English. Portfolios often include reflective entries or annotations from the learner that offer insight into their thinking.

Rubrics

Rubrics have been called many things depending on how they look – performance checklists, scoring criteria, rating scales. Regardless of the term used, they usually state the factors from which a learner's work or performance can be evaluated. These criteria can be informed by the curriculum, teachers' own knowledge/experience or learning progressions. Rubrics are not used to generate assessment information or evidence – they are used to evaluate them to support teacher inferences and judgements. Sometimes (particularly when grading essays), rubrics can be used to decide on a grade. These rubrics include descriptions indicating standards of attainment for different levels of performance, success or competency (Brookhart, 2015). Two broad categories of rubrics exist – holistic and analytic. A holistic rubric is one in which each category of performance (e.g. excellent, very good, good, satisfactory) contains several criteria to help give an overall rating. An analytic rubric is one in which each 'feature' of the performance is identified and scored separately. The purpose of the assessment should help determine which form of rubric could be used. Both have advantages and disadvantages. The following box shows how the same performance-based assessment could be evaluated using an analytic or a holistic rubric.

Think about ... Rubrics

Imagine that you are evaluating learners' performance in a debate on the motion 'Animals should not be in zoos'. Consider each of the following rubrics.

Rubric 1 (Analytical)

	Excellent	Good	Satisfactory	Needs improvement
Delivery	Speaks consistently and clearly with excellent volume, variation and inflection. Uses several persuasive techniques to excellent effect (e.g. humour, rhetorical questions). *10 points*	Speaks clearly with good volume, variation and inflection. Uses some persuasive techniques effectively (e.g. humour, rhetorical questions). *7 points*	Speaks relatively clearly with appropriate but inconsistent volume, variation and inflection. Shows knowledge of persuasive techniques but with little effect or impact (e.g. humour, rhetorical questions). *4 points*	Speaks in a low volume with little variation and inflection. Inadequate use or absence of persuasive techniques (e.g. humour, rhetorical questions). *2 points*
Organisation	Begins with a clear and purposeful statement of position. Provides multiple, highly relevant arguments. Contains an effective logical flow and structure. *10 points*	Begins with a statement of position. Provides relevant arguments. Contains a reasonably logical flow and structure. *7 points*	Statement of position is somewhat unclear. Small number of arguments provided; not all are relevant. Flow and structure are poorly organised. *4 points*	Does not begin with a clear position. Provides few or no real and relevant arguments. Difficult to understand the flow of the presentation due to inadequate structure and flow. *2 points*
Content	All arguments had specific evidence to support them (e.g. examples, statistics). All information was highly accurate and clear. *10 points*	Most arguments had some evidence to support them (e.g. examples, statistics). Information was accurate and clear but further elaboration was needed. *7 points*	Few arguments had evidence to support them (e.g. examples, statistics). Some inaccuracies in the information provided. *4 points*	Inadequate evidence provided to support arguments or statements (e.g. examples, statistics). Significant number of inaccuracies in the information provided. *2 points*

Preparation	Includes a wide range of sources. Provides well considered, elaborate and in-depth counterarguments.	Includes a range of sources. Provides appropriate counterarguments with varying levels of depth.	Includes a limited number of sources. Provides rudimentary counterarguments provided with little depth.	Includes very few, if any, sources. Provides no counterarguments.
	10 points	7 points	4 points	2 points

Rubric 2 (Holistic)

Performance levels	Success criteria
Excellent 30–40 points	Speaks clearly and consistently using a wide range of well-supported, evidence informed arguments. Presentation is very well organised and effectively includes a range of persuasive techniques. Offers excellent counterarguments and defends position very well when asked questions.
Good 20–29 points	Speaks clearly using a range of well-supported arguments. Presentation is organised and includes some persuasive techniques. Offers appropriate counterarguments and can defend position when asked questions.
Satisfactory 10–19 points	Speaks relatively clearly using a small number of arguments that had limited evidence to support them. Presentation is somewhat disorganised and includes very few persuasive techniques. Offers some counterarguments but can only offer a limited defence of their position when asked questions.
Needs improvement <10 points	Does not speak clearly or consistently with little reference to any arguments or evidence. Presentation is poorly organised and contains few or no persuasive techniques. Offers no counterarguments and is unable to defend position when asked questions.

Think...
1 Do you think rubrics can eliminate teacher bias?
2 What are you going to learn about each learner's performance using the analytic or the holistic rubrics? Do you favour one more than the other and why?

Standardised assessments and examinations

When people think of summative assessments, they usually think of public examinations or standardised assessments. While they can be useful to classroom teachers' practice (e.g. identifying learners who have specific needs), certain authors (e.g. McMillan, Shepard) do not consider these tools to be relevant to the field of classroom assessment as teachers often have very little to do with their creation or selection, i.e. they are obliged to do it for accountability reasons rather than for learning. However, it is still important for teachers to have a clear understanding of them.

Standardised tests assess the abilities of learners under very controlled conditions, e.g. strict administration, scoring and interpretation guidelines. These tests also have to follow careful rules in terms of their construction. How these tests are constructed can help teachers to understand the *meaning* of learner outcomes in accordance with the interpretative frameworks used. Two main interpretative frameworks are associated with standardised tests: norm-referenced and criterion-referenced. Some tests can use both frameworks. Norm-referenced tests allow teachers to compare their students' performance to a 'norming group' using test norms. The following steps are involved in creating norms:

1. Select a relatively large and representative sample of students from the country, i.e. students who are similar in age and other characteristics to those who will be using the test in the future. This is the norming group.
2. Administer the test to the norming group.
3. Score the test and examine the appropriateness of the content.
4. Analyse the scores and use them to represent the performance of all learners who will be taking the test.

For example, if learners in Mr. Murphy's class take a norm-referenced standardised maths test at the end of Key Stage 1, their performance will be compared to the performance of students who helped 'norm' this test. Performance in a norm-referenced test can be summarised using percentile ranks, scaled scores or standard scores (see the next box for a brief explanation of two of these measures). Criterion-referenced standardised tests use 'proficiency levels' or 'performance bands' to score students, e.g. 'meets expected standards'. The Phonics Check performed at the end of Key Stage 1 in England uses a criterion-referenced score to identify what children have or have not met the expected standard for phonics decoding.

Think about ... Standardised tests

Performance on a standardised test can be summarised in different ways. We will just explain two in this box.

A student's **percentile rank** summarises the percent of students in the norming group that the learner outperformed. It does *not* represent the amount they got correct in the test. For example, if Jack received a percentile score of 80, then that means he performed better than 80 percent of the students in the norming group.

A student's **standard score** summarises the distance of a student's performance from the mean. Lots of tests use standard scores that range from 55 to 145 and have a mean of 100 (with a standard deviation of 15). Scores between 85 and 115 are within the average range. If Lottie received a standard score of 109, then we can say that Lottie's performance is within the average range when compared to peers of the same age.

Think...

What if the norming group of a test is very different from the learners who take that test? Can a valid interpretation be made about the learners from their scores? Why or why not?

Isaacs et al. (2013: 52) define examinations as 'an attempt to measure a learner's knowledge, understanding or skills within a certain subject or sector domain in a limited amount of time'. They can be used to certify students (e.g. getting a 'license' to practice medicine), select candidates for third-level or further education (e.g. A-Levels being used by universities to select students for courses) or for accountability reasons. While exams allow learners the opportunity to demonstrate their knowledge under the same conditions as their peers, the fairness of this assessment approach can be influenced by several inter-related factors that should be borne in mind when considering the appropriateness of the interpretations that can arise from them.

SUMMATIVE ASSESSMENT AND REPORTING: CURRENT POLICY

The most visible form of summative assessment used in England are the Standard Assessment Tests (SATs). These tests are based on the national curriculum and are only administered in England. They are currently completed at the end of Key Stage 2 (KS2) (end of primary phase) and take place annually. Schools are statutorily obliged to administer them in state-funded schools. There are three specific SATs: (i) *Reading*, (ii) *Grammar, Punctuation and Spelling* and (iii) *Mathematics*. In addition, a selected sample of pupils countrywide also participate in biennial assessments in science. The purpose of these forms of summative assessments is to monitor student progress and attainment. They are also used by the Department for Education to hold schools accountable for their performance.

The SATs are considered 'high-stakes' assessments as they are reported to the local authorities and can be published at local authority, regional and national levels (as they were in 2022). This allows for the development of league tables where a school's results can be measured against the results of all schools nationally as well as other schools in its similar catchment area. Schools are ranked in these league tables in order of their success in the assessments. These results are reported on school websites, within school prospectuses and can also be reported in the media generally. The use of statutory assessments at the end of KS2 to create league tables are subject to critique, given they only provide a narrow picture of what is occurring in the school (Gardner et al., 2010). However, it can also be argued that these league tables equip parents with important information on how to select a school that caters for their children (Roberts, 2022).

Alongside the national curriculum assessment at the end of KS2, children also undertake a range of other summative tests and assessments during their primary schooling in England. In the first year of primary education, known as Reception, children undertake the Reception Baseline Assessment (RBA) within their first six weeks. This baseline assessment looks at (i) *maths* and (ii) *language, communication, and literacy*. The scores are not publicly available but are instead used within schools to monitor the progress pupils make from Reception until the end of KS2. Schools are also required to administer the criterion-referenced *Phonics Screening Check* in Year 1. The purpose of this assessment is to check if all children have learned decoding skills to an age-appropriate level. They complete the screen again in Year 2 if they do not reach the expected standard. While the results of individual schools are not published in the performance tables, the results will be made available to Ofsted (inspectorate) and to local authorities so that schools will be able to benchmark the performance of their children.

In Year 2, schools can administer the Key Stage 1 (KS1) SAT in *English reading, Grammar, Punctuation and Spelling* and *Mathematics*. Since 2023, these assessments are optional for schools. They do not need to be published but can be used by teachers as a way of reporting progress to parents. In Year 4, English schools are also statutorily obliged to administer the *Multiplication Tables Check (MTC)*. The purpose of this assessment is to determine whether pupils can fluently recall their times tables. Like the *Year 1 Phonics Screening Check*, the results of individual schools are not published in performance tables but are made available to national and local authorities. Table 5.2.1 summarises some of the tests that are undertaken in primary schools in England as of 2023.

TABLE 5.2.1 Assessments in English primary schools

Name	When	Content	Reporting
Reception Baseline Assessment (RBA)*	Within first 6 weeks of beginning Reception	Maths Language, Communication and Literacy	Results used by teachers within schools Not publicly available
Phonics Screening Check*	Year 1 (and Year 2 if necessary)	Word reading skills (decoding)	Reported at local authority level Reported to Ofsted
KS1 Standard Assessment Tests (SATs)	Year 2	English reading English grammar, punctuation and spelling Mathematics Science (for a sample of schools)	Results used by teachers within schools Can be reported at local authority level
Multiplication Tables Check	Year 4	Times tables up to 12	Reported at local authority level
KS2 Standard Assessment Tests (SATs)*	End of Key Stage 2 (Year 6)	Reading Grammar, punctuation and spelling Mathematics Science (for a sample of schools)	Can be published at local authority, regional and national levels.

Source: see Roberts, 2022

* All English primary schools are obliged to administer these assessments.

> **Think about … Publishing test results**
>
> England is unique in that it is the only jurisdiction in the UK that produces league tables based on the performance of individual schools at primary level. For example, while it is a statutory requirement for schools in Wales to annually administer online assessments in reading and numeracy for learners in Years 2 to 9, test results are not publicly available. Instead, the central purpose of these assessments is to help teachers plan next steps and to support learner progress.
>
> *Think …* Do you think league tables for primary schools are a good idea? What are some advantages and disadvantages for teachers, children and parents?

SUMMATIVE AND FORMATIVE ASSESSMENT: KEY COMMENT

While summative and formative assessment have been considered separately in this book, harshly categorising an assessment tool as 'formative' or 'summative' may be somewhat counterproductive. For example, an end-of-week assessment designed by a teacher to measure addition skills in mathematics may have been originally conceived as a summative measure of learning but it can *also* be used to identify areas for future learning and instruction, e.g. renaming within 100. Therefore, it may be better to acknowledge that 'supportive links can be forged' between summative and formative assessment as both support the production of judgements about student learning (Black and Wiliam, 2018: 569). While some assessment tools are better suited for summative purposes (e.g. tests) and others are better for formative purposes (e.g. self-assessment), it is important to remember that it is the judgements or inferences arising and **not** the assessments themselves that are formative or summative. Therefore, any assessment tool that is controlled by the teacher can potentially be used for formative or summative purposes, or a combination of both.

SUMMARY

In this unit, we have sought to define and describe summative assessment and its role in classrooms. We spoke about three key characteristics of assessment – validity, reliability and fairness. We discussed some common approaches to summative assessment as well – classroom tests, performance-based assessments, rubrics and standardised tests and exams. To recap the major points of the unit, we suggest that you revisit the learning objectives we noted on the first page. As you do this, you might consider the different ways in which you could demonstrate your understanding and knowledge of the topic.

ANNOTATED FURTHER READING

Murchan, D. and Shiel, G. (2017) *Understanding and Applying Assessment in Education*, Thousand Oaks, CA: SAGE Publications.
> This book provides an excellent overview of assessment across all levels of the education system. It is a 'one-stop-shop' for all issues in summative and formative assessment using examples of practice from the UK, Ireland and other international contexts. It goes into more detail on many of the topics outlined here in an easy-to-read, highly accessible manner.

Elwood, J. and Murphy, P. (2015) 'Assessment systems as cultural scripts: A sociocultural theoretical lens on assessment practice and products', *Assessment in Education: Principles, Policy & Practice*, 22(2): 182-192.
> This editorial to a special issue on sociocultural perspectives on assessment, along with its accompanying articles, offers a challenging and theorised account of assessment research, policy and practice that is worth studying to sharpen your thinking and invite you to challenge some current practices.

Black, P. and Wiliam, D. (2018) 'Classroom assessment and pedagogy', *Assessment in Education: Principles, Policy & Practice*, 25(6): 551-575. https://doi.org/10.1080/0969594X.2018.1441807
> This piece from Black and Wiliam outlines how assessment, pedagogy, instruction and learning all relate to each other. Of particular interest is how the authors speak about the relationship between formative and summative assessment.

FURTHER READING TO SUPPORT M-LEVEL STUDY

Guo, W. Y. and Yan, Z. (2019) Formative and summative assessment in Hong Kong primary schools: students' attitudes matter. *Assessment in Education: Principles, Policy & Practice*, 26(6): 675-699. 10.1080/0969594X.2019.1571993
> This study investigates the relationship between primary students' attitudes towards formative assessment and summative assessment. It unpacks some of the common perceptions of both formative and summative assessment that students' hold and whether gender or age have any influence on these attitudes.

Brownlie, N., Burke, K. and van der Laan, L. (2024a) Quality indicators of effective teacher-created summative assessment. *Quality Assurance in Education*, 32(1): 30-45. http://dx.doi.org/10.1108/QAE-04-2023-0062

    This paper extends the discussion on summative assessment by identifying five key principles – validity, reliability, fairness, authenticity, and flexibility – that contribute to high-quality, teacher-designed summative assessments. This meta-analysis provides valuable insights for primary teachers seeking to refine their summative assessment practices.

Schildkamp, K. (2019) Data-based decision-making for school improvement: Research insights and gaps. *Educational Research*, 61(3): 257-273. DOI 10.1080/00131881.2019.1625716

    This paper goes beyond the definitions and explanations of summative assessment discussed in this chapter by exploring a broader, more iterative approach to data use in education. It offers an interesting discussion on how summative assessment data can be used in conjunction with other evidence to enhance teaching and learning in primary classrooms.

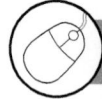

RELEVANT WEBSITES

https://www.blooket.com/

    Blooket can support summative assessment through the use of interactive, game-based quizzes that assess students' knowledge and understanding in a dynamic way, while providing teachers with instant performance data to inform final evaluations.

https://seesaw.com/

    Seesaw supports summative assessment by enabling students to build digital portfolios that showcase their learning over time, using a variety of tools – such as voice recordings, drawings, videos and written reflections – to capture a rich and diverse range of assessment data for teachers to evaluate.

REFERENCES

Black, P. and Wiliam, D. (2018) 'Classroom assessment and pedagogy', *Assessment in Education: Principles, Policy & Practice*, 25(6): 551-575. https://doi.org/10.1080/0969594X.2018.1441807

Brookhart, S. M. (2015) *Performance Assessment: Showing What Students Know and Can Do*. Learning Sciences International.

Burke, P. and Lehane, P. (2023) *Weaving the Literature on Integration, Pedagogy and Assessment: Insights for Curriculum and Classroom*. National Council for Curriculum and Assessment. Retrieved from: https://ncca.ie/media/6371/weaving-the-literature-on-integration-pedagogy-and-assessment.pdf

Gardner, J., Harlen, W., Hayward, L., Stobart, G. and Montgomery, M. (2010) *Developing Teacher Assessment*, New York and London: McGraw-Hill Education.

Isaacs, T., Zara, C., Herbert, G., with Coombes, S. J. and Smith, C. (2013) *Key Concepts in Educational Assessment*, SAGE Publications.

Murchan, D. and Shiel, G. (2017) *Understanding and Applying Assessment in Education*, SAGE Publications.

Niemann, D., Martens, K. and Teltemann, J. (2017) 'PISA and its consequences: Shaping education policies through international comparisons', *European Journal of Education*, 52: 175-183. https://doi.org/10.1111/ejed.12220

Pizmony-Levy, O. and Bjorklund, P., Jr. (2018) 'International assessments of student achievement and public confidence in education: Evidence from a cross-national study', *Oxford Review of Education*, 44(2): 239-257. https://doi.org/10.1080/03054985.2017.1389714

Roberts, N. (2022) *Assessment and Testing in Primary Education (England)*, House of Commons Library. Retrieved from: https://researchbriefings.files.parliament.uk/documents/CBP-7980/CBP-7980.pdf

SECTION 6
DIVERSITY AND INCLUSION

UNIT 6.1

UNDERSTANDING AND IMPLEMENTING ADAPTIVE TEACHING

Sarah Leonard

INTRODUCTION

Adaptive teaching has recently become a more familiar part of discussion about classroom practice, and there is much positivity about how it might be positioned to inform the learning and teaching choices made to meet the needs of all learners (Quigley, 2023). In turn, those choices will secure better learning for all children, especially those whose needs are often not well met in our current education system. But the adoption of a new term is not enough to change practice, even if the language helps us modify thinking. Therefore, this unit endeavours to translate the term into effective provision by exploring what adaptive teaching means, to which children it might apply and, crucially, how it might be enacted in the classroom.

OBJECTIVES

By the end of this unit you should:

- understand why adaptive teaching is central to high quality, inclusive practice;
- recognise for which pupils adaptive practice might be particularly helpful;
- make connections between adaptive teaching practices and what is known about how children learn, including those who might find learning more challenging;
- have more knowledge of some adaptive teaching strategies which can be included in your practice.

THE 'WHY' AND 'WHAT' OF ADAPTIVE TEACHING

Research suggests that teachers enter the profession because they are altruistically motivated and want to contribute to the learning of children and young people (Fray and Gore, 2018). A significant part of this motivation is the desire to meet the needs of every pupil, recognising that these different needs can be permanent or temporary, and may range from extremely complex to relatively straightforward. This intention – identified as central to the role of a teacher in both the Teachers' Standards (Department for Education [DfE], 2011) and the Initial Teacher Training and Early Career

DOI: 10.4324/9781032691794-30

Framework (ITTECF; DfE, 2024a) – becomes increasingly important because classrooms are more diverse, and teaching more multifaceted, than ever before. Before exploring what adaptive teaching might be, it is helpful first to consider the factors that might contribute to this diversity and the continued imperative to embed adaptive practice in every classroom.

> **Task 6.1.1 Understanding differences in outcomes for some groups of pupils**
>
> Which groups of pupils are you aware of who are vulnerable to underachievement in the primary phase of school? Make a list of these.
>
> In your experience, which pupils have been the focus of closer monitoring of progress and attainment? Which approaches and strategies have you observed or used yourself?

Why we need adaptive teaching: Meeting the needs of diverse classrooms

The number of children identified as having a special educational need or disability (SEND) has grown significantly since 2016 for those with both 'higher level' needs (supported with an education, health and care plan – EHCP) and 'lower level' needs (mostly supported with adjustments to learning managed in-school) (DfE, 2024b, 2024c). This group of pupils does not attain well in the educational system, with a large and persistent attainment gap (of around 40 percentage points) existing between pupils with SEND and their peers without identified SEND (DfE, 2024d). The SEND code of practice (DfE and Department of Health and Social Care [DHSC], 2014) categorises four broad areas of need and there has been a rise in the numbers of each. Social, emotional and mental health needs have increased over this time period (DfE, 2024c), for instance, and there is good evidence that such needs affect children's engagement with learning and the ability to both retain and recall knowledge (EEF, 2020; Immordino-Yang, 2015). Equally, the number of pupils with speech, language and communication needs has risen (DfE, 2024c), with evidence that the pandemic has amplified these needs (Byrne et al., 2023). As language is the main medium of learning – both in terms of processing knowledge and demonstrating what is understood – children with such needs may need adaptations in practice.

Moving away from SEND, additional language needs may also arise for children with English as an additional language (EAL). They equate to roughly a fifth of the total pupil population (DfE, 2024e) and there is huge diversity in this group. Strand and Lindorff (2020) identify that EAL status alone does not predict academic attainment; instead, the ease with which multilingual children can engage with learning is affected by a range of factors including proficiency in English, age of arrival in the school system, prior educational experience and other socio-economic factors. Since this is the case, it becomes even more important that learning strategies are adapted to recognise these influences and thus minimise the potential impact that learning in another language might present.

The data tells us that there are other groups of pupils potentially vulnerable to underachievement. Hunt (2023) notes, 'The disadvantage gap at the end of primary school widened in 2022 to above its 2012 level, wiping out a decade of progress in narrowing the gap' with the DfE recognising that it may take a decade to return the gap to its 2019 level. Such a gap affects increasing numbers of pupils as the past few years have seen a rise in the percentage of children falling into this 'disadvantaged' category; it has grown each year over the last decade to around one in four currently, with no expectation that this number will decline soon (Hunt, 2023).

Of course, this list of groups of pupils who add to the diversity of our classrooms is not close to exhaustive and teachers speak, rightly, of the need to avoid labels and to know and understand the needs of everyone in a class. Whilst true, the data highlights a legitimate case for thinking about adaptive teaching as relevant for every pupil, especially those vulnerable to underachievement, yet more strongly making the case for adopting adaptive approaches.

What is adaptive teaching?

For many years, the term differentiation was commonly used when considering how best to create inclusive teaching practice. Whilst potentially a vital concept, it has since been argued that it may have produced some unintended consequences because of its focus on finding differences between children and the learning opportunities they are exposed to (Eaton, 2022; Mould, 2021). For example, interpretations of differentiation may have been behind the expectation that children should do completely different activities to help them consolidate learning, or even that the content to which some children are exposed should be different (Eaton, 2022). In the mainstream setting, some pupils (most commonly those with complex SEND) may need access to additional resources and/or an adjustment in curriculum focus (see the SEND code of practice, DfE and DHSC, 2014, para.1.24), but a key word from the latest EEF (2020) guidance seems crucial – these reasonable adjustments should be *complementary* to high quality teaching.

The Teachers' Standards (DfE, 2011) include Standard 5, which provides a clear definition of adaptive teaching: teachers should 'adapt teaching to respond to the needs of all pupils'. The ITTECF (DfE, 2024a) document is equally clear: adaptive teaching is not about creating artificial groups of pupils (5.4) or responding to learning styles (5.6). Instead, it is about 'seeking to understand pupils' differences' (5.3) to 'adapt teaching in a responsive way' (5.1). This helps us move away from ideas that pupils' needs are met through the preparation of endless different learning activities (which may also impact teachers' workload) that can 'exclude certain learners from a positive classroom experience because of adverse labelling by ability, or by diagnosis' (National Association for Special Educational Needs [NASEN], 2020: 34) and towards a position where teachers maximise learning for all.

Adaptive teaching can be thought of as a response to this by making the learning process more accessible for all, taking children's diversity and needs (be they long or short term, complex or more straightforward) into account.

In Wales …

Effective pedagogy is paramount to supporting progression. The pedagogical approaches used by practitioners should be selected to support progression and these will need to adapt to learners' needs.

Support for progression should provide space for diversion, reinforcement and reflection as a learner develops over time to new levels. Progression will require learners to revisit the concepts outlined in the statements of what matters, developing a more sophisticated understanding and application of these as they progress. Consequently, this is not linear, or simply moving from one topic to another, without making connections between learning and developing understanding of the underlying, shared fundamental concepts.

(Welsh Government, 2023)

> **In Northern Ireland ...**
>
> **Inclusive education is more than a concern about any one group of pupils.** It is about providing opportunities for all children and young people in the community to learn together and where schools nurture learners by providing inclusive systems which are open, participatory and flexible. Inclusive systems work to remove barriers to learning and address issues that relate to all individuals who are vulnerable to exclusion from education.
>
> (Council for Curriculum Examinations and Assessment [CCEA], n.d.)

> **In Scotland ...**
>
> The General Teaching Council sets standards for provisional and full registration. Adaptive teaching is seen to be part of teacher professionalism which asks preservice and qualified teachers to regularly examine the connections between their values and actions.
>
> Autonomy and agency are seen as having a key role in developing teacher professionalism and prompting professional learning that positions children, families and communities at the heart of learning and teaching.
>
> Source: General Teaching Council for Scotland (2021a, 2021b)

THE 'HOW' OF ADAPTIVE TEACHING

If we want to support every child's learning, then thinking about what is known about learning processes is a good place to start. Adaptive teaching can help refine practice in core areas of our teaching (see Figure 6.1.1) which are central to high quality learning for all but which might prove more challenging for some children.

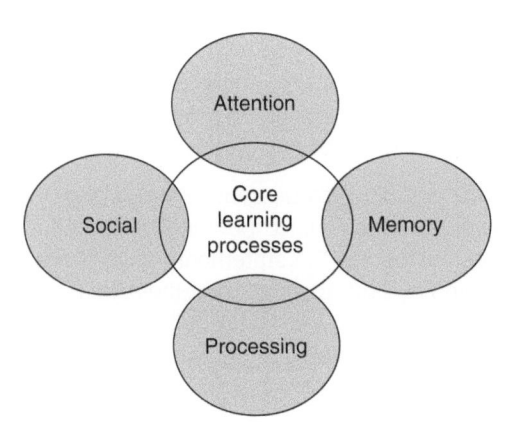

FIGURE 6.1.1 Core learning processes

The next section of this unit is divided up to allow exploration of each of the elements of the core learning processes, including:

- a short summary of how challenges in these areas might present in a child;
- a brief overview of what is known about each learning process;
- suggestions for teaching practice choices to support learners, linked with what is known about the learning process (Tables 6.1.1–6.1.4).

Attention

> **Case study 1**
>
> Avery is enthusiastic and keen to tell you about their interests and what they do outside school. In group tasks, they participate with plenty of energy and creativity, keeping other children motivated and demonstrating resilience when there are obstacles. However, they can also find it difficult to get started with a task and to follow instructions. You find that they can sometimes get distracted in the middle of learning.

The first step in learning is attention. The environment is full of sensory information which is taken in by the body's sensory receptors by seeing, hearing, touching, tasting and smelling. Sensory memory is the first mechanism of understanding the world; endless incoming stimuli are interpreted so that sense can be made of them. The capacity of the sensory memory is actually very large (to accommodate the multitude of information coming from the environment all the time) but it has relatively short duration, lasting for between half a second (for visual input) and three seconds for auditory input (McInerney and Putwain, 2016). Numerous factors influence to what and how we attend, and theorists have proposed four different types of attention: selective, sustained, alternating and divided:

- *Selective attention* is the ability to control attentional mechanisms and to focus on one thing. Younger children demonstrate less selective attention – brain development means that they are more easily distracted by stimuli and can easily move attention from one thing to another (Woolfolk, Hughes and Walkup, 2013). This does not mean that they cannot attend for longer periods, but this 'selective attention' tends to get easier as children mature. However, it is different across individuals.
- *Sustained attention* is the ability to focus on what has been attended to. Sustained attention is affected by the complexity of the task, which is influenced by what the learner already knows, what they might want to know, as well as what they need to learn, the latter of which is usually the main focus for the teacher (Woolfolk, Hughes and Walkup, 2013).
- Being able to *alternate attention* is vital because the brain is unable to process all information in parallel. It involves a shift of both focus and task, and the ability to engage and reengage attention depending on incoming information and the response to what is happening environmentally (Commodari, 2017). Much classroom practice involves children's ability to switch attention, perhaps from group discussion to individual tasks, or from copying the learning objective from the board to undertaking the learning activity provided.
- *Divided attention* occurs when there are lots of environmental stimuli or tasks being attended to. As sensory memory has a limited capacity, the more that is being attended to, the harder it becomes to do this effectively.

TABLE 6.1.1 Adaptive teaching strategies to support attention

Learning strategy	Understanding the approach
Short and succinct instructions, using visuals where appropriate.	Keeps attention focussed on the most important aspects of the task.
Using pictures or colours to highlight key points.	Can help draw attention to important ideas and knowledge.
Access to sound-cancelling headphones.	Can reduce the possibility of divided attention from unwanted, external stimuli. Access to sound-cancelling headphones should be available to all children.
Low stimulus areas in the classroom. Consider how many potential distractions there are in areas where children are frequently focussed, such as the whiteboard or where they work independently.	A focus on the noise, light and visual complexity of an area can provide a space where there are fewer stimuli to divide attention. These spaces can also help manage arousal levels, reducing stress and anxiety.
Concentration aids (such as fidget toys) and movement breaks.	Movement as an intervention works with many children but can be especially helpful for those who find attention and staying task-focussed more difficult.
Redirection of a pupil's attention. For example, teacher participation in a group or paired discussion to facilitate sustained attention.	Asking a pupil to refocus may be unhelpful if key information has been missed and the learning seems inaccessible. Refocussing and revisiting key knowledge is required.

Memory

> ### Case study 2
>
> Mahari started in a Key Stage 2 class six weeks ago with no prior knowledge of English. They have established friendships, are highly sociable and have already picked up some key phrases which help navigate the school day. They appear to have secure curriculum knowledge, however, concentrating for extended periods of time is challenging, and they find the repetition of key information helpful even when they seem to have the skills to do the task.

When a learner's attention is oriented towards incoming information, this can be further processed through memory. Memory itself involves a series of processes: making sense of information and how this relates to what is already known (encoding); retaining information (storage); accessing information that is stored when it is needed (retrieval) (Woolfolk, Hughes and Walkup, 2013).

Working memory is a crucial part of learning as it is the system which can *attend to and manipulate* information within short-term memory (McInerney and Putwain, 2016). For example, these processes help a child use times table knowledge up to 10x10 to solve the calculation 27x3 through partitioning, or to remember which ingredients they have already put into the meal they are cooking in a food technology lesson. It also contributes to the concept of cognitive load theory (Sweller, 1988), which highlights that *working memory has limited capacity* for all learners but that this capacity may be further limited for some children. Adaptive teaching takes account of this variance.

TABLE 6.1.2 Adaptive teaching strategies to support memory

Learning strategy	Understanding the approach
Recording devices. This can be through class tablets/laptops, or through very simple, portable technology such as sound buttons or 'talking postcards' which record up to 30 seconds of sound.	Presents the opportunity to revisit and have further chances to retain key information. Recordings can be of the teacher (for example, providing instructions) or a child/group of children, recording their ideas or key points for learning. Where possible, children should record and access what they need themselves, as this adds an important element of autonomy for learners.
Provide opportunities for over-learning and encourage automaticity. Aim for procedural (skills-based, such as cursive writing) as well as declarative (knowledge-based, such as number facts) automaticity.	Repeated practice produces automaticity; where information is quickly and easily recalled, it leads to less demand on working memory securing more capacity for new learning.
Provide prompts to support if automaticity has not yet been achieved, e.g. number facts, key vocabulary, writing scaffolds, information in first language.	Scaffolding of this nature supports working memory because children are not having to manipulate too much new or unfamiliar information at the same time.
Employ multi-sensory approaches to learning. For example, children could try cursive writing in shaving foam or use giant chalk to record tricky spelling or number facts on the playground.	Different structures in the brain are specialised for encoding information, but making connections between these structures supports learning. Here, the physical and visual link together to establish more neural connectivity.

Another key element of the memory system is *long-term memory*. Learning is dependent on *long-term memory, which has unlimited capacity*. As Ofsted (2019) notes, 'Learning can be defined as an alteration in long-term memory. If nothing has altered in long-term memory, nothing has been learned'. Transfer to long-term memory is supported by different factors. The first is semantics (meaning making), as the more the learner can make sense of information, the more likely it is to be stored long term. The second is the multi-sensory encoding of information. Where 'children are taught new information using a variety of senses, learning will be stronger' because the knowledge is represented through more neural connections making the learning both more secure and more easily retrieved (Goswami, 2011: 22). This links with the final point that teachers must support learners to recall information from long-term memory, otherwise it becomes irretrievable and cannot support subsequent learning (McInerney and Putwain, 2016).

Processing

Case study 3

Perryn is extremely hard working, has a close-knit group of friends and shows great kindness to others. They are keen to please and often help with classroom jobs. You have noticed that although they appear to be listening carefully in lessons, they can lose concentration and do not always fully understand the content or the task given. They usually let others lead in paired or group discussions. Sometimes independent work suggests understanding, but not always, and the patterns of success in learning seem inconsistent.

In 1972, Craik and Lockhart researched the importance of *processing* in remembering, identifying that successful processing was the result of learners successfully extracting meaning from information presented, rather than simply the number of times they encountered that information. This confirms the idea that sense-making is central in how information is learnt and reiterates what is known about semantic understanding, improving how learners commit information to long-term memory.

As teachers working to promote sense-making, it is useful to consider strategies which can support better processing. One helpful practical approach is *elaboration*, the process of connecting new and existing information which adds and extends meaning (Woolfolk, Hughes and Walkup, 2013). This can be done by encouraging pupils to make connections and to compare and contrast when learning; for example, in a mathematics lesson, thinking about how two numbers are the same or different from each other, or in RE teaching how the practices in one religion are the same or different from those in another. Such elaborative approaches allow children to activate prior knowledge and create more complex, integrated (and therefore better learned) memories (Kirschner and Hendrick, 2020).

A final point about this aspect of learning is that children can find processing difficult at different stages of learning: *input* (processing incoming information); *cognition* (working with the information that is being presented); and *output* (demonstrating what has been learnt, which in the classroom is usually done verbally or in written tasks). Some learning strategies are applicable to all three, and some relate to one or two of these.

TABLE 6.1.3 Adaptive teaching strategies to support processing

Learning strategy	Understanding the approach
Lengthen the 'think' element of think-pair-share.	Learners may need more time to make connections between information and prior knowledge (*input and cognition*). They may also need more time to structure ideas before answering questions or talking in pairs or groups (*output*).
Present information in small chunks.	Chunking helps children to find connections because the amount of information is not overwhelming and can be fully processed (*input and cognition*).
Use colours and visual prompts to provide additional semantic information. For example, present odd and even numbers in two different colours on a number line or connected vocabulary on the same-coloured section of a display/table prompt.	Colour, or other visual prompts, can help with the meaning extracted from information. In the examples given, colour becomes another way of connecting information and meaning (*cognition and output*).
Use mind mapping and mnemonics to make connections with prior learning.	Mnemonics aid processing because associations are made to more established, meaningful information. They can also help organise thinking or information that might appear abstract (*cognition*).
Use scaffolds for writing and talking and display these so that they are easily accessible for all pupils.	Provide support for *output* in the same way that input is often scaffolded. For example, sentence stems can help activate meaning and support idea sharing.

Social

> **Case study 4**
>
> Shia is lively and charismatic with plenty of ideas and a keen sense of right and wrong. They will defend others when they perceive any form of injustice. Sometimes they can struggle to manage their emotions and they seem to get frustrated easily. They seem not always to recognise their own positive attributes and can need considerable praise and encouragement to keep going if a task is challenging.

Social and emotional learning (SEL) refers to the development of a range of key skills: building relationships, making decisions, identifying goals, empathising and managing emotions (EEF, 2019). SEL promotes the development of executive functions (attentional and cognitive flexibility, working memory and inhibitory control) which allow an individual to plan and organise, to manage and to regulate emotions and behaviours; in short, their readiness to learn (Whitebread et al., 2019). It is notable that children from more disadvantaged backgrounds have poorer social and emotional skills than their peers from more socially advantaged backgrounds (Goodman et al., 2015), which may consequently make learning harder.

Effective teachers promote and explicitly teach SEL skills to create an environment which supports pupils to access learning. This includes both the physical experience of learning - the place that learning happens (see sections on attention and processing) - and the emotional context, such as the learner's mood and sense of security (Woolfolk, Hughes and Walkup, 2013). Teachers have a crucial role in establishing security by ensuring that events in the school day are predictable and well-established to support engagement with the core purpose of learning. Kern and Clemens (2007: 67) identified that 'When students can predict the events throughout their school day, they are more likely to be engaged'. By establishing predictable routines, and for some children exploring what might happen if there are changes (through, for example, social stories), teachers free up children's processing for learning rather than trying to second-guess systems, expectations and routines.

TABLE 6.1.4 Adaptive teaching strategies to support social and emotional aspects of learning

Learning strategy	Understanding the approach
Use visual timetables. Ensure that images are of high quality and actively use the timetable, e.g. removing completed sessions. Involve children in putting the timetable up. (Some children will additionally need a short-term version of the visual timetable with a 'now and next' board.)	Predictability ensures that children feel safe and that their attention, memory and processes can be directed towards learning rather than working out the organisation of the school day.
Help children to practise planning, using mind maps or coloured stickers to set out key tasks. Access to building or craft activities can also help children learn to plan.	Supports the development of executive functions which inform a range of learning skills.
Use timers for activities and give children control of these. The autonomy reduces anxiety as well as helping keep track of time to meet goals.	Managing goals supports the development of self-regulation.

(Continued)

TABLE 6.1.4 (Continued)

Learning strategy	Understanding the approach
Teach children both to express emotions (e.g. emotion thermometers, circle time, worry boxes) and manage emotions (e.g. the 5,4,3,2,1 grounding activity where children identify five things they can see, four they can hear, etc.)	Supports children's self-awareness (the recognition of emotion and thought) which can reduce some difficulties in social functioning and 'externalising' feelings through, for example, aggression. It can also promote a child's awareness of their strengths, increasing the sense of self-efficacy.
Be a clear, consistent and positive presence.	It is imperative to model the social and emotional skills that children should adopt. Relentless, over-the-top enthusiasm can cause over-arousal in some children and is hard to sustain, which can produce emotional inconsistency in teachers.

Task 6.1.2 Final reflection task

Review the strategies in Tables 6.1.1–6.1.4. Notice how many of them would work to support *more than one* core process of learning. Why might these approaches be especially helpful to include in your teaching repertoire early on in your career?

Are there other strategies you have seen in action you would add to these lists?

SUMMARY

Adaptive teaching is a more recent term in teaching which addresses the requirement that teachers meet the needs of all learners, especially when classrooms are more complex and diverse than ever before. Adaptive teaching will be supportive for all children at some points in their learning and could be especially powerful for groups of pupils who are known to be vulnerable to underachievement, a key focus for individual teachers and the education system. Adaptive teaching moves away from finding differences between children based on labelling by ability or diagnosis and towards a closer analysis of how children learn, and which aspects of the learning process might be more difficult. Thinking about attention, memory, processing and social and emotional aspects of learning is a good starting point as these are central to learning. When adaptive practice sits at the heart of teaching, as our first focus, then children are likely to experience higher quality learning which will impact their outcomes.

NOTE

My thanks to Dr. Helen Fisher whose knowledge, insight and guidance has significantly shaped this unit.

ANNOTATED FURTHER READING

Westwood, P. (2018) *Inclusive and Adaptive Teaching: Meeting the Challenge of Diversity in the Classroom*, Routledge: Oxon.
> This book covers aspects of diversity and adaptive teaching in more detail than is possible in a single unit. It draws together concepts of adaptive teaching and inclusion and provides examples of good practice.

Education Endowment Foundation (EEF). (2020) *Special Educational Needs in Mainstream Schools*. Retrieved from: https://d2tic4wvo1iusb.cloudfront.net/production/eef-guidance-reports/send/EEF_Special_Educational_Needs_in_Mainstream_Schools_Guidance_Report.pdf?v=1701702020 (accessed 1 December 2023).
> This key summary of research aligns effectively with discussions of adaptive teaching, looking particularly at how pupils with SEND may be supported through mainstream classroom practice. It also provides useful guidance about when and how to use additional interventions and maximise the impact of additional adults involved in children's learning.

Ellis, P., Kirby, A. and Osborne, A. (2023) *Neurodiversity and Education*, UK: Corwin.
> Adaptive teaching allows us to think differently about practice – moving away from seeking differences and instead focussing on core elements of learning. The concept of neurodiversity is an extremely useful piece of this approach to practice, focussing less on labels for children and instead on understanding the strengths and overlapping challenges that pupils experience.

FURTHER READING TO SUPPORT M-LEVEL STUDY

Webster, R. (2022) *The Inclusion Illusion*, London: UCL Press. Retrieved from: www.uclpress.co.uk/products/152465 (accessed 1 December 2023).
> This text explores the structural challenges of inclusion for pupils with the highest level of need and the experiences of these children in mainstream settings. It provokes questions which promote deep thinking about adaptive teaching.

Francis, B., Taylor, B. and Tereshchenko, A. (2019) *Reassessing 'Ability' Grouping: Improving Practice for Equity and Attainment*, Oxon: Routledge.
> A critical perspective on the use of attainment grouping for pupils. Whilst the research is focussed on secondary schools, the conclusions and guidance for making effective use of grouping is equally relevant to primary settings.

RELEVANT WEBSITES

National Association for Special Educational Needs (NASEN): https://nasen.org.uk/
> Free to join, NASEN provides access to guidance and advice and training, as well as the NASEN teachers' handbook, which has subject-specific suggestions for classroom practice. It also provides links to SEND-specific sites (such as the National Autistic Society) and the resources they produce which align with the core areas of need outlined in this chapter.

The Bell Foundation: www.bell-foundation.org.uk/teaching-resources/
> The Bell Foundation seeks to break down language barriers in schools and support multilingual learners to fulfil their academic potential. The excellent collection of teaching resources is multi-purpose, supporting all aspects of classroom practice within the adaptive teaching framework.

REFERENCES

Byrne, S., Sledge, H., Franklin, R., Boland, F., Murray, D. M. and Hourihane, J. (2023) 'Social communication skill attainment in babies born during the COVID-19 pandemic: a birth cohort study', *Archives of Disease in Childhood*, 108(1): 20–24.

Commodari, E. (2017) 'Novice readers: The role of focused, selective, distributed and alternating attention at the first year of the academic curriculum', *i-Perception*, 8(4): 2041669517718557. https://doi:10.1177/2041669517718557

Council for Curriculum Examinations and Assessment (CCEA). (n.d.) *Inclusion*, Belfast: CCEA. Retrieved from: https://ccea.org.uk/sen-inclusion/inclusion-general-strategies/inclusion

Craik, F. I. and Lockhart, R. S. (1972) 'Levels of processing: A framework for memory research', *Journal of Verbal Learning and Verbal Behavior*, 11(6): 671–684.

Department for Education (DfE). (2011) *Teachers' Standards*. Last updated 2021. Retrieved from: www.gov.uk/government/publications/teachers-standards (accessed 9 February 2025).

Department for Education (DfE) (2024a) *Initial Teacher Training and Early Career Framework*. Retrieved from: https://www.gov.uk/government/publications/initial-teacher-training-and-early-career-framework (accessed 9 February 2025).

Department for Education (DfE). (2024b) *Education, Health and Care Plans*. Retrieved from: https://explore-education-statistics.service.gov.uk/find-statistics/education-health-and-care-plans (accessed 9 February 2025).

Department for Education (DfE). (2024c) *Special Educational Needs in England*. Retrieved from: https://explore-education-statistics.service.gov.uk/find-statistics/special-educational-needs-in-england (accessed 9 February 2025).

Department for Education (DfE). (2024d) *Key Stage 2 Attainment*. Retrieved from: https://explore-education-statistics.service.gov.uk/find-statistics/key-stage-2-attainment (accessed 9 February 2025).

Department for Education (DfE). (2024e) *Schools, Pupils and Their Characteristics*. Retrieved from: https://explore-education-statistics.service.gov.uk/find-statistics/school-pupils-and-their-characteristics (accessed 9 February 2025).

Department for Education (DfE) and Department of Health and Social Care (DHSC). (2014) *Special Educational Needs and Disability Code of Practice: 0–25 Years*. Last updated 2024. Retrieved from: www.gov.uk/government/publications/send-code-of-practice-0-to-25 (accessed 9 February 2025).

Eaton, J. (2022) *EEF Blog: Moving From Differentiation to Adaptive Teaching*. Retrieved from: https://educationendowmentfoundation.org.uk/news/moving-from-differentiation-to-adaptive-teaching (accessed 1 December 2023).

Education Endowment Foundation (EEF). (2019) *Improving Social and Emotional Learning in the Primary School*. Retrieved from: https://educationendowmentfoundation.org.uk/education-evidence/guidance-reports/primary-sel (accessed 1 December 2023).

Education Endowment Foundation (EEF). (2020) *Special Educational Needs in Mainstream Schools*. Retrieved from: https://educationendowmentfoundation.org.uk/education-evidence/guidance-reports/send (accessed 1 December 2023).

Fray, L. and Gore, J. (2018) 'Why people choose teaching: A scoping review of empirical studies, 2007–2016', *Teaching and Teacher Education*, 75: 153–163. https://doi.org/10.1016/j.tate.2018.06.009

General Teaching Council for Scotland. (2021a) *The Standard for Provisional Registration: Mandatory Requirements for Registration with the General Teaching Council for Scotland*. Retrieved from: https://assets-global.website-files.com/653fc30601a80aefd5668009/65de10ce9d1436edbc53b787_GTCS_The%20Standard%20for%20Provisional%20Registration.pdf

General Teaching Council for Scotland. (2021b) *The Standard for Full Registration: Mandatory Requirements for Registration with the General Teaching Council for Scotland*. Retrieved from: https://cdn.prod.website-files.com/653fc30601a80aefd5668009/65de1052167fdf3d4d70eeda_GTCS_The%20Standard%20for%20Full%20Registration.pdf

Goodman, A., Joshi, H., Nasim, B. and Tyler, C. (2015) *Social and Emotional Skills in Childhood and Their Long-term Effects on Adult Life*. Retrieved from: www.eif.org.uk/report/social-and-emotional-skills-in-childhood-and-their-long-term-effects-on-adult-life (accessed 1 December 2023).

Goswami, U. (2011) 'What cognitive neuroscience really tells educators about learning and development', in J. Moyles, J. Payler and J. Georgeson (eds) *Beginning Teaching, Beginning Learning: In Early Years and Primary Education*, UK: McGraw-Hill Education, pp. 18-29.

Hunt, E. (2023) *EPI Annual Report 2023*. Retrieved from: https://epi.org.uk/publications-and-research/annual-report-2023/ (accessed 1 December 2023).

Immordino-Yang, M. H. (2015) *Emotions, Learning, and the Brain: Exploring the Educational Implications of Affective Neuroscience (the Norton Series on the Social Neuroscience of Education)*, New York: WW Norton & Company.

Kirschner, P. and Hendrick, C. (2020) *How Learning Happens: Seminal Works in Educational Psychology and What They Mean in Practice*. Oxon: Routledge.

Kern, L. and Clemens, N. H. (2007) 'Antecedent strategies to promote appropriate classroom behavior', *Psychology in the Schools*, 44: 65-75. https://doi.org/10.1002/pits.20206

McInerney, D. and Putwain, D. (2016) *Developmental and Educational Psychology for Teachers: An Applied Approach*, Oxon: Taylor & Francis.

Mould, K. (2021) *EEF Blog: Assess, Adjust, Adapt – What Does Adaptive Teaching Mean to You?* Retrieved from: https://educationendowmentfoundation.org.uk/news/eef-blog-assess-adjust-adapt-what-does-adaptive-teaching-mean-to-you (accessed 1 December 2023).

National Association for Special Educational Needs (NASEN). (2020) *Teacher Handbook: SEND*. Retrieved from: https://nasen.org.uk/news/teacher-handbook-launched (accessed 1 December 2023).

Ofsted. (2019) *Education Inspection Framework 2019: Inspecting the Substance of Education*. Retrieved from: www.gov.uk/government/consultations/education-inspection-framework-2019-inspecting-the-substance-of-education/education-inspection-framework-2019-inspecting-the-substance-of-education (accessed 1 December 2023).

Quigley, A. (2023) 'Differentiation is dead, long live adaptive teaching', *TES* (21 February). Retrieved from: www.tes.com/magazine/teaching-learning/general/adaptive-teaching-vs-differentiation-inclusive-teaching (accessed 1 December 2023).

Strand, S. and Lindorff, A. (2020) *English as an Additional Language: Proficiency in English, Educational Achievement and Rate of Progression in English Language Learning*. Retrieved from: www.bell-foundation.org.uk/eal-programme/research/english-as-an-additional-language-proficiency-in-english-educational-achievement-and-rate-of-progression-in-english-language-learning/ (accessed 1 December 2023).

Sweller, J. (1988) 'Cognitive load during problem solving: Effects on learning', *Cognitive Science*, 12(2): 257-285.

Welsh Government. (2023) *Designing Your Curriculum: Developing a Vision for Curriculum Design*. Retrieved from: https://hwb.gov.wales/curriculum-for-wales/designing-your-curriculum/enabling-learning/ (accessed 26 April 2024).

Whitebread, D., Grau, V., Kumpulainen, K., McClelland, M., Perry, N. and Pino-Pasternak, D. (2019) *The SAGE Handbook of Developmental Psychology and Early Childhood Education*, London: SAGE Publications Ltd. https://doi.org/10.4135/9781526470393

Woolfolk, A. E., Hughes, M. and Walkup, V. (2013) *Psychology in Education*, 2nd edn, Pearson Education.

UNIT 6.2

SPECIAL EDUCATIONAL NEEDS AND INCLUSION

Noel Purdy and Adam Boddison

INTRODUCTION

> Teachers are responsible and accountable for the progress and development of the pupils in their class, including where pupils access support from teaching assistants or specialist staff ... Where a pupil is identified as having SEN, schools should take action to remove barriers to learning and put effective special educational provision in place.
>
> (Department for Education [DfE] and Department of Health [DoH], 2015: sections 6.36, 6.44)

It is clear from many influential reports over recent years that much more is now expected of mainstream teachers than in the past in relation to meeting the needs of children and young people with special educational needs (SEN). For instance, the Bercow Report (Department for Children, Schools and Families [DCSF], 2008) into children with speech, language and communication needs; the Lamb Inquiry into parental confidence and SEN (DCSF, 2009) and the Cambridge Primary Review (2010) all made recommendations that teachers should be better equipped to meet the needs of pupils with a wide range of different SEN. This sentiment was echoed more recently in the SEND (special educational needs and disabilities) and Alternative Provision Green Paper, which champions the role of teacher development to improve mainstream provision for children with SEN (DfE, 2022). The need for quality preparation for teachers is clear, given that census data for 2022-23 show that more than 17 per cent of pupils across all schools in England have SEN, up from 14 per cent in 2015-16, with 57 per cent of children with an Education, Health and Care Plan (EHCP) educated in state-funded mainstream settings (DfE, 2013).

OBJECTIVES

By the end of this unit, you should have:

- an awareness of the policy context of SEN over recent years across the UK;
- an understanding of current standards and expectations for primary teachers in relation to SEN;
- an understanding of the main principles involved in seeking to meet the needs of children with SEN in primary schools.

It is far beyond the scope of this unit to provide detailed practical guidance in relation to meeting the needs of children with specific SEN; however, student teachers are advised to follow the general principles at the end of the unit and to consult the texts suggested in the annotated further reading section.

THE DEVELOPMENT OF UK POLICY IN RELATION TO SEN

Perhaps the most significant report to date in relation to SEN in the UK was the *Report of the Committee of Enquiry into the Education of Handicapped Children and Young People* (Department of Education and Science [DES], 1978), commonly referred to as *The Warnock Report*, after the chair of the committee, Professor Mary Warnock. This influential report led to legislation in the 1981 Education Act in England and led to the reconceptualisation of special education right across the UK by advocating a focus by teachers on addressing children's individual 'special educational needs' as a means to giving them access to the curriculum, rather than categorising their 'handicap' or disability.

The Warnock Report not only coined the term 'special educational needs', but is important for a number of other reasons: it rejected once and for all the notion that some children with the most severe disabilities are 'ineducable' and asserted that 'education, as we conceive it, is a good, and specifically a human good, to which all human beings are entitled' (section 1.7); it suggested that 'up to one in five' (section 3.3) children will require a form of special educational provision at some stage during their school careers, thus broadening the term and removing the notion of a fixed or irreversible label; it endorsed the policy of 'integration' (now more commonly referred to as the 'inclusion') of children with SEN into mainstream schools; it introduced the principle that parents should be engaged in meaningful dialogue as 'equal partners' in the education of their children; and it safeguarded educational provision for the small minority of children with more severe or complex needs by laying an obligation on local authorities to make special educational provision for any child judged to be in need of such provision.

There have been many subsequent policy developments, but perhaps the most significant was the introduction of the National Curriculum (Her Majesty's Stationary Office [HMSO], 1988), which established the notion that all children were entitled to have access to the same curriculum. However, this also marked the beginning of the standards and performance agendas in schools, which are often perceived to have had a negative impact on the inclusion of children with SEN.

Although significant SEN policy reforms were introduced in 2014-15 (HMSO, 2014; DfE and DoH, 2015) with the aim of empowering families and providing greater protections for children with SEN, these are generally deemed to have been unsuccessful (Ofsted, 2021). Consequently, further significant policy reform is planned to transform a 'vicious cycle of late intervention, low confidence and inefficient resource allocation' into a financially sustainable system that delivers effective provision for children with SEN (DfE, 2022).

In Wales ...

Effective environments should celebrate and value diversity and demonstrate inclusivity. They should promote a sense of belonging so all learners feel valued and represented.

The rate of acquisition of skills and knowledge will differ for all learners, as well as differing across an individual learner's progress. Practitioners should use observation and knowledge of child development to plan learning experiences that support and challenge all learners.

(Welsh Government, 2023)

Schools should be aware of the needs and circumstances of all their learners when designing their own curriculum, considering equity of opportunity when putting into place support and interventions or making reasonable adjustments … to be inclusive of all learners, including those with additional learning needs (ALN) … the pace at which learners progress along the continuum may differ – allowing for a diversion, repetition and reflection as each learner's thinking, knowledge and skills develop over time. Schools and practitioners have discretion when planning for progression, giving due regard to all learners in their settings/schools.

Irrespective of the national approach to ALN (Additional Learning Needs) policy or the profile of needs in the classroom, it is hard to argue against the benefits of knowing individual children better and putting personalised provision in place. As part of the suite of learning resources for those supporting children with ALN, the Welsh Government has published a practical guide containing person-centred thinking tools.

(Welsh Government, 2019)

> **Task 6.2.1 'Breaking down' special educational needs**
>
> Professor Mary Warnock (2005) argued that her own concept of SEN must be 'broken down' and that we must abandon the common practice of referring to children with SEN (or 'SEN pupils') as one homogeneous group. Think of three pupils you have come across who have SEN. To what extent are their needs and their barriers to learning the same/different? Why might a single label of SEN be unhelpful in planning to meet the needs of these children?

LEGAL DEFINITION OF SEN

The term 'special educational needs' was first defined in the Education Act 1981 (HMSO, 1981) and more recently in the Education Act 1996 (HMSO, 1996), and the Children and Families Act 2014 (HMSO, 2014):

When a child or young person has special educational needs

1. A child or young person has special educational needs if he or she has a learning difficulty or disability which calls for special educational provision to be made for him or her.
2. A child of compulsory school age or a young person has a learning difficulty or disability if he or she –
    a. has a significantly greater difficulty in learning than the majority of others of the same age, or
    b. has a disability which prevents or hinders him or her from making use of facilities of a kind generally provided for others of the same age in mainstream schools or mainstream post-16 institutions.

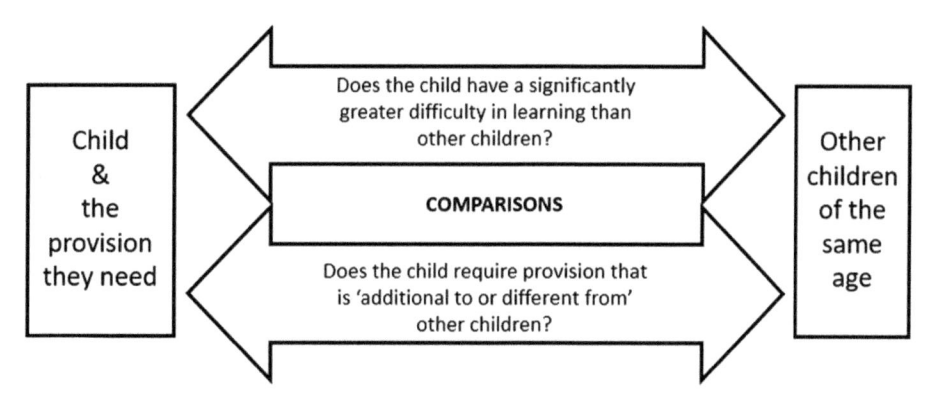

FIGURE 6.2.1 Comparisons informing the identification of SEND
Source: Boddison (2020: 6)

3 A child under compulsory school age has a learning difficulty or disability if he or she is likely to be within subsection (2) when of compulsory school age (or would be likely, if no special educational provision were made).
4 A child or young person does not have a learning difficulty or disability solely because the language (or form of language) in which he or she is or will be taught is different from a language (or form of language) which is or has been spoken at home.

(HMSO, 2014: 20)

As Figure 6.2.1 shows, the determination about whether or not a child or young person has SEND is relative as well as being dependent on the level of ordinarily-available provision. In practice, this means that for two children with similar profiles of needs attending different schools, one might be deemed to have SEND and the other not.

The broader term of 'additional support needs' (ASN) was introduced in Scotland (Scottish Government, 2004) and this refers to any child or young person who requires additional short- or long-term support to benefit from their school education. This definition encompasses any factor that might relate to social, emotional, cognitive, linguistic, health, disability or family and care circumstances.

The rights of children with ASN are enshrined in law through the Education Scotland 2004 Act, which is commonly referred to as the Additional Support for Learning Act. In 2009, the Act was amended to ensure that additional support could be drawn from multiple agencies including education, health, social care and the voluntary sector (Scottish Government, 2009). The Act was updated again in 2016 with the aim of extending certain rights already in place for those aged 16 to 18 and still in school children as young as 12. This includes the right to ask for an assessment of additional support needs, making placement requests for special schools and requesting or reviewing a Coordinated Support Plan (CSP), which is the equivalent of an EHCP in England (Scottish Government, 2016). Despite these apparent improvements in legislation in Scotland, there remains some doubt about whether they deliver on their intent in a way that is compliant with human rights expectations (Equality and Human Rights Commission [EHRC], 2016).

THE INCLUSION DEBATE

There has been considerable focus in recent years on *where* children with SEN should be taught, whether wholly in mainstream classes or special schools or in dual placements where children can be integrated at certain times or for certain subjects, according to their individual needs. The polarity of opinion on this subject is often very evident. Some would argue (for instance, Rustemier, 2002) that although the UK has signed up to pro-inclusion international agreements, such as the *United Nations Convention on the Rights of the Child* (United Nations, 1989), the *Salamanca Statement* (United Nations Educational, Scientific and Cultural Organization [UNESCO], 1994) and the *United Nations Convention on the Rights of Persons with Disabilities* (United Nations, 2006), financial and legislative support for separate special schooling continues as before. Others, including Mary Warnock herself, would contend that inclusion has not always worked and indeed can, at times, be experienced as a 'painful kind of exclusion' for some children (Warnock, 2005: 39), and that there remains a need for separate schooling for children with the most severe and complex needs.

Another perspective has proposed that the focus should rest, not on *where* children with SEN are taught, but rather on *how* they are taught. Frederickson and Cline (2009: 8), for instance, argue that the concept of SEN must be seen as 'the outcome of an interaction between the individual characteristics of learners and the educational environments in which they are learning', emphasising the degree to which the child has responded to their current learning environment and suggesting how the environment might be adapted to meet those learning needs more effectively. This is confirmed by Ofsted's survey report, *The Special Educational Needs and Disability Review* (Ofsted, 2010), which found that the most significant factor in promoting the best outcomes for pupils with learning difficulties and disabilities was not the *type* but the *quality* of provision. The review found, further, that pupil progress depended less on whether the placement was in a mainstream or special school or a combination of both, and more on the availability of high-quality teaching and learning, close monitoring of pupil progress and regular evaluation of the effectiveness of interventions.

The experiences of James (next) illustrate the difference that a supportive placement context can make to successful inclusion:

> James is 8 and attends a mainstream primary school. He has hemiplegia (partial paralysis of one side of his body) and moderate learning difficulties. Two years ago his parents felt that they had no choice but to remove him from his previous school due to bullying by other pupils who mocked his disability which they did not understand ('You're just weird', 'You shouldn't be in this school'), resulting in severe anxiety and aggressive behaviour by James both at school and at home. In his new school James has made a fresh start with a very capable teacher, Mrs Thompson, who met James and his parents several times before the new school year, and has worked hard to differentiate her teaching, allowing James to be much more fully integrated into all classroom lessons, including physical education. With his and his parents' permission, Mrs Thompson explained James' impairment to the other pupils in the class at the start of the year, which helped them to understand his disability and behaviours and has also led to much greater acceptance of him. Just a few weeks ago an increasingly confident and happy James volunteered to create and deliver a presentation to the rest of the class on hemiplegia.

Tutt (2016) has argued that inclusion should be seen as a *process* by which children can be properly included in education to prepare them for life after school. She advocates a 'continuum of provision' so that all children can be included 'in a meaningful sense' in education, irrespective of the setting. For Tutt, 'equality is not about giving everyone the same experiences, but about recognising that, while everyone is different, they should be equally valued and educated in an environment where they feel they belong' (p. 10).

Over time, Ofsted have attempted to regulate and monitor the effectiveness of SEND and inclusion in schools. For example, the notion that for a school to be rated as outstanding, it must be outstanding for all pupils, including those with SEND (Whittaker, 2018). In 2025, Ofsted set out its ambition to explicitly grade schools' effectiveness on inclusion in an open consultation on proposed reforms to its inspection framework (Ofsted, 2025).

THE *CODE OF PRACTICE*

Needless to say, in working with children with SEN, teachers are often more interested in practical guidance rather than legal definitions. In this regard, students in England are referred to the most recent *Code of Practice* (DfE and DoH, 2015), which was a direct outcome of the Children and Families Act 2014. The *Code of Practice* sets out practical advice to local authorities, early years settings, schools and post-16 providers on how best to carry out their statutory duties in relation to provision for children with SEN, through the graduated approach of 'assess, plan, do and review' (DfE and DoH, 2015: 100-102). Although the *Code* itself is not a piece of legislation, all relevant education and health settings 'must have regard to [it]' and 'cannot ignore it' (DfE and DoH, 2015: 12). The *Code of Practice* is underpinned by a set of general principles (DfE and DoH, 2015: 19) that are designed to support:

- the participation of children, their parents and young people in decision-making;
- the early identification of children and young people's needs and early intervention to support them;
- greater choice and control for young people and parents over support;
- collaboration between education, health and social care services to provide support;
- high-quality provision to meet the needs of children and young people with SEN;
- a focus on inclusive practice and removing barriers to learning;
- successful preparation for adulthood, including independent living and employment.

In the spirit of *The Warnock Report*'s recommendations, the *Code of Practice* acknowledges that, 'the purpose of identification is to work out what action a school needs to take, not to fit a pupil into a category' (DfE and DoH, 2015: 97). The spirit of the *Code of Practice* is clear that each child is unique, and that there is a wide spectrum of needs that are often interrelated. Nonetheless, the *Code of Practice* does indicate that children will have needs and requirements that may fall into at least one of four broad areas (see sections 6.28-6.35):

- communication and interaction;
- cognition and learning;
- social, emotional and mental health;
- sensory and/or physical needs.

In Scotland …

Teachers are encouraged to think about ways in which children feel included by interactions, experiences, and spaces. Children's rights as human rights are enshrined in law.

Sources: The Stationery Office (TSO; 2024); GTC Scotland (2022); Scottish Government (2017, 2020, 2024a, 2024b)

In Northern Ireland …

Inclusive education is more than a concern about any one group of pupils. It is about providing opportunities for all children and young people in the community to learn together and where schools nurture learners by providing inclusive systems which are open, participatory and flexible. Inclusive systems work to remove barriers to learning and address issues that relate to all individuals who are vulnerable to exclusion from education.

(Council for Curriculum Examinations and Assessment [CCEA], n.d.)

CHANGING POLICY AND SUPPORT IN MAINSTREAM PRIMARY SCHOOLS

Since January 2015, there have been two levels of SEN in England, SEN Support and EHCPs, each of which will now be considered in turn.

SEN support

SEN support refers to a level of support that can be met from within a school's existing resources. For each individual pupil, the school is required to keep a record of what SEN they have identified, the provision to be put in place to meet those needs and the expected outcomes as a result of the provision. Although the overall responsibility for SEN provision lies with the Special Educational Needs Co-ordinator (SENCO; called the Additional Learning Needs Co-ordinator in Wales), the *Code of Practice* is clear that the main class teacher is responsible for all the pupils they teach, including those with SEN:

> The class or subject teacher should remain responsible for working with the child on a daily basis. Where the interventions involve group or one-to-one teaching away from the main class or subject teacher, they should still retain responsibility for the pupil. They should work closely with any teaching assistants or specialist staff involved, to plan and assess the impact of support and interventions and how they can be linked to classroom teaching.
>
> (DfE and DoH, 2015: section 6.52)

Census data for 2022-23 show that almost 1.1 million pupils in England (12.9 per cent of the total pupil population) have been identified as requiring provision at the level of SEN support to meet their needs (DfE, 2023). Provision at the SEN support level might typically include a personalised learning programme, additional help from a teacher or a teaching assistant or targeted educational interventions. At the heart of this level of provision is the principle that high-quality teaching and differentiation can remove barriers to learning so that children can 'achieve the best possible educational and other outcomes' (DfE and DoH, 2015: section 19d). Schools are required by the *Code of Practice* to publish a SEN Information Report on their website, which details their arrangements for providing a 'graduated approach to children's SEN' (DfE and DoH, 2015: 69). This includes how schools will use the cyclic process of 'assess, plan, do, review' to meet the needs of children identified as needing SEN support.

EHCPs

If a school does not have the expertise or resources to meet the needs of a particular child, then an Education, Health and Care (EHC) needs assessment is undertaken by the local authority, as shown in Figure 6.2.2.

The assessment should provide a holistic picture of the needs of the child and contains information such as (DfE and DoH, 2015: 161-162):

- the views, interests and aspirations of the child and their parents;
- the child's educational, health and social care needs that relate to their SEN;
- the outcomes sought for the child (including outcomes for life);
- the special educational provision required by the child.

EHC needs assessment process

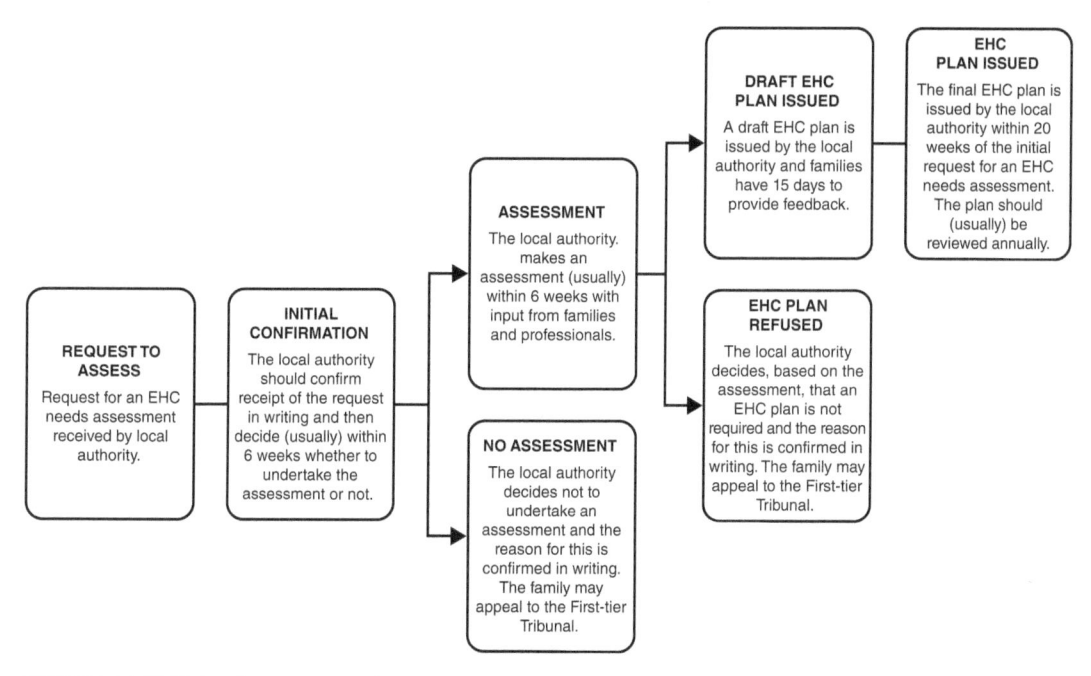

REQUEST TO ASSESS
Request for an EHC needs assessment received by local authority.

INITIAL CONFIRMATION
The local authority should confirm receipt of the request in writing and then decide (usually) within 6 weeks whether to undertake the assessment or not.

ASSESSMENT
The local authority makes an assessment (usually) within 6 weeks with input from families and professionals.

NO ASSESSMENT
The local authority decides not to undertake an assessment and the reason for this is confirmed in writing. The family may appeal to the First-tier Tribunal.

DRAFT EHC PLAN ISSUED
A draft EHC plan is issued by the local authority and families have 15 days to provide feedback.

EHC PLAN REFUSED
The local authority decides, based on the assessment, that an EHC plan is not required and the reason for this is confirmed in writing. The family may appeal to the First-tier Tribunal.

EHC PLAN ISSUED
The final EHC plan is issued by the local authority within 20 weeks of the initial request for an EHC needs assessment. The plan should (usually) be reviewed annually.

FIGURE 6.2.2 EHC needs assessment process
Source: Boddison (2020:21)

At the heart of this process are the wishes of the child and their parents, and both should be considered as equal partners in determining the provision required to meet the SEN. Once an EHCP is in place, the SENCO works with all of those organisations named to ensure that the provision detailed is delivered. EHCPs must be reviewed at least annually, and more regularly (every 3–6 months) for children under 5 years old. It should be made clear that, regardless of the complexity of the needs or the number of external agencies involved, the accountability for the educational progress and outcomes of the child remains firmly with the classroom teacher.

Census data for 2022–23 show that more than 360,000 pupils in England (4.2 per cent of the total pupil population) have been identified as requiring provision at the level of an EHCP to meet their needs (DfE, 2013).

In Scotland ...

Where lead professionals are working with children or young people with additional support needs then, in addition to the points set out below, they also have a responsibility to be familiar with the Act and, in particular, to ensure that parents and young people themselves are aware of their rights when they have concerns or disagreements about the provisions being made under the Act.

(Scottish Government, 2017: 30)

TEACHERS' STANDARDS

The preamble of the current Teachers' Standards for England (DfE, 2011) makes it clear that teachers must 'make the education of their pupils their first concern'. Part One comprises the Standards for Teaching, which are set out under eight main objectives, each of which has several elements:

A teacher must:

1. set high expectations that inspire, motivate and challenge pupils;
2. promote good progress and outcomes by pupils;
3. demonstrate good subject and curriculum knowledge;
4. plan and teach well-structured lessons;
5. adapt teaching to respond to the strengths and needs of all pupils;
6. make accurate and productive use of assessment;
7. manage behaviour effectively to ensure a good and safe learning environment;
8. fulfil wider professional responsibilities.

Although *all* of these standards are evidently relevant to the teaching of children with SEN, the fifth standard is of particular importance. Under this standard, in adapting their teaching to respond to the strengths and needs of all pupils, teachers must:

- know when and how to differentiate appropriately, using approaches that enable pupils to be taught effectively;
- have a secure understanding of how a range of factors can inhibit pupils' ability to learn, and how best to overcome these;
- demonstrate an awareness of the physical, social and intellectual development of children, and know how to adapt teaching to support pupils' education at different stages of development;
- have a clear understanding of the needs of all pupils, including those with special educational needs; those of high ability; those with English as an additional language; those with disabilities; and be able to use and evaluate distinctive teaching approaches to engage and support them.

Part Two of the Standards relates to teachers' personal and professional conduct. Here, too, it is important that when working with children with SEN, teachers maintain high standards of ethics and behaviour by 'treating pupils with dignity, building relationships rooted in mutual respect' and 'having regard for the need to safeguard pupils' well-being' (DfE, 2011).

SENCO

The SENCO in a primary school has day-to-day responsibility for coordinating the specific SEN provision within a school. Although SENCO is the legal title, in recent years many alternative titles have emerged in England, such as director of inclusion, inclusion manager and head of learning support. In Wales, the title of ALNCO is used (additional learning needs coordinator), and in Northern Ireland, the role is to be renamed 'learning support coordinator'.

TEACHING ASSISTANTS

Student teachers also need to learn to manage teaching assistants (in NI, classroom/learning support assistants) effectively to support the learning of children with SEN. The role of teaching assistants has come under close scrutiny in recent years. In a primary phase-specific study of adult support for children with statements of SEN (for children with moderate learning difficulties and behavioural, emotional and social difficulties), Webster and Blatchford (2013) found that the role of teaching assistants could actually create a barrier between the child receiving support and the person with lead responsibility for her or his learning, the class teacher. Unfortunately, research findings have been wilfully misinterpreted by some commentators, who argue that they point to the need for schools to stop employing teaching assistants (Robertson, 2013). In fact, as Russell, Webster and Blatchford (2012) are careful to note, the real challenge is for school leaders, SENCOs and teachers to examine how best they can optimise the skills of teaching assistants, with a clear focus on teaching.

PARENTS AND CARERS

Student teachers can sometimes feel daunted by the prospect of working 'in partnership' with parents/carers of children with SEN. This is not surprising, given that some parents/carers may, for a variety of reasons, have concerns about their child that might be expressed in terms of what can be perceived as blaming the teacher or school. Reading the *Lamb Inquiry* report (DCSF, 2009) or the *Too Little, Too Late* report (Purdy *et al.*, 2020) on parental experiences of the special educational system in England and Northern Ireland, respectively, helps to explain why some parents/carers can feel angry or upset about provision for their child, the lack of it or bureaucratic assessment procedures. It is also worth noting, however, that relatively straightforward approaches to honest communication can be used by teachers, SENCOs and head teachers to make a positive difference to the education of children with SEN, as Robertson (2010) and Laluvein (2010) make clear.

MEETING THE NEEDS OF CHILDREN WITH SEN: WHERE DO I BEGIN?

In Northern Ireland ...

Although it is not a teacher's duty to diagnose SEN, it is important that they know the fundamentals behind the disorder to offer the most effective differentiated teaching.

Source: Department of Education Northern Ireland (DENI, 2023)

Many trainee teachers express apprehension at the prospect of teaching children with so many different learning needs (Richards, 2010). However, in seeking to support a move from fear to confidence, the following additional advice is offered:

- Take advantage of the courses available during your training on the most common and challenging SEN (e.g. speech, language and communication difficulties; autism; dyslexia), and thus try to develop your understanding of the particular learning needs of different children with SEN.
- Consider the need to make adaptations to the learning environment, the task set and your teaching style, rather than focusing solely on the child's learning characteristics. The English *Code of Practice* stresses the importance of high-quality differentiated teaching as the first step in responding to pupils with SEN and adds that, 'Additional intervention and support cannot compensate for a lack of good quality teaching' (DfE and DoH, 2015: section 6.37).
- Be aware of the particular targets set in a child's support plan and plan your teaching to facilitate the meeting of those targets. This necessitates knowledge and understanding of the particular child, their needs and the barriers to their learning, as well as the particular targets themselves.
- Realise that you are not alone: ask for advice and support from more experienced teachers, and especially from the school SENCO.

- Always seek the support of the child's parents/carers as 'equal partners', as they can offer unrivalled insights into the child's needs and also help to reinforce at home the strategies you are implementing in class.
- Take every opportunity to develop your own skills and understanding through professional development courses and/or membership of professional organisations (e.g. nasen – the National Association for Special Educational Needs).
- Remember that each child with SEN is unique. It is crucial that you take time to get to know the strengths and needs of each individual child with SEN in your primary classroom, including an understanding of their lives outside school.

Task 6.2.2 What SEN knowledge do I need?

The Cambridge Primary Review (2010) concludes that expert teachers should possess knowledge of *children*, knowledge of *subject*, but also knowledge of children's *context* (recognising the importance of family and community). Think of two pupils with SEN. Explain the nature of the children's SEN, how the barriers to their learning depend on the curricular area in question (are the barriers different in mathematics, history, art and design?) and the extent of contact you or the school had with the pupils' families. If you have no knowledge of the children's context, how might you develop that in the future?

SUMMARY

In this unit, we have examined the current levels of SEN provision in schools and provided guidance on how planning should be used to support children with SEN in meeting learning targets. The policy context for SEN is changing rapidly, and in this unit we have considered the development of the concept of SEN, from its origins in *The Warnock Report* (DES, 1978) to the most recent policy changes across the four jurisdictions of the UK. Notwithstanding recent developments in SEN policy, we have concluded that nothing is more important than a teacher's willingness to engage with an individual child and to seek to meet their learning needs, while drawing on the support of parents, teachers and other professionals.

APPENDIX: ADDITIONAL MATERIAL ON REGIONAL VARIATIONS

Scotland

The Education (Additional Support for Learning) (Scotland) Act 2004 placed new duties on education authorities to provide for children with ASN, and this was most recently updated in 2016 along with a revised version of the *Supporting Children's Learning: Code of Practice* (Scottish Government, 2017). In some respects, the Scottish *Code* shares many similarities with the English *Code* – for example, a four-stage process of 'assessment, planning, action and review' and a focus on preparation for adulthood. However, there are some clear differences between the two *Codes*. The Scottish focus on additional learning support needs is much broader than special educational needs and includes additional groups of children such as highly able children, children being bullied and those with English as an additional language. This, in turn, means that the terminology is somewhat different, with 'Additional Support Needs Coordinator' being used instead of SENCO and 'Coordinated Support Plan' instead of EHC plan. The 2017 *Code of Practice* states that ASN occur 'where, for whatever reason, the child or young person is, or is likely to be, unable without the provision of additional support to benefit from school education' (Scottish Government, 2017: 17).

Wales

Until 2002, provision for additional learning needs (ALN) in Wales followed a very similar pattern to that in England. Following devolution, Wales published its own *SEN Code of Practice* alongside a report, *Special Educational Needs: A Mainstream Issue* (Audit Commission, 2002). The Additional Learning Needs and Education Tribunal (Wales) Bill was introduced to the National Assembly for Wales in December 2016. The Bill replaced the terms 'special educational needs' and learning difficulties and/or disabilities (LDD) with the term 'additional learning needs' (ALN) to encompass children and young people aged 0-25. The Bill replaced SEN statements with individual development plans (IDPs). IDPs place the emphasis on making provision that delivers tangible outcomes contributing to the fulfilment of the child/young person's potential. The Additional Learning Needs and Education Tribunal (Wales) Act came into force in 2018 creating a single statutory framework for ALN, expanding the remit of the SEN Tribunal to education more broadly (Welsh Government, 2018). Section 5(4)(a) of the 2018 Act required the Welsh Assembly to issue an ALN Code, which was published in 2021, setting out the responsibilities of public sector providers of ALN services and the rights of children and young people with ALN (Welsh Government, 2021).

Northern Ireland

A lengthy period of review of SEN in Northern Ireland began in August 2009, with the DE consultation on *The Way Forward for Special Educational Needs and Inclusion* (DENI, 2009), and led to the passing of new legislation by the Northern Ireland Assembly. While the Special Educational Needs and Disability (SEND) Act received Royal Assent in 2016, the full implementation of the new SEND framework has been hindered by the collapse of the Northern Ireland Executive and Assembly for two lengthy periods (2017-20 and 2022-24). Several highly critical reports have subsequently been published (e.g. Purdy *et al.*, 2020; Northern Ireland Audit Office [NIAO], 2020; DENI, 2023) and have led to the establishment of a SEND Transformation Programme within the Education Authority, and most recently, an End to End Review of SEND led by DENI. Following the latest restoration of the Northern Ireland Executive, Education Minister Paul Givan has published an ambitious Special Educational Needs (SEN) Reform Agenda and five-year Delivery Plan (DENI, 2025).

ANNOTATED FURTHER READING

Westwood, P. (2020) *Commonsense Methods for Children with Special Needs and Disabilities*, 8th edn, London: Routledge.
> This fully revised and updated publication offers sound practical advice on assessment and intervention in relation to a wide range of SEND, embedded within a clear theoretical context supported by current research and classroom practice. This most recent edition features new material on the importance of digital technology in supporting the learning of children with SEND.

Sobel, D. and Alston, S. (2021) *The Inclusive Classroom: A New Approach to Differentiation*, London: Bloomsbury.
> In this innovative guide, Daniel Sobel and Sara Alston help teachers understand the barriers to children's learning through an emphasis on the importance of meeting needs rather than focusing on diagnosis.

M FURTHER READING TO SUPPORT M-LEVEL STUDY

Dunsmuir, S., Frederickson, N. and Cline, T. (2024) *Special Educational Needs, Inclusion and Diversity*, 4th edn, Maidenhead: Open University Press.
> This new edition covers a broad range of themes, grounded in research evidence but illustrated by practical activities and case studies. This comprehensive text would make essential, insightful yet accessible reading for Master's students.

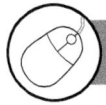

RELEVANT WEBSITES

2015 *Code of Practice*: www.gov.uk/government/publications/send-code-of-practice-0-to-25
> The 2015 *Code of Practice* provides statutory guidance for organisations in England that work with and support children and young people who have special educational needs or disabilities.

nasen: www.nasen.org.uk
> nasen is a leading national and international SEN membership organisation for education professionals, offering a wealth of publications, training and resources.

REFERENCES

Audit Commission. (2002) *Special Educational Needs: A Mainstream Issue*, London: Audit Commission.

Boddison, A. (2020) *The Governance Handbook for SEND and Inclusion: schools that work for all learners*, London: Routledge.

Cambridge Primary Review. (2010) *Children, Their World, Their Education – Final Report and Recommendations of the Cambridge Primary Review* (ed. R. Alexander), London: Routledge.

Council for Curriculum Examinations and Assessment (CCEA). (n.d.) *Special Educational Needs and Inclusion – Inclusion and General Strategies*, Belfast: CCEA. Retrieved from: https://ccea.org.uk/sen-inclusion/inclusion-general-strategies/inclusion

Department for Children, Schools and Families (DCSF). (2008) *The Bercow Report: A Review of Services for Children and Young People (0-19) with Speech, Language and Communication Needs*. Retrieved from: www.education.gov.uk/publications/eOrderingDownload/Bercow-Report.pdf (accessed 30 October 2017).

Department for Children, Schools and Families (DCSF). (2009) *Lamb Inquiry: Special educational needs and parental confidence*. Retrieved from: www.education.gov.uk/publications/standard/publicationDetail/Page1/DCSF-01143-2009 (accessed 30 October 2017).

Department for Education (DfE). (2011) *Teachers' Standards*. Last updated 2021. Retrieved from: www.gov.uk/government/publications/teachers-standards (accessed 9 January 2023).

Department for Education (DfE). (2022) *SEND Review: Right Support, Right Place, Right Time*. Last updated 2023. Retrieved from: https://assets.publishing.service.gov.uk/media/624178c68fa8f5277c0168e7/SEND_review_right_support_right_place_right_time_accessible.pdf (accessed 21 October 2023).

Department for Education (DfE). (2023) *Statistics: Special Educational Needs in England: January 2023*. Last updated 2024. Retrieved from www.gov.uk/government/collections/statistics-special-educational-needs-sen (accessed 9 February 2025).

Department for Education (DfE) and Department of Health (DoH). (2015) *Special Educational Needs and Disability Code of Practice: 0-25 Years*. Retrieved from: www.gov.uk/government/uploads/system/uploads/attachment_data/file/398815/SEND_Code_of_Practice_January_2015.pdf (accessed 30 October 2017).

Department of Education and Science (DES). (1978) *Report of the Committee of Enquiry into the Education of Handicapped Children and Young People (The Warnock Report)*, London: HMSO.

Department of Education for Northern Ireland (DENI). (2009) *The Way Forward for Special Educational Needs and Inclusion*. Retrieved from: www.education-ni.gov.uk/publications/every-school-good-school-way-forward-special-educational-needs-consultation-document (accessed 30 October 2017).

Department of Education Northern Ireland (DENI). (2023) *Independent Review of Special Educational Needs Services and Processes*, Bangor: DENI/IPSOS. Retrieved from: www.education-ni.gov.uk/sites/default/files/publications/education/SEN%20Review%20Report%20For%20Publication%202023%20May%202023.pdf

Department of Education Northern Ireland (DENI). (2025) *SEN Reform Agenda*. Retrieved from: https://www.education-ni.gov.uk/publications/sen-reform-agenda (accessed 16 March 2025).

Equality and Human Rights Commission (EHRC). (2016) *New Year, New Rights: Upcoming Changes to Additional Support for Learning Legislation and the Impact on Children's Rights*. Retrieved from: www.equalityhumanrights.com/sites/default/files/new_year_new_rights.pdf (accessed 17 October 2023).

Frederickson, N. and Cline, T. (2009) *Special Educational Needs, Inclusion and Diversity*, 2nd edn, Maidenhead, UK: Open University Press.

GTC Scotland. (2022) *National Framework for Inclusion*, 3rd edn. Retrieved from: www.gtcs.org.uk/knowledge-base/articles/national-framework-for-inclusion

Her Majesty's Stationary Office (HMSO). (1981) *Education Act*, London: HMSO.

Her Majesty's Stationary Office (HMSO). (1988) *Education Reform Act*, London: HMSO.

Her Majesty's Stationary Office (HMSO). (1996) *Education Act*, London: HMSO.

Her Majesty's Stationary Office (HMSO). (2014) *Children and Families Act*, London: HMSO.

Laluvein, J. (2010) 'Variations on a theme: Parents and teachers talking', *Support for Learning*, 25(4): 194-199.

Northern Ireland Audit Office (NIAO). (2020) *Impact Review of Special Educational Needs*, Belfast: NIAO. Retrieved from: www.niauditoffice.gov.uk/files/niauditoffice/media-files/242135%20NIAO%20Special%20Education%20Needs_Fnl%20Lw%20Rs%20%28complete%29.pdf

Ofsted. (2010) *The Special Educational Needs and Disability Review*. Retrieved from: www.gov.uk/government/uploads/system/uploads/attachment_data/file/413814/Special_education_needs_and_disability_review.pdf (accessed 30 October 2017).

Ofsted. (2021) *SEND: Old Issues, New Issues, Next Steps*. Retrieved from: www.gov.uk/government/publications/send-old-issues-new-issues-next-steps/send-old-issues-new-issues-next-steps (accessed 21 October 2023).

Ofsted. (2025) *Improving the way Ofsted inspects education: consultation document*. Retrieved from: https://www.gov.uk/government/consultations/improving-the-way-ofsted-inspects-education/improving-the-way-ofsted-inspects-education-consultation-document

Purdy, N., Beck, G., McClelland, D., O'Hagan, C., Totton, L. and Harris, J. (2020) *Too Little, Too Late – The Views of Parents/Carers on Their Child's Experiences of the Special Educational Needs (SEN) Process in Mainstream Schools*, Stranmillis University College, Belfast: Centre for Research in Educational Underachievement. Retrieved from: www.niccy.org/media/3516/niccy-too-little-too-late-summary-report-march-2020-web-final.pdf

Richards, G. (2010) '"I was confident about teaching but SEN scared me": Preparing new teachers for including pupils with special educational needs', *Support for Learning*, 25(3): 108-115.

Robertson, C. (2010) 'Working in partnership with parents', in F. Hallett and G. Hallett (eds) *Transforming the Role of the SENCO: Achieving the National Award for SEN Coordination*, Maidenhead, UK: Open University Press, pp. 194-201.

Robertson, C. (2013) 'Future of teaching assistants: Let's wilfully misinterpret the evidence', *SENCO Update*, 147(July): 6.

Russell, A., Webster, R. and Blatchford, P. (2012) *Maximising the Impact of Teaching Assistants: Guidance for School Leaders and Teachers*, London: Routledge.

Rustemier, S. (2002) *Social and Educational Justice: The Human Rights Framework for Inclusion*, Bristol, UK: Centre for Studies in Inclusive Education.

Scottish Government. (2004) *Education (Additional Support for Learning) (Scotland) Act*, Edinburgh: Scottish Government.

Scottish Government. (2009) *Education Additional Support for Learning Scotland Act*, Edinburgh: Scottish Government.

Scottish Government. (2016) *Education Additional Support for Learning Scotland Act*, Edinburgh: Scottish Government.

Scottish Government. (2017) *Supporting Children's Learning: Code of Practice*. Retrieved from: www.gov.scot/binaries/content/documents/govscot/publications/advice-and-guidance/2017/12/supporting-childrens-learning-statutory-guidance-education-additional-support-learning-scotland/documents/00529411-pdf/00529411-pdf/govscot%3Adocument/00529411.pdf (accessed 22 October 2023).

Scottish Government. (2020) *The United Nations Convention on the Rights of the Child (Incorporation Scotland) Bill*, Edinburgh: Scottish Government.

Scottish Government. (2024a) *Statutory Guidance on Part 2 of the UNCRC (Incorporation) (Scotland) Act 2024*. Retrieved from: www.gov.scot/publications/statutory-guidance-part-2-uncrc-incorporation-scotland-act-2024/

Scottish Government. (2024b) *United Nations Convention on the Rights of the Child – Concluding Observations 2023: SG Initial Response*. Retrieved from: www.gov.scot/publications/united-nations-convention-rights-child-scottish-government-initial-response-concluding-observations-issued-un-committee-rights-child/documents/

The Stationery Office (TSO). (2024) *United Nations Convention on the Rights of the Child (Incorporation) (Scotland) Act 2024*, Norwich: TSO. Retrieved from: www.legislation.gov.uk/asp/2024/1/pdfs/asp_20240001_en.pdf

Tutt, R. (2016) *Rona Tutt's Guide to SEND and Inclusion*, London: Sage.

United Nations. (1989) *The United Nations Convention on the Rights of the Child*. Retrieved from: http://treaties.un.org/pages/viewdetails.aspx?src=treaty&mtdsg_no=iv-11&chapter=4&lang=en (accessed 30 October 2017).

United Nations. (2006) *Convention on the Rights of Persons with Disabilities*. Retrieved from: www.un.org/development/desa/disabilities/convention-on-the-rights-of-persons-with-disabilities.html (accessed 30 October 2017).

United Nations Educational, Scientific and Cultural Organization (UNESCO). (1994) *The Salamanca Statement and Framework for Action*. Retrieved from: www.unesco.org/education/pdf/SALAMA_E.PDF (accessed 30 October 2017).

Warnock, M. (2005) *Special Educational Needs: A New Look* (Impact 11), Salisbury, UK: Philosophy of Education Society of Great Britain.

Webster, R. and Blatchford, P. (2013) *The Making a Statement Project Final Report: A Study of the Teaching and Support Experienced by Pupils with a Statement of Special Educational Needs in Mainstream Primary Schools*, London: Institute of Education/Nuffield Foundation.

Welsh Government. (2018) *Additional Learning Needs and Education Tribunal (Wales) Act*. Retrieved from: www.gov.wales/additional-learning-needs-and-education-tribunal-wales-act (accessed 21 October 2023).

Welsh Government. (2019) *Person-Centred Practice in Education: A Geode for Early Years, Schools and College*, Cardiff: Welsh Assembly Government (WAG). Retrieved from: www.gov.wales/sites/default/files/publications/2019-01/person-centred-practice-in-education-a-guide-for-early-years-schools-and-colleges-in-wales.pdf (accessed 22 October 2023).

Welsh Government. (2021) *The Additional Learning Needs Code*. Retrieved from: www.gov.wales/additional-learning-needs-code (accessed 21 October 2023).

Welsh Government. (2023) *Designing Your Curriculum: Enabling Learning*. Retrieved from: https://hwb.gov.wales/curriculum-for-wales/designing-your-curriculum/enabling-learning/ (accessed 26 April 2024).

Whittaker, N. (2018) *High standards - and highly inclusive*. Retrieved from: https://educationinspection.blog.gov.uk/2018/09/10/inspecting-special-educational-needs-and-disabilities-provision/

UNIT 6.3

TEACHING FOR SOCIAL JUSTICE

Creating equity for pupils living in poverty and those from black and minority ethnic backgrounds

Hanneke Jones and Heather Smith

INTRODUCTION

The UK is one of countries in the western world with the greatest levels of inequality (Pickett and Vanderbloemen, 2015), and this is reflected in very unequal outcomes in education. We, the authors of this unit, are committed to the concept of equity. This recognises that extra resources are needed to support pupils whose lives are disadvantaged, in order to achieve more justice in education. However, providing resources is not enough. We must also counter any prejudices in ourselves and others, so that we can begin to counter inequalities at a deeper level. In this unit we focus on children who are disadvantaged through poverty and/or race discrimination. These forms of disadvantage are largely created by socio-cultural factors and the economic system in which we live; can often be exacerbated by schooling as we will discuss; and can have a huge bearing on children's educational success and their wellbeing.

Although many of the causes of disadvantage are structural, we also know that there are forms of education and teacher behaviour that can empower pupils, break down elements of disadvantage and create more equity at school and contribute to a more just society. Teaching for social justice from this viewpoint involves having a clear commitment to maximising equity for our pupils in our schools and classrooms. It also means having a clear understanding of the risks of making things worse for some of the most disadvantaged pupils if we don't engage seriously with these issues.

In the first section of this unit, we will discuss issues in relation to poverty, and in the second section, we will discuss issues in relation to race and racism. Although these are distinct issues, it is important to be aware that many pupils are disadvantaged by both. Intersectionality between the two will also be addressed.

OBJECTIVES

By the end of this unit, you should:

- understand the nature of poverty and race discrimination and their impact on education;
- be aware of the ways in which education can further increase inequalities;
- know how you can minimise this in your own practice, and maximise equity.

DOI: 10.4324/9781032691794-32

SUPPORTING PUPILS LIVING IN POVERTY

This section will start with some definitions, figures and some of the causes of poverty in our society. This is followed by a section describing some of the experiences of children living in poverty. We will then look at some barriers to learning that these pupils may experience at school, before we discuss what can be done to counter these injustices, in classrooms, in schools and beyond. Throughout, be aware that many children living in poverty have skills, knowledge and understandings that are likely to be well beyond those of children in more affluent circumstances, and that many children who grow up in poverty do well at school, despite the odds that are stacked against them. Although we will make some generalisations and discuss structural issues, remember that the lives and needs of no two children are the same.

Some definitions, figures and causes of poverty

The government publishes yearly figures regarding poverty, in which the terms 'relative poverty' and 'low income' are used for households with incomes that are below 60% of the median UK household. Child Poverty Action Group (shortened as CPAG) explains that families living in relative poverty do not have the resources to eat, participate in activities and have the living conditions that are seen as normal and encouraged in the societies in which they live. This mean that a child may have warm clothes and three meals a day, but live in poverty, as there may not be enough money to heat the house adequately, to provide access to a computer or to go on school trips (CPAG, 2023).

According to the Department of Work and Pensions (GOV.UK, 2022a), 4.2 million children (or 29% of all children) were living in poverty in the UK in 2021-22. CPAG (2023) reports that based on these figures, 44% of children living in lone-parent families were in poverty in 2021; 48% of children from black and minority ethnic groups were growing up in poverty; and 71% of children in poverty were living in a household with at least one person in work. CPAG (2023) identifies a number of causes for poverty, such as low-paid, insecure jobs; the high cost of housing; and barriers to employment such as (chronic) ill health, the cost of childcare or caring responsibilities. Benefit cuts and the cost-of-living crisis have, in recent years, further exacerbated these factors.

Destitution is an extreme form of poverty, when people are not able to meet the most basic physical needs: to stay warm, dry, clean and fed. Shockingly, in 2022, 3.8 million people in the UK were living in destitution, including around one million children (Fitzpatrick et al., 2023).

Children whose parents are entitled to Universal Credit and have a net annual income which was, in 2023, no more than £7,400 (GOV.UK, 2023b) are eligible for Free School Meals (or FSM), and the percentage of children on FSM is commonly used as an indicator of levels of material deprivation of a school population. In 2023, 23.8% of all pupils in the UK (or just over 2 million pupils) were eligible for FSM (GOV.UK, 2023c). Although not all of the 4.2 million children living in poverty attend school - this number includes, for example, children of pre-school age - it is interesting that only just over 2 million pupils are eligible for FSM. It is also important that not all children who are eligible for FSM have them. Their parents, for example, may not know how to apply, or the children may not want a FSM, for fear of being stigmatised. In other words, the number of pupils in your class who live in poverty will almost certainly be higher than that of the pupils who receive FSM.

Poverty and school achievement

Behind these numbers lie a vast range of extremely challenging experiences. As many of these families must choose between eating and heating, children's access to food supplies can be scarce, especially during holidays. The Trussell Trust (2023) reports a 37% increase on the year before in the number of food parcels supplied in 2022-23 - more than 1 million of which were used to feed children in the UK. Homes are often cold, damp, insecure and may be temporary, which for some children leads to moving school repeatedly. Parents may have work involving unsociable hours, so that time itself can be a scarce commodity. Unsurprisingly, physical and mental health issues can affect families living in poverty, and chronic ill health and disability can in themselves be causes of poverty, as mentioned earlier. Transport can add extra pressures - families may not own a car, and public transport can be expensive and time-consuming. In many families, there is no money for trips or holidays away, no money to buy books or have a computer at home or have access to the internet, all of which have both social and academic consequences.

Many children who live in poverty succeed at school, despite the challenges they face. However, it is clear that there are a host of factors which make it difficult for children from poor backgrounds to achieve as highly as they might have done had they been living in more affluent circumstances. They may come to school hungry, tired and worried. They may be worried about the state of their uniform, and worried about being bullied. As a result, they may find it difficult to concentrate on your lessons, or do the homework you set. Poverty is statistically the main predictor of low school achievements (Pickett and Vanderbloemen, 2015; National Education Union [NEU], 2023): the NEU reports that by Year 6, many pupils living in poverty are nine months behind their peers in English and maths (2023).

In order to improve educational outcomes for disadvantaged pupils, the government introduced the pupil premium. At the time of writing, state-funded primary schools receive £1,455 for each child who is, or has, in the last 6 years been recorded as eligible for FSM (GOV.UK, 2023d). Again, it is important to note that not all eligible parents apply for FSM, so pupil premium cannot be claimed for pupils who might benefit. Schools are required to provide evidence to Ofsted on how this funding has specifically benefitted those pupils for whom the pupil premium was received. This can be very hard to demonstrate, as there is rarely a direct link between investment in specific resources on the one hand, and achievement by individual children on the other. This can unfortunately lead schools and teachers to narrow the curriculum further for these pupils, and focus overtly on summative assessment, which of course does little to engage these children, and creates a risk that these pupils are publicly identified in class as belonging to one group. This can have disastrous consequences, because of the very great stigma attached to being poor.

Task 6.3.1 Putting yourself in the shoes of the poorest child

Based on your placement experiences, imagine what life might be like if you were one of the poorest children in the school. What physical, social and academic challenges might you experience on your way into school, in class, in the playground and in the dining hall?

Then, consider what the school could do to make going to school fairer and easier. You may want to look at 'Turning the Page on Poverty' (NEU, 2023) for ideas.

Another important disadvantage that may be experienced by pupils living in poverty is stereotyping by teachers. Prejudices and misconceptions might include the idea that families are in poverty because of their own shortcomings; or that people living in poverty lack aspiration and interest in education. This can, disastrously, lead to low expectations of pupils living in poverty, and grouping them together in lower sets, or not fully involving some parents. Teachers who, consciously or less consciously, have such prejudiced deficit views create real barriers to the education of their most vulnerable pupils (Gorski, 2016).

In addition to the points made earlier, there may be other reasons why children from poorer backgrounds don't do as well as they might otherwise have done. Unless engaging forms of teaching are used, the nature of the current National Curriculum may not be experienced as very meaningful to many pupils who live in the circumstances described earlier. In addition, the language used in most schools is that of the 'middle classes' and resources used tend to reflect life in affluent families, whereas working-class families may have less awareness of the 'dominant culture' and be less knowledgeable about how to be successful at school (Hatcher, 2012).

Task 6.3.2 Class and values portrayed as 'normal' in school resources

Consider a range of educational materials, for example, textbooks, reading scheme books, assessment materials, and so on. What messages are given here of a 'normal' lifestyle? How might this come across to a child living in poverty? Consider if it would be right to adapt these materials for pupils from poorer backgrounds, and how you could do this.

Countering the impact of poverty

It is clear that in order to counter the inequality related to poverty in our schools, we need to start by looking at our own expectations, at an individual and whole-school level, and think of ways to avoid, and counter, prejudice and stigmatisation.

Merilyn Cochran-Smith (2004) has put forward six important principles of pedagogy to counter inequality:

- We must make sure to provide *all* pupils with challenging learning opportunities.
- We must challenge and expand the knowledge and interests of our pupils, while at the same time respecting their culture and language.
- If particular skills are lacking, we need to teach those.
- We must work *with*, rather than around, poorer pupils' families and communities.
- We must use diverse forms of assessment that are able to acknowledge the strengths of all pupils.
- We must make equity, power and activism part of the curriculum wherever relevant.

A wealth of practical information can be found in 'Turning the Page on Poverty', an online guide published by the NEU, with many suggestions to support children living in poverty, including the Poverty Proofing the School Day, and the UK Cost of the School Day projects (NEU, 2023). Measures taken as a result of these projects include reorganising dinner times, so that it is not possible to detect whose meal is free; a ban on brand items such as trainers; discrete support with payment for school trips and uniforms and consideration given to more equity on non-uniform days.

However, underachievement by pupils living in poverty is a symptom of economic injustice, which schools cannot be expected to solve (Gorski, 2016). Although the suggestions made in this unit will support children growing up in poverty, there is a limit to what individual teachers and schools can achieve: ultimately, child poverty and the underachievement that goes with it can only be reduced and eradicated at a political and structural level. Teacher activism can of course contribute to such changes.

> **Vignette about Mantle of the Expert and Philosophy for Children**
>
> Two pedagogies which can provide all pupils with challenging and engaging learning opportunities are *Philosophy for Children* and *Mantle of the Expert*, and there is much evidence that these can be of real benefit to children from poorer backgrounds. Websites for both pedagogies are provided under the 'Relevant websites' section at the end of this unit, and both websites have sections on research findings.
>
> In Philosophy for Children, pupils are encouraged to ask philosophical questions based on a stimulus, one of which is chosen by the class to discuss in a community of enquiry. The aim is to develop caring, critical, creative and collaborative thinking.
>
> In Mantle of the Expert, drama is used through a process of imaginative enquiry to enable pupils (and teachers!) to experience new realities, take on the role of responsible experts and become completely immersed in deep learning across the curriculum.
>
> You do not need to use full-blown versions of these pedagogies – any opportunities you can give your pupils to be engaged, to enquire, to imagine and to be listened to will be helpful!

RACE, RACISM AND EDUCATION

Background: Untangling an acronym

The teaching world is flooded with acronyms, so, before we begin our exploration of racism in education, let's begin by questioning the meaning of the acronym 'BME'.

> **Task 6.3.3 What does BME *mean*?**
>
> The following sketch represents the sort of typical conversation we, as teacher educators, often find ourselves holding with student teachers regarding the common acronym BME:
>
> *Teacher:* What does BME *mean*?
> *Student 1:* Does it stand for British something?
> *Teacher:* No it stands for black minority ethnic, but what does minority ethnic *mean*?
> *Student 1:* Does it mean not British?
> *Student 2:* No it means not white.
> *Teacher:* But what does white mean?
> *Student 1:* Does it mean you're British? Like you speak English?

In other words, some student teachers conflate race, ethnicity, nationalism, language status and often religion too. This conflation is largely reflective of the current sociopolitical climate created by politicians and powerful media representations (Smith, 2016, 2021). And, as we shall see later, this imagining of some children as British and others as either not British or not quite British enough along the axes of race, ethnicity, religion and linguistic norms can have powerful consequences for teachers and pupils, not least because racism can be enacted through affiliated factors such as language, immigration status and culture (Kohli, 2009). But first, let's continue our investigation.

If black means not white (as in student 2 in Task 6.3.3), we are back to the question: What does white mean? If you are white, are you always white, everywhere? Is race a fixed, incontrovertible, biological truth? Although our eyes tell us that people look different, as phenotypic features vary, the scientific reality is that there are no sets of genetic markers that occur in everybody of any one specific race but in nobody of another race:

> There are no genetic characteristics possessed by all Blacks but not by non-Blacks; similarly, there is no gene or cluster of genes common to all Whites but not to non-Whites.... The data compiled by various scientists demonstrate, contrary to popular opinion, that intra-group differences [in genetic coding] exceed inter-group differences. That is, greater genetic variation exists *within* the populations typically labelled Black and White than *between* these populations. This finding refutes the supposition that racial divisions reflect fundamental genetic differences.
>
> (López, 2000: 166)

So how is race defined by social scientists? Gillborn (2008: 3) describes race as 'a system of socially constructed and enforced categories that are constantly recreated and modified through human interaction'. This has meant that sometimes people defined as white in one context are not quite so white in another. For example, there are echoes of the treatment of Irish immigrants to America in the early nineteenth century, by the white protestant elite, as an inferior race in today's sociopolitical representations of Eastern European immigrants to the UK, particularly those from poorer countries such as Romania, including and especially Gypsy Roma Traveller (GRT) communities. In May 2023, the Council of Europe reported shocking and troubling levels of discrimination in education and the media against GRT communities in the UK (Siddique, 2023).

So, if race isn't real in a biological sense, why mention it at all? Colourblindness, or the putting aside of race in a focus on social inequities, although comfortable from a liberal perspective (many of us are taught that it's rude to even mention race), has not and will not lead to racial equality, including in education. As Mazzei (2008: 1130) so powerfully puts it:

> As progressive as she [the teacher] may be in her attitudes towards those from different backgrounds, what are the effects upon students when she 'doesn't see colour', or is silent as to the effects of colour and treats all students the same, thereby denying the fact that the students in her classroom are shaped and acted on by others because of their colour.

In short, although race isn't real, racism is. Racism here does not refer solely to more obvious, crude acts of racial hatred, but to 'the more subtle and hidden operations of power that have the effect of disadvantaging one or more minority ethnic groups' (Gillborn, 2008: 27). Racism is also to be understood as a relational practice; it acts to disadvantage, but also to advantage, even when those benefitting from this are unaware of or do not seek advantages. This process of racial (dis)advantaging occurs through that which critical race theorists refer to as whiteness, which is defined 'not as an attribute of identity adhering to a white body, but as a process, a performance, or a constantly shifting location upon complex maps of social, economic, and political power' (Levine-Rasky, 2000: 287).

Although not fixed, 'whiteness has come to be associated with reproduction, dominance, normativity and privilege' (Solomon et al., 2005: 159). So, if the practice of racism is real in all its forms, leading to certain advantages and disadvantages, what are the consequences for children's education? One way of investigating this is to refer to statistics. You may find this brief video useful for understanding race, racism and anti-racism: https://blogs.ncl.ac.uk/anti-racism/being-anti-racist/

A brief sojourn in statistics

Although it is beyond the scope of this unit to fully interrogate education statistics, even a cursory glance at the latest government report shows a complex web of intersectionality where race, gender and poverty impact together on children's exam success in school in the UK. The African American Policy Forum (AAPF; 2013) describes intersectionality as:

> a concept that enables us to recognize the fact that perceived group membership can make people vulnerable to various forms of bias, yet because we are simultaneously members of many groups, our complex identities can shape the specific way we each experience that bias.

See Hopkins (2018) for a useful short video clip explaining the concept of intersectionality.

Looking at government statistics for outcomes at age 11 exemplifies the concept of intersectionality. Key Stage 2 SATs results from 2018-19 (the last year these intersectional figures were made available on the government's ethnicity facts and figures website) revealed that 47% of all pupils entitled to FSM met the expected standard in reading, writing and maths, compared with 68% of non-FSM pupils. Pupils from the Chinese ethnic group entitled to FSM were most likely out of all ethnic groups to meet the expected standard (at 75%), whereas White Gypsy and Roma pupils entitled to FSM were least likely out of all ethnic groups to meet the expected standard (at 17%).

Although an intersectional lens is not applied to the data on school suspensions and permanent exclusions, the statistics are certainly worthy of note. In the period 2020-21 (i.e. during covid), the overall suspension rate was 4.25%, meaning around 425 suspensions per 10,000 pupils, compared to 15.00%, or 1,500 suspensions per 10,000 pupils of Gypsy Roma heritage, and 7.41% or 741 suspensions per 10,000 Black Caribbean pupils. A similar stark picture is presented for permanent exclusions where five white pupils per 10,000 were permanently excluded, compared to 18 or 12 pupils per 10,000 Gypsy Roma and mixed white black Caribbean heritage respectively.

Unless we consider that some pupils are somehow *naturally* 'less able to achieve' or 'more at risk of being excluded', then we must continue to explore why such inequities exist. Let us do so from three perspectives: the effect of racism on pupils' lives; the effects of teacher stereotyping and resulting prejudiced and discriminatory behaviour; and education structures and systems.

Countering racial inequality

Perhaps it is easier to understand the effects of racism on pupils when considering overt acts of racism (verbal or physical). This is certainly the focus of many school policies and anti-discrimination materials (Rollock, 2012). However, for the purposes of this unit and in line with the definition of racism provided earlier, let us consider the impact of a particular manifestation of whiteness known as racial micro-aggressions, or 'brief and commonplace daily verbal, behavioural and environmental indignities, whether intentional or unintentional, that communicate hostile, derogatory, or negative racial slights and insults to the target person or group' (Sue et al., 2009). The cumulative nature of such indignities is of most concern here. Let us illustrate this by considering an example that, on its own, may appear inconspicuous. How many times have you heard, or indeed have yourself used, phrases such as, 'wow, that's a hard name to pronounce; it's so exotic compared to mine; is there a shorter version I can use?' Kohli and Solórzano (2012) investigated the effect of the mispronunciation, change or disrespect of pupils' names by teachers in American high schools. Evidence suggested that when this happens to black minority ethnic pupils, coupled with numerous other daily micro-aggressions, pupils begin to hear a message that they don't belong, and, crucially, 'start to believe the message, and begin to doubt their place or cultural worth in … society. This can impact their aspirations, motivation, and love for their culture and themselves' (Kohli and Solórzano, 2012: 449). The resurgence of notions of Britishness and the intrusion of British values into education policies in England can only heighten prejudicial notions of belonging in the minds of both pupils and teachers (Smith, 2016, 2021).

If teachers hold damaging stereotypes of children (unconscious or not) based on associations relating to race, gender, assumed nationality and religion, then they are more likely to be perpetrators of such racialised micro-aggressions. This is because stereotypes, which abound in society and often remain unnoticed and unchallenged, are accompanied by prejudices (emotions) leading to discriminatory acts, however small and unconscious, such as micro-aggressions. For example, if a teacher believes purple people are devious (after all, the newspapers are full of stories of devious purple people), they are more likely to feel wary of the acts of purple people (a prejudice). When Peter (a purple boy) reports being called nasty names for being purple by some non-purple boys, rather than treating the incident as important, the teacher fails to believe Peter and tells him to stop telling tales and trying to get 'other' (i.e. non-purple) children into trouble (i.e. to stop playing the purple (race) card) – a discriminatory act against Peter and unhelpful too for the boys committing the racist bullying, who need an anti-racist education. This issue has led critical race theorists to argue that student teachers need to 'examine their overall understanding of their racial identity; the ideologies with which they enter the classroom; explore the impact of those ideologies on their teaching practices and their interactions with students' (Solomon *et al.*, 2005: 149).

But this is not just about individual acts by teachers or pupils, it is about the structures and systems of schooling in which teachers teach and in which pupils learn.

Here is an imagined sketch on how this might work, based on recent conversations we or others we know have been privy to. It takes place in a primary school with a higher than national average intake of black and working-class pupils:

> *Head teacher (to teacher):* We must improve the SATs results this year or we will be faced with another visit from Ofsted.
> *Teacher:* Well we have to be realistic; there are a lot of challenging children in Year 6 this year.
> *Head teacher (later to deputy head teacher):* I really don't want us to fail our next Ofsted visit. We need to think of ways to change the student intake to improve results.

The word 'challenging' is a euphemism often used in education to signal not just the reality of the challenging circumstances some children face, but a lack of belief that education can change anything for these children. The pressures on schools to raise results of ever-more-demanding tests have real effects for schools and teachers. We are writing this unit at an unprecedented moment in time when Ofsted inspections have been temporarily suspended by Ofsted's new chief inspector in order for Ofsted staff to receive training on mental health. This follows intense pressure after Ofsted was criticised for insensitivity and intimidation by a coroner investigating the death by suicide of Headteacher Ruth Perry. This pressure can act to shift the focus of school improvement away from providing a transformational education for the pupils in their school to, as in the imagined sketch earlier, transformation of a school population itself.

If you want to start your journey towards becoming an anti-racist teacher, read the NEU's Anti-racism Charter (NEU, 2024), and the Anti-racism Framework for Initial Teacher Education/Training (NEU, n.d.).

CONCLUSION

In conclusion, we all need to be aware of, and then act to challenge, deeply ingrained prejudices in ourselves and in others, including our pupils. Prejudices related to poverty are often bound up with preconceptions related to ability and aspiration, whereas racial prejudices are often bound up with prejudices around nationalism, culture, religion and language status. We must be aware of the slippery and intersectional nature of these prejudices and their often covert operation to maintain hierarchies of power. We must understand such operations as acting from the level of interpersonal communication to systems and structures (including the curriculum) and, hence, we must educate ourselves and our students to resist them whenever and wherever they occur. However, we also need to understand that inequity is rooted in the historical, racial and socio-economic order of society and it therefore cannot be alleviated by schools and teachers alone. Encouraging children and young people to engage critically and actively with political matters within and beyond formal education remains vital to achieving a better world for all children.

SUMMARY

In this unit, we have discussed a number of challenges faced by pupils living in poverty or belonging to black minority ethnic groups, mindful of the fact that many pupils belong to both. For both groups, we have provided some statistical data highlighting the disadvantages faced and we have explored these issues in relation to the effects of poverty and racism on pupils' lives, the impact of teacher stereotyping and the education system as a whole. In relation to the latter, a number of suggestions have been made to maximise equity in the classroom.

In our conclusion we have highlighted the need to become aware of, and challenge, our own prejudices and those of others. We have also argued, however, that many sources of inequality are structural and, therefore, less penetrable by individuals. Finally, we have suggested that teaching for equity involves questioning and challenging power structures in and outside school, and encouraging pupils to do the same.

ANNOTATED FURTHER READING

National Education Union (NEU). (2023) *Turning the Page on Poverty*. Retrieved from: https://neu.org.uk/latest/library/turning-page-poverty

> The NEU's No Child Left Behind campaign is aimed at breaking down the barriers to education created by poverty. As part of the campaign, the NEU has, together with Children North East and Child Poverty Action Group, published this helpful booklet, which is packed with information, advice and resources.

Pearce, S. (2005) *You Wouldn't Understand: White Teachers in Multiethnic Classrooms*, Stoke-on-Trent, UK: Trentham.

> Sarah Pearce kept a diary over the five years she taught in an inner-city multi-ethnic primary classroom in England. She began to trace how her own 'race' influenced her attitudes and relationships in the classroom.

FURTHER READING TO SUPPORT M-LEVEL STUDY

Reay, D. (2007) 'The zombie stalking English schools: Social class and educational inequality', *British Journal of Educational Studies*, 54(3): 208-307.
> The focus of this article is social class, rather than poverty. Although the educational landscape has changed since Diane Reay wrote this, many of the points she raises are at least as valid as they were in 2007.

Allard, A. C. and Santoro, N. (2006) 'Troubling identities: Teacher education students' constructions of class and ethnicity', *Cambridge Journal of Education*, 36(1): 115-129.
> Andrea Allard and Ninetta Santoro explore how Australian student teachers understand ethnicity and socio-economic status. They ponder the significance of this in the classroom and in teachers' relations with pupils.

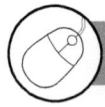

RELEVANT WEBSITES

Some websites and videos on this topic which you may want to explore are as follows:

Poverty

Child Poverty Action Group: www.cpag.org.uk

Mantle of the Expert: www.mantleoftheexpert.com/

NEU Child Poverty campaign: https://neu.org.uk/campaigns/child-poverty

Philosophy for Children: www.sapere.org.uk/

Race/racism

The School that tried to end racism: www.amazon.co.uk/School-that-Tried-End-Racism/dp/B0D9MJ39BW (your institution may also have access to this programme via Box of Broadcasts).

The Black Curriculum: https://theblackcurriculum.com
> This is a social enterprise which provides programmes for all young people aged 3-25. It aims to equip young people with a sense of identity, and the tools to navigate a diverse landscape. It also aims to embed black history in the English national curriculum to include a wide range of contextual examples of black British histories.

How to be an anti-racist educator: www.thersa.org/blog/2020/10/anti-racist-educator
> This is a blogpost with many very useful links for teachers.

Project Implicit: https://implicit.harvard.edu/implicit/Study?tid=-1
> Test your racial biases with Harvard University's implicit association test.

REFERENCES

African American Policy Forum (AAPF). (2013) *Intersectionality*. Retrieved from: www.aapf.org/2013/2013/01/intersectionality?rq=intersectionality (accessed 30 October 2017).

Child Poverty Action Group (CPAG). (2023). Retrieved from: https://cpag.org.uk (accessed December 2023).

Cochran-Smith, M. (2004) *Walking the Road – Race, Diversity and Social Justice in Teacher Education*, New York: Teachers College, Columbia University.

GOV.UK. (2022a) *Households Below Average Income, Statistics on the Number and Percentage of People Living in Low Income Households for Financial Years 1994/95 to 2021/22*. Retrieved from: www.gov.uk/government/statistics/households-below-average-income-for-financial-years-ending-1995-to-2022 (accessed 10 December 2023).

GOV.UK. (2023b) *Free School Meals: Guidance for Local Authorities, Maintained Schools, Academies and Free Schools*, London. Retrieved from: www.gov.uk/government/publications/free-school-meals-guidance-for-schools-and-local-authorities (accessed 7 December 2023).

GOV.UK. (2023c). *Academic Year 2022/23 Schools, Pupils and Their Characteristics*. Retrieved from: https://explore-education-statistics.service.gov.uk/find-statistics/school-pupils-and-their-characteristics (accessed 6 December 2023).

GOV.UK. (2023d) *Guidance. Pupil Premium: Overview*. Retrieved from: www.gov.uk/government/publications/pupil-premium/pupil-premium#service-pupil-premium (accessed 10 December 2023).

Fitzpatrick, S., Bramley, G., Treanor, M., Blenkinsopp, J., McIntyre, J., Johnsen, S. and McMordie, L. (2023) *Destitution in the UK 2023*, Joseph Rowntree Foundation. Retrieved from: www.jrf.org.uk/report/destitution-uk-2023 (accessed 6 December 2023).

Gillborn, D. (2008) *Racism and Education. Coincidence or Conspiracy?*, London: Routledge.

Gorski, P. C. (2016) 'Poverty and the ideological imperative: A call to unhook from deficit and grit ideology and to strive for structural ideology in teacher education', *Journal of Education for Teaching*, 42(4): 378–386.

Hatcher, R. (2012) 'Social class and schooling – Differentiation or democracy?', in M. Cole (ed.) *Education, Equality and Human Rights – Issues of Gender, 'Race', Sexuality, Disability and Social Class*, London: Routledge, pp. 239–267.

Hopkins, P. (2018) *What is Intersectionality?* YouTube, 22 April. Retrieved from: www.youtube.com/watch?v=O1isIMOytkE

Kohli, R. (2009) 'Critical race reflections: Valuing the experiences of teachers of color in teacher education', *Race Ethnicity & Education*, 12(2): 235–251.

Kohli, R. and Solórzano, D. G. (2012) 'Teachers, please learn our names! Racial microaggressions and the K-12 classroom', *Race Ethnicity & Education*, 15(4): 441–462.

Levine-Rasky, C. (2000) 'Framing Whiteness: Working through the tensions in introducing whiteness to educators', *Race, Ethnicity and Education*, 3(3): 271–292.

López, I. F. H. (2000) 'The social construction of race', in R. Delgado and J. Stefancic (eds) *Critical White Studies: Looking Behind the Mirror*, Philadelphia: Temple University Press, pp. 163–177.

Mazzei, L. (2008) 'Silence speaks: Whiteness revealed in the absence of voice', *Teaching & Teacher Education*, 24: 1125–1136.

National Education Union (NEU). (2023) *Turning the Page on Poverty*. Retrieved from: www.neu.org.uk/latest/library/turning-page-poverty (accessed December 2023).

National Education Union (NEU). (2024) *Anti-racism Charter: Framework for Developing an Anti-racist Approach*. Retrieved from: https://neu.org.uk/latest/library/anti-racism-charter

National Education Union (NEU). (n.d.) *Anti-racism Framework for Initial Teacher Education/Training*. Retrieved from: www.ncl.ac.uk/mediav8/humanities-research-institute/files/LBU.pdf

Pickett, K. and Vanderbloemen, L. (2015) *MIND THE GAP Tackling Social and Educational Inequality – The Effect of Poverty on Cognitive Development*, CPR Trust. Retrieved from: http://cprtrust.org.uk/research/equity-and-disadvantage

Rollock, N. (2012) 'Unspoken rules of engagement: Navigating racial microaggressions in the academic terrain', *International Journal of Qualitative Studies in Education*, 25(5): 517–532.

Siddique, H. (2023) 'Gypsy, Roma and Travellers suffer "persistent" discrimination in UK', *The Guardian*, 25 May. Retrieved from: www.theguardian.com/world/2023/may/25/gypsy-roma-travellers-suffer-persistent-discrimination-uk?CMP=share_btn_link

Smith, H. J. (2016) 'Britishness as racist nativism: A case of the unnamed "other"', *Journal of Education for Teaching*, 42(3): 298–313.

Smith, H. J. (2021) 'Britishness and "the outsider within": Tracing manifestations of racist nativism in education policy in England', *Prism Journal*, 3(2): 62–79.

Solomon, R. P., Portelli, J. P., Daniel, B. and Campbell, A. (2005) 'The discourse of denial: How white teacher candidates construct race, racism and "white privilege"', *Race, Ethnicity & Education*, 8(2): 147–169.

Sue, D. W., Lin, A. I., Torino, G. C., Capodilupo, C. M. and Rivera, D. P. (2009) 'Racial microaggressions and difficult dialogues on race in the classroom', *Cultural Diversity & Ethnic Minority Psychology*, 15(2): 183–190.

The Trussell Trust. (2023) *What We Do*. Retrieved from: www.trusselltrust.org (accessed 6 December 2023).

UNIT 6.4

RESPONDING TO CULTURAL DIVERSITY AND CITIZENSHIP

Des Bowden

INTRODUCTION

> Education for diversity is fundamental if the United Kingdom is to have a cohesive society in the twenty-first century.
>
> (Ajegbo, 2007)

This unit is for teachers who are hoping to develop an understanding of, and who are ready to implement a real commitment to, cultural diversity in their teaching. It explores the issues, challenges and opportunities that face schools, teachers and children in an ever-diverse, multicultural, twenty-first-century classroom.

OBJECTIVES

By the end of this unit, you will have understood:

- the issues surrounding diversity;
- entitlements to diversity;
- obstacles to entitlement to diversity;
- the value of diversity awareness;
- challenges in the classroom;
- teacher attitudes to diversity.

The population of the UK continues to be diverse in terms of ethnicity, religion, language and culture. This diversity was characterised in Professor Kwame Anthony Appiah's 2016 BBC Reith lectures as being by creed, country, colour and culture, to which might also be added community and indeed class (the four lectures are available on a podcast from the BBC website: www.bbc.co.uk/programmes/b081lkkj). The Census 2021 data (Office for National Statistics [ONS], 2023) showed that England and Wales have become more ethnically diverse, with increasing numbers of people identifying with minority ethnic groups. The white ethnic group has decreased in size; although it is still the majority, the trend is apparent: in 2021, 82% of the people living in England and Wales were classified as white and 18% belong to black, Asian mixed or other ethnic group. In 2011, 86.0% were white, a change from 91.3% in 2001 and 94.1% in 1991. According to the 2021 Census, London has become the

DOI: 10.4324/9781032691794-33

most ethnically diverse region in England and Wales so that the white ethnic group is no longer in the majority: Newham is the most ethnically diverse borough in England and Wales, with 30.8% classified as white. It is a clear sign of this great diversity that London claims some 300 languages are spoken throughout its streets (Johnson, 2012). The countries of Scotland (95.4% white), Wales (93.8% white) and Northern Ireland (96.8% white) are less diverse than England.

Religious affiliations are also changing. The 2021 Census reported a drop in the number of Christians from 59.3% in 2011 to 46.2%; at the same time, the number of Muslims increased from 4.8% to 6.5%, and those reporting no religion increased from 25.1% to 37.2%. Those classifying as Hindu rose from 1.5% in 2011 to 1.7%.

One in six usual residents of England and Wales were born outside the UK; the top four countries are India, Poland, Pakistan and Romania. Over half the population growth between 2011 and 2023 (from 56m to 59.5m) is the result of positive net migration. This diversity also has a great spatial and locality variation (Figure 6.4.1). For example, 92% of the population in the north-east are white, whereas in the London Borough of Newham, 30.8% are white. Annual school census data, e.g. School Workforce in England 2023 (GOV.UK, 2024) suggest that UK primary schools are becoming increasingly diverse in their ethnic composition, although there are variations in numbers at a national scale.

In primary schools in England, 86% of teachers are female and 14% are male, yet male teachers progress more rapidly to leadership roles. Some 74% of primary heads are female; only 7% of primary heads are from ethnic minorities. Ethnic minority teachers, leaders and pupils are concentrated in London and the West Midlands. So, in general, primary schools are less diverse than the general population with the teaching and leadership roles being filled by white British females, with ethnic minorities being less represented.

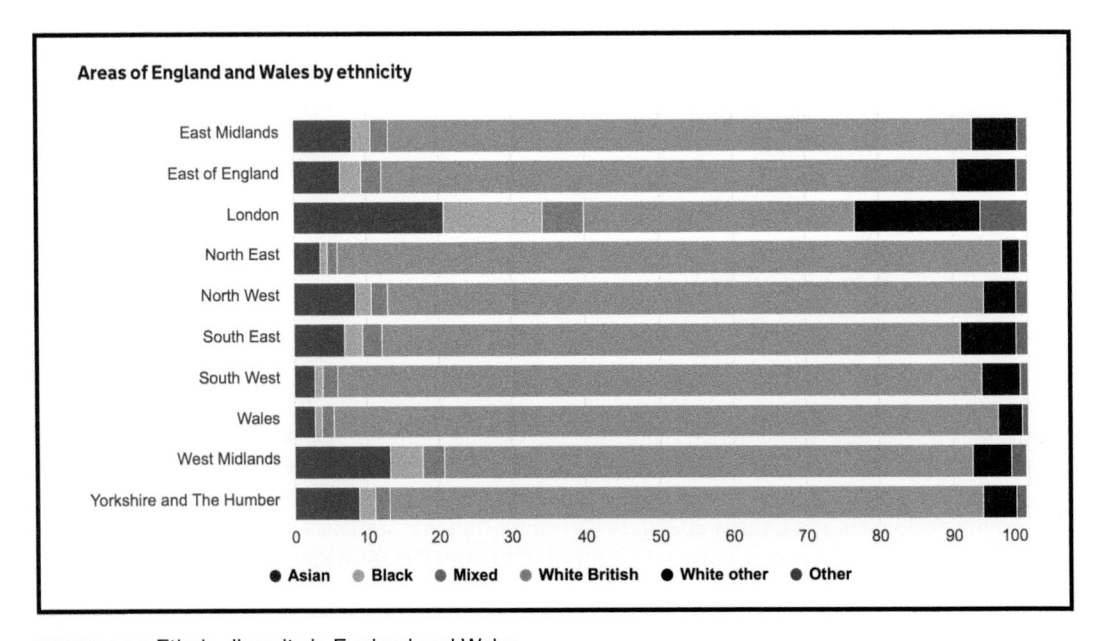

FIGURE 6.4.1 Ethnic diversity in England and Wales
Source: GOV.UK (2021)

The degree to which diverse populations should be integrated is often a matter of debate, but there are societal drivers that interact to encourage segregation. This is partly a cultural issue, but also controlled by social (e.g. language, housing allocation) and economic (e.g. job market) factors. Cantle and Kaufmann (2016) highlight that segregation has been linked to prejudice and intolerance of the 'other' owing to the lack of contact and interaction across social and cultural boundaries.

This cultural diversity is highlighted in Hall's study – 'Super-diverse street' (2015). This research explored streets that are located in ethnically diverse and comparatively deprived urban places (streets in Leicester, Bristol, Manchester and Birmingham), where urban retail spaces shape and are shaped by migrant investments. Over time, integration does seem to occur more or less organically; for example, great concentrations of Jewish people in the East End of London and the central area of Birmingham are no longer clearly identifiable. These people have prospered, developed and integrated into wider society. Catney et al. (2023: 73) conclude from their study of the 2021 Census data that '… residential segregation of all ethnic groups – White and minority – is declining. … many more neighbourhoods are ethnically diverse, and diversity has been spreading out to new locales.'

This unit develops strategies for use in school for identifying, sharing and working with this wealth of difference. It develops an understanding of the issues concerned with identities that children inhabit. It tries to promote an understanding of the different people in the UK today, and how children contribute to this diverse society. Teachers and schools have the difficult task of helping their children challenge and evaluate standpoints different from their own, and educating them to develop an informed view of diversity and, hopefully, become part of a more cohesive society.

Children in the UK can inhabit a range of identities that are as confusing as they are defining, not only for themselves, but also for others. It is for teachers to gain an understanding of these dilemmas and to devise appropriate learning episodes that contribute to a curriculum tailored to the individual needs of the children in their unique setting. This should be their entitlement for education for diversity.

There is much encouragement from government educational policies to work towards the goal of a more cohesive and united society. The Ajegbo Report (2007) and Ofsted (2024) are strong in their encouragement of understanding diversity and working towards a cohesive curriculum that reflects, understands and celebrates the values of today's multicultural society, and indeed there is a UNESCO convention on the protection and promotion of the diversity of cultural expressions (2005).

For schools, spiritual, moral, social and cultural development is a significant focus in all lesson Ofsted observations, as well as overall school effectiveness (Ofsted, 2024)

In Wales …

The four purposes should be the starting point and aspiration for schools' curriculum design. Ultimately, the aim of a school's curriculum is to support its learners to become:

- ambitious, capable learners, ready to learn throughout their lives
- enterprising, creative contributors, ready to play a full part in life and work
- ethical, informed citizens of Wales and the world
- healthy, confident individuals, ready to lead fulfilling lives as valued members of society

Ethical, informed citizens who:

- find, evaluate and use evidence in forming views
- engage with contemporary issues based upon their knowledge and values
- understand and exercise their human and democratic responsibilities and rights
- understand and consider the impact of their actions when making choices and acting
- are knowledgeable about their culture, community, society and the world, now and in the past
- respect the needs and rights of others, as a member of a diverse society
- show their commitment to the sustainability of the planet.

(Welsh Government, 2022)

The Foundation Phase supports the cultural identity of all children, to celebrate different cultures and help children recognise and gain a positive awareness of their own and other cultures. Positive attitudes should be developed to enable children to become increasingly aware of, and appreciate the value of, the diversity of cultures and languages that exist in a multicultural Wales.

(Learning Wales, 2015: 9)

In Wales ...

Learners should be grounded in an understanding of the identities, landscapes and histories that come together to form their cynefin. This will not only allow them to develop a strong sense of their own identity and well-being, but to develop an understanding of others' identities and make connections with people, places and histories elsewhere in Wales and across the world.

It is important for this to be inclusive and to draw on the experiences, perspectives and cultural heritage of contemporary Wales. Confidence in their identities helps learners appreciate the contribution they and others can make within their different communities and to develop and explore their responses to local, national and global matters.

It also helps them to explore, make connections and develop understanding within a diverse society. This also recognises that Wales, like any other society, is not a uniform entity, but encompasses a range of values, perspectives, cultures and histories: that includes everybody who lives in Wales.

(Welsh Government, 2022)

Key Stage 2:

builds upon the Personal and Social Development, Well-Being and Cultural Diversity Area of Learning in the *Foundation Phase framework for children's learning for 3 to 7-year-olds in Wales* and progresses into the 14–19 Learning Core components that relate to PSE such as Personal, Social, Sustainability and Health Matters, Attitudes and Values, and Community Participation.

(Department for Children, Education, Lifelong Learning and Skills [DCELLS], 2008: 3)

There is evidence from the recent analysis of ethnicity and attainment in primary schools (Department for Education [DfE], 2022) that attainment has ethnic and social controls. Attainment levels were seen to vary by ethnic group and deprivation (represented by Free School Meals [FSM] which are taken by 15.8% of school population). Chinese and Indian ethnic minority groups perform consistently strongly, whereas white and black pupils tend to have poorer outcomes. Pupils who are eligible for FSM have much lower average performance.

Teachers were found to show evidence of implicit bias (unconscious bias) in the way they act towards race including those ethnic groups that are consistently out-performing white British pupils. This is an important reminder that even those groups performing well in school may still face prejudice (see Task 6.4.2).

In Scotland ...

Responding to cultural diversity and citizenship are at the heart of the General Teaching Councils standards. The Scottish Government sees this as a high priority within education and wider society.

Sources: General Teaching Council for Scotland (GTC Scotland; n.d.); Scottish Government (n.d.; 2023)

CASE STUDIES IN MODERN DIVERSITY

The following case studies demonstrate the challenges and benefits of living in a plural society. The example of Newham shows the plurality of a modern British city. The study of Gascoigne Primary School highlights the benefits and richness that a multicultural school can offer. The individual study of George Alagiah shows how people may have a range of identities, determined by racial, cultural, social and economic circumstances.

Case study 1: Urban diversity – the London Borough of Newham

In the 2021 Census, the London Borough of Newham was found to be the most ethnically diverse place in the UK with 30.8% of the population of 351,000 identifying as white British and 48% having been born outside of the UK. Yet the number of people identifying their nationality as British increased from 39.4% in 2011 to 56.4% in 2021. Beyond London, Slough, Luton, Birmingham and Leicester were the most 'blended' places. The raw 2021 Census increased anxieties about 'minority majority' towns and cities. However, these places are better understood as highly ethnically diverse, 'rainbow settlements' home to a great variety of people. Newham Borough has developed a positive social integration strategy because they realise that the local people face racism, inequality and disproportionality. The strategy requires engagement with and trust between all groups, for example older people, LGBT people, those defined by a faith and other beliefs, disabled people, people of different genders and those financially vulnerable people, with and without children. Several organisations and initiatives are supporting the Borough's plans for even greater integration (Newham Council, 2022). Although employment rates in Newham are high (56% of working age), there is still much deprivation in the borough, but the fact that the increasing proportion of people identifying as British nationality would seem to be evidence for less segregation and more integration (ONS, 2023).

Case study 2: School diversity

Gascoigne Primary School in Barking (East London) has been recognised as the largest primary school in the UK, with 160 staff and a challenging mix of some 1,200 pupils, ranging in age from 3 to 11 (www.gascoigneprimaryschool.co.uk). The diversity is evidenced by more than 60 different languages being spoken, and only 10% of children have English as their first language. There is a high turnover, but the school is short of space for learning, teaching and play. It is located in one of Britain's most deprived areas (45% of children qualify for Pupil Premium). It was the focus of a Channel 5 TV documentary series in the spring of 2015 (www.channel5.com/show/britains-biggest-primary-school).

Notwithstanding the challenges facing this school, it continues to be judged 'good' at its last inspection (Ofsted, 2022). Table 6.4.1 illustrates the diversity of the school population and the sensitivity of the school.

The school strives to establish close links with its community and celebrates its diversity. Albanian, Lithuanian and Portuguese groups use its facilities regularly. Pupils appreciate the varied experiences and opportunities the school offers them enjoying visits to London museums, local places of worship, and theatres. Pupils are encouraged to become responsible citizens.

As part of its action for diversity programmes it also fully and sensitively implements the Prevent strategy (a safeguarding requirement for schools to refer children for support if at risk of radicalisation) (GOV.UK, 2023).

Case study 3: Personal identities – George Alagiah

George Alagiah was born in Colombo, Sri Lanka, on 22 November 1955, to Tamil parents. The Tamils were a minority group in Sri Lanka. His father was an engineer, and the family moved to Ghana in 1961, where George completed his primary education. They then moved to the UK and lived in Portsmouth, at a time when there was an unhappy intrusion of race into politics. After reading politics at Durham, he followed a career as a journalist and author, which led to him becoming a prominent BBC presenter. He married Frances Robathan, from a British family, with whom he has two sons. He wrote of the gentle clash of cultures, as his mother wore a red sari, and his mother-in-law

TABLE 6.4.1 Diversity in action: The class names in the seven most spoken languages at Gascoigne Primary School

	English	Albanian	Bengali	Yoruba	Portuguese	Somali	French
Nursery	White	Ebardhe					Blanc
Reception	Yellow	Everdhe	Holud	Ofeefee	Amarelo	Jaalleah	Jaune
Year 1	Blue	Blu	Nil	Bulu	Azul	Buluug	Bleu
Year 2	Red	Kuq	Lal	Pupa	Vermelho	Cas	Rouge
Year 3	Purple	Vjollce	Benguni	Popu	Roxo	Iyo guduud	Violet
Year 4	Green	Gjelber	Shobuj	Awo Ewe	Verde	Cagaaran	Vert
Year 5	Orange	Portokalli	Komola	Osan	Laranja	Oranjo	Orange
Year 6	Gold	Ari	Shonali	Wura	Ouro	Dahab	Or

a floral-patterned suit. He claimed not to have found race an impediment: 'If you're hungry enough, you work that much harder'. But he recognised that multiculturism may not be the answer, as it results in almost ghetto-like communities of poor and isolated people (Alagiah, 2011). His was the kind of extended rainbow network of relationships, spanning countries and continents, that has become a conventional feature of the migrant experience. George Alagiah passed away in 2023, aged 67, after a battle with bowel cancer.

ENTITLEMENT TO DIVERSITY EDUCATION

> Multi-cultural education that celebrates diversity is an important part of responding to the kaleidoscope of cultural attributes in the school and the community. Children will be living in a more globalised world where the old barriers of geography will no longer be relevant. Children in all parts of UK (rural, inner-city, suburban) need to understand and respect a range of different cultural heritages.
>
> (Claire, 2006: 308)

Schools are under a legal obligation to promote good race relations and provide full equality of opportunity for all children (Race Relations (Amendment) Act 2000). Ajegbo (2007) recommended that schools recognise the 'pupil voice' and have systems in place so these voices can be heard (such as school councils and other mechanisms for discussion). The National Professional Qualification (NPQ) for Headship (GOV.UK, 2024) highlights the importance of ensuring partnership with parents and families and making sure that there is 'positive two way dialogue' (p.36). Schools can audit their curriculum to establish their provision for diversity and multiple identities and should build active links between and across communities, with diversity understanding as the focus.

The extensive Cambridge Primary Review (Alexander, 2010) was a major independent survey and analysis of primary school education that had been ongoing since 2004. It warned that recognising diversity in school may not be straightforward, as often differences are constructed which might lead to simplistic categorisations. This review went on to encourage individual schools to develop approaches to diversity that meet the needs of their children and the local community.

The Ofsted inspectors' handbook (2024) attempts to ensure that the school provides effectively for pupils' broader development and that the school's work to enhance pupils' spiritual, moral, social and cultural development is of a high quality. There are also developments that do not owe their origins to governmental initiatives. Some schools have formalised their commitment to diversity education through the Rights Respecting Schools Award, developed by UNICEF (see www.unicef.org.uk/rights-respecting-schools/). Schools can apply to register for this award, gathering evidence that demonstrates they have embedded children's rights in the practice and the ethos of the school.

The Headteacher (2023) (an online publication), suggests three techniques for fostering inclusion in the diverse classroom:

- 'Allyship' gives strength and support to isolated learners.
- Offer 'equity' which recognises fundamental differences, then allows and caters for this difference appropriately to the learner.
- Attempt to 'usualise' the presence of different cultures (whereas normalising suggests there is a standard into which everyone should fit). This is to get the pupils to accept what is usual.

> **Task 6.4.1 Provision for diversity**
>
> Use these questions to consider the provision for diversity in a school known to you:
>
> 1. Do you think that primary schools effectively and equitably address the diverse learning needs and cultural backgrounds of all children?
> 2. Are all children given equal access to high-quality primary education?
> 3. If disparities exist, what strategies can be implemented to enhance access and equity?
> 4. How can a national education system best respond to the rich mixture of cultures, faiths, languages and aspirations that define modern British society?
> 5. How can primary schools best support children with a wide range of abilities, interests and learning styles?
> 6. What approaches can primary schools take to engage children and families who are traditionally the most difficult to reach?

OBSTACLES TO ENTITLEMENT TO DIVERSITY

Ajegbo (2007) recognises that the quality of education across the nation is uneven and suggests the following issues may prevent a coherent diversity curriculum being implemented:

- insufficient clarity about flexibility and customising the curriculum;
- lack of confidence in schools to engage in diversity issues;
- lack of diversity training opportunities;
- lack of proper consideration for the 'pupil voice';
- tenuous or non-existent links to the community.

Other challenges facing teachers wishing to develop diversity awareness include:

- embedding it in a single subject, such as religious education, and not in others;
- lack of planning for integration of newcomers into the learning environment;
- concentration on famous British people;
- narrow selection of reading materials in the library;
- stereotypes in school displays;
- stereotypes in geography (e.g. all Africans are starving and live in mud huts);
- lack of empathy in questioning children who are different from the teacher;
- not recognising that some children do not have Christian names;
- exoticising minority children;
- tokenism;
- language;
- unwillingness to face controversial issues;
- not recognising their own unconscious biases.

> ### Task 6.4.2 Unconscious bias
>
> A riddle:
>
> *A father and his son are in an accident. Badly injured, they are rushed to hospital. In the operating room the surgeon looks at the boy and says, 'I can't operate on this boy, he is my son'.*
>
> Who is the surgeon?
>
> The answer is that the surgeon is the boy's mother. Many people struggle to give this answer because their brain automatically associates surgeon with males. This is because the brain deals with so much information that it uses short cuts to provide rapid (automatic/unconscious) responses like flinching from pain. However, there is a slower, more conscious system which allows people to make informed decisions about the actions to take. The automatic system makes decisions which may end up as unconscious biases, which can be side-stepped with conscious thought, but in the rush of classroom activities, teachers may treat the polite, well-mannered child differently to the noisy, scruffy child.
>
> Teachers can use a simple test to measure their unconscious bias by taking an implicit association test such as the one developed at Harvard. This test is tried and tested over 25 years. It is free, but teachers should carefully consider the biases that it may reveal. Test your own unconscious bias using The Harvard implicit association test: https://implicit.harvard.edu/implicit/takeatestv2.html
>
> Adapted from Davenport (2020)

VALUE OF DIVERSITY AWARENESS: BEYOND TOKENISM

If children are to develop as successful learners, confident individuals and responsible citizens, it is essential for them to understand and have respect for cultures, religions and identities. The most successful teaching and learning for diversity occur when there is a whole-school commitment. This includes governors and staff, children, support staff and the local community, working together on the whole-school ethos, which includes the taught and learned curriculum as well as the hidden curriculum. Too many schools celebrate cultural diversity without really understanding the nature of that diversity.

> ### In Northern Ireland ...
>
> The Council for the Curriculum, Examinations, and Assessment (CCEA) offers resources to help schools implement inclusive education, focusing on cultural diversity (CCEA, 2024). The NI curriculum sets out guidelines for promoting equality and diversity through teaching and learning (CCEA, 2024). There are specific model equality policies available for schools to draw on (Education Authority [EA], 2024)
>
> Other support for N.I. primary schools include anti-bullying policies, the availability of bilingual classroom assistance, and the promotion of intercultural education.
>
> Recent policy recognises that for the nearly 400 controlled primary schools in Northern Ireland there is a proud tradition of mutual respect and inclusion, welcoming children of all faiths and denominations.

FLEXIBILITY AND THE CURRICULUM

Since 2002, schools have been encouraged to adopt more flexible approaches to the curriculum by customising the basic entitlement to learning to create their own distinctive and unique curricula (Qualifications and Curriculum Authority [QCA], 2002). Some schools have shown innovative ways to include this flexibility, by:

- using appropriate resources, such as artefacts and images, to show diversity within and between cultures and groups:
    - ensuring choice of examples provides balance;
- presenting a broad and balanced view of culture, identity and diversity:
    - giving learners accurate and objective views;
    - avoiding presenting minority groups as problematic;
    - looking for commonalities between groups;
- questioning commonly held opinions and stereotypes (e.g. migration in the UK is a recent occurrence):
    - challenging media portrayal of different countries and peoples;
- creating an open climate (using ground rules and distancing techniques when dealing with controversial issues):
    - encouraging learners to take pride in their identity and culture;
    - encouraging learners to draw on their own experience.

DIVERSITY AND INCLUSION

These two ideas are often regarded as virtual similes, but this is not the case. Diversity in the primary classroom is a fact (there are pupils of different genders, ethnicities and more), whereas inclusion is a choice (maybe informally made by the pupils and more formally planned and designed by the teacher). In the famous words of Verna Myers (2016), 'Diversity is being invited to the party. Inclusion is being asked to dance'.

Task 6.4.3 Racism

Consider the influence of such people on dispelling racialist myths:

- Mary Seacole – black nurse during the Crimea war;
- Nelson Mandela – anti-apartheid activist who eventually became president of South Africa;
- Anne Frank – Jewish refugee from Nazism;
- Anton Wilhelm Amo Afer – a Ghanian boy 'given' to the Duke of Brunswick-Wolfenbüttel in 1707, who became a professor of philosophy during the European Renaissance;
- Rosa Parkes – US activist against segregation who refused to give up her seat in a bus to a white passenger, galvanizing the Civil Rights Movement;
- Stephen Lawrence – victim of racist murder in London in 1993;
- Asquith Xavier – railway worker who challenged the colour bar on employment at Euston Station in 1966 (Figure 6.4.2).

Develop a scheme of work to include activities that will enhance learners' empathy.

FIGURE 6.4.2 Memorial plaque to Asquith Xavier, a railway guard who broke the colour bar on employment at Euston Station as recently as 1966

SCHOOL CONFIDENCE IN ADDRESSING DIVERSITY ISSUES

Many teachers feel that they do not have the experience or understanding to deal with diversity issues. At one level, it is treating individuals with politeness and respect, but this can be confounded by language difficulties. In some cases, female teachers may not be shown the same sort of respect as male teachers by certain minority groups. Schools need to develop their staff to feel confident in their approach to dealing with controversial issues and to be aware of their own unconscious biases and intersectionality.

Task 6.4.4 Intersectionality

The term intersectionality was coined to help describe the distinct discrimination faced by people because of multiple facets of their lives meeting at an 'intersection'. For example, 'black Afro-Caribbean boys' are spoken of as a category, but in primary school any individual member of this group will have other characteristics like being in receipt of FSM, may be of Muslim faith, may or may not have special needs, and may have another nationality. All these traits may combine to compound discrimination and heighten a feeling of exclusion. Teachers need to understand this intersectionality and how to make their classes inclusive.

Watch the TED talk by Prof Kimberly Crenshaw, the originator of the term 'intersectionality': https://youtu.be/M2z7FCPnxQQ?si=AN79uGM4xi59e6Ux

Consider how the concept of intersectionality may influence the way you teach in the primary classroom.

The children's voice

This is concerned with giving children a real say in what goes on in school. Most schools now have a school council. Some of these are strong and allow children to join in by making decisions on the nature of the school and its curriculum. In these schools, children are seen as part of the solution, not part of the problem.

Developing community links

These may be addressed by engaging children, their parents and the wider community in the daily life of the school. The extended school day, with breakfast clubs and after-school activities, offers opportunities for more people to come into school and for the school to play a more important role in the community. Some schools, like Gascoigne, have developed successful strategies for involving the wider community in the life of their school. St Brigid's Catholic Primary School in Northfield, Birmingham, for example, has been able to involve members of its diverse community in extracurricular school activities (www.stbrigid.bham.sch.uk).

POSSIBLE CHALLENGES AND OPPORTUNITIES IN THE CLASSROOM

Various languages

Languages may be both barriers and bridges to learning. There are dangers that some teachers confuse not understanding a language with low ability. The child receiving language help and the other children need to be informed about the nature of the EAL support in the classroom (see Unit 6.5 for further information).

Transient populations

Some schools receive more or less transient children, such as those from Gypsy, Roma and Irish Traveller communities, army children or the children of short-term migrants. Their inclusion in the classroom needs to be sensitively managed, and their learning needs need to be catered for and recorded.

Task 6.4.5 Watching children

When you are in school, take time to watch specific children who might be vulnerable, in the playground and on those occasions where children choose partners or group members. Isolation and marginalisation can be a signpost to more overt bullying away from teachers' eyes. Who is being left out? Who is hanging around on the sidelines?

- Can you find out why some children are popular and others are not?
- Does the school's equal opportunities policy have anything to say about bullying and name-calling? How is this monitored and dealt with?

Source: Adapted from Claire (2006)

BULLYING AND NAME-CALLING OF MINORITY ETHNIC GROUPS

Name-calling is probably one of the more frequently encountered expressions of racial hostility. Picking on individuals or small groups is also seen as bullying. Children need to be made aware that this type of behaviour is unacceptable, and they also need to understand why it is unacceptable. They may need to consider what their feelings might be if the situation were reversed. Moralising tends not to work in the face of opposing attitudes. Just to forbid such behaviour is controlling rather than educating. No Name-Calling Week is a week of educational activities aimed at ending name-calling in school and supporting schools to work on practice for eliminating bullying (see Relevant websites section).

It is hard to counter entrenched attitudes of racism, possibly learned from the family; nevertheless, racism is illegal, and children need to be made aware of their right not to be bullied. Teachers need to be vigilant about bullying in their school, and it may be a suitable topic for the school council to consider.

CONTROVERSIAL ISSUES

Teachers must deal with controversial issues for many reasons, and sometimes they are unavoidable. They may result in exciting classroom learning and, indeed, reflect partly what it means to be human, and they may help children make connections between areas of learning. They will help children develop value positions.

The former QCA suggested that, 'Education should not attempt to shelter our nation's children from even the harsher controversies of adult life, but should prepare them to deal with such issues knowledgeably, sensibly, tolerantly and morally' (QCA, 1998: 56).

A strategy for dealing with controversial issues is for the teacher to take a known stance and argue the issue from there. The teacher may:

- be an impartial chairperson (procedural neutrality);
- speak from his or her viewpoint (stated commitment);
- present a wide variety of views (balanced approach);
- take an opposing position (devil's advocate).

Task 6.4.6 Tokenistic gestures or real understanding?

Consider these issues:

- Is learning a Caribbean song in music really improving diversity awareness?
- Does circle time raise awareness of difference?
- Are travellers' children ethnic minorities?
- Do all children in your school celebrate Christmas?
- Does making a curry make you more culturally aware?
- Does dressing up in 'native' clothes improve understanding of other people?

TEACHER ATTITUDES

Sometimes, it is the teacher's attitude that is the concern in the classroom. Teachers need to acknowledge and decide how to deal with their own prejudices and viewpoints, and to consider how to represent their personal opinions in the classroom (see Task 6.4.7). Low expectations of certain children and perceived typical behaviour problems are often associated with teachers' own stereotypical views and unconscious bias.

> ### Task 6.4.7 Teachers' viewpoint
>
> Teachers should ask themselves:
>
> - What are the different ways in which children at my school are categorised by others? (This might include categories such as ethnic groups, pupils with disabilities, new immigrants, residents of public housing, looked-after children.)
> - What characteristics first come to mind when I think of each group?
> - Where did these impressions come from (such as peers, media, family, religion)?
> - How reliable are these sources and my impressions?
> - Can I remember a time when someone made assumptions about me based on a group I belong to?
> - How did that make me feel?
>
> Source: Ross (n.d.)

SUMMARY

Encouraging multicultural education to be an integral part of the school ethos and embedding it in the curriculum are the first stages towards real inclusion and equal opportunity for all children. It should be part of the whole-school ethos, embraced by all members of the school community. There is a need to directly tackle racism and racial and other stereotyping, so that a relevant, meaningful and coherent curriculum can flourish. This curriculum needs to be designed to be appropriate for the whole school, in its local context, and help all concerned to develop a cohesive society, based on mutual understanding, tolerance and respect.

ANNOTATED FURTHER READING

Centre for Studies on Inclusive Education. (2016) *Equality Making it Happen*, Bristol, UK: CSIE.
   A succinct and user-friendly guide to help schools address prejudice, reduce bullying and promote equality holistically. Created with schools for schools, the guide is sponsored by the NASUWT.

Claire, H. and Holden, C. (eds) (2008) *The Challenge of Teaching Controversial Issues*, Stoke-on-Trent, UK: Trentham.
   This is an authoritative book that offers much practical support in teaching controversial issues, including diversity, in the primary school.

Elton-Chalcraft, S. (2009) *It's Not Just About Black and White, Miss: Children's Awareness of Race*, Stoke-on-Trent, UK: Trentham.
> This book provides research-based evidence on what children themselves think about cultural diversity and about efforts to counter racism in their schools. It is empirical, child-centred research that tells educators what they need to know. The book offers children's voices and their surprising and challenging ideas.

Richards, G. and Armstrong, F. (eds) (2016) *Teaching and Learning in Diverse and Inclusive Classrooms*, London: Routledge.
> This provides a guide for those teachers and other staff who are wanting to make their classrooms more inclusive spaces. The contributors consider how alienation may happen through ethnicity, gender and sexuality and suggest ways in which interaction and participation may take place.

M — FURTHER READING TO SUPPORT M-LEVEL STUDY

Manzoni, C. and Rolfe, H. (2019) *How Schools Are Integrating New Migrant Pupils and Their Families*, National Institute of Economic and Social Research, Report.
> This paper explores the ideology of social justice through links between equality and equity within early years. It investigates the issues facing early years specialists working in mono- and multicultural settings.

Ford, R., Morrell, G. and Heath, A. (2012) '"Fewer but better"? Public views about immigration', in A. Park, E. Clery, J. Curtice, M. Phillips and D. Utting (eds) *British Social Attitudes: The 29th Report*, London: National Centre for Social Research. Retrieved from: www.bsa-29.natcen.ac.uk (accessed 31 October 2017).
> This is a detailed investigation of the data collected on British attitudes to immigration showing a sophisticated and nuanced view of the issues pertaining to immigration, multiculturalism and integration

RELEVANT WEBSITES

Equality and Human Rights Commission: www.equalityhumanrights.com/
> The Commission enforces equality legislation on age, disability, gender reassignment, marriage and civil partnership, pregnancy and maternity, race, religion or belief, sex and sexual orientation – these are known as protected characteristics.

No Name-Calling Week: www.nonamecallingweek.org
> Runs annually in January and is a week of educational activities aimed at ending name-calling in school and providing schools with the tools and inspiration to launch a continuing dialogue about ways of eliminating bullying

Mixed Britannia: www.bbc.co.uk/programmes/b015skx4/episodes/guide
> Telling the story of mixed-race Britain, this is a BBC2 documentary series hosted by George Alagiah (through BBC iPlayer).

Sophie Thompson (2024) 'Diversity in schools – How to diversify your curriculum', *The Headteacher*, January. Retrieved from: www.theheadteacher.com/attainment-and-assessment/teaching-practice/how-to-diversify-your-curriculum (accessed 31 January 2024).
> A concise article suggesting ways of developing a diverse but happy and tolerant school community.

Controlled School's Support Council (CSSC) Northern Ireland: Celebrating diversity in controlled schools as admissions open for 2022: www.csscni.org.uk/news/celebrating-diversity-in-controlled-schools-as-admissions-open-for-2022

REFERENCES

Ajegbo, K. (2007) *Diversity and Citizenship in the Curriculum: Research Review*, London: DfES.

Alagiah, G. (2011) 'What it's like to be mixed-race in Britain', *BBC News Magazine*, 2 October. Retrieved from: www.bbc.co.uk/news/magazine-15019672 (accessed 2 January 2014).

Alexander, R. (2010) *The Cambridge Primary Review Research Surveys*, London: Routledge.

Cantle, E. and Kaufmann, E. (2016) *Is Segregation on the Increase in the UK?* Retrieved from: www.opendemocracy.net/wfd/ted-cantle-and-eric-kaufmann/is-segregation-on-increase-in-uk (accessed 31 October 2017).

Catney, G., Lloyd, C. D., Ellis, M., Wright, R., Finney, N. and Jivraj, S. (2023) 'Ethnic diversification and neighbourhood mixing: A rapid response analysis of the 2021 Census of England and Wales', *Geographical Journal*, 189: 63–77.

Claire, H. (2006) 'Education for cultural diversity and social justice', in J. Arthur and T. Cremin (eds) *Learning to Teach in the Primary School*, London: Routledge, pp. 307–317.

Council for Curriculum Examinations and Assessment (CCEA). (2007) *The Northern Ireland Curriculum – Primary*, Belfast: CCEA. Retrieved from: https://ccea.org.uk/downloads/docs/ccea-asset/Curriculum/The%20Northern%20Ireland%20Curriculum%20-%20Primary.pdf

Davenport, C. (2020) 'Unconscious bias and primary schools', *Primary Science*, 165(Nov/De): 6–8.

Council for Curriculum Examinations and Assessment (CCEA). (2024) *The Northern Ireland Curriculum – Primary*, Belfast: CCEA. Retrieved from: https://ccea.org.uk/learning-resources/supporting-shared-education/primary#section-27344

Department for Children, Education, Lifelong Learning and Skills (DCELLS). (2008) *Personal and Social Education Framework for 7 to 19-Year-Olds in Wales*, Cardiff: Welsh Assembly Government (WAG). Retrieved from: http://learning.gov.wales/docs/learningwales/publications/130425-personal-and-social-education-framework-en.pdf (accessed 14 November 2017).

Department for Education (DfE). (2022) *Outcomes by Ethnicity in Schools in England* – Topic Note Reference: RR1216 ISBN: 978-1-83870-379-0.

Education Authority (EA). (2024) *Equality and Diversity Policy for Schools*. Retrieved from: www.eani.org.uk/school-management/policies-and-guidance/equality-and-diversity-policy-for-schools

General Teaching Council for Scotland (GTC Scotland). (n.d.) *Equality and Diversity*. Retrieved from: www.gtcs.org.uk/registrant-resources/equality-and-diversity.

GOV.UK (2021) *Areas of England and Wales by Ethnicity*. Retrieved from: www.ethnicity-facts-figures.service.gov.uk/uk-population-by-ethnicity/national-and-regional-populations/regional-ethnic-diversity/latest/#areas-of-england-and-wales-by-ethnicity

GOV.UK (2023) *The Prevent Duty: An Introduction For Those With Safeguarding Responsibilities*. Available from: www.gov.uk/government/publications/the-prevent-duty-safeguarding-learners-vulnerable-to-radicalisation/the-prevent-duty-an-introduction-for-those-with-safeguarding-responsibilities

GOV.UK (2024) *School Workforce in England 2023*. Retrieved from: https://explore-education-statistics.service.gov.uk/find-statistics/school-workforce-in-england

Hall, S. (2015) 'Super-diverse street: A "trans-ethnography" across migrant localities', *Ethnic & Racial Studies*, themed issue on 'Cities, diversity, ethnicity', 38(1): 22–37.

Johnson, B. (2012) 'Let's not dwell on immigration but sow the seeds of integration', *Daily Telegraph*, 15 December.

Learning Wales. (2015) *Curriculum for Wales: Foundation Phases Framework*, Cardiff: Welsh Government (WG). Retrieved from: http://learning.gov.wales/docs/learningwales/publications/150803-fp-framework-en.pdf (accessed 30 October 2017).

Office for National Statistics (ONS). (2023) *How Life Has Changed in Newham: Census 2021*. Retrieved from: www.ons.gov.uk/visualisations/censusareachanges/E09000025 (accessed 20 November 2023).

Ofsted (2022) *Gascgoine Primary School*. Retrieved from: https://reports.ofsted.gov.uk/provider/21/131775

Myers, V. (2016) 'How to overcome our biases? Walk boldly toward them', *TED*. Retrieved from: www.ted.com/talks/verna_myers_how_to_overcome_our_biases_walk_boldly_toward_them

Newham Council (2022) *Building a Fairer Newham, Corporate Plan*. Retrieved from: www.newham.gov.uk/council/building-fairer-newham-corporate-plan

Ofsted. (2024) *School Inspection Handbook*. Retrieved from: www.gov.uk/government/publications/school-inspection-handbook-eif/school-inspection-handbook-for-september-2023

Qualifications and Curriculum Authority (QCA). (1998) *Education for Citizenship and the Teaching of Democracy in Schools*, London: QCA.

Qualifications and Curriculum Authority (QCA). (2002) *Designing and Timetabling the Primary Curriculum*, London: QCA.

Race Relations (Amendment) Act. (2000) Retrieved from: www.legislation.gov.uk/ukpga/2000/34/contents.

Ross, L. (n.d.) *Connect With Kids and Parents of Different Cultures*. Retrieved from: www.scholastic.com/teachers/articles/teaching-content/connect-kids-and-parents-different-cultures-0/ (accessed 31 October 2017).

Scottish Government. (n.d.) *Anti-racism in Education Programme*. Retrieved from: www.gov.scot/groups/race-equality-and-anti-racism-in-education-programme-stakeholder-network-group/

Scottish Government. (2023) *Anti-racism in Scotland: Progress Review 2023*. Retrieved from: www.gov.scot/publications/anti-racism-scotland-progress-review-2023/

The Headteacher. (2023) *Diversity in Schools – How to Diversify Your Curriculum*. Retrieved from: www.theheadteacher.com/attainment-and-assessment/teachingpractice/how-to-diversify-your-curriculum (accessed 22 November 2023).

UNESCO. (2005) *Convention on the Protection and Promotion of the Diversity of Cultural Expressions*, Paris: UNESCO, 20 October.

Welsh Government. (2022) *Designing Your Curriculum: Developing a Vision for Curriculum Design*. Retrieved from: https://hwb.gov.wales/curriculum-for-wales/designing-your-curriculum/developing-a-vision-for-curriculum-design/ (accessed 26 April 2024).

UNIT 6.5

RESPONDING TO LINGUISTIC DIVERSITY

Virginia Bower

INTRODUCTION

The intention of this unit is to convey two key messages:

- that responding to linguistic diversity means more than merely acknowledging the languages spoken in our class and a consideration of what support might be required; rather, it involves celebrating, utilising and capitalising on this diversity to the benefit of all children in the setting;
- that bilingual learners should be seen as having something 'extra' in terms of the linguistic and cultural diversity they bring to the classroom, and not as a problem that needs to be managed.

With these key messages in mind, the frequently observed tendency towards the 'deficit' model (Carruthers and Nandi, 2021), which perceives bilingual learners as 'lacking' something – that *something* being the English language – might be replaced by an appreciation of what bilingual children and their families can contribute to classroom life.

This unit will use the term 'bilingual learners' (in schools in England, Scotland and Wales the term usually used is children and families with English/Welsh as an additional language [EAL/WAL]; in Northern Ireland 'newcomers' is now in common usage) in an attempt to further emphasise the linguistic power these learners possess. However, it is important to clarify what is meant, in this sense, by bilingual. It certainly does not mean that a child or adult is necessarily proficient and fluent in more than one language. The Cambridge Assessment International Education (CAIE) definition helps to clarify this, referring to: 'individuals or groups who routinely use two or more languages for communication in varying contexts' (CAIE, 2017: 1).

Children might be fully literate in their first language, with very little knowledge of English. Others, such as very young children or children who have had no formal education, will have limited literacy in *any* language. Some children will be literate in their own language and can speak some/a great deal of English. Others will speak English in school and language 1 (L1) at home. Responding to linguistic diversity involves identifying these differences and ensuring that a whole school ethos is promoted that enables the creative use of pedagogies and practices to support all needs. This unit will examine these notions and will offer practical ideas and activities for everyday practice.

OBJECTIVES

By the end of this unit you should:

- have an understanding of the historical and current context for bilingual learners;
- know how to respond to and promote linguistic diversity;
- have an appreciation of bilingual children's knowledge and skills;
- have an understanding of practical strategies that might be implemented to support bilingual learners and capitalise on their existing knowledge and understanding.

HISTORICAL BACKGROUND: HOW DID WE GET TO WHERE WE ARE NOW?

An understanding of the historical, political, research and educational background underpinning current theories and practices relating to linguistic diversity is necessary if we are to comprehend the context in which we work. This section will provide an overview of the issues and perspectives that have emerged since the mid-twentieth century, with reference to both policy and research. The policy relates to England, as within this nation, there is a tendency towards 'monolingualising or assimilationist policy orientations' (Gundarina & Simpson, 2022: 524), whereby English is seen as the high status, legitimate language through which to learn. In contrast, Wales, Scotland and Northern Ireland arguably demonstrate more of an appreciation of bilingualism in terms of positive commitments to Gaelic, Welsh and Irish, although it is likely that challenges remain in multilingual settings.

1920s–1950s: At this time, it was suspected that learning more than one language was likely to have a detrimental effect on the brain, and that it would lead to confusion, low academic achievement, language delay and 'suboptimal cognitive development' (Antoniou, 2019: 396).

1960s and 1970s: From the late 1960s onwards, there was increasing recognition of the advantages of being bilingual, reflected in Section 11 of the Local Government Act (1966), which decreed that funding was to be made available to support bilingual learners. This usually followed the model of providing out-of-class interventions, either within the school setting or in a separate language centre (The Bell Foundation, n.d.), although the Bullock Report (Department of Education and Science [DES], 1975) recognised that allowing children to use their first language (L1) in the classroom might be beneficial.

1980s: This decade saw some significant changes, some of which arose from the Swann Report (DES, 1985). This report advanced, in the most positive of terms, a respect for cultural diversity, the importance of language learning and the need for bilingual learners to be integrated into all aspects of classroom life, rather than excluded through interventions. Funding was to be used, therefore, for in-class support, provided by language specialists. However, the Swann Report rejected the idea that minority languages should be taught or were useful to maintain. In fact, 'the promotion of biliteracy was seen as a threat to social cohesion' (Bower, 2016: 48), despite a renewed interest in theories relating to 'cross-linguistic transfer' and 'contrastive analysis', whereby bilingual learners are perceived to use what they know of L1 to support their development of the second language (L2).

1990s: This decade saw growing centralisation, with budgets increasingly controlled by schools rather than local authorities, leading to a reduction in funding for supporting bilingual learners. Schools had competing priorities, and responding to linguistic diversity was rarely on the top of the list. There was, however, the introduction of the Ethnic Minority Achievement Grant (1999) allocated to Local Education Authorities, with the aim of narrowing achievement gaps and providing support for bilingual learners. Despite this, any benefits gained were arguably lost through the educational direction of travel at this time. A rising focus on the 'standards agenda' (Williams-Brown & Jopling, 2021: 49), which emerged in the late 1980s with the Education Reform Act (1988), introduced a competitive market for schools which included statutory testing and the publication of league tables and parental choice over schools. This had a profound effect on provision for and the experience of bilingual learners. It has been suggested that children from diverse backgrounds who had English as a second language began to be perceived as having the potential to lower school test results, with the consequence that 'it was no longer in a school's interest to welcome refugee children and other newcomers to England' (Rampton, Harris and Leung, 2001: 6). The introduction of the National Curriculum, National Literacy Strategy (Department for Education and Employment [DfEE], 1998) and the Literacy Hour, promoted a focus on Standard English as the only acceptable mode of oral and written communication in primary schools. Rather than responding to linguistic diversity, arguably this promoted the idea of 'English only' in primary classrooms.

2000s: Encouragingly, however, research studies into bilingual learners – including research based on new technologies and neuro-imaging – continued to indicate the extensive benefits of being bilingual. Advisory materials produced by the English government in this decade appeared to recognise these benefits and the importance of supporting bilingual learners. Among these, the Primary National Strategy materials (Department for Education and Skills [DfES], 2006), including *New Arrivals Excellence Programme Guidance* (Department for Children, Schools and Families [DCSF], 2007) and *Excellence and Enjoyment: Learning and Teaching for Bilingual Children in the Primary Years* (Department for Education and Skills [DfES], 2007), explicitly promoted the use of children's first language to support their learning and recognised the value of making links to the child's home culture and individual experiences. There was still the sense, however, that use of L1 should be temporary; rather than capitalising on the diversity in English primary schools and using it to commit to a bilingual approach to the benefit of all children, the support was to ensure proficiency in English and slowly replace the mother tongue. Conteh and Brock (2011) refer to this as 'transitional' bilingualism where speaking L1 is perceived as an acceptable bridge to speaking good English, but, once English is established, a second language is not necessary.

2010s: This decade saw the revised National Curriculum in England (Department for Education [DfE], 2014), which included no specific guidance; instead, it highlighted the responsibility of all teachers for ensuring the progress of bilingual learners, subsuming this support within the idea of general inclusion. This is reflected in the ITT Core Content Framework, which provides generic guidance on pedagogy and practice, with no particular direction for teacher trainees in terms of providing support to those learning to learn in a new language (Richardson, 2020).

Current day: In England, 22% of pupils in primary school are bilingual learners (DfE, 2024). In Wales, the figure is 7.5% (primary and secondary), Scotland 6.7% (primary and secondary) and Northern Ireland 4.9% (primary and secondary). There is ongoing debate as to the benefits of bilingualism in terms of executive functions, cognitive aging and the delay of incidence of neuropathology (dementia, for example), but the evidence suggests that 'the effect of bilingualism is real, and it contributes to the robustness of cognitive ability' (Bialystok, 2021: 4). It is with this message in mind that I would like you to read the remainder of this unit, considering ways that you can promote language in your classroom.

Task 6.5.1 Examining your own context

Think about a school context you know well. This might be a setting where you have had a placement, where you work or, indeed, where you went to school. Make notes on the following questions:

- How does your context reflect the timeline just illustrated?
- What have you noticed about support and funding for bilingual learners?
- To what extent do you feel prepared to ensure that bilingual learners are included in all aspects of classroom life?
- What might you do to further improve your confidence in this area?

KNOWLEDGE OF CHILDREN'S BACKGROUNDS: HOW THIS CAN SUPPORT US TO RESPOND POSITIVELY TO LINGUISTIC DIVERSITY

The preceding section examined the macro perspective, in terms of the historical and current context, setting the scene for a more local and personal examination of bilingual children in our classrooms. If we are to be successful in responding to linguistic diversity, an understanding is needed of children's backgrounds, so that we can recognise what they bring to the classroom and the areas where they might need support.

Imagine that a Nepalese child is enrolled in your class, and you are told they are from a military background, the family having recently been posted to England. Immediately, this provides you with useful context: the child may be accustomed to moving from country to country, school to school. It is likely that they can speak some English, and that their parents will have at least a basic knowledge of the English language. A little more investigation might inform you that Nepalese families are often very keen on supporting their child's education and will be happy to engage with learning activities at home. You might discover that although the child can switch between spoken languages with ease, they are not confident to write in either Nepali or English. It does not take much effort to find out useful details such as these, by speaking to family members or the military community, looking at any records that accompany the child, researching the culture, ethos and traditions of the Nepalese community or speaking with bilingual personnel within the school or local community.

This information not only provides a starting point for planning, teaching and adapting practice to meet individual needs (DfE, 2019: 20), it also reminds us of the significant advantages bilingual learners have in terms of the social, cultural, linguistic and cognitive benefits (Bailey and Marsden, 2017: 299), and how this enriches our classrooms. Next is a list of suggestions relating to how you might be proactive in terms of finding out as much as possible about children's backgrounds:

- Find out what language/s is/are spoken at home and, if possible, if parents are literate/biliterate.
- Read any documentation that might have accompanied the child, so that you are aware of previous educational experiences.
- Research aspects of the child's culture, traditions, language and so forth to help avoid misunderstandings or actions that might prove to be disrespectful or alienating.

- Investigate the education system in the child's home country and the prevalent pedagogies and practices – this can help you assess why a child might, for example, be reluctant to engage in a 'talk partners' activity or to raise their hand. I remember, in my first year of teaching, a girl in my class would stand up every time she answered a question. She soon realised that this was not expected within the English classroom culture, but, had I known this in advance, I could have talked to her about it and prevented potential embarrassment for her.
- Take time to discuss and celebrate different cultural practices and linguistic variances. Children will very soon realise if their language and culture are not valued and may even feel ashamed (Cummins, 2005). This is not only de-motivating and damaging to self-esteem but might also cause tensions for them between home and school. Learning key words yourself – in a child's language – demonstrates that you are interested and value all languages.

As well as gleaning as much information as possible about the linguistic diversity of the children in our class, much can be learned from finding out about the families and the communities to which they belong.

Case study

One school that I worked in went beyond an 'open door' policy for parents and organised specific activities to promote engagement, interaction and ongoing communication between the school and its families. Examples of this were regular coffee mornings, where parents were invited to come along and meet members of staff and other parents. Classes were organised for parents for whom English was not their first language, so that they themselves could learn English. Other sessions were organised where parents could join sessions to find out about the curriculum their children were studying; the topics for that term, the objectives and some of the pedagogies and practices that were likely to be employed. Often, if parents and children are from different countries, the education system they will have experienced and the way it is delivered will be very different and they may feel alienated and excluded from the discourse surrounding learning. These informative, yet social, events were highly successful in breaking down barriers and developing a sense of belonging.

Task 6.5.2 Considering children's backgrounds

Look at the following list, which provides examples of possible backgrounds of bilingual learners:

- refugees;
- Gypsy, Roma and Traveller children;
- children from well-established local communities;
- children of short-stay business families.

Consider how these diverse backgrounds might have an impact on the children's linguistic, cognitive and social development. Conduct a little research into the types of experience these children might already have encountered. List some ways by which you might ensure that the diversity they bring is acknowledged and celebrated, while their needs are met.

LEARNING A SECOND LANGUAGE: WHAT DOES THIS ENTAIL?

If we are to respond successfully to linguistic diversity, an understanding of what learning a second language entails is required. In fact, not only this, we need also to appreciate how it feels to *learn to learn* in a new language. Learning a second language has similarities and differences to learning our first language. The similarities include the following:

- Language learning often happens in recognisable stages and patterns, with the gradual accumulation of words enabling increasingly complex sentences to be created and utilised.
- When speaking, pronunciation is crucial to meaning-making.
- When writing, grammatically correct sentences are crucial to meaning-making.
- There are connections between words (morphology) and when we make these connections, language learning moves forward; making the connections between 'comfortable' and 'uncomfortable' and 'beauty' and 'beautiful' for example. I am currently learning Portuguese and it has helped me immensely to realise that 'ment' in Portuguese is the equivalent of 'ly' in English - for example 'lentement' = 'slowly' and that 'ção' in Portuguese is a word ending equivalent to 'ion' in English e.g. 'estação' = 'station'.
- The realisation of the power of language in different contexts.

Task 6.5.3 Using knowledge about language learning to ensure a positive response to linguistic diversity

Consider the five bullet points just mentioned. Choose two of these and think about pedagogies and practices you might utilise which reflect an understanding of how children learn language and enable you to respond to linguistic diversity. For example, the fourth bullet point has a focus on morphology. If you were teaching about adverbs or suffixes, you could take a bilingual approach (using your knowledge of a language other than English spoken in your class) and introduce an activity like this:

Example of a 'cloze procedure' activity to support identification of adverbs, with accompanying bilingual word bank:

The sun was shining -------- in the sky.

The boy whispered ------- to his mother.

--------, she started her exam.

English	Portuguese
quietly	silenciosamente
nervously	nervosamente
brightly	brilhantement

There are also *differences* between learning our first language and learning a second:

- When learning a first language, a child is usually surrounded by others who speak that language, and they are immersed in the sounds and cadences. If bilingual learners are in an English-speaking primary school, they will certainly be immersed in English, but they might be the only individual who has a different L1.
- When children learn their first language, those interacting with them tend to adjust and simplify their language. In the classroom, bilingual learners are having to keep up with the pace of those who have English as their first language, and, more often than not, the language used is not modified, e.g. the use of more grammatically minimal sentence structures or avoiding the use of idioms.
- With a second language, the learner already possesses an understanding of how language works and some of the rules of spoken and written language.
- There is often a self-consciousness or embarrassment attached to speaking or writing in a second language, particularly if you are the only bilingual learner.

Becoming familiar with a second language usually begins with recognising and utilising everyday words and phrases – what might be referred to as 'survival' language which allows us to negotiate the routines of life. These are known as basic interpersonal communication skills (BICs) (Cummins, 2001), which can take at least two years to acquire and feel confident with. Although basic skills begin with straightforward words and phrases, interpersonal communication can of course become extremely complex, as often it includes the use of colloquial expressions, idioms and culturally based language, which can be difficult to master. In Liu *et al.*'s (2017: 384) study into the multilingual pedagogies employed in two schools, one of the identified principles underpinning practice was 'simplifying tasks to cater to individual needs and contexts'. A teacher in the study noted the importance of being aware of the language we use in the classroom – avoiding colloquialisms, for example – and the speed we deliver information.

Alongside the more basic language skills, bilingual learners in English primary schools are also obliged to learn to learn through the 'medium of a new language' (Kelly, 2010: 76). To succeed within a monolingual assessment system, children need to rapidly acquire cognitive academic language proficiency (CALP) (Cummins, 2001), to enable successful engagement with the curriculum. CALP can take at least five to seven years to achieve. Think about this in relation to the previous section, where children's backgrounds were discussed. If a bilingual learner enters the education system age 7, for example, they may be into their secondary school years before they are reaching a level of CALP. This, of course, depends on many factors, but it certainly should raise our awareness of the enormity of bilingual children's achievements.

Bilingual children will often be observed engaging in what is sometimes referred to as 'codeswitching' between L1 and L2, more often in spoken than written language. By this, we mean moving from one language to another, sometimes within sentences or, at other times, to suit a particular context or situation. A more recent and potentially more useful term, 'translanguaging', is described by Wei (2017: 23) as a situation whereby 'different languages are used in a dynamic and functionally integrated manner to organize and mediate mental processes in understanding, speaking, reading, writing and, not least, learning.' For many families, translanguaging is a way of life, as some members might speak two or more languages, whereas others may be monolingual. Parents and children might be literate in more than one language, or they might be proficient with regards to BICs, but not with CALP. Sometimes, children are required to translate for their parents and switch between languages to ensure effective communication. One of my primary teacher colleagues once reported an instance at a parent consultation meeting where the child was translating for his mother. The news about the child's progress was not altogether positive, and yet the mother was smiling and seemed delighted.

It was then that my colleague realised the translation might not be wholly accurate! Although this is a humorous anecdote, it emphasises the responsibility that is often on young children's shoulders.

Children might predominantly use L1 in play, but then switch to L2 for more formal classroom activities. Given the opportunity, children and adults will use the language most suited to them for particular situations and practices. Wei (2017: 25) coined the term 'Translanguaging space' wherein there is not merely co-existence between people's identities, their values and their practices; instead these elements 'combine together to generate new identities, values and practices.' The following case study, taken from my doctoral research, seems to encapsulate Wei's idea of a 'Translanguaging space'. In this example, the children were all sitting on the carpet and, one at a time, were invited to the front to put a decoration on the Christmas tree.

Case study

Suresh tapped the teaching assistant for attention and said 'Sujit said can he have his bottle?' She nodded, and he and Sujit went to their bottles and had long drinks and a little chat in Nepali. They lingered there for some time, patting their stomachs and clearly demonstrating the amount of water they were consuming by pushing out their stomachs as far as possible. There was quite a bit of very gentle contact between them. Then Sujit pointed at the Christmas decorations and said 'Star!' and Suresh pointed and said 'Wow!' They sat back down, side by side, and for a few minutes, watched the other children decorating the tree. Then, whilst the tree was still being decorated, they rolled up their sleeves and compared muscles and pinched each other's muscles (in a friendly way!) in what looked like a macho contest. They started talking about red and white Ninjas very quietly, moving back and forth between Nepali and English. They had an extended conversation for over five minutes about who they were going to invite to play with them. Then they kissed each other on the shoulder and turned to me and started telling me about the rewards board they had in the classroom.

What is so significant for me about this incident is how the inherent sociability of the two boys enabled them to have one eye on the classroom activity, whilst supporting each other linguistically and engaging in conversation about their shared interests. Wei (2017: 25) writes that, 'Human beings' knowledge of language cannot be separated from their knowledge of human relations and human social interaction which includes the history, the context of usage and the emotional and symbolic values of specific socially constructed languages.' In the case study example, Sujit recognises that Suresh might not have the confidence or linguistic competence to ask the assistant for his water bottle, so he does this for him, thus modelling the language needed. The boys then acknowledge the Christmas tree and decorations – using English – before engaging in several sociable interactions, moving between languages to suit their needs. Finally, the boys see me observing and engage me in conversation, in English, recognising that Nepali would not be appropriate. This whole incident was based on trust, friendship and a sense of belonging, and is an excellent model for our own responses to linguistic diversity. Allowing time for children to discuss and explore ideas, time where they can move between languages without anxiety or self-consciousness, is a step towards creating an ethos and educational climate that reflects superdiversity (Vertovec, 2007) within our classrooms. This is further explored in the following section.

CELEBRATING AND CAPITALISING UPON LINGUISTIC DIVERSITY: DEVELOPING GOOD PRACTICE AND IMPROVING THE LEARNING EXPERIENCE FOR ALL

The idea of celebrating and capitalising upon linguistic diversity is encapsulated effectively in the Northern Ireland policy document, *Every School a Good School: Supporting Newcomer Pupils*. Here they observe that inclusive practice 'not only welcomes newcomer pupils but turns the linguistic, cultural and ethnic diversity to the educational advantage of all' (Department of Education for Northern Ireland [DENI], 2011: 21). The social, cognitive and linguistic benefits of expanding and deepening our language repertoires and knowledge about language are well-documented and, as teachers, we are in a prime position to promote these benefits. Taking a principled approach, built on the wealth of research into bilingualism and learning in a new language, empowers us to celebrate and capitalise on the linguistic diversity in our classrooms, improving the learning experience for all.

In a project undertaken by Liu *et al.* (2017), which examined multilingual pedagogies in two schools, ten principles were identified from observations and interviews with teachers. The ten principles are:

1. drawing on professional expertise to make informed professional judgements;
2. using bilingual resources and strategies for specific teaching purposes;
3. employing multimodal aids to reduce the language demands in learning;
4. simplifying tasks to cater to individual needs and contexts;
5. using home language for academic and social purposes;
6. making cultural and contextual references to create resonance and rapport;
7. combining mainstreaming with individual-focused support to ensure that no one is left behind;
8. 'buddying' to provide peer support for learning and social integration;
9. using dialogic tasks for effective content and language integration;
10. using flexible and continuous assessment to promote learning.

For the purposes of this section, I have focused on numbers 2 and 5 suggesting some practical ideas which reflect these principles. However, I would recommend reading the article in full and examining all ten principles in more depth. The research is undertaken in secondary schools but is wholly relevant to all settings.

Principle 2: Using bilingual resources and strategies for specific teaching purposes

There are so many effective resources and strategies which will help you respond to linguistic diversity in your classroom. Once you allow yourself to be creative and innovative, ideas will begin to flow! However, it is important to avoid feeling overwhelmed in terms of planning and resourcing lessons. I always refer to the 'drip drip' approach - using just one new approach/pedagogy/resource each week perhaps - this adds up to a bucket full of drips over a term and a year! Here, I am going to outline two ideas to get you started:

- dual language picture books;
- lexical sets and language mats.

Dual-language picture books

Dual-language picture books are an invaluable resource - of enormous benefit to both bilingual and monolingual learners. These texts demonstrate a respect for and interest in another language. They enable children to see their own language written down (even if they are not able to read it) and to share and delight in the shapes of the letters and words and explore the differences and similarities. In 2000, Edwards, Monaghan and Knight conducted research into the use of multimedia bilingual books, focusing on the effectiveness of these as tools for teaching. The teachers noticed a growth in metalinguistic awareness, not just for bilingual learners, but also for weaker, monolingual readers. Not only this, but discussions held with the children after they had engaged with the bilingual texts were invaluable in terms of assessing their reading progress and their language comprehension.

Here are some ways you might integrate the use of dual-language texts into your daily practice:

- Put children in pairs – one Bulgarian and one English, for example – and they could read to each other in their own languages. If they are not yet reading, they could look at the pictures and discuss what they think the story is about.
- Encourage parents to come in and read to children in different languages.
- Plan for book-making sessions where children can explore their personal identity and heritage through creating their own texts. This activity reflects a dialogic approach to teaching and learning (see Principle 9), where children could work in pairs or groups to produce dual-language texts, each contributing their own language.
- Use, for example, a Turkish/English version of a traditional tale with an accompanying audio version. This will help a Turkish-speaking child to follow the story when it is used in class, to participate in activities and to start reading in English. The two written texts will be particularly supportive if the child is already literate in Turkish.

You can find a dual-language booklist on the National Literacy Trust website:

https://literacytrust.org.uk/resources/dual-language-booklist/
Mantra lingua is very useful for dual-language picture books:
https://uk.mantralingua.com/

Approach your senior leadership team and ask if there is any budget to invest in these wonderful resources.

Lexical sets and language mats

Learning relies on language and access to a wide range of vocabulary. Lexical sets are words associated with a subject, for example the weather, and having prior knowledge of words that might be used in a lesson provides 'hooks' for children's learning, enabling them to engage. They can be used to pre-teach vocabulary before a lesson (either to a small group or the whole class), particularly when the lexicon of a topic or subject is complex. They are beneficial during the initial input of a new topic and can then be used throughout the lesson if and when children need them. These are valuable to ALL children in your class; they are valuable even if you do not have bilingual children in your class! Here is an example of a dual-language lexical set (English/Portuguese):

in the sea	no mar
water	a água
fish	o peixe
shark	o tubarão
jelly fish	a água-viva
boat	o barco
rocks	as rochas

It takes no time at all to translate some of the key words you intend to use in your lesson into another language. However, if you have many different languages spoken in your class then this can be time-consuming, and you could perhaps encourage parents to support with producing these lexical sets. Alternatively, children in the later primary years could have this as a project for homework – creating resources for their peers and for younger children in the school. Lexical sets can be presented in the form of language mats. Here is a bilingual (English/Portuguese) example, where the words are supported by pictures:

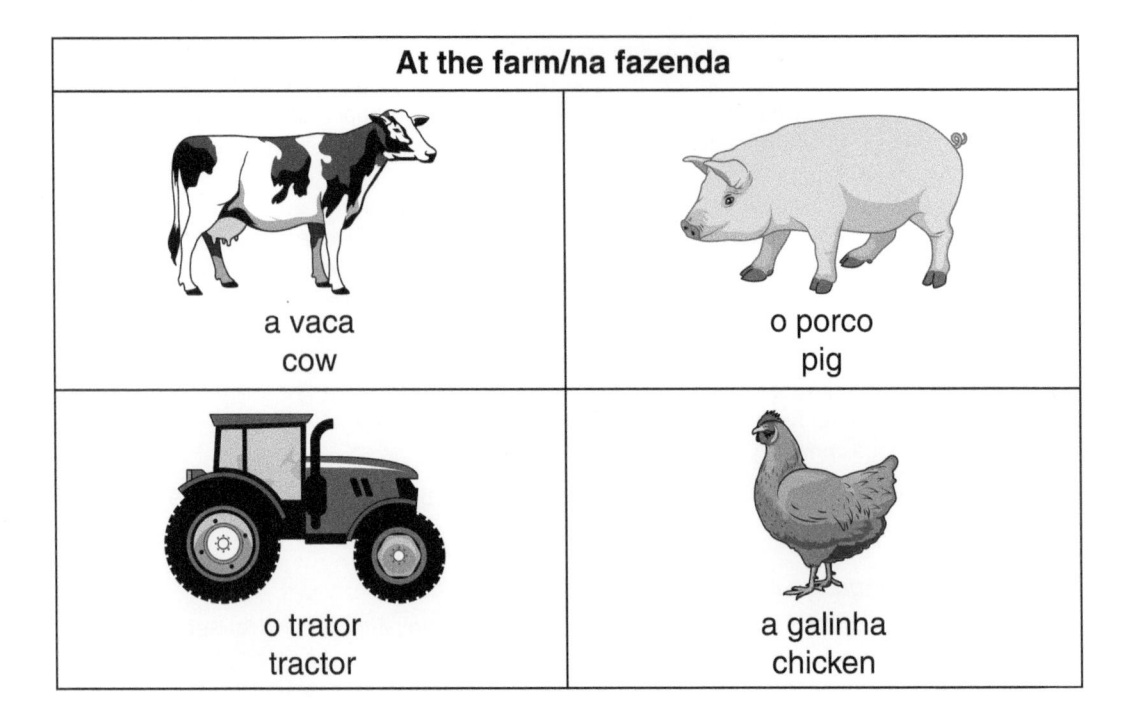

At the farm/na fazenda	
a vaca cow	o porco pig
o trator tractor	a galinha chicken

Having pictures gives children an extra cue when they are learning new vocabulary. If you have A4 paper, divided into 12 squares, children and their families can enjoy creating language mats for different subjects and topics, and these can then be laminated and used repeatedly.

Task 6.5.4 Creating lexical sets and language mats

Think of a topic which you have taught/observed recently. List the key words relating to this topic, creating a lexical set. Now translate this list into a language of your choice and create a language mat, with accompanying images. Once you have started doing these, you will probably be keen to produce more!

Principle 5: Using home language for academic and social purposes

Vygotsky (1962: 110) writes that a child needs 'to see his native language as one particular system among many', and this is true for all the children in your class. Early awareness and appreciation of different languages and cultures are fundamental to a society that has an authentic interest in and respect for human diversity. Children need to realise that their home language is valued and respected in the classroom and that it is good practice to use L1 if they feel it supports them. Gundarina and

Simpson (2022) noted the severely damaging effects on the subject of their research – a 7-year-old Russian girl – when denied access to L1 in the classroom; indeed, she was punished for using it.

Bailey and Marsden (2017: 284) highlight three strong reasons for promoting the use of L1:

- a means of helping bilingual learners access English and the curriculum
- a way of celebrating diversity and recognising children's home lives
- a way of welcoming or integrating pupils into the classroom.

It is not enough to 'allow' children to use L1. If it is not actively promoted, children will be very quick to realise that English is the only valued language, and that maintaining their L1 holds no material advantage. Here are some ways to ensure that children feel comfortable in using L1, socially and academically:

- Use other languages yourself, regularly, and encourage pupils to do the same. This could be answering the register in another language; using key phrases in different languages – instructional, imperative language is effective here as it is short, sharp and easy to remember, for example 'Fetch your coats'.
- If you have bilingual learners in the class who are confident and happy to speak in front of their peers, they could be encouraged to teach some words and phrases of their language. This does not need to be specifically planned for in a particular lesson. Instead, it is likely to be more powerful if it is spontaneous and authentic, responding to something that happens in a lesson, for example in maths you might ask, 'How do you say triangle in Polish?'.
- Displays can be routinely produced to reflect the range of languages in the class. Most displays tend to have nouns identified, and these are relatively easy to translate. Small voice recorders can be attached to displays, and children could be encouraged to record themselves explaining an element of the display in their L1. For example, if several children have Nepali as L1, they could contribute to a maths display on shape by naming the shape and describing it in Nepali. These translation activities are beneficial in a number of ways. They raise the status of all languages spoken; they can potentially involve all children and their parents; they enable children to use and hear their L1, promoting a safe and stimulating, language-rich environment; and they enhance the linguistic experience of monolingual children, exposing them to the sounds and rhythms of different languages.

SUMMARY

If practitioners are to respond effectively to linguistic diversity, a recognition is needed that each child will arrive in school with useful and potentially transformative knowledge and experience. Within the confines of the curriculum, flexible and innovative approaches are required that provide a space for bilingual children to develop both L1 and L2 and work collaboratively to promote a rich learning environment for all. Wei (2017: 19), suggests that 'the complex linguistic landscape of the 21st century calls for new approaches to multilingualism and linguistic diversity' and part of this means that, rather than problematising children's bilingualism, it might be more appropriate to problematise our own monolingualism (Palmer and Martinez, 2013), and seek ways by which to embrace and capitalise on linguistic diversity within our classrooms. Imaginative approaches to planning, teaching, resourcing and assessment will raise our own levels of practice, while enhancing the learning experience for all our pupils.

ANNOTATED FURTHER READING

Conteh, J. (2012) *Teaching Bilingual and EAL Learners in Primary Schools*, London: Sage.
> Jean Conteh has a wealth of experience working with and researching the lives of bilingual children and their families. In this text, she addresses beliefs and misconceptions relating to bilingual learners and provides ideas and strategies for supporting their needs. This is a very readable and engaging text that draws on a wide range of research within the field.

Creese, A. and Blackledge, A. (2018) *The Routledge Handbook of Language and Superdiversity*, London: Routledge.
> The abstract to this book states that, '"superdiversity" has the potential to contribute to an enhanced understanding of mobility, complexity, and change, with theoretical, practical, global, and methodological reach'. From this, you can see the value of this text, and its chapters cover a vast range of topics relating to linguistic diversity.

FURTHER READING TO SUPPORT M-LEVEL STUDY

Safford, K. and Drury, R. (2013) 'The "problem" of bilingual children in educational settings: Policy and research in England', *Language & Education*, 27(1): 70-81.
> This is a very readable article that includes a very useful timeline relating to how approaches to ethnic minority children have changed over the years. The authors promote the importance of understanding what bilingual children bring to the classroom, rather than seeing them as a problem.

Bialystok, E. (2021) 'Bilingualism as a slice of Swiss cheese', *Frontiers in Psychology*, 12: 1-6.
> Bialystok has for many years been a key researcher into the impact of bilingualism. This very timely article uses the pandemic to illustrate how finding a 'one size fits all' solution to major, global issues is never likely and that the 'Swiss cheese model' is often needed – 'each slice has holes, but the holes are in different places, so when the slices are stacked together, all the holes are blocked' (p. 1) and applies this to the debates around bilingualism – a fascinating article!

RELEVANT WEBSITES

National Association for Language Development in the Curriculum: https://naldic.org.uk/
> This website has a wealth of information. Some of this is accessible without joining the association, but I would highly recommend joining. There is a very low subscription, and this then allows you access to all the online resources and journals.

The Bell Foundation: www.bell-foundation.org.uk/
> The Bell Foundation's key message is: 'Changing lives and overcoming exclusion through language education': something for all of us to aspire to. Their website is invaluable. The Bell Foundation has resources, webinars, research and a great deal of other support which you can draw on, whatever your role in school.

REFERENCES

Antoniou, M. (2019) 'The advantages of bilingualism debate', *Annual Review of Linguistics*, 5(1): 395-417.

Bailey, E. G. and Marsden, E. (2017) 'Teachers' views on recognising and using home languages in predominantly monolingual primary schools', *Language and Education*, 31(4): 283-386.

Bialystok, E. (2021) 'Bilingualism as a slice of Swiss cheese', *Frontiers in Psychology*, 12: 1-6.

Bower, V. (2016) 'Supporting Nepalese children with English as an additional language in the English primary school'. Unpublished PhD thesis, Canterbury Christ Church University, UK.

Cambridge Assessment International Education (CAIE). (2017) *Bilingual Learners and Bilingual Education*, Cambridge: UCLES.

Carruthers, J. and Nandi, A. (2021) 'Supporting speakers of community languages: a case study of policy and practice in primary schools', *Current Issues in Language Planning*, 22(3): 269-289.

Conteh, J. and Brock, A. (2011) '"Safe spaces"? Sites of bilingualism for young learners in home, school and community', *International Journal of Bilingual Education & Bilingualism*, 14(3): 347-360.

Cummins, J. (2001) *Language, Power and Pedagogy*, Clevedon, UK: Multilingual Matters.

Cummins, J. (2005) 'A proposal for action: Strategies for recognising heritage language competence as a learning resource with the mainstream classroom', *The Modern Language Journal*, 898(4): 585-592.

Department for Children, Schools and Families (DCSF). (2007) *New Arrivals Excellence Programme Guidance*. Retrieved from: www.naldic.org.uk/Resources/NALDIC/Teaching%20and%20Learning/naep.pdf

Department for Education (DfE). (2014) *The National Curriculum in England: Framework Document*. Retrieved from: https://assets.publishing.service.gov.uk/media/5a7db9e9e5274a5eaea65f58/Master_final_national_curriculum_28_Nov.pdf

Department for Education (DfE). (2019) *Initial Teacher Training (ITT): Core Content Framework*, London: DfE. Last updated 2024.

Department for Education (DfE). (2024) *Schools, Pupils and Their Characteristics*. Retrieved from: https://explore-education-statistics.service.gov.uk/find-statistics/school-pupils-and-their-characteristics

Department for Education and Skills (DfES). (2007) *Excellence and Enjoyment: Learning and Teaching for Bilingual Children in the Primary Years*. Retrieved from: https://dera.ioe.ac.uk/id/eprint/6560/7/DFES-00068-2007_Redacted.pdf

Department of Education and Science (DES). (1975) *The Bullock Report: A Language for Life*, London: HMSO.

Department of Education and Science (DES). (1985) *Education for All: Report of the Committee of Inquiry into the Education of Children from Ethnic Minority Groups (Swann Report)*, Cmnd. 9453, London: HMSO.

Department of Education for Northern Ireland (DENI). (2011) *Every School a Good School: Supporting Newcomer Pupils*, Bangor, NI: DENI.

Department for Education and Employment (DfEE). (1998) *The National Literacy Strategy: Framework for Teaching*, London: DfEE.

Department for Education and Skills (DfES). (2006) *Primary National Strategy Excellence and Enjoyment: Learning and Teaching for Bilingual Children in the Primary Years*, London: DfES.

Education Reform Act (1988). Retrieved from: www.legislation.gov.uk/ukpga/1988/40/contents

Edwards, V., Monaghan, F. and Knight, J. (2000) 'Books, pictures and conversations: Using bilingual multimedia storybooks to develop language awareness', *Language Awareness*, 9(3): 135-146.

Gundarina, O. and Simpson, J. (2022) 'A monolingual approach in an English primary school: practices and implications', *Language and Education*, 36(6): 523-543.

Kelly, C. (2010) *Hidden Worlds*, Stoke-on-Trent, UK: Trentham.

Liu, Y., Fisher, L., Forbes, K. and Evans, M. (2017) 'The knowledge base of teaching in linguistically diverse contexts: 10 grounded principles of multilingual classroom pedagogy for EAL', *Language and Intercultural Communication*, 17(4): 378-395.

Palmer, D. and Martinez, R. A. (2013) 'Teacher agency in bilingual spaces: A fresh look at preparing teachers to educate Latina/o bilingual children', *Review of Research in Education*, 37: 269-297.

Rampton, B., Harris, R. and Leung, C. (2001) 'Education in England and speakers of languages other than English', *Working Papers in Urban Language and Literacies*, London: King's College London.

Richardson, S. (2020) *Quality Teaching for EAL Learners in the ITT Core Content Framework*. Retrieved from: www.bell-foundation.org.uk/news/blog-quality-teaching-for-eal-learners-in-the-itt-core-content-framework/ (accessed 6 November 2023).

The Bell Foundation (n.d.) *Historical Background to EAL Provision in England*. Retrieved from: www.bell-foundation.org.uk/eal-programme/guidance/eal-provision/(accessed 4 November 2023).

Vertovec, S. (2007) 'Super-diversity and its implications', *Ethnic and Racial Studies*, 30(6): 1024–1054.

Vygotsky, L. S. (1962) *Thought and Language*, Cambridge, MA: MIT Press.

Wei, L. (2017) 'Linguistic (super) diversity, post-multilingualism and translanguaging moments', in A. Creese and A. Blackledge (eds.) (2018) *The Routledge Handbook of Language and Superdiversity*, London: Routledge, pp. 16–29.

Williams-Brown, Z. and Jopling, M. (2021) '"Children are more than just a statistic. Education is more than government outlines": Primary teachers' perspectives on the standards agenda in England', *Educationalfutures*, 12(1): 48–72.

UNIT 6.6

GENDER MATTERS

Respectful approaches to gender equity in primary school

Jayne Osgood

INTRODUCTION

Contemporary public debate about gender is often highly charged, playing out across social media, policy arenas, educational institutions and family homes in vitriolic and sometimes unhelpful (and confusing) ways. Whilst gender in childhood incites a wide range of (often staunchly opposed) views and opinions, too often teachers find themselves caught in a seemingly impossible position. In 2019, the Department for Education (DfE) in the UK published guidance on Relationship and Sex Education (RSE), which stipulated that pupils must be taught about gender identity in age-appropriate and inclusive ways. This guidance was met with a degree of resistance, with critics arguing that teaching children about gender identity is inconsistent with the Education Act 1996, which prohibits 'political indoctrination'. However, supporters of teaching gender identity in schools argue that pupils must be given accurate and timely information about sexualities, healthy relationships and gender identity, which is especially needed in the current social and cultural environment. Neglecting to educate children about gender identity will lead to ignorance and misunderstanding, which will then contribute to discrimination and prejudice.

Therefore, teachers have a legal and ethical duty to take gender seriously and to find ways in which to appropriately embed gender equity into their daily practices at school – both in and out of the classroom. For many, a whole-school approach is adopted that involves curricular revisions, addressing the accessibility of school spaces (e.g. toilets, changing rooms); reappraising uniform guidelines and challenging cultures of gender stereotyping (or worse gender harassment and/or abuse). Yet many schools feel caught up in the gender 'culture wars' where conservative forces are hostile to these recent policy moves; but other organised parent and campaign groups demand more LGBT+ inclusive content, all of which frequently plays out against a backdrop of inadequate resources. For teachers caught up in this maelstrom, becoming literate in how best to address gender is not systematically addressed within initial teacher training programmes, Inservice Education and Training (INSET) and Continuing Professional Development (CPD). This unit offers insights, evidence and practical strategies that can make the task of addressing gender in our teaching and day-to-day interactions with young people less daunting.

This unit seeks to provide an orientation into the field of gender studies in childhood with the intention of exploring the reasons why gender remains crucially important and to consider theories of gender that shed light on how we come to think of gender in the ways that we do, and what that might

DOI: 10.4324/9781032691794-35

mean for how we interact with young children. Research shows that in many areas of life, gender is hugely important. Stereotyped ideas about how children ought to behave according to gender can be limiting and harmful. This is a powerful influence upon all children, and may be particularly challenging for those who are perceived not to fit in with certain gendered expectations. Therefore, it is vital that teachers feel equipped in how to empower pupils, create greater equity and ultimately contribute to broader shifts in society. Teaching for gender inclusivity involves developing capacities to critically appraise ourselves; our pedagogical approaches; our school environment and home-school relations. It involves challenging preconceived ideas and inviting open, sometimes uncomfortable, conversations that can make schools places that challenge restrictive ideas about gender that can make schools feel unsafe or hostile.

OBJECTIVES

By the end of this unit, you should:

- be aware of how ideas about children impact upon approaches to gender equity in school;
- identify ways to pursue gender equity in your everyday interactions with children;
- know how you can address RSE in ways that are inclusive and respectful.

BACKGROUND

Some questions that might usefully frame this unit include:

- How do you conceptualise children/childhood?
- How much thinking have you done about gender?
- How inclusive, safe and unbiased is your school, your classroom, your playground?
- How can you go about actioning positive change to best support your pupils?

These are not questions that have immediate or simple answers; they are intended as a starting place for critical self-reflection regarding ourselves, our schools and our classrooms that are worth regularly revisiting. Gender too often falls off the agenda because it seems too difficult, or irrelevant or simply too contentious.

In the contemporary context in which we teach, pupils are grappling with challenges around gender and sexualities. The language used with children, the (conflicting) messages they receive from books, the media and the home environment can have a powerful impact on how children feel about themselves and others. Teachers are key figures within children's lives from whom reliable, accurate and age-appropriate guidance can be provided as young people navigate their emerging identities. It is through assessing our own practice – the language used, the nature of our interactions, the resources chosen and the seemingly benign organisation of bodies and spaces – that a deeper appreciation of how gender comes to matter can find expression.

SHIFTING IDEAS ABOUT GENDER IN CHILDHOOD

Feminist researchers have made significant contributions to the ways gender and childhood are thought about; questioning long-established ideas that gender binaries are inevitable, 'natural' and determined by biology (e.g. Davies, 1989; Walkerdine, 1990; Robinson, 2012). Rather, gender and sexuality in children's everyday lives come about through social interactions and through cultural messages best understood as constantly negotiated, continuously emerging and taking shape. Therefore, children should not be understood as passively soaking up messages about gender binaries, but rather active in constructing their own gendered identities and regulating and policing those of others. Shifting the focus in childhood studies to a place that recognises children as exercising agency and producing/performing their gender as multiple and shifting is significant and informs contemporary conceptualisations. Recognising children as agentic beings who are persistently navigating (often competing, sometimes confusing, but always evolving) discourses about gender is a significant advance and has important implications for pedagogical practice and everyday life in school.

To practically support children's social and emotional capacities it is important for them to learn about respect, consent and well-being from the earliest age (Osgood, 2019). It is important that children feel able to learn how to understand themselves and others, and how to navigate the world around them. Young children undertake identity work starting in the early years (Robinson, 2013; Osgood and Robinson, 2019) by observing and making sense of the world as they encounter it and using their environment to facilitate the process (Green, Kalvaitis and Worster, 2016). This continues throughout childhood, adolescence and into adulthood, but it has been noted that towards the end of primary school gender becomes more heavily regulated through a desire to fit into normative expectations (Renold, 2004). Therefore, it is especially important for primary pupils to have opportunities to ask difficult questions about the world as they encounter it. Therefore, exposure to diversity is important (Amer, 2019) as it presents myriad possibilities for self-expression as children continue to explore their forming identity. Practical strategies in this respect are offered later in the unit.

Too frequently, though, significant adults in a child's life (parent, carer, teacher) fail to fully appreciate children's perceptive capacities. From birth, children will encounter countless gender assumptions and gender identities; by the time adults explicitly address these topics with them, ideas are already taking shape (Staley and Leonardi, 2019). Media, books, peers and people that children observe in everyday life generate curiosity about gender. There is an imperative for significant adults to engage in open conversations to avoid confusion and reliance upon inappropriate or inaccurate sources of information. Children need safe learning environments where they can explore gender issues, such as non-normative families and diverse gender identities.

Children's innate curiosity deserves to be taken seriously. The words uttered most frequently by young children are 'why' and 'how'; adults have a responsibility to explore the answers to these (sometimes difficult) questions with them. However, seemingly taboo topics (such as gender and sexuality) are a source of embarrassment for some parents and other adults hearing the questions (Robinson, 2013). Exploring the question openly rather than avoiding it demonstrates respect for children's rights. Young children notice and internalise the ways in which role-models (parents and teachers, amongst others) react. Embarrassment or unwillingness to answer questions can be interpreted that the topic is to be distrusted or feared, which may result in prejudice (Gidinski, 2019). Towards the end of this unit, direction to a selection of practical resources to help in this respect is offered.

PRIMARY SCHOOL AND THE 'HETEROSEXUAL MATRIX'

Primary school is an important site in which ideas about gender can be reinscribed, challenged or left largely unaddressed. They have also been identified as contexts that (perhaps unwittingly) tend to operate upon heteronormative logic. Butler (1990) wrote of the 'heterosexual matrix' which argues that only 'natural' and 'normalised' bodies, genders and desires are rendered culturally intelligible through processes of heterosexualisation. Heterosexuality provides such an everyday backdrop to contemporary childhood that it goes largely unnoticed (Robinson, 2013). As such, children come to understand themselves as gendered in relation to heteronormative discourses of gender through everyday language they encounter; the organisation of classroom space; sporting activities; games played in designated areas of the playground and so on – all of which are left unquestioned because *'that is the way it has always been done here'*, or *'it's quicker to organise them by gender'*, or *'that's just children being children'*, or *'boys need to let off steam'*, or *'girls are just more studious/quiet/compliant'*. This routine heteronormativity in schools frequently goes overlooked, but it has implications for children's sense of belonging. Such approaches are also markedly out of touch with the broader cultural context in which children are situated with more complex and sophisticated accounts of gender fluidity and diversity, discrimination and exclusion. The RSE guidance underlines the imperative for schools to consciously engage in teaching gender identity, but it allows for a narrow and contained engagement, rather than considering gender as permeating all aspects of contemporary schooling. As teachers, it is possible to embed a concern with how the heterosexual matrix works throughout all aspects of schooling and to actively call it to account through critical self-appraisal.

This section highlighted that children must be thought of as curious and capable, and their questions are worthy of respectful engagement. It has also underlined that gender is an issue that permeates all aspects of schooling, and whilst teaching gender identity through RSE is a progressive step it is not without tensions and challenges. It also does not go far enough to support children who are actively processing and negotiating their gendered identities daily, not only in designated RSE lessons. Unfortunately, ideas about gender identities remain stereotyped and schools play a significant part in perpetuating this. Gender is best understood as persistently taking shape; endlessly being questioned and processed, in fluid ways (Renold *et al*., 2017). Gender in primary school emerges through performances and interactions – it is not a static identity that is assigned and fixed throughout time. This section started with a series of questions that invite critical self-reflection. It concludes by adding to those questions to ask: *How can schools become places that challenge the gender binary and its restrictive stereotypes that limit how children think about themselves (and others)? How can schools be supportive, safe spaces where children can ask pertinent questions about gender identity?*

Task 6.6.1 Gender equity audit

Reflect upon how gender identities take shape in your school, your classroom, your practice.

Take a tour of the school to identify gendered practices:

Focus on displays; queuing systems; areas of the playground. Who takes up which spaces? When? Who is represented? Who is welcome? How? Could it be different?

Undertake a classroom audit:

Take a critical look at your bookshelves. Undertake a sorting exercise; make a note of the gender of authors, protagonists. (See Stonewall resources in the Relevant websites section at the end of this unit to assist in refreshing the literature that is available to children and how schemes of work might be organised differently to be more gender inclusive.)

Take stock of how children are organised. Are they seated by gender? Lined up by gender? Put in teams according to gender?

Map your school: Where, when and how does gender stereotyping routinely take shape throughout the school day? Across different areas of the school: inside/outside? During lunchbreaks? Assemblies?

CLASSROOM MATTERS

To address inequality we must start with critical personal reflection and map our prejudices and gendered practices onto what happens within our classrooms. This involves questioning our own expectations and identifying ways in which pupils are (unwittingly) stereotyped. Using gender stereotypical language is so deeply ingrained in everyday speech that it can go unnoticed. Stereotypical language contributes to divisions and hierarchies within the classroom; and for gender non-conforming pupils, or those questioning their gender identity (Lee, 2019), it is especially likely to be experienced negatively.

Classrooms are highly gendered spaces – classroom interactions are shaped by gender from designated learning areas, seating patterns, friendship groups and (perceived) willingness to participate. Boys' physical domination of classroom space has long been extensively researched (see Davies, 1989; Francis, 2006, and more recently, Lyttleton-Smith, 2019; Prioletta, 2022), revealing it be the source of disruption, sometimes aggressive, and often disruptive to learning. Dominant boys occupy more of the teachers' attention – in preventing or disciplining such behaviour. Although these gendered patterns are complicated by social class and ethnicity, research in primary schools nevertheless reveals that girls, less powerful boys and gender diverse pupils are often silenced through ridicule or by sexist/misogynistic/homophobic and/or transphobic abuse (Bragg et al., 2018). Gendered classroom behaviour implicitly teaches pupils about gendered hierarchies. Hypermasculine domination of space, attention and verbal interaction by some boys quickly becomes normalised and patterns of classroom interaction become established and maintained. This phenomenon has been noted from reception age through to secondary school (Equimundo, 2022) and often goes unnoticed by classroom teachers when pragmatic demands of getting through the taught curriculum are most pressing.

When gender is placed squarely on the agenda that underpins classroom interactions it becomes much more possible to identify when and where these gendered patterns emerge. It is important to question whether disproportionate time is spent with particular groups of children and the nature of those interactions. *Do we harbour gender stereotypical expectations for different pupils? What sort of language is used with different children? Is this gendered? What sort of language are children using? Is it sexist, misogynistic, homophobic, transphobic?*

Having these questions in mind facilitates change from greater attunement to difference among pupils whilst avoiding imposing stereotypical categorisations. Being aware of power dynamics within the classroom and considering the organisation of space and resources (Lyttleton-Smith, 2019; Prioletta, 2022) will reveal how gendering practices are enabled by more than only the teacher. A whole-class approach to how gendered identities are performed and imposed involves collective critical reflection which requires creative, teacher-led activities that allow the issue to be explored.

Language matters

Vignette about BBC Documentary: *No More Boys and Girls: Can Our Kids Go Gender Free?*

In 2017, I advised the production team of a two-part BBC documentary series concerning gender in the primary school. The documentary filmed a six-week experiment with primary school teacher, Mr Andre, to address the gendered patterns that were notable in his classroom. I directed the production team to research-informed interventions that could be implemented that would alter relationships within the class; pupil interactions; levels of esteem and compassion. This involved several, very practical, changes to classroom organisation and interaction, involving the entire class. For example, everyone was invited to publicly call out Mr Andre whenever he used language that was highly gendered; or when he devoted more classroom time to boys than girls. Making gendered classroom interactions highly visible in this way drew to everyone's attention how deeply engrained this unwitting gendered teaching practice had become.

Link to documentary: https://youtu.be/3PyQS94Pfa8?si=r2T1TsXxqxV7llYc

IN-BETWEEN SPACES AND PLACES MATTER

Work done in the classroom to address gendered patterns of interaction and perpetuation of stereotypes can come quickly undone during the in-between times and spaces at school. When pupils are moving around the school, passing through corridors or playing outdoors, heightened heteronormative gendered patterns of behaviour surface, and adherence to agreed rules can be overshadowed by peer-group dynamics. Playground areas and activities quickly become gender stereotyped and exclusionary. Huuki and Renold (2015) noted the ways in which gendered violence can surface during children's playtimes, with boys exerting control over space and the direction of games that work to actively marginalise girls. Research with 6- to 11-year-olds in London primary schools (Hall, 2020) found that within front-stage spaces like classrooms, pupils align with inclusive narratives around gender, sex and sexuality. However, in back-stage spaces, including school corridors, playgrounds and toilets, heteronormative discourses of gender, sex and sexuality that circulate outside school (e.g. at home, across media sources, in public spaces) find expression with heteronormativity resurfacing as the *modus operandi*. As with gendered classroom interactions, involving pupils in auditing the situation in playgrounds and in-between spaces is an effective way to take a whole-school/class approach to tensions arising from misogyny, heteronormativity and exclusionary gendered practices. *Lifting Limits* has demonstrated that interventions in primary schools involving the whole-school, which place children at the forefront, raise awareness and confidence in challenging stereotypes and increase acceptance of diverse gender roles across leaders, staff and parents/carers, as well as children (Horvarth, 2019).

Task 6.6.2 Space matters: 'Mapping the in-between'

Invite pupils to engage in research to determine what and where gender equity issues reside in the in-between times and spaces – this is an important means of ensuring their active engagement to address an issue of injustice and to afford them opportunities to critically appraise the spatial organisation of their school.

Devise a map of the playground(s), corridors and other in-between spaces which can then be divided amongst the class so that specific sections can be systematically monitored by small groups of pupils, at different times of the day and observational records compiled.

Through this exercise, gendered patterns will quickly become identified and provide the focus of ongoing whole-school/whole-class debate that may result in the physical or temporal reorganisation of aspects of the school day that call into question who plays what, where and when. It may also involve redesigning areas of the playground to be more gender inclusive.

'TEACHING' RSE

Embedding a concern with gender equity throughout all aspects of primary schooling is being advocated in this unit. However, it is likely that specific times will be dedicated to 'teaching RSE', which causes great anxiety for everyone involved (Meyer *et al.*, 2019). As outlined in the introduction, teaching RSE at primary school has been met with controversy, and therefore places teachers in a contested space.

A common argument against teaching primary aged children about gender identity and the LGBTQ+ community is that they are too young or that the content is not age-appropriate (Pettway, 2016). Teachers share these worries; studies have found only half of primary teachers were comfortable including these topics in their lessons (Meyer *et al.*, 2019). Children do not live in a vacuum; as outlined earlier, they are exposed to a wide range of messages from many sources making them curious about gender diversity. Tuning into children's curiosity, and approaching gender and sexuality education that aligns with that curiosity in respectful ways, offers the hesitant teacher a sound starting place. Sensitive and open conversations are necessary if we are to provide children with the support needed to navigate their place within the world, and to process the ways in which inequities take shape and crucially how we can (all) be active in preventing/addressing them. It is our responsibility to use the feelings of discomfort that we might encounter as a reminder to remain critical and reflective of our own practices (Staley and Leonardi, 2019).

RSE in practice

There is a growing range of toolkits and frameworks publicly available to schools and teachers to pursue gender inclusivity work with primary aged children (see Relevant websites section at the end of this unit for examples from organisations including *Lifting Limits*; *Stonewall* and *Welcoming Schools*). Another particularly innovative and effective example is *Primary AGENDA* (Renold, 2019), introduced across Wales as a resource intended to support teachers in their work with primary aged children to make positive relationships matter in school and the local community. The emphasis is very much on a positive, affirmative approach which accepts children's experiences and enables them to be explored sensitively. The approach foregrounds a concern with consent, rights and respect by giving children a range of creative ways to express feelings and ideas, which can be empowering to understand that they are not alone, and that others are grappling with similar questions. *Primary AGENDA* encourages a collective approach to RSE that invites children to forge alliances with others and act on injustices as they experience them. The toolkit invites teachers and pupils to explore inclusive, rights-based approaches to feelings and emotions; friendships and relationships; body image; consent; gender and sexuality equity.

The approach draws upon some of the feminist scholarship outlined earlier that underlines the idea that children are agentic, curious people deserving of respectful responses to their questions about gender and sexuality. By starting with curiosity, *Primary AGENDA* recognises what matters to children when RSE is being taught at school. Refusing a didactic, instructional approach, *AGENDA* provides opportunities to create interactive and agentic spaces that invite children to engage in dialogue, debate and action for change. The toolkit provides interactive examples of creative methods and pedagogies, e.g. storytelling, crafting, movement and music to work with children in ways that raise awareness whilst also respecting rights and advocating a whole-school approach to RSE. Teachers are provided with ideas for safely and creatively exploring the impact of uneven power relations in society with children. Many of the case studies are about advancing gender equity and equality.

> ### Task 6.6.3 'What Jars You?'
>
> One of the activities offered in the *Primary AGENDA* toolkit is an arts-based activity entitled *'What Jars You?'* which invites pupils to contemplate 'Jar' as a verb: as something that jolts or sends a shock; something that disrupts or unsettles.
>
> Pupils are asked to think about what is unequal or unfair in society when it comes to relationships, gender and sexuality.
>
> They then work on their own or in pairs, and write down what jars them on paper slips, which are then placed within a glass jar.
>
> When they have finished, they each take a comment from the jar in turn and think about what needs to change; to turn what is unfair to fair, for an equal and more inclusive world.
>
> They are then invited to decorate the jar with a message for change.
>
> This is one of many activities that work together – creatively and cumulatively – to invite reflection and to open up for discussions about how gender and sexualities are deeply embedded in everyday life, and that everyone has experiences of and thoughts about.
>
> Source: https://issuu.com/croatoan/docs/agendaonline

HOME MATTERS

As this unit has sought to demonstrate, gendered identities are constantly in flux and under persistent negotiation and revision. Primary aged children are actively navigating shifting norms and ideals surrounding gender every day. Therefore, schools and teachers have a crucial role in supporting children to negotiate the complexities of gender and how and what it means to them as they grow. Families and parenting practices are also significant forces that can both suppress and support shifting gender identities and norms that regulate children's behaviours and attitudes. As the *No More Boys and Girls* documentary, and other research-informed initiatives (such as *Lifting Limits* and *AGENDA*) attest, it is crucially important that schools and families work together to support children to explore gender issues.

Working closely with families involves transparent and clear lines of communication about what gender equity means, and how it is being approached by the school, and by individual teachers. As this unit has sought to advocate, it is possible for teachers to safely, creatively and, in age-appropriate ways, explore the implications of gender inequities and prejudices, and seek practical ways to pursue greater equity in school. This unit encourages making rights-based, respectful approaches, that start with children's curiosity, transparent to parents and carers. This can involve invitations for parents/carers to come into school and become aware of books and other resources that are being used; and by making the school equality policy available on the school website; and by making curriculum content (including plans of how and when gender equity will be explicitly addressed) openly available. The 'tasks' outlined in this unit (and others that teachers might be inspired to devise themselves) can be a cause for celebration. Projects that make visible the processes involved in exploring gender inclusivity and equity offer important opportunities for pupils to get involved in creating artwork on the theme of celebrating difference – that make visible their views and opinions about how and why gender matters to them.

The emphasis stressed throughout this unit concerns an urgent need to reappraise how children are conceptualised (as agentic, knowing, critical subjects) and therefore how pupils in primary school might best be related to, educated and supported. This necessarily involves critical reflection on where teacher perceptions and expectations come from and how they can impact upon pedagogical practices. The example of the *Primary AGENDA* toolkit underlines that 'sensitive topics', whilst at first might appear too difficult or contentious to 'teach', can be approached in playful, creative, collaborative ways that give pupils a sense of ownership as they explore and debate what gender equity, diversity and healthy relationships mean to them. Actively involving the entire school, and notably making pupils central to processes of critical reflection – through audits, mapping, debating and creating – offers teachers ways to embed a concern with gender equity throughout their practices, in collaboration with children, both in and out of the classroom.

SUMMARY

In this unit, the challenges involved in addressing gender equity in primary schools have been discussed.

Reflecting upon where ideas about childhood and gender come from is a crucial first step in establishing a sound foundation upon which more inclusive approaches to interacting with children in primary school can be developed.

Taking children's innate curiosity as a basis upon which to approach more equitable and inclusive approaches has been proposed that involves treating children as inquisitive subjects, with rights to explore what it means to navigate gendered identities. Foregrounding rights, consent and respect is fundamental to implementing more creative and collaborative approaches that enable sensitive topics to be addressed in open and inclusive ways.

Finally, the unit has suggested that the pursuit of gender equity permeates primary schooling in the broadest sense and that creating more equitable and inclusive educational communities involves whole-class/whole-school in ongoing exploration and questioning.

ANNOTATED FURTHER READING

Bragg, S., Renold, E., Ringrose, J. and Jackson, C. (2018) 'More than boy, girl, male, female': Exploring young people's views on gender diversity within and beyond social contexts', *Sex Education*, 18(4): 420-434. DOI: 10.1080/14681811.2018.1439373
> This report provides a detailed account of research that was undertaken with pupils and makes the case for celebrating gender diversity from the perspectives of children themselves.

Meyer, E. J., Quantz, M., Taylor, C. and Peter, T. (2019) 'Elementary teachers' experiences with LGBTQ-inclusive education: Addressing fears with knowledge to improve confidence and practices', *Theory into Practice*, 58(1): 6-17.
> This article provides useful insights from Canada regarding how primary teachers have overcome their fears of approaching gender in their teaching and interactions within school.

Osgood, J. (2019) 'Gender in the nursery: Learning lessons from an early age', in L. Rycroft-Smith and G. Andre (eds) *The Equal Classroom: Life-Changing Thinking About Gender*, London: Routledge, pp. 53-60.
> This brief chapter offers guidance on practical strategies that can be employed with very young children to support their curiosity about gender.

FURTHER READING TO SUPPORT M-LEVEL STUDY

Lyttleton-Smith, J. (2019) 'Objects of conflict: (Re) configuring early childhood experiences of gender in the pre-school classroom', *Gender and Education*, 31(6): 655–672.

> This journal paper provides a theorised account of how the organisation of space and materials in an early childhood classroom works upon how gender is performed by children and offers some practical suggestions for teachers.

Robinson, K. H. (2013) *Innocence, Knowledge and the Construction of Childhood: The Contradictory Nature of Sexuality and Censorship in Children's Contemporary Lives*, London: Routledge.

> Writing from the Australian context, this book offers a lively and insightful account of how adults (teachers, parents, carers) unwittingly censor children's explorations of gender. It offers useful guidance on how it is possible to become more confident in interactions with children that are shaped by curiosity.

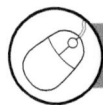

RELEVANT WEBSITES

Lifting Limits: Delivering gender equality through education: https://liftinglimits.org.uk/resources-for-schools-and-families/

> Lifting Limits offers a whole-school approach that integrates gender equality into the school curriculum, ethos and routines: equipping staff and pupils to recognise, discuss and challenge stereotypes and inequalities wherever they find them.

No More Boys and Girls – Can Our Kids Go Gender Free? Episode 1 [Video file]: www.youtube.com/watch?v=wN5R2LWhTrY

> This two-part BBC documentary film asks whether the way boys and girls are treated explains why true equality between men and women in adult life has not been achieved. Through a bold but simple experiment with Year 3 pupils, a term of gender-neutral practice reveals that gender differences in self-confidence and emotional intelligence are evened out.

Primary AGENDA: Supporting Children in Making Positive Relationships Matter: https://agendaonline.co.uk/download-agenda/

> AGENDA is a research-informed resource that offers information and stories to help build safe, supportive, inclusive and engaging environments for children and young people to speak out and share what matters to them. The resource offers multiple examples of what is possible to explore and how, and clear signposting on support and advice on safe-guarding issues. AGENDA demonstrates that good RSE provision is all about listening to children and young people and working in partnership with other agencies.

Stonewall: Inclusive Primary School: www.stonewall.org.uk/resources/creating-lgbt-inclusive-primary-curriculum

> This inclusive curriculum guide for primary school teachers is a key part of Stonewall's work addressing LGBTQ+ inclusion in primary schools; it offers practical, step-by-step guidance on how to approach more inclusive practices with young children in school.

Welcoming Schools: Developing a Gender Inclusive School: www.welcomingschools.org/pages/framework-for-developing-a-gender-inclusive-school/

> This framework for developing gender inclusive schools offers practical guidance intended to educate staff to understand the complexities of gender as well as specific methods to stop gender based harassment, bullying and hurtful teasing. The framework emphasises the importance of providing training for all school personnel – from teachers, assistants and counsellors to administrative staff, bus drivers, lunchtime supervisors and canteen staff.

REFERENCES

Amer, L. (2019) *Why Kids Need to Learn About Gender and Sexuality* [Video file]. Retrieved from: www.ted.com/talks/lindsay_amer_why_kids_need_to_learn_about_gender_and_sexuality

Bragg, S., Renold, E., Ringrose, J. and Jackson, C. (2018) 'More than boy, girl, male, female': Exploring young people's views on gender diversity within and beyond social contexts', *Sex Education*, 18(4): 420–434. DOI: 10.1080/14681811.2018.1439373

Butler, J. (1990) *Gender Trouble: Feminism and the Subversion of Identity*, New York: Routledge.

Davies, B. (1989) *Frogs and Snails and Feminist Tales: Preschool Children & Gender*, Sydney: Allen & Unwin.

Department for Education (DfE). (2019) *Relationships Education, Relationships and Sex Education (RSE) and Health Education: Statutory Guidance for Governing Bodies, Proprietors, Head Teachers, Principals, Senior Leadership Teams, Teachers*, London: HMSO. Retrieved from: https://assets.publishing.service.gov.uk/media/62cea352e90e071e789ea9bf/Relationships_Education_RSE_and_Health_Education.pdf

Education Act (1996) *The Stationery Office*, The National Archives. Online. Retrieved from: www.legislation.gov.uk/ukpga/1996/56/contents

Equimundo. (2022) *State of UK Boys: An Urgent Call for Connected, Caring Boyhoods*, Washington, DC: Equimundo.

Francis, B. (2006) 'Heroes or zeroes? The discursive positioning of "underachieving boys" in English neo-liberal education policy', *Journal of Education Policy*, 21(2): 187–200.

Gidinski, B. (2019) *How Young Can SOGI Go?* Retrieved from: www.edcan.ca/articles/how-young-can-sogi-go/

Green, C., Kalvaitis, D. and Worster A. (2016) 'Recontextualizing psychosocial development in young children: A model of environmental identity development', *Environmental Education Research*, 22(7): 1025–1048.

Hall, J. J. (2020) '"The word gay has been banned but people use it in the boys' toilets whenever you go in": Spatialising children's subjectivities in response to gender and sexualities education in English primary schools', *Social & Cultural Geography*, 21(2): 162–185.

Horvarth, T. (2019) *Lifting Limits Pilot: Impact Evaluation Report*, London: Tessa Horvarth Research.

Huuki, T. and Renold, E. (2015) 'Crush: Mapping historical, material and affective force relations in young children's hetero-sexual playground play', *Discourse*, 37(5): 754–769.

Lee, L. (2019) *A Framework for Supporting Gender-diverse Students*. Retrieved from: www.edutopia.org/article/framework-supporting-gender-diverse-students (accessed 16 October 2020).

Lyttleton-Smith, J. (2019) 'Objects of conflict: (Re) configuring early childhood experiences of gender in the pre-school classroom', *Gender and Education*, 31(6): 655–672.

Meyer, E. J., Quantz, M., Taylor, C. and Peter, T. (2019) 'Elementary teachers' experiences with LGBTQ-inclusive education: Addressing fears with knowledge to improve confidence and practices', *Theory into Practice*, 58(1): 6–17.

Osgood, J. (2019) 'Gender in the nursery: Learning lessons from an early age', in L. Rycroft-Smith and G. Andre (eds) *The Equal Classroom: Life-Changing Thinking About Gender*, London: Routledge, pp. 53–60.

Osgood, J. and Robinson, K. (2019) *Feminists Researching Gendered Childhoods: Generative Entanglements*, London: Bloomsbury.

Pettway, A. (2016) 'The new sex ed', *Teaching Tolerance*, 53(1): 23–26.

Prioletta, J. (2022) 'Unearthing gender violence with/in kindergarten play environments', *Gender and Education*, 34(8): 973–990. DOI:10.1080/09540253.2022.2118441

Renold, E. (2004) '"Other" boys: Negotiating non-hegemonic masculinities in the primary school', *Gender and Education*, 16(2): 247–265.

Renold, E. (2019) *Primary AGENDA: Supporting Children in Making Positive Relationships Matter*, Cardiff: Children's Commissioner for Wales, NSPCC.

Renold, E., Bragg, S., Ringrose, J. and Jackson, C. (2017) *How Gender Matters to Children and Young People Living in England*, Cardiff: Cardiff University, University of Brighton, Lancaster University and University College London, Institute of Education. Available from: http://orca.cf.ac.uk/id/eprint/107599

Robinson, K. H. (2012) 'Difficult citizenship: The precarious relationships between childhood, sexuality and access to knowledge', *Sexualities*, 15(3/4): 257-276.

Robinson, K. H. (2013) *Innocence, Knowledge and the Construction of Childhood: The Contradictory Nature of Sexuality and Censorship in Children's Contemporary Lives*, London: Routledge.

Staley, S. and Leonardi, B. (2019) 'Complicating on what we know: Focusing on educators' processes of becoming gender and sexual diversity inclusive', *Theory into Practice*, 58(1): 29-38.

Walkerdine, V. (1990) *Schoolgirl Fictions*, London: Verson.

SECTION 7
WIDER CURRICULUM ASPECTS

UNIT 7.1

LISTENING TO PUPILS

Developing mutually respectful teacher–pupil relationships to enhance pupils' learning

Carol Robinson

INTRODUCTION

Listening to children and young people about issues that matter to them and that affect their experiences in school is important if we are to understand the needs and preferences of pupils and build positive relationships with them. This unit focuses on outlining ways in which adults in schools can support pupils to voice their opinions, and the benefits of this for both teachers and pupils. Within the unit we start by considering the terms used when referring to pupil voice work, we consider the importance of building mutually respectful teacher-pupil relationships, and we identify factors for teachers to consider to facilitate eliciting the voices of those they teach. We draw attention to how implementing strategies focused on listening to pupils can make learning and other school experiences more meaningful and enjoyable for children and young people in schools.

OBJECTIVES

By the end of this unit, you should:

- understand the terms 'pupil voice', 'pupil participation' and 'pupil engagement';
- be familiar with school practices that promote eliciting pupils' voices;
- be aware of the benefits of listening to pupils for both teachers and pupils;
- understand how listening to pupils' views can make lessons more meaningful and enhance pupils' enjoyment of school.

PUPIL VOICE, PUPIL PARTICIPATION AND PUPIL ENGAGEMENT: WHAT DO THESE TERMS MEAN?

You are likely to come across the terms 'pupil voice', 'student voice' and 'learner voice', as well as pupil, student and learner 'participation' and 'engagement'. Each of these terms broadly relates to the move to consult pupils and provide opportunities for pupils to voice their opinions about matters that concern them and that affect their learning and other school experiences.

DOI: 10.4324/9781032691794-37

The term 'pupil voice', often used synonymously with the terms 'student voice' and 'learner voice' (Robinson and Taylor, 2007), refers to working with pupils to elicit their perspectives on matters relating to any aspect of school life. It is about teachers and other adults in schools placing importance on pupils' views and wanting to develop an environment in which children feel at ease to express their views. In extreme cases, if schools were to fully embrace pupil voice work, this would result in schools being run in a democratic way, with pupils' voices holding equal weight to those of the adults in the school.

The notion of 'pupil participation' strongly resonates with that of pupil voice. The Welsh Government's *Children and Young People's Participation in Wales ... Good Practice 2016* guide states: 'participation is about children and young people having their voices heard when decisions are being made that affect their lives, and being actively involved in decision-making processes' (Welsh Government, 2016: 2). Additionally, Mannion and Sowerby (2018) assert that 'learner participation' requires 'adults, children, and young people to engage in communications which are two-way, voluntary, sustained, deal with real concerns, and [are] based on mutual respect and children's rights' (Mannion and Sowerby, 2018: 2).

The term 'pupil engagement' commonly has two meanings attributed to it. It can relate to pupils being active partners in shaping their experiences of school. Pupil engagement in this sense has similarities with the earlier definition of pupil voice. It is concerned with listening to individual and collective perspectives about matters that relate to pupils' experiences of school, including issues of teaching and learning – this work may be the outcome of institution-driven or pupil-driven agendas (Robinson, 2012). However, 'pupil engagement' can also refer to the excitement and investment a pupil feels towards an issue that is of interest to them (Cheminais, 2008). During the Covid-19 pandemic, the term tended to relate more to this latter definition and there were reports of pupils having significantly lower levels of engagement with learning, mainly due to not being able to access in-school learning (Lucas, Nelson and Sims, 2020; Nelson and Sharp, 2020).

From the definitions mentioned, it is clear that there are overlaps between the various terms. For the purpose of our work in this unit, we will focus in particular on pupil voice work and the importance of listening to pupils with a view to enhancing their experiences of learning and teaching in school.

LEGISLATION PROMOTING PUPIL VOICE WORK IN SCHOOLS

The increasing importance placed on listening to the voices of children and young people has stemmed from the United Nations Convention on the Rights of the Child (UNCRC; United Nations [UN], 1989). Part 1 of Article 12 of the UNCRC states that:

> ... the child who is capable of forming his or her own views [has] the right to express those views freely on all matters affecting the child, the views of the child being given due weight in accordance with the age and maturity of the child.

Part 1 of Article 12, therefore, comprises two key elements – the right for children and young people to (i) express their views and (ii) have their views be given due weight (Lundy, 2007: 927). It gives children the right to freedom of opinion and the right to be heard and take part in decisions that affect them; this was a major factor that contributes to the positive recognition of practices that support listening to and engaging with pupils in schools.

Following the UNCRC, in 1991 Fullan posed the question 'What would happen if we treated the student as someone whose opinion mattered?' (Fullan, 1991: 170). At this time the notion of taking pupils' opinions into account was relatively new for most teachers; however, this idea, coupled with the implications of the UNCRC, served to open up spaces for consideration to be given as to how the whole school community might benefit through listening to the voices of the pupils within it.

Over the past 25 years, although educational reforms within England have largely focused on raising pupils' measurable academic achievements, there have also been a number of Acts and reforms that have recognised and promoted the importance of engaging with pupils. For example, the 2002 Education Act (Department for Education and Skills [DfES], 2002) required that schools consult with pupils; the 2003 DfES (2003) document, *Working Together: Giving Children and Young People a Say*, provided guidance on pupil participation; and the 2004 *Every Child Matters: Change for Children* legislation (DfES, 2004) provided a national framework outlining ways in which public services could work together to bring about improved outcomes for children, young people and families; central to this was the view that all children should have a say in decisions affecting their lives.

In 2007, the voices and views of children and young people informed the government's *Children's Plan* (Department for Children, Schools and Families [DCSF], 2007); and, in 2008, *Working Together: Listening to the Voices of Children and Young People* (DCSF, 2008) made specific reference to the UNCRC and stated that schools should ensure the views of children and young people are 'heard and valued in the taking of decisions which affect them, and ... are supported in making a positive contribution to their school and local community' (p.5). Furthermore, statutory guidance, *Listening to and Involving Children and Young People* (DfE, 2014: 1), asserted that schools are 'strongly encouraged to pay due regard to the convention', and that local authorities and maintained schools should have regard to the guidance when 'considering how best to provide opportunities for pupils to be consulted on matters affecting them or contribute to decision-making in the school'.

In addition to these legislative documents, regulations relating to teachers' standards have implications for the extent to which teachers prioritise listening to pupils. In September 2011, new *Teachers' Standards* (DfE, 2011) were introduced, and these are still relevant today. The standards set a clear baseline of expectations for the professional practice and conduct of teachers from the point of qualification, and apply to almost all teachers, regardless of their career stage. They are used to assess all trainees working towards Qualified Teacher Status (QTS), teachers completing their statutory induction period, and all teachers with QTS who are subject to The Education (School Teachers' Appraisal) (England) Regulations 2012.

The *Teachers' Standards* require teachers to 'Set high expectations which inspire, motivate and challenge pupils' (DfE, 2011: 10) and 'manage classes effectively, using approaches which are appropriate to pupils' needs in order to involve and motivate them' (DfE, 2011: 12). Implicit within these standards is the expectation that teachers will have built positive relationships with pupils, gained insights into individual pupils' interests, capabilities and preferred ways of learning and be aware of and understand the sort of work and activities that are most likely to inspire, motivate and challenge pupils.

The recent Office for Standards in Education (Ofsted) *Education Inspection Framework* (2023a) reinforces the requirement for teachers to build positive relationships with pupils. Inspectors make judgements about the extent to which 'relationships among learners and staff reflect a positive and respectful culture' (Ofsted, 2023a: 10). Additionally, within the *Ofsted School Inspection Handbook* (Ofsted, 2023b) it is stated that judgement is made about whether the school has been successful in 'fostering a positive and respectful school culture in which staff know and care about pupils' (Ofsted, 2023b: 68, point 289).

> **Task 7.1.1 Why is it so important to listen to pupils?**
>
> Imagine a classroom in which teachers teach only what they think learners ought to know, where there is no space for pupils to ask questions or voice opinions on areas of interest to them, where pupils are not encouraged to learn through discovery, where teacher–pupil relationships are not positive, and where pupils are simply passive recipients within a process. Alternatively, imagine a classroom in which teacher–pupil relationships are based on mutual respect, where pupils feel listened to and valued as individuals, where teachers want to know what interests and motivates the pupils and where pupils feel confident about taking responsibility for aspects of their learning – a classroom in which pupils are encouraged to participate in assessing their work and setting future goals and where they feel a sense of belonging to the classroom and the wider school.
>
> Of the two situations described, in which of these would you expect pupils to thrive? Why?

HOW CAN LISTENING TO PUPILS BE OF BENEFIT TO THEM?

Children tend to enjoy school more when they are listened to and their views are taken seriously, when they are treated with respect and when they feel valued and included. Findings from research reported in the Cambridge Primary Review Research Report, *Children, Their Voices and Their Experiences of School: What Does the Evidence Tell Us?* (Robinson, 2014: 5-6), indicate that positive pupil-teacher relationships are a significant factor in contributing to primary pupils' enjoyment of school and, where such relationships dominate in schools, this contributes to pupils feeling a sense of security within the school. The involvement of pupils in school decision-making also encourages them to become active participants in a democratic society, contributes to their achievement and attainment, promotes increased confidence and increases their motivation and engagement with learning (DfE, 2014).

Rudduck and McIntyre (2007: 152) found that pupil consultation tends to enhance pupils' commitment to, and capacity for, learning through strengthening self-esteem and enhancing attitudes towards school and learning. Moreover, disregarding pupils' voices diminishes their sense of autonomy and can reduce their motivation to learn (Murray and Cousens, 2020). Not listening to pupils also conveys messages to children that we do not value or place importance on their views.

LISTENING TO PUPILS: VIGNETTE 1

Year 5 teachers in one primary school in England were grappling with how best to support individual pupils with challenging behaviour to engage in lessons, having already tried implementing various strategies. The pupils concerned included some who had been excluded from previous primary schools due to behavioural issues. Teachers engaged in one-to-one conversations with individual pupils about specific incidents in which teachers considered the pupil had displayed aggression or been particularly uncooperative. Teachers invited pupils to reflect on what prompted them to respond to a situation in the way they did, and on the approach taken by teachers to support them. Through these reflective discussions teachers were able gain a deeper understanding of pupils' perspectives about specific situations. For example, one pupil commented how standing in the lunch queue made her feel anxious as she did not like being next to people who she doesn't know very well. In the build up to lunch time this anxiety increased, which in turn led to her displaying aggressive or uncooperative behaviour. She knew by behaving in this way the teacher was likely to ask her to remain behind at the beginning of lunch time and, crucially, the outcome would be that she would have less time in the lunch queue. Talking openly about this issue with the pupil increased the teacher's insights into the pupil's experiences and perspectives, and informed future approaches to supporting them.

HOW CAN LISTENING TO PUPILS BENEFIT TEACHERS?

Listening to pupils' views, considering their needs and interests, and involving them as active participants in their learning and other school activities can help schools to become learning communities, rather than knowledge factories, that serve the needs of the majority of the pupils within them (Busher, 2012). Florian and Beaton (2018) highlight that where teachers listen to pupils, they can use what they learn from pupils to inform their future practice. Where pupils' views are listened to about teaching and learning issues, teachers can gain an insight into pupils' perspectives on what enhances and what inhibits their learning. Finding out about pupils' perspectives of their school experiences, including learning, may take you outside your comfort zone in terms of the sort of dialogue in which you want to engage with pupils. The outcomes, however, can be hugely beneficial through increasing your awareness of the preferences and learning needs of those you teach, and this can be helpful when analysing and reflecting on your own practices and pedagogical approaches. Merrick (2020) found that talking to pupils and gaining an understanding of their thoughts, feelings and priorities also helped to develop insights into how best to manage pupils' behaviour.

A further benefit of listening to pupils is that a more collaborative relationship between teachers and pupils tends to develop and, the better you are able to understand pupils, the more effective your teaching and their learning will be. Practices that support listening to pupils' perspectives, therefore, have the potential to transform teacher–pupil relationships and lead to improvements in teachers' practices, through teachers learning from pupils about how they can make learning and other school experiences more meaningful for pupils.

LISTENING TO PUPILS: VIGNETTE 2

A Year 6 teacher from a primary school in England shared her experience of how listening to comments from one pupil in her class changed the way she approached question-and-answer sessions with the class. This teacher quoted the following, said to her by a Year 6 pupil, to illustrate her point:

> Miss, when you ask us questions, like what the answer to something is in maths or science, you ask different people until you get the right answer, and then you go on to the next question. But that doesn't really help us – just because someone has said the right answer, that doesn't mean that the rest of us understand why it's the right answer, so we never actually learn that.

This simple comment by one pupil prompted this teacher to reflect on her teaching and to include more in-depth explanations in future lessons during question-and-answer activities.

WAYS TO FACILITATE LISTENING TO PUPILS IN SCHOOL

If schools are to develop an ethos in which it is the norm for staff to listen to pupils, and for staff and pupils to work together in a mutually respectful way, this requires teachers to work with pupils to develop insights into pupils' needs, interests, likes and dislikes, and factors that motivate and demotivate pupils. Listening to pupils involves encouraging pupils to voice their opinions and providing opportunities for pupils to be active participants in their learning and in decision-making processes in school. Wall *et al.* (2019) identified eight factors for consideration when supporting voice work with children from birth to age 7. These factors, however, are equally applicable with children in older age groups. The eight factors are as follows:

1. *Definition.* It is important to define what you understand by 'voice' and to acknowledge that 'voice' refers to far more than the spoken word. We need to be mindful that 'voice' can incorporate different forms of communication, including 'behaviour, actions, pauses in action silences, body language, glances, movement and artistic expression' (Wall *et al.*, 2019: 268).
2. *Power.* There are likely to be power imbalances between teachers and pupils, and between pupils themselves, and these can inhibit children and young people's voices. Consideration, therefore, needs to be given to how these imbalances can be reduced to ensure pupils have equal opportunity to express their views.
3. *Inclusivity.* To create an inclusive school environment, equal value needs to be placed on the voices of all pupils, including those who express alternative and non-conformist views, and teachers need to be receptive to 'listening' to voices expressed through non-verbal, as well as verbal, means.
4. *Listening.* Actively listening to pupils is fundamental when supporting pupils to voice their opinions. Consideration needs to be given to whether there are situations in which the attitudes and actions of teachers convey to pupils that their voices are not important.
5. *Time and space.* Time and opportunities need to be available for pupils to express their views, and we need to be aware of which spaces within school encourage, and which inhibit, the voices of different children.
6. *Approaches.* Teachers need to adopt flexible approaches when listening to pupils and be receptive to listening to a range of voices and modes of expression.
7. *Processes.* When creating a listening school environment, it is important that school processes and structures provide 'opportunities for consultation, collaboration and dialogue' (Wall *et al.*, 2019: 274).
8. *Purposes.* To ensure that pupils are listened to in an authentic way, teachers need to know why they are listening to pupils and be prepared to take action as an outcome of pupils voicing their perspectives.

In order for an inclusive listening environment to be built, the development of positive working relationships between teachers and pupils is crucial; however, it takes time and perseverance by the whole school community to build such relationships. A 'listening school' is one in which children's voices are taken seriously (Cassidy *et al.*, 2022) and all voices are respected and valued. As part of building a listening environment, adults in schools need to be attuned to listening to different voices and to the different ways pupils choose to communicate (Glazzard, 2012).

Task 7.1.2 Listening to pupils in your classroom

Reflect on the following in relation to listening to pupils:

- Define what you understand by the term 'voice' in the context of our classroom.
- Identify examples of where you consider a classroom environment has supported pupils to express their views. Can you think of examples where teachers' actions have signalled to pupils that their views about a particular matter are not important?
- Consider whether you listen to some pupils more than others. Are there any pupils who you seldom listen to? If so, why is this? How could you address these issues?

- Where pupils remain silent, what meaning do you give to these silences? Does this vary from pupil to pupil?
- Identify different approaches you could adopt to listen to pupils about an area of teaching, or other school experiences. Which methods of 'listening' to pupils do you consider would suit the needs and preferences of different pupils?
- How will you ensure that pupils know they have been listened to?

The eight factors listed earlier as areas for consideration when developing a listening school ethos can be used alongside specific strategies commonly employed by teachers for listening to pupils. These may include, for example, setting up a school council or holding 'circle times'. In addition, you, as the teacher, can pose simple questions to pupils during your day-to-day working with them in order to determine their perceptions of what motivates/demotivates them, what enhances/diminishes their enjoyment of lessons and what increases/reduces barriers to learners engaging in learning. For example, you might ask pupils: 'What activities help you to learn best? Why?'; 'Which activities do you enjoy the most? Why?'; 'What stops you from learning? Why?'; 'What would your ideal lesson be like? Why?'.

Pupils can also be encouraged to express their views through any of the following ways:

- drawing, painting, taking photos of, or role-playing different situations – for example, situations that they either like or dislike in school;
- posting their opinions in a postbox – pupils can remain anonymous if they wish;
- writing a log about, for example, what aspects of lessons they enjoy and why;
- completing questionnaires, sentence-completion exercises or surveys on an aspect of their school experiences. Pupils could be involved in the writing and administering of these;
- taking part in ballots and elections.

GUIDING PRINCIPLES FOR LISTENING TO PUPILS

To avoid tokenistic ways of listening to pupils schools could develop a pupil voice policy, taking into consideration the following principles:

- There should be a genuine desire by staff to listen to pupils' opinions.
- Pupils and staff should understand what is meant by 'pupil voice', and staff should understand the benefits of this for individual pupils, for staff and for the whole school community.
- Pupils and staff should work together in ways that enable pupils to influence the conditions for their own learning.
- Teacher–pupil relationships should be based on mutual respect, and adults in the school should acknowledge that pupils have the right to express their views on matters affecting them.
- It should be acknowledged that there are as many voices as there are pupils, not just one unified voice.
- *All* pupils should be encouraged to have an active involvement in discussions and decision-making.
- Pupils should feel confident that they can speak freely about what is on their mind, rather than feeling they ought to say what they think you or other adults want to hear.
- Pupils need to know that if they express their views they will be taken seriously, and this won't be held against them, no matter how controversial their views are.
- It should be acknowledged that pupils may express their views through more than the spoken word.

SUMMARY

This unit has provided an introduction to how you can listen to pupils within everyday classroom practices and has outlined that listening to pupils and building an awareness of ways of working that interest, motivate and challenge pupils, individually and collectively, will help to improve their learning and experiences of school. There are no set ways of listening to pupils, with teachers adopting different approaches depending on the pupil and the situation. If teachers are to listen to pupils in genuine and meaningful ways, appropriate ways of doing so need to be developed. There needs to be a recognition that one size may not fit all, and that different approaches will be needed for different pupils. However, once facilitating pupils to voice their views becomes the norm, and mutually respectful teacher–pupil relationships are built, teachers will benefit from developing a better understanding of pupils' needs and interests, and pupils will benefit from feeling an enhanced sense of motivation and engagement with learning.

ANNOTATED FURTHER READING

John-Akinola, Y. O., Gavin, A., O'Higgins, S. E. and Gabhain, S. N. (2014) 'Taking part in school life: Views of children', *Health Education*, 1114(1): 20-42.
> This paper reports findings from research relating to the views of children about participation in school. The study involved 248 primary school pupils aged 9–13 years.

Merrick, R. (2020) 'Pupil participation in planning provision for special educational needs: teacher perspectives', *Support for Learning*, 35(1): 101-118.
> This paper reports on findings from a study of 64 teachers with an interest in special educational needs. It highlights their perspectives of the impact of pupil participation on pupil motivation. The findings are equally applicable to all pupils, and not only those considered to have special educational needs,

Robinson, C. (2014) *Children, Their Voices and Their Experiences of School: What Does the Evidence Tell Us?*, York, UK: Cambridge Primary Review Trust.
> This report draws on evidence from empirical studies in the United Kingdom that explore pupils' own perspectives of their primary school experiences.

Sebba, J. and Robinson, C. (2010) *Evaluation of UNICEF UK's Rights Respecting Schools Award*, London: UNICEF UK.
> UNICEF UK's Rights Respecting Schools Award helps schools use the United Nations Convention on the Rights of the Child as their values framework. A major part of working towards the award involves schools listening to the voices of their pupils and developing a culture of respect in all aspects of school life, as well as developing a culture of respect in pupils outside of school.

FURTHER READING TO SUPPORT M-LEVEL STUDY

Busher, H. (2012) 'Students as expert witnesses of teaching and learning', *Management in Education*, 26(3): 113-119.
> Within this article, the author advocates that student voice is a key component in constructing discourse, empowerment and citizenship in schools, and that listening to and acting upon the views of students can lead to improvements in pedagogical and organisational practices. The article takes the position that students are expert observers of school life and teachers' practices and draws on

research with students in primary and secondary schools to explore students' perspectives in relation to such practices.

Robinson, C. and Taylor, C. (2007) 'Theorising student voice: Values and perspectives', *Improving Schools*, 10(1): 5-17.

This article explores the core values that underpin and inform student voice work. The authors argue that student voice work is an inherently ethical and moral practice, and that at the heart of student voice work are four core values: a conception of communication as dialogue; the requirement for participation and democratic inclusivity; the recognition that power relations are unequal and problematic; and the possibility for change and transformation. Throughout the article, complexities that arise in theorising student voice work are highlighted.

Wall, K., Cassidy, C., Robinson, C., Hall, E, Beaton, M., Kanyal, M. and Mitra, D. (2019) 'Look who's talking: Factors for considering the facilitation of very young children's' voices' *Journal of Childhood Research*, 17(4): 263-278.

This article presents the outcome of an international collaboration between academics working in the field of early childhood education. Grounded in the field of children's rights, the paper outlines eight factors identified as pivotal for consideration when facilitating the voices of children.

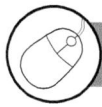

RELEVANT WEBSITES

Look Who's Talking: Eliciting the Voices of Children from Birth to Seven. https://www.voicebirthtoseven.co.uk/talking-point-posters/

Young Children have powerful voices https://education.gov.scot/resources/young-children-have-powerful-voices/

The National Council for Curriculum and Assessment (NCCA), Ireland https://ncca.ie/en/about-ncca/collaborations-and-partnerships/student-voice/

REFERENCES

Busher, H. (2012) 'Students as expert witnesses of teaching and learning', *Management in Education*, 29(3): 113-119.

Cassidy, C., Wall, K., Robinson. C., Arnott, L., Beaton, M. and Hall, E. (2022) 'Bridging the theory and practice of eliciting the voices of young children: Findings from the *Look Who's Talking* project', *European Early Childhood Education Research Journal*, 30(1): 32-47.

Cheminais, R. (2008) *Engaging Pupil Voice to ensure that Every Child Matters: A Practical Guide*, London and New York: Routledge.

Department for Children, Schools and Families (DCSF). (2007) *The Children's Plan: Building Brighter Futures: Summary*, Norwich, UK: The Stationery Office.

Department for Children, Schools and Families (DCSF). (2008) *Working Together: Listening to the Voices of Children and Young People*, DCSF-00410-2008, London: DCSF.

Department for Education (DfE). (2011) *Teachers' Standards*. Last updated 2021. Retrieved from: www.gov.uk/government/publications/teachers-standards (accessed 11 October 2023).

Department for Education (DfE). (2014) *Listening to and Involving Children and Young People (Statutory Guidance)*, London: DFE.

Department for Education and Skills (DfES). (2002) *The Education Act Statutory Instrument 2002*, London: DfES.

Department for Education and Skills (DfES). (2003) *Working Together: Giving Children and Young People a Say*, DfES/0492/2003, Nottingham, UK: DfES.

Department for Education and Skills (DfES). (2004) *Every Child Matters: Change for Children*, DfES/1081/2004, Nottingham, UK: DfES.

Florian, L. and Beaton, M. (2018) 'Inclusive pedagogy in action: Getting it right for every child', *International Journal of Inclusive Education*, 22(8): 870-884.

Fullan, M. (1991) *The New Meaning of Educational Change*, New York: Teachers College Press.

Glazzard, J. (2012) 'Tuning into children's voices: Exploring the perceptions of primary aged children about their education in one primary school in England', *International Journal of Education*, 4(3): 49-66.

Lucas, M., Nelson, J. and Sims, D. (2020) *Schools' Responses to Covid-19: Pupil Engagement in Remote Learning*, Slough: NFER.

Lundy, L. (2007) '"Voice" is not enough: Conceptualizing Article 12 of the United Nations Convention of the Rights of the Child', *British Educational Research Journal*, 33(6): 927-942.

Mannion, G. and Sowerby, M. (2018) *Learner Participation in Educational Settings (3-18)*, Livingstone: Scottish Government/Education Scotland. Retrieved from: https://education.gov.scot/improvement/Documents/learner-participation.pdf (accessed 11 October 2023).

Merrick, R. (2020) 'Pupil participation in planning provision for special educational needs: Teacher perspectives', *Support for Learning*, 35(1): 101-118.

Murray, J. and Cousens, D. (2020) 'Primary school children's beliefs associating extra-curricular provision with non-cognitive skills and academic achievement', *Education 3-13: International Journal of Primary, Elementary and Early Years Education*, 48(1): 37-53.

Nelson, J. and Sharp, C. (2020) *Schools' Responses to Covid-19: Key Findings from the Wave 1 Survey*, Slough: NFER.

Office for Standards in Education (Ofsted). (2023a) *Education Inspection Framework for September 2023*, London: Ofsted. Retrieved from: www.gov.uk/government/publications/education-inspection-framework/education-inspection-framework-for-september-2023 (accessed 11 October 2023).

Office for Standards in Education (Ofsted). (2023b) *School Inspection Handbook for September 2023*, London: Ofsted. Retrieved from: www.gov.uk/government/publications/school-inspection-handbook-eif/school-inspection-handbook-for-september-2023 (accessed 11 October 2023).

Robinson, C. (2012) 'Student engagement: What does this mean in practice in the context of higher education institutions?', *Journal of Applied Research in Higher Education*, 4(2): 94-108.

Robinson, C. (2014) *Children, Their Voices and Their Experiences of School: What Does the Evidence Tell Us?*, York, UK: Cambridge Primary Review Trust.

Robinson, C. and Taylor, C. (2007) 'Theorising student voice: Values and perspectives', *Improving Schools*, 10(1): 5-17.

Rudduck, J. and McIntyre, D. (2007) *Improving Learning through Consulting Pupils*, London: Routledge.

The Education (School Teachers' Appraisal) (England) Regulations (2012). Retrieved from: www.legislation.gov.uk/uksi/2012/115/contents

United Nations (UN). (1989) *UN Convention on the Rights of the Child: General Assembly Resolution 44/25*, New York: United Nations.

Wall, K., Cassidy, C., Robinson, C., Hall, E, Beaton, M., Kanyal, M. and Mitra, D. (2019) 'Look who's talking: Factors for considering the facilitation of very young children's voices' *Journal of Childhood Research*, 17(4): 263-278.

Welsh Government. (2016) *Children and Young People's Participation in Wales ... Good Practice 2016*. Retrieved from: www.gov.wales/sites/default/files/publications/2019-06/good-practice-guide.pdf#:~:text=The%20 Standards%20identify%20the%20key%20issues%20that%20all,integral%20to%20working%20 with%20children%20and%20young%20people (accessed 11 October 2023).

UNIT 7.2

CREATIVITY AND CREATIVE TEACHING AND LEARNING

Teresa Cremin and Jonathan Barnes

INTRODUCTION

In a world dominated by technological innovation and rapid change, creativity is a critical component; human skills and people's imaginative and innovative powers are key resources and the ability to live sustainably with uncertainty is essential (Robinson, 2009, 2022). Global issues like climate change, environmental damage and increasing violence require creative thinking at every level. So, organisations and governments all over the world are now more concerned than ever to promote creativity (World Intellectual Property Organisation [WIPO], 2023).

As primary professionals, it is our responsibility to steer the creative development of young people in our care. In the first decade of the twenty-first century, creativity was given a high profile in education policy and the media, and children were expected to think creatively, make connections and generate ideas, as well as problem-solve (Craft, 2011). Whilst the Early Years Foundation Stage Framework (Department for Education [DfE], 2014) in England recognises that 'the development of children's artistic and cultural awareness supports their imagination and creativity', references to creativity in the primary curriculum (DfE, 2013) and the Ofsted Education Inspection Framework (2023) are limited. Nonetheless, professionals recognise that developing the creativity of the young cannot be left to chance.

Academic explorations of creative teaching and teaching for creativity are extensive (e.g. Chappell et al., 2021; Cremin, 2017; Craft et al., 2014; Barnes, 2021), and teachers still seek innovative ways to shape the curriculum in response to children's needs. Creative teaching should not be placed in opposition to the teaching of essential knowledge, skills and understandings in the subject disciplines; neither does it imply lowered expectations of challenge or behaviour. Rather, creative teaching involves teaching the subjects in contexts that explicitly invite learners to connect, engage imaginatively and that stretch their generative, evaluative and collaborative capacities (Barnes, 2021).

However, many teachers still feel constrained by perceptions of a culture of accountability. You too may already be aware of the classroom impact of an assessment-led and highly standardised system. Such pressures can limit opportunities for creative endeavour and may tempt you to stay within the safe boundaries of the known. Recognising that tensions exist between the drive to raise measurable standards and the impulse to teach more creatively is a good starting point, but finding the energy and enterprise to respond flexibly is a real challenge. To do so, you need to be convinced that creativity has an important role to play in education and believe that you can contribute, both personally and professionally. You may also need to widen your understanding of creativity and creative practice in order to teach creatively and teach for creativity.

DOI: 10.4324/9781032691794-38

> **OBJECTIVES**
>
> By the end of this unit, you should have:
>
> - an increased understanding of the nature of creativity;
> - an awareness of some of the features of creative primary teachers;
> - a wider understanding of creative pedagogical practice;
> - some understanding of how to plan for creative learning.

CREATIVE PRACTICE

A class of learners engage with interest as they collaborate to create three-dimensional representations of Egyptian gods to add to their classroom museum. Earlier that morning, at this Northamptonshire primary school, the 6–7-year-olds had generated and discussed their ideas and listened to others. Then, in groups, they turned these ideas into action. Operating independently of their teacher, they found resources in their classroom and others, monitored their activities and talked about their work. A variety of representations were created, and new ideas celebrated and appraised. Later, the children wrote instructions for making their images and added them to a huge class book, which recorded other cross-curricular projects. However, their ability to recall, explain and discuss the finer points of this carefully planned and executed project two terms later was an even richer testimony to the enjoyment and depth of creative learning involved.

In this school, as in many others, the staff had adopted a creative approach to the curriculum, influenced in part by the significant achievements of what were then called 'creative schools' (Ofsted, 2009). This trend was encouraged by many initiatives, including the report *Nurturing Creativity in Young People* (Roberts, 2006) and Creative Partnerships (2002–11), a government-funded initiative that encouraged schools to develop innovative ways of teaching. It showed that creative and collaborative projects inspired and fostered creative skills and raised children's and young people's confidence and aspiration (Eames et al., 2006).

The focus on creative learning has since shifted; a 'cultural education' agenda is now evident and creativity is not foregrounded in education policies in England, although Arts Council England has developed the Creativity Collaboratives initiative. Nonetheless, creativity plays a key role economically, and recent research evidences strong relationships between creative activity and well-being (e.g. Fancourt and Finn, 2019; Acar et al., 2020; Tan et al., 2021). In the light of new awareness of the value of creativity, teachers continue to seek innovative ways of teaching to increase motivation and develop creative learners.

SO WHAT IS CREATIVITY?

Creativity is not confined to special people or to arts-based activities, nor is it undisciplined play. It is, however, notoriously difficult to define. It has been described as 'a state of mind in which all our intelligences are working together', involving 'seeing, thinking and innovating' (Craft, 2000: 38) and as 'imaginative activity fashioned so as to produce outcomes that are both original and of value' (National Advisory Committee on Creative and Cultural Education [NACCCE], 1999: 29). Creativity is possible wherever human intelligence and imagination are actively engaged and is an essential part of an effective education: it includes all areas of understanding and all children, teachers and others working in primary education. Indeed, it can be demonstrated by anyone in any aspect of life, throughout life.

It is useful to distinguish between 'big C creativity' (exemplified in some of Gardner's (1993) studies of highly creative individuals, such as Picasso, Einstein and Graham) and 'little c creativity'. This latter form focuses on the individual agency and the resourcefulness of ordinary people to innovate and take action. Csikszentmihalyi suggests that each of us is born with two contradictory sets of instructions – a conservative tendency and an expansive tendency, but warns us that, 'If too few opportunities for curiosity are available, if too many obstacles are put in the way of risk and exploration, the motivation to engage in creative behaviour is easily extinguished' (1996: 11).

In the classroom, developing opportunities for children to 'possibility think' their way forwards is, therefore, critical (Craft et al., 2012; Cremin, Chappell and Craft, 2013). This will involve you in immersing the class in an issue or subject and helping them ask questions, be imaginative and playfully explore options, as well as innovate. At the core of such creative endeavour is the child's identity. Their sense of self-determination and agency and their understanding of themselves as unique thinkers able to solve life's problems are essential ingredients of their success, resilience and general health (Marmot et al., 2020). From this perspective, creativity is not seen as an event or a product (although it may involve either or both), but a process or a state of mind involving the serious play of ideas and possibilities. This generative, problem-finding/problem-solving process may involve rational and non-rational thought and may be fed by the intuitive, by daydreaming and pondering, as well as by the application of knowledge and skills. In order to be creative, children may need considerable knowledge in a domain, but creativity and knowledge are not in opposition, they enrich each other.

Imaginative activity can take many forms; it draws on a more varied range of human functioning than linear, logical and rational patterns of behaviour (Claxton, 2006; Lucas et al., 2023). It is essentially generative and may include physical, social, reflective, musical, aural or visual thinking, involving children in activities that produce new and unusual connections between ideas, domains, processes and materials. When children and their teachers step outside the boundaries of predictability and are physically engaged, this provides a balance to the sedentary and too often abstract, apparently context-free nature of school education.

Creative learning is often collaborative and uses mind and body, emotions, eyes, ears and all the senses, in an effort to face a challenge or solve a problem. In less-conventional contexts, new insights and connections may be made through analogy and metaphor, and teachers become the 'meddlers in the middle' (McWilliam, 2008), not the 'sage on the stage' of more transmissive modes of education. Modes of creative thinking, such as the 'imaginative-generative' mode, which produces outcomes, and the 'critical-evaluative' mode, which involves consideration of originality and value (NACCCE, 1999: 30), operate in close interrelationship and need to be consciously developed in the classroom.

The process of creativity, Lucas et al. (2023) suggest, involves the ability to move freely between the different layers of our memories to find solutions to problems. Others see the creative mind as one that looks for unexpected likenesses and connections between disparate domains (Bronowski, 1978). Csikszentmihalyi (1996) wisely suggests, however, that creativity does not happen inside people's heads, but in the interaction between an individual's thoughts and the sociocultural context. When one considers examples of both big C and little c creativity, this explanation makes the most sense, as the social and cultural context of learning is highly influential.

> **In Wales ...**
>
> The four purposes should be the starting point and aspiration for schools' curriculum design. Ultimately, the aim of a school's curriculum is to support its learners to become:
>
> - ambitious, capable learners, ready to learn throughout their lives
> - enterprising, creative contributors, ready to play a full part in life and work
> - ethical, informed citizens of Wales and the world
> - healthy, confident individuals, ready to lead fulfilling lives as valued members of society
>
> enterprising, creative contributors who:
>
> - connect and apply their knowledge and skills to create ideas and products
> - think creatively to reframe and solve problems
> - identify and grasp opportunities
> - take measured risks
> - lead and play different roles in teams effectively and responsibly
> - express ideas and emotions through different media
> - give of their energy and skills so that other people will benefit.
>
> (Welsh Government, 2022)

Task 7.2.1 Ownership of learning

Relevance, ownership and control of learning, as well as innovation, are key issues in creative learning in children. Imaginative approaches involve individuals and groups in initiating questions and lines of enquiry, so that they are more in charge of their work, and such collaboration and interaction help to develop a greater sense of autonomy in the events that unfold.

- To what extent have you observed children taking control of their learning, making choices and demonstrating ownership of their learning? Think of some examples and share these in small groups.
- To what extent was the work also relevant to the lives of the children? Were they emotionally or imaginatively engaged, building on areas of interest, maintaining their individuality and sharing ideas with one another?
- If you have seen little evidence of these issues, consider how you could offer more opportunity for relevance, ownership and control of learning in the classroom.

It is clear, too, that creativity is not bound to particular subjects. At the cutting edge of every domain of learning, creativity is essential and always present. It depends in part on interactions between feeling and thinking across boundaries and ideas. It also requires a climate of trust, respect and support; an environment in which individual agency and self-determination are fostered and ideas and interests are valued, discussed and celebrated. Yet we have all experienced schools that fail to teach the pleasure and excitement to be found in science or mathematics, for example, or that let routines and timetables, subject boundaries and decontextualised knowledge dominate the daily diet of the young. In such sterile environments, when formulae for learning are relied upon, and off-the-shelf curriculum packages are delivered, children's ability to make connections and to imagine alternatives is markedly reduced. So, too, is their capacity for curiosity, for enquiry and for creativity itself.

CREATIVE TEACHING AND TEACHING FOR CREATIVITY

The distinction between creative teaching and teaching for creativity is helpful in that it is possible to imagine a creative teacher who engages personally and creatively in the classroom, yet fails to provoke and provide for children's creative learning. Responsible creative professionals are not necessarily flamboyant performers, but teachers who use a range of approaches to create the conditions in which the creativity of others can flourish. Creative teachers also recognise and make use of their own creativity, not just to interest and engage the learners, but also to promote new thinking and learning. Their confidence in their own creativity enables them to offer the children stronger scaffolds and spaces for emotional and intellectual growth.

> ### In Northern Ireland ...
>
> The importance of creativity, both in pedagogy and as a theme that underpins the learning experiences of pupils, is regarded by educationalists as fundamental to the teaching and learning process. With this in mind, the competences have been designed to enhance professional autonomy, both at an individual and collective level, in a way that encourages creative and innovative approaches to teaching and which, in turn, develops in pupils the ability to think creatively. Indeed, the ability to think creatively, and the innovation it encourages, is central to any modern education system that strives to enhance the life chances of children and young people.
>
> (General Teaching Council for Northern Ireland [GTCNI], 2011: 8)

Research undertaken in higher education, with tutors teaching music, geography and English, suggests that creative teaching is a complex art form - a veritable 'cocktail party' (Grainger, Barnes and Scoffham, 2004). The host gathers the ingredients (the session content) and mixes them playfully and skilfully (the teaching style), in order to facilitate a creative, enjoyable and worthwhile party (the learning experience). Although no formula was, or could be, established for creative teaching, some of the ingredients for mixing a creative cocktail were identified, albeit tentatively, from this work. The elements are not necessarily creative, but the action of shaking and stirring the ingredients and the individual experience of those attending are critical if the 'cocktail party' is to be successful. The intention to promote creative learning appeared to be an important element in this work.

The session content included placing current trends in a wider context and extensive use of metaphor, analogy, humour and personal anecdotes to make connections. The teaching style included multimodal pedagogic practices, pace, humour, the confidence of the tutors and their ability to inspire and value the pupils. In relation to the learning experience, the themes included involving the pupils affectively and physically and challenging them to engage and reflect. Together, these represent some of the critical features of creative teachers and creative teaching that combine to support new thinking.

> **Task 7.2.2 Teaching as a cocktail party**
>
> - Consider the metaphor of teaching as a cocktail party for a moment. In what ways do you think it captures the vitality of teaching – the dynamic interplay between teachers, children and the resources available? Select one or two of the features, such as humour or personal anecdotes. Do you make extensive use of either? Remember, the research indicates that such features are employed *with others* at the 'cocktail party'.
> - Consider your previous teachers. Which were the most creative? Did they create successful cocktail parties in which you felt valued and engaged, took risks, made connections and developed deep learning? How did they achieve this?

PERSONAL CHARACTERISTICS OF CREATIVE TEACHERS

It is difficult to identify with any certainty the personal characteristics of creative teachers. Research tends to offer lists of propensities that such teachers possess (e.g. Beetlestone, 1998; Sternberg and Chowkase, 2021). Common elements include:

- enthusiasm, passion and commitment;
- risk-taking;
- deep curiosity or a questioning stance;
- willingness to be intuitive and/or introspective;
- gregariousness and introspectiveness;
- a clear set of personal values;
- awareness of self as a creative being.

This list encompasses many of the personal qualities you might expect in any good teacher, except perhaps the last. Sternberg and Chowkase (2021) suggest that creative teachers are creative role models themselves – professionals who continue to be self-motivated learners, who value the creative dimensions of their own lives and who make connections between their personal responses to experience and their teaching. In addition, a clear set of values, reflecting fair-mindedness, openness to evidence, a desire for clarity and respect for others, are important and among the attitudinal qualities embedded in creative teaching. So, too, is a commitment to inclusion and a belief in human rights and equity. Such attitudes and values have a critical role in creative teaching and are, perhaps, best taught by example.

FEATURES OF A CREATIVE PEDAGOGICAL STANCE

The intention to promote creativity is fundamental. There are a number of features of a creative pedagogical stance that you may want to consider in relation to your teaching and observation of other creative professionals.

A learner-centred, agency-oriented ethos

Creative teachers tend to place the learners above the curriculum and combine a positive disposition towards creativity and person-centred teaching that actively promotes pupils who learn and think for themselves (Sawyer, 2011; Robinson, 2022). Relaxed, trusting educator-learner relationships exist in creative classrooms, and the role of affect and children's feelings play a central role in learning. These relationships foster children's agency and autonomy as learners and enable, for example, children to respond to literature personally, imaginatively and affectively (Kuzmičová and Cremin, 2021). A learner-oriented ethos will also involve you showing patience and openness, reinforcing children's creative behaviour, celebrating difference, diversity and innovation, as well as learning to handle different views. If you adopt such a person-centred orientation, you will be shaping the children's self-esteem and enhancing their intrinsic motivation and agency. You might, for example, explicitly plan for small groups to shape and plan for themselves how they might investigate melting, by giving them enormous 'ice eggs' (made from balloons filled with water and frozen) and telling an imaginary tale of how these came to be in your possession (see Craft et al., 2012).

A questioning stance

Creativity involves asking and attempting to answer real questions; the creative teacher is seen by many as one who uses open questions and who promotes speculation in the classroom, encouraging deeper understanding and lateral thinking (Cremin, Barnes and Scoffham, 2009; Barnes, 2023). Both teachers and children need to be involved in this process of imaginative thinking, encompassing the generation of challenging and unusual questions and the creation of possible responses. The questioning stance of the teacher has also been noted as central to children's possibility thinking (Chappell et al., 2008). You could, for example, play with the idea of 'book zips', new books that have invisible zips that prevent children opening them! (Zipped plastic bags or magical tales often help to extend the patience necessary!) Groups can generate questions about characters, plot and setting and respond to other groups' questions.

Creating space, time and freedom to make connections

Creativity requires space, time and a degree of freedom. Deep immersion in an area or activity allows options to remain open, and persistence and follow-through to develop. Conceptual space allows children to converse, challenge and negotiate meanings and possibilities together. For example, through imaginatively adopting the role of the unknown sibling of the star of a popular video you could, for example, trigger historical, geographical or scientific enquiry and exploration (see Cooper, 2017).

Employing multimodal, intuitive teaching approaches

A variety of multimodal teaching approaches and frequent switching between modes in a playlike and spontaneous manner support creative learning. The diversity of pattern, rhythm and pace used by creative teachers is particularly marked, as is their use of informed intuition. As you teach, opportunities will arise for you to use your intuition and move from the security of the known. Give yourself permission to go beyond the 'script' you have planned and allow the children to take the initiative and lead you; such spontaneity will encourage you to seize the moment and foster deeper learning (Cremin, Craft and Burnard, 2006; Burnard and Loughray, 2021). In geography, for example, you might nurture creative play through opportunities for transforming and adapting places, making dens, yurts, shelters or tree houses (see Scoffham, 2017).

Prompting full engagement, ownership and ongoing reflection

In studying a curriculum area in depth, children should experience both explicit instruction and space for exploration and discovery. Try to provide opportunities for choice and be prepared to spend time developing their self-management skills so that they can operate independently. Their engagement can be prompted by appealing to their interests and passions, by involving them in imaginative and sensory experiences and by connecting learning to their lives (Cremin et al., 2009). A oscillation between physical/emotional involvement and reflection will become noticeable in the classroom as you work to refine, reshape and improve learning. The ability to give and receive criticism is also an essential part of creativity.

Modelling risk-taking and enabling the children to take risks too

The ability to tolerate ambiguity is an example of the 'confident uncertainty' to which Claxton (2021) refers when discussing creative teachers – those who combine subject and pedagogical knowledge, but leave space for uncertainty and the unknown. You will gain in confidence through increased subject knowledge, experience and reflection, but your assurance will also grow through taking risks and having a go at expressing yourself. Risk-taking is integral to creativity, and one that you will want to model and foster and support the children in too.

To be a creative practitioner, you will need more than a working knowledge of creativity and the curriculum. You will need a clear idea of your own values, secure pedagogical understanding and a knowledge base, supported by a passionate belief in the potential of creative teaching to engage, inspire and educate. Such teaching depends, in the end, upon the human interaction between teachers and pupils and is also influenced by the teacher's state of mind. The creative teacher is one who is aware of, and values, the human attribute of creativity in themselves and actively seeks to promote this in others. The creative teacher has a creative state of mind that is both exercised and developed through their creative practice and personal/professional curiosity, connection-making, originality and autonomy (Cremin, Barnes and Scoffham, 2009; Barnes, 2018). Such practice is, of course, influenced by the physical, social, emotional and spiritual environments in which teachers and children work.

Task 7.2.3 Creative engagement

- Make a list of the times when you feel deeply engaged – in 'flow', as Csikszentmihalyi (1996) describes it, or in your 'element', as Robinson (2009) does. What are the characteristics of this engagement?
- How do these relate to the aspects of creative practice described earlier – are there parallels, and, if not, what might this reveal about the degree to which creative engagement can be prescribed or fostered?

CREATING ENVIRONMENTS OF POSSIBILITY

You may have been to a school where creativity is planned for and fostered, and where there is a clear sense of shared values and often a real buzz of purposeful and exciting activity. Such schools have a distinctive character that impacts upon behaviour, relationships, the physical and ethical environment and the curriculum. An ethos that values creativity will, according to most definitions, promote originality and the use of the imagination, as well as encourage an adventurous attitude to life and learning. In such environments of possibility, packed with ideas and experiences, resources and choices, as well as time for relaxation and rumination, physical, conceptual and emotional space is offered. Schools offering such spaces are, Robinson (2015) argues, revolutionising education from the ground up. They are not alone: there is considerable interest in such pedagogical practice internationally (Cremin and Chappell, 2019).

The social and emotional environment

Taking creative risks and moving forward in learning are heavily dependent upon an atmosphere of acceptance and security. Children's well-being is widely recognised as important, in its own right and to support their creativity, but can only be fostered by a secure ethos. However, creative schools may display apparently contradictory characteristics. The ethos may be simultaneously:

- highly active and relaxed;
- supportive and challenging;
- confident and speculative;
- playful and serious;
- focused and fuzzy;
- individualistic and communal;
- understood personally and owned by all;
- non-competitive and ambitious.

Since Plato, many have argued that there are links between involvement in creative acts and a general sense of well-being. More recent research in cognitive neuroscience (Abraham, 2018) and positive psychology (Fredrickson, 2010) has suggested that a state of well-being promotes optimum conditions in mind and body, and ensures secure relationships. A perceived link between discovering one's own creativity and feeling a sense of well-being (Barnes, Hope and Scoffham, 2008) suggests that frequent, planned and progressive creative opportunities are needed across the curriculum (Barnes, 2018, 2023).

The physical environment

The physical environment in a school that promotes creativity is likely to celebrate achievement and individuality and can be a valuable teaching resource. Children's views on this are important and deserve to be taken into account. Projects have shown how creative thinking in the context of focused work on improving the school building, grounds or local areas can achieve major citizenship objectives and high-level arts and literacy targets in an atmosphere of genuine support and community concern (Barnes, 2007, 2023).

Active modes of learning and problem-solving approaches that include independent investigation require accessible resources of various kinds, so the richer and more multifaceted a range you can offer, the better. This supports genuine choice, speculation and experimentation, happy accidents and flexibility. An environment of possibility in which individual agency and self-determination are fostered and children's ideas and interests are valued, shared and celebrated depends upon the presence of a climate of trust, respect and support in your classroom/school. Creativity can be developed when you are confident and secure in both your subject knowledge and your knowledge of creative pedagogical practice; then, you will seek to model the features of creativity *and* develop a culture of creative opportunities in school.

PLANNING FOR CREATIVITY

Open-ended learning opportunities that offer space for autonomy, collaboration and have real-world relevance can be created through extended and creative units of work, encompassing multiple subjects. These can be enriched by regularly involving the expertise of partners from the creative and cultural sector; Galton (2015) argues such partnerships can enrich learning and raise children's expectations and achievements. In planning creative units of work, you will want to build on insights from research. The following ten research-informed suggestions are worth considering:

1. Create a *positive, secure atmosphere* in which risks can be taken (Barnes, 2023).
2. Profile a *questioning stance* and frame the work around children's interests and questions (Cremin and Chappell, 2019).
3. Ensure a range of *practical and analytical, open-ended* activities (Craft *et al.*, 2014).
4. Emphasise *learner agency* and individual and cooperative thinking and learning (Craft *et al.*, 2014).
5. Agree *clear goals*, some of which are set and owned by the learners (Jeffrey and Woods, 2009).
6. Build *emotionally relevant links* to the children's lives, offering opportunities for *engagement and enjoyment* (Barnes, 2018).
7. Integrate a manageable number of *relevant subjects/areas of learning* (Barnes, 2015).
8. Involve developmentally appropriate *progression* in skills, knowledge and understanding.
9. Set the work in a wider framework that includes *concepts, content and attitudes* (Cremin, 2009).
10. Provide supportive *assessment* procedures that build security and include time and tools for reflection (Lucas, 2022).

CREATIVE CURRICULA IN ACTION

Two examples bring such a curriculum, centred upon creative learning, to life. A whole-school community from Tower Hamlets made a winter visit to Canary Wharf, not far from the school. Many pupils had never been there. The event was grasped as an opportunity to collect as much information as possible. None of the collected impressions could have been gathered from websites or written sources, and so the visit was a genuine investigation, involving every age group in traffic surveys; rubbings; observations of people walking; collections of geometric shapes; still images framed by 'key' describing words; moving images; sensory descriptions of sights, sounds and smells; intricate 360° drawings; mosaics and photos of trees imprisoned in stainless steel; stone and scaffolded containers. Every moment, morning or afternoon, was fully used in information-gathering. Children and adult supporters collected digital, drawn, listed, tallied, acted and heard data from a variety of contrasting sites around the wharf.

The library of collected and remembered objects, images and sensations was brought back to school and formed the basis of the curriculum for the next few weeks. Creating responses from these disparate sources involved very different paths in each class, from Nursery to Year 6. One Year 2 class made a 'sound journey' using mapping and musical skills and knowledge. Groups of five or six composed music to capture different places on their journey and linked them with their own 'walking music'. Separate teams then mapped their journeys using previously learned techniques, and the resultant maps were used as graphic musical scores. A mixed group created large, imaginative abstract constructions from bamboo and tissue and applied decoration from rubbings and drawings, expressing their experience of the towering buildings at the wharf.

Children, along with their co-learning teachers, presented their compositions, artworks, mathematical investigations, stories and dramas to the rest of the school in a series of assemblies. These were especially appreciated because everyone had shared in the same initial experience. The whole project was evaluated through a continuous blog kept by children, teachers, artists and teaching assistants. Their challenge, like yours, is to take account of individual differences in learning, help each child become a self-regulated learner and ensure appropriate coverage of the areas of learning and their attendant knowledge bases.

In another context, a combined Year 3/4 class in a school on England's south coast reflected on and learned about refugees. Most children knew that a boat carrying a large number of asylum seekers had landed on a beach near the school. Their classes had already welcomed refugees from Ukraine, Syria and Sudan. Teachers decided on a week-long, cross-curricular unit of work on refugees to support the development of understanding in their community. Initially, the class divided into teams of six and followed a carousel of starter projects: with an artist they constructed tiny origami boats with their own written personal messages for newly-arrived refugees; they shared time with a refugee who told the story of their journey; they found the geographical details of refugee journeys from maps, news reports, videos and photographs; and learned how to make a blog and the words and music of a welcome song from The Congo.

Bursts of creativity occurred as groups were introduced to different ways of responding to the theme. When the paper boats were collected, the children were keen to see what others had written. They discovered words like *care, love, welcome, safe, secure, kind, peace* had been used by most of their classmates. As the artist gathered the boats to make an installation in the town hall, a group of children unexpectedly asked if they could tally certain words and suggested making a bar graph of these 'values words'. They wanted mathematically to share their feelings about refugees with the rest of the school. As children listened to a story of escape from Ethiopia on foot, many responded with detailed questions, and all wrote single word notes to remind them of important details – they wanted to use them to help compose collaborative blogs about the refugee's journey. A group of singers devised ways of making their welcome song more communicative by improvising a rhythmic backing track, devising actions and emphasising facial expressions. These ideas were expanded with others and in the following days the teacher assisted groups in developing a final presentation to the school.

Different kinds of creativity were involved as children worked towards this. Some *redefined* their existing thinking about community through exposure to new information and relationships. Others demonstrated creativity as *forward momentum* as they took their existing understanding further in the direction it was already moving – for example, as they imaginatively refined the presentation and performance of the song they learned. One group *redirected* their mathematical skills as they expressed their feelings about refugees in statistics and graphs. Several groups *integrated* thinking from different disciplines to produce demonstrably original responses in their design, geography and English skills in the refugee journey blogs. In time, you will feel confident to plan such creative work; what is critical now is that you recognise its value and aspire to this.

SUMMARY

Creative teaching is a collaborative enterprise that capitalises on the unexpected and variously involves engagement, reflection and transformation, patterned at such a rate as to invite and encourage a questioning stance and motivate self-directed learning. Creative learning involves asking questions, exploring options and generating and appraising ideas, as the learner takes risks and imaginatively thinks their way forwards, making new or innovative connections in the process. New thinking happens at the meeting places of different minds, ideas and approaches, and it also takes place when new links occur between people. Many of the examples in this unit show both adults and children involved in thinking and learning together, which can be a key generator of creativity. We hope you will choose to teach creatively and promote creativity through your planning, and will build in choice and autonomy, relevance and purpose in engaging environments of possibility – environments both inside and outside the classroom.

For more ideas on teaching creatively across the curriculum, see the series that accompanies this handbook. Edited by Cremin, it includes books on teaching: *English* (Cremin, 2023), *Mathematics* (Pound and Lee, 2021), *Science* (Davies, 2015), *History* (Cooper, 2017), *Geography* (Scoffham, 2017), *Music* (Burnard and Murphy, 2013), *Physical Education* (Pickard and Maude, 2021), *Religious Education* (Elton-Chalcraft, 2015), *Outdoors* (Pickering, 2017), *Design and Technology* (Benson and Lawson, 2017), *Creatively*, as well as creatively teaching *Cross-curricular Learning* (Barnes, 2018).

ANNOTATED FURTHER READING

Barnes, J. (2023) *Positive Pedagogy across the Primary Curriculum*, London: Sage.
   This book explicates the benefits of creativity in schools and stresses the importance of placing creative learning within a real-world, moral context, alongside its role in addressing sustainability, climate change, environmental degradation, inequality and violence.

Cremin, T. (ed.) (2017) *Creativity and Creative Pedagogies in the Early and Primary Years*, Abingdon, UK: Routledge.
   This edited international collection reveals the possibilities and complexities of creative pedagogies in different cultural contexts and offers practical evidence of practice from around the world.

Sawyer, R. (ed.) (2011) *Structure and Improvisation in Creative Teaching*, New York: Cambridge.
   This US collection provides practical advice for teachers wishing to become creative professionals. It highlights the need for teachers to respond artfully to curricula and the unexpected demands of classroom interactions.

FURTHER READING TO SUPPORT M-LEVEL STUDY

Craft, A., Cremin, T., Hay, P. and Clack, J. (2013) 'Creative primary schools: Developing and maintaining pedagogy for creativity', *Ethnography & Education*, 9(1): 16–34.
   This paper is a case study of three schools; it documents their creative practice and the tenets underpinning this.

Cremin, T. and Chappell, K. (2019) 'Creative pedagogies: A systematic review', *Research Papers in Education*, 36(3): 299–331.
   This paper, drawing on the findings of a systematic review of studies from around the world, identifies seven characteristics of creative pedagogies.

RELEVANT WEBSITES

The Global Institute of Creative Thinking: www.gioct.org/
   Established as a UK institute, it is now a registered charity focused on fostering creative thinkers, and empowering those we teach, and inspire futures.

Creativity Collaboratives: www.artscouncil.org.uk/developing-creativity-and-culture/children-and-young-people/creativity-collaboratives
   This Arts Council England funded programme is seeking to build networks of schools in order to test innovative practices in teaching for creativity and facilitating system wide change.

REFERENCES

Abraham, A. (2018) *The Neuroscience of Creativity*, Cambridge: Cambridge University Press.

Acar, S., Tadik, H., Myers, D., Sman, C. van der and Uysal, R. (2020) 'Creativity and well-being: A meta-analysis', *Journal of Creative Behavior*, 55(3): 738-751.

Barnes, J. (2007) *Cross Curricular Learning 3-14*, 1st edn, London: Sage.

Barnes, J. (2015) *Cross-Curricular Learning 3-14*, London: Sage.

Barnes, J. (2018) *Applying Cross-Curricular Approaches Creatively*, London: Routledge.

Barnes, J. (2021) 'Intimations of Utopia' in V. Bower (ed.) *Debates in Primary Education*, London: Routledge, pp. 15-34.

Barnes, J. (2023) *Positive Pedagogy Across the Primary Curriculum*, London: Sage.

Barnes, J., Hope, G. and Scoffham, S. (2008) 'A conversation about creative teaching and learning', in A. Craft, T. Cremin and P. Burnard (eds) *Creative Learning 3-11 and How We Document It*, London: Trentham, pp. 125-134.

Beetlestone, F. (1998) *Creative Children, Imaginative Teaching*, Buckingham, UK: Open University Press.

Benson, C. and Lawson, L. (2017) *Teaching Design and Technology Creatively*, London: Routledge.

Bronowski, J. (1978) *The Origins of Knowledge and Imagination*, New Haven, CT: Yale University Press.

Burnard, P. and Loughray, M. (2021) *Sculpting New Creativities in Primary Education*, London: Routledge.

Burnard, P. and Murphy, R. (2013) *Teaching Music Creatively*, London: Routledge.

Chappell, K., Craft, A., Burnard, P. and Cremin, T. (2008) 'Question-posing and question-responding: At the heart of possibility thinking in the early years', *Early Years: An International Journal of Research & Development*, 28(3): 267-286.

Chappell, K., Redding, E., Crickmay, U., Stancliffe, R., Jobbins, V. and Smith, S. (2021) 'The aesthetic, artistic and creative contributions of dance for health and wellbeing across the life course: A systematic review', *International Journal of Qualitative Studies of Health and Wellbeing*, 16(1).

Claxton, G. (2006) 'Mindfulness, learning and the brain', *Journal of Rational Emotive & Cognitive Behaviour Therapy*, 23: 301-314.

Claxton, G. (2021) *The Future of Teaching*, London: Routledge.

Cooper, H. (2017) *Teaching History Creatively*, 2nd edn, London: Routledge.

Craft, A. (2000) *Creativity across the Primary Curriculum: Framing and Developing Practice*, London: RoutledgeFalmer.

Craft, A. (2011) *Creativity and Education Futures: Learning in a Digital Age*, London: Trentham.

Craft, A., Cremin, T., Burnard, P., Dragovic, T. and Chappell, K. (2012) 'Possibility thinking: An evidence-based concept driving creativity?', *Education 3-13*: 1-19.

Craft, A., Cremin, T., Hay, P. and Clack, J. (2014) 'Creative primary schools: Developing and maintaining pedagogy for creativity', *Ethnography & Education*, 9(1): 16-34.

Cremin, T. (2009) 'Creative teaching and creative teachers', in A. Wilson (ed.) *Creativity in Primary Practice*, Exeter, UK: Learning Matters, pp. 36-46.

Cremin, T. (ed.) (2017) *Creativity and Creative Pedagogies in the Early and Primary Years*, Abingdon, UK: Routledge.

Cremin, T. (2023) *Teaching English Creatively*, 3rd edn, London: Routledge.

Cremin, T. and Chappell, K. (2019) 'Creative pedagogies: A systematic review', *Research Papers in Education*, 36(3): 299-331.

Cremin, T., Barnes, J. and Scoffham, S. (2009) *Creative Teaching for Tomorrow*, Margate, UK: Future Creative.

Cremin, T., Chappell, K. and Craft, A. (2013) 'Reciprocity between narrative, questioning and imagination in the early and primary years: Examining the role of narrative in possibility thinking', *Thinking Skills & Creativity*, 9: 135-151.

Cremin, T., Craft, A. and Burnard, P. (2006) 'Pedagogy and possibility thinking in the early years', *Journal of Thinking Skills & Creativity*, 1(2): 108-119.

Csikszentmihalyi, M. (1996) *Creativity: Flow and the Psychology of Discovery and Invention*, New York: Harper.

Davies, D. (2015) *Teaching Science Creatively*, 2nd edn, London: Routledge.

Department for Education (DfE). (2013) *National Curriculum in England: Primary Curriculum*. Last updated 2015. Retrieved from: www.gov.uk/government/publications/national-curriculum-in-england-primary-curriculum

Department for Education (DfE). (2014) *Statutory Framework for the Early Years Foundation Stage*, London: DfE. Last updated 2024.

Eames, A., Benton, T., Sharp, C. and Kendall, L. (2006) *The Impact of Creative Partnerships on the Attainment of Young People*, Slough, UK: NFER.

Elton-Chalcraft, S. (ed.) (2015) *Teaching RE Creatively*, London: Routledge.

Fancourt, D. and Finn, S. (2019) *What is the Evidence on the Role of the Arts in Improving Health and Well-being? A Scoping Review*, Copenhagen: WHO Regional Office for Europe.

Fredrickson, B. (2010) *Positivity: Groundbreaking Research to Release Your Inner Optimist and Thrive*, London: Oneworld.

Galton, M. (2015) 'It's a real journey: A life changing experience', *Education 3-13*, 43(4): 433-444.

Gardner, H. (1993) *Frames of Mind: The Theory of Multiple Intelligences*, London: Fontana Press.

General Teaching Council for Northern Ireland (GTCNI). (2011) *The Reflective Practitioner*, Belfast, GTCNI. Retrieved from: https://gtcni.org.uk/cmsfiles/Resource365/Resources/Publications/The_Reflective_Profession.pdf

Grainger, T., Barnes, J. and Scoffham, S. (2004) 'Creative teaching: A creative cocktail', *Journal of Education & Teaching*, 38(3): 243-253.

Jeffrey, B. and Woods, P. (2009) *Creative Learning in the Primary School*, London: Routledge.

Kuzmičová, A. and Cremin, T. (2021) 'Different fiction genres take children's memories to different places', *Cambridge Journal of Education*, 52(1): 37-53.

Lucas, B. (2022) *A Field Guide to Assessing Creativity in Schools*, Perth: FORM.

Lucas, B., Spencer, E., Stoll, L., Fisher-Naylor, D., Richards, N., James, S. and Milne, K. (2023) *Creative Thinking in Schools: A Leadership Playbook*, Bancyfelin: Crown House.

McWilliam, E. (2008) 'Unlearning how to teach', *Innovations in Education & Teaching International*, 45(3): 263-269.

Marmot, M., Allan, J., Boyce, T., Goldblatt, P. and Morrison, J (2020) *Health Equity in England: The Marmot Review 10 Years On*, London: Institute of Health Equity.

National Advisory Committee on Creative and Cultural Education (NACCCE). (1999) *All Our Futures: The Report of the NACCE*, London: DfEE/DCMS.

Ofsted. (2009) *Twenty Outstanding Primary Schools: Excelling Against the Odds*, Manchester, UK: Ofsted.

Ofsted. (2023) *Education Inspection Framework*. Retrieved from: www.gov.uk/government/publications/education-inspection-framework/education-inspection-framework-for-september-2023 (accessed 13 November 2023).

Pickard, A. and Maude, T. (2021) *Teaching Physical Education Creatively*, London: Routledge.

Pickering S. (2017) *Teaching Outdoors Creatively*, London: Routledge.

Pound, L. and Lee, T. (2021) *Teaching Mathematics Creatively*, 3rd edn, Abingdon, UK: Routledge.

Roberts, P. (2006) *Nurturing Creativity in Young People: A Report to Government to Inform Future Policy*, London: DCMS.

Robinson, K. (2009) *The Element: How Finding Your Passion Changes Everything*, London: Allen Lane.

Robinson, K. (2015) *Creative Schools*, New York: Allen Lane.

Robinson, K. (2022) *Imagine If: Creating a Future For Us All*, London: Penguin.

Sawyer, R. (ed.) (2011) *Structure and Improvisation in Creative Teaching*, New York: Cambridge.

Scoffham, S. (ed.) (2017) *Teaching Geography Creatively*, 2nd ed, London: Routledge.

Sternberg, R. J. and Chowkase, A. (2021) 'When we teach for positive creativity, what exactly do we teach for?', *Education Sciences*, 11(5): 237.

Tan, C. Y., Chuah, C. Q., Lee, S. T. and Tan, C. S. (2021) 'Being creative makes you happier: The positive effect of creativity on subjective well-being', *Int J Environ Res Public Health*, 18(14):7244. doi: 10.3390/ijerph18147244

Welsh Government. (2022) Developing a Vision for Curriculum Design. Retrieved from: https://hwb.gov.wales/curriculum-for-wales/designing-your-curriculum/developing-a-vision-for-curriculum-design/ (accessed 26 April 2024).

World Intellectual Property Organisation (WIPO). (2023) *Sustainable Development Goals and Intellectual Property*. Retrieved from: www.wipo.int/sdgs/en/ (accessed 13 November 2023).

UNIT 7.3

TEACHING THINKING

Developing children's thinking skills and metacognition

Robert Fisher

INTRODUCTION

> We need to think better if we are to become better people.
>
> (Paul, aged 10)

In recent years, there has been growing interest across the world in ways of developing children's thinking and learning skills (Kerslake and Wegerif, 2018). This interest has been fed by new knowledge about how the brain works and how people learn, and evidence that specific interventions can improve children's thinking and intelligence. The particular ways in which people apply their minds to solving problems are called *thinking skills*. Many researchers suggest that thinking skills are essential to effective learning, although not all agree on the definition of this term (Moseley *et al.*, 2005). If thinking is how children make sense of learning, developing their thinking skills will help them get more out of learning and life. This unit looks at the implications of research into ways to develop thinking children, thinking classrooms and thinking schools.

OBJECTIVES

By the end of this unit, you should be able to:

- inform your understanding of 'thinking skills' and metacognition and their role in learning;
- understand some key principles that emerge from research into teaching thinking;
- identify the main approaches to developing children's thinking;
- see how you might integrate a 'thinking skills' approach into classroom teaching and research.

WHAT ARE THINKING SKILLS?

Thinking skills are not mysterious entities existing somewhere in the mind. Nor are they like mental muscles that have a physical presence in the brain. What the term refers to is the human capacity to think in conscious ways to achieve certain purposes. Such processes include remembering, questioning, forming concepts, planning, reasoning, imagining, solving problems, making decisions and judgements, translating thoughts into words, and so on. Thinking skills are ways in which humans exercise the *sapiens* part of being *Homo sapiens*.

Some critics claim that there are no general thinking skills, and that all thinking must be about specific aspects of knowledge or linked to a particular subject in the school curriculum. However, different fields of learning can have shared aspects, and, although a subject such as history may have a particular content, this does not mean it has no links to thinking in other subjects – for example, in the need to give reasons and analyse evidence.

Nor does a focus on thinking mean ignoring the role of knowledge. Knowledge is necessary, but simply knowing a lot of things is not sufficient, if children are to be taught to think for themselves. Children need knowledge, but they also need to know how to acquire it, assess it and use it. 'Knowledge comes from other people', said Leo, aged 11, 'but thinking comes from yourself, or should do.'

It is true that thinking must be about something, but people can do it more or less effectively. The capacity, for example, to assess reasons, formulate hypotheses, make conceptual links or ask critical questions is relevant to many areas of learning. As Gemma, age 10, put it: 'To be a good learner you need to practice training your mind'.

We usually refer to skills in particular contexts, such as being 'good at cooking', but 'skills' can also refer to general capacities in cognitive performance, such as having a logical mind, a good memory, being creative or analytical, and so on. A thinking skill is a practical ability to think in ways that are judged to be more or less effective or skilled. However, learning a skill is not enough, for we want children to use their skills on a regular basis and get into the habit of thinking critically, creatively and with care (Grigg and Lewis, 2018). Good thinking requires that cognitive skills become habits of intelligent behaviour learned through practice, and children tend to become better at, for example, giving reasons or asking questions, the more they practise doing so.

Psychologists and philosophers have helped to extend our understanding of the term 'thinking' by emphasising the importance of *dispositions*, such as attention and motivation, commonly associated with thinking. This has prompted a move away from a simple model of 'thinking skills' as isolated cognitive capacities, to a view of thinking as inextricably connected to emotions and dispositions, including 'emotional intelligence', which is our ability to understand our own emotions and the emotions of others (Goleman, 2020), or what Lipman, founder of Philosophy for Children, describes as 'caring thinking'.

The curriculum is no longer seen simply as subject knowledge, but also as the habits of intelligent behaviour and the skills of lifelong learning. Good teaching is about achieving curriculum objectives, but is also about developing general capacities to think, remember and learn. The last 50 years have seen a burgeoning of research across the world into the teaching of thinking, developing 'teaching for thinking' approaches in new directions, integrating them into everyday teaching to create 'thinking classrooms' and developing whole-school policies to create 'thinking schools'.

If thinking skills are the mental capacities we use to investigate the world, to solve problems and make judgements, to identify every such skill would be to enumerate all the capacities of the human mind, and the list would be endless. Many researchers have attempted to identify the key skills in human thinking, and the most famous of these is Bloom's taxonomy (Fisher, 2005). Bloom's taxonomy of thinking skills (what he called 'the cognitive goals of education') has been widely used by teachers in planning their teaching. He identifies a number of basic, or 'lower-order', cognitive skills – knowledge, comprehension and application – and a number of 'higher-order' skills – analysis, synthesis and evaluation. Table 7.3.1 shows the various categories identified by Bloom and the processes involved in the various thinking levels.

TABLE 7.3.1 Bloom's taxonomy

Cognitive goal	Thinking cues
1 Knowledge (knowing and remembering)	Say what you know, or remember, describe, identify, say who, when, which, where, what
2 Comprehension (interpreting and understanding)	Describe in your own words, tell how you feel about it, what it means, explain, compare, relate
3 Application (applying, making use of)	How can you use it, apply what you know, use it to solve problems, demonstrate
4 Analysis (taking apart, being critical)	What are the parts, the order, the reasons why, the causes/problems/solutions/consequences
5 Synthesis (connecting, being creative)	How might it be different, how else, what if, connecting developing, improving, creating
6 Evaluation (judging and assessing)	How would you judge it, what is good about it, how might it be improved?

Bloom's taxonomy has been criticised as being too simple a representation of levels of thinking and many more complex taxonomies have been created since his pioneering work in the 1950s, but many teachers over the years have found it a simple and useful tool for creating questions that offer increasing levels of cognitive challenge. Bloom's taxonomy was built on earlier research by Piaget and Vygotsky that suggested that thinking skills and capacities are developed by *cognitive challenge*. Good teachers ask challenging questions and set challenging work. As Tom, aged 10, put it: 'A good teacher makes you think even when you don't want to'. One way good teachers do this is by asking questions that probe and challenge children's thinking.

Task 7.3.1 Questions for thinking

Choose a story, poem, text or topic that you would like to use with children as a stimulus for their thinking. Using Bloom's taxonomy, create a series of questions to think about and discuss after you have shared the stimulus with them. List your questions under Bloom's six categories: knowledge, comprehension, application, analysis, synthesis and evaluation.

WHY ARE THINKING SKILLS IMPORTANT?

Thinking skills are important because mastery of the 'basics' in education (literacy, maths, science, etc.), however well taught, is not sufficient to fulfil human potential, nor to meet the demands of the labour market or of active citizenship. Countries across the world are recognising that a broad range of competencies is needed to prepare children for an unpredictable future. These higher-order thinking skills are required, in addition to basic skills, because individuals cannot 'store' sufficient knowledge in their memories for future use. Information is expanding at such a rate that individuals require transferable skills to enable them to address different problems, in different contexts, at different times, throughout their lives. The complexity of modern jobs requires people who can comprehend, judge and participate in generating new knowledge and processes. Modern, democratic societies require citizens to assimilate information from multiple sources, determine its truth and use it to make sound judgements.

The challenge is to develop educational programmes that enable all individuals, not just an elite, to become effective thinkers, because these competencies are now required of everyone. A 'thinking skills' and metacognitive approach suggests that young learners must develop awareness of themselves as thinkers and learners, practise strategies for effective thinking and develop the habits of intelligent behaviour that are needed for lifelong learning (Fisher, 1998). As Paul, aged 10, said: 'We need to think better if we are to become better people'.

WHAT DOES RESEARCH TELL US ABOUT THINKING?

Research in cognitive science and psychology is providing a clearer picture of the brain and the processes associated with thinking. This brain research has some important implications for teachers. For example, we now know that most of the growth in the human brain occurs in early childhood: by the age of 6, the brain in most children is approximately 90 per cent of its adult size. This implies that intervention, while the brain is still growing, may be more effective than waiting until the brain is fully developed. Cognitive challenge is important at all stages, but especially in the early years of education.

Dialogue is the primary means for developing intelligence in the human species. The large human brain evolved to enable individuals to negotiate, through dialogue, the complexities of social living. The capacity for dialogue is central to human thinking. Human consciousness originates in a motivation to share emotions, experience and activities with others. This 'dialogic' capacity is more fundamental than writing or tool use. It is through dialogue that children develop consciousness, learn control over their internal mental processes and develop the conceptual tools for thinking (Fisher, 2009). No wonder recent research emphasises that teacher-pupil interaction is the key to improving standards of teaching (Alexander, 2020; Hattie, 2012).

Psychologists and philosophers have helped to extend our understanding of the term 'thinking' by emphasising the importance of *dispositions*, such as attention and motivation, commonly associated with thinking (Claxton, 2002). This has prompted a move away from a simple model of 'thinking skills' as isolated cognitive capacities to a view of thinking as inextricably connected to emotions and dispositions, including 'emotional intelligence', which is our metacognitive ability to understand our own emotions and the emotions of others (Goleman, 2006).

THE IMPORTANCE OF METACOGNITION

There has been much research in recent years into the teaching of metacognitive strategies in schools. Metacognitive strategies are teaching approaches which make learners think about their learning in explicit ways, for example in planning, monitoring and evaluating their own learning. These metacognitive habits do not just happen. Children need teachers who cue metacognitive responses, make explicit the habits of good thinking and make clear the value of those habits. A summary of research commissioned by the Sutton Trust found that 'Meta-cognitive approaches have consistently high levels of impact with meta-analyses reporting impact of between seven and nine months additional progress ... and is particularly helpful for low achieving pupils' (Higgins, Kokotsaki and Coe, 2011).

Metacognition involves thinking about one's own thinking. It includes knowledge of oneself: for example, what one knows, what one has learned, what one can and cannot do, and ways to improve one's learning or achievement.

Metacognition involves two levels of reflection:

1 knowledge of thinking: includes awareness of self, task and strategy;
2 self-regulated thinking: includes ability to self-evaluate, and self-manage learning.

Metacognition is promoted by helping pupils to reflect on their thinking and decision-making processes. It is developed when pupils are helped to be strategic in organising their activities and are encouraged to reflect before, during and after problem-solving processes. The implication is that you need to plan time for debriefing and review in lessons, to encourage children to think about their learning and how to improve it. This can be done through discussion in a plenary session, or by finding time for reflective writing in their own thinking or learning logs.

In practice, we prompt metacognitive thinking by asking metacognitive questions at different levels of cognitive challenge. First is the level of *cognitive description*, when we ask children to describe what they have been thinking and learning, as when we ask: 'What have you read/learned?'. We then seek *cognitive extension*, by probing their thinking more deeply, as when we ask: 'What does & mean?'. We should also encourage their *cognitive regulation* by asking them, for example, 'What does a good learner/reader/writer do?'

In teaching for metacognition, we want to strengthen children's belief that their intelligence and ability to learn can improve, and teach them to set goals, plan, monitor and evaluate their own learning and, as far as possible, be self-directed in their thinking and learning. There is a need therefore for teachers to infuse teaching for metacognition into their lesson planning (Tarrant and Holt, 2016; Mughal, 2021; Webb, 2021).

Task 7.3.2 Creating a metacognitive classroom

Ask the children to illustrate a poster that says 'Stop … and think'.

Infuse the key metacognitive questions into your teaching: What do I/you think?

Other metacognitive questions to ask children include:

Before a task: What do I need to do? What should I remember? What might help?
During a task: Is it working? What is difficult? Is there another way?
After a task: What went well? What have I learned? What do I need to do next?

Choose and display three metacognitive questions you want your children to ask themselves.

KEY PRINCIPLES IN TEACHING FOR THINKING

The research and the pioneering work of Reuven Feuerstein (who created a programme called Instrumental Enrichment), Matthew Lipman (who founded Philosophy for Children) and other leading figures have inspired a wide range of curriculum and programme developments (Fisher, 2005). Key principles that emerge from this research include the need for teachers and carers to provide:

- *cognitive challenge*: challenging children's thinking from the earliest years;
- *collaborative learning*: extending thinking through dialogue and work with others;
- *metacognitive discussion*: reviewing what children think and how they learn.

Pioneers in the research into the teaching of thinking include Reuven Feuerstein, who created a programme called Instrumental Enrichment (Howie, 2019), Matthew Lipman, who founded Philosophy for

Children (Lipman, 2003), and other leading figures who have inspired a wide range of curriculum and programme developments (Fisher, 2005).

HOW DO WE TEACH FOR THINKING AND METACOGNITION IN THE CLASSROOM?

Researchers have identified a number of teaching strategies you can use to help stimulate children's thinking and metacognition in the classroom. These approaches to teaching thinking can be summarised as:

- thinking programmes aimed at cognitive development;
- thinking strategies across the curriculum.

Thinking programmes aimed at cognitive development

Cognitive Acceleration through Science Education (CASE) and Maths (CAME)

Cognitive Acceleration through Science Education (CASE) applies the theories of Piaget on 'cognitive conflict' to the teaching of science (Shayer and Adey, 2002). Their work now extends into Cognitive Acceleration in Mathematics Education (CAME) and all age groups with teaching materials entitled 'Let's Think!' (see https://letsthink.org.uk).

Children are first given a challenge and then required to work collaboratively in order to plan and evaluate their own and others' thinking strategies, and are encouraged to state whether they agree or disagree with each other by giving a reason. Activities are designed as problems to be solved, thus creating a context for developing thinking. The teacher then gets the children to think about their thinking (metacognition) through asking such questions as, 'What do you think we are going to have to think about?' and 'How did you get your answer?', rather than, 'Is your answer correct?'. This teaching strategy can also be applied to any area of the curriculum.

Accelerated learning

Accelerated learning approaches draw on research that the brain processes information in different ways, such as applying VAK learning styles to teaching. VAK stands for:

- *visual* – learning through pictures, charts, diagrams, video, etc.;
- *auditory* – learning through listening;
- *kinaesthetic* – learning through being physically engaged in a task.

'*Brain Gym*' uses simple but challenging aerobic exercises to focus the mind and stimulate the brain; see Relevant websites section).

Philosophy for children

A pioneer of the 'critical thinking' movement in America is the philosopher Matthew Lipman who developed, with colleagues, a programme called Philosophy for Children, used in more than 40 countries around the world (see www.icpic.org). Lipman believes that children are natural philosophers, because they view the world with curiosity and wonder (Lipman, 2003). It is children's own questions, stimulated by philosophical stories, that form the starting point for enquiry or discussion. The aim, through using stories and other kinds of stimulus for philosophical discussion, is to create a *community of enquiry* in the classroom. Encouraging children to question and discuss what they do not understand is fundamental to this teaching method, which can be applied across the curriculum (Shorer and Quinn, 2023). Researchers have reported striking cognitive gains through this approach in the classroom, including enhanced verbal reasoning, self-esteem and dialogic skills (see www.sapere.org.uk).

Stories for thinking

Many resources have been developed that adapt Matthew Lipman's approach to Philosophy for Children to the needs of children and teachers in the UK. 'Stories for Thinking' is one such approach (Fisher, 1996).

Teachers note that in Stories for Thinking lessons – in which they may also use poems, pictures, objects or other texts for thinking – the children have become more thoughtful, better at speaking and listening to each other, better at questioning and using the language of reasoning, more confident in posing creative ideas and in judging what they and others think and do, and more confident about applying their thinking to fresh challenges in learning and in life (Fisher, 2013).

What stories or other forms of stimulus could you use to really engage your children in thinking? How could you create an enquiring classroom?

Task 7.3.3 Creating a thinking classroom

What would a thinking classroom look like?

- Collect words to describe what a thinking classroom might look like. These might include some reference to the teacher's behaviour, children's behaviour, classroom environment or kinds of activity that help children to think and learn well.
- Sort your ideas into small groups and give each group a heading that you think is appropriate.
- Choose one idea from each group and consider how you could develop this in your classroom.

TEACHING THINKING ACROSS THE CURRICULUM

The Teachers' Standards (UK) argues that teachers should demonstrate knowledge and understanding of how pupils learn and how this impacts on teaching and the National Curriculum (Department for Education [DfE], 2013) has a useful section on how spoken language relates to learning and teaching for understanding in all subjects:

> Pupils should be taught to speak clearly and convey ideas confidently using Standard English. They should learn to justify ideas with reasons; ask questions to check understanding; develop vocabulary and build knowledge; negotiate; evaluate and build on the ideas of others; and select the appropriate register for effective communication.
>
> (DfE, 2013: 10)

It also notes that they should be taught to 'give well-structured descriptions and explanations and develop their understanding through speculating, hypothesising and exploring ideas'. This will enable young people clarify their thinking and organise their ideas, which are key aims of teaching for thinking. On reading, the National Curriculum notes that 'pupils must be encouraged to read widely across both fiction and non-fiction to develop their knowledge of themselves and the world in which they live' (DfE, 2013: 10). Research has shown that teaching for thinking, metacognition and self-regulation can help in developing higher-order reading skills (Moir, Boyle and Woolfson, 2020).

Teaching thinking can be infused into all subjects of the curriculum, for example:

English – explaining why in all their comprehension answers.
Maths – being able to explain how they reach an answer.
Science – hypothesising and giving reasons for their conclusions.
History and Religious Education – discussing, explaining and understanding key concepts.
Geography – discussing big ideas like global warming and environmental issues.
Art and Design – understanding how artists and designers develop their ideas.
Music too can provide a stimulus for critical and creative thinking (Liptai, 2005).
Computers – used to encourage critical and creative thinking and discussion.

In all areas of learning understanding, children's concepts should be developed through discussion and extended through writing.

> ### Task 7.3.4 Create a think book
>
> Children's thinking can be extended through writing and drawing.
>
> Give each child a personal notebook to write their personal thoughts, feelings, ideas and questions. Decide what to call it or discuss possible names and let children decide; for example, it could be called a think book, note book, journal, learning log or jotter. It could be an all-purpose book or a subject-based book like a reading 'think book' for them to record ideas about books they have read. Or with young children create a large class think book or question book for children, or the teacher, to add to or stick in ideas (with their names attached).

Teaching strategies

The following teaching strategies can help stimulate children's thinking across the curriculum:

Thinking time (or 'wait time')

How long do you wait for children's answers? Research shows that if teachers spend longer waiting for an answer, a child will give longer, more thoughtful answers and ask more questions about what they do not understand about the question.

How long do you spend thinking about a child's answer? The more teachers model taking their time to think about what a child says, the more their pupils will.

Think aloud

Teachers are the models for thinking in the classroom. Think aloud when introducing a problem or showing a problem-solving process. Ask questions about the process, for example by saying 'Which way is best, x or y?' 'How do I start?' or 'What should I do now?' Model the questions you want the children to ask themselves or the process you want them to follow.

Think-pair-share

Extend thinking time after you have presented a stimulus or problem, by dividing the class into thinking partners, who are given time to think about and discuss the particular question or problem you or a child have posed.

Question time

Invite questions about the topic you are teaching, display children's questions and create a questioning classroom. For example, test their questioning power by choosing an everyday object and see how many questions they can think of about the object, list them, then discuss how they might be answered. Or create a Question Board for children to add questions later. Young children may need to be shown some question starters like 'Why...?' 'What...?' 'How. ?' or 'Which.?'

Mind mapping: Making thinking visual

'Mind maps' or 'concept maps' involve drawing a central idea in a circle and adding related ideas that radiate out from the centre, then adding more branching ideas and connections between the ideas. Mapping knowledge in this way can help them understand and remember new information (Buzan, 2009). A simple concept map, for example, might be used to map out the connections between characters in a story.

Starters for thinking

A 'starter for thinking' is an open-ended challenge aimed at focusing attention and activating the child's brain, often used by teachers at the start of the day or prior to a lesson. They could include a puzzle, problem, design challenge or topic for writing, for example: 'Write 5 things that make you happy and say why' (Fisher, 2006).

Task 7.3.5 What do good teachers do to stimulate thinking?

Investigate and record what good teachers do to stimulate children's thinking in the classroom, and link this to what good learners do.

Think what stimulating children's thinking and learning looks like in the classroom. Record in the following chart what good teachers do to stimulate thinking and what good learners do.

What do good teachers do?	What do good learners do?
•	•
•	•
•	•
•	•
•	•

Collect data by observing teachers in the classroom and record examples of how they stimulate children's thinking. Interview teachers and children to discover what answers they would give to the questions earlier.

Think about ways your teaching practice might be modified by your research.

Action research

Every lesson provides a research opportunity for the teacher in investigating ways to improve their practice through action research. Action research is aimed at both investigating and solving an issue or problem at the same time. For example, as a young teacher, my problem was getting my class of restless inner-city children to focus at the start of lessons on what I was teaching. I decided to see if teaching them meditation would help them improve self-management by the practice in stilling their bodies and focusing their attention. I found my meditation sessions were surprisingly successful in helping them to focus their attention on thinking and learning. I later published an article based on my research (Fisher, 2006).

Recent test results show that standards in schools are rising – but slowly. Could the teaching of thinking provide a key to raising achievement? The experience of many teachers suggests that when pupils are taught the habits of effective thinking, they grow in confidence, their learning is enriched and they are better prepared to face the challenges of the future. Children think so too – as Arran, aged 9, put it: 'When you get out in the real world you have to think for yourself; that's why we need to practise it in school'. There still remains much scope for action research into the practice of teaching thinking in the classroom.

SUMMARY

In recent years, there has been much research into ways of developing children's thinking and metacognitive skills. This has been informed by growing knowledge about how the brain works, people learn and teaching approaches can help improve children's ability to think and learn. Thinking and metacognitive skills refer to many of the capacities involved in thinking and learning, skills fundamental to lifelong learning, active citizenship and emotional intelligence. Metacognition is the ability to think about our own thinking and learning and is about the self-awareness that helps us become better thinkers and learners. Research shows that the key to raising standards in education is through teaching that promotes cognitive challenge, interactive dialogue with and between children and metacognitive review. These and other teaching strategies can help raise standards of achievement and create thinking children, thinking classrooms and thinking schools.

ANNOTATED FURTHER READING

Fisher, R. (2005) *Teaching Children to Think*, 2nd edn, Cheltenham, UK: Stanley Thornes.
  This book discusses the nature of thinking and thinking skills and explores the development of thinking skills programmes and how they can be implemented in the classroom.

Fisher, R. (2009) *Creative Dialogue: Talk for Thinking*, London: Routledge.
  This is a guide to dialogic learning, presenting practical, research-based ways of teaching children to be more thoughtful and creative and to learn more effectively through talk for thinking in the classroom. It includes advice on using dialogue to support Assessment for Learning (AfL) and ideas for developing listening skills and concentration.

Fisher R. (2013) *Teaching Thinking: Philosophical Enquiry in the Classroom*, 4th edn, London: Continuum.
  A guide to using philosophical discussion in the classroom to develop children's thinking, learning and literacy skills.

M FURTHER READING TO SUPPORT M-LEVEL STUDY

Kerslake, L. and Wegerif, R. (eds) (2018) *Theory of Teaching Thinking: International Perspectives*, London: Routledge.

>The authors discuss what is meant by 'thinking' in the context of teaching and the book takes a global perspective, including contributions from neurocognitive, technological, Confucian, philosophical and dialogical viewpoints.
>
>Questions explored throughout this edited book include: What is thinking? How can thinking be taught? What does 'better thinking' mean, and how can we know it if we see it? What is the impact on wider society when thinking is taught in the classroom?

Hattie, J. (2008) *Visible Learning: A Synthesis of Over 800 Meta-analyses Relating to Achievement*, London: Routledge.

>This, the largest-ever overview of education research, suggests that raising the quality of teacher–pupil interaction is the key to improving education.

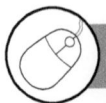

RELEVANT WEBSITES

Society for Advancing Philosophical Enquiry and Reflection in Education (SAPERE): www.sapere.org.uk/for philosophy for children throughout the UK and for international perspectives see: www.icpic.org.

The Sutton Trust Toolkit: www.cem.org/attachments/1toolkit-summary-final-r-2-.pdf

>The *Toolkit of Strategies to Improve Learning* evaluates teaching strategies, including teaching for metacognition.

Thinking Skills and Creativity: www.journals.elsevier.com/thinking-skills-and-creativity/

>A journal of peer-reviewed articles on teaching for thinking and creativity.

Brain Gym: www.braingym.org.uk

>Simple but challenging aerobic exercises to focus the mind and stimulate the brain.

REFERENCES

Alexander, R. (2020) *A Dialogic Teaching Companion*, London: Routledge.

Buzan, T. (2009) *The Mind Map Book*, London: BBC Active Publications.

Claxton, G. (2002) *Building Learning Power: Helping Young People Become Better Learners*, Bristol, UK: TLO.

Department for Education (DfE). (2013) *National Curriculum in England: Primary Curriculum*. Last updated 2015. Retrieved from: www.gov.uk/government/publications/national-curriculum-in-england-primary-curriculum

Fisher, R. (1996) *Stories for Thinking*, Oxford, UK: Nash Pollock.

Fisher R. (1998) 'Thinking about thinking: Developing metacognition in children', *Early Child Development and Care*, 141: 1–13.

Fisher, R. (2005) *Teaching Children to Think*, 2nd edn, Cheltenham, UK: Stanley Thornes.

Fisher, R. (2006) 'Still thinking: The case for meditation with children', *Thinking Skills and Creativity*, 1(2): 146–151.

Fisher, R. (2009) *Creative Dialogue: Talk for Thinking*, London: Routledge.

Fisher, R. (2013) *Teaching Thinking: Philosophical Enquiry in the Classroom*, 4th edn, London: Continuum.

Goleman, D. (2006) *Social Intelligence*, New York: Arrow.

Goleman, D. (2020) *Emotional Intelligence*, London: Bloomsbury.

Grigg, R. and Lewis, H. (2018) *Teaching Creative and Critical Thinking in Schools*, London: Sage.

Hattie, J. (2012) *Visible Learning for Teachers: Maximizing Impact on Learning*, London: Routledge. See also Visible Learning website: http://visible-learning.org/

Higgins, S., Kokotsaki, D. and Coe, R. J. (2011) *Toolkit of Strategies to Improve Learning: Summary for Schools Spending the Pupil Premium*, Sutton Trust. Retrieved from: www.researchgate.net/

Howie, D. (2019) *Thinking about the Teaching of Thinking: The Feuerstein Approach*, London: Routledge.

Kerslake, L. and Wegerif, R. (eds) (2018) *Theory of Teaching Thinking: International Perspectives*, London: Routledge.

Lipman, M. (2003) *Thinking in Education*, 2nd edn, Cambridge, UK: Cambridge University Press.

Liptai, S. (2005) 'Creativity in music and art', in R. Fisher and M. Williams (eds) *Unlocking Creativity: Teaching Across the Curriculum*, London: David Fulton.

Moir, T., Boyle, J. and Woolfson, L. (2020) 'Developing higher-order reading skills in mainstream primary schools: A metacognitive and self-regulatory approach', *British Educational Research Journal*, 46(2): 399–420.

Moseley, D., Baumfield, V., Elliott, J., Higgins, S., Miller, J. and Newton, D. P. (2005) *Frameworks for Thinking: A Handbook for Teaching and Learning*, Cambridge, UK: Cambridge University Press.

Mughal, A. (2021) *Think!: Metacognition-powered Primary Teaching*, London: Corwen UK.

Shayer, M. and Adey, P. (2002) *Learning Intelligence*, Buckingham, UK: Open University Press.

Shorer, A. and Quinn, K. (2023) *Philosophy for Children Across the Primary Curriculum; Inspirational Themed Planning*, London: Routledge.

Tarrant, P. and Holt, D. (2016) *Metacognition in the Primary Classroom: A Practical Guide to Helping Children Understand How They Learn Best*, London: Routledge.

Webb, J. (2021) *The Metacognition Handbook: A Practical Guide for Teachers and School Leaders*, Melton: John Catt.

UNIT 7.4

MENTAL HEALTH AND WELLBEING IN INITIAL TEACHER EDUCATION

Jonathan Glazzard

INTRODUCTION

This unit explores mental health and wellbeing in initial teacher education. There are two fundamental assumptions that underpin this unit. The first assumption is that children are unlikely to thrive academically if their mental health or wellbeing are adversely affected. The second assumption is that teachers who have poor mental health or wellbeing are not in an ideal position to support children's emotional needs and are likely to have a detrimental impact on children's learning. These assumptions are explored in greater detail throughout this unit.

It is estimated that one in five pupils currently has a diagnosable mental health condition. Prior to the Covid-19 pandemic, the figure was one in ten. A decade ago, children's mental health was rarely discussed in the context of schools. Arguably, although it is undeniable that schools are facing very difficult challenges, evidence of a mental health crisis should be treated cautiously given that society is now better at identifying mental ill-health and significant progress has been made in relation to reducing the stigma associated with it. Although the number of cases is serious, it must not be assumed that mental ill-health in children and young people did not exist in the past.

Staff mental health is also important, given the challenges that colleagues working in the education sector experience daily. In recent years, school leaders have started to prioritise staff wellbeing, and this is certainly a step in the right direction. This unit will help you to reflect on ways to look after your own mental health and wellbeing and support you to be resilient so that you can confidently address any challenges that you face during your career.

This unit will explore the mental health of children, young people and staff, including trainee teacher mental health. It will provide strategies for supporting mental health and wellbeing and it will identify significant factors which influence mental health and wellbeing.

OBJECTIVES

By the end of this unit, you will:

- understand the whole school approach to mental health;
- learn some strategies for supporting children's mental health;
- learn strategies for supporting your own mental health during your teacher training.

DOI: 10.4324/9781032691794-40

MENTAL HEALTH AND WELLBEING

The definition of mental health by the World Health Organisation (WHO) is a useful reference point:

> Mental health is a state of mental well-being that enables people to cope with the stresses of life, realize their abilities, learn well and work well, and contribute to their community. It is an integral component of health and well-being that underpins our individual and collective abilities to make decisions, build relationships and shape the world we live in. Mental health is a basic human right. And it is crucial to personal, community and socio-economic development. Mental health is more than the absence of mental disorders. It exists on a complex continuum, which is experienced differently from one person to the next, with varying degrees of difficulty and distress and potentially very different social and clinical outcomes.
>
> (WHO, 2022)

Some definitions of mental health focus on describing mental health as a disorder. The WHO definition is particularly useful because of its focus on mental health as a continuum. Therefore, within the WHO definition, mental ill-health is viewed as only one facet of overall mental health. An individual who is mentally healthy is experiencing a positive state of mental health, but an individual who is experiencing mental ill-health is experiencing a negative state of mental health. The dynamic nature of mental health is emphasised in the WHO definition and thus, the definition acknowledges that mental health can fluctuate and is influenced by a range of factors.

Mental health is only one component of overall wellbeing. Wellbeing is multi-dimensional, and these dimensions include, but are not limited to, the following:

- **Physical wellbeing:** This relates to our physical health. An individual who has good physical wellbeing is likely to be physically active.
- **Social wellbeing:** This relates to our need, as humans, for social connections. An individual who has good social wellbeing is likely to have access to social networks, including friends and/or family connections.
- **Emotional wellbeing:** This relates to our emotions. Individuals with good emotional wellbeing are likely to experience a range of positive emotions but if they experience negative emotions, they can regulate these adequately.
- **Psychological wellbeing:** Psychological wellbeing is used to describe an individual's emotional health and overall functioning. Emotional and psychological wellbeing are closely related and align with mental wellbeing.
- **Spiritual wellbeing:** Spiritual wellbeing is often a misunderstood concept. It does not refer to any religious or spiritual practice or ideology but to the human need for meaning, purpose and connection to something greater than ourselves. This could include connection to the environment or to animals.

(Glazzard, 2018)

In Wales...

> Feeling connected, secure and safe is essential for positive well-being. Learners are influenced by the adults, experiences and environments they encounter. These three enablers should work together to provide learners with the opportunities to develop their emotional, social and physical health to create a strong sense of well-being.

> Practitioners should create emotionally safe environments that support learners to begin to recognise and manage their feelings and behaviours in positive ways. They can also help learners to begin to understand that actions have consequences.
>
> Practitioners should provide opportunities for learners to develop secure attachments and relationships, so that they can feel confident in themselves and be better able to make choices, take risks, show greater resilience and independence, and participate positively in everyday activities.
>
> (Welsh Government, 2023)

In Scotland ...

Health and wellbeing is the responsibility of all. The curriculum is organised into six areas:

Mental, emotional, social and physical wellbeing
Planning for choices and changes
Physical education, physical activity and sport
Food and health
Substance misuse
Relationships, sexual health and parenthood

Sources: Education Scotland (2017); Scottish Government (n.d.; 2023)

RISK AND PROTECTIVE FACTORS

The causes of mental ill-health are complex and multi-faceted. Risk and protective factors exist in individuals, the home, school and community. Individuals with disabilities are more likely to experience mental ill-health (Glazzard, 2018). This is a risk factor within the individual, but it may also be influenced by other people's attitudes towards disabled people and a disabled person's experience of discrimination. Children who develop insecure attachments with parents or carers are more likely to develop mental ill-health (House of Commons, 2018). Additionally, children who witness domestic abuse, or those who experience child abuse, parental separation and parental criminality, are also at a heightened risk of developing poor mental health (Glazzard, 2018; House of Commons, 2018). Conversely, protective factors exist within the home and include exposure to nurturing, caring and loving environments, which reduces the risk of mental ill-health. School-related risk factors might include bullying, exam-related stress and being suspended/excluded (Institute for Public Policy Research [IPPR], 2017). Community-related factors include poverty. Children living in areas of social deprivation are more likely to experience mental ill-health because socio-economic disadvantage acts as a psychosocial stressor (Education Policy Institute [EPI], 2018). In addition, the adverse effects of social media on young people's mental health have been documented (Frith, 2017; Royal Society for Public Health [RSPH], 2017). These multiple and overlapping factors demonstrate that providing children with access to clinical interventions does not address the underlying factors which result in mental ill-health.

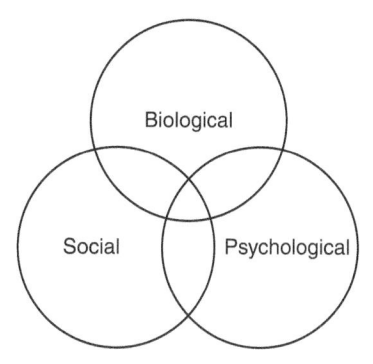

FIGURE 7.4.1 Biopsychosocial model of health
Source: Engel (1977)

The biopsychosocial model of health

The biopsychosocial model of health was developed by George Engel in 1977. It outlines the biological, social and psychological factors which determine overall health. Within the model, mental health is the intersection of all three circles. Thus, mental health is affected by a combination of biological, social and psychological factors.

Look at the model of the biopsychosocial model of health.

- What **biological factors** could influence health?
- What **social factors** might influence health?
- What **psychological factors** might influence health?
- Give examples of how the factors might overlap, for example between social and psychological factors.

The wellbeing see-saw

As a trainee teacher you will experience a range of psychological, social and physical challenges which can adversely affect your wellbeing. You might experience a difficult placement in which you struggle to develop effective relationships with your mentor and other colleagues in school. You might experience a class of children with a high level of social and emotional needs. This might impact on your self-esteem, particularly if you are struggling to manage their behaviour. Inevitably, you will have good days and bad days. We have all experienced teaching lessons which do not go well. Most teachers have experienced difficult interactions with parents or children. Even when things are going well, there is the constant pressure of workload which is typically associated with courses which lead to qualified teacher status. However, if you have the resources to balance out some of these challenges, it is possible to keep your wellbeing in equilibrium. Dodge *et al.* (2012) developed the model as shown in Figure 7.4.2.

Resources which you can draw on might include support from your social connections. Talking to friends, family and other trainee teachers can help to maintain your wellbeing. These are social

```
         ┌──────────────┐  ┌──────────────┐
         │Psychological │  │Psychological │
         │  resources   │  │  challenges  │
         └──────────────┘  └──────────────┘
         ┌──────────────┐  ┌──────────────┐
         │   Physical   │  │   Physical   │
         │  resources   │  │  challenges  │
         └──────────────┘  └──────────────┘
         ┌──────────────┐  ┌──────────────┐
         │    Social    │  │    Social    │
         │  resources   │  │  challenges  │
         └──────────────┘  └──────────────┘
        ═══════════════════════════════════
                         △
```

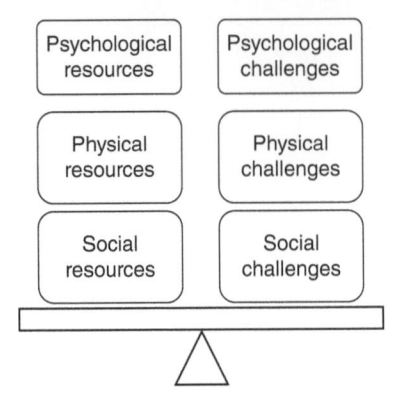

FIGURE 7.4.2 Wellbeing see-saw
Source: Adapted from Dodge et al. (2012)

resources and are very important when you are experiencing social challenges (for example, a breakdown in your relationship with your mentor). You can also reach out and talk to staff who are employed by your Initial Teacher Training/Education (ITT/ITE) provider. When individuals have more challenges than resources, the see-saw dips, along with their wellbeing, and vice-versa.

- What challenges have you experienced so far in your journey as a trainee teacher? Try to group these into physical, social and psychological.
- What resources do you have, or have used, to address the specific challenges?

Scenario 1

Task 7.4.1 Reflecting on James' experience as a trainee teacher

James is a trainee teacher with dyslexia. He is experiencing anxiety because he is struggling to keep on top of his workload. To address this, his mentor provided James with some useful strategies. These included writing a daily list of tasks that need to be completed and using a simple numbering system so that urgent tasks are completed first and less urgent tasks are completed later. His mentor discussed the use of live feedback during lessons and within-class marking to reduce the amount of work that James needed to complete after lessons. His mentor also introduced James to a more efficient way of planning lessons.

- What other resources might James draw upon to stabilise his anxiety?
- James is particularly anxious when teaching phonics because he has dyslexia. What might help to reduce his anxiety in relation to this aspect of the curriculum?

Scenario 2

> ### Task 7.4.2 Reflecting on Ned's experience as a trainee teacher
>
> Ned is a trainee teacher. They are finding their teaching placement challenging because they are struggling to manage pupils' behaviour. This has started to adversely affect their mental health. Ned spoke to their mentor about this, and the mentor reassured them that all teachers experience this situation. Ned then spoke to other teachers who also provided similar reassurance and provided them with some useful strategies to try out. Ned also spoke to other trainees who provided reassurance and they explained to Ned that they were also experiencing similar challenges. Ned and the mentor identified the children who needed additional behaviour support in class and the mentor agreed to provide some support to these pupils during Ned's lessons. Ned's resilience gradually improved, and they completed their placement successfully.
>
> - What social support did Ned draw on to support their resilience?
> - What action did the school take to reduce the daily challenges that Ned faced?

Supporting wellbeing and mental health during your ITE/ITT journey

The following strategies will support you to maintain good mental health and wellbeing during your ITT/ITE phase:

- Keep a diary, note deadlines and stay organised.
- Try to complete tasks as quickly as possible rather than allowing them to build up.
- Use schemes to support lesson planning and the sourcing of resources.
- Mark work in class with pupils.
- Provide pupils with live feedback in lessons.
- Do not spend time making resources that will only be used once.
- Ask colleagues and peers to share resources with you.
- Talk to your friends, family and teacher educators.
- Ensure that you build in time for relaxation, physical activity and try to eat healthily.
- Get enough sleep. Go to sleep early.
- Work efficiently during the day, so that you have less work to do in the evenings.
- Limit your alcohol intake if this is appropriate to you.
- Remember that a three-page lesson plan will not help you teach a lesson better. Quickly get used to planning lessons concisely.
- Do not waste time writing things up neatly.
- Learn to prioritise – which tasks need to be completed urgently and which tasks can wait?

Transitions

Educational and life transitions impact adversely on mental health, particularly when the process of adaptation to change is not smooth (Jindal-Snape, 2016). Some transitions are linear and occur at a certain time within a sequence (for example, moving from primary school to secondary school). These are *normative* transitions. However, multiple transitions can occur at the same time (Jindal-Snape, 2016). These are *non-normative transitions* in that they do not occur at a specific time within a sequence of other linear transitions. Examples include academic, social, cultural and psychological transitions. These transitions for individuals are also *multi-dimensional* because they trigger transitions for others. These are outlined in Scenario 3.

Scenario 3

> ### Task 7.4.3 Reflecting on transitions for a child refugee
>
> A Ukrainian child has come to the UK with his family. The journey from the Ukraine to the UK took several months and the child has witnessed war, death and threat. The family have settled into a community in the UK and they are safe and the child has been in his new school for five days. He speaks very little English, and he appears to be withdrawn. He can say some common nouns (table, coat, etc.) and his understanding of English is also very limited at this stage.
>
> - What transitions has the child and his family experienced?
> - How might these transitions have affected the child's mental health?
> - What transitions might this trigger for the school?
> - Supporting children who have experienced trauma can result in teachers experiencing secondary trauma. How can teachers protect themselves from trauma when they are supporting pupils who have experienced trauma?

The whole school approach to mental health

In 2017 the government published its five-year strategy on the role of schools in addressing mental health challenges in children and young people (Department for Education [DfE] and Department of Health [DoH], 2017). It was titled *Transforming Children and Young People's Mental Health Provision*. The document made the case for schools taking greater ownership for supporting children and young people's mental health, through the implementation of a whole school approach. A whole school approach to mental health may enable early identification and ongoing support for children (PHE, 2022).

The whole school approach to mental health was developed by Public Health England (PHE, 2022). It is a preventative model which is designed to reduce the number of referrals to NHS services. The model is shown in Figure 7.4.3.

The elements of the model are summarised as follows:

- **Leadership and management:** The model requires schools to make mental health a strategic priority and to appoint a designated senior lead for mental health who has responsibility for implementing, monitoring and evaluating the whole school approach to mental health.
- **Ethos and environment:** The model requires school leaders to establish positive school cultures which foster a sense of belonging and enable children and staff to thrive.
- **Curriculum, teaching and learning:** Central to the whole school approach is the provision of a mental health curriculum in schools which is designed to develop pupils' mental health literacy, reduce the stigma associated with mental ill-health and improve wellbeing.
- **Student voice:** Working in partnership with children and young people through a range of initiatives, including developing the roles of mental health champion, peer mentor and peer buddies, is a key part of the whole school approach.
- **Staff development:** The model requires leaders to invest in staff professional development in mental health and to develop approaches to supporting staff wellbeing.

Whole school approach to mental health

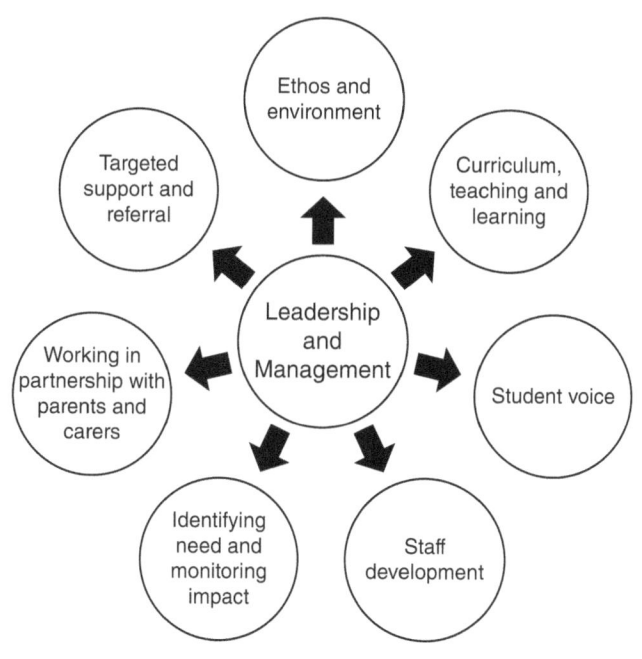

FIGURE 7.4.3 Whole school approach to mental health
Source: Adapted from PHE (2022)

Components (around Leadership and Management):
- Ethos and environment
- Curriculum, teaching and learning
- Student voice
- Staff development
- Identifying need and monitoring impact
- Working in partnership with parents and carers
- Targeted support and referral

- **Identifying need and monitoring impact:** The model assumes that a range of interventions will be required, including a mental health curriculum for all pupils, group and individual interventions. These interventions should be systematically evaluated. School leaders need to develop systems for identifying mental ill-health, for example universal mental health screening for all pupils.
- **Working in partnership with parents and carers:** The model acknowledges that parents may also require support to manage their child's (and their own) mental health.
- **Targeted support and referral:** Children with the most complex and enduring needs will need to be referred to Child and Adolescent Mental Health Services (CAMHS) run by the NHS and referral to social care and other organisations may also be required.

(PHE, 2022)

In Wales...

The Health and Well-being Area of Learning and Experience (Area) provides a holistic structure for understanding health and well-being. It is concerned with developing the capacity of learners to navigate life's opportunities and challenges. The fundamental components of this Area are physical health and development, mental health, and emotional and social well-being. It will support learners to understand and appreciate how the different components of health and well-being are interconnected, and it recognises that good health and well-being are important to enable successful learning.

(Welsh Government, 2021)

EDUCATION AND MENTAL HEALTH PRACTITIONERS

It is important to state that teachers are not health professionals and therefore clinical interventions can only be delivered by appropriately trained staff who are employed in the health sector. Following the government strategy document (DfE and DoH, 2017), the government invested in developing mental health support teams. Education Mental Health Practitioners (EMHPs) are employed by the NHS but work in schools to support teachers, individual children, parents and groups of pupils. They are qualified to deliver a range of low-intensity clinical interventions. EMHPs are responsible for managing a caseload of schools and not all schools benefit from this resource.

Identifying mental ill-health

Developing a clear process for identifying mental ill-health in children and young people is not straightforward. Many schools rely on reactive approaches for identification (Glazzard, 2018). This might include noticing small changes in a child's mood or behaviour or spotting signs such as declining attendance or punctuality. The problem with relying on noticing visible changes, such as the ones described here, is that some children who are experiencing mental ill-health could go unnoticed. It is a reasonable assumption that children may be experiencing mental ill-health, but they may not display any outward indicators that this is the case. Universal screening is one approach to addressing this issue because it requires all children to undertake a mental health assessment. There are a range of tools available for this, including the wellbeing measurement frameworks that have been published on the Anna Freud website (see relevant websites section), although the use of these screening tools tends to rely on pupil self-reporting, which is, in itself, problematic. An alternative approach is to carry out wellbeing conversations on a regular basis with each child, although this is time consuming. Teachers and teaching assistants can use these conversations to support children to reflect on how they are feeling and how they are managing their emotions. Designated Senior Leads for Mental Health in Schools can support staff to structure these conversations.

The mental health curriculum

The mental health curriculum should be systematically sequenced so that pupils develop greater knowledge of mental health as they learn the curriculum. A mental health curriculum develops pupils' *mental health literacy* (Jorm et al., 1997) and reduces stigma (Glazzard, 2018). The mental health curriculum usually starts by developing pupils' emotional literacy and emotional regulation skills in the early years and then it progresses to introduce more complex knowledge as pupils move through it. The curriculum must be age-appropriate, and teachers should be aware of specific cultural, religious or social sensitivities. Schools may decide to teach the mental health curriculum through Personal, Social and Health Education (PSHE) or through Relationships and Sex Education (RSE).

Working in partnership with pupils and parents

Working in partnership with pupils can help them to feel that they belong in the school, provide them with agency and develop their independence (PHE, 2022). Some schools develop peer mentoring schemes as part of the whole school approach to mental health. Older pupils are trained to provide support to younger pupils with social and emotional needs, including developing the role of peer listeners. However, although this approach is beneficial in providing children with agency, it is not unproblematic. Peer mentors who are acting as 'sympathetic ears' to younger pupils will need adequate training and supervision, including opportunities for debriefing. Some schools provide parent workshops to develop parents' knowledge of mental health and most schools now signpost parents to services in the community so that parents with mental ill-health can also get the support that they need.

> **Peer Mentoring in Action**
>
> A school in the North-East of England developed a peer mentoring intervention using physical activity. Older pupils (mentors) were trained to plan and run physical activities with younger pupils who had been identified as having social, emotional and mental health needs (mentees). Mentors and mentees developed positive relationships and the mentors also provided a sympathetic listening ear to mentees who needed someone to talk to. The intervention benefitted the mentors as they developed leadership skills. It also led to improvements in wellbeing for some of the mentees. The mentors received training in mental health, safeguarding and were provided with debriefing opportunities by the member of staff who led the intervention.

Mental health interventions

It is important to emphasise that schools can only provide educational interventions which develop pupils' knowledge of mental health, and which also have a positive impact on pupils' wellbeing. Teachers are not qualified to implement therapeutic/clinical interventions. It is also important to emphasise that teachers are not qualified to diagnose mental ill-health. A clinical diagnosis of mental ill-health can only be made by a clinician. Teachers and other staff working in education can identify signs of mental ill-health, but they cannot provide an official diagnosis.

> Schools offer a range of interventions, which are supported by research. These include:
>
> - **Trauma-informed approaches:** In trauma-informed schools, staff recognise that childhood trauma can have a lasting impact on the lives of pupils. Trauma-informed practice adopts a variety of approaches to help children and young people to feel safe and develop trusting relationships with adults.
> - **Mindfulness:** Mindfulness is the ability to be aware of experiences as they are happening through an appreciation of the present, rather than a preoccupation with the past or the future.
> - **Solution-focused approaches:** Solution-focused approaches focus on raising the child's self-esteem by focusing on their strengths and setting them small, achievable and realistic goals. They are useful when working with children with social, emotional and mental health needs. One strategy is *scaling* where children rate their behaviour on a scale of 1–10 (10 being excellent). Through a supported conversation, children are then encouraged to consider what their behaviour might look like if they moved up the scale from one number to another.

Teacher mental health

This section relates to staff mental health. The prevalence of mental ill-health in teachers has been explored in several studies (Dolton *et al.*, 2018; Education Support, 2021, 2022; Organisation for Economic Co-operation and Development [OECD], 2020). Burgeoning research has explored concerns related to teacher stress (Nathaniel *et al.*, 2016; National Education Union [NEU], 2019), teacher supply, burnout and retention (e.g. Billingsley and Bettini, 2019; Chambers Mack et al., 2019; Madigan and Kim; 2021; Nguyen et al., 2020; Sutcher, Darling-Hammond and Carver-Thomas, 2019). The challenge of maintaining adequate teacher supply has been evident for some time (Sibieta, 2020). A third of teachers in the UK leave the profession within the first five years of qualifying (Foster, 2019). Issues related to workload, poor work-life balance, accountability pressures and poor school leadership are cited by former teachers as reasons for leaving the profession (National Audit Office [NAO], 2016; Towers et al., 2022; Worth et al., 2018). Reports in the media have highlighted a 'teacher supply crisis' (Fearn, 2017) which has been described as 'severe' (Coughlan, 2018) and 'alarming' (Hazell, 2018). The detrimental effects of increased workloads and high-stakes accountability that impact on teachers' job satisfaction and wellbeing have been well documented in the international literature (e.g. Burkhauser, 2017; Gray, Wilcox and Nordstokke, 2017; Holloway, Sørensen and Verger, 2017).

Improving your wellbeing

Teaching is a challenging career. However, there are steps you can take that will improve your wellbeing and help you to remain in the profession (Falecki and Mann, 2021). The following list builds on some of the strategies highlighted earlier in the unit as useful during your training and offers some new possibilities for your ongoing teaching career:

- Set boundaries on the start and end of your working day.
- Identify a cut off time each evening when you will stop working.
- Ensure that you take the time to rest and recharge, particularly at weekends.
- Talk to colleagues, friends, family and your training provider when you are experiencing challenges.
- Keep a 'to-do' list and prioritise tasks.
- Plan some lessons which do not result in pupils generating work which needs to be marked.
- Make sure you have time to undertake regular physical activity.
- Develop strategies to help relax, for example, listening to music.
- Always keep a sense of perspective: you don't need to be perfect and being consistently good is good enough.
- Accept that you will make mistakes and learn from them.
- Invest in your friendships and your social life. Teaching is a job; it does not need to be your whole life.
- Try not to compare yourself to others.

- What factors other than workload may contribute to poor wellbeing in teachers?
- What other steps can teachers take to improve their mental health and wellbeing?

LOOKING FORWARD: BECOMING AN EARLY CAREER TEACHER

Workload is an important factor influencing teachers' decisions to leave the profession and a significant threat to retention (Worth et al., 2018). However, other factors also influence attrition and poor mental health, including personal/family circumstances, school culture and motivation. Although the challenges of teaching during the early phase of a teaching career are not dissimilar to the challenges experienced during the initial training phase, there are different factors which may contribute to mental ill-health once you are qualified. First, you are now accountable for the pupils you teach, not only for the standards they achieve, but also the quality of your teaching, the safety of your pupils and the behaviour of pupils in your class. Now that you are being paid to teach, it is inevitable that you will experience a heightened degree of accountability. Working in a school with a positive school culture is essential to good overall wellbeing and positive mental health (Glazzard, 2018). If you think you are being bullied or if the culture is not conducive to good mental health, there is no shame in resigning and starting again somewhere else. Sometimes, a change of school is all that is needed to balance your wellbeing. If you are struggling, talk to your mentor and don't 'bottle things up' - in most cases, people will be happy to help you. Remember that you are still learning to be a teacher and you do not need to be perfect.

A range of studies have explored teacher resilience (Greenfield, 2015; Kyriacou, 2011; Tait, 2008). Greenfield's (2015) model of teacher resilience demonstrates the factors which affect resilience in teachers (see Figure 7.4.4).

The model demonstrates that there are some *innate characteristics* which influence teacher resilience. These are located in the centre of the model. Teachers who have a sense of hope, purpose and good self-efficacy (i.e. they feel that they are competent) are more likely to be resilient than those who do not have these characteristics. Teachers who take positive actions are also more likely to be resilient compared to those who do not. However, resilience operates within a socio-ecological framework and is therefore influenced by access to *social networks* and relationships, *daily challenges* and the *wider policy context* which influences schools and teachers. Multiple challenges in the job role, without access to adequate resources to address these, can adversely affect resilience. In addition, the neoliberal education climate and the strong accountability culture can adversely affect teacher resilience. However, teaching unions and the national charity, Education Support, can provide advice, help and guidance to teachers, particularly when they experience professional challenges.

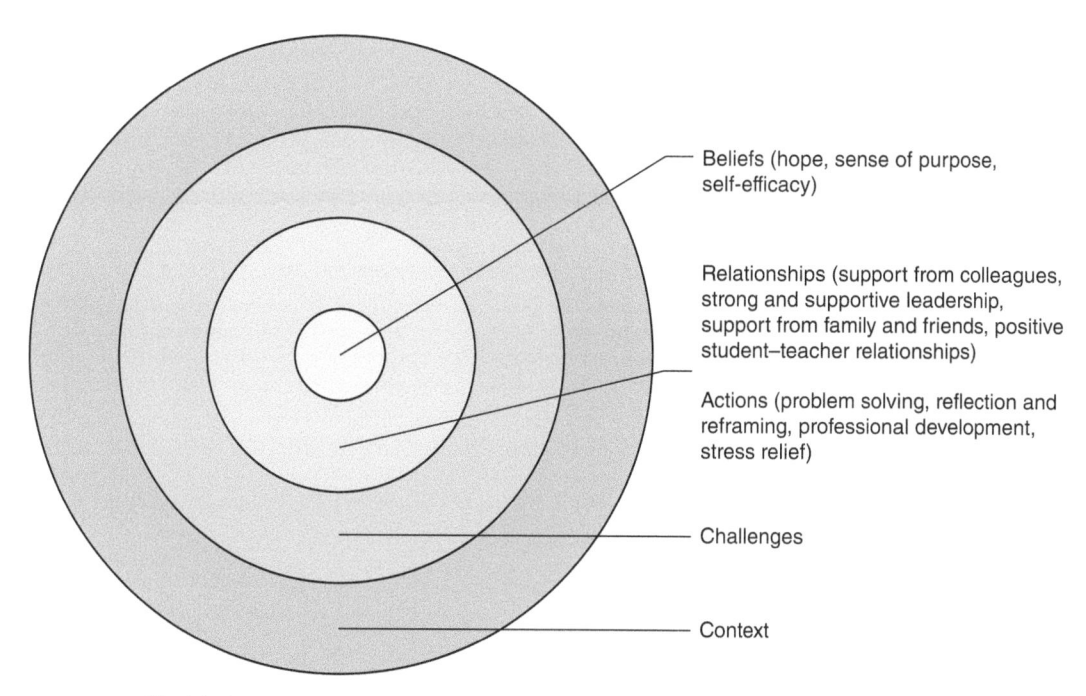

- Beliefs (hope, sense of purpose, self-efficacy)
- Relationships (support from colleagues, strong and supportive leadership, support from family and friends, positive student–teacher relationships)
- Actions (problem solving, reflection and reframing, professional development, stress relief)
- Challenges
- Context

FIGURE 7.4.4 Model of teacher resilience
Source: Adapted from Greenfield (2015)

Teachers with access to supportive social networks and supportive school leaders are likely to be more resilient than those who do not have this. It is important to remember that more teachers stay in the profession than those who leave. It is also important to remember that, despite the challenges, teaching is a rich and rewarding career. High quality education improves life outcomes and teachers play a transformative role in children's lives.

SUMMARY

In this unit, you have been introduced to the factors which affect children and young people's mental health and the mental health of their teachers. You have been introduced to theoretical models of wellbeing and teacher resilience. You have also learned some strategies for managing your own mental health.

ANNOTATED FURTHER READING

Brady, J. and Wilson, E. (2021) 'Teacher wellbeing in England: Teacher responses to school-level initiatives', *Cambridge Journal of Education*, 51(1): 45-63, DOI: 10.1080/0305764X.2020.1775789
> This article explores teacher responses to a range of school-based initiatives designed to improve staff wellbeing.

Glazzard, J. and Rose, A. (2020) 'The impact of teacher well-being and mental health on pupil progress in primary schools', *Journal of Public Mental Health*, 19(4): 349-357. https://doi.org/10.1108/JPMH-02-2019-0023
> This article explores the impact of teacher wellbeing on pupils' learning in primary schools.

FURTHER READING TO SUPPORT M-LEVEL STUDY

Greenfield, B. (2015) 'How can teacher resilience be protected and promoted?', *Educational and Child Psychology*, 32: 51-68.
> This article presents a new conceptual model of teacher resilience.

Kim, L. E., Oxley, L. and Asbury, K. (2021) '"My brain feels like a browser with 100 tabs open": A longitudinal study of teachers' mental health and wellbeing during the COVID-19 pandemic', *British Journal of Educational Psychology*, 92(1): 299-318. https://doi.org/10.1111/bjep.12450
> This article explores the impact of the Covid-19 pandemic on teachers' mental health and wellbeing.

Madigan, D. J. and Kim, L. (2021) 'Towards an understanding of teacher attrition: A meta-analysis of burnout, job satisfaction, and teachers' intentions to quit', *Teaching and Teacher Education*, 105, [103425]. https://doi.org/10.1016/j.tate.2021.103425
> This article explores the issue of teachers leaving the profession, the factors which impact on job satisfaction and the concept of teacher burnout.

RELEVANT WEBSITES

Young Minds: www.youngminds.org.uk/professional/resources
> This website provides useful statistics and mental health research.

MindEd: www.minded.org.uk/
> This website provides access to free videos and webinars to further develop your knowledge of mental health.

Mentally Healthy Schools: https://mentallyhealthyschools.org.uk/
> This website provides information on the whole school approach to mental health and specific mental health conditions.

Trauma Informed Schools UK: www.traumainformedschools.co.uk/
> This website provides information on trauma informed approaches in schools.

Mindfulness: https://mindfulnessinschools.org/wp-content/uploads/2018/10/Weare-Evidence-Review-Final.pdf
> This website provides information on mindfulness and specifically research on the use of mindfulness in schools.

Anna Freud website: www.annafreud.org/schools-and-colleges/resources/wellbeing-measurement-framework-for-schools/
> Website containing wellbeing measurement frameworks.

REFERENCES

Billingsley, B. and Bettini, E. (2019) 'Special education teacher attrition and retention: A review of the literature', *Review of Educational Research*, 89: 697-744.

Burkhauser, S. (2017) 'How much do school principals matter when it comes to teacher working conditions?' *Educational Evaluation and Policy Analysis*, 39(1): 126-145.

Chambers Mack, J., Johnson, A., Jones-Rincon, A., Tsatenawa, V. and Howard, K. (2019) 'Why do teachers leave? A comprehensive occupational health study evaluating intent-to-quit in public school teachers', *Journal of Applied Biobehavioral Research*, 24.

Coughlan, S. (2018) 'England's schools face 'severe' teacher shortage', *BBC*. Retrieved from: www.bbc.co.uk/news/education-45341734 (accessed 13 August 2022).

Department for Education (DfE) and Department of Health (DoH). (2017) *Transforming Children and Young People's Mental Health Provision: A Green Paper*, London: DfE. Last updated 2018.

Dodge, R., Daly, A. P., Huyton, J. and Sanders, L. D. (2012) 'The challenge of defining wellbeing', *International Journal of Wellbeing*, 2: 222-235.

Dolton, P., Marcenaro, O., De Vries, R. and She, P-W. (2018) *Global Teacher Status Index 2018*. Varkey Foundation, University of Sussex. Retrieved from: www.varkeyfoundation.org/media/4867/gts-index-13-11-2018.pdf (accessed 13 August 2022).

Education Policy Institute (EPI). (2018) *Written Evidence from the Education Policy Institute*. SGP0007.

Education Scotland. (2017) *Health and Wellbeing*. Last updated 2023. Retrieved from: https://education.gov.scot/curriculum-for-excellence/curriculum-areas/health-and-wellbeing/

Education Support. (2021) *Teacher Wellbeing Index 2021*, London: Education Support.

Education Support. (2022) *Teacher Wellbeing Index 2022*, London: Education Support.

Engel, G. L. (1977) 'The need for a new medical model: A challenge for biomedicine', *Science*, 196(4286): 129-136. https://doi.org/10.1126/science.847460

Falecki, D. and Mann, E. (2021) 'Practical applications for building teacher wellbeing in education', in C. F. Mansfield (ed.) *Cultivating Teacher Resilience*, Singapore: Springer, pp. 175-194.

Fearn, H. (2017) 'Teachers are leaving the profession in droves', *Independent*. Retrieved from: www.independent.co.uk/voices/teachers-crisis-education-leaving-profession-jobs-market-droves-who-would-be-one-a7591821.html (accessed 13 August 2022).

Foster, D. (2019) *Teacher Recruitment and Retention in England*. House of Commons Briefing Paper Number 7222, 12 February.

Frith, E. (2017) *Social Media and Children's Mental Health: A Review of the Evidence*, London: Education Policy Institute.

Glazzard, J. (2018) 'The role of schools in supporting children and young people's mental health', *Education and Health*, 36(3): 83–88.

Gray, C., Wilcox, G. and Nordstokke, D. (2017) 'Teacher mental health, school climate, inclusive education and student learning: A review', *Canadian Psychology/Psychologie Canadienne*, 58(3): 203–210.

Greenfield, B. (2015) 'How can teacher resilience be protected and promoted?', *Educational and Child Psychology*, 32(4): 52–69.

Hazell, W. (2018) 'Alarming new stats show teacher recruitment down by a third', *Times Educational Supplement*, 4 January. Retrieved from: www.tes.com/news/alarmingnew-stats-show-teacher-recruitment-down-third (accessed 13 August 2022).

Holloway, J., Sørensen, T. B. and Verger, A. (2017) 'Global perspectives on high-stakes teacher accountability policies: An introduction', *Education Policy Analysis Archives*, 25(85): 1–18.

House of Commons. (2018) *The Government's Green Paper on Mental Health: Failing a Generation*, House of Commons Education and Health and Social Care Committees.

Institute for Public Policy Research (IPPR). (2017) *Making the Difference: Breaking the Link Between School Exclusion and Social Exclusion*, IPPR.

Jindal-Snape, D. (2016) *A–Z of Transitions*, London: Palgrave.

Jorm, A., Korten, A., Jacomb, P., Christensen, H., Rodgers, B. and Pollitt, P. (1997) '"Mental health literacy": A survey of the public's ability to recognise mental disorders and their beliefs about the effectiveness of treatment', *Medical Journal of Australia*, 166: 182–186.

Kyriacou, C. (2011) 'Teacher stress: From prevalence to resilience', in J. Langan-Fox and C. L. Cooper (eds) *Handbook of Stress in the Occupations*, Cheltenham: Edward Elgar Publishing, pp. 161–173.

Madigan, D. J. and Kim, L. E. (2021) 'Towards an understanding of teacher attrition: A meta-analysis of burnout, job satisfaction, and teachers' intentions to quit', *Teaching and Teacher Education*, 105.

Nathaniel, P., Sandilos, L. E., Pendergast, L. and Mankin, A. (2016) 'Teacher stress, teaching-efficacy, and job satisfaction in response to test-based educational accountability policies', *Learning and Individual Differences*, 50: 308–317.

National Audit Office (NAO). (2016) *Training New Teachers*, Report No: HC 798 SESSION 2015-16. Retrieved from: www.nao.org.uk/wpcontent/uploads/2016/02/Training-new-teachers.pdf

National Education Union (NEU). (2019) *Tackling Stress*, London: NEU.

Nguyen, T. D., Pham, L. D., Crouch, M. and Springer, M. G. (2020) 'The correlates of teacher turnover: An updated and expanded meta-analysis of the literature', *Educational Research Review*, 31, 100355.

Organisation for Economic Co-operation and Development (OECD). (2020) *TALIS 2018 Results (Volume II) Teachers and School Leaders as Valued Professionals*. Retrieved from: www.oecd-ilibrary.org/education/annex-bmainbreakdown-variables_d1ba43b3-en

Royal Society for Public Health (RSPH). (2017) *#StatusOfMind Social Media and Young People's Mental Health and Wellbeing*, Royal Society for Public Health.

Public Health England (PHE). (2022) *Promoting Children and Young People's Mental Health and Wellbeing: A Whole School or College Approach*, London: Public Health England.

Scottish Government. (n.d.) *Health and Wellbeing in Schools*. Retrieved from: www.gov.scot/policies/schools/wellbeing-in-schools/

Scottish Government. (2023) *Mental Health and Wellbeing Strategy*. Retrieved from: www.gov.scot/binaries/content/documents/govscot/publications/strategy-plan/2023/06/mental-health-wellbeing-strategy/documents/mental-health-wellbeing-strategy/mental-health-wellbeing-strategy/govscot%3Adocument/mental-health-wellbeing-strategy.pdf

Sibieta, L. (2020) *Teacher Shortages in England: Analysis and Pay Options*, London; Education Policy Institute.

Sutcher, L., Darling-Hammond, L. and Carver-Thomas, D. (2019) 'Understanding teacher shortages: An analysis of teacher supply and demand in the United States', *Education Policy Analysis Archives*, 27: 1–36.

Tait, M. (2008) 'Resilience as a contributor to novice teacher success, commitment, and retention', *Teacher Education Quarterly*, 35: 57-75.

Towers, E., Gewirtz, S., Maguire, M. and Neumann, E. (2022) 'A profession in crisis? Teachers' responses to England's high-stakes accountability reforms in secondary education', *Teaching and Teacher Education*, 117.

Welsh Government (2021) *AREA OF LEARNING AND EXPERIENCE: Health and Well-being*. Retrieved from: https://hwb.gov.wales/curriculum-for-wales/health-and-well-being/ (accessed 26 April 2024).

Welsh Government (2023) *Designing Your Curriculum: Enabling Learning*. Retrieved from: https://hwb.gov.wales/curriculum-for-wales/designing-your-curriculum/enabling-learning/ (accessed 26 April 2024).

World Health Organisation (WHO). (2022) *Looking After Our Mental Health*. Retrieved from: www.who.int/news-room/fact-sheets/detail/mental-health-strengthening-our-response

Worth, J., Lynch, S., Hillary, J., Rennie, C. and Andrade, J. (2018) *Teacher Workforce Dynamics in England*, Slough: NFER.

UNIT 7.5

SUSTAINABILITY AND CLIMATE CHANGE EDUCATION

Verity Jones and Joanna Farbon

INTRODUCTION

Young climate activists such as Nyombi Morris of Uganda, Greta Thunberg of Sweden, Xiye Bastida of Mexico and Mya Rose Craig of England have campaigned tirelessly for the voices of young people to be listened to and governments to act at a time of climate and ecological emergency. Since 2018, children and young people have taken to the streets to protest and demand a global response to the images of melting icebergs and stranded polar bears, failed crops and hungry people, dried out reservoirs and flooded homesteads that fill our media feeds (Neas, Ward and Bowman, 2022). However, these young people have often been treated as though they are too inexperienced, naïve, young and ultimately powerless to make a difference (Hickman *et al.*, 2021). Yet, the children in our classrooms are often eager and alert to themes of learning around these issues, and schools have a key role to play in preparing learners for the challenges that are to come.

With growing calls for action (Howard-Jones *et al.*, 2021), the Department for Education (DfE) published its Strategy for Sustainability and Climate Change in 2022. The national strategy's first aim is to prepare young people for a world impacted by climate change through learning and practical experience. This unit begins to think about how this might be planned for and practised in the primary classroom, drawing on examples from schools.

OBJECTIVES

By the end of this unit you should have:

- developed an awareness of what sustainability and climate change education is and why we need it in primary schools;
- understood the importance of being sensitive to how sustainability and climate change education might be approached in the primary classroom to support both learning and wellbeing;
- reflected on how you can develop your pedagogy for achieving successful sustainable and climate change education in your classroom.

SUSTAINABILITY AND CLIMATE CHANGE EDUCATION – ON YOUR BIKE!

The United Nations (UN) defines sustainable development as the development that meets the needs of the present without compromising the ability of future generations to meet their own needs (Brundtland, 1987). This definition goes far beyond turning off the lights when you leave a room or recycling your cereal packets as it looks at the needs of people's quality of life. This includes: water and food access, economic prosperity, quality education and so much more. Changes in our climate due to human industrialisation are a major challenge to sustainability. By their very nature, human activities that contribute to climate change are not sustainable – they alter the planet we depend on. The consequences are more complex than complicated and interconnect social, cultural, political, economic, historical and environmental challenges. For example, shifting climate conditions alter biodiversity which alters soil health, the success of harvests, sea levels, the design of our cities and so much more.

Sustainable and climate change education, like the underlying problems, is complex and not just about knowledge acquisition and transfer. Just knowing about sustainability and climate change is not enough to ignite the changes required. Cantell *et al.* (2019) offers the 'bicycle model' to help describe the interconnected elements required of this type of education. Scientific knowledge is represented by the bicycle's front wheel; this is essential for understanding, but alone the bicycle would topple over. Effective sustainable and climate education relies on thinking skills (the back wheel), motivation (the saddle), future orientation (the handle bars), identity, world view and values (the frame), actions (the pedals), operational barriers (the brakes) and emotions, including hope (the front light).

For many it may be action for the climate and sustainability that is a useful lens through which to think about education as we sit on our bicycle. We might be motivated to put energy into pedalling towards mitigation strategies at a local, national or international scale. Recycling, walking instead of taking the car to school and having solar power installed to provide electricity and/or heating are positive actions that we need our knowledge and thinking skills for. However, unless governments and businesses make it easy to recycle, safe to walk and cheap enough to install solar panels, these personal acts come to a halt as the brakes are put on through operational barriers that need to be lifted (Newell, Daley and Twena, 2022). The bicycle cannot go forward but has to find alternative routes.

We want to start with a focus on how sustainable and climate education can be framed in schools and reflect on the successes and challenges of how international policy can inform the route schools take to implementation.

In Wales …

Developing an understanding of how human actions in the past and present can affect interrelationships between the natural world and people will heighten learners' awareness of how the future sustainability of our world and climate change is influenced by the impact of those actions. It will also encourage learners to understand, as producers and consumers, their own impact on the natural world. In addition, an exploration of a range of beliefs, philosophies and worldviews about the natural world can help learners realise how these influence people's interactions with the world.

This aspect of the Area encourages learners to explore concepts, including the inter-relationships between humans and the natural world, cause and effect, change and continuity, significance, place, space and physical processes.

This Area will encourage learners to understand the interconnected nature of economic, environmental and social sustainability; justice and authority; and the need to live in and contribute to a fair and inclusive society that confronts and addresses racism. Experiences in this Area will also help learners develop an awareness of their own rights (including those protected in the United Nations Convention on the Rights of the Child (UNCRC) and United Nations Conventions on the Rights of Persons with Disabilities (UNCRPD), as well as their needs, concerns and feelings, and those of others, and of the role such an awareness plays in the creation of a sustainable and interconnected world.

(Welsh Government, 2021)

In Northern Ireland …

Education is one of the most important keys to tackling the climate change emergency. The Northern Ireland Curriculum will continue to play a vital role in supporting the green economy and nurturing environmentally conscious citizens. Through the integration of topics related to sustainability, climate change, and green growth, schools can equip children and young people with the knowledge, understanding, skills, and values necessary to contribute actively to a greener future; a curriculum that emphasizes the green economy can also prepare our children for future careers in sectors such as renewable energy, sustainable agriculture, and green technology.

To support the above, the Department for Education is considering how best green growth and climate change can be enhanced in the curriculum. Education acts as a catalyst, enabling the widespread adoption of sustainable practices, encouraging responsible consumption, and inspiring our children and young people as the next generation of environmental leaders and change-makers.

(Department of Education Northern Ireland, n.d.)

Task 7.5.1 Mapping the Sustainable Development Goals in school

In 2015, the United Nations published the Sustainable Development Goals (SDGs) – 17 interlinked objectives overlying 169 targets to be reached by 2030. These goals work towards peace and prosperity for people and planet. The goals are:

1. No poverty
2. Zero hunger

3   Good health and wellbeing
4   Quality education
5   Gender equality
6   Clean water and sanitation
7   Affordable and clean energy
8   Decent work and economic growth
9   Industry, innovation and infrastructure
10 Reduced inequalities
11 Sustainable cities
12 Responsible consumption and production
13 Climate action
14 Life below water
15 Life on land
16 Peace, justice and strong institutions
17 Partnerships for the goals

a   Ask colleagues, friends and family what they think the term 'sustainable' relates to. How does this compare to the themes of the SDGs?
b   If you are working in a school, check for policies that refer to themes relating to the SDGs. How do they relate to your work in the classroom?
c   Think back to our metaphorical bicycle. What are the operational barriers (brakes), the knowledge and thinking skills (wheels) and actions (pedals) a teacher might need to think about if they wished to embed the SDGs into their pedagogical practice?

Case study: Beginning a journey to embed the Sustainable Development Goals in School

Merdon Junior School in Hampshire is a two-form entry school for 7-11-year-olds. In 2022, three teachers were involved in the development of primary geography resources through which they were introduced to the SDGS. Initially, lessons relating to the SDGS were planned for pupils in Year 5 (9-10 year olds) and Year 6 (10-11 year olds). Teachers found that framing learning through the Goals connected with pupils' interest in contemporary issues and they saw interest and engagement in lessons. This work led the Geography Lead to map where the school's curriculum overlapped with the 17 SDG themes and provided the teaching team with a new climate and sustainable education lens through which to think about their practice. For example, which were themes of life on land and in water linked through the termly class reading books in literacy? How was sustainable consumption and production linked with the design and technology relating to food, textiles and resistant materials? School grounds saw the building of deep beds to allow children opportunity to grow more plants (including for food) and align with the goal of zero hunger.

SUSTAINABILITY AND CLIMATE EDUCATION IN THE CURRICULUM

Schools such as Merdon Juniors are informing their planning with the SDGs. As a school in England, the current National Curriculum (DfE, 2013), which it delivers, has no specific reference to sustainability and climate change. It is not until Key Stage 3 (for 11-13 year olds), when children will have left this school, that learners are expected to explore these themes in Science and Geography. Across the UK, reference to sustainability and climate change education differs. The Curriculum for Wales has explicit reference to the climate emergency and sustainability, where schools are encouraged to provide a rich context through which to explore these themes. Similarly, the curriculum for Northern Ireland and Scotland's Curriculum for Excellence both have a range of opportunities for learners to be taught about climate change and sustainability issues. As a significant contemporary issue, primary schools across the UK (whether their curriculums demand it or not) are responding to sustainability and climate change themes in their schools in a variety of ways.

What constitutes effective sustainable and climate education and how to teach this has yet to be clarified (see Reid, 2019, for a discussion of this). As we have seen, to get on our metaphorical bikes and ride the sustainable and climate education course, we need more than just knowledge about the issues. England's Sustainability and Climate Change Strategy (DfE, 2022) plans for every school to have a nominated sustainability lead by 2025. These individuals or working groups have the task of developing a climate action plan. Having a leadership team with the authority, knowledge and commitment to take sustainable and climate education forward it is hoped that a holistic approach to sustainable and climate change in school will emerge. This approach would include: improving energy (including heat) and water efficiency, prioritising sustainable purchasing practices, enhancing the biodiversity on the school's grounds, as well as helping learners to develop the skills and knowledge that will be needed for resilience and success in a time of climate and ecological emergency.

As a teacher, you have the opportunity to draw on themes of sustainable and climate education in your classroom. However, many teachers feel constrained by perceptions of accountability and the toll of an assessment led system. Cremin and Barnes, unit 7.2 in this volume, talk about how these issues impact creative education and we would argue they similarly impact sustainable and climate education. Research has shown that many teachers feel underprepared for the challenges of teaching sustainable and climate education (Howard-Jones et al., 2021). This, in part, comes with a lack of confidence relating to subject knowledge. Finding the time to develop subject and pedagogical knowledge around the complex themes of a world in climate and ecological emergency, whilst being mindful of your wellbeing and the wellbeing of children in your classroom, can be a real challenge. We would suggest following your interests initially – being an 'expert' in everything is an impossible task. So, if you are interested in animal welfare and extinction, or are passionate about food waste and recycling, or think knowing who and how your clothes are made is important or where your food waste ends up, then start there.

Whatever the theme you may decide to explore, there are always options on how this is presented in practice. For example, a primary school in Bristol takes one day a term for whole school cross curricula events relating to sustainable and climate education. Amongst their activities they have worked with parents to reduce the amount of parking outside the school and set up more active transport activities like walking buses and Walk to School Week celebrations. A school in Pembrokeshire focussed on a whole school project that explored where food came from and how to reduce the impact it has on people and planet across a term. This was a cross curricula activity where children visited local shops, cooked and prepared food as well as explored packaging design (see Jones, Ruge and Jones, 2022, for a discussion of how schools across Europe are embedding food education). In addition to these, the place of eco/green/sustainable awards might be something you or your school want to consider.

Case study: School awards for climate change and sustainable education

Icknield Primary School is a large primary school which hosts the Luton Primary Deaf Provision, including a Deaf Provision Nursery for children aged 2 to 4 years old. The school has been awarded the John Muir Award. The award 'encourages awareness and responsibility for the natural environment through a structured yet adaptable scheme, in a spirit of fun, adventure and exploration' (John Muir Trust, 2024).

Set on the Luton/Bedfordshire border, the school site has a large playing field, a nature garden with pond that is a haven for wildlife, including badgers and foxes. Pupils also have access to local nature reserves set alongside the River Lea that further enhance their understanding of the wildlife, flora and fauna in their local area.

All pupils, including pupils who are deaf or have special educational needs or disabilities, are invited to take part in meeting the challenges set by the John Muir award. This has deepened both pupils' and staff understanding of the opportunities the local area offered to develop behaviours in their everyday lives that support a sustainable way of living. For example, pupils have created their own litter picking group to ensure the school grounds and local area are free of litter. Year 5 pupils (9-10 years old) lobbied Senior Leaders to allow rewilding of areas around the school site to attract more pollinators. Achieving the award provided the school with the momentum to continue and keep climate and sustainable education a focus. Staff have continued to take part in continuous professional development and learning opportunities that were held in the local area with time to plan for activities that maintain the focus on appreciating their local environment and how children can understand and care for it for future generations.

Task 7.5.2 Reflecting on education for sustainability

a   Reflect on where you would expect to see education for sustainability explicitly referenced in the National Curriculum.
b   Critically consider where you have seen or heard about education for sustainability in practice.
c   What were/might be the impacts on children's learning and wellbeing?

SUPPORTING WELLBEING AND EDUCATION FOR SUSTAINABLE DEVELOPMENT

For many, sustainable and climate education may have its core goal in being 'for' the environment, to give learners the tools in which to make a difference. However, research shows that simply providing information about climate change is a relatively ineffective way of encouraging pro-environmental behaviour (Whitmarsh, Poortinga and Capstick, 2021) and our bicycle model supports that view: we need more than a front wheel to drive us towards change in order to support people and planet. Knowledge about the environment may not only prove to be ineffective to behaviour change, but also have negative impacts on young people's wellbeing. Concern had been voiced that young people are experiencing a loss of hope in relation to the future of the planet; that they perceive the future as a threat rather than a promise (Levrini et al., 2021) and struggle to create positive future worlds. Without hope, young people may stick their head in the growing metaphorical sands of climate change deserts and ignore or deny the situation. Alternatively, a growing number of young people find the situation a source of distress (Martin et al., 2021). There is evidence that children and young people feel let down and betrayed by government (in)action (Walker, 2020; Hickman et al., 2021) - when in class with children as young as 6, and asked if they have heard about climate change, those children have shouted out 'we're all going to die!'.

Research in the field of futures literacy (Miller, 2010) and sustainable and climate education pedagogy has brought new insights into how we can develop young people's ability to understand more fully the role that the future plays in what they see and do in the present, recognising that the way we think about the future will influence our decision making in the present (Pouru and Wilenius, 2018). Active engagement with the future is something that can be taught (Häggström and Schmidt, 2021) and by developing young people's ability to think about possible futures can allow them to develop a sense of agency and purpose with which to address the challenges of the climate crisis, in a way which supports their wellbeing. Hicks (2019) outlined four critical stages that teachers should plan for in their practice:

1. up to date acquisition of appropriate knowledge;
2. exploration of children's feelings;
3. identification of relevant choices for positive change;
4. opportunities to engage in that change.

This four-stage approach provides a framework for planning within which we would argue good news stories are essential. The acquisition of knowledge should not be limited to the doom and gloom of our current context, but also the mitigation already underway. Whilst we may identify problems and crises, we can equally identify how individuals, communities, organisations and governments are working to ensure fairer, more sustainable systems for people and planet – these hopeful pedagogies are critical. For example, when learning about the impact of fast fashion (one of the top polluting industries with ongoing concerns over the welfare of garment workers), classes of 9–11-year-olds have not only been told about environmental and social problems, but also how businesses have been encouraged to sign up to the Bangladesh Accord. This policy ensures the safe and fair working conditions for garment workers. Children have been introduced to the work of the international charity Fashion Revolution, which raises awareness and petitions for industrial change. In addition, companies that support a circular economy approach to production were also highlighted. This approach provides opportunity for deliberative engagement, situated in dialogue (Roper and Hurst, 2019) and allows the young people to see their views and actions as being a contribution to a larger social issue where local, national and international organisations are engaged, rather than based around their actions alone (see Jones and Podpadec, 2023, for an overview of this work).

On a final note in relation to wellbeing, we remember, when growing up, being told that it was up to us, as the new generation, to sort out the mess of previous generations. For us in the 1980s, one of the largest threats to humankind was the growing hole in the ozone layer which we all feared would spread across the world and ultimately fry us. Laying the future of the world in the hands of children is not a new idea and we can often see how children are positioned as saviours in the texts we share in school. Just look at how Harry Potter has to battle against the all-time evil Voldermort in order to save the world. Or, to come back to a popular story relating to climate and sustainable education themes, how in Dr Zeus's *The Lorax* it is up to a single child to save a tree from extinction (see Boggs et al., 2016, for a discussion of this). To be positioned as the saviour can be empowering for some and terrifying for others, potentially encumbering more climate distress. Positioning young people as saviours is also an unrealistic goal. For climate and sustainable practices to be successful, we require engagement at every level, from the individual, the class, school, local community right through to international leaders in politics and industry. As such, teachers might benefit from being *critical identifiers* of children's sustainable and climate education on behalf of their pupils. In particular, you might consider how the books you share present questions and potential enquiry regarding the placement, use and positioning of young people within a narrative (see Jones and Macleod, 2024, for a discussion of this in respect to three children's books).

> **Task 7.5.3 Analysis of a case study**
>
> Read the international climate change and sustainable education case study next and analyse it in terms of how it was planned for and put into practice. Does it follow Hicks' (2019) four-stage approach? How might you adapt this approach to be relevant to your school community context? Then, think carefully about the effect of this experience on the children's learning and wellbeing – is it similar or different to your responses from Task 7.5.2?

Case study: International climate change and sustainable education

Researchers from the University of Central Lancashire linked schools in the UK with schools in other parts of the world. The intention was to provide children the opportunity for conversations with one another to learn about the contexts of each other's lives and how climate change is affecting them. Children became experts in their own lives and by seeing 'first-hand' the varying effects in different settings, the children could begin to acquire a sense of climate injustice. Ultimately this work provided an opportunity for children to have a say in how and what they learn about the climate crisis.

As a starting point, the children learned about one another – their interests, daily lives and perspectives on climate change – through asking and answering questions either by video messages via WhatsApp, writing letters and sending them by post, or writing, illustrating and telling stories. Subsequently, the children decided, together, what they would like to do next.

Through this process the children have enjoyed the novelty of talking to other children on the opposite side of the world, and their perspectives on climate change broadened. For example, children in the UK learnt that their peers experience hurricanes, cyclones and landslides and are worried about rising sea levels. Children in the South Pacific were interested in learning about UK children's urban environments and have shared anxieties about sea defences with children living on UK islands. Whilst potentially distressing, sharing thoughts and engaging in activities together was found to help children to feel they are not alone with their concerns. Nonetheless eco-distress was an important consideration in all aspects of the project, and the wellbeing of pupils was paramount.

When undertaking international education programmes such as this, the team were reflective of ethical considerations. This included reciprocity and mutual benefit across countries. Collaborative relationships were established with partner schools, and care was taken so that the direction of the project was jointly agreed by participants in all settings.

SUMMARY

Sustainability and climate education can draw on themes that engage and enable learners to develop understanding and skills to work towards the mitigation of planetary destruction, whilst simultaneously support wellbeing. Such education relies on subject knowledge, critical questioning and exploration at the local, national and international scale, where new links between people and planet can be developed. Many of the examples in this unit show how schools work towards embedding sustainability and climate change education with the support of the senior leadership team. We have drawn on examples of how eco-awards can bring focus to school curriculum and presented ideas of how young people can become enabled as active citizens: this might be promoting sustainable travel to school or planting vegetables to eat. Such practical activities can be a significant hook into talking about wider issues and allowing young people the time and space to make sense of complex issues.

We hope you will promote sustainability and climate change education in your planning and pedagogical practice, building in subject knowledge, skills, good news stories and opportunities for your school community to make a difference.

In Scotland …

Learning for Sustainability (LfS) is a crosscutting theme underpinning the GTCS Professional Standards for Teachers and is interdependent with the other crosscutting themes of values and leadership.

The Scottish Government published strategic goals for LfS as part of its 'strategic vision 2030' that align with the United Nations Convention on the Rights of the Child (UNCRC) and the General Teaching Council for Scotland (GTCS) Professional Standards.

Sources: GTC Scotland (2021; n.d.); Scottish Government (2023)

ANNOTATED FURTHER READING

Doull, K. and Ogier, S. (2023) *Teaching Climate Change Education in the Primary Curriculum*, Exeter: Learning Matters.
> This book offers a practical insight for new teachers to help develop knowledge and understanding of climate change and sustainable education across the curriculum.

Jones, V. and Podpadec, T. (2023) 'Young people, climate change and fast fashion', *Environmental Education Research*, 10.1080/13504622.2023.2181269.
> A research paper with a practical example of how fast fashion and sustainability might be used in the primary classroom to frame future thinking with young people.

FURTHER READING TO SUPPORT M-LEVEL STUDY

Monroe, M., Plate, R., Oxarart, A., Bowers, A. and Chaves, W. (2019) 'Identifying effective climate change education strategies: A systematic review of the research', *Environmental Education Research*, 25(6): 791–812. DOI: 10.1080/13504622.2017.1360842
> A really useful paper to explore effective educational strategies relating to climate education and the gaps that require further exploration.

Malone, K., Truong, S. and Gray, T. (eds) (2017) *Reimagining Sustainability in Precarious Times*, Singapore: Springer.
> An interesting volume to explore theoretical perspectives and research methodologies applied to sustainability and education.

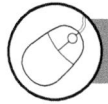

RELEVANT WEBSITES

Department for Education's Sustainability and Climate Change Education Strategy: www.gov.uk/government/publications/sustainability-and-climate-change-strategy
> The DfE's Sustainability and Climate Change Education Strategy (2022) for the education and children's services systems.

Teacher Development Trust: https://tdtrust.org/wp-content/uploads/2022/07/Sustainability-and-Climate-Change-Education-Report-Final-Pages-1.pdf
> The Teacher Development Trust's response to the Sustainability and Climate Change Education Strategy, offering insights into effective implementation. Written by Leigh Hoath and Heena Dave (2022).

UNESCO's Sustainable Development Goals: https://en.unesco.org/themes/education/sdgs/material/

Resources for educators

Global Goals Centre: https://globalgoalscentre.org/
> An educational charity with a growing database of information, activities and educational resources.

REFERENCES

Boggs, G. L., Wilson, N. S., Ackland, R. T., Danna, S. and Grant, K. B. (2016) 'Beyond the Lorax: Examining children's books on climate change', *The Reading Teacher*, 69(6): 665-675.

Brundtland, G. (1987) *Our Common Future: Report of the World Commission on Environment and Development*. Geneva, UN-Document A/42/427. Retrieved from: www.un-documents.net/our-common-future.pdf

Cantell, H., Tolppanen, S., Aarnio-Linnanvuori, E. and Lehtonen, A. (2019) 'Bicycle model on climate change education: Presenting and evaluating a model', *Environmental Education Research*, 25(5): 717-731. https://doi.org/10.1080/13504622.2019.1570487

Department for Education (DfE). (2013) *National Curriculum in England: Primary Curriculum*. Last updated 2015. Retrieved from: www.gov.uk/government/publications/national-curriculum-in-england-primary-curriculum

Department for Education (DfE). (2022) *Sustainability and Climate Change Strategy – Policy Paper*. Last updated 2023. Retrieved from: www.gov.uk/government/publications/sustainability-and-climate-change-strategy

Department of Education Northern Ireland (n.d.) *Climate Change and Green Growth*. Available at: www.education-ni.gov.uk/articles/climate-change-education-and-green-growth

GTC Scotland. (2021) *Learning for Sustainability: A Professional Guide for Teachers*. Retrieved from: www.gtcs.org.uk/documents/learning-for-sustainability-a-professional-guide-for-teachers

GTC Scotland. (n.d.) *Learning for Sustainability*. Retrieved from: www.gtcs.org.uk/registrant-resources/learning-for-sustainability

Häggström, M. and Schmidt, C. (2021) 'Futures literacy – To belong, participate and act!: An educational perspective', *Futures*, 132.

Hickman, C., Marks, E., Pihkala, P., Clayton, S., Lewandowski, R. E., Mayall, E. E., ... and van Susteren, L. (2021) 'Climate anxiety in children and young people and their beliefs about government responses to climate change: A global survey', *The Lancet Planetary Health*, 5(12).

Hicks, D. (2019) 'Climate change: Bringing the piece together', *Teaching Geography*, 44(1): 20-23.

Howard-Jones, P., Sands, D., Dillon, J. and Fenton-Jones, F. (2021) 'The views of teachers in England on an action-oriented climate change curriculum', *Environmental Education Research*, 27(11).

John Muir Trust (2024) *John Muir Award 2023 Landmarks*. Retrieved from: www.johnmuirtrust.org/whats-new/news/1645-john-muir-award-2023-landmarks

Jones, M., Ruge, D. and Jones, V. (2022) 'How educational staff in European schools reform school food systems through "everyday practices"', *Environmental Education Research*, 28(4): 545–559.

Jones, V. and Podpadec, T. (2023) 'Young people, climate change and fast fashion futures', *Environmental Education Research*, 29(11): 1692–1708. DOI: 10.1080/13504622.2023.2181269

Jones, V. and MacLeod, C. (2024) 'Why children need to read about plants at a time of climate change', *Children's Literature in Education*, 55: 416–431. https://doi.org/10.1007/s10583-022-09511-x

Levrini, O., Tasquier, G., Barelli, E., et al. (2021) 'Recognition and operationalization of *Future-Scaffolding Skills*: Results from an empirical study of a teaching–learning module on climate change and futures thinking', *Science Education*.

Martin, G., Reilly, K., Everitt, H. and Gilliland, J. A. (2021) 'Review: The impact of climate change awareness on children's mental well-being and negative emotions – a scoping review', *Child and Adolescent Mental Health*, 27: 59-72.

Miller, R. (2010) 'Futures literacy – embracing complexity and using the future', *Ethos*, 10: 23–28.

Neas, S., Ward, A. and Bowman, B. (2022) 'Young people's climate activism: A review of the literature', *Frontiers in Political Science*, 4.

Newell, P., Daley, F. and Twena, M. (2022) *Changing Our Ways: Behaviour Change and the Climate Crisis* (Elements in Earth System Governance), Cambridge: Cambridge University Press.

Pouru, L. and Wilenius, M. (2018, June) 'Educating for the future: How to integrate futures literacy skills into secondary education', in *Session Futures Proficiency for Society. 6th International Conference on Future-Oriented Technology Analysis (FTA). Future in the Making*, pp. 6–8.

Reid, A. (2019) 'Climate change education and research: Possibilities and potentials versus problems and perils?" *Environmental Education Research*, 25(6): 767–790. doi:10.1080/13504622.2019.1664075

Roper, J. and Hurst, B. (2019) 'Public relations, futures planning and political talk for addressing wicked problems', *Public Relations Review*, 45(5): 101828. https://doi.org/10.1016/j.pubrev.2019.101828

Scottish Government (2023) *Learning for Sustainability: Action Plan 2023 to 2030*. Retrieved from: www.gov.scot/publications/target-2030-movement-people-planet-prosperity/

United Nations (UN). (2015) *Transforming Our World: The 2030 Agenda for Sustainable Development*. Resolution Adopted by the General Assembly on 25 September 2015, 42809, 1–13.

Walker, C. (2020) 'Uneven solidarity: The school strikes for climate in global and intergenerational perspective', *Sustain Earth*, 3(5).

Welsh Government (2021) *AREA OF LEARNING AND EXPERIENCE: Humanities: Statements of What Matters*. Retrieved from: https://hwb.gov.wales/curriculum-for-wales/expressive-arts/ (accessed 26 April 2024).

Whitmarsh, L., Poortinga, W. and Capstick, S. (2021) 'Behaviour change to address climate change', *Current Opinion in Psychology*, 42: 76–81.

UNIT 7.6

PRIMARY EDUCATION IN A DIGITAL AGE

John Potter

INTRODUCTION

One of the key debates in primary education is around the location and nature of its work in the digital age. This debate, held in the press, on TV, in schools, on social media and in teacher education, takes in a vast range of issues and responsibilities. These range from the statutory obligation to teach the computing curriculum to attempts to link other subject areas, such as literacy, with digital practices, such as film-making, animation, video games and social media. It is further complicated by the messy and problematic issues of both safety and access, with some schools taking a pragmatic position and encouraging a wider integration with the online world and wider, popular media culture, and others taking the view that children need to be protected at all costs from the inherent risks of digital activity. A further connected range of issues concerns the extent to which 'big data' are used or misused in the context of schools, with so much information collected about children from the minute they enter formal education. Indeed, there are widely differing views about whether or not the reductive nature of a curriculum based on testing is being manipulated at some level in the various algorithms and datasets, to produce policy outcomes over learning gains for our children (Selwyn and Facer, 2013). Thinking about education in the digital age means also, therefore, thinking about the relationship of home to school, of information knowledge and of what counts as 'learning' in an age in which so much is available on-screen to discover. It also asks us to think about the spaces in which we learn and how many of these are in school, how many out of school, in a 'third space' of an after-school club or other space between educational settings and home. These aspects have all been highlighted in a report for the Cambridge Primary Review exploring the implications of the digital for primary schools, which states that:

> The digital age has implications for curriculum, pedagogy and schools' wider role in supporting children's emotional and social life, and indeed raises questions about the purpose and nature of schools themselves, and how schools' work relates to the wider political, economic and commercial context.
>
> (Burnett, 2016: 3)

Around the world, 'digital education' is an area that is addressed in many different ways. Sometimes, this is directly in policy documents, in the way a country will set out its message for parents, carers, children and educators, as a set of policy requirements, expectations or simply aspirations. Sometimes, as for other age groups, this is referred to as learning for the twenty-first century, with a set of skills presented that are assumed to be the goal of any digitally or technologically enhanced

DOI: 10.4324/9781032691794-42

education system. Indeed, the degree to which technology enhances any educational outcomes is the subject of much debate, with the most frequent conclusion being that it *can* work in the right context, with the right amount of support and the appropriate pedagogy. There will be changes to education as a result of these seismic shifts in how we do things, though a surprising amount will remain the same, not least in societies in which assessment, often in highly traditional forms, plays such a huge part in determining both the curriculum and its outcomes.

It is worth stating at the outset that it is no longer tenable to think of the 'digital' as synonymous with 'technology'. The 'digital' connects us to themes and approaches that are cultural. When we think of the 'digital', we need to think of more than just 'technology' and its associated artefacts; we need to think about its use in the world, the media that get made and distributed on it and how we use it. In doing this, we will begin to think more widely about what it means to be literate in the digital age. We may also begin to think of ways in which children can be enabled to think of themselves as makers, learning by being active and by crafting all kinds of media (Cannon, 2016).

One issue that will come up at some stage in your work with children is the notion that all young people are essentially 'native' to the digital world, and all adults are 'immigrants'. Teachers are out of touch with these millennial young people. This is a very popular and contagious pattern of thought about children and young people, derived from writing by Marc Prensky (2005). Once you start working with children and young people and talking to other adults in the school setting, you will discover that life is more complex than this and that the issues are not so easily divided into generational differences. This argument is not tenable in the face of digital economic divides, nor the great differences between people's circumstances and lived experience. The children you teach and the adults you work with will all have varying experiences of life online and digital competence of various kinds that are not age-dependent, and have much more to do with their habitus in the world and their experience in the various online spaces which they live and spend huge amounts of time, or very little. Dave White and Alison Le Cornu (2011) have a much more nuanced way of looking at this issue that positions all learners and teachers in digital environments as either 'visitors' or 'residents'; either you are, every day, navigating your Instagram, Facebook and Twitter feeds, or you are using them sparingly, occasionally or just for work, or just for home. And these are subtle variations that reflect more accurately the world in which the children you teach will be living. The important thing to remember is that digital media are part of everyday, material and virtual culture and have complexity, depth and richness in people's lives. Indeed, in many senses, life has become 'postdigital' and we can no longer separate ourselves from the artefacts, texts and practices which surround us and with which we, and the children we teach, are imbricated (Jandrić et al., 2018).

In Scotland ...

Educators across all sectors are encouraged to support digitally literate learners to use school devices and services; access learning activities and resources; find share & evaluate information online; securely access and use devices and online platforms; use digital literacy to create responses or express their thinking on subjects that matter to them.

Sources: Education Scotland (2021; 2023); https://blogs.glowscotland.org.uk/glowblogs/digilearn/

OBJECTIVES

By the end of this unit, we will have:

- explored how we define digital and/or media literacy, broadening the definition beyond print literacy;
- considered children's rights concerning 'datafication' and 'the digital';
- explored how AI might be addressed in the context of education;
- considered social media and how this can be used, and how it impacts primary school life in a range of ways, before considering aspects of safety and daily use of technology;
- addressed the biggest official curriculum change about primary education and the digital, which has come in the form of the computing curriculum, and we will devote a substantial section to this towards the end of the unit;
- reviewed some further reading and sources of help in navigating teaching with technology and media, and with 'digital education'.

ARTIFICIAL INTELLIGENCE (MACHINE LEARNING)

A key current issue for all educators is the impact of Artificial Intelligence (AI) on teaching and learning. This is felt in different ways at all levels, though the emphasis in media commentary is usually around the impact on assessment in schools and universities where students may be relying on large language modelling tools such as 'Chat GPT' to generate text for assignments. However, there is potentially far more going on than machine-assisted plagiarism, with AI also active behind the scenes in the gathering, analysis and use of very large datasets for commercial purposes, in the design of apps for learning, the surveillance of pupil and teacher activity and the shaping of curriculum development. For those of us interested in the primary school years and AI, good starting points include the work of the Council of Europe, which has modelled policy statements and compiled a report on the necessary safeguards for AI in Education (Holmes et al., 2022) whilst academic researchers like Selena Nemorin have provided useful critical commentary on the discourse and 'hype' around AI in Education, particularly with regards to development issues (Nemorin et al., 2023).

Regarding talking with pupils, there is great potential in having discussions around 'good and bad' technology use, including AI; children have an innate interest in fairness, rules and systems around them. Generating live text from large language models, such as Chat GPT, is a good way to start discussions in classrooms with older children around the subject. Inviting children to imagine what Chat GPT or a similar remote ChatBot looks like will stimulate all sorts of interesting representations and discussions. The main point of this is to surface awareness of these technologies which will impact every aspect of their lived experience. Further resources for introducing children to concepts around AI are listed at the end of the unit and more can be found online (see, for example, Lane, 2023).

SCREEN USE, DATAFICATION AND CHILDREN'S DIGITAL RIGHTS

Older children, in particular, are aware of the debates about screen use which will be going on around them. For those from more economically privileged backgrounds, there will most likely be opportunities to have these discussions daily. In less affluent homes there is more likely to be a struggle for screen time of any kind. In all cases, children will have something to say about this issue because of how central technology has become in most aspects of daily life. Some older primary-age children from resource-rich backgrounds will be transitioning soon to mobile device use (if they don't already use them) and will have things to say about how their use is regulated or not. At the time of writing in late 2023, the move to ban devices permanently in secondary schools in England is once again surfacing, though this approach has as many adherents as detractors, and learning how to manage screen use is arguably something that adults need to pay attention to themselves, before legislating on adolescent use.

Datafication, the extent to which childhood has become measured and circumscribed by statistics from the point of entry to the school, to the time they leave, is a controversial area which has been addressed in recent research and writing (Bradbury and Roberts-Holmes, 2017). Children's rights in this respect, in the digital age, are front and centre in some organisations. In recent years, the 5Rights Foundation (2023) has been active in producing resources for children and adults who are having serious conversations about these matters. Their work is based on the United Nations General Comment No. 25 which has been appended to the UN Convention on the Rights of the Child (United Nations [UN], 2021). Again, with older children in the primary school years, there are potential opportunities for discussions on these topics.

DIGITAL TEXTS AND MEDIA LITERACY

Children, their carers, parents and teachers are living in a world in which media generally, and digital still and moving images in particular, are the dominant modes of communication and meaning-making. And yet, in schools in England, there is no formal requirement to study media in primary schools as a separate subject, to explore the codes and conventions of moving image literacy. This is not the case in other parts of the world, where there are developed, or developing, media literacy curricula, some of them based on a synthesis of ideas produced for UNESCO (Wilson et al., 2011). In England, the use of media in the form of moving image texts has a tradition of being integrated into subject areas, although, in the most recent version (Department for Education [DfE], 2013a), reference to it has been removed from the English curriculum, where it had long resided as a way of looking at different kinds of narrative and of exploring links between popular culture and writing. Instead, there is a vestigial presence in the computing curriculum, which sets out that children should become:

> responsible, competent, confident and creative users of information and communication technology [and] able to use, and express themselves and develop their ideas through information and communication technology – at a level suitable for the future workplace and as active participants in a digital world.
>
> (DfE, 2013a: 178)

The implication at least is that children should become competent at reading and understanding media, as well as producing it (echoing Buckingham, 2003 and, more recently in 2019). Without space in a crowded curriculum, it can be all too easy to forget or leave out these encounters with digital media and the opportunities to make and interpret moving image texts together. And yet, many teachers and researchers find that even the simplest activities around film-making and animation can bring many curriculum subjects alive and open a portal to the lived experience and popular culture of children and young people, on to their funds of knowledge and cultural experience, which, in turn, produce huge benefits in terms of motivation, engagement and learning (Buckingham, 2003; Buckingham, 2019; Burn and Durran, 2007; Cannon, 2018; Marsh, 2009; Bazalgette, Parry and Potter, 2011; Potter, 2012; Parry, 2013). This is not something that detracts from their experience of the literacy 'basics', but something that suggests a rather more ambitious curriculum experience that both enhances and produces contexts for learning the reading and writing of print. In more recent work, authors have begun to argue that a lack of formal media education constitutes a violation of children's rights under the UN convention (Cannon, Connolly and Parry, 2022).

Research connecting the use of touchscreen devices in a primary school after-school club took place in the context of learning about film-making (Potter and Bryer, 2016). Here, working with a device that is at the heart of everyday practices around technology was most important to its success. The work, with Year 5 students aged around 10, was based on the idea that the reading of images that children had been engaged with all their lives could be productively analysed and turned into production quite rapidly on touchscreen devices. It was not unproblematic, owing to the constraints around file handling and other issues, but, compared with forays into this kind of work in previous years, involving cameras and cables, it was a far less technically intimidating experience for those teaching it, and for the children exploring it. Children moved through the experiences of reviewing clips, making short practice exercises, learning about shaping moving image stories and more into iteratively making them. The touchscreen devices – in this case, iPad minis – enabled a shorter time frame between such activities and allowed the children to engage directly with shaping and crafting the scenes that they shot. This way of working is encouraged in the frameworks for screen literacy produced by the European Film Literacy Advisory Group (FLAG, 2014), which connects the creative to the cultural and the critical. It is also the basis for some of the innovative practices in moving image education undertaken by the British Film Institute Education Department, Into Film and the Film Space, all of which have resources and contacts to support teachers in primary schools, but perhaps, more importantly, all have accounts, complete with films, of the kinds of work it is possible to do (Cannon and Reid, 2010; Cannon, 2018; Into Film, 2015; BFI, 2016; The Film Space, 2016).

During the pandemic, the 'Play Observatory' project explored children's experiences of lockdown in the UK and included aspects of digital play and media production which became part of everyday experience in ways that are not usually in the formal curriculum (Cannon, Connolly and Parry, 2022; Cowan et al., 2021; Potter, Cannon and Cowan, 2024). The researchers have subsequently argued that there are lessons which can be learned in formal education about changing the curriculum and moving it closer to children's lived experience of media, popular culture and the development of skills and dispositions towards the digital (Cannon et al., 2023).

Task 7.6.1 A short film describing a mood or emotion (no longer than 10 seconds)

Working with a friend or two and using your mobile phone, or a tablet device, or one you can borrow from a friend, open the camera app and switch to video. Take three shots, one of which must be a close-up of a face, the other two of which must show an encounter between two people. The way that you frame the shots or move the camera must describe an emotion that a viewer can take away from watching it. Negative emotions or attributes tend to be easier to work with in this kind of activity – for example, jealousy, fear, embarrassment or hate. Positive emotions are harder to represent but include feelings of friendship, kindness and empathy. Watch the sequences back. Which work? How much of each do you need to show? Open the shots in an editor on your phone or tablet device and cut them to improve the impact. What did you need to know to do this? Consult a source of advice on shooting for education online (such as Learn about Film – see the Relevant websites section at the end of the unit).

SOCIAL MEDIA AND EDUCATION

We've looked earlier in this unit at some examples of digital making, drawn from the worlds of computing, media production and more. Throughout, we have tried to illustrate that these facets of life in digital culture are a central part of lived experience and cannot be excluded from a curriculum vision for the digital age. The world of social media, in the form of micro-blogging sites, blogging and wiki authoring and sharing of digital material, is a further realm in which children, even those as young as primary age, are immersed, like many of their adult carers and teachers. There is an argument that the flow of self-publishing online and exhibiting aspects of identity in social and other media is like a form of 'curation' of the self (Potter, 2012), a new literacy practice with digital media in which children and parents are engaged, either individually or in groups and communities (Potter and McDougall, 2017: Chapter 4). Even younger children are aware of these activities having, for example, taken selfies or seen older siblings, friends and family doing this and posting online or having shared media that they are excited by and find interesting, which they know will reflect their representation of themselves: pictures of toys, cats and family members, and so on.

Exploring these areas with children has the potential to provide contexts for a vast array of learning opportunities. Martin Waller's experience with Twitter (now known as X, as of 2023) in his class of Year 1 children a few years ago provided some insight into how the social practice of communication in micro-blogs can lift and frame writing and identity (Waller, 2013). In other projects that are worth following up online, collaborative writing in the form of blogging is something that has been shown to lift learning to write in important ways for younger learners (Barrs and Horrocks, 2014; Hawley, 2016). And, although there are important safety concerns associated with these forms of work in the digital age, there is no shortage of ways of modelling how to integrate social media sensitively and safely into a programme for teaching and learning in the digital age that can be accessed using the links and references at the end of the unit.

A NOTE ON SAFETY

Teachers bear considerable responsibility for promoting safe practices around technology, with the most usually cited aspect being preventing the unauthorised sharing or distribution of images of children. This is recognised in the National Curriculum document in the requirement to ensure that children 'use technology safely, respectfully and responsibly; recognise acceptable/unacceptable behaviour; identify a range of ways to report concerns about content and contact' (DfE, 2013a: 179).

This is something that can appear daunting to parents, carers, teachers and beginner teachers, particularly in a culture whose media outlets encourage panic, outrage and blame, rather than considered thinking in this area. Nevertheless, schools are expected to guide children and their carers and are at risk themselves if they do not have a policy about digital safety that is part of lived practice and experience, and not simply something that is covered by written statute and regulation alone. Indeed, there are significant projects, resources and spaces that are dedicated to advising on this issue, along with guidance in the form of policies, research and teaching about it (Livingstone, 2009; UK Safer Internet Centre, 2016), and no beginner teacher should feel that they are alone in dealing with potential issues such as access to inappropriate images or cyberbullying and more.

That said, the process of both educating about digital media and safeguarding children can be made to work by application of the principles we have tried to establish throughout the unit of recognising that digital education is part of lived experience and material, everyday culture. It is not something that stands apart from everyday life; it is bound up in everyday social practices.

With this in mind, conversations that establish a safe space in which to exchange information and support are important; simple, regular, short dialogues that bring the everyday into the classroom, rather than separate, large-scale interventions, are likely to inculcate positive and autonomous strategies and dispositions towards safety online. Examples of such conversations might include talking about when and where pictures are shared and by whom; things that children might have seen online that make them feel uncomfortable in some way; feeling bullied or harassed in an online space; and so on.

Task 7.6.2 Social media reflections

Reflect on any time you have posted in an online social media space, either in print or in text, on a blog or a micro-blog, and felt uncomfortable over any consequences. What happened? Was an image shared without your consent? Did someone miss the point or get angry as a result of something you wrote? How did you handle it? What techniques or tools did you use? Did you defuse the situation with humour? Did you find a way to block the person from your social media space? If you are not currently a user of social media, find someone who is and interview them about these aspects of life online. How does this translate into dealing with such issues in school? Are adults better or worse at dealing with social media?

In Northern Ireland ...

Pupils should be provided with opportunities to develop knowledge and understanding of e-safety and acceptable online behaviour.

In today's digital world, children require knowledge and skills to be digital citizens and digital workers and to enable them to have the prerequisite skills to access technology and to use it safely, keeping themselves, their personal information and their money safe.

CCEA have produced the following overview as guidance for ICT coordinators and teachers to use to address issues that they may want to cover with their pupils. The overviews cover the following issues:

- Digital Wellbeing and Online Safety;
- Digital Etiquette and Identity;
- Digital Security and Privacy;
- Digital Consumer;
- Digital Law; and
- Digital Proficiency.

The overviews are not prescriptive but cover a range of important areas that face our children and young people in a digital world.

(Council for Curriculum Examinations and Assessment [CCEA], 2024)

FINAL THOUGHTS AND A NOTE ON THE COMPUTING CURRICULUM

Although so far in the unit we have established that we will consider the wider picture of the digital about primary school teaching, children's formal engagement with the digital within the school curriculum is prescribed by the subject orders for computing (DFE, 2013b).

In everyday practice, we should ask: what is different about the computing curriculum, and what does it mean for teaching and learning in schools in the digital age? First, it is worth noting that although the computing subject document is minimal in form and runs only to a few pages inside the larger curriculum document (DFE, 2013a), its implications are *potentially* revolutionary in how it positions children, and teachers to an extent, as people who can experiment, try things out and even make things in an educational context.

One of the key advisers to the government on the computing curriculum helpfully identifies three components in a freely available guide for primary school teachers (Berry, 2013). These are *computer science*, *information technology* and *digital literacy*, separated as follows:

> The core of computing is *computer science*, in which pupils are taught the principles of information and computation, how digital systems work and how to put this knowledge to use through programming. Building on this knowledge and understanding, pupils are equipped to use *information technology* to create programs, systems and a range of content. Computing also ensures that pupils become *digitally literate* – able to use, and express themselves and develop their ideas through, information and communication technology – at a level suitable for the future workplace and as active participants in a digital world.
>
> (Berry, 2013: 5)

The emphasis on *activity* and *action on the world* comes through in the document in the choice of words such as 'building', 'develop', 'use' and, ultimately, 'active' itself. It is *not* intended as a rote learning curriculum, and, if the curriculum itself is short on detail, documents such as Berry's guide, and the many supplementary websites to which it refers, offer opportunities to provide rich experiences in very accessible language, for both teachers and children.

In Northern Ireland ...

CCEA is currently creating a framework to integrate digital skills across the different stages of the Northern Ireland education system, building thinking skills into the process of learning about digital devices and creating qualifications that are unique to Northern Ireland. The CCEA framework addresses all the statutory requirements for using ICT in Foundation Stage, Key Stage 1 and Key Stage 2, through a new, optional digital skills curriculum for primary schools. This curriculum is delivered through three strands and will be supported by the publication of teaching and learning resources for different types of ICT and a progression of skills appropriate for each key stage in the primary. The strands are called:

- Becoming a Digital Citizen
- Becoming a Digital Worker
- Becoming a Digital Maker

Source: CCEA (n.d.)

> **In Wales ...**
>
> Learners will engage with what it means to be a conscientious digital citizen who contributes positively to the digital world around them and who critically evaluates their place within this digital world. They will be prepared for and ready to encounter the positive and negative aspects of being a digital citizen and will develop strategies and tools to aid them as they become independent consumers and producers.
>
> Learners will look at methods of electronic communication and know which are the most effective. Learners will also store data and use collaboration techniques effectively.
>
> The cyclical process of planning (including searching for and sourcing information), creating, evaluating and refining digital content. Although this process may apply to other areas of the framework, it is of particular importance when creating and producing digital content. It is also essential to recognise, however, that producing digital content can be a very creative process and this creativity is not intended to be inhibited. Digital content includes the production of text, graphics, audio, video and any combination of these for a variety of purposes. As such, this will cover multiple activities across a range of different contexts.
>
> Computational thinking is a combination of scientific enquiry, problem-solving and thinking skills. Before learners can use computers to solve problems they must first understand the problem and the methods of solving them.
>
> Through these elements learners will understand the importance of data and information literacy, and they will explore aspects of collection, representation and analysis. Learners will look at how data and information links into our digital world and will provide them with essential skills for the modern, dynamic workplace.
>
> (Welsh Government, 2023)

What do you need to know to teach this area of the curriculum? What do you need to know and do to look beyond what you see and play with every day, to gain an understanding of how it works and to have the opportunity to make things? Teachers could be forgiven for imagining that all children are somehow innately gifted in this regard and regularly exposed to the world of making things at home and in the wider world. And yet, although there is a vast and growing community of younger users of the software and associated online spaces, such as Minecraft and Scratch (MIT, 2016), it would be wrong to assume that all children we teach are developing as sophisticated programmers beyond the classroom. As with all areas of the curriculum, part of the role of the primary school teacher in this respect is to try and develop these skills, by finding out and building on what children already know and can do.

SUMMARY

Finally, as Burnett observes: 'Responding to the digital age involves more than just skills' and 'Digital practices vary, linked to social, emotional, cultural, economic and political circumstances' (2016: 9). As we ponder how we should work with children in the primary years in the context of digital education, we should be mindful of the fact that technology itself is neither fixed nor stable, and the meanings that are made in media created by users with that technology are always contingent and based in specific contexts, whether these are programs and procedures, films or animation, or more. As in other areas of the curriculum, we should begin by finding out where our children are starting from, in terms of their abilities, knowledge, skills and dispositions. We should work with the funds of knowledge they bring with them, but develop them further along the lines suggested by the curriculum and by the many examples of creative work available to support that work.

ANNOTATED FURTHER READING

Burnett, C. (2016) *The Digital Age and Its Implications for Learning and Teaching in the Primary School*, York, UK: Cambridge Primary Review Trust.
> This gives a critical perspective and a wide-ranging review of the literature and research into primary education in the digital age.

Buckingham, D. (2019) *The Manifesto for Media Education*, Cambridge: Polity.
> This is a persuasive and highly readable argument for media education in schools from a leading media researcher.

Turvey, K., Potter, J. and Burton, J. (2016) *Primary Computing and Digital Technologies*, 7th edn, London: Sage.
> This has detailed examples of classroom practice, research and digital education in primary schools.

Berry, M. (2015) *Quick Start Computing: A CPD Toolkit for Primary Teachers*, Swindon, UK: BCS.
> See this for guidance on computing and computational thinking specifically, a toolkit for learning for teachers by one of the people behind the curriculum orders.

FURTHER READING TO SUPPORT M-LEVEL STUDY

Lynch, J. and Redpath, T. (2014) '"Smart" technologies in early years education: A meta-narrative of paradigmatic tensions in iPad use in an Australian preparatory classroom', *Journal of Early Childhood Literacy*, 14(2): 147-174.
> This article explores some of the issues and contradictions teachers face when integrating digital technologies within classrooms.

Selwyn, N. (2015) 'Data entry: Towards the critical study of digital data and education', *Learning, Media & Technology*, 40(1): 64-82.
> This is a discussion of the complex debates surrounding the role of digital data in education.

RELEVANT WEBSITES

Educational AI Resources for Children: https://machinelearningforkids.co.uk/#!/links
> 'Machine Learning for Kids' gathers many accessible and useful sites for teaching about the latest developments in Artificial Intelligence in Education.

Learn about Film: learnaboutfilm.com
> A very helpful resource for all kinds of hands-on work making moving image media with children.

BFI Education: www.bfi.org.uk/education
> A source of project links from moving-image education work throughout the UK.

MIT Scratch Project: scratch.mit.edu/about
> One of the most widely used resources for teaching programming, with freely downloadable materials.

Computing at School: www.computingatschool.org.uk
> The home of many excellent resources to support teachers and children in learning programming.

The Safer Internet Centre: www.saferinternet.org.uk
> Essential advice on safety issues around using the internet with children and families.

REFERENCES

5Rights Foundation. (2023) *5Rights Foundation: Creating a Digital Environment Fit for Children and Young People*. Retrieved from: https://5rightsfoundation.com (accessed 1 March 2023).

Barrs, M. and Horrocks, S. (2014) *Educational Blogs and Their Effects on Pupil's Writing*, London: CFBT.

Bazalgette, C., Parry, B. and Potter, J. (2011) *Creative, Cultural and Critical: Media Literacy Theory in the Primary School Classroom*. Creative Engagements 7, Oxford, UK: Mansfield College, Oxford University.

Berry, M. (2013) *Computing in the National Curriculum: A Guide for Primary School Teachers*. Retrieved from: www.computingatschool.org.uk/data/uploads/CASPrimaryComputing.pdf (accessed 5 November 2017).

BFI. (2016) *BFI Education*. Retrieved from: www.bfi.org.uk/education (accessed 19 November 2016).

Bradbury A. and Roberts-Holmes G. (2017) *The Datafication of Primary and Early Years Education*, London: Routledge.

Buckingham, D. (2003) *Media Education: Literacy, Learning and Contemporary Culture*, Cambridge: Polity.

Buckingham, D. (2019) *The Media Education Manifesto*, Cambridge: Polity.

Burn, A. and Durran, J. (2007) *Media Literacy in Schools*, London: Paul Chapman.

Burnett, C. (2016) *The Digital Age and Its Implications for Learning and Teaching in the Primary School*, York, UK: Cambridge Primary Review Trust.

Cannon, M. (2016) 'Media-making matters: Exploring literacy with young learners as media crafting, critique and artistry'. PhD thesis, Bournemouth University, Bournemouth, UK.

Cannon, M. (2018) *Digital Media in Education: Teaching, Learning and Literacy Practices with Young Learners*, London: Palgrave.

Cannon, M., Connolly, S. and Parry, R. (2022) 'Media literacy, curriculum and the rights of the child', *Discourse: Studies in the Cultural Politics of Education*, 43(2): 322-334. https://doi.org/10.1080/01596306.2020.1829551

Cannon, M., Potter, J., Olusoga, Y. and Cowan, K. (2023) 'Lessons from the Play Observatory: Re-imagining learning through film-making and transludic practices in children's pandemic play', *Education 3-13*: 1-17. https://doi.org/10.1080/03004279.2023.2186970

Cannon, M. and Reid, M. (2010) *BFI/Cinematheque Blog*. Retrieved from: http://markreid1895.wordpress.com/ (accessed 12 July 2012).

Council for Curriculum Examinations and Assessment (CCEA). (n.d.) *Digital Skills Hub*, Belfast: CCEA. Retrieved from: https://ccea.org.uk/learning-resources/digital-skills-hub

Council for Curriculum Examinations and Assessment (CCEA). (2024) *Digital for Life and Work*, Belfast: CCEA. Retrieved from: https://ccea.org.uk/learning-resources/digital-life-and-work

Cowan, K., Potter, J., Olusoga, Y., Bannister, C., Bishop, J. C., Cannon, M. and Signorelli, V. (2021) 'Children's digital play during the COVID-19 pandemic: Insights from the Play Observatory', *Journal of E-Learning and Knowledge Society*, 17(3): 8-17. https://doi.org/10.20368/19718829/1135583

Department for Education (DfE). (2013a) *National Curriculum Programmes of Study*, London: DfE.

Department for Education (DfE). (2013b) *Computing Programmes of Study for Key Stages 1 and 2*, London: DfE.

Education Scotland. (2021) *Promoting Digital Learning and Teaching*. Last updated 2023. Retrieved from: https://education.gov.scot/about-education-scotland/what-we-do/promoting-digital-learning-and-teaching/

Education Scotland. (2023) *Teacher Digital Literacy Framework*. Retrieved from: https://education.gov.scot/media/gsrczkd0/teacher-digital-literacy-framework-jan23-draft.pdf

Film Literacy Advisory Group (FLAG). (2014) *A Framework for Film Education*, London: British Film Institute.

Hawley, S. (2016) *Presentation: The Sociomateriality of Literacy*. Language, Literacy and Identity Conference, Educational Studies, Sheffield University, Sheffield UK.

Holmes, W., Persson, J., Chounta, I.-A., Wasson, B. and Dimitrova, V. (2022) *Artificial Intelligence and Education: A Critical View Through the Lens of Human Rights, Democracy and the Rule of Law*, Strasbourg: Council of Europe. Retrieved from: https://rm.coe.int/artificial-intelligence-and-education-a-critical-view-through-the-lens/1680a886bd

Into Film. (2015) *Into Film: FAQs*. Retrieved from: www.intofilm.org/faqs (accessed 19 November 2016).

Jandrić, P., Knox, J., Besley, T., Ryberg, T., Suoranta, J. and Hayes, S. (2018) 'Postdigital science and education', *Educational Philosophy and Theory*, 50(10): 893-899. https://doi.org/10.1080/00131857.2018.1454000

Lane, D. (2023) *Educational AI Resources for Children*. Retrieved from: https://machinelearningforkids.co.uk/#!/links (12 December 2023).

Livingstone, S. (2009) *Children and the Internet*, Cambridge, UK: Polity.

Marsh, J. (2009) 'Productive pedagogies: Play, creativity and digital cultures in the classroom', in R. Willett, M. Robinson and J. Marsh (eds) *Play, Creativity and Digital Cultures*, New York: Routledge, pp. 200-218.

MIT. (2016) *About Scratch*. Retrieved from: https://scratch.mit.edu/about (accessed 21 September 2016).

Nemorin, S., Vlachidis, A., Ayerakwa, H. M. and Andriotis, P. (2023) 'AI hyped? A horizon scan of discourse on artificial intelligence in education (AIED) and development', *Learning, Media and Technology*, 48(1): 38-51. https://doi.org/10.1080/17439884.2022.2095568

Parry, B. (2013) *Children, Film and Literacy*, London: Palgrave MacMillan.

Potter, J. (2012) *Digital Media and Learner Identity: The New Curatorship*, New York: Palgrave MacMillan.

Potter, J. and Bryer, T. (2016) '"Finger flowment" and moving image language: Learning filmmaking with tablet devices', in B. Parry, C. Burnett and G. Merchant (eds) *Literacy, Media, Technology: Past, Present and Future*, London: Bloomsbury, pp. 111-128.

Potter, J. and McDougall, J. (2017) *Digital Media, Culture and Education: Theorising Third Space Literacies*, London: Palgrave Macmillan/Springer.

Potter, J., Cannon, M. and Cowan, K. (2024) 'Children's production of place and (third) space during Covid 19: Den building, filmmaking and the postdigital in the Play Observatory', *Global Studies of Childhood*, [Online First]. https://doi.org/10.1177/20436106241231810

Prensky, M. (2005) 'Listen to the natives', *Educational Leadership*, 63(4): 8-13.

Selwyn, N. and Facer, K. (eds) (2013) *The Politics of Education and Technology: Conflicts, Controversies and Connections*, London: Palgrave MacMillan.

The Film Space. (2016) www.thefilmspace.org (accessed 20 October 2016).

UK Safer Internet Centre. (2016) *UK Safer Internet Centre: Page for Teachers and Education Professionals* (Online). Childnet International/Internet Watch Foundation/European Union Connecting Europe. Retrieved from: www.saferinternet.org.uk/advice-centre/teachers-and-professionals (accessed 20 November 2016).

United Nations (UN). (2021) *UN General Comment No. 25 (Digital Rights of the Child) 25 20 § 14*. Retrieved from: https://tbinternet.ohchr.org/_layouts/15/treatybodyexternal/Download.aspx?symbolno=CRC%2fC%2fGC%2f25&Lang=en

Waller, M. (2013) 'More than tweets: Developing the "new" and "old" through online social networking', in G. Merchant, J. Gillen, J. Marsh and J. Davies (eds) *Virtual Literacies: Interactive Spaces for Children and Young People*, Abingdon, UK: Routledge, pp. 126-141.

Welsh Government. (2023) *Cross-curricular Skills Framework: Digital Competence Framework*. Retrieved from: https://hwb.gov.wales/curriculum-for-wales/cross-curricular-skills-frameworks/digital-competence-framework/ (accessed 26 April 2024).

White, D. and Le Cornu, A. (2011) 'Visitors and residents: A new typology for online engagement', *First Monday*, 16(9). Retrieved from: http://firstmonday.org/article/view/3171/3049 (accessed 15 May 2014).

Wilson, C., Grizzle, A., Tuazon, R., Akyempong, K. and Cheung C.-K. (2011) *Media and Information Literacy Curriculum for Teachers*, Paris: UNESCO.

SECTION 8
PARTNERSHIP IN PRACTICE

UNIT 8.1

WORKING EFFECTIVELY WITH TEACHING ASSISTANTS

Carrie Winstanley

INTRODUCTION

Teachers who collaborate effectively with support staff not only reap the benefits personally, in terms of efficient and improved work, but also contribute positively to the overall ethos of their class, school and community. While managing relationships is often complex and challenging, understandings from education research, practitioners' experiences and personal reflection can all help equip you with the tools, mindset, habits and attitudes needed to optimise and mutually benefit from positive working relationships in school. A number of significant research papers have been published since the beginning of the 21st century, delving into the evolving role of the TA, parallel to the substantial increase in the number of support staff in schools. Some of these changes include role titles, so please note that in this unit, 'TA' or 'Teaching Assistant' is used to refer to a wide range of classroom support roles. These include (but are not limited to): Learning Support Assistants (LSAs); Special Needs Assistants; Classroom Assistants; Higher-Level Teaching Assistants (HLTA).

Despite some reservations about the role when poorly implemented (Blatchford *et al.*, 2009; Webster, Blatchford and Russell, 2013), there is consensus that TAs generally add significant positive value to the education experiences of pupils. Among significant points around the importance of strategic school leadership in managing TAs (Education Endowment Foundation [EEF], 2021; Lewis, 2023, etc.), and salary issues, various findings are beyond the remit of the teacher to implement. However, you can still make a positive impact, and this unit will assist you. For example, one notable common finding is that TAs should support, but not supplant, teachers (Giangreco, 2021), since the roles are distinctly different, yet complementary (EEF, 2021). Through defining responsibilities clearly, you can ensure you and the TA are working to your strengths.

This unit examines roles and responsibilities of TAs, in classroom and school contexts, providing you with helpful practical strategies for effective collaboration. You will also be equipped to manage potentially complex challenges, such as setting professional boundaries, helping you retain the distinctiveness of both teacher and TA roles, whilst addressing essential wellbeing issues. Throughout, you will find information, questions, ideas and examples to help you think critically about working with TAs, with the ultimate goal of supporting learners in your care.

DOI: 10.4324/9781032691794-44

> **OBJECTIVES**
>
> By the end of this unit, you should:
>
> - understand and appreciate the roles and responsibilities of TAs;
> - acquire practical strategies for working relationships and collaboration;
> - have considered how to overcome challenges and set professional boundaries;
> - cultivate awareness of wellbeing.

THE (CHANGING) ROLES AND RESPONSIBILITIES OF TEACHING ASSISTANTS

The number of TAs in UK schools has increased almost every year since 2011, reaching their highest levels since the introduction of 'auxiliary staff' in the late 1960s. However, the landscape of teaching support is shifting and dynamic. For example, in the 1990s and early 2000s, the employment of TAs in English schools significantly increased, propelled by two major policy developments. Aiming to alleviate the teacher recruitment and retention crisis, the 2002 Education Act expanded the TA role, thereby providing increased support for teachers. Then, in 2004, Labour's 'Every Child Matters' initiative sought to ensure support for students with additional needs within mainstream classrooms. The continuing mix of initiatives, reports and findings published over the subsequent two decades are adeptly discussed by Lewis, who exposes the 'contradictions, complexities, tensions and moral dilemmas' (2023: 13) inherent in understanding the complexity of the TA role. He stresses the importance of understanding specific needs with local contexts. Given that the effectiveness of TAs hinges upon these specific factors, adept management of teacher–TA relationships is essential, as this has a direct bearing on pupils' learning and their overall school experience.

In response to worries about the efficacy of the TA role (see British Educational Research Association [BERA], 2013), interventions and projects have explored improvements in school and classroom TA deployment (Webster, Blatchford and Russell, 2013; Wren, 2017, etc). Consequently, we can now make research-backed recommendations likely to result in positive experiences for teachers, TAs and pupils. As concerns about potentially adverse effects from the over-use of TAs continued to swirl within the education sphere, the pandemic abruptly brought the TA role into sharp relief. Covid-19 has 'remade the role of the TA - potentially forever', claimed Webster and Hall (2022: 3), as additional duties assigned during school lockdowns revealed the extent of the school system's reliance on support staff. TAs described their job as 'more intense' than before' (Webster and Hall, 2022: 3), with an increased workload and more significant emotional load.

> Amid the pandemic, the teacher was managing in-school key workers' children, so I joined forces with the other Y5 teachers for maths. We shared safe doorstep home visits to engage with individual children and their families. Combined with online sessions and resources, we had quite well-targeted tasks. The visits were a lot of work, but showed families our dedication to their children's learning, plus, it was lovely to see them in person!
>
> (Winstanley, 2023: Conversation with Y5 TA)

Emerging from the pandemic, a cost-of-living crisis has exacerbated challenges in education, and coupled with poor remuneration, many TAs have found it tough to remain in post (Fazackerley, 2023). Researchers accentuate the need to address this, for the TAs themselves, but more pressingly 'to ensure pupils with SEND continue to be included and supported in mainstream classrooms, and to avert bigger and costlier problems for schools and their local communities' (Webster and Hall, 2022: 19). Antoniazzi (2023) reports that low pay and difficult under-resourced schools are finding it challenging for schools to attract new TAs and retain existing staff who can earn more in less demanding jobs. Understanding these pressures helps in building positive working relationships, the matter to which we now turn.

WORKING RELATIONSHIPS AND COLLABORATION

If you have spent any time at all in school, you will be aware that fostering positive working relationships is essential. While teachers have ultimate classroom authority, decisions on assigning roles are best made in consultation with TAs. Giangreco stresses this, confirming 'We cannot appropriately determine the roles of TAs in isolation or before the roles of accountable educators [teachers] have been determined' (2021: 298). Cockroft and Atkinson also corroborate the importance of teacher-LSA co-operation, for 'maximising pupil outcomes' (2015: 101).

You might not be entirely clear about what tasks you can allocate to TAs working with you, which is understandable, given the variability of the role. Typically, it would be expected that TAs may be on hand to scribe for you or a pupil, reinforce instructions, ensure comprehension, help with displaying children's work and assist with preparing or using practical materials. They may encourage discussion and participation, challenging pupils through questioning and addressing misconceptions. If assessing learning through observation and discussion, they can also help pupils reflect on their work, identifying next learning steps and actions together. This range of tasks is only indicative. (See Department for Education [DfE], 2024, for more details of expected tasks for teachers and TAs.)

Task 8.1.1 Prioritising the TA's activities

It's important that you consider how to prioritise the tasks that you allocate to TAs. Imagine that you have access to a few hours of support with one TA, but you have several tasks you need to accomplish. Consider which task you would ask the TA to do and the reasons for making that choice. There is no 'right' answer to find here; the skill is in being able to rationalise your reasons for your order of priorities.

Review the tasks, decide on the priority order and explain your reasoning for assigning the TA:

a   Work with a group of six pupils who need more consolidation of a new concept in maths.
b   Put up a specific display to meet a looming, urgent whole-school deadline.
c   Work one-to-one with a child with an Educational, Health and Care Plan (ECHP) for challenging behaviour whose key helper is away sick.
d   Check that family and carer consent letters have been collated for a school trip next week.

What did you decide? Might it be important to focus directly on supporting children who are currently in school? Which tasks could be pushed to non-teaching time? Do health and safety issues outweigh other concerns? Have you considered the impact of not completing each task? If so, which could have the most significant impact if not addressed?

There may also be activities where TAs should not be used. The very first of the seven EEF (2021) recommendations states: 'TAs should not be used as an informal teaching resource for low attaining pupils' (based on Blatchford *et al.*, 2009). However, newer research is showing contradictory results, which, whilst tentative, highlight the need for on-going investigation and adaptation of TA-teacher roles (Glazzard, 2018; Hodgen, Adkins and Ainsworth, 2023).

In practice, establishing harmonious TA and teacher roles may need negotiation. Making use of evidence-based guidance materials (e.g. EEF, 2021; Open University – see Relevant websites section at the end of the unit) is useful, but may lack the nitty-gritty detail needed to ensure shared teacher–TA understandings. For example, the third EEF recommendation urges: 'Use TAs to help pupils develop independent learning skills and manage their own learning'. What might that mean in practice? While TAs can encourage children's independent learning, it is a subtle process. How might it work? The EEF suggestions are based on sources that provide more depth. For this example, Bosanquet, Radford and Webster (2016) specify good-practice guidelines which could be useful for teacher–TA discussion:

Self-scaffolding: TAs observe, allowing pupils processing and thinking time.
Prompting: TAs provide prompts, encouraging pupils to draw on their own knowledge, nudging them into deploying self-scaffolding techniques.
Clueing: Clues worded as questions provide a hint for pupils who often know, but cannot immediately recall, a required strategy.
Modelling: TAs model while pupils actively watch and listen and then immediately try out the same steps.
Correcting: If modelling, clueing and prompting are not sufficient, correcting can be appropriate.

(Adapted from Bosanquet, Radford and Webster, 2016)

Expectations (of enforcing school behaviour policies, etc., as well as pedagogies) need to be consciously articulated; shared understanding should not be assumed. The aim is to establish and maintain consistency, thus supporting pupils' learning.

Task 8.1.2 Observing TAs in action

To gain a better understanding of TAs' activities, delve into this investigation, observing TA(s) in different classrooms, or other relevant settings. Next is an Observation Schedule, with a list of features to look out for. Remember to check with teachers and TAs for permissions both to undertake the observations and also to take notes.

Observation Schedule				
Classroom/Age Group:		**Date/Time:**	**Session Duration:**	
Contextual Notes:				
Nature of pupil(s) being supported (attainment level, SEND, EAL, etc.)				
Teacher's role during the observation period				
Predominant activity of TA:	**Time Spent on Activity**	**Features of TA-to-pupil talk (open/closed questions, etc.)**	**How independent are pupils? Do they take responsibility for their learning?**	**Task differentiation (e.g. different content)**
Working one-to-one with pupil				
Working with a group				
Roving around the classroom				
Listening to teacher				
Other tasks (tidying/admin)				

Adapted from EEF (2021)

OVERCOMING CHALLENGES AND SETTING PROFESSIONAL BOUNDARIES

This section highlights the vital role of establishing and maintaining professional boundaries in the teacher-TA relationship, offering practical guidance for effective collaboration. Challenges, such as TA pay, impacts from understaffing of qualified teachers and even issues of violence, are beyond your direct scope, but many aspects can be addressed through sensitive collaboration. Initially, relationships tend to be formal, however, this dynamic may change as your work together evolves. Table 8.1.1 is intended as a starting point, offering you a flexible framework. Remain receptive to the potential for growing informality in your relationship and adjust accordingly.

TABLE 8.1.1 Promoting positive teaching assistant and teacher work relationships

Strategy	Description	Explore Further
Clear Communication Channels	Arrange regular check-ins and facilitate open dialogues. Clearly outline expectations for response times and respect preferred communication methods.	Giangreco, 2021.
Role Clarity; Alignment of Expectations	Clearly articulate roles and responsibilities, negotiating, not dictating, using open dialogue to address uncertainties, ensuring a reciprocal understanding and distribution of professional duties.	Ravalier, Walsh and Hoult, 2021; Webster Blatchford and Russell, 2013.
Recognition of Expertise	Acknowledge and appreciate the unique strengths of each professional. Advocate for continuous professional development for both teachers and TAs to remain well-informed and to strengthen collaborative partnerships.	Cockroft and Atkinson, 2015.
Confidentiality; Safeguarding; Boundaries	Establish and communicate unambiguous protocols for managing sensitive information to build trust and uphold ethical standards. Acknowledge the necessity for boundaries beyond school, promoting a balanced work–life dynamic and nurturing a respectful working relationship.	Wigford and Higgins, 2019.
Promoting Appreciative Cultures	Implement strategies fostering recognition and acknowledging everyone's contributions. Emphasise initiatives prioritising wellbeing, encompassing mindfulness practices and stress management, building a positive working environment.	Yang et al., 2023; Greenway and Edwards, 2021.

Another aspect of working relationships within your control is that of communication. Tone, in conjunction with empathy and clarity, plays a pivotal role, influencing the overall effectiveness and reception of your messages and shaping their emotional impact. In the midst of a hectic day, when tempers can fray, it is all too easy to snap, potentially causing upset. It is imperative, therefore, that you are mindful and conscious of how you communicate. One way to help yourself would be to anticipate possible tricky moments and think about reframing conversations.

> ### Task 8.1.3 Rewriting the script
>
> In the following (imagined) dialogue, let's explore how to create a constructive conversation between a Teacher (T) and Teaching Assistant (TA) who are facing a bit of tension due to a misunderstanding. The task is to revise this script, perhaps together with a peer. Can you find ways to de-escalate the tension, transforming a rather tetchy dialogue to something with a more collaborative spirit? In place of agitation and anxiety, it's possible to build some effective communication strategies and bring about a positive resolution.
>
> T: *(visibly frustrated)* Look, I clearly said I'm leading the planning for this maths lesson on place value. And where are the counting cubes? I shouldn't have to worry about this!
>
> TA: *(defensively)* Well, I thought we were supposed to be a team, but if you want to be in total charge of absolutely everything, fine.
>
> T: *(sighs)* Just make sure the materials are here. I need your input on the lesson plan.
>
> TA: *(irritated)* Hey, I was just trying to help. I already gave you my ideas for the lesson plan – have you forgotten? If you don't like my ideas, I can leave you to it.
>
> T: *(softening slightly)* I appreciate your help, but I need to keep control over this lesson to meet the objectives. I just wanted some practical help. I still need you to get the counting cubes.
>
> TA: *(angrily)* Fine, whatever you want. Someone else is using the counting cubes. Not my fault.
>
> T: *(firmly)* It's still your responsibility to find some type of counting materials. Sort it out, please, and I'll finish the planning – *(muttering)* even though that was supposed to be a shared task.
>
> *TA leaves the room, noisily.*
>
> Here follow some possible suggestions for improvements. Did you have these ideas? What more could you add?
>
> - A lack of role clarity is giving rise to misunderstandings so establish clear expectations.
> - Respectful communications need to be modelled and shared; soften the language.
> - Both people need to express appreciation for one another's contributions.
> - Collaborative and flexible mindsets help with problem-solving, so should be adopted.
> - It's important to cultivate emotional intelligence in order to manage emotions in a professional setting.

Everyday minor conflicts are generally manageable, and you are likely to encounter these, but thinking about how to communicate effectively will be really helpful. Thankfully, it is very unlikely that you will be exposed to more serious concerns and conflicts in the classroom with staff or pupils; low-level disruption is the most typical issue and there are many ways to manage your work to reduce these concerns. However, unfortunately, instances of negative behaviour do exist in schools, and it is generally the TAs who tend to bear the brunt of these difficult instances. There can even be occasional violence against TAs in schools, but this happens more typically in secondary settings and is still a very unusual occurrence. Holt and Birchall (2023) report instances of unpleasant behaviours, reinforced in reports to parliament from TAs, sharing experiences of working with challenging pupils, noting that 'It falls on TAs to work with these children without any training' (Antoniazzi, 2023).

As a teacher, it is helpful and supportive if you can be aware of these concerns. It is likely that difficult behaviours are more prevalent among children being frequently supervised by TAs; there *can sometimes* be a link between the need for additional support and some negative behaviours (not always, of course). Your school should have procedures in place for managing serious incidences of violent behaviours, which hopefully you will never need to use. However, as a teacher, you should be aware of the possibility of a serious incident and be equipped to safely follow protocol, providing support to any TA who may have been harmed. For example, in their recommendations, Holt and Birchall specifically call upon teachers to support their colleagues, noting, 'there needs to be a culture change that addresses current "us and them" divisions between teaching staff and support staff, which is damaging to an inclusive school ethos' (2022: 8). To support this, we move on to consider wellbeing.

WELLBEING

While we typically recognise wellbeing intuitively, defining the notion in research terms can pose a challenge. Dodge *et al.* (2012) describe stable wellbeing as when individuals have a sound balance of resources and challenges. When psychological, social and/or physical resources are insufficient to match the challenges at hand difficulties can arise. When individuals have more challenges than resources, the disequilibrium results in anxiety and stress.

However, despite difficult conditions, poor pay and low status (Cockroft and Atkinson, 2015), TAs generally do derive a lot of job satisfaction from their work, as explored in this unit. Holt and Birchall define common TA intersectionalities as a combination of 'gender, income, education, social class and professional status' (2023: 54). However, other aspects may also intersect, such as having a minority ethnic background, neurodivergence or a disability. For example, an additional stress factor arising from a non-dominant background is the continual requirement to manage the deficit beliefs held by some teaching colleagues. 'Deficit thinking stems from the notion that the beliefs and standards of the dominant group are inherently correct' (Bamgbose *et al.*, 2023: 489). TAs from diverse backgrounds distinct from teacher-colleagues, but shared with pupils from their own minority communities, may find it challenging to witness stereotypical and negative views in school. Continually advocating for pupils from their own background is emotionally draining.

Unsurprisingly, TAs face an elevated risk of stress, necessitating colleagues to be vigilant, looking out for problems and providing support. Ravalier, Walsh and Hoult cite 'organisational factors such as job demand, available support, and role clarity [as] significant predictors of stress in TAs' (2021: 787). They also note that 'high demands, in particular, were consistently found to be a significant predictor of stress levels, and the impact of these demands on wellbeing is likely exacerbated by poor peer and management support structures' (Ravalier, Walsh and Hoult, 2021: 800). Fortunately, this is an aspect that you can directly address and you can help reduce stress factors through positive collaborative working and also through positive appreciation. For more ideas around building a supportive ethos for pupils and staff alike, see Winstanley (2019).

Wigford and Higgins provide further positivity, showing that personal feelings of pride, passion, enjoyment and a sense of purpose all help with wellbeing. TAs benefit from witnessing students' progress, and 'being present for "light bulb moments when students grasp a concept"'(2019: 53). They highlight the importance of belonging to the school community but note that this is likely to be more intense in the international sector – the context of their research – since people tend to be living away from their original home community. Improving the broader community's understanding of the TA role can also help TAs' sense of worth. Back in 2008, Wilson and Bedford highlighted the need for relevant research. They noted that the impact of teacher-TA partnerships on pupil achievement has been comprehensively studied, along with projects harnessing TA voices, but 'there remains a persistent gap in understanding parental and pupil perceptions of TA and HLTA roles' (2008: 137). Recent research supports this lack of clarity. Wren (2017) explored pupils' understanding of the TA's role, finding that pupils refer vaguely to non-specific help, failing to identify support activities undertaken by TAs, considering them instead as friends, suggesting '"playing" as a key role of the TA' (2017: 17).

As if the personal wellbeing of TAs was not persuasive enough, some research shows pupil wellbeing can also be directly enhanced. See, for example, Hills 2016 Emotional Literacy Support Assistant programme, which would surely have resonance in helping address the social, emotional and personal development deficiencies caused by the pandemic. The link between TA and pupil wellbeing is also noted by this Y3 TA:

> I started noticing that my unhappy time in Reception was impacting on the pupils. I raised it with Deputy and although it took a while to arrange, I moved to a role where I felt better, less stressed and more comfortable. I find Y3 less frustrating than Reception. This made a big difference in how much help and support I could provide and I think they benefited a lot too. I was happier and they seemed excited about their learning in a more supportive atmosphere; I genuinely think that if the TA is happy, the pupils benefit.
>
> (Winstanley, 2023: Conversation with Y3 TA)

Contrary to common belief, not all primary TAs aspire to become teachers. The TA role is not merely a stepping-stone but is valuable in itself. Calls for renaming TAs as 'paraprofessionals' are increasing (Yang et al., 2023: 2), reframing the role as complementary, rather than subordinate to the teacher. Webster and Hall echo this, suggesting that 'treating TAs as part of a community of professionals may be an effective way of encouraging them to stay in post as the cost-of-living crisis continues' (2022: 20). They also posit a national TA strategy including pay increases, better training and other ways to boost morale. As a teacher, you cannot easily impact national strategies, but you can be aware of your colleagues' needs and advocate for them. Review the jigsaw-model in Figure 8.1.1 and identify aspects you can act on directly in practice, plus those you need to be aware of, even if you do not have a direct influence.

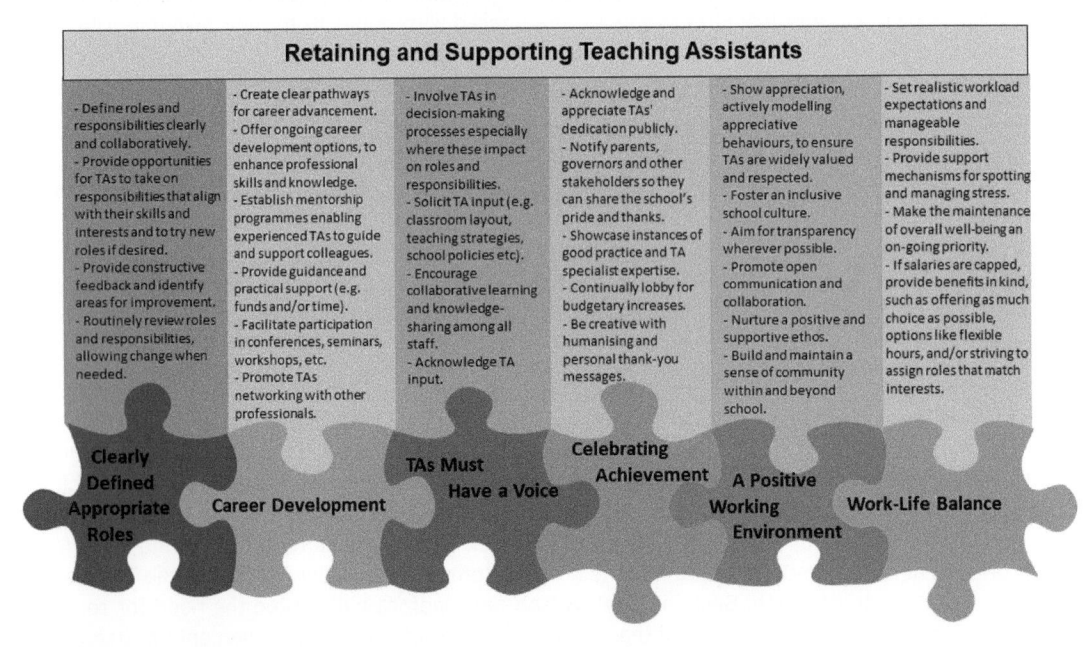

FIGURE 8.1.1 Jigsaw model: Retaining and Supporting Teaching Assistants
Source: Winstanley (2023)

Here are some further suggestions of positive strategies for building and enhancing a professional and positive ethos between teachers and TAs. You will know your own school context. Familiarise yourself with support colleagues and collaborate with other teachers and managers to initiate and implement ideas of this nature:

- ✓ Express gratitude with personalised thank-you notes, a recognition board, flexible break times and rotated parking privileges.
- ✓ Provide professional development opportunities.
- ✓ Showcase TAs in newsletters; host informal celebration lunches.
- ✓ Ensure TAs have essential school materials, including items like stickers and pocket-money prizes for incentives.
- ✓ Offer coffee vouchers, virtual shout-outs, or dedicate a book in the school library.
- ✓ Sponsor professional memberships, brighten workspaces with plants or flowers and provide customised school merchandise, along with thoughtful certificates of recognition.

SUMMARY

This unit empowers you to establish effective relationships with support staff by cultivating an understanding and appreciation of their pivotal roles in your classroom and the broader school context. Explore practical strategies to glean valuable insights into fostering effective working relationships and collaboration, acknowledging the vital role of teamwork in enhancing the overall educational experience.

Through navigating the complexities of the TA role, you will be in a stronger position to overcome challenges and set professional boundaries, ensuring a healthy and productive working environment. A key focus of the unit has been the importance of wellbeing, and now you have strategies to maintain and enhance the wellbeing of the TAs who, in turn, support your wellbeing.

Despite persistent queries about the value of TAs, researchers suggest that 'deliver[ing] short, structured, time-limited individual or small group interventions, this can have a positive impact on attainment' (Glazzard, 2018, echoed by Hodgen, Adkins and Ainsworth, 2023). Similarly, the value of TAs is emphasised by MP Antoniazzi when urging the government to ensure a fair pay deal: '[TAs] are all too often the only reason a student will stay in school. Their nurturing nature and patience is priceless, their ability to break down work so a student can understand is phenomenal' (Antoniazzi, 2023; Hansard HC Deb., 2023). The final remarks in this unit are from an apposite quotation. Although the source article primarily concentrates on pupils with ADHD, its content is more broadly applicable, neatly encapsulating the overarching findings from the scholarship and other evidence reviewed:

> Despite the apparent challenges described above, the TAs in the present study showed great enthusiasm and love for their job. The dedication, willingness to learn and desire for others to learn exhibited by TAs should be celebrated, and this calls for investment in the professional development of all those involved in the care and education of children with ADHD. Finally, there is a real need to create mandatory and statutory guidelines that clearly define the TA's role to ensure effective classroom practice.
>
> (Greenway and Edwards, 2021: 364)

ANNOTATED FURTHER READING

Bosanquet, P., Radford, J. and Webster, R. (2021) *The Teaching Assistant's Guide to Effective Interaction: How to Maximise Your Practice*, 2nd edn, London: Routledge.

> This book emphasises scaffolding as the primary role for TAs, covering assessment, group work and intervention management. The authors provide practical details, including thought-provoking tasks and reflection boxes with carefully crafted questions to engage with key ideas.

Glazzard, J. (2018) *Effectively Deploying Teaching Assistants to Support Pupils with Special Educational Needs and/or Disabilities (SEND)*, 2 February, BERA. Retrieved from: www.bera.ac.uk/blog/effectively-deploying-teaching-assistants-to-support-pupils-with-special-educational-needs-and-or-disabilities-send

> This blog, succinct yet comprehensive on issues related to TAs working with pupils with special educational needs and/or disabilities (SEND), includes references in Glazzard's bibliography to additional papers worth exploring.

Gray, A. and Wright, M. (2020) *The Effective Teaching Assistant: A Practical Guide to Supporting Achievement for Pupils with SEND*, London: Routledge.

> Since TAs frequently dedicate time to supporting students with additional needs, a book specifically addressing the practical aspects of this role proves valuable. Drawing from their firsthand experience, the authors offer a wealth of constructive, practical strategies and suggestions deeply rooted in scholarly research.

FURTHER READING TO SUPPORT M-LEVEL STUDY

Hills, R. (2016) 'An evaluation of the Emotional Literacy Support Assistant (ELSA) project from the perspectives of primary school children', *Educational and Child Psychology*, 33(4): 50–65.

> This fascinating paper describes a professional development intervention designed for TAs working in partnership with Educational Psychologists undertaking an Emotional Literacy Support project. You will find an insightful focus showing children's perspectives, highlighting the importance of listening to children and gathering their views through alternative methods, such as drawing.

Lewis, G. (2023) 'The classroom deployment of teaching assistants in England: A critical review of literature from 2010 to 2020', *Educational Review*. DOI: 10.1080/00131911.2023.2184773

> This comprehensive meta-synthesis critically examines a substantial decade of literature on the value of TAs, providing a thorough evaluation. In addition to reviewing the DISS study highlighted in this unit, it offers a commendable model for analysing literature. Lewis strategically reassesses the literature thematically, through new lenses, offering a fresh perspective that unveils new insights.

RELEVANT WEBSITES

Education Support: www.educationsupport.org.uk and www.educationsupport.org.uk/resources/for-individuals/guides/wellbeing-resources-for-teaching-assistants/

> Education Support provides a charitable, free helpline (available 24/7) for all education staff, along with a paid employee assistance service. Of particular relevance to this unit are the downloadable free resources focusing on general wellbeing and specifically tailored for teaching assistants.

Teaching Assistants: Support in Action: www.open.edu/openlearn/education-development/education/teaching-assistants-support-action/content-section-0/?printable=1

> A free course offered by the Open University as part of 'OpenLearn'. It complements the themes in this unit and is illustrated with helpful examples from scholarly literature, vignettes and direct quotations from children and TAs, as well as tasks and activities.

The Education Endowment Foundation: https://educationendowmentfoundation.org.uk/education-evidence/teaching-learning-toolkit/teaching-assistant-interventions

> An independent charity sharing evidence and information about interventions to ameliorate education. Their work on TAs is wide-ranging and includes a lot of downloadable resources.

European Journal of Special Needs Education 2021 Vol.36 Issue 2: www.tandfonline.com/toc/rejs20/36/2

> This is a Special Edition of the journal, in which all nine articles are devoted to concerns around TA issues and inclusive education. The edition is edited and curated by Webster, R. & de Boer, A.A.

REFERENCES

Antoniazzi, T. (2023) *Teaching Assistant Pay Debate, Hansard*. Retrieved from: https://hansard.parliament.uk/Commons/2023-07-17/debates/00104CAB-7B8B-4CBB-AA47-67A200EBCE04/TeachingAssistantPay (accessed 10 November 2023).

Bamgbose, O. O., Toms, O. M., Kranz, L. J. and Owen, M. P. (2023) 'Assessing the cultural knowledge of pre-service professionals, faculty, and staff on the journey toward developing cultural competence', *Teacher Development*, 27(4): 487–505.

Blatchford, P., Bassett, P., Brown, P., Koutsoubou, M., Martin, C., Russell, A., Webster, R. and Rubie-Davies, C. (2009) *The Impact of Support Staff in Schools. Results from the Deployment and Impact of Support Staff (DISS) Project* (Strand 2 Wave 2), London: DCSF.

Bosanquet, P., Radford, J. and Webster, R. (2016) *The Teaching Assistant's Guide to Effective Interaction*, London: Routledge.

British Educational Research Association (BERA). (2013) *40@40 – A Portrait of 40 Years of Educational Research Through 40 Studies*. BERA. Retrieved from: www.bera.ac.uk/project/40at40 (accessed 10 November 2023).

Cockroft, C. and Atkinson, C. (2015) 'Using the wider pedagogical role model to establish learning support assistants' views about facilitators and barriers to effective practice', *Support for Learning*, 30(2): 88–104.

Department for Education (DfE). (2024) *Workload Reduction Taskforce: Initial Recommendations*. Retrieved from: https://assets.publishing.service.gov.uk/media/65a10648e8f5ec000d1f8c2f/Workload_reduction_taskforce_-_initial_recommendations.pdf (accessed 12 February 2024).

Dodge, R., Daly, A. P., Huyton, J. and Sanders, L. D. (2012) 'The challenge of defining wellbeing', *International Journal of Wellbeing*, 2(3): 222–235.

Education Act (2002). Retrieved from: www.legislation.gov.uk/ukpga/2002/32/contents

Education Endowment Foundation (EEF). (2021) *Making Best Use of Teaching Assistants*. Retrieved from: https://educationendowmentfoundation.org.uk/education-evidence/guidance-reports/teaching-assistants (accessed 17 November 2023).

Fazackerley, A. (2023) 'Low pay "forcing teaching assistants out of UK classrooms"'. *The Guardian*, 14 May. Retrieved from: www.theguardian.com/education/2023/may/14/low-pay-teaching-assistants-uk-classrooms (accessed 10 November 2023).

Giangreco, M. F. (2021) 'Maslow's Hammer: Teacher assistant research and inclusive practices at a crossroads', *European Journal of Special Needs Education*, 36(2): 278–293.

Glazzard, J. (2018) *Effectively Deploying Teaching Assistants to Support Pupils with Special Educational Needs and/or Disabilities (SEND)*, 2 February, BERA. Retrieved from: www.bera.ac.uk/blog/effectively-deploying-teaching-assistants-to-support-pupils-with-special-educational-needs-and-or-disabilities-send

Greenway, C. W. and Edwards, A. R. (2021) 'Teaching assistants' facilitators and barriers to effective practice working with children with ADHD: A qualitative study', *British Journal of Special Education*, 48(3): 347–368.

Hansard HC Deb. (17 July 2023) Vol. 736, Col. 205. Retrieved from: https://hansard.parliament.uk/Commons/2023-07-17/debates/00104CAB-7B8B-4CBB-AA47-67A200EBCE04/TeachingAssistantPay (accessed 10 November 2023).

Hills, R. (2016) 'An evaluation of the Emotional Literacy Support Assistant (ELSA) project from the perspectives of primary school children', *Educational and Child Psychology*, 33(4): 50-65.

Hodgen, J., Adkins, M. and Ainsworth, S. E. (2023) 'Can teaching assistants improve attainment and attitudes of low performing pupils in numeracy? Evidence from a large-scale randomised controlled trial', *Cambridge Journal of Education*, 53(2): 215-235.

Holt, A. and Birchall, J. (2022) *Violence Towards Teaching/Classroom Assistants in Mainstream UK Schools: Research Findings and Recommendations*, University of Roehampton, UK.

Holt, A. and Birchall, J. (2023) 'Student violence towards teaching assistants in UK schools: A case of gender-based violence', *Gender and Education*, 35(1): 53-68.

Lewis, G. (2023) 'The classroom deployment of teaching assistants in England: A critical review of literature from 2010 to 2020', *Educational Review*. Advance online publication. DOI: 10.1080/00131911.2023.2184773

Ravalier, J. M., Walsh, J. and Hoult, E. (2021) 'The impact of working conditions on the UK's teaching assistants', *Oxford Review of Education*, 47(6): 787-804.

Webster, R. and Hall, S. (2022) *From Covid to the Cost of Living: The Crises Remaking the Role of Teaching Assistants*, Education Research, Innovation and Consultancy Uni, University of Portsmouth, September.

Webster, R., Blatchford, P. and Russell, A. (2013) 'Challenging and changing how schools use teaching assistants: Findings from the Effective Deployment of Teaching Assistants project', *School Leadership & Management*, 33(1): 78-96.

Wren, A. (2017) 'Understanding the role of the teaching assistant: Comparing the views of pupils with SEN and TAs within mainstream primary schools', *Support for Learning*, 32(1): 4-19.

Wigford, A. and Higgins, A. (2019) 'Wellbeing in international schools: Teachers' perceptions', *Educational and Child Psychology*, 36(4): 46-64.

Wilson, E. and Bedford, D. (2008) 'New partnerships for learning: Teachers and teaching assistants working together in schools – the way forward', *Journal of Education for Teaching*, 34(2): 137-150.

Winstanley, C. (2019) 'Developing a supportive ethos for all learners', in S. Ogier (ed.) *A Broad and Balanced Curriculum in Primary Schools: Educating the Whole Child*, 1st edn, London: Sage, pp. 87-101.

Winstanley, C. (2023) *Informal Conversations with Teaching Assistants (TAs and HLTAs)*. Personal communications.

Yang, L., Chi-Kin Lee, J., Zhang, D. and Chen, J. (2023) 'Examining the relationships among teaching assistants' self-efficacy, emotional well-being and job satisfaction', *Teachers and Teaching*. Advance online publication. DOI: 10.1080/13540602.2023.2265825

UNIT 8.2

PARTNERSHIPS WITH PARENTS

Stephen Griffin

INTRODUCTION

This unit focuses on building effective, purposeful and long-lasting relationships with parents/carers. For the purposes of this unit, the term 'parents' should be taken to include carers also - single parents, grandparents, foster carers or older siblings, acting *in loco parentis*. After the Education Reform Act 1988, Education (Schools) Act 1992 and Education Act 2011, parents have been increasingly described as 'partners' in their children's education. Coupled with the move towards greater parental choice in terms of the schools parents can send their children to, such as academy and free primary schools, there has also been an increased transparency of school performance data, via Ofsted reports, league tables and the publication of exam results; parents are viewed as key stakeholders in the educational process and, more recently, the choice of schools. Historically, in England, the home and the school have been two distinct and separate realms of a child's life. The role that parents have as educators has, therefore, been underdeveloped in the past. Indeed, the Hadow Report (1931) highlighted the importance of a child-centred curriculum, but it was not until the Plowden Report (Department of Education and Science [DES], 1967) that recognition was attributed to the vital role that parents can play in their child's education: 'One of the essentials for educational advance is a closer partnership between the two parties (i.e. schools and parents) to every child's education' (DES, 1967: 102). The power of parental involvement should not be underestimated - in 2018, PISA studies highlighted the impact of positive parental involvement in children's education in terms of pupil educational outcomes (OECD, 2012; 2018). Therefore, it is evident that greater collaboration with parents needs to be a key aim in improving educational outcomes for children and as such should be a priority for all primary school teachers.

OBJECTIVES

By the end of this unit, you should:

- have an understanding of the need to ensure that you develop secure relationships with the parents of pupils in your class, during school placement, the first year of teaching and subsequent years of teaching;
- recognise and understand the importance of purposeful and structured working relationships with parents;
- know of effective ways of liaising and communicating with parents;
- have an appreciation of the need for trust and understanding as the foundation for successful relationships between parents and school;
- begin to have some strategies as a student teacher or early careers teacher (ECT) and begin to establish sound home–school links.

DOI: 10.4324/9781032691794-45

PROFESSIONAL REQUIREMENTS: STATUTORY EXPECTATIONS

It is important to recognise that not only is parental involvement desirable in achieving positive educational outcomes, but it is also a professional requirement of all teachers, as detailed in the *Teachers' Standards* (Department for Education [DfE], 2011). Furthermore, it is reflected in the Initial Teacher Training Core Content Framework standard 8 (DfE, 2019: 29) and Early Career Framework which states that: 'Building effective relationships with parents, carers, and families can improve pupils' motivation, behaviour and academic success'.

The Qualified Teacher Status (QTS) standards are divided into three sections:

- professional attributes;
- professional knowledge and understanding;
- professional skills.

The implementation of a concise set of standards, which apply to teachers at the point of entry to the profession, as well as to experienced practitioners, will, according to the government: 'define the minimum level of practice expected of trainees and teachers from the point of being awarded QTS', furthermore they 'are used to assess an ECT's performance at the end of their induction period in employment' (DfE, 2011). Running through all these standards is a theme of being respectful towards all learners and considerate and committed to raising their achievement. The standards are organised as separate headings, numbered 1-8. Under each section, there are bullets and subheadings. These subheadings should not be referenced as separate standards and should be used advisedly. For example, under Section 8, we see the introduction of the role of parents for the first time. Despite the government's acknowledgement of the importance of schools working effectively with parents, the standards have only one reference to parental engagement. However, included in Standard Q8 is an emphasis on the need for all teachers to ensure the importance of working alongside parents: 'Communicate effectively with parents with regard to pupils' achievements and well-being, young people, colleagues, parents and carers' (DfE, 2011: Q8).

Under successive governments, there has been increasing concern regarding the teaching of reading, mathematic strategies and basic skills generally. These now form an integral part of Ofsted inspections and Initial Teacher Training (ITT) provision. As such, parents' understanding of pedagogical approaches in primary school, such as the teaching of synthetic phonics as the preferred method for teaching reading and a move towards an instrumental approach for the teaching of mathematics, has now increased.

ADVANTAGES OF SECURE RELATIONSHIPS WITH PARENTS

Research (Bastiani, 2003; Desforges and Abouchaar, 2003; Department for Children, Schools and Families [DCSF], 2008; Lee and Bowen, 2006; Ofsted, 2011; Carroll and Alexander, 2016; Robinson, Bingle and Howard, 2016; Tan, Lyu and Peng, 2020) has shown that involving parents in their children's education can help remove barriers to learning, raise attainment and improve attitudes and behaviour. It is widely believed that primary schools, working in partnership with parents to support their children's learning and development, can expect significant and lasting benefits. Among these are improved, as well as consistent, levels of attainment, coupled with a more positive attitude towards behaviour and attendance. However, it is important to be aware that not all parents have access to the same levels of resources to support this partnership, hence communication becomes especially important for families that are experiencing challenges. Leenders *et al*. (2019: 12) highlight the importance of two-way communication between teachers and parents as a means of 'building a relation of trust before there is anything substantial to talk about'. In particular, informal conversations and occasional sharing of positive stories to parents about their children's progress can encourage a dialogue and challenge the more traditional and directive relationship whereby teachers report to parents formally.

O'Hara (2008: 14) highlights the importance of communicating with parents and suggests six practical ways to ensure that teachers and parents have effective dialogue:

1. regular parent-teacher contact (such as PTA);
2. joint teaching/work in the classroom;
3. home visits;
4. whole-school events;
5. school handbooks/prospectuses;
6. letters, notices and circulars.

As well as highlighting parental involvement, he also suggested strategies as to how this could be implemented, the most significant being Parent Teacher Associations (PTAs) - a common feature of our schools today. Desforges and Abouchaar discussed the obvious link between input from home and attainment in school: 'Parental involvement has a significant effect on children's achievement and adjustment even after all other factors (such as social class, maternal education and poverty) have been taken out of the equation' (2003: 9.2.2). However, involving parents requires 'strong leadership and thoughtful and sustained communication' and can be crucial as a means of 'levelling up' achievement for all pupils in school (OECD, 2018). Furthermore, PISA (OECD, 2022) emphasised that parental engagement is especially important for disadvantaged pupils. Despite this, they also noted that 'parental involvement in students' learning at school decreased substantially between 2018 and 2022' (OECD, 2024). The UK government's own data notes that the percentage of persistent absentees was 21.2% across autumn and spring in the year 2022 to 2023 (Gov.uk, 2023b). Unsurprisingly, the challenges of the pandemic underscore the critical need for teachers and parents to engage with one another in relation to pupils' education.

In a survey by Lewis *et al.* (2007: 2), primary head teachers were asked what were the most effective ways of involving parents in their child's education. The findings indicated that more than 90% of primary schools used the following:

- school newsletters;
- special events for parents (e.g. information/discussion evenings);
- gathering parents' views as part of school self-evaluation;
- encouraging parents to contact/or visit the school.

As teachers, you need to ensure that such opportunities are constructively built upon and you have a secure understanding of pupils' cultural capital (Bourdieu, 1986). This can be understood as the set of dispositions that enable certain groups of pupils to succeed more readily at school than others; that is, they receive linguistic ability from their parents and have access to certain forms of culture, such as the theatre and the 'arts', which are reflected heavily in the school curriculum. In the most recent inspection framework, Ofsted (2023) highlights the importance of cultural capital being reflected in the curriculum, especially for 'the most disadvantaged and those with special educational needs and/or disabilities (SEND) or high needs'. This presents a significant challenge to teachers and schools. It is worth considering how you might support disadvantaged children who might find it harder to access the school curriculum for the reasons to do with access to cultural capital. In particular, contemplate how to better understand and support parents to talk with their children about learning and the curriculum. Corsaro and Fingerson (2006) and Hart and Risley (1995) outline that parents who engage children in their learning and talk to their children about learning before their children begin school ensure that their children are actually ready for school. It is these predisposed skills that give them the advantage, whereas pupils from less privileged backgrounds, or with parents who need support to ensure their children are ready to begin school, may struggle to access the curriculum for this very reason.

When considering the behaviour of pupils in the classroom, Rogers (2000) contends that there are some behavioural issues outside the school or classroom environment that teachers or the school cannot influence. Similarly, Charlton and David (1993: 207) state that, 'much behaviour at school seems to be independent of home influences'. It could, therefore, be argued that some children's lives are split into two distinct parts: home and school. Thus, it is vital that, in order to provide a consistent and effective approach to the education of children in primary-phase education, both academically and socially, parents and teachers cooperate and form what Cooper and Olson (1996) term a healthy 'alliance'. The Steer Report (2005) and Ofsted (2023) placed similar emphasis on this crucial relationship, asserting that good, as well as effective, communication between the school and home is essential for appropriate behaviour.

Research by Miller and Rollnick (2002) outlined that many teachers have rather a negative view of parents of children in their class. This chimes with findings from the Elton Report (1989: 133), which concluded: 'our evidence suggests that teachers' picture of parents is generally very negative. Many teachers feel that parents are to blame for much misbehaviour in schools'. Yet the value of healthy parent–teacher relations has been strongly emphasised within the behavioural discourse (Cooper and Olson, 1996; Barnard, 2004; Addi-Raccah and Ainhoren, 2009; Robinson, Bingle and Howard, 2016; Leenders et al., 2019), and Selwyn (2011a, 2011b) observes that, 'the notion of the "engaged parent" has become a key element of governmental policy efforts to improve educational standards and reduce inequalities' (Selwyn et al., 2011: 314). Despite this, these potential relationships are not always fully utilised and realised, and, as a teacher new to the profession, it could be advantageous for you to be proactive in forming appropriate and effective relationships with parents.

The survey also described how the majority of primary schools actively sought strategies to involve their PTAs. However, the survey highlighted that socio-economic factors influenced the amount of involvement from the PTA or even whether the school had a PTA. Whether before or after qualifying as a teacher, you need to ensure that you know the strategies employed by the school to ensure that parents are involved in their child's education. Recently, online communication and virtual learning environments (VLEs) have been used increasingly to involve parents in school life. This is going to have an impact on your daily routine, and you may be requested to contribute to such forums, so you need a confident and capable approach to Information and Communication Technology (ICT). Lewis et al.'s (2007: 3) survey also outlines other strategies that head teachers feel they use to actively involve parents in primary education:

- parents' forums/focus groups;
- online communication/VLEs;
- family learning/parent–child workshops;
- as parent governors.

The latest government guidance on communication with parents proposes that schools utilise letters, emails, text messages and phone calls to engage with parents over attendance issues (Gov.uk, 2023a).

FIRST IMPRESSIONS: MANAGING THE NARRATIVE

Recent initiatives at both a national and local level have encouraged greater collaboration between the two (schools and parents). For example, many schools now offer parents the opportunity to observe lessons and to discuss the new teaching methods employed.

To this end, it is essential that you seek out opportunities to forge meaningful and appropriate links with parents of the children in your class. Outside formal meetings such as parents' evenings, this can be done effectively by taking the opportunity to be 'seen' at key times. It is often the case that many home-school partnerships never reach their potential because the school is seen as being remote and distant from the home. When you also consider that there may be significant numbers of parents whose own experience of schooling was negative, it is not surprising that they are reticent to 'cross the threshold' and approach teachers comfortably. For these parents, school may still represent an unhappy and less-than-productive period of their lives. Also, demands on parents, who may work full time or look after younger children, may mean that they are less active than they would like to be regarding the teaching and learning of their children. Therefore, it is your duty as teachers to reach out and open up the possibilities of home-school partnerships in a positive and proactive manner.

A key time to achieve this aim is at the beginning and end of the school day. Although you need to be mindful of ensuring a prompt start to lessons, if you are visible and welcoming in the morning, it sends a clear message to parents and children alike. This is especially important at the beginning of a new school year. Both the parents and the children will be keen to meet the new teacher, and your presence will ensure that you have a positive influence throughout the year. As formal parents' meetings may not take place until later in the school year, a quick personal introduction is an effective means of establishing a relationship sooner.

Task 8.2.1 Relationships with parents

- *Action point*: Introduce yourself to parents at either the beginning or end of the school day – make a point of remarking positively on an achievement each child has made.
- *Task*: During your non-contact time (or ECT time), visit other schools (or compare approaches while on school placements) to research how they ensure that parents are involved with their children's education. Report your findings to your mentor, line manager or tutor.

DEALING WITH DIFFICULT SITUATIONS

As discussed previously, as teachers we are aware of the benefits that supportive parents have for the achievement of their children. Research (Edwards and Warin, 1999; Desforges and Abouchaar, 2003; Corsaro and Fingerson, 2006; Feiler, 2010; Robinson, Bingle and Howard, 2016) also highlights the enormous benefits that parents can bring to school when the values and ethos are shared between home and school. However, we need to be aware of the problematic nature of school when this is not the case. The work of Edwards and Warin (1999) and Feiler (2010) raises many issues concerning the assumptions that schools make considering adequate and appropriate support from parents. They reached the conclusion that many schools were keen to utilise parents as 'long arms' for the schools' own purposes, and not as equal partners. They concluded that the ways in which schools enhance parental involvement is rather one-sided. This can be problematic if parents and the school have opposing views and values. As an ECT, you may find that not all parents are as supportive as you would hope.

A shared language concerning the nature of school is vital, and staff in primary schools have to be aware that this may not be the case for the majority of parents, so that schools have to take steps to ameliorate the feeling of failure, the feeling that education is of little or no value, and that school represents a legitimate target for verbal and physical abuse. It is vital that, if you are abused physically or verbally, your line manager, mentor or a senior teacher is informed immediately. It is against this background that your role as an ECT or trainee student teacher may sit. When you are appointed, you will need local knowledge of the school and an understanding of the issues that families may bring: domestic violence, child protection, alcohol and substance abuse, teenage pregnancies, joblessness and so on. Despite this, it is important to state that, you should not make assumptions about parents and families that are unfounded.

You will also need a working knowledge of agencies and training opportunities for parents. The role of any ECT in a whole-school context is that of supporting families and children. This is crucial in building and developing a shared vision, where the outcomes ensure that every day matters for every child, and where parents and staff are given the tools, knowledge and understanding to enable this.

Task 8.2.2 Managing pupil absence

How would you respond to the following?

- In your first term of teaching you note that Josh in your class is consistently absent from school and has missed more than 10% of lessons.
- When beginning the school year you are notified that Evie has struggled with anxiety since the pandemic and is now refusing to attend school. Her parents are unable to get her to leave the house.
- Isiah's parents withdraw him from school for a week early in June for a family holiday every year.

Discuss these with a fellow ECT or your school mentor or tutor and decide upon a clear, structured course of action. Consider how you would engage with the parents in each instance. What other stakeholders might need to be involved here?

Consider, in particular, how these issues can be dealt with in a measured and sensitive manner.

One of the most challenging, yet rewarding, aspects of being an ECT, after teaching and learning, is the relationship between yourself and parents. Research (Bastiani, 2003; Desforges and Abouchaar, 2003; Robinson, Bingle and Howard, 2016) shows that, where the partnership between home and school is supportive, with shared values and expectations, this contributes greatly to the outcomes for the child. In order for this to happen, there needs to be a good relationship between home and school that facilitates open and honest communication. This does not just mean 'talking' to parents when there are concerns about the pupil, but taking the time to celebrate the child's achievements on a day-to-day basis, so that, when the difficult conversations have to take place, they do so against a background of 'perceived fairness'. It is imperative, therefore, that all school policies are consistently adhered to by all staff. Such policies may include the following, which you should find and read:

- safeguarding policies;
- behaviour policy;
- SEND policy;
- teaching and learning policy;
- whole-school policy;

- assessment policy;
- emotional literacy policy;
- homework policy.

All policies should be followed with transparency, so that parents are kept informed about their children's behaviour and attainment at every stage.

All primary schools need to work hard to develop positive relationships with parents. This can be a challenge. It is, therefore, important that as part of the induction process or while on placement, you as an ECT or trainee teacher have the opportunity to sit in at both formal and informal parent discussions. This will provide you with an opportunity to observe how such a meeting is structured, to observe the body language and the language used by the teacher, and to see how any issues are resolved. It is suggested that, should an ECT need to have a 'difficult conversation' with a parent, they discuss it with their mentor or line manager first, in order to 'rehearse' the points, and that the mentor or line manager should also be at the meeting with the ECT, whether this is formal or informal. There should be some reflection following the meeting, to critically analyse your responses and set common agreements after such meetings.

If appropriate, it would be extremely useful for ECTs to attend any parents' coffee mornings (or similar activities) from time to time. This allows parents to get to know the ECT in a different setting and also provides ECTs with the opportunity to observe the other staff's relationships with parents. Experienced staff may know the parents very well and may well have information about the whole family that the ECT needs to be aware of, on a need-to-know basis, before seeing the parents. You should be careful of making generalisations or labelling parents unduly.

PARENTS' EVENINGS

Parents' evenings form part of a teacher's statutory duties (Department for Education and Skills [DfES], 2009) and are an important fixture of the school year. Many schools will operate a termly parents' evening, where parents are invited in to discuss their child's progress. It is also worth mentioning that parents' evenings may vary in their nature. Pastoral parents' evenings are often held at the start of the academic year to allow discussion around specific issues of transition and settling into a new class. These meetings may well be held with the acknowledgement that it is too early to discuss academic progress, and, as such, the discussion will centre on the happiness and disposition of the child and friendship groupings. It may also be an opportunity for the teacher to share information regarding the curriculum. As was mentioned previously, these early meetings are particularly useful as a means of building purposeful relationships.

Whilst traditionally parents' evenings are held as face-to-face meetings, the recent pandemic necessitated a move to online video calls. Furthermore, this has led to the emergence of commercial software programs, such as SchoolCloud, that can facilitate virtual parents' evenings for schools. Many schools, especially secondary schools, have retained these virtual meetings as they are seen as a more efficient means of meeting with parents and ensuring that evenings do not overrun (controversially, some software programs time out automatically after 5 minutes). Irrespective of the modality of the meeting, parents' evenings require careful planning to ensure success. Obviously, parents will expect to see their children's work marked effectively, with purposeful, formative comments if they are attending in person. Also, it will help to make a few notes about each child prior to the meeting and be prepared to make notes during the meeting, should the need arise. Often, parents may use the meeting to air particular concerns about their child that you may not be able to respond to immediately without some investigation (e.g. a bullying issue). In this case, it is important that you offer the parents a particular time to meet at a later stage, when you have more information at hand.

It is always worth opening the meeting by asking the parents whether they have any particular concerns that they wish to discuss. This will allow for an open and frank dialogue. You must also be mindful that parents themselves are useful sources of information, as the Cambridge Primary Review (Alexander, 2009) suggests: 'Teachers need to establish more fruitful links between home and school which build on the support for children's learning that already exists in the home and community'. This highlights the need for the partnership between teachers and parents to be a two-way process.

Remember that the purpose of the meeting with parents is to report on the child's progress, but it is also an opportunity to enhance pupil learning by empowering the parents with knowledge that will help them support their child. Therefore, you will need to communicate pupil targets clearly and make suggestions as to how these can be supported at home. As these meetings operate (for the most part) on scheduled appointments, it is necessary to keep an eye on the time – online systems can support this. It is inevitable that you will, on occasion, run over time, but, in the interests of all parents, it is important to keep an eye on the clock. If you find that a particular issue requires more time, you may have to arrange to meet at a later date.

Task 8.2.3 Parents' evenings

Case studies

1) During your first parents' evening as an ECT you find that one of your meetings has over-run by 5 minutes and you are aware that parents who are waiting are getting impatient. You have discussed the child's progress and how well they have settled into the new year, but their parents continue to ask questions about what the next term's topics will be. Consider how you can politely draw the meeting to a close using one of the following approaches – what are the advantages and disadvantages of each strategy?

1. Thank you for coming – we must end now so that I can talk to the next family.
2. Good to see you this evening, we must end now.
3. If you have any other queries, then please do send me an email – otherwise, regretfully, I must move on.
4. Time's up I'm afraid.
5. I think it would be helpful if we arranged a follow up meeting to continue our discussion as I am conscious of time. Please let me know your availability.

2) In preparation for parents' evening you have ensured that all of the children's work has been placed out on their desks for parents to look at. This is normal school practice, and you speak to parents individually at your desk at allocated times. While talking to a parent, you notice that another parent is looking at his daughter's work and is now comparing her work with other children on her table. He then proceeds to look at the work of other children in the class on different tables.

- How do you deal with this situation?
- How could this situation have been avoided?
- What will you do to avoid a similar situation in the future?

Discuss these with your mentor or tutor.

PARENTAL EXPERTISE

Another strategy to encourage closer relationships between parents and schools is to maximise on the expertise of parents and other members of the community. Contributions to the development of the curriculum by support from outside agencies and parents has become increasingly common over recent years. The willingness of parents to share their experiences with a group of children can provide a renewed vigour and inspiration to an existing unit or scheme of work. Parents who are, for example, nurses, postal workers, police officers, community artists, technicians or workers for the fire service may be willing to support schools to enhance learning. Parents with particular interests or hobbies, or who have visited places of interest, or who have lived in different countries, could also be involved by being invited to the class (or a small group of children, if the whole class is too daunting) as visiting speakers.

It is vital that, if you are going to use the suggestions mentioned, you arrange a meeting before any planned activities, in order to ensure that the work or talk that any visitor is going to lead is appropriate for the children in your class. You will also need to refer to the school's policy on Disclosure and Barring Service checks, to ensure that the correct protocols for adult visitors in class are followed. It is also important that follow-up work is planned for, and shared with, such parents, in order to celebrate the impact that their expertise may have had on a group of children. This work does not necessarily have to be in written form, thus encouraging all children to express their engagement with the visiting speakers.

Such an approach could ensure that you value as well as respect parents' contributions, and the children in your class will notice that you have a two-way relationship with parents.

Task 8.2.4 Using critical reflection to support positive teacher/parent relationships

There are many different models of reflective practise that are valuable to teaching practitioners (Brookfield, 1998; Gibbs, 1998; Kolb, 1984; Jasper, 2013). Ghaye (2011: 6) suggests that reflection can be categorised broadly in the following way:

Reflection *in* action whereby you respond in the moment; Reflection *on* action that occurs after the event; Reflection *for* action when you are planning for a specific purpose and Reflection *with* action whereby you consciously act, either alone or with others, after considering a range of possibilities.

Use Ghaye's categorisation to reflect on the following scenarios.

a   You are teaching a P.E. lesson in the school hall when a dinner supervisor asks you a question about their child. How would you respond in the moment?
b   At a parents' evening you notice that a parent repeatedly criticises their child in front of you – the child is visibly anxious. You also notice that Millie's parent, who you especially wanted to meet to discuss her anxiety, has failed to make their appointment. With a busy schedule you have little time to consider these issues. What would your reflections be once the evening finishes?
c   The next day you know you will be on home duty by the school gates and both parents may be present. How might you plan to informally start a conversation with them?
   - What might be the best course of action here for A, B and C? Consider discussing this your mentor or other supportive colleagues.

SUMMARY

In this unit, we have endeavoured to highlight the importance of purposeful, open and structured relationships with parents as a means of ensuring the best possible education for the children in school. At the heart of this is the acknowledgement that parents are partners in their children's education and, as such, are key educators themselves. The need to develop effective professional relationships is vital for all primary school teachers. We have suggested that there are many ways in which these partnerships can be developed and supported in school, and the tasks are a good starting point for this. We have established that, if links between parents and the school are strong, then children achieved more, both academically and in terms of behaviour. We have outlined that, when working with parents, you need to adopt a professional and understanding approach. It is our view that establishing strong home–school links is essential when it comes to ensuring that the individual potential of pupils is realised.

ANNOTATED FURTHER READING

PISA. (2012) *The Role of Families in Shaping Students' Engagement, Drive and Self-Beliefs*. Retrieved from: www.keepeek.com/Digital-Asset-Management/oecd/education/pisa-2012-results-ready-to-learn-volume-iii/the-role-of-families-m-shapmg-students-engagement-drive-and-self-beliefs_9789264201170-10-en#page1 (accessed 6 November 2017).

> This report from PISA 2012 provides a helpful insight into the impact that families have on pupils' engagement with their education. From considerations of the significance of the home environment, parental behaviour and involvement with their children's education, this report gives an overview of the relationship between educational achievement and parental expectation and support. It is helpful, in particular, to consider the key themes that emerge here from the data and the role that the school and teachers can play in promoting positive home–school relationships.

Hampden-Thompson, G. and Galindo, C. (2017) 'School-family relationships, school satisfaction and the academic achievement of young people', *Educational Review*, 69(2): 248-265.

> Drawing upon data from more than 10,000 students in England, this journal article examines the role of home–school relationships and the impact that these have on educational achievement. The data suggest, unsurprisingly, that positive school-family relationships are a 'predictor of achievement', but that the degree of parental satisfaction with the school has a significant role to play also. In particular, this highlights the importance of schools actively considering how they can enhance parental satisfaction in order to facilitate positive working relationships and increase educational achievement.

FURTHER READING TO SUPPORT M-LEVEL STUDY

Abdullah, A. G. K., Seedee, R., Alzaidiyeen, N. J., Al-Shabatat, A., Alzeydeen, H. K. and Al-Awabdeh, A. H. (2011) 'An investigation of teachers' attitudes towards parental involvement', *Educational Research*, 2(8): 1402-1408.

> This journal article discusses teachers' attitudes towards parents and their involvement in their children's education in Jordan, and whether individual teacher characteristics (such as age, qualifications and experience) have an impact upon these relationships. It will be useful for you to analyse the findings of the research and consider whether we might find parallels in England. What cultural differences might impact upon the teacher–parent relationship?

Selwyn, N., Banaji, S., Hadjithoma-Garstka, C. and Clark, W. (2011) 'Providing a platform for parents? Exploring the nature of parental engagement with school learning platforms', *Journal of Computer Assisted Learning*, 27(4): 314–323.

> This journal article considers how the utilisation of digital platforms can further support parental involvement in children's education. It will be useful for you to consider carefully just how such technologies might provide a support for parents. The report suggests that most learning technologies used for this purpose provide mostly 'one way traffic' from the school to the home. What might the barriers to engagement be? How might these be overcome?

RELEVANT WEBSITES

Department for Education: www.education.gov.uk
> Type 'parent support advisers' into the search box and follow the links.

Department for Education Teaching Agency: www.education.gov.uk/get-into-teaching
> This merged with the National College for School Leadership from 1 April 2013.

REFERENCES

Addi-Raccah, A. and Ainhoren, R. (2009) 'School governance and teachers' attitudes to parents' involvement in schools', *Teaching & Teacher Education*, 25(6): 805–813.

Alexander, R. (ed.) (2009) *Children, Their World, Their Education: Final Report and Recommendations of the Cambridge Primary Review*, London: Routledge.

Barnard, W. (2004) 'Parent involvement in elementary school and educational attainment', *Children & Youth Service Review*, 26(1): 39–62.

Bastiani, J. (2003) *Materials for Schools: Involving Parents, Raising Achievement*, London: DfES.

Bourdieu, P. (1986) 'The forms of capital', in J. G. Richardson (ed.) *Handbook of Theory and Research for the Sociology of Education*, Santa Barbara, CA: Greenwood Press, pp. 241–258.

Brookfield, S. (1998) 'Critically reflective practice', *Journal of Continuing Education in the Health Professions*, 18(4): 197–205. DOI: 10.1002/chp.1340180402

Carroll, J. and Alexander, G. (2016) *The Teachers' Standards in Primary Schools*, London: Sage.

Charlton, T. and David, K. (1993) *Managing Misbehaviour in Schools*, New York: Routledge.

Cooper, K. and Olson, M. (1996) 'The multiple "I's" of teacher identity', in M. Kompf, T. Boak, W. R. Bond and D. Dworet (eds) *Changing Research and Practice: Teachers' Professionalism, Identities and Knowledge*, London: Falmer Press, pp. 78–89.

Corsaro, W. and Fingerson, L. (2006) 'Development and socialisation in childhood', in J. DeLamter, *Handbook of Social Psychology*, New York: Kluwer Academic/Plenum, pp. 125–155.

Department for Children, Schools and Families (DCSF). (2008) *The Impact of Parental Involvement in Children's Education*, Nottingham, UK: DCSF.

Department for Education (DfE). (2011) *Teachers' Standards*. Last updated 2021. Retrieved from: www.gov.uk/government/publications/teachers-standards

Department for Education (DfE). (2019) *Initial Teacher Training (ITT): Core Content Framework*. Last updated 2024. Retrieved from: www.gov.uk/government/publications/initial-teacher-training-itt-core-content-framework

Department for Education and Skills (DfES). (2009) *School Teachers' Pay and Conditions Document 2009*, London: DfES.

Department of Education and Science (DES). (1967) *Children and Their Primary Schools (Plowden Report)*, London: HMSO.

Desforges, C. and Abouchaar, A. (2003) *The Impact of Parental Involvement, Parental Support and Family Education on Pupil Achievement and Adjustment: A Literature Review* (Research Report RR433), London: DfES.

Education Act (2011). Retrieved from: www.legislation.gov.uk/ukpga/2011/21/contents

Education Reform Act (1988). Retrieved from: www.legislation.gov.uk/ukpga/1988/40/contents

Education (Schools) Act (1992). Retrieved from: www.legislation.gov.uk/ukpga/1992/38/contents

Edwards, A. and Warin, J. (1999) 'Parental involvement in raising the achievement of primary school pupils: Why bother?', *Oxford Review of Education*, 25(3): 325–341.

Elton, R. (1989) *Discipline in Schools*, London: HM Stationery Office.

Feiler, A. (2010) *Engaging 'Hard to Reach' Parents Teacher-Parent Collaboration to promote Children's Learning*, Chichester: Wiley-Blackwell.

Ghaye, T. (2011) *Teaching and Learning Through Reflective Practice: A Practical Guide for Positive Action*, London: Routledge.

Gibbs, G. (1998) *Learning by Doing: A Guide to Teaching and Learning Methods*, Oxford: Further Education Unit, Oxford Polytechic.

Gov.uk (2023a) *Guidance Toolkit for Schools: Communicating With Families to Support Attendance*. Retrieved from: www.gov.uk/government/publications/working-together-to-improve-school-attendance/toolkit-for-schools-communicating-with-families-to-support-attendance (accessed 28 December 2023).

Gov.uk (2023b) *Autumn and Spring Term 2022/23: Pupil Absence in Schools in England*. Retrieved from: https://explore-education-statistics.service.gov.uk/find-statistics/pupil-absence-in-schools-in-england (accessed 28 December 2023).

Hadow, W. H. (1931) *Report of the Consultative Committee on The Primary School*, London: HM Stationery Office.

Hart, B. and Risley, T. (1995) *Meaningful Differences in the Everyday Experience of Young American Children*, Baltimore, MD: Paul H. Brookes.

Jasper, M. (2013) *Beginning Reflective Practice*, Andover: Cengage Learning.

Kolb, D. (1984) *Experiential Learning: Experience as the Source of Learning and Development*, Upper Saddle River: Prentice Hall.

Lee, J. S. and Bowen, N. K. (2006) 'Parent involvement, cultural capital, and the achievement gap among elementary school children', *American Educational Research Journal*, 43(2): 193–218. Retrieved from: www.jstor.org/stable/3699418

Leenders, H., de Jong, J., Monfrance, M. and Haelermans, C. (2019) 'Building strong parent–teacher relationships in primary education: The challenge of two-way communication', *Cambridge Journal of Education*, 49(4).

Lewis, K., Chamberlain, T., Riggall, A., Gagg, K. and Rudd, P. (2007) *How Are Schools Involving Parents in School Life? Annual Survey of Trends in Education 2007: Schools' Concerns and their Implications for Local Authorities (LGA Research Report 4/07)*, Slough, UK: NFER.

Miller, W. R. and Rollnick, S. (2002) *Motivational Interviewing: Preparing People for Change*, 2nd edn, New York: Guilford Press.

OECD. (2012) *Parental Involvement in Selected PISA Countries and Economies*, OECD Education Working Paper no. 73. Retrieved from: www.oecd.org/officialdocuments/publicdisplaydocumentpdf/?cote=EDU/WKP(2012)10&docLanguage=En (accessed 19 December 2023).

OECD. (2018) *Insights and Interpretations*. Retrieved from: www.oecd.org/pisa/PISA%202018%20Insights%20and%20Interpretations%20FINAL%20PDF.pdf (accessed 19 December 2023).

OECD. (2022) *PISA 2022 Results: The State of Learning and Equity in Education*. Retrieved from: https://read.oecd-ilibrary.org/view/?ref=1235_1235421-gumq51fbgo&title=PISA-2022-Results-Volume-I (accessed 19 December 2023).

OECD (2024) *PISA 2022 Results (Volume V): Learning Strategies and Attitudes for Life*, PISA, Paris: OECD Publishing. Retrieved from: https://doi.org/10.1787/c2e44201-en

Ofsted. (2011) *Schools and Parents*. Retrieved from: www.gov.uk/government/uploads/system/uploads/attachment_data/file/413696/Schools_and_parents.pdf (accessed 6 November 2017).

Ofsted. (2023) *Guidance: Education Inspection Framework*. Retrieved from: www.gov.uk/government/publications/education-inspection-framework/education-inspection-framework-for-september-2023 (accessed 22 December 2023).

O'Hara, M. (2008) *Teaching 3-8 (Reaching the Standard)*, 3rd edn, London: Continuum.

Robinson, C., Bingle, B. and Howard, C. (2016) *Surviving & Thriving as a Primary NQT*, Northwich, UK: Critical Publishing.

Rogers, B. (2000) *Behaviour Management: A Whole-School Approach*, Thousand Oaks, CA: Sage.

Selwyn, N. (2011a) *Education and Technology: Key Issues and Debates*, London: Continuum.

Selwyn, N. (2011b) *Schools and Schooling in the Digital Age: A Critical Perspective*, London: Routledge.

Selwyn, N., Banaji, S., Hadjithoma-Garstka, C. and Clark, W. (2011) 'Providing a platform for parents? Exploring the nature of parental engagement with school learning platforms', *Journal of Computer Assisted Learning*, 27: 314-323.

Steer, A. (2005) *Learning Behaviour: The Report of the Practitioners' Group on School Behaviour and Discipline*, Nottingham, UK: DfES.

Tan, C. Y., Lyu, M. and Peng, B. (2020) 'Academic benefits from parental involvement are stratified by parental socioeconomic status: A meta-analysis', *Parenting: Science and Practice*, 20(4): 241-287.

UNIT 8.3

UNDERSTANDING THE TEACHER'S PASTORAL ROLE

Helen Childerhouse

INTRODUCTION

> A child centred approach to safeguarding … is fundamental to safeguarding and promoting the welfare of every child. A child centred approach means keeping the child in focus when making decisions about their lives and working in partnership with them and their families.
>
> (HM Government, 2018: 9)

This unit explores the pastoral role of the teacher. It recognises the important links between a child's social and emotional well-being and their academic progress. As a teacher, you will need to be aware of the challenges some children face and how this can have an impact on how well they can access the teaching and learning in school. By developing an understanding of these challenges, you will be able to shape your teaching approaches and strategies. *Working Together to Safeguard Children* identifies children's perspectives of what they need: 'vigilance … understanding and action … stability … respect … information and engagement … explanation … support … advocacy … protection' (HM Government, 2018: 10). These aspects provide practitioners with insights into what children regard as important to them, and can be used to shape effective practice.

The current focus of the Primary National Curriculum (Department for Education [DfE], 2013), in particular, is subject-specific. This knowledge-based curriculum provides a breadth of opportunities for children to develop their skills and understanding. However, the pastoral element of learning, which promotes well-being and personal development, is not as explicit as curricular guidance. In this unit, you will be able to reflect on what you can do to incorporate experiences for children that address areas such as safeguarding and emotional and social well-being. An overview of expectations of, and guidance for, teachers identified in legislation will be discussed. Case studies will be used to demonstrate how personal issues can impact on a child's school life and what the teacher needs to consider, and do, to support the child through challenging circumstances.

OBJECTIVES

By the end of this unit, you will:

- understand how children's personal, social and emotional needs can have an impact on their learning;
- understand the legal framework associated with pastoral provision in schools;
- begin to identify the strategies and practices for developing pastoral provision in your teaching.

WHAT IS THE TEACHER'S PASTORAL ROLE, AND WHY IS IT IMPORTANT FOR EFFECTIVE TEACHING?

Throughout the school year, the teacher builds a good rapport with the children in the class. They will come to learn about the children's likes, dislikes, preferred ways of learning and their home lives. They recognise when children are happy, healthy, enthusiastic and engaged in their learning. They must also be able to spot any changes to their usual ways of behaving and demeanours. Through noticing these changes, such as a child becoming quiet, withdrawn, unusually emotional or exhibiting excessive and challenging behaviours, the teacher can be alerted to possible problems and the need for them to intervene to find out what is wrong.

The pastoral needs of children may arise from relationships with other children in the class or school, events at home, or social and emotional issues, and/or may be related to special educational needs or disability. Some children may become involved with bullying, or be affected by problems faced within the family, such as poverty, illness or domestic violence. Pastoral needs may also arise following events that occur during the school day, and these may lead to more serious concerns if a child is at risk owing to their general health and well-being or because of relationships with others, adults or children. By having a good understanding of the children in your class, you will be an important adult in their lives who can ensure that they receive any support they need.

TRANSITION THROUGH SCHOOL

Typical times in school when children can find it difficult and may need more reassurance and support can be during periods of transition (O'Connor, 2017). Moving into a new class or new school can be daunting for some children, and one aspect of your role is to ensure that children are well prepared for moving out of, or into, your class. This can be achieved by good preparation and information-sharing about what to expect; you will need to be available to address any questions or concerns the children may have. Similarly, children can become worried or feel uncomfortable during the school day, when in transition between different lessons or at break times. It may be helpful to introduce a visual timetable in your class; examples of these, together with tools for creating your own, can be found in the relevant websites section. This will help children to know what is happening at each point in the day and can enable them to prepare for what is to happen next. You need to be aware that, for some children, lunchtimes or break times can be difficult, and you can support them by ensuring they can seek peer support to help them feel more socially and emotionally confident during these times. One way of implementing peer support is to establish a 'buddy system' in your class (Tzani-Pepelasi et al., 2019). It is useful for the children to be able to identify another child who they can approach at break times when they are feeling lonely or nervous or simply need someone to be with.

LOOKED-AFTER CHILDREN

There may be children in your school who are regarded as 'looked after', whereby they are currently living with a new family, owing to foster care or adoption. These children will have been allocated a professional from a social services team who has a responsibility for 'looked-after children'. There will also be a member of staff in the school who oversees the provision for these children. If you have a 'looked-after child' in your class, you will be expected to liaise with these people to ensure that the child is receiving the necessary support. You need to be aware of any issues the child may be experiencing to ensure you are sensitive in your expectations of them. An example of this could be in setting homework or when reading particular stories. It might be difficult for a child to read or write about relationships with their parents if they have recently been moved into foster care, or if they have experienced difficult relationships in the home. Many children who have moved into foster homes may have to travel into school by taxi, and so it helps to be aware that their arrival and departure from school will be shaped by this. This might prevent them from taking part in after-school activities and from building out-of-school friendships with their peers. You could address this by helping them to establish a group of friends to be with during the day.

> **Task 8.3.1 How do you know if the children in your class are happy?**
>
> Drawing on your experience of working with children in schools, consider the social and emotional needs of the children:
>
> - How do you know if the children are happy, confident and able to learn?
> - How might children behave if they do not feel happy and confident?
> - Can you identify possible reasons for why children's social and emotional well-being may be affected?

THE DEVELOPMENT OF UK POLICY IN RELATION TO PASTORAL PROVISION IN SCHOOLS

Every teacher must be aware of the legislation and policy that have been implemented to ensure children are safe, happy and well. The Teachers' Standards (DfE, 2011: 11-14) make it clear that teachers must:

- have a secure understanding of how a range of factors can inhibit pupils' ability to learn, and how best to overcome these;
- demonstrate an awareness of the physical, social and intellectual development of children;
- safeguard pupils' well-being.

Every teacher must take responsibility for identifying any child whose welfare and personal development are affected or at risk. The non-statutory guidance in the Personal, Social, Health and Economic section of the *National Curriculum* (DfE, 2021) identifies the importance of 'drug education, financial education, sex and relationship education (SRE) and the importance of physical activity and diet for a healthy lifestyle'. These elements will be incorporated into teaching and planning and are usually delivered alongside other curriculum subjects and lessons. However, it is important that the teacher also considers the broader holistic elements of welfare and well-being.

> **In Wales ...**
>
> In the 'Health and Well-being' area of the Curriculum for Wales, it is stated that:
>
> > The Health and Well-being Area of Learning and Experience provides a holistic structure for understanding health and well-being. It is concerned with developing the capacity of learners to navigate life's opportunities and challenges. The fundamental components of this Area are physical health and development, mental health, and emotional and social well-being.
> >
> > (Education Wales, 2020)

In Northern Ireland …

Public awareness of matters relating to safeguarding and child protection continues to grow, as the whole context rapidly expands due to changes in society and, particularly, new technology. Recent safeguarding and child protection cases have highlighted the need for everyone to take responsibility for protecting children as well as the necessity for those in key positions to have a clear understanding of their role in adhering to policies and procedures.

Safeguarding is more than child protection. Safeguarding begins with preventative education and activities which enable children and young people to grow up safely and securely in circumstances where their development and well being is promoted. It includes support to families and early intervention to meet the needs of children and continues through to child protection, which refers specifically to the activity that is undertaken to protect individual children or young people who are suffering, or likely to suffer harm.

(DENI, 2017, Section 1.1)

SAFEGUARDING

Ensuring that children are safe from harm is one of the most important elements of your role. Table 8.3.1 shows the key government legislation that has been issued to ensure all teachers know and understand the role they play. The expectations outlined within it identify how children could be vulnerable and how teachers must respond in order to address concerns.

TABLE 8.3.1 Key legislation and documentation for safeguarding in schools

Document	Key points
Children and Families Act (HM Government, 2014)	This legislation focuses on adoption, special educational needs and disabilities, child care in the early years, and statutory rights for parents and carers. It identifies the support and guidance that parents and carers are entitled to from education, health and social services.
Special Educational Needs and Disability Code of Practice (DfE and DoH, 2015)	This document outlines the education, care and support that 0–25-year-olds identified with special educational needs and disabilities are entitled to. It addresses areas including identification of needs, barriers to learning, working together with parents, carers and other professionals, and the statutory assessment process.
Supporting the Attainment of Disadvantaged Pupils (DfE, 2015)	This research report commissioned by the government describes the practices and strategies that schools use to improve pupil achievement and outlines the barriers that teachers describe when working with children and young people who are considered to be disadvantaged. The report identifies pupils from ethnic minority groups, those who have special educational needs and disabilities, those who live in socially and economically impoverished environments and those who have low levels of school attendance as being vulnerable or disadvantaged.

(Continued)

TABLE 8.3.1 (Continued)

Document	Key points
Working Together to Safeguard Children (HM Government, 2018)	This statutory guidance identifies the need for safeguarding children and young people. It describes the role and support available from the Local Safeguarding Children Boards and calls for effective multi-agency working of professionals involved in education, health and social services, and also those working within the police and housing services.
Keeping Children Safe in Education (DfE, 2023a)	This provides specific guidance for schools in terms of safeguarding and specifies the duties of staff in relation to recruitment, management of safeguarding strategy and policy, how to deal with allegations and the role of the 'safeguarding lead' member of staff.
The Prevent Duty (DfE, 2023b)	This non-statutory guidance outlines the possible risks that children in schools may face in relation to terrorism and radicalisation. Further information and discussion regarding safeguarding can be found in Unit 1.2.

Your immediate responsibility is to ensure that you know which member of staff to refer to if you have any concerns. You must read and understand the school's safeguarding and child-protection policies as soon as you begin working in any school, and it is your duty to liaise with this member of staff if there is anything you do not understand.

Although instances of abuse and risk are thankfully rare, you may find that a child in your class confides in you. Children who are living in difficult circumstances and who have not developed supportive relationships with their parents may see you as being the reliable, constant and trustworthy adult in their lives. They may choose to share their questions, personal thoughts and worries with you, and, as their advocate, you will be expected to share such confidences with the colleague in school responsible for safeguarding.

In Wales …

The role of the adult is integral to all learners' progress, but is particularly significant in this period of learning. It is the enabling adult who sets the expectation for learning by creating emotionally safe environments that support learners to begin to express and regulate their feelings and behaviours in positive ways. They are consistent in their care, and model compassion and kindness. They support learners to cope with uncertainty and change, preparing them to manage transitions and changes in daily routines.

Enabling adults create an environment that is communication rich, modelling multiple ways of expression. They support learners' understanding through skilful interactions, expanding on learners' existing knowledge to support and encourage them in making connections with people, places and things. They model appropriate use of context-specific language and concepts.

It is essential for enabling adults to support learners' skills development through varied experiences and opportunities. It is the role of the practitioner to recognise

> opportunities to make the most of cross-curricular connections that draw on learners' previous knowledge and experiences. They maintain quality of provision, and adapt their plans to meet the needs and interests of all learners.
>
> (Welsh Government, 2023)
>
> Safeguarding is about protecting children and adults from abuse or neglect and educating those around them to recognise the signs and dangers. The Social Services and Well-being (Wales) Act introduces a strengthened, robust and effective partnership approach to safeguarding. One of the most important principles of safeguarding is that it is everyone's responsibility. Each professional and organisation must do everything they can, to ensure that children and adults at risk are protected from abuse.
>
> (Welsh Government, n.d.)

E-SAFETY

Access to the Internet during lessons in schools is a common element of teaching. Teachers use digital media to support their teaching, and children are increasingly familiar with using computers and mobile phones to support their learning. Guidance such as *Keeping Children Safe in Education* (DfE, 2023a) has been issued; it recognises that children may be at risk when accessing the Internet owing to the availability of websites that provide content purely for adults. The school will have a policy outlining how they prevent children from accessing such sites, and you are responsible for ensuring these are followed in your class.

Issues such as cyber-bullying, which Lechner, Crăciun and Scheithauer (2023) describe as 'hostile communication via messaging' (p.1), and the grooming of children through social network sites may put children at risk. Even though there are age restrictions for some social network sites, it is possible for children to claim they are older than they are, or to access them anyway. The more knowledge and understanding a teacher has about the possible risks, the more they can put measures into place to avoid children using such websites. You may find *The Internet and Today's Children* (Perkel, 2022) a useful text for raising your awareness of the concerns and for identifying strategies that you could put into place, such as working with parents to monitor, advise and support children as they use social networking. The National Society for the Prevention of Cruelty to Children (NSPCC, 2023) also provides up to date guidance and advice for keeping children safe online.

ATTENDANCE

Children's attendance at school also relates to the teacher's pastoral role. *Working Together to Improve School Attendance* (DfE, 2022) provides guidance for schools and school governing bodies. This provides the statutory expectations for attendance at schools and outlines the measures schools can take to ensure that children do not miss their education. The document states that teachers must take two registers during the day, one in the morning and one in the afternoon. This information is included in the school's census, which is collated by the Department for Education. You must ensure that you understand your role for registering pupils. In addition, if you have any concerns regarding a child's attendance, then it is your duty to bring this information to the member of staff responsible. Continued absences may indicate that the child is unwell or failing to attend owing to problems inside or outside school, and if you share this information, the situation can be investigated.

Task 8.3.2 Safeguarding children: Your role

Ensure you are aware of the legislative documentation regarding safeguarding children in schools.

- Reflect on the Teachers' Standards (2011), which outline your responsibilities. Make a list of specific activities and tasks that you can put into practice to help you to meet the expectations.
- Read the *Working Together to Safeguard Children* document (HM Government, 2018). What are your role and responsibilities as a teacher in relation to each of the sections?
- Read the school's e-safety policy. What role do you play in implementing this policy? How can you ensure that the strategies you put into place meet the policy requirements?

SCENARIO 1[1]

Molly, a 10-year-old who is in your Year 5 class, is normally happy and cheerful and eager to take part in the lessons. She arrives one morning looking tired and refuses to answer the register. She does not want to work with the other children in her group, and you see that she is standing by herself in the playground and refusing to play with the others when asked. During a lesson, another child comes over to you and says that Molly is crying. You go over and ask her if she is all right, but she wipes her eyes and says that she is fine and that she has something in her eye. Later in the day, the same thing happens, but again Molly says she is fine. Molly is usually met at the school gate by her mum, a single parent with three other, younger children in the school. You look out for her at home time so that you can check everything is OK, but a neighbour collects Molly and her siblings on that day. The following day, Molly arrives late. She is not in uniform and has not brought her lunch box with her. When you ask her what she is going to eat for lunch, she cries. Molly settles down after you reassure her that she can have a school lunch. For the rest of the day, she remains quiet and withdrawn but rebuffs your efforts to talk. That afternoon, you receive a phone call from Molly's aunt, her mum's sister, who informs you that mum has been diagnosed with an aggressive form of breast cancer. She explains that Molly knows her mum is poorly, but does not know why or that the diagnosis is that she is terminally ill. Over the next few days, Molly's work deteriorates, she is often late and goes into the playground for the younger children to find her younger siblings each day. During the register on the Friday afternoon, Molly blurts out in front of the class that her mum is dying.

Task 8.3.3 Identifying approaches to support specific needs in Scenario 1

- Reflect how Molly's situation will impact on her social, emotional, physical and academic well-being. Make a list of these possible impacts and consider her immediate needs.
- Consider who you need to liaise with in school to make sure everyone who needs to know is aware of the situation.
- You know that Molly's outburst has upset some of the other children. What can you do to support them?

In this scenario, Molly's teacher identified her needs, and support was put into place to help her through the school day. She was allocated a teaching assistant (TA) who met her and her siblings at the school gate each morning, and she and the TA took each child to their classrooms and ensured they were settled. The teachers were kept informed of events regarding the mother's health and the children's experiences at home. The member of staff responsible for safeguarding was notified, and additional support focusing on the children's social and emotional needs was put into place. Each of the children was provided with tea and toast during the morning registration period, and they sat together with the TA so they could talk about their concerns if they needed to. A meeting with mum's sister was arranged, and she was appointed as the point of contact with the school. As Molly's mum became more ill, the social services support team was notified, and a multi-agency team (Cheminais, 2009), including the teacher for safeguarding, worked together to support the family. Molly's teacher ensured that she was provided with a buddy during the school day; she maintained consistency in her teaching and expectations to ensure that there were no additional changes to her life; she was sensitive to her emotional needs; and established a set time during each day when she and Molly could talk, if Molly wanted to. In addition to this, her teacher provided a time for the rest of the class to share their concerns and ask any questions they had. This was arranged with the permission of Molly, her mum and her aunt, and was done while Molly was out of the classroom.

SCENARIO 2

You are preparing your classroom one morning when the Head teacher arrives with a very distressed and bewildered 6-year-old child and his father. They arrived in the country four days earlier following a traumatic journey and are seeking asylum due to their refugee status as a result of living in their country, which is at war. The child, Hamza, will be joining your class. He does not speak English and his father explains that Hamza's mother and two sisters are still in their home country but he hopes to bring them over as soon as he and his son are settled. They are living in temporary accommodation near the school, but hope to move into somewhere more permanent in the next few months. They are receiving support from a refugee charity and the local council. Hamza's father explains that his son is a good student who got high marks in his previous school, and that he wants him to gain stability and continue with his studies. He also says that there is another child in their accommodation who is in the same class as Hamza and that he hopes they can become friends. The child is crying and becomes even more upset when his father tells him in Kurdish that he must leave him at school so that he can go to work, but that he will see him at the end of the school day.

Task 8.3.4 Identifying approaches to support specific needs in Scenario 2

- Write down the situation as you see it from Hamza's perspective. What do you think Hamza's main concerns are?
- As you see it from your perspective as a teacher, what do you feel are the main concerns and challenges you would face in teaching Hamza? What do you think Hamza's short-term and medium-term needs are?
- Who do you think you could talk to, and work with, to help you ensure Hamza settles into your class effectively?

In this scenario, the class teacher worked closely with the member of staff responsible for supporting children with English as an Additional Language (EAL) to identify ways of communicating with Hamza in the early days when his knowledge and use of English was minimal. This meant that Hamza could communicate his needs and understanding without the frustrations of not being able to make himself understood. The class teacher arranged for Hamza to sit with the other child from his accommodation so that he had a buddy who understood his experiences, language and social and emotional challenges. The child would stay with Hamza throughout the day, translate when necessary, explain the structure of the school day and explain the food they were eating during lunchtime – most of which was new to Hamza. The Head teacher arranged for a TA to welcome and work with Hamza each morning to help ensure a settled start to each day. A member of staff from the charity supporting refugee families visited the class teacher and Hamza. They explained some of the challenges and experiences familiar to Hamza and his family and talked about how particular times or events during the school day might be difficult for Hamza, such as home time when Hamza would see the other children being greeted by their mothers, listening to other children talking about family events or the lack of material possessions, particularly toys and clothes. Regular 'Team Around the Child' meetings (Siraj-Blatchford, Clarke and Needham, 2007) were arranged so that all those involved in supporting Hamza and his father could talk about ongoing needs and concerns and a support plan was put in place. Hamza began to settle into his school life and as his knowledge and use of the English language developed, he soon began to show his very impressive mathematics and science skills.

STRATEGIES TO SUPPORT THE TEACHER'S PASTORAL ROLE

From your own experiences and the examples in each scenario, you can see how helpful it can be to provide a holistic response to ensure that the whole child – physical, language, social, emotional and academic – can develop and make progress. There are practices you can implement to enhance the pastoral provision in your class. Creating a safe and stimulating learning environment will provide a feeling of security for the children. You will need to establish good relationships with children, so that they feel confident that you are going to listen carefully to what they tell you and are more likely to regard you as approachable.

You will also need to set up a system to record and monitor the welfare and needs of the children in your class. Most schools encourage teachers to use a journal or electronic recording system such as the Child Protection Online Monitoring System (CPOMS) to record issues or concerns. The entries in a journal could identify when a child is late, if they share any worries with you, ask you unusual questions or if they appear unkempt, hungry or upset. Individual entries in the journal that record that the child has arrived at school without having breakfast may not seem serious on one occasion, but when this is recorded many times over weeks or months, the teacher can recognise a pattern that may indicate concern about care and well-being.

WHOLE-SCHOOL STRATEGIES TO SUPPORT THE TEACHER'S PASTORAL ROLE

There are a range of strategies that many schools use to support teachers with their pastoral role. Table 8.3.2 lists some of the additional support that schools often provide. It provides information about their aims and purposes and gives websites that you may want to access to find out more about them.

TABLE 8.3.2 School strategies for supporting your pastoral role

Provision	Aims and purpose	Additional information
Circle Time	Circle Time is used in many schools. It gives children the opportunities to talk and be heard. Children share their thoughts and ideas about a specific focus and can choose to contribute or not. This gives the class teacher an opportunity to address concerns and to identify any children they feel may need further support at another time	Circle Time, devised by Jenny Mosely, has a designated website for further information. It provides guidance, training and ideas for use in schools: www.circle-time.co.uk/
Lunchtime or after-school groups	For all children, or for those identified as needing social support at particular times during the day. Examples include Lego, science, books, games or craft clubs	
Small-group or one-to-one support groups	To provide support for children identified as having difficulties in their classrooms. This may include behavioural, social or emotional needs. These are often provided by TAs or specialist support staff	
Diary entries or video rooms and suggestion or worry boxes	Accessible to all children. They can leave comments, notes or small videos to inform staff of their concerns. The messages are confidential	
Nurture groups	Identifies the importance for children to experience effective attachments, good communication and a safe place during their early years. Nurture groups are designed to address possible developmental 'gaps' due to poor experiences in early childhood. First established by Boxall in the 1960s (Boxall and Lucas, 2010). Children with social and emotional difficulties are usually recommended by their teachers for inclusion in the nurture group	Nurture Group Network provides further information and training: www.nurtureuk.org/

SUMMARY

In this unit, the teacher's pastoral role has been considered on two levels: generic daily practice and responses to specific children's needs. Strategies and suggestions have been provided that can be used by all teachers in their classrooms. The importance of a safe and stimulating learning environment has also been discussed; a teacher with an effective pastoral provision will establish an ethos in which children feel comfortable and confident to share their views, and in which they know that they will be listened to. Specific examples of times when additional pastoral support may be needed have also been provided in order to emphasise the importance of providing safeguarding and ensuring the well-being of children experiencing difficult circumstances or relationships. Every teacher has a duty to know how children could be at risk and how they must respond to the concerns they have.

By ensuring that you know every child in the class, you can be confident that your pastoral teaching will be enhanced. Your planning and teaching will be more personalised and responsive because of the knowledge you have of each child. This will mean that you can include their social and emotional needs, which will have a positive impact on their holistic development.

NOTE

1   The author would like to thank Sean Woolley for the scenario and his general contribution to this unit.

ANNOTATED FURTHER READING

Goepel, J., Sharpe, S. and Childerhouse, H. (2015) *Inclusive Primary Teaching*, 2nd edn, Northwich, UK: Critical Publishing.

> This text is written for trainee and early career teachers and focuses on special educational needs and disability. However, it identifies good practice for supporting all learners, and many of the scenarios and suggestions are applicable to the teacher developing a pastoral role. The chapters 'Understanding learners who are vulnerable' and 'Working with children' are particularly useful and relevant.

Dowling, M. (2010) *Young Children's Personal, Social and Emotional Development*, 3rd edn, London: Sage.

> Although this book is written with learners in the early years in mind, it is useful for providing an in-depth understanding of the holistic needs of children. By developing knowledge about their social, emotional, physical and cognitive growth and skills, the teacher will have a sound understanding of how this can impact on their long-term well-being.

FURTHER READING TO SUPPORT M-LEVEL STUDY

Clark, A. and Moss, P. (2011) *Listening to Young Children: The Mosaic Approach*, 2nd edn, London: NCB.

> The focus of this text is research with children. At M-level study, you may choose to develop your knowledge of the views and feelings of the children in your class so that you can enhance pastoral provision. The authors provide guidance and suggestions for how you can give children a 'voice' that can inform your understanding and improve your practice.

Howard, C., Burton, M. and Levermore, D. (2019) *Children's Mental Health and Emotional Well-being in Primary Schools: A Whole School Approach*, 2nd edn, Exeter, UK: Learning Matters.

> This text provides valuable insights and points for consideration for teachers supporting learners in primary schools; it identifies ways to build good mental health for all children and also intervention strategies for those who need additional support. The reflective practice activities will enable you to reflect on your experiences of teaching and learning in schools and consider your and your colleagues' provision. Do you consider academic and mental health and well-being teaching to be different aspects of your role? How do you feel you can develop a balance between the two?

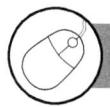

RELEVANT WEBSITES

National Association for the Pastoral Care of Education: www.napce.org.uk/
    This is an excellent website that provides guidance and suggestions relating to many issues, such as bullying, peer counselling, relationships and vulnerability.

EU Kids Online: www.lse.ac.uk/media-and-communications/research/research-projects/eu-kids-online/eu-kids-online-2020
    Provides guidance, research findings and recommendations for policy with regards to children's use of the Internet.

NSPCC: www.nspcc.org.uk/services-and-resources/working-with-schools/
    The NSPCC provides guidance and resources for schools to help teachers provide support for children who may need pastoral support or who may be considered vulnerable.

Looked-after Children: www.gov.uk/topic/schools-colleges-childrens-services/looked-after-children
    This government website provides further information and guidance regarding the care and education of 'looked-after children'.

Twinkl: www.twinkl.co.uk/resources/visual-timetable
    Visual timetable.

REFERENCES

Boxall, M. and Lucas, S. (2010) *Nurture Groups in Schools: Principles and Practice*, 2nd edn, London: Sage.

Cheminais, R. (2009) *Effective Multi-Agency Partnerships: Putting Every Child Matters into Practice*, London: Sage.

Department for Education (DfE). (2011) *Teachers' Standards*. Last updated 2021. Retrieved from: https://assets.publishing.service.gov.uk/media/61b73d6c8fa8f50384489c9a/Teachers__Standards_Dec_2021.pdf (accessed 18 November 2023).

Department for Education (DfE). (2013) *National Curriculum*. Updated 2014. Retrieved from: www.gov.uk/government/publications/national-curriculum-in-england-framework-for-key-stages-1-to-4/the-national-curriculum-in-england-framework-for-key-stages-1-to-4 (accessed 18 November 2023).

Department for Education (DfE). (2015) *Supporting the Attainment of Disadvantaged Pupils*. Retrieved from: www.gov.uk/government/uploads/system/uploads/attachment_data/file/473974/DFE-RR411_Supporting_the_attainment_of_disadvantaged_pupils.pdf (accessed 18 November 2023).

Department for Education (DfE). (2021) *Personal, Social, Health and Economic Education*. Retrieved from: www.gov.uk/government/publications/personal-social-health-and-economic-education-pshe/personal-social-health-and-economic-pshe-education (accessed 18 November 2023).

Department for Education (DfE). (2022) *Working Together to Improve School Attendance*. Retrieved from: https://assets.publishing.service.gov.uk/government/uploads/system/uploads/attachment_data/file/1099677/Working_together_to_improve_school_attendance.pdf (accessed 18 November 2023).

Department for Education (DfE). (2023a) *Keeping Children Safe in Education*. Retrieved from: https://assets.publishing.service.gov.uk/government/uploads/system/uploads/attachment_data/file/1181955/Keeping_children_safe_in_education_2023.pdf (accessed 18 November 2023).

Department for Education (DfE). (2023b) *The Prevent Duty*. Retrieved from: www.gov.uk/government/publications/the-prevent-duty-safeguarding-learners-vulnerable-to-radicalisation/the-prevent-duty-an-introduction-for-those-with-safeguarding-responsibilities (accessed 18 November 2023).

Department for Education (DfE) and Department of Health (DoH). (2015) *Special Educational Needs and Disability: Code of Practice 0 to 25 Years*. Retrieved from: www.gov.uk/government/uploads/system/uploads/attachment_data/file/398815/SEND_Code_of_Practice_January_2015.pdf (accessed 18 November 2023).

Department of Education for Northern Ireland (DENI). (2017) *Safeguarding and Child Protection in Schools: A guide for Schools*, Belfast: DENI. Retrieved from https://www.eani.org.uk/publications/safeguarding-and-child-protection/pastoral-care-in-schools-child-protection (accessed 18 November 2023).

Education Wales. (2020) *Curriculum for Wales: Health and Well-being*, Cardiff: Welsh Government. Retrieved from: https://hwb.gov.wales/curriculum-for-wales/health-and-well-being/ (accessed 18 November 2023).

HM Government. (2014) *Children and Families Act*. Retrieved from: www.legislation.gov.uk/ukpga/2014/6/contents/enacted (accessed 18 November 2023).

HM Government. (2018) *Working Together to Safeguard Children*. Retrieved from: https://assets.publishing.service.gov.uk/media/5fd0a8e78fa8f54d5d6555f9/Working_together_to_safeguard_children_inter_agency_guidance.pdf (accessed 18 November 2023).

Lechner, V., Crăciun, I. C. and Scheithauer, H. (2023) 'Barriers, resources, and attitudes towards (cyber-)bullying prevention/intervention in schools from the perspective of school staff: Results from focus group discussions', *Teaching and Teacher Education*, 135: 1–9.

NSPCC. (2023) *Keeping Children Safe Online*. Retrieved from: www.nspcc.org.uk/keeping-children-safe/online-safety/ (accessed 27 November 2023).

O'Connor, A. (2017) *Understanding Transitions in the Early Years*, 2nd edn, Abingdon, UK: Routledge.

Perkel, J. (2022) 'The internet and today's children', in *Children in Mind: Their Mental Health in Today's World and What We Can Do To Help Them*. Johannesburg: Wits University Press, Chapter 6.

Siraj-Blatchford, I., Clarke, K. and Needham, M. (eds) (2007) *The Team Around the Child: Multiagency Working in the Early Years*, Stoke-on-Trent, UK: Trentham Books.

Tzani-Pepelasi, C., Ioannou, M., Synnott, J. and McDonnell, D. (2019) 'Peer support at schools: The buddy approach as a prevention and intervention strategy for school bullying', *International Journal of Bullying Prevention*, 1: 111–123.

Welsh Government. (2023) *Designing Your Curriculum: Enabling Learning*. Retrieved from: https://hwb.gov.wales/curriculum-for-wales/designing-your-curriculum/enabling-learning/ (accessed 26 April 2024).

Welsh Government. (n.d.) *Safeguarding*. Retrieved from: www.gov.wales/safeguarding-guidance (accessed 18 November 2023).

SECTION 9
YOUR PROFESSIONAL DEVELOPMENT

UNIT 9.1

READY, STEADY, TEACH…

Anna Harrison and Paula Moses

INTRODUCTION

Day five of my first week in my teaching career… 'Miss, there's a pigeon in the room'… Hearing those words and spotting mister pigeon perched near the ceiling was literally terrifying! I remember clocking that all 30 children were out of their seats and standing up. 'All's fine, I'll go and open a window, please sit down' and then moving purposely but with shaking hands to the window area and opening those windows as fast as I could. Nothing from your teacher training prepares you for a pigeon in your classroom on day five … and yet, arguably, my training had kicked in.

Let's think it through. For all unplanned events, children and their safety come first, and resolving problems calmly is highly desirable. If the pigeon had not obliged me in flying out of the window, option two was to enlist two children to fetch an office person who might then contact the caretaker. Meanwhile, my role was to reassure the children to stay calm and remain seated as this would help the bird in the classroom stay calm, too. The pigeon happily flew away. We moved on to lunchtime! Whilst we hope you never have pigeons entering your classroom spaces, we do know that unplanned events happen. Reflecting on the skills you have already developed to cope with planned and unplanned teaching and learning experiences will help you to think about the kind of teacher you are and help you to prepare for the next steps in your teaching career. In this unit, we set out steps for applying for your first teaching role and considerations for your induction phase.

OBJECTIVES

By the end of this unit, you will:

- identify key skills and experiences that will support your application for your first teaching post;
- reflect on what you are looking for in your first teaching post;
- consider the key features of a successful CV or application letter;
- plan for answers to possible interview questions;
- be aware of the support you need to be a successful Early Career Teacher (ECT).

In Wales …

The purpose of statutory induction is to:

- contribute to building an excellent teaching workforce for the benefit of all learners
- support NQTs to have the best start to their teaching career
- provide all NQTs with the opportunity to develop their practice by focusing on the requirements set out in the professional standards
- prepare all NQTs for their career as a teacher by establishing the skills and behaviours that they need to build on throughout their career
- ensure that all NQTs focus on national priorities
- ensure that NQTs focus their professional learning on the most effective methods and approaches, including reflective practice, effective collaboration, coaching and mentoring, and effective use of data and research evidence
- build on the experiences gained in initial teacher education (ITE) to support career-long professional growth.

Source: Welsh Government (2023)

In Scotland…

Eligible students graduating from university with a teaching qualification can enrol on the Teacher Induction Scheme (TIS). The scheme allows provisionally registered teachers to undertake a training post in a local education authority with the view to gaining full registration within one school year.

Source: General Teaching Council for Scotland (GTCS) n.d.a; n.d.b

APPLYING FOR YOUR FIRST TEACHING ROLE

During your training, you may well begin to think about and plan for your first teaching role and to be well prepared, you need to make a few key decisions. Aspfors and Bondas' (2013) study involved working with newly qualified teachers in Finland with a key focus on relationships. One decisive factor for new teachers was how the leadership of the school welcomed and cared for new teachers. When applying for your first job, do ask the school about how they envisage their mentoring commitment. What does the mentoring relationship look like in their school? Try to find out if their focus is on the quality of mentoring rather than quantity in terms of time allocation.

Jerrim's (2021) research showed how important it is that new teachers feel that their own effort and ideas are valued. In addition, Aspfors and Bondas (2013: 250) call for 'a permissive and open atmosphere, where everybody is equal, shows mutual respect, takes responsibility and helps each other'. These authors emphasise the tension that many teachers feel between a joy in 'caring for' pupils and that feeling of making a difference with the 'the exhaustion and tiredness it may cause simultaneously' (p.251). Jerrim (2021: 22) also stresses that although many new teachers express a high work satisfaction compared to their contemporaries in other industries, it is vital that school leaders 'make greater efforts to show junior teachers that their hard work and dedication to the job is highly valued and sincerely appreciated'.

One of the first decisions you may need to make is the age or stage of the pupils you will be teaching. It is likely that you will have gained some valuable experience working with children of different ages. You may have decided to prioritise a particular age group, for example, children aged 6 to 8 years which then spans three possible year groups, 2, 3 and 4 (or upper KS1 and lower KS2 in England). It is useful to do some research about this but also to keep an open mind. I remember thinking that I wouldn't want to teach children younger than Year 5 (10 yrs old) but when I reluctantly moved to Year 3 (7 yrs old) I realised very quickly that this was where I was happiest as a teacher! You should talk to colleagues, tutors and friends about their experiences.

The second decision is likely to concern the type of school you feel comfortable in. Some trainee teachers prefer smaller schools such as one-form entry because they perceive it could offer a greater opportunity for trying out a few different roles for subject leadership at the school, and more emphasis on individual planning of lessons rather than shared lesson planning with other teachers in your year group. Alternatively, some trainee teachers may prefer a larger two- or three-form entry school, where whole year groups share planning, and you may feel less isolated. Perhaps, your training involved preparing for a specialist role of teaching children with Special Education Needs and Disabilities (SENDs) and this is the direction you want to take.

Alongside the size of the school, you may also want to consider whether you prefer to teach in a faith school, which aligns with your own background and set of values, or a community school that doesn't have a faith focus. You may want to work as part of an Academy Chain, Free School, specialist school or a local authority school. You can read about the different types of primary schools (www.gov.uk/types-of-school) and find out about schools in your area through the Local Authority websites.

The final piece of the jigsaw, and perhaps the most important one, is to consider the practical decisions about **where** to teach in terms of distance from where you will be living. It is vital that your journey to and from school doesn't run the risk of contributing unnecessary stress or expense to an already demanding role. It is always worth mapping out routes to and from a school and evaluating commuting times and transport links. If you are planning to cycle to work, it is worth finding out if schools provide bike racks or staff showers to help. Research suggests that finding optimal conditions for your first role can help with job satisfaction and positively influence your enthusiasm and relationships in school, potentially helping you to stay motivated to succeed (Høigaard, Giske, and Sundsli, 2012: 348).

In terms of finding out about teaching jobs, there is a range of options to consult. On a wider national scale, there are three main options: the UK Government site (https://teaching-vacancies.service.gov.uk) Guardian Jobs (https://jobs.theguardian.com/jobs/schools) and the TES (www.tes.com/jobs/). The TES operates a large database of teaching roles where you can search using key terms, location and distance from your own home. Alternatively, local authorities and academy groups can advertise on their own websites.

It is also sometimes worth sending your CV and a speculative application directly to schools where you would like to teach, explaining what you love about the school and could contribute to their vision and ethos. You may have already made good relationships with schools where you completed a training experience so keep in touch with the schools to be first to find out about positions as they occur.

Schools in the Independent sector advertise their teaching positions on The Independent Schools Council (https://jobs.isc.co.uk/) and The Independent Association of Prep Schools (https://iaps.uk/jobs.html). If applying abroad, it is worth planning decisions carefully using available information such as from Generate (https://generate-fs.co.uk/the-guide-to-teaching-abroad/) and agencies such as Teaching Abroad Direct (www.teachingabroaddirect.co.uk/teaching-jobs). One key factor to ask is whether international schools can support your ECT training years.

CREATING AND MAKING A JOB APPLICATION

Applications for teaching roles provide an opportunity for you to show your prospective employer all that you can bring to the role. Completing an application form can feel daunting, but breaking it down into manageable chunks can really help and once you have completed one then you will always have a starting point which you can adapt for subsequent applications. Like any successful form filling, make sure you read and answer the questions as clearly as possible. Teaching roles often include a personal specification or list of essential and desirable skills. During your application, there may either be space for a supporting statement or a letter of application. Follow the guidance in front of you. Your writing needs to address which prior experience matches the skills required. There may be some areas where you feel you have less experience to draw upon to fulfil the specification. However, there are many jobs where there are applicable skill sets. If you have gained previous retail or catering experiences, this will often involve working with a range of people and utilising a variety of communication skills. Demonstrating good communication skills for a teaching role is vital as you will interact with a range of parents and carers as well as other educational professionals in a school setting. Follow the order of the Job and Person Specifications in your written statement to make sure that you have answered everything but not repeated yourself. Your answers need to assertively promote your abilities truthfully, steering the balance between being too modest to being an Olympic athlete in all things! Allow ample time for proofreading and check that your writing is Standard English, avoiding abbreviations and colloquialisms. It is always worth reading it out loud to yourself or a trusted person before sending it off. Finally, if there are questions you cannot answer then write N/A (not applicable) rather than leave them blank and if you have gaps in your work history due to caring responsibilities or travelling then do not be afraid to include this information.

Headteachers and governors of schools are looking for teachers who not only meet the specifications of the role but also can offer something individual or special for their school, such as running a gardening club, coaching a sports team or offering musical and theatrical expertise. Your previous and current hobbies or outside interests may be relevant to include if you want them to be part of your teaching journey. Your ECT years are unlikely to require you to coordinate a subject area, however, you may decide to indicate on your application or interview where you see your specialism areas developing and offer to get involved with aspects of subject area roles, for example, helping to run a school library, offering to lead a times tables club, co-leading a science experiment club or showing an interest in teaching using the outside environment. Within your application, there will be space for you to offer details of previous school placements or any other voluntary work with children. Make sure that the names of schools and the details about time spent and age groups are always accurate and prioritise answering any questions on safeguarding as all children need safe adults to be working with them (Department for Education [DfE], 2015).

Task 9.1.1 Creating a CV for teaching

Spend some time thinking about your previous work, training or voluntary experiences and jot down the skills you gained through them. Look at the CV template. First make sure you have all the relevant information you need, then consider what experiences and skills set you apart from other applicants. How can you briefly convey this on your CV?

Example:

Volunteer teaching assistant: communication and organisational skills, running a chess club.

Waitress/Waiter: working with a range of members of the public which will help me work well with parents and carers

Babysitting: caring for young children and communicating clearly with adults, appreciating the role of play for learning and story times for reading development

---

[Your name]
[Address]
[Phone number]
[Email address]

Education
[Degree, year obtained]
[School]

Professional experience
[Employer]
[Job title | Years worked]
[A bullet list of responsibilities and achievements]

Skills and qualifications
[A bullet list of best skills and qualifications]

Awards and honours
[A bullet list of relevant awards and honours]

Publications and presentations
[The authors, (year) 'Title or presentation name.' Journal or publisher. Volume, page and DOI number.]

Professional associations and affiliations
[A bullet list of relevant memberships or associations]

FIGURE 9.1.1 CV template

VISITING SCHOOLS BEFORE APPLYING

It is important to take up opportunities to visit schools before applying. This gives you a chance to find out more about the role, try out the journey and explore whether the school's ethos aligns with your values.

Generally, you will gain a sense of whether the school is a 'good fit' for you and what you are able to bring to the teaching role. Research by the National Education Union (NEU; 2023) shows that teachers are happiest at schools where they 'know that they can make a difference and they have a strong sense of personal and professional agency' so it is important that you try to find out if the school you are visiting is able to provide this. You can ask the people you meet on the visit what they enjoy about working at the school and look out for displays and mentions on the websites of teachers and signs that they are valued by the leadership team. Do not underestimate the influence of your own formative years, when you were at school, when choosing a workplace that feels like a 'good fit'. Flores' research (2001) mentions these recurring themes of 'Feeling like a teacher', 'being one of them [students]', 'being on the other side' in new students' accounts of settling into a new teaching environment (p.145).

On this visit not only will you be gathering impressions of the school, but you will also be making first impressions. Before the visit, learn the names of key people who might take you around. Make sure you dress appropriately as this is a professional role you are undertaking. It is better to be too smart than not smart enough. Make sure you have calculated ample time for travelling to the school. Be ten minutes early. Being late will not make a good first impression. Have some questions ready to ask about the school and the teaching position. Some people might say that the interview starts the minute you enter the school so don't forget to smile!

Table 9.1.1 gives some of the questions you might want to ask but make sure you tailor them to things that you are genuinely interested in or relate to the job that you are applying for:

TABLE 9.1.1 Some questions to consider asking when visiting a primary school before interview

- What would you say is special or different about this school?
- What's your approach to behaviour management?
- What after-school clubs and extracurricular activities do you run?
- Do you organise any social activities for staff outside of work?
- Which phonics/maths/English/RE scheme do you use?
- Do you have teachers with any specialisms?
- How are the TAs allocated?

YOUR FIRST INTERVIEW

Getting an interview is a real achievement and the fact that you have been shortlisted means that your application and interactions with the school so far have been positive. Therefore, you are in a good position, and you can go into the interview feeling confident and happy.

However, first interviews are best managed with the right preparation. You have already started the preparation by completing a successful application form so make sure you read this through carefully. This will help you remember to refer to good examples of your experience and skills during the interview. Your preparation should also include thorough research of the school's website so that you can come across as someone who knows and likes the school. For example, I once got a job because I talked about the outdoor learning photographs on the school's website and how I would like to contribute to that work beyond my classroom role.

On the day of the interview, make sure you allow plenty of time to get to the school. If your interview is at 9am make sure you don't get caught up in the traffic of parents dropping off their children – get there early as the worst that can happen is that you need to sit and wait for a bit. If you are using public transport, plan your route and go earlier than you would normally. If you need to park when you get there, then it would be polite to check with the school where would be best – it would be a shame if you accidentally parked in the Headteacher or Caretaker's spaces.

Dress smartly – as if you were doing the job – and wear something that you will feel comfortable in in case you are asked to teach a lesson. When you arrive make sure you smile and say hello to the people in the office – this shows that you are a respectful person and will be someone they would like to work with. Even if you are nervous, try to put across a relaxed and happy but professional persona.

If you have been asked to teach a sample lesson, then make sure that you have all the information you need before the day. You can normally send an email to the person who has invited you to interview so make sure you think ahead about what you want to ask so you only need to send one message. You might want to check what resources will be available to you, if you will be able to use a computer and smartboard or if you need to bring your own laptop. You may also want to ask if there will be a general teaching assistant support as part of the lesson that you can plan for, or if they are working with a specific pupil. It is also always good to ask ahead if there are any specific or special needs within the group of students you will be teaching so that you can be prepared. At the end of this email don't forget to thank them again for inviting you to interview.

Finally, double check the email that has invited you to interview. There might be attachments that you need to read or complete before the day. You may also be asked to bring specific paperwork or certificates that validate the qualifications on your application. Once, I was also asked to bring something which I could talk about in the interview that reflected me as a teacher.

In the interview, there are certain subjects that will normally come up. The first subject is normally your suitability to work with young children. There will always be a safeguarding question so be ready to draw upon your training in this area. Other curriculum areas will also be covered, such as how you will support your class with their reading including how systematic synthetic phonics fits within a broad, rich literacy environment. Any other subjects may be included, and it is good to have a few examples of connections between your teaching and pupil progress that you can draw upon from previous school experiences. Other questions might include how to keep children safe in school, for example, your experience of PE lessons using apparatus or how you would organise your classroom. You may well have examples of projects which promote cross-curricular links.

So, we have covered safeguarding and some curriculum questions. The role of being a teacher involves good communication with a range of adults, both parents and carers and other educational professionals. Therefore, a question on how you communicate well is likely to occur. In terms of communication, a key factor to remember is knowing about the range of school policies on areas such as behaviour management and curriculum to know about and feel confident to communicate.

There will be times as a new teacher when you will not know all the answers and the key point here is that you do know who in the school to ask for advice. Your ECT mentor, Deputy Head or Headteacher will all include a support team to turn to for advice. I remember as a young teacher in my 20s feeling a huge responsibility when navigating public transport for school trips and managing parent volunteers to help with this. However, the Headteacher I worked with gave me all the support needed to make sure that the children were safe, and the trips were a success. This topic about how to manage school trips may come up, too. Your answers will include checking the school policy on how to manage school trips and making substantial preparations to make sure all areas are covered. Being prepared for a school trip will include making sure that children with individual educational and medical needs are well supported. You may also need to order packed lunches to take with you so check how much notice the kitchen needs to be able to get these ready for you.

Being a teacher involves leading teaching and learning for a range of pupils. Another key area for first interviews will be how you adapt your teaching to support different children. Often, working closely with teaching assistants and other educational professionals is involved with doing this well. The best advice is again to draw on your previous recent experiences within school and have some concrete examples that you can draw upon.

The other factor to consider is 'selling yourself'. This does not mean overstating what you can contribute but it does include communicating your strengths. These strengths may be connected to your personality such as being patient, kind, enthusiastic and positive. These strengths may also include extra qualities you can offer such as first aid skills, and hobbies such as music, cooking, art, sport and music.

The interview is likely to feel very quick and it is easy to forget key information if you are thinking hard to answer each question. Therefore, write a list of your strengths and have this to hand on a piece of paper. If you get to the end of the interview and there are strengths which you want to raise, then it is worth saying that 'other areas I would like you to know about are…'. You could also think ahead about one or two questions that you would like to ask at the end of the interview. Keep in mind that the interviewers do not expect this part of the interview to take a long time so don't feel under pressure to ask lots of questions but one or two can be a useful chance to reinforce your interest in the school. Finally, try not to put the people interviewing you on the spot or in an embarrassing position through your questions. Instead use it as an opportunity to leave a positive lasting impression.

Task 9.1.2 Preparing for an interview

Select a job you have applied for, or a school you have previously trained/volunteered in. Work through the following interview questions and prompts, noting down the answers you would give if being interviewed there.

Some sample interview questions (and thoughts) you might want to consider.

How do you think today's lesson went? What was good and what could have gone better? (This is if you have been asked to teach a sample lesson.)

Be honest but specific. If you think it went well or badly then it is important to say that, but try to stay balanced between the two. Most school leaders understand that things can go wrong when you are nervous – what they are looking for is a reflective, curious person who can learn from their mistakes and respond well to feedback.

Why did you apply for the job at our school?

This should be a <u>specific reason</u> about <u>this specific school</u> – perhaps it has a good reputation for something in particular?

Tell us about yourself. What strengths and experience can you bring to our school?

Plan this answer carefully but make it seem natural! You can share 'lessons learned' but keep it succinct and meaningful.

Do you have any extracurricular skills we could benefit from?

Only mention something here that you would like to share. Be aware that you might be asked to run a club in it once you have finished your Early Career Framework (ECF)!

How would you describe your teaching style?

Plan this answer carefully but make it seem natural! You might want to link this to the reason you like the school – perhaps they teach in a certain way that you admire?

What are your areas of strength in the National or our wider school curriculum?

Plan this answer carefully but make it seem natural!

What are your areas of development in delivering the National or our wider school curriculum?

Plan this answer carefully but make it seem natural! Try to think of something that won't concern the interview panel and would be easily solvable with some guidance from your mentor.

How would you react to a safeguarding situation in school?

The answer is always to follow the safeguarding policy of the school so make sure you have read this. Common sense would normally involve: 1. Write down a verbatim account straight away and do not make any promises to keep secrets, 2. Report your concerns straight away/as soon as possible to the Safeguarding lead, 3. Do not discuss the incident with anyone else.

What behaviour management experience do you have, and can you give us an example of how you have used specific techniques successfully?

Plan this answer carefully but make it seem natural! If you mention individual teachers or children, then do not mention names. Always finish with a positive outcome or lesson learned.

What experiences do you have of including learners with special educational needs or disabilities?

Plan this answer carefully but make it seem natural! If you mention individual teachers or children, then do not mention names. Always finish with a positive outcome or lesson learned.

Over to you: some questions you could ask:

How would you measure success in this role?

What are the school's goals for the future?

What support do you offer new starters?

What development opportunities are available?

If I were successful in this role, how do you see me contributing to the wider school community?

CONGRATULATIONS, YOU ARE NOW AN EARLY CAREER TEACHER

Congratulations! You have secured your first teaching job as an Early Career Teacher (ECT). In England, you will now work with a mentor and follow the Early Career Framework (ECF) (DfE, 2019) which is a mandatory structured programme designed to provide essential support and professional development for early career teachers in England. The ECF covers a two-year period and seeks to provide you with all the necessary tools and guidance to thrive in the teaching profession. One of the key components of the ECF is that all ECTs receive access to a structured curriculum that covers various aspects of teaching, including behaviour management, curriculum planning, assessment and special educational needs. These materials are designed to be accessible and relevant, equipping you with evidence-based practices that can be immediately applied in the classroom. The ECF's focus on evidence-based practices aligns with the government's broader agenda to raise educational standards and ensure that students receive the best possible education.

Mentorship plays a central role in the ECF, with all ECTs being assigned an in-school mentor to provide guidance and support throughout their first two years of teaching. Mentors are experienced teachers who have received specific training to fulfil this role effectively. They help ECTs navigate the challenges of the classroom, offer feedback on their teaching and facilitate professional development opportunities. Working with your mentor will be covered in more detail in the next section.

Word cloud containing: communication, encouragement, ect, guidance, growth, role, learning, wellbeing, mentor, support, collaboration, training, sharing, community, resources, pedagogy, feedback, teaching, classroom, development, coaching, planning, assessment, lesson, modeling, observation

FIGURE 9.1.2 The ECT mentoring relationship

Moreover, the ECF places a strong emphasis on ongoing assessment and reflection. ECTs are required to complete assessments at key points during their induction period, with their mentor playing a crucial role in this process. These assessments help to identify areas for improvement and allow for targeted professional development. The ECF encourages a reflective practice, where teachers continually evaluate their teaching methods and adapt to meet the needs of their students.

> **In Northern Ireland …**
>
> Induction and EPD normally take 3 years to complete (possibly longer depending on your employment circumstances). You will be supported through this process by the Induction and EPD team at the Education Authority. You will also receive advice, guidance and support from your Teacher Tutor and other colleagues in the school(s) in which you may be working.
>
> (Education Authority [EA], 2024)

WORKING CLOSELY WITH YOUR MENTOR

Working with a mentor as an ECT is a pivotal aspect of the teaching profession, offering invaluable support, guidance and opportunities for growth during the early stages of your career. The mentorship relationship can be transformative, helping you to acclimatise to the demands of the classroom, navigate the intricacies of school culture and develop the skills and confidence needed to excel in your teaching career. Your mentor is normally an experienced teacher who has taken part in specific training to provide support and mentorship to ECTs. Your mentor should also serve as a trusted advisor and ally, offering a wealth of knowledge and experience. A blog from the Chartered College of Teaching (Barker, 2023) described good mentoring as the 'lynchpin of educational communities' and research shows that mentoring can not only have a positive impact on mentees, their learning, classroom practice and their well-being, but also a positive impact on mentors themselves (Maxwell, Hobson and Manning, 2022; Gager and Percival, 2022).

One of the primary benefits of working with a mentor is the personalised support they will give you in line with the criteria of the ECF in England, or other expectations for new teachers set out in your home nation. However, the type and quality of mentoring can vary from school to school. The mentor should be able to make the time to understand your individual needs and challenges within the complex and varied role of being a teacher (Jerrim, 2021; Cowley, 2023). This personalised approach is essential because no two new teachers are alike, and each may require different areas of focus and development. Whether it's classroom management, lesson planning or adapting to the school's unique environment, the mentor's guidance is specific to the new teacher's circumstances.

Your mentor will also have a crucial role in helping you develop your teaching skills. They will offer you constructive feedback on lesson plans, teaching style and classroom strategies. This feedback should be invaluable for you and help you refine your practice and make continuous improvements. This feedback will also help you develop your ability to be reflective, which is an essential skill for any successful teacher. Although feedback can sometimes be hard to take, especially if you are feeling under pressure, see it as a gift which you can learn from. Lamb (2017: 101) carried out a small case study to find out how teachers reflect on their practice and he recommended that 'schools help teachers that are new to a school establish a good rapport with colleagues, so reflective discussions can be utilised' and highlighted the positive impact 'of schools establishing a whole school approach to reflection which could encourage teachers to ask colleagues for feedback on their practice'.

Beyond the classroom, mentors can help ECTs to understand the broader school context. They should help you understand school policies, procedures and expectations from the leadership team. This knowledge can be especially valuable in ensuring that you can integrate smoothly into the school community and comply with important guidelines. Gager and Percival (2022: 5) provide useful guidance for ECTs and their mentors by explaining that for the relationship to be successful then there needs to be a 'collective responsibility' for ECTs throughout the school instead of a focus by the mentor on 'the new teacher's developmental needs in isolation'. New teachers benefit from knowing about the wider networks available to them throughout the school where they can benefit from 'frequent supportive learning conversations with colleagues'.

Mentors can also serve as a source of emotional support. The transition into teaching can be challenging, and new teachers often face a range of emotions, from excitement to anxiety. Mentors lend a sympathetic ear and offer encouragement, helping new teachers build their confidence and resilience. Knowing that there is someone experienced to turn to for advice can alleviate the stress that can come with the demands of teaching. Teacher well-being is organised differently between schools and Cotson and Kim (2024) explain that some teachers can sometimes feel that well-being initiatives are not always effective and can feel tokenistic. The mentorship relationship should foster a sense of camaraderie within the school community. It promotes a culture of collaboration, where experienced teachers actively share their expertise with newcomers. This not only benefits the new teacher but also enhances the overall quality of instruction within the school. Therefore, if you do not feel supported by your mentor then it is important that you know who else you can speak to in the school; other teachers can also support you and sometimes a change of mentor might be needed. In addition to the day-to-day support, mentors can often be asked to facilitate professional development opportunities for new teachers. They may recommend workshops, conferences or resources to help new teachers continue their learning journey. This commitment to ongoing professional growth is normally useful for you as a new teacher to stay motivated and committed to your career.

In conclusion, working with a mentor as a new teacher should be an enriching and essential experience. However, if you do not feel supported by your mentor, please make sure you know who else you can speak to. The relationship with your mentor should provide you with tailored guidance, instructional support, emotional reassurance and a sense of belonging within the school community. This mentorship relationship should not only accelerate the professional development of you as an ECT, but it is also a partnership that has the potential to shape your future career which will ultimately benefit the students you serve.

CONSOLIDATING YOUR PROFESSIONAL IDENTITY

Consolidating your professional identity as a primary school teacher in England is a journey that involves continuous self-reflection, ongoing learning and a commitment to the well-being and development of your students. Here are key steps to help you strengthen your professional identity:

1 **Reflect on your teaching philosophy:** It is always worthwhile to think about your personal teaching philosophy. Do you have a clear idea about your core beliefs about education, teaching and learning? Clarifying your values and principles can help you make informed decisions about how and where you want to teach. You might also want to discuss this with your mentor as their own philosophy about education could inform how they interact and view your skills and abilities.

2 **Look after yourself:** Teaching can be demanding, so prioritise your physical and mental well-being because a healthy teacher is better equipped to support students. However, it can be tricky to maintain a healthy work-life balance when you are starting out in any new role so try not to let this become another way to put pressure on yourself. It is important though to think carefully about setting boundaries that are right for you, for example, setting a regular bedtime or having a walk round the block at lunchtime if this is possible.

3 **Collaborate:** Your colleagues can be a useful source of support, guidance and feedback. It is normally a useful and positive experience to join in with any opportunities to plan with colleagues and sharing ideas with your fellow teachers can enrich your teaching experience and professional identity.

4 **Build good relationships:** Building strong positive relationships with all your colleagues, pupils, parents and carers can enhance your effectiveness as a teacher and often take the stress out of difficult situations when they arise. Regular professional communication with families so they feel involved in their child's education can also contribute to a positive classroom environment and the achievement of your pupils.

5 **Stay informed:** Staying up to date with latest educational research and approaches can not only expand your knowledge and skills but also help you keep your teaching fresh and innovative. You might also want to join professional organisations which can connect you with other teachers and provide you with access to good quality training, conferences and online learning. There are some useful links at the end of this unit, and see Unit 9.2 about planning your continuing professional development.

6 **Take time to reflect:** Being a teacher is a rewarding but demanding profession so making time to reflect is vital. Choose a method that works for you: writing notes or talking to colleagues or simply giving yourself time to think. Some of the questions you could consider are:
   - **Am I looking after myself?**
   - **Am I still able to enjoy my job in line with my teaching philosophy?**

- **Am I contributing to a positive environment for those around me – my pupils, their families and my colleagues?**
- **What is my plan for the future?**

Finally, take time to celebrate your successes, however small, and never underestimate the positive impact you are having on the lives of your students every day!

BUILDING YOUR PROFESSIONAL NETWORKS

Building professional networks as a primary school teacher in England is a valuable activity that can enhance your career, provide support and open up opportunities for collaboration and growth. Effective networking can help you stay informed about the latest educational trends, exchange ideas and connect with colleagues who share your passion for teaching. Here are strategies to help you build and nurture professional networks in the field of primary education:

1. Attend conferences, workshops and local teacher groups (online and in person) as they can be helpful for improving your teaching as well as making you feel more connected and inspired.
2. Find out if there are professional associations or unions that are interesting to you. Speak to your colleagues and do your research before you pay to join. Sometimes you can get a free trial if you are not sure.
3. Share your expertise – there might be opportunities to join in with school committees or extra-curricular activities and community events. If you feel that you can do this without it negatively affecting your core job and work-life balance, then these can be fun. They can also build your network outside the classroom and demonstrate your commitment to the school and local community.
4. You will probably be advised to join a Union. This is a very personal decision, so it is worth doing your research and find one you feel comfortable with. You might also get a good deal as an ECT. Here are some places to start:
   - NASUWT: www.nasuwt.org.uk
   - National Education Union (NEU): https://neu.org.uk
   - EDAPT – (Edu-legal support for teachers): www.edapt.org.uk

AND FINALLY

Remember that you have already demonstrated great skill and determination by completing your Initial Teacher Training – Well done! The next stage of your career is very exciting but can be challenging so try not to get disillusioned if things don't work out exactly as planned.

SUMMARY

This unit was designed to give you the information you need to get started in your first job in a primary school, but it is impossible to describe everyone's potential journey so always do lots of research. Perhaps the best piece of advice is to stay approachable, curious and open minded as this will help you feel part of a community full of trust and strong professional relationships. By actively seeking opportunities for collaboration, sharing your expertise and staying engaged with other teachers, you can enrich your teaching practice and stay connected to the dynamic field of primary education. And watch out for pigeons!

FIGURE 9.1.3 Watch out for pigeons!
Source: Moondot Creative

ANNOTATED FURTHER READING

Department for Education (DfE). (2024) *Early career framework* (England). Retrieved from: https://www.gov.uk/government/publications/early-career-framework (accessed 30 March 2025).

> The early career framework (ECF) sets out what early career teachers are entitled to learn about and learn how to do when they start their careers.

Welsh Government Initial Teacher Education: *Career entry profile* (CEP) Retrieved from: https://www.gov.wales/career-entry-profile (accessed 30 March 2025).

> Once you have gained QTS and are a Newly Qualified Teacher (NQT) you will need to complete a career entry profile (CEP) and undertake your induction.

Scottish Government *Initial Teacher Education: Induction* Retrieved from: https://www.gov.scot/policies/schools/teachers/#initialeducation (accessed 30 March 2025).

> All new teachers have access to the services of an experienced teacher as a mentor. Following induction, teachers should be ready to gain full registration with the General Teaching Council for Scotland (GTCS).

Northern Ireland Early Career Teacher Programme Retrieved from: https://www.eani.org.uk/sites/default/files/2022-09/Early%20Career%20Teacher%20Supply%20Teaching%20Leaflet.pdf (accessed 30 March 2025).

> All newly qualified teachers are required to complete Induction and Early Professional Development (EPD).

FURTHER READING TO SUPPORT M-LEVEL STUDY

Hatley, J. and Kingston, A. (2021) The influence of support for early career teachers on their decision to remain in the teaching profession, *Impact*, Issue 13: Professional Development https://my.chartered.college/impact_article/the-influence-of-support-for-early-career-teachers-on-their-decision-to-remain-in-the-teaching-profession/

Antonsen, Y., Aspfors, J. and Maxwell, G. (2024) 'Early career teachers' role in school development and professional learning', *Professional Development in Education*, 50(3): 460-473. doi: 10.1080/19415257.2024.2306998.
   Note* although this context is Norwegian, the article still poses interesting themes to discuss within ECT professional development initiatives

Curtis, E., Nguyen, H., Larsen, E., and Loughland, T (2024) 'The positioning tensions between early career teachers' and mentors' perceptions of the mentor role', *BERJ British Educational Research Journal*, Vol 50, Issue 3, June 2024: 1327-1349. https://doi.org/10.1002/berj.3974

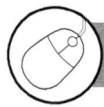

RELEVANT WEBSITES

A small selection of key websites for information about teaching vacancies are as follows:

Scotland: https://teachinscotland.scot/find-a-job/

England: https://teaching-vacancies.service.gov.uk/

Northern Ireland: www.eani.org.uk/jobs

Wales: https://educators.wales/

REFERENCES

Aspfors, J. and Bondas, T. (2013) 'Caring about caring: Newly qualified teachers' experiences of their relationships within the school community', *Teachers and Teaching: Theory and Practice*, 19(3): 243-259.

Barker, H. (2023) *Recognising the Power of Mentoring for Teacher Development*. Retrieved from: https://chartered.college/2023/02/17/recognising-the-power-of-mentoring-for-teacher-development/

Cotson, W. and Kim, L. E. (2024) 'Are schools doing enough? An exploration of how primary schools in England support the well-being of their teachers', *Psychology in the Schools*, 61(2): 435-454. https://doi.org/10.1002/pits.23061

Cowley, S. (2023) *How to Survive your First Year in Teaching*, 4th edn, London: Bloomsbury Education.

Department for Education (DfE). (2015) *Keeping Children Safe in Education*. Last updated 2024. Retrieved from: www.gov.uk/government/publications/keeping-children-safe-in-education-2

Department for Education (DfE). (2019) *Early Career Framework*. Last updated 2024. Retrieved from: www.gov.uk/government/publications/early-career-framework

Education Authority (EA). (2024) *Early Career Teachers Induction and Early Professional Development*. Retrieved from: www.eani.org.uk/services/early-career-teachers-induction-and-early-professional-development

Flores, M. A. (2001) 'Person and context in becoming a new teacher', *Journal of Education for Teaching*, 27(2): 135-148. DOI: 10.1080/02607470120067882

Gager, A. and Percival, J. (2022) 'More than just workload: factors influencing the success and retention of new teachers', *Teacher Education Advancement Network (TEAN) Journal*, 14(1).

General Teaching Council for Scotland (GTCS). (n.d.a) *Teacher Induction Scheme*. Retrieved from: www.gtcs.org.uk/knowledge-base/sections/teacher-induction-scheme

General Teaching Council for Scotland (GTCS). (n.d.b) *Student Teachers*. Retrieved from: www.gtcs.org.uk/join-the-register/student-teachers

Høigaard, R., Giske, R. and Sundsli, K. (2012) 'Newly qualified teachers' work engagement and teacher efficacy influences on job satisfaction, burnout, and the intention to quit', *European Journal of Teacher Education*, 35(3): 347-357. https://doi.org/10.1080/02619768.2011.633993

Jerrim, J. (2021) 'How is life as a recently qualified teacher? New evidence from a longitudinal cohort study in England', *British Journal of Educational Studies*, 69(1): 3–26. https://doi.org/10.1080/00071005.2020.1726872

Lamb, J. (2017) 'How do teachers reflect on their practice? A study into how feedback influences teachers' reflective practice', *The STeP Journal (Student Teacher Perspectives)*, 4(4): 94–104.

Maxwell, B., Hobson, A. and Manning, C. (2022) *Mentoring and Coaching Trainee and Early Career Teachers: Conceptual Review*. National Institute of Teaching. Retrieved from: https://niot.s3.amazonaws.com/documents/Conceptual_Review_Mentoring_-_Nov_22.pdf

National Education Union (NEU). (2023) *National Education Union Research: Place and Belonging in School: Why it Matters Today*. Retrieved from: https://neu.org.uk/advice/classroom/behaviour/creating-sense-place-and-belonging-schools

Welsh Government. (2023) *Induction for Newly Qualified Teachers in Wales*. Retrieved from: https://hwb.gov.wales/professional-learning/career-long-professional-learning/induction/induction-guidance-and-related-documents/induction-for-newly-qualified-teachers-in-wales#introduction (accessed 26 April 2024).

UNIT 9.2

UNDERSTANDING AND PLANNING YOUR CONTINUING PROFESSIONAL DEVELOPMENT

Alison Fox

INTRODUCTION

In this unit, we consider how continuing professional development (CPD) is provided, reflect on what it could and should be and highlight a teacher's role in their own development. Wherever you are based, professional development and/or learning should be linked to your experience of entering the profession. Reflecting on your strengths, interests and areas for skill, knowledge or practice development should be an ongoing process to identify how you can make the best use of opportunities for development. Across the four UK nations this fits in with reviews of how you continue to meet the teacher standards you were assessed as meeting on entry. Evidence of your commitment to professional development (England and Northern Ireland) and professional learning (Wales and Scotland) is embedded in these frameworks. You will see later in the unit how CPD is connected with annual appraisal of your progress as a professional teacher. In England, this process bridges teacher training providers and schools employing beginning teachers, through jointly applying the *Standard for Teachers' Professional Development* (Department for Education [DfE], 2016) embedded in an *Early Career Teacher Framework* (DfE, 2019b). In Scotland and Wales the teacher standards are linked directly to national curricula – Education Scotland's *Curriculum for Excellence* (n.d.) and the Welsh Government's *Curriculum for Wales Framework* (n.d.). In this unit you will see how inspection systems monitoring school performance against such policy frameworks pay attention to evidence of your professional development as part of their evaluations.

Apart from arguably in Scotland, where teachers are offered a national *Professional Standards and Professional Learning* model (Education Scotland/Foghlam Alba, 2022), web materials and access to local development of communities of practice and programmes, the UK PD context has deviated from the notions of a 'bottom-up' self-improving system as advocated by Hargreaves (2012) to the UK government. Whilst the mechanisms he advocated are no longer apparent, the principles of 'disciplined innovation', which see teachers developing evidence-informed practices through collaborative working, remain. Examples of these are explored in this unit.

DOI: 10.4324/9781032691794-49

> **OBJECTIVES**
>
> By the end of this unit, you should:
>
> - understand what CPD could and should encompass;
> - recognise the links between CPD, teacher standards and performance management/appraisal;
> - understand how reflective practice can be developed into sustainable CPD;
> - appreciate the role of enquiry and others in effective CPD.

WHAT IS CPD OR WHAT COULD IT BE?

There are three aspects to CPD, as the words imply. It:

1. connects with being a 'professional' teacher;
2. involves a teacher's 'development' within the profession; and
3. needs to be 'continuing' or 'continuous'.

Professionalism and implications for CPD

Professionalism can be viewed as externally imposed, relying on society's perceptions and expectations of a profession's (e.g. teaching, nursing, social work) remit and responsibilities (Evans, 2011). This sees professions in a kind of service-level agreement with those who hold the profession to account. In the UK, as with many education systems globally, schools are judged on the attainment of their pupils in national and international tests, monitored by a government inspection body. Accountability extends to parents, further and higher education sectors and wider society for producing a highly educated workforce. The pressures of such external accountability help explain the performativity culture judged to have developed in UK schools (Edgington, 2016). This is demonstrated by schools' searching for quick-fix forms of PD aimed to help individual teachers address immediate issues, identified through analysis of performance data, and the trend, in some settings, towards providing teachers with approved lesson plans, tools and resources based on evaluations of 'what works' (Biesta, 2010).

Alternatively, professionalism can be defined as 'the attitudes and behaviour one possesses toward one's profession' (Boyt, Lusch and Naylor, 2001: 322. This grass-roots vision connects with professional culture and collective identity development. Baker (2019) argues that the teaching profession needs to capture this sense of control-from-within to overcome the culture of compliance threatening its development. Given the landscape of high-stakes testing and history of top-down policy-making driving such compliance, teachers need to develop self-confidence and self-efficacy to cope in order to remain enthusiastic and innovate (Bangs, MacBeath and Galton, 2011). This is important, not just for individuals but for the whole profession; a shared sense of what it is to be a teacher, based on agreed values, is needed. This assumes a teacher's identification with the profession, something not all training teachers feel they have developed as they take on their first post (Pillen, Beijaard and Brok, 2013). This is not surprising when a teacher's professional identity can be considered multifaceted – for example:

1. as a subject matter expert, based on self-perceptions of his/her subject matter knowledge and skills;
2. as a didactic expert, based on self-perceptions of his/her knowledge and skills related to planning, executing and evaluating teaching and learning;
3. as a pedagogic expert, based on self-perceptions of his/her knowledge and skills to support students' social, emotional and moral development

(Beijaard, Verloop and Vermunt, 2000)

Understanding and planning your CPD

Professional identity, however, is more complex than this (Schellings et al., 2023). Think about, for example, your classroom management and how this involves how you think about yourself, perceptions of you by your students and evaluations of your professionalism by the team/organisation you are working within. Still, these three facets are useful in thinking about becoming a teaching professional.

> ### Task 9.2.1 Reflecting on your expertise
>
> Reflect on how you see your developing expertise as a professional using Beijaard, Verloop and Vermunt's (2000) three facets to professional identity development.
>
> Rank yourself on a scale of 1–10:
>
> - as subject expert (which, in primary settings, covers the full range of subjects you are expected to teach);
> - as didactic expert (as defined earlier, rather than its more recent usage referring to a teacher-led teaching style);
> - as pedagogic expert (again, as defined earlier, rather than its more recent usage referring to knowledge and skills about teaching approaches).
>
> Mark your value on the sides of a triangle, with each side representing one facet, scaled from 1 to 10. Join your chosen values to help visualise your identity. Figure 9.2.1 illustrates what a 7, 3, 4 evaluation would look like. Add words to each facet describing how confident you are in each expertise. Use one colour for words associated with how you feel now and another colour for your aspirations for the future.
>
> **FIGURE 9.2.1** Visualising your professional identity

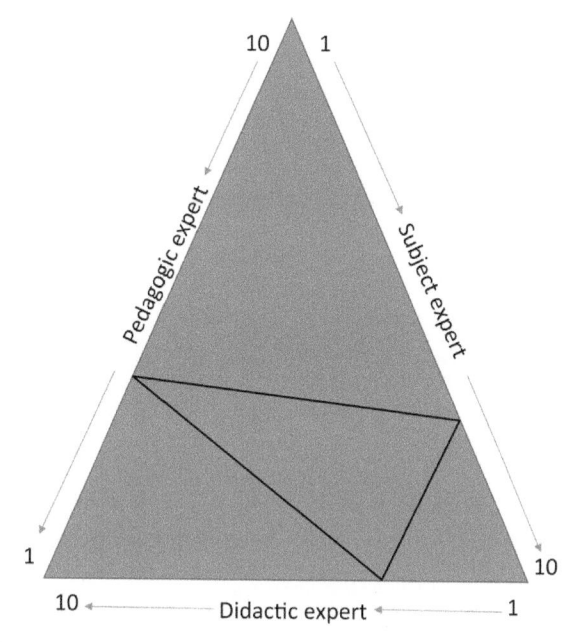

So, what does *development* within the profession encompass, and how are teachers supported to develop?

TABLE 9.2.1 Schools as professional learning environments

An expansive learning environment has:	A restrictive learning environment has:
Close collaborative working between colleagues, demonstrating mutual support	Individuals working in isolation
Opportunities to work beyond current role in other departments, working groups and school activities	No chance to boundary cross into other areas of school life, without a major job change
Support for personal development, beyond school or government priorities	Targets for development limited to external accountability agendas
A supportive atmosphere accepting diverse ways of working and learning	An expectation of standardised ways of working and learning
Opportunities to work beyond the school to experience different perspectives	Limited chance to work out of school, other than short training sessions

Source: Adapted from Figure 3.1, Fuller and Unwin (2006: 53)

Development as part of CPD

The Teacher Professional Standards across the four UK nations are linked to notions of 'Professional Development' (PD) and/or 'Professional Learning' (PL). Practically, the term 'development' remains within policy documentation and, hence, the vocabulary of schools. In the best cases, PD will exceed its traditional roots as a set of fragmented activities designed to transfer knowledge and will be effective in supporting sustained learning. We retain reference to PD in this unit, although what is being discussed is better described as professional learning for individual teachers and the school: one relies on the other.

One way to evaluate a school's CPD provision is to rate it as a professional learning environment on a continuum from restrictive to expansive; see Table 9.2.1.

When this framework was applied to beginning teachers' reported experiences (Fox, Wilson and Deaney, 2011), it was revealed that individual teachers can perceive the same school differently and engage differently with its CPD opportunities. This evidences the role teachers can play in their own development, by proactively making connections with others, rather than passively relying on a workplace to provide opportunities. Effective PD is fundamentally social and requires a commitment to working alongside, listening to, watching and, most significantly, talking with other professionals and members of a school community. The roles of mentors (formal and informal) in supporting new teachers are over and again reported as helpful in navigating, as well as being part of, an effective learning environment (e.g. in Welsh schools by Milton *et al.*, 2022).

Task 9.2.2 Reflecting on your learning opportunities

Who do you refer to and rely on to develop your thinking and practice as a teacher?

Consider creating a learning opportunities map of those from whom you gain support, placing yourself at the centre and drawing links to all those you identify, such as shown in Figure 9.2.2. This could extend beyond how you develop your expertise, as evaluated in Task 9.2.1, to those who keep you motivated, inspired and support your wellbeing.

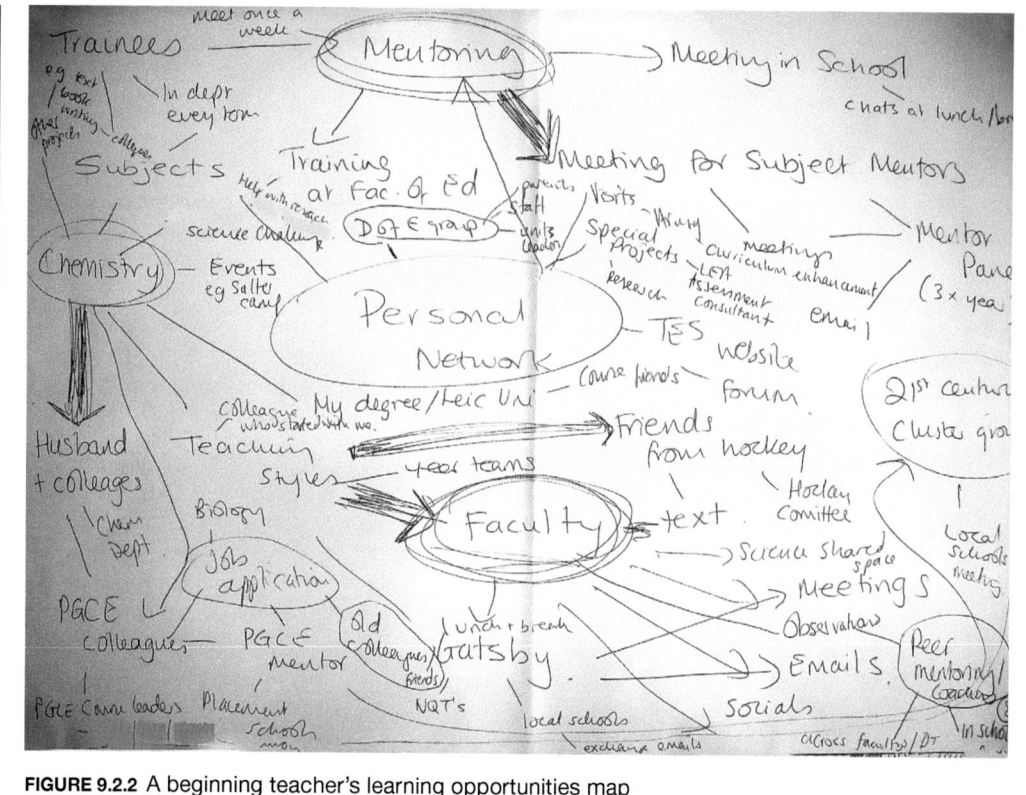

FIGURE 9.2.2 A beginning teacher's learning opportunities map
Source: Alison Fox (unpublished)

How is CPD continuing?

In-service CPD activities are seen as central to the professionalisation of teaching (OECD, 2019). Participation in CPD is one metric for marking success towards the United Nations Sustainable Development Goal 4: Quality Education (UN, 2015). So school leaders need to create a culture of continuous improvement in their settings. Impactful PD, as experienced and reported by teachers across 48 countries in the 2018 OECD TALIS survey…

> provided opportunities to practise/apply new ideas and knowledge in [their] own classroom (86%);
> provided opportunities for active learning (78%);
> provided opportunities for collaborative learning (74%); and
> focused on innovation in [their] teaching (65%).
>
> (OECD, 2019)

These teachers recognise the need for PD to be personalised and opportunities to be creative, which are not served well by a one-size-fits-all approach. Your development as a teacher needs to be an ongoing, continuing endeavour. It also needs to be a collective one.

Effective workplaces are those that can be considered learning organisations (Senge, 2006) or professional learning communities (Lieberman and Miller, 2011) in which the whole organisation learns as individual members of staff learn and teachers model lifelong learning for their students.

'We used to learn to do the work, now learning is the work' (Schleicher, 2018). When looking for posts in schools, seek out those that offer an expansive learning environment for you to grow (Fuller and Unwin, 2006).

THE SCOPE OF CPD ACTIVITIES

Traditionally, PD has taken the form of courses. Course attendance is still very much part of teachers' lives, whether part-day, full-day or run on consecutive days. Less often, they are more sustained, requiring participation between linked days. Courses can be offered by external providers off-site or as visitors to school, school cluster, alliance, trust or chain venues. Increasingly, courses are organised within school collectives drawing on expertise from within, rather than buying in external input. Digital learning opportunities mean any course can include online components, such as drawing on multimedia resources and web platforms or utilising online collaborative and interactive tools. They can be run entirely online at a distance from the provider. This opens up opportunities for teachers to think globally about their PD.

There is nothing intrinsically wrong with courses. They can be beneficial and fulfil specific needs. Longer courses run by external providers might offer accreditation, either professionally – for example, as part of the National College for Teaching and Learning (NCTL)'s modular leadership curriculum or accreditation through the Chartered College of Teaching – or academically, at Masters or Doctoral level, by universities. These can support career development and ways of thinking and tools to critically reflect on a teacher's values and practice. However, less formal in-house, in-work opportunities for PD are vital for ongoing reflection and enquiry.

Importantly, activities should be relevant and meaningful and lead to changes in your thinking and practice. The question 'What makes great PD that leads to consistently great pedagogy?' was examined by 31 Teaching School Alliances as part of a national NCTL project (Stoll, Harris and Handscombe, 2012) and evidenced nine claims.

> Effective PD …
>
> … starts with the end in mind;
> … challenges thinking as part of changing practice;
> … is based on assessment of individual and school needs;
> … connects work-based learning with external expertise;
> … opportunities are varied, rich and sustainable;
> … uses enquiry as a key tool;
> … is enhanced through collaborative learning and joint practice development;
> … is enhanced by creating professional learning communities within and between schools;
> … requires leadership to create the necessary conditions.
>
> (Nelson, Spence-Thomas and Taylor, 2015)

Nelson, Spence-Thomas and Taylor's (2015) report offers a vision. Look for this in schools you work in or seek to work in.

SCHOOLS' RESPONSIBILITIES FOR PROFESSIONAL DEVELOPMENT: THE POLICY CONTEXT

The aspirations for the standards teachers should meet are set out in national policies. Once judged as competent to join the profession, teachers are expected to evidence that they continue to meet these standards and, in so doing, provide high quality education for learners. Conversely, teachers should expect that all schools will provide them with an effective environment for their learning and development. To support teachers (as well as learners and their parents), schools are independently monitored and advised. This role lies with inspection agencies, with different attention paid to PD depending on national context.

In England the PD focus of the Office for Standards in Education, Children's Services and Skills (Ofsted) inspection is on alignment with the curriculum, and teachers' development of content and pedagogical content knowledge (Ofsted, 2023, para 335). A broader approach by the Scottish equivalent inspectorate, Education Scotland/Foghlam Alba, looks for enquiry, coherence, sustainability and a role for critical reflection, with teachers expected to show evidence of professional learning over time. Like Scotland, the Welsh inspectorate, Estyn (2022), places professional learning centrally, looking for a breadth of opportunities for teachers' professional learning and championing research to provide evidence to inform professional decision-making. Here, a broad view of professionals is taken, recognising the multiple practitioners who support schools as places of learning and whose learning needs to be supported. The Northern Ireland Teacher Competences (General Teaching Council for Northern Ireland [GTCNI], 2011) are similarly underpinned by teachers' responsibilities to become reflective practitioners, who engage in enquiry, extending to see professional learning *as* leadership, placing teachers as 'agents of change' (Priestley, Biesta and Robinson, 2013).

SETTING AGENDAS FOR PROFESSIONAL DEVELOPMENT: LINKS WITH APPRAISAL

Whilst the Scottish *Review and Development* process feeds directly through self-evaluation and evidence of professional learning, into an annual update on the General Teaching Council of Scotland (GTCS) register, teacher appraisal in England is quite clearly a mechanism for establishing teacher competences against the Teacher Capability model (DfE, 2019a), without explicit reference to professional learning. UK teacher unions, such as the National Education Union (NEU) and NASUWT: The Teacher Union, produce a range of guidance to assist teachers in taking control of their performance management, in whatever UK national setting you work. Their checklists are particularly helpful in understanding your rights and how the principles of the policies should be interpreted e.g. the NEU Policy (2019).

HOW DOES REFLECTIVE PRACTICE RELATE TO MY PROFESSIONAL DEVELOPMENT?

Reflective practice (Schön, 1983) builds on reflective thinking, traced back to Dewey in the 1930s, to challenge teachers to go beyond routinised ways of thinking to develop as a teacher, and potentially challenge 'the way we do things around here'.

Being a 'reflective practitioner' involves a commitment to reflecting on problems, tensions or curiosities experienced in practice – for example, children unable to settle to a task or fully embrace and be able to apply a new concept or skill – to identify the underpinning issue(s) and consider the options for future actions. This goes beyond one-off problem-solving (sometimes termed single-loop learning), to identify how such problems can be prevented or solved in the future (double-loop learning; Argyris and Schön, 1974). It involves reflection-on-action as well as reflection-for-action (Schön, 1983) by revealing and challenging a teacher's assumptions, in order to develop theories to guide future practice, and is termed 'reflexivity' (Pollard *et al.*, 2023).

Vignette 1 reports how a group of teachers were supported in developing reflective thinking to guide future practice.

> **Vignette 1: The value of reflective diaries**
>
> (With thanks to Elizabeth Hewitt, PGCE Lecturer, University of Leicester)
>
> Three Year 4 teachers (with children aged 8 and 9 years old) were trying to develop more interactive teaching in their science lessons. After selected lessons, they audio-recorded short reflections to form a year's oral diary. These diaries revealed teachers' shifting beliefs and helped to capture their developing understanding of the value children gain from becoming involved in peer-group discussion. These spaces are not easy to incorporate into the general busyness of school life, and teachers benefited from being prompted to recount illustrative excerpts and analyse significant moments. As this was part of a research project, transcripts of pupils in class discussions and group interviews provided further stimulus for reflection, allowing teachers to hear the reality of group talk and gain insights into the pupils' perspectives.
>
> The oral diary revealed teachers openly questioning their views and their practice to develop plans for their future practice, as illustrated by sequenced extracts from Emma's diary:
>
>> They [the children] didn't really question what they had produced necessarily and again looking ahead … that could be … peers being able to look at their work together.
>>
>> But I want them to be ready to do it themselves next time and I think if I keep giving it to them they are not going to make that step.
>>
>> I am more aware of not talking too much … The hardest thing was not to get involved but at the same time not to let them go off at the totally wrong tangent.
>>
>> I said to them I've not taught like this before and thought I'd just see what questions they could come up with and I was a bit unsure but I was just, go on, go with it … It gave them the courage and the opportunity to almost fly with it, to just have a go and learn from each other.
>
> The diaries revealed how teachers brought into consciousness their beliefs.

Reflective practice has become a central tenet of teacher professionalism embedded in initial teacher education (ITE) in the UK and referred to in UK Teacher Standards, either explicitly or implicitly. Beyond informing future practice, reflective journalling can also support a teacher's identity development (Schellings et al., 2023). However, there is a threat to this potential if reflexivity is overly prescribed, top-down. To be able to exert their agency, teachers need an awareness of the constraints and enablers to possibilities for future action (Priestley et al., 2015).

Studies have evidenced that teachers' practice is not easily aligned with what they value and believe about teaching. A values-practice-gap survey of more than 1,000 teachers from 338 primary and secondary schools, as part of the 'Learning How to Learn' project (Pedder and Opfer, 2013), identified this gap across a range of classroom and PD activities. If what teachers value is not revealed and discussed, practices will remain un-evaluated, and value-practice gaps will remain unidentified in schools. An international variant of this survey captured the influences of cultural and political agendas on the ways both value and practice are evaluated (Warwick, Shaw and Johnson, 2015). This evidences how those in schools with top-down approaches to teacher PD are in danger of staff developing routinised ways of thinking (and practising), as Dewey feared. We hope you find spaces and support in the schools you work in, for you and colleagues to challenge assumptions and develop reflective practice. Teachers can make active choices about which schools to work in, to allow them to find a 'level of fit' (Kelchtermans, 2017).

THE ROLES OF ENQUIRY AND OTHERS IN DEVELOPING AS A REFLECTIVE PRACTITIONER

The value of enquiry

Whilst research about teachers and teaching has been cited throughout this book, the power of individual and collaborative practitioner research is also promoted, in particular in the following unit. Being involved in enquiry is well evidenced as the most effective approach to CPD, as it allows evidence to inform practice development (Stoll, Harris and Handscombe, 2012; Gilchrist, 2018).

Together, teacher enquiry can collectively inform school development, which relates back to Hargreaves's notion of schools becoming self-improving. Enquiry is written explicitly into the expectations of education professionals in Wales and Scotland. For example, teachers are engaged in collaborative research networks connecting schools with universities across Wales, and the criteria for professional learning in Scotland is supported by the GTCS providing regular advice about practitioner enquiry (Education Scotland/Foghlam Alba, 2022). In Vignette 2, we illustrate the significance of enquiry for a beginning teacher's development.

Vignette 2: Reflections on the value of enquiry as CPD

(With thanks to Emily Smith, John Mayne C of E Primary School, part of Tenterden Schools Trust)

When I started as an early career teacher, I wanted to focus on behaviour management and enhance my skills. I began by researching different behaviour strategies and how to support children with social, emotional, and mental health difficulties, which led me towards 'emotion coaching' (Gus, Rose and Gilbert, 2015). This was inspired from reading Paul Dix's book '*When the adults change, everything changes*' (Dix, 2017).

As a Year 1 teacher, I use emotion coaching as a crucial aspect of my teaching approach. It is vital to create a safe and supportive environment where students can recognise and regulate their emotions. When difficulties arise, through one-to-one discussions, I can help the child to recognise their feelings, validate their experiences and offer approaches for self-regulation (Dignath, Buettner and Langfeldt, 2008).

Self-regulation for the 5- to 6-year-olds in my classroom includes breathing techniques, mindfulness and becoming aware of themselves and their surroundings. I have integrated this into our daily routine so that all children can re-centre themselves which gets them in the right frame of mind to focus and engage in the lesson. Through our daily routine, the students have learned to identify and manage their emotions when faced with academic and social challenges. A child that I have taught, who would struggle when conflicts would arrive with other children, would express his upset by throwing objects or lashing out at other children. However, after getting into the routine of self-regulation now before he gets to that point, he can self-regulate, he will find his 'calm box' which consists of colouring, a blanket and bubble wrap which are all things that he finds calming and once he has calmed down, he can express his feelings to an adult and will rejoin the rest of the class.

This approach not only supports emotional intelligence but also promotes a positive and empathetic classroom atmosphere.

Overall, implanting emotion coaching and regulation skills in my classroom has been instrumental in promoting a positive and productive learning environment for my students.

Collaborative enquiry into how to develop practice cannot be assumed to take place simply by teachers being put together and expected to collaborate. For teachers to feel able to challenge themselves, trust and a supportive environment are prerequisites (Nelson, Spence-Thomas and Taylor, 2015).

The importance of others

In Task 9.2.2 you will have reflected on the potential role of others in your development as a teacher. Some of these might be the mentors or coaches all early career teachers should be offered. Is there a distinction between mentoring and coaching support?

A *mentoring* approach is intended to be directive, suggesting a relationship between a more experienced and a more novice practitioner. The support given through mentoring relates to passing on essential knowledge and skills developed from years of experience, ideally using their experience and pedagogic skills to model teaching and learning.

Coaching can be seen as at another end of a continuum (see Figure 9.2.3), where a coach could be anyone trained in coaching skills. A teacher can be 'coached' by being encouraged to talk about the issues they are facing in a non-directive way and, using a variety of strategies, supported to find solutions to their own problems. This approach is also a powerful way to develop a teacher's reflective skills and increase teacher independence.

The two approaches are not mutually exclusive, as Anne and Shauna explain in Vignette 3.

Vignette 3: An effective coaching relationship with a mentor

(With thanks to Anne Kagoya and Shauna Donno, Class teachers at Our Lady and Saint George Catholic Primary School, London)

Anne was teaching a Year 4/5 composite class of children aged between 8 to 10 years and Shauna was teaching a Year 5 class (of 9–10 year olds) in a Catholic Primary School. Anne had been teaching 25 years and Shauna had been teaching 5 years. In order to cover the RSE (Relationships and Sexuality Education) national curriculum requirements, which were new to us and potentially challenging to implement, we chose to team teach the Year 5 cohort of 50 children together whilst our Year 4 children joined the other Year 4 class for their RSE lessons.

From Shauna's point of view, it was a rare opportunity to learn and question who she is as a teacher. It gave her a chance to reflect on what learning can look like. Shauna was able to consider the importance of making sure each child had a voice in real time. It was genuine teaching rather than 'simply getting the job done'. It was relaxed, calm and non-performative. We, as teachers, built a stronger learning community where there was open communication, mutual reflection and respect between both adults and children.

From Anne's point of view, learning from Shauna, the values of the Catholic Faith, a younger teacher's perspective of Safeguarding and *Keeping Children Safe in Education* (DfE, 2023), helped her to analyse her own standpoints, opinions and values. Anne also appreciated learning how a colleague filtered what could have been quite dictatorial material and used her professional knowledge of the children to keep it relevant and meaningful. As the weeks progressed, the trust between them grew and consequently grew between the children and themselves. Both Anne and Shauna felt having to find a practical solution to a logistical problem led to this shared coaching experience.

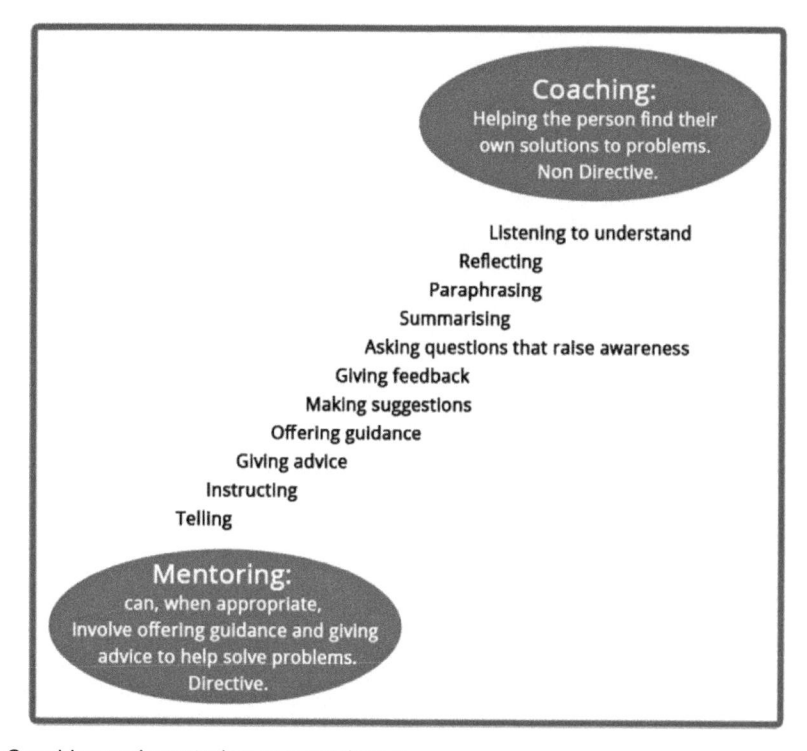

Coaching:
Helping the person find their own solutions to problems. Non Directive.

Listening to understand
Reflecting
Paraphrasing
Summarising
Asking questions that raise awareness
Giving feedback
Making suggestions
Offering guidance
Giving advice
Instructing
Telling

Mentoring:
can, when appropriate, involve offering guidance and giving advice to help solve problems. Directive.

FIGURE 9.2.3 Coaching and mentoring as a continuum
Source: GTCS (2016)

Mentoring, rather than coaching, is most commonly employed and embedded within teacher training and induction, especially since the establishment of the Early Career Framework in England and Wales. However, concerns have been raised about the dangers, in 1:1 situations, of this becoming overly judgemental – termed 'judgementoring' (Hobson, 2016). Schools are encouraged to consider a more equable coaching-like or 'onside mentoring' provision, as illustrated by Anne and Shauna in Vignette 3. This should offer holistic support, paying attention to wellbeing and empowering the mentee to become agentic in their next steps, including engaging in enquiry (Hobson, 2016). In Vignette 4, Amber reflects on how she navigated the different opportunities afforded her and identified what she feels she still needs in her first year of teaching.

Vignette 4: Amber's reflections on learning from and with others

(Amber Hall, Class teacher, Our Lady and Saint George Catholic Primary School, London)

When writing this piece I have just begun my second ECT year and am using *UCL-extend* (an online platform that aims to develop your teaching skills through tasks and readings[1]) to guide my CPD and mentoring sessions. During my first year as an ECT, participating in this course, I believe I have made significant progress in my understanding and knowledge of what it is to be an 'outstanding' teacher. I participated in weekly discussions with my mentor (another teacher in my school) at the end of the school day, who helped me better understand the teacher standards and how to implement them in my everyday practice. I have had multiple opportunities to observe other professionals and ask questions about their practices, giving me the opportunity to take on some of these learning techniques. My mentor has shown me how to practise different learning scenarios in the classroom.

When observed, I am given targets to work on and support on how to achieve these targets which I believe has made a significant difference in my practice, boosted my confidence and has helped me ensure the pupils in my class are learning. I believe my mentoring experience was positive due to the feelings of having continuous support from my mentor and having someone to turn to when things do not go as planned. If I were to change something about my mentoring experiences as an ECT, it would be having greater access to examples of how different teacher standards could be met in a class more similar to my own. While *UCL-extend* provides lots of information on what to do, it gives less information on how to directly apply that knowledge to different year groups and groups of children (such as those with special educational learning needs and English as a foreign language, etc.).

Task 9.2.3 Engaging with your professional development planning

Having read this unit, you will have seen how you can be active in your own PD.

To help you contribute to your appraisal/performance management meetings, it might be helpful to prepare some reflections:

Step back for a moment and …

Celebrate!

Identify the things you feel proud of, have enjoyed doing and/or have given you satisfaction.

Analyse!

List the skills and attributes you have used to make these activities successful. Note skills it would be useful to have or be stronger in.

Imagine!

Imagine what will be expected of you at the end of the coming year. How confident or excited do you feel about achieving these? Note down any constraints you are aware of. What else do you want to have achieved? And why?

Request!

Identity and be prepared to ask for advice about CPD opportunities which could help you.

You might start by reviewing the Professional Teacher Standards relevant to your context and colour code those you think you:

i   are achieving well (colour *green*);
ii could develop further over the coming year (colour *amber*); or
iii should prioritise (colour *red*).

To help, ask others, refer to feedback you have received and look at evidence you have collected. A professional portfolio is a great way to collate evidence of your achievements and progress. Base your evaluations on the assumption that you are meeting all the standards, but are committing to a serious and honest self-evaluation of where you want to focus your efforts in the coming year.

SUMMARY: THE BENEFITS OF CPD

As you join the profession, you will be assessed as competent to teach against the relevant Teachers' Standards. This is not a one-off judgement and you are expected to continue the process started during teacher training of:

- setting targets;
- meeting with a mentor;
- keeping records of CPD;
- taking a full part in school life.

You should find you are provided with opportunities to share experiences:

- with other teachers;
- with other early career professionals;
- and/or in working groups with teachers across the career stages;
- during formal or informal training.

These can be important spaces for self-reflection and self-evaluation. Consider keeping a reflective diary. Working alongside other, more experienced staff (including, but not limited to, mentors) can help you feel welcomed into the profession, offering opportunities to talk about practice and learn individually and collectively. Working within a school culture where staff are committed to professional learning offers the ideal conditions for support and challenge to develop practice and build professional relationships. Collaborative enquiry, where teachers undertake research in their settings, offers the chance to understand the reasons why particular approaches do or don't work and identify new pedagogical or assessment strategies to try. This can help understand the factors at play in a profession as complex as teaching: a powerful element of CPD. Be alert to avoiding routinised thinking and be open to challenging assumptions and beliefs. This requires your commitment to being proactive about your development, and for school leaders to commit to offering you an 'expansive' learning environment.

NOTE

1   www.ucl.ac.uk/isd/services/learning-teaching/learning-teaching-services/online-learning-and-short-courses/ucl-extend (accessed 31 January 2025)

ANNOTATED FURTHER READING

Guskey, T. R. and Yoon, K. S. (2009) 'What works in professional development?', *Leading Edge Series, Phi Delta Kappan*, 90(7): 495-500. Retrieved from: https://keystoliteracy.com/wp-content/pdfs/orc-implement-science/What%20works%20in%20PD.pdf (accessed 31 January 2025).

> In this accessible paper, more than 1,300 studies identifying connections between PD and student learning outcomes are reviewed. The conclusions re-evaluate the importance of workshops, external experts and time in offering effective teacher CPD and reinforce the value of enquiry.

Lieberman, A. and Miller, L. (2011) 'Learning communities: The starting point for professional learning is in schools and classrooms', *The Learning Professional*, 32(4): 16-20. https://learningforward.org/wp-content/uploads/2011/08/lieberman.pdf (accessed 31 January 2025).

> This article brings together five research studies to illustrate the ways schools can provide teachers with opportunities for collaborative PD, framed as professional learning. It concludes by summarising what it terms 'essential practices' as well as identifying key challenges.

Menter, I. and McLaughlin, C. (2015) 'What do we know about teachers' professional learning?' in C. McLaughlin, P. Cordingley, R. McLellan and V. Baumfield (eds) *Making a Difference: Turning Teacher Learning Inside-Out*, Cambridge: Cambridge University Press, pp. 41-51. Retrieved from: www.researchgate.net/profile/Colleen-Mclaughlin-8/publication/282246057_Making_a_difference_-_Turning_teacher_learning_inside_out/links/560a76b508ae840a08d564ee/Making-a-difference-Turning-teacher-learning-inside-out.pdf#page=41 (accessed 31 January 2025)

> This book chapter offers an overview of changes in policy contexts supporting professional learning, conceptualises teacher learning and the needs for community support and covers different stages of career development and models of professional learning.

FURTHER READING TO SUPPORT M-LEVEL STUDY

Livingston, K. and Hutchinson, C. (2017) 'Developing teachers' capacities in assessment through career-long professional learning', *Assessment in Education: Principles, Policy and Practice*, 2492: 290-307. Retrieved from: https://eprints.gla.ac.uk/123823/1/123823.pdf (accessed 31 January 2025)

> This paper explores professional learning as a career-long commitment and illustrates this through the development of assessment practices. It covers: the skills teachers need to understand the role of assessment in supporting learning, the opportunities teachers have for developing such skills and understanding and how these can be offered from a local through to national scale. Whilst international evidence is drawn upon, the paper is focused on teachers in the Scottish context.

Milton, E., Daly, C., Langdon, F., Palmer, M., Jones, K. and Davies, A. J. (2022) 'Can schools really provide the learning environment that new teachers need? Complexities and implications for professional learning in Wales', *Professional Development in Education*, 48(5): 878-891. Retrieved from: https://pure.aber.ac.uk/ws/portalfiles/portal/37261211/Milton_Daly_et_al.pdf (accessed 31 January 2025).

> Mentoring is so important to supporting professionals into the profession. The paper is based on the views of nearly 100 school leaders and teachers across Wales who reveal their experiences of mentoring from both mentee and mentor perspectives. Insights into the 'complexities of schools as sites of professional learning for new teachers' offer directions for further enquiry and practice change whether in Wales or beyond.

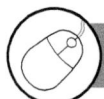

RELEVANT WEBSITES

Teacher Development Trust: https://tdtrust.org/
> The Teacher Development Trust is a charity set up to support and promote effective teacher professional development, with a free database and live updates.

The Chartered College of Teaching: https://chartered.college/
> Whilst based in the UK the Chartered College invites teachers internationally to join, with a range of categories of membership, offering an accreditation pathway to gain full Chartered Member status, as well as providing resources through podcasts, publications and events.

International Professional Development Association: www.ipda.org.uk
> The International Professional Development Association is a membership organisation of an international community of academics and professionals committed to exploring effective approaches to CPD, offering a programme of seminars and a journal.

REFERENCES

Argyris, M. and Schön, D. (1974) *Theory in Practice. Increasing Professional Effectiveness*, San Francisco, CA: Jossey-Bass.

Bangs, J., MacBeath, J. and Galton, M. (2011) *Reinventing Schools: Reforming Teaching*, London: Routledge.

Baker, J. (2019) 'Teachers – Being in Control or Being Controlled?' Education International blog post, 30 October. Retrieved from: www.ei-ie.org/en/item/23111:teachers-being-in-control-or-being-controlled-by-jim-baker (accessed 31 January 2025).

Beijaard, D., Verloop, N. and Vermunt, J. D. (2000) 'Teachers' perceptions of professional identity: An exploratory study from a personal knowledge perspective', *Teaching & Teacher Education*, 16(2): 749-764.

Biesta, G. J. (2010) 'Why 'what works' still won't work: From evidence-based education to value-based education', *Studies in Philosophy and Education*, 29: 491-503.

Boyt, T. E., Lusch, R. F. and Naylor, G. (2001) 'The role of professionalism in determining job satisfaction in professional services: A study of marketing researchers', *Journal of Service Research*, 3(4): 321-330.

Department for Education (DfE). (2016) *Standard for Teachers' Professional Development*, London: Crown Copyright. Retrieved from: www.gov.uk/government/publications/standard-for-teachers-professional-development (accessed 31 January 2025)

Department for Education (DfE). (2019a) *Teacher Appraisal and Capability Model Policy*, London: Crown Copyright. Retrieved from: https://assets.publishing.service.gov.uk/media/5c8a576940f0b640d0dc049d/Teacher_appraisal_and_capability_model_policy.pdf (accessed 31 January 2025).

Department for Education (DfE). (2019b) *Early Career Framework. Last updated 30 January 2024*. London: Crown Copyright. Retrieved from: www.gov.uk/government/publications/early-career-framework (accessed 31 January 2025).

Department for Education (DfE). (2023) *Keeping Children Safe in Education*, London: Crown Copyright. Retrieved from: https://assets.publishing.service.gov.uk/government/uploads/system/uploads/attachment_data/file/1181955/Keeping_children_safe_in_education_2023.pdf (accessed 31 January 2025).

Dignath, C., Buettner, G. and Langfeldt, H. P. (2008) 'How can primary school students learn self-regulated learning strategies most effectively? A meta-analysis on self-regulation training programmes', *Educational Research Review*, 3(2): 101-129.

Dix, P. (2017) *When the Adults Change, Everything Changes: Seismic Shifts in School Behaviour*, Carmarthen: Crown House Publishing Ltd.

Edgington, U. (2016) 'Performativity and accountability in the UK education system: A case for humanness', *Pedagogy, Culture & Society*, 24(2): 307-312.

Education Scotland (n.d.) *Curriculum for Excellence*. Retrieved from: https://home.scotlandscurriculum.scot/ (accessed 31 January 2025)

Education Scotland/Foghlam Alba. (2022) *Professional Standards and Professional Learning*, Edinburgh: Education Scotland, Retrieved from: https://education.gov.scot/professional-learning/national-approach-to-professional-learning/the-national-model-of-professional-learning/ (accessed 31 January 2025)

Estyn. (2022) *Guidance Handbook for the Inspection of Local Government Education Services*, Cardiff: Estyn. Retrieved from: www.estyn.gov.wales/system/files/2022-08/Guidance%20handbook%20for%20the%20 inspection%20of%20LGES%202022.pdf (accessed 31 January 2025).

Evans, L. (2011) 'The "shape" of teacher professionalism in England: Professional standards, performance management, professional development and the changes proposed in the 2010 White Paper', *British Educational Research Journal*, 37(5): 851–870.

Fox, A., Wilson, E. and Deaney, R. (2011) 'Beginning teachers' workplace experiences: Their perceptions and use of support', *Vocations & Learning*, 4(1): 1–24.

Fuller, A. and Unwin, L. (2006) 'Applying the expansive-restrictive framework', in K. Evans, P. Hodkinson, H. Rainbird and L. Unwin (eds) *Improving Workplace Learning*, London: Routledge, pp. 49–67.

General Teaching Council for Northern Ireland (GTCNI). (2011) *Teaching: The Reflective Profession*, Belfast: GTCNI. Retrieved from: www.gtcni.org.uk/professional-space/professional-competence/teaching-the-reflective-profession (accessed 31 January 2025).

General Teaching Council of Scotland (GTCS). (2016) *Coaching and Mentoring*, Edinburgh: GTCS. Retrieved from: www.gtcs.org.uk/professional-update/coaching-and-mentoring/ (accessed 31 January 2025).

Gilchrist, G. (2018) *Practitioner Enquiry: Professional Development with Impact for Teachers, Schools and Systems*, London: Routledge.

Gus, L., Rose, J. and Gilbert, L. (2015) 'Emotion coaching: A universal strategy for supporting and promoting sustainable emotional and behavioural well-being', *Educational & Child Psychology*, 32(1): 31–41.

Hargreaves, D. H. (2012) *A Self-Improving School System: Towards Maturity*, Nottingham, UK: National College for School Leadership.

Hobson, A. J. (2016) 'Judgementoring and how to avert it: Introducing ONSIDE Mentoring for beginning teachers', *International Journal of Mentoring and Coaching in Education*, 5(2): 87–110.

Kelchtermans, G. (2017) '"Should I stay or should I go?": Unpacking teacher attrition/retention as an educational issue', *Teachers and Teaching*, 23(8): 961–977.

Lieberman, A. and Miller, L. (2011) 'Learning communities: The starting point for professional learning is in schools and classrooms', *The Learning Professional*, 32(4): 16–20. Retrieved from: https://learningforward.org/wp-content/uploads/2011/08/lieberman.pdf (accessed 31 January 2025).

Milton, E., Daly, C., Langdon, F., Palmer, M., Jones, K. and Davies, A. J. (2022) 'Can schools really provide the learning environment that new teachers need? Complexities and implications for professional learning in Wales', *Professional Development in Education*, 48(5): 878–891. Retrieved from: https://pure.aber.ac.uk/ws/portalfiles/portal/37261211/Milton_Daly_et_al.pdf (accessed 31 January 2025).

National Education Union (NEU). (2019) *Appraisal Policy Checklist*, London: NEU. Retrieved from: https://neu.org.uk/sites/default/files/2023-02/Appraisal%20Policy%20Checklist_0.pdf (accessed on 31 January 2025).

Nelson, R., Spence-Thomas, K. and Taylor, C. (2015) *What Makes Great Pedagogy and Great Professional Development: Final Report*, London: NCTL. Retrieved from: https://dera.ioe.ac.uk/id/eprint/22157/1/What_makes_great_pedagogy_and_great_professional_development_final_report.pdf (accessed 31 January 2025).

OECD. (2019) *TALIS 2018 Results (Volume I): Teachers and School Leaders as Lifelong Learners*, Paris: OECD. Retrieved from: www.oecd.org/education/talis/talis-2018-results-volume-i-1d0bc92a-en.htm (accessed 31 January 2025).

Ofsted. (2023) *School Inspection Handbook: Ofsted Guidance on Inspecting Maintained Schools and Academies in England Under the Education Inspection Framework*, London: UK Government. Retrieved from: www.gov.uk/government/publications/school-inspection-handbook-eif (accessed 31 January 2025).

Pedder, D. and Opfer, V. D. (2013) 'Professional learning orientations: Patterns of dissonance and alignment between teachers' values and practices', *Research Papers in Education*, 28(5): 539–570.

Pillen, M., Beijaard, D. and Brok, P. D. (2013) 'Tensions in beginning teachers' professional identity development, accompanying feelings and coping strategies', *European Journal of Teacher Education*, 36(3): 240–260.

Pollard, A., Wyse, D., Craig, A., Daly, C., Harmey, S., Hayward, L., Higgins, S., McCrory, A. and Seleznyov, S. (2023) *Reflective Teaching in Primary Schools*, London: Bloomsbury Publishing.

Priestley, M., Biesta, G. and Robinson, S. (2013) 'Teachers as agents of change: Teacher agency and emerging models of curriculum', *Reinventing the Curriculum: New Trends in Curriculum Policy and Practice*, 1: 187–206.

Priestley, M., Biesta, G. J. J., Philippou, S. and Robinson, S. (2015) 'The teacher and the curriculum: Exploring teacher agency', *The SAGE Handbook of Curriculum, Pedagogy and Assessment*, pp. 187–201.

Schellings, G., Koopman, M., Beijaard, D. and Mommers, J. (2023) 'Constructing configurations to capture the complexity and uniqueness of beginning teachers' professional identity', *European Journal of Teacher Education*, 46(3): 372–396.

Schleicher, A. (2018) *Implementing Education Policies—Schools as Learning Organisations*, Paris: OECD Publishing. Retrieved from: www.youtube.com/watch?time_continue=25&v=hVDmF8XIWV4 (accessed 31 January 2025).

Schön, D. A. (1983) *The Reflective Practitioner: How Professionals Think in Action*, London: Basic Books.

Senge, P. M. (2006) *The Fifth Discipline: The Art and Practice of the Learning Organization*, London: Random House Business.

Stoll, L., Harris, A. and Handscombe, G. (2012) *Great Professional Development which Leads to Great Pedagogy: Nine Claims from Research*, London: NCSL.

United Nations (UN). (2015) *Transforming our World: The 2030 Agenda for Sustainable Development*, New York,: United Nations. Retrieved from: https://sdgs.un.org/2030agenda (accessed 31 January 2025).

Warwick, P., Shaw, S. and Johnson, M. (2015) 'Assessment for learning in international contexts: Exploring shared and divergent dimensions in teacher values and practices', *Curriculum Journal*, 26(1): 39–69.

Welsh Government (n.d.) *Curriculum for Wales Framework*. Retrieved from: https://hwb.gov.wales/curriculum-for-wales (accessed 31 January 2025)

UNIT 9.3

RESEARCH AND PROFESSIONAL LEARNING

Using research and enquiry to develop practice through asking 'What if?', 'What else?' and 'What for?' as well as 'What might work?'

Cathy Burnett

INTRODUCTION

One of the most exciting – and perhaps challenging – dimensions of learning to teach is that the learning never stops. We cannot underestimate the complexity of teaching, of developing inclusive approaches to facilitate all our pupils' learning while responding to their emotional and social needs, and organising classes of children, given limited space and resources. Moreover, we find that approaches that work well for one child or in one context do not work for others, that policy changes place new demands on us as professionals or that there are broader shifts in society – such as developments in new technologies – that have implications for education. Being a teacher involves ongoing reappraisal as we review, interrogate and re-evaluate how we are supporting children's learning, and the values and beliefs that underpin what we do.

This unit explores how engaging with research, possibly through further qualification, can help you reflect on your practice more deeply and make informed decisions about your work. It is likely that you will engage with research and enquiry during initial teacher education, for example through conducting small-scale investigations or child studies or reading and reflecting on published research. This unit describes how research can support you throughout your career. Research will help you gain new insights, build your confidence to refine or innovate and sometimes generate the evidence to justify why you should continue to do what you are already doing. After discussing different perspectives on teacher-led research and enquiry, this unit explores how you can challenge your own assumptions about practice. It also provides guidance on critical engagement with the research that others produce. Finally, it explores how you can become involved in research and considers the benefits of collaboration and belonging to professional communities within and beyond your school or trust.

OBJECTIVES

By the end of this unit, you will be able to:

- identify how engagement with research will support ongoing critical reflection on your practice;
- engage critically with the work of other researchers;
- consider how your practice is underpinned by certain ways of thinking, values and beliefs;
- identify how you can use research to explore children's perspectives;
- recognise the value of engaging in collaborative, research-focused activities.

In Northern Ireland ...

Teachers cannot be developed passively. They develop actively. It is vital, therefore, that they are centrally involved in decisions concerning the direction and processes of their own learning.

(Galanouli, 2009: 11)

In Scotland ...

Teaching Scotland's Future recognises key strengths in Scotland as we continue to build a culture of career-long professional learning, owned by individual teaching professionals and supported by coherent and sustained systems. That includes the 35 hour per year commitment of every teacher in Scotland to continuing professional development (CPD), alongside other opportunities for professional learning across the working week and through in-service days.

(Scottish Government, 2011: 13)

WHAT IS RESEARCH, AND WHY IS IT IMPORTANT TO PROFESSIONAL DEVELOPMENT?

Teachers constantly make choices and decisions. In doing so, they gather evidence through talking to children, observing what they do and analysing what they produce. As they make sense of all this, they draw conclusions about how children are learning. Teachers work in busy, complex environments, and consequently much of this sense-making is tacit, and decisions about how to respond are often rapid. These processes of gathering evidence and drawing conclusions are very similar to those we associate with research. Engaging in research is essentially about engaging in these processes more systematically. It means slowing down to look more deeply and perhaps differently at what is happening. This process involves being explicit about the questions you want to investigate and deciding which research methods will generate the kinds of understanding you need to answer these questions. It means collecting and analysing data in an organised manner and considering different interpretations of what you find. Ultimately, it means communicating the results to others, so that they can learn from what you have found out. Much teacher research involves *action research* or *practitioner enquiry* through which teachers research and develop their own practice, collecting evidence and using what they learn from this to inform what they do. Jenni Newton, for example, conducted an action research project as part of her Masters degree:

> I carried out an enquiry for my Masters in my third year of teaching. I had started working in a new school and was given responsibility for Music, which was the subject I had studied for my undergraduate degree. I wanted to find out about the school's vision for teaching music and how this connected with other approaches that I had read about in the research literature. I developed a questionnaire which helped me to understand staff perspectives on the subject. Finding out that some of my colleagues lacked confidence in this area (understandably), I led some CPD which included a chance to explore how music teaching could be linked to other curriculum areas. I also produced a curriculum booklet that addressed their concerns and introduced new ways of teaching music. When I evaluated the outcomes, I found that this work seemed to have made a real difference to how colleagues felt about the subject.
>
> Undertaking this analysis really helped me in a number of ways. First of all, the fact that I was studying a Masters (part-time) seemed to open the door to having professional discussions with colleagues. This was important, as I was new to the school and relatively inexperienced. Doing the enquiry made me feel like I was on a 'level playing field' with colleagues and that I could discuss what was happening in school – beyond my own classroom. I also enjoyed the opportunity to engage with a mixture of research, policy and practice and reflect on what was happening, what might be happening, and what could be happening in relation to Music provision. It gave me the confidence to become more 'outward looking' and not just consider what was happening in my classroom, and see what was happening across the school. I now have a leadership role within an academy and this ability to look outwards – to explore different avenues of theory and practice – is crucial to what I do as a teacher, as well as a leader.

The terms 'practitioner enquiry' and 'action research' have been used to describe investigations conducted in different ways and for different purposes. Sometimes these focus on developing and refining effective approaches to teaching a specific topic or skill whereas sometimes they delve into an aspect of children's or teachers' experiences – into how children or teachers approach or feel about certain kinds of activity, for example. Sometimes investigations are driven by the priorities of schools or trusts and sometimes by teachers' own interests and concerns. Sometimes they are conducted by an individual and sometimes by a team or through partnerships between teachers and academics or other interested organisations (Rutton, 2021). Action research involves a process through which a problem or question is identified, explored and addressed, leading to new questions or a refinement of the existing question which, in turn, leads to new cycles of enquiry (Mertler, 2019). Perhaps most importantly engaging in research can enable teachers to take charge of what they do.

With this in mind, a *critical* stance is important. Teacher research is not just about finding 'what works' to raise attainment in relation to existing frameworks, but about interrogating the assumptions, values and beliefs that underpin policy and practice (Carr and Kemmis, 1986). A critical stance emphasises the relationship between the specific contexts in which teachers work and broader social, cultural and political contexts. As White *et al.* (2021) argue:

> Positioning 'agentive' teachers to both determine their own place in the world and prepare their students for living in such a world requires teachers who: are research literate in that they continue with their own learning; know how to identify problems related to their practice, their students' learning and education more generally; and can think beyond the 'accepted wisdom' to pose new questions about these problems and to harness a set of skills and capabilities that enables them to implement change.
>
> (p. 348)

> **In Scotland ...**
>
> The Scottish Government will ask the National Partnership Group to consider how Masters level work can be built into ITE courses, induction year activities and ongoing CPD activity. Alongside this the Government encourages universities to set up Masters accounts for students studying on ITE courses.
>
> (Scottish Government, 2011: 29)

Task 9.3.1 Considering relationships between research and teaching

Lankshear and Knobel suggest that a teacher who is involved in research is also a 'thinker, troubleshooter, creator, designer and practitioner' (Lankshear and Knobel, 2004: 11).

Discuss what you feel is meant by each of these terms in relation to your teaching role, using examples from your own experience or of practice you have observed or read about.

Next, order the terms from 'most' to 'least' to represent the extent to which you feel you have had opportunities to fulfil each of these roles in your teaching experience to date. Consider what has enabled you to do so, and any barriers you have faced.

Discuss how you think research might support you in carrying out these different roles as you embark on your career.

Importantly, when individual teachers and researchers look at evidence, they often notice very different things and have different ways of interpreting what they do notice. In her seminal book *Listening to Stephen Read*, Kathy Hall (2003) illustrated this powerfully by presenting interviews with four experts on the teaching of reading, all of whom had different beliefs about what reading involves and, consequently, how children can best be supported to become readers. The interviews focus on their analysis of evidence of 8-year-old Stephen's reading. They each draw different conclusions about him as a reader and the kinds of experience that might be appropriate for him. The book not only helps us understand different perspectives on reading, but also illustrates how different theoretical understandings can lead us to different conclusions when we analyse evidence. Just like researchers, all teachers draw on theories as they interpret what learners are doing and what they need. These theories may be explicit (based on values and beliefs that they clearly express) or implicit (evident in what they do and the assumptions they make as they do so). Research can help you re-examine some of the implicit theories that underpin everyday practice and understand what happens in your classroom from other perspectives.

In a project, led by Teresa Cremin and colleagues (2015), teachers researched children's 'literacy lives' outside school in order to better understand 'the cultural, linguistic and social assets' they brought to school. Drawing on work by Moll *et al.* (1992) on 'funds of knowledge', they supported teachers to recognise and investigate what children *could* do and *did* know, rather than what they could not do. The project shifted teachers' perceptions about schools and parents, strengthened relationships between teachers and families, and generated new approaches to working in partnership.

As part of a British Academy funded project, *Doing Data Differently* (Clarke-Allan et al., 2021), seven primary teachers set out to collect data on aspects of literacy teaching that mattered to them. They did this in various ways: some observed what children were doing and recorded this visually, some logged what happened in a school day while some used visual metaphors to capture what they saw, felt or did. They all found creative and imaginative ways to present their data. One teacher spent time observing children during a session in the library and systematically logged children's interactions, where they went and the books they chose. She found that this opportunity to observe gave her new insights into her children as readers:

> It was just really interesting because so often I think as teachers you're hands on, you're constantly doing things, spinning plates. I took the conscious decision to just sit back and just watch and not intervene, not interfere and just let them make the choices, and particularly with the ones where I think I'd underlined a few where they were the children that took three, four, maybe five minutes to find a book because normally I'd be like, come on, get a move on, you need to begin reading but they did, they settled in their own time and still had ten minutes reading time afterwards. It was that social aspect that really struck me.
>
> (cited in Burnett, Merchant and Guest, 2022: 153)

Another teacher in the group commented more generally about the value of taking time to reflect on what they were trying to achieve as a teacher:

> I think it's something that as teachers we always come back to because you can have all your Ofsteds and all your testing and everything but actually those 30 children that are sitting in front of you on a day-to-day basis, are you meeting their needs and are you doing the right thing for them? [...] it just evoked so much conversation which, again, as professionals it's not something we often get a chance to do, just to reflect and have that time to sit back and think am I doing the right thing? Am I doing the best thing for the children? Is there another way to do it?
>
> (Burnett, Merchant and Guest, 2022: 153)

Task 9.3.2 Reflecting on your own assumptions when analysing practice

With a group of colleagues, watch a video of children interacting around a shared task. This could be a video of children you have taught or one of the many videos of classroom practice found on the Teachers TV video archive, available via YouTube. Individually, jot down what you notice about how the children interact and how this is supporting their learning.

Afterwards, draw two conclusions about these children's interactions based on what you have noted. Take turns with your colleagues to share and justify your observations.

Discuss reasons for any differences – both in what you noticed and in your explanations. Which theories – implicit or explicit – did you draw on as you made sense of what you observed? For example, did these relate to assumptions about each individual child, or to features such as the task or the setting?

Another way of gaining a different perspective is to research children's perspectives of school. Children will learn what counts in classrooms from what happens when they enter them, the resources they can access, the way their spaces are bounded and regulated and the responses given to what they do and say. It can, however, be hard to elicit children's experiences as they may find it difficult to express what they feel or be reluctant to speak candidly. Clark and Moss (2011) recommend using participatory methods to enable parents, children and practitioners to build a 'mosaic' of a child's experiences. This might involve, for example, inviting children to take photographs, give tours, create maps or role-play. The range of evidence can then be used to stimulate reflection and dialogue about children's experiences and feelings and how to respond to these as a teacher. You will also find it valuable to explore parents' experiences of their children's time at school.

Anne Kellock and Julia Sexton (2018) drew on visual narratives created with eight children using annotated photographs they took of their classroom environment. The narratives gave unexpected insights into what these children felt about their classroom space. This led to changes in classroom routines and organisation.

Jill Pluquailec, Gill O'Connor and Emma Sadler (2023) interviewed parents about their response to the government's SEND Review (Department for Education [DfE], 2022) which was a consultation on provision for children and young people identified as having special educational needs and disabilities. Their report (Pluquailec, O'Connor and Sadler, 2023) highlights a number of concerns arising from parents' experiences of their children's schooling and of wider policy. It also raises broader questions about how schools and teachers communicate and learn from the parents and families of the children they teach.

Task 9.3.3 Thinking differently about a focus area

Identify an aspect of your teaching experience to date that has caused you concern or raised questions for you. This could, for example, be linked to an area of the curriculum, the experiences of a particular group of children or the broader school environment. Summarise the evidence you currently have that has led you to identify this issue. Identify what you think you already know about this and your possible explanations for how things are. Try to represent these in diagrammatical form. Now consider what you could investigate to help you gain a deeper understanding of this area. Whose perspectives might you investigate? How might you involve children or parents and carers in this process? What kind of evidence might you collect? How might the wider context – such as school, local or national policy – be relevant here? Annotate your initial diagram with these areas for further investigation. It will help to talk through your ideas with a friend – can they provide other possible explanations? Or suggest other areas for enquiry?

'EVIDENCE' AND THE EDUCATION ENDOWMENT FOUNDATION

The previous sections have suggested that carrying out your own research and enquiry can play an important role in your ongoing professional learning. You will also find it valuable to draw on published educational research and other writing done by researchers in universities and/or commissioned by organisations. Such work can provide new insights or introduce new approaches. In doing so it is worth noting that different kinds of research may speak to practice in different ways.

In recent years it has become increasingly common to hear policy makers calling for schools to build on 'the best available evidence of what works' and this reflects wider discussions about the need to draw more effectively on research evidence in policy and practice (OECD, 2023). Various organisations are dedicated to distilling what can be learned from educational research and presenting summaries that are accessible to schools. You may find, therefore, that you encounter *reviews* of research that make recommendations based on the findings of multiple studies on a single topic. Research reviews or summaries vary in purpose and in approach. When reading them it is worth remembering that all reviews are selective, whether or not they make their selection criteria transparent. They may, for example, focus on certain aspects of a topic or on certain age groups. They may draw on research conducted using a limited set of methodologies, or feature research only within a certain time scale. These choices will frame the research that is deemed to be relevant and, consequently, the reviews' conclusions. Different reviews conducted on the same topic may well lead to quite different conclusions.

One organisation which plays a central role in producing and mediating research evidence for education in the UK is the Education Endowment Foundation (EEF), which is an independent charity in receipt of government funding. EEF has been designated as the government's trusted source of evidence on effective approaches to education in England (Zahawi, 2022: 9). A key part of EEF's work involves funding randomised controlled trials (RCTs) to measure the impact of particular approaches, strategies or interventions. An RCT has an experimental design through which a group is split into two. One sub-group receives an intervention (a new teaching approach or a programme of support, for example) while a second sub-group – 'the control group' – continues as usual. The effects of the intervention are measured by comparing the outcomes of both groups after a given period (usually through a test). EEF is engaged in various activities designed to support schools in building on research evidence. As well as funding RCTs and producing research reviews and guidance, EEF co-ordinates a network of 'research schools' to provide support to other schools in working with evidence for the purposes of school improvement.

EEF has contributed to a range of government policy documents and frameworks that you are likely to encounter as a teacher. These include the Core Content Framework (DfE, 2019) which sets out what trainees must learn through initial teacher training and into the early years of teaching. The Framework is described as building on the 'best available evidence' and includes an approved bibliography. It is important to know that the EEF has developed and applies a particular set of criteria for what counts as 'best evidence'. These take account of variables like sample size and the consistency of the intervention or approach being evaluated. Much of the evidence cited draws on RCTs or quasi experimental studies.

BEYOND WHAT WORKS

Ideas about which kinds of evidence or research might be useful to schools and to teachers has been the subject of a great deal of debate. Many have argued that RCTs and other experimental studies can never provide us with straightforward evidence of 'what works' (Biesta, 2016). Learning is always highly contextualised, and what 'works' in one context may not in others. There are also various practical and ethical concerns when conducting RCTs in educational contexts (Cartwright, 2019; Fives et al., 2015; Joyce, 2019). While these questions have been the subject of considerable debate, it is likely that you will find different kinds of research useful to you in different ways. It may sometimes be useful to draw on large-scale studies which arrive at generalisations of what might be most effective, but at others it may be more valuable to work with studies that have explored the experiences of just a few children or teachers in depth. Research using qualitative methods, for example, aims to describe and analyse children's experience rather than measure it. Such work can raise important questions for you as a teacher. Examples include:

- Interview studies that explore experiences or perspectives, e.g. an interview study of 8-9-year-old boys' reading by Laura Scholes, Nerida Spina and Barbara Comber (2021) which challenges some common assumptions about what boys choose to read.
- Ethnographic work which sets out to provide rich descriptions of classroom life. E.g. Jacqueline D'warte investigated language use by 6-8-year-old bilingual children who had recently moved to Australia. She invited the children to create maps showing the languages they used and how and where they used them. She then worked with the teachers to recognise and build on children's linguistic repertoires in school (D'Warte, 2020).
- Discourse analysis that provides detailed insights into classroom interactions, e.g. Lauran Doak used multimodal analysis to explore the communication of children who did not use spoken language (Doak, 2018). She explored how they used gesture, movement and sound to communicate for a range of purposes. Her work highlights the diverse ways in which these children used different modes of communication, challenging some of the assumptions that are often made of children labelled as 'non verbal'. It highlights the kinds of interactions that the children enjoyed and which seemed to enable them to communicate what they wanted. It also highlighted barriers to their communication.

Such studies may well involve small numbers of children but can provide rich and detailed insights into classroom life and the experiences of individual children and teachers. As such they may well provide a valuable starting point for reflecting on practice. The studies described could, for example:

- **Provide inspiration and/or guidance** for how to plan and provide for children in ways that they find enabling and empowering and which recognise and value their varied experiences and strengths.
- **Stimulate critique of established ways of doing things**, helping to reflect on how everyday classroom practices and assessment arrangements might disadvantage some children.
- **Provide insight** into experiences or processes, helping to understand children's perspectives on what happens in class and to learn more about their experiences outside school and how these might be valued and feed into school based learning.
- Be used as inspiration for **imagining otherwise**. These studies could lead to broader discussions about how a curriculum could be devised that recognises and values children's different communications preferences, experiences and repertoires.
- Suggest **methods** that could be used to investigate your own classroom. The participatory mapping used in D'Warte's study, for example, could be used with children to explore different aspects of their experiences within or outside school.

Research evidence, therefore, is not only useful in signalling approaches that might 'work' but can also be helpful in providing ways to think about: 'What else...?', 'What if...?', 'Why...?', 'What's going on?' and 'How can I find out?' (Burnett et al., 2023).

Activity – Making sense of research

Take a research report or article and arrange to share your thoughts on this with a colleague. You could take one of those mentioned in this unit or elsewhere in this handbook. Before you start reading, reflect on the topic of the article (based on the title or abstract) and jot down what you already know and/or believe about this topic.

Once you have read the article, reflect on the key ideas presented and how these relate to the notes you wrote before you began reading. Is there anything that reflects your initial thoughts? Anything that contradicts? Anything that adds to your thinking or understanding?

Consider:

- the kinds of questions the article *addresses*;
- the kinds of questions the article *raises* for you as a teacher.

Consider whether, or how, the article leads to: guidance or inspiration, insights, critique, methods or imagining otherwise.

It may help to use different question starters to generate different kinds of questions: 'What might work?', What else…?', 'What if…?', 'Why…?', 'What's going on?' and 'How can I find out?'

CRITICAL ENGAGEMENT WITH PUBLISHED RESEARCH

Just as it is important to adopt a critical orientation when enquiring into your own practice, so it is important to engage critically with published research, particularly when that research is being used to justify local or national policy developments. Consider how researchers' assumptions, values and beliefs shaped what they tried to find out, how they went about this and what they concluded. One aspect of being critical involves evaluating how the study was conducted and judging whether or not the ideas presented seem justified. This involves considering whether methods used were well chosen to generate the insights the researchers claim to have gained. You might review, for example, the research tools used, the range of participants or the scale of the study. As discussed earlier, different kinds of research offer different sorts of insights. Consequently, they need to be evaluated in different ways. It is important not to dismiss a study simply because it is small-scale or because it used qualitative approaches. Critical evaluation of qualitative studies includes deciding whether the researchers' approach to the study enabled them to gain rich and detailed insights into the experiences or practices of the individuals, groups, classes or schools studied. In any case, as explored earlier, you need to try to identify the values, beliefs and assumptions (implicit and explicit) that informed the study and decide whether you feel these are appropriate.

Some questions to support critical reading of research articles and reports:

- Which research questions did the researchers set out to answer? How far did their research approaches and methods enable them to answer these questions?
- Which claims do they make, based on their findings? How far are these justified by the evidence presented?
- How do the findings connect to your current understanding and beliefs relating to this area, or to existing research?
- What implications do they have for your and others' practice?
- Do any issues or questions remain unresolved?
- Which values, beliefs and assumptions have informed the choice of research question, research approaches, methods, data analysis and conclusions?

> **Task 9.3.4 Critical review of research**
>
> Identify a report or journal article based on a recent study that has been linked to a policy development at local, regional or national level. For example, you could choose an article listed in the Reading List of one of the units in this handbook.
>
> Use the questions earlier to support your critical reading of the report or article.
>
> Next, search for any mentions of the report on social media. How far do these 'mentions' reflect the conclusions you have drawn through your own critical reading?

GETTING INVOLVED IN RESEARCH

There are lots of ways in which you may participate in research and/or enquiry. These include postgraduate programmes of professional development such as a Masters in Education or a course accredited through another organisation such as the Chartered College for Teaching, which is the professional body for teachers in England (https://chartered.college). You may gather credits towards a Masters degree during initial teacher education and have opportunities to gain further credits through modules aimed at early career teachers. Universities run a variety of Masters courses, including generic programmes with a broad range of options and those with a specific focus, such as literacy, inclusion or leadership. During a Masters programme, you are likely to engage in enquiries designed to research aspects of your work. Programmes will support you in reflecting critically on your practice, exploring it from different perspectives and developing your skills as a teacher-researcher. A Masters also provides you with an opportunity to read widely about research connected to topics you are interested in or concerned with.

Other opportunities for research arise when schools become involved in major projects or lead research themselves, for example through participating in large-scale trials conducted by the Education Endowment Foundation or collaborating with researchers in research/practice partnerships (McGeown *et al.*, 2023). Trusts and teaching school alliances may coordinate research activity and enquiry-based activities designed to benefit all their schools. Sometimes, schools take a national role in initiating and coordinating such developments. Working with colleagues to investigate and develop practice can be very rewarding. Indeed research seems to be most useful to teachers when they are given time and space to discuss it and to make connections between research findings and their professional experience (Cain *et al.*, 2019).

COLLABORATION BEYOND SCHOOLS

Many teachers access and exchange ideas through following teachers' blogs, signing up for email alerts from various organisations and using social media to connect with other teachers across the UK and overseas (Guest, 2018). As part of this, they may come across links to reports, blog posts and podcasts which are informed by research. There is also a wide array of other forms of online support available, such as webinars, conferences or training modules. These diverse formats can provide rich opportunities to exchange ideas, call for help, provide mutual support and develop professional relationships. Navigating online sources has therefore become a significant part of professional practice (Burnett *et al.*, 2023).

This access to a vast array of information and inspiration can be hugely supportive but it can also be overwhelming. This is partly due to the sheer volume of resources, alerts, sites and online spaces available, but also because, even though many claim that their work is 'evidence-based', it is often difficult to evaluate the credibility of underpinning research. As individuals and organisations compete for attention and/or business, it is increasingly common to see the claim that recommendations are 'evidence based' and it can be hard to work out where research comes from, which research is used as the basis of these claims and indeed whether they are based on any research at all. As a teacher you will find seemingly endless sources of inspiration online but you will need to weigh sources carefully and critically. This will become particularly important as artificial intelligence becomes more established as a way of gathering information. Artificial intelligence can offer rapid access to summaries of research to specific questions. However, just like any individual piece of research, these summaries will be selective, building on certain assumptions about what is relevant to your query and what is not.

Activity: Reflecting on the use of artificial intelligence to support professional learning

Generative artificial intelligence, such as Chat GPT, can summarise the findings of a range of sources rapidly. However, like any summary, it will be selective. Investigate this by entering a question into Chat GPT. You could try, 'What is the most effective way to teach literacy?', or something else that reflects your current interests and concerns. Once you have done this and made a copy of the results, try the same question again to generate another response, and then another. You will find that each time a slightly different response is given because it draws on different sources of information. Reflect on what is different about these results and what it suggests about the different ways in which a question can be defined, understood and/or investigated.

THE VALUE OF PROFESSIONAL ASSOCIATIONS

As well as opportunities that arise to engage with research and professional development within a school, trust or alliance, there are also many organisations that work with teachers across the country. These include professional or subject associations committed to the promotion and development of a particular subject or aspect of teaching. Joining an association or attending an association conference can provide you with rich opportunities to learn about recent research and/or present your own research, meet colleagues from elsewhere and even work with others to play an active part in influencing policy. Subject associations also sometimes offer small grants for research projects. Next, Vikki Varley reflects on her involvement with the United Kingdom Literacy Association (UKLA) and Simon Collis on his experience of the Geographical Association.

> **Vikki Varley:** UKLA is a community of people knowledgeable in various aspects of research and practice. Being part of UKLA can feel like being part of an extended family with lots of people who you can ask for advice. It's helpful to be part of an organisation beyond your school to meet likeminded people and to find out what's happening in other settings and what's working for them. It helps you form connections and ask questions if you don't have that expertise in school.
>
> Through UKLA I joined a Teachers Reading Group and this led to presenting at the UKLA conference in Birmingham. I talked about how this had made an impact in the classroom and how I took it further to make it a whole school initiative. I also focused on this for my Masters dissertation. The conference was a really good opportunity to be part of a research community. Presenting something gives you confidence.

I've been invited to be on the judging for the UKLA Book Awards and that's leading to my increased knowledge of children's literature. I also take part in the UKLA Hashtag chats and I led one of them on spelling with another UKLA member. This was a good opportunity to refresh my own knowledge beforehand and to reflect on my own ideas. It was also good to hear from others and to hear about research you hadn't encountered and to reassure yourself you're doing OK.

Simon Collis: Joining the Geographical Association (GA) began as an opportunity to build on knowledge and skills from my degree, but over time has grown into a much richer experience. It has given me the chance to be part of a broader educational community that encompasses professional researchers, teacher trainers, university lecturers and teachers from very different backgrounds to my own. This diverse group of people are all passionate about sharing a geographical vocabulary that allows children to articulate their place in the world and use a geographical lens to identify global and local challenges and offer possible solutions. Being part of this community allows individual teachers to 'zoom out' from their own context and approach teaching and learning from an alternative perspective.

The GA has also allowed me to write for their *Primary Geography* journal – to conduct small scale studies and then articulate them to a wider audience. Education is oftentimes a contested space, where teachers' experience can be mediated or crowded out by broader political or accountability frameworks. These links with the wider educational community allow an authentic voice for teachers.

Task 9.3.5 Investigating subject associations

In a group, each select a subject association from the following list. Visit its website and investigate the support and opportunities the association provides. Report back to the rest of the group.

- Association for Physical Education: www.afpe.org.uk
- Geographical Association: www.geography.org.uk
- NAACE – the IT association: www.naace.co.uk
- National Association for Language Development in the Curriculum: www.naldic.org.uk
- National Association for Primary Education: www.nape.org.uk
- National Association for Special Educational Needs: www.nasen.org.uk
- National Association for the Teaching of English: www.nate.org.uk
- National Drama: www.nationaldrama.org.uk/nd
- The Association for Science Education: www.ase.org.uk
- The Association of Teachers of Mathematics: www.atm.org.uk
- The Design and Technology Association: www.data.org.uk
- The Historical Association: www.history.org.uk
- The National Society for Education in Art & Design: www.nsead.org/home/index.aspx
- United Kingdom Literacy Association: www.ukla.org

You can also identify subject associations through the Council for Subject Associations website: www.subjectassociation.org.uk

> **In Northern Ireland ...**
>
> The Chief Inspector of the Education and Training Inspectorate, Stanley Goudie, stated:
>
> > There is proportionately insufficient investment in the development of the teachers and the educational workforce compared with that invested in changing structures and systems. The need to ensure a range of continuing professional development for those who lead, manage and teach has never been greater.
> >
> > (ETI, 2009: 59)

SUMMARY

This unit has explored the role of research in supporting ongoing critical reflection on practice. It has emphasised that this involves asking questions and collecting and analysing evidence as well as being prepared to examine the values and beliefs that underpin what you do and how you think about your work. It has suggested that collaborating with others is an important part of this process and also highlighted the need to keep up to date with research conducted by others and review this critically. Research has an important role in professional development, and it is hoped that the examples provided here will inspire you to keep investigating and interrogating practice throughout your career.

ANNOTATED FURTHER READING

Clark, A. (2017) *Listening to Young Children: A Guide to Understanding and Using the Mosaic Approach*, 3rd edn, London: Jessica Kingsley Publishers.
> This book explores how to conduct research in ways that are sensitive to the needs of very young children. The examples and approaches used are relevant to working with older children, too, and provide inspiration for thinking about how to explore children's perspectives on learning and their wider experience of school.

Cohen, L., Manion, L. and Morrison, K. (2017) *Research Methods in Education*, 8th edn, London: Routledge.
> This book gives practical guidance on designing and conducting research, including a very useful overview of research methods.

Perry, T. and Morris, R. (2023) *A Critical Guide to Evidence-Informed Education*, London: McGraw Hill.
> This book takes a critical look at the use of 'evidence' in education and raises questions to ask when encountering evidence as a teacher.

FURTHER READING TO SUPPORT M-LEVEL STUDY

Carter, C. and Nutbrown, C. (2016) 'A pedagogy of friendship: Young children's friendships and how schools can support them', *International Journal of Early Years Education*, 24(4): 395–413.
> This article uses participatory methods (including drawings, persona dolls) to investigate 5–6-year-old children's experiences of friendship. The article is an example of research into children's experiences that raises questions for teachers about their role beyond the curriculum.

Hardy, I., Rönnerman, K. and Edwards-Groves, C. (2018) 'Transforming professional learning: Educational action research in practice', *European Educational Research Journal*, 17(3): 421–441.
> This article explores how action research can support professional learning and highlights personal, political and professional aspects of this process.

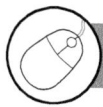

RELEVANT WEBSITES

Education Endowment Foundation (EEF): https://educationendowmentfoundation.org.uk/
> EEF's website includes reviews of research findings on a range of topics as well as summaries of education research projects it has funded, usually by conducting randomised control trials.

Monash Q project: www.monash.edu/education/research/projects/qproject
> The Monash Q project, based in Australia, explored how to support teachers to use research evidence to support their practice. Their website provides links to a range of useful resources and webinars.

That's a Claim: https://thatsaclaim.org/educational/introduction/
> Website designed to support educators in assessing whether the claims made about the effects of educational interventions stand up to scrutiny.

Using Research Evidence: https://educationendowmentfoundation.org.uk/support-for-schools/using-research-evidence
> EEF's guide to critical use of research evidence in education.

Research Mobilities in Primary Literacy Education: https://research.shu.ac.uk/rmple/
> This website features resources designed to support teachers' critical engagement with research, developed through the *Research Mobilities in Primary Literacy Education* project.

ACKNOWLEDGEMENTS

Some of the ideas in this unit were developed through the *Research Mobilities in Primary Literacy Education* project which was supported by the Economic and Social Research Council (grant number ES/W000571/1).

REFERENCES

Biesta, G. (2016) 'Improving education through research? From effectiveness, causality and technology to purpose, complexity and culture', *Policy Futures in Education*, 14(2): 194–210.

Burnett, C., Merchant, G. and Guest, I. (2022) 'Postcards from literacy classrooms: Possibilities for teacher-generated data visualisation', *Education 3-13*, 50(2): 145–158.

Burnett, C., Adams, G., Gillen, J., Thompson, T. L., Cermakova, A., Shannon, D. and Shetty, D. (2023) *Research Mobilities in Primary Literacy Education: How Does Research Reach Teachers in an Age of Evidence-Informed Education*, London: Routledge.

Cain, T., Brindley, S., Brown, C., Jones, G. and Riga, F. (2019) 'Bounded decision-making, teachers' reflection and organisational learning: How research can inform teachers and teaching', *British Educational Research Journal*, 45(5): 1072–1087.

Carr, W. and Kemmis, S. (1986) *Becoming Critical: Education, Knowledge and Action Research*, Lewes, UK: Falmer.

Cartwright, N. (2019) 'What is meant by "rigour" in evidence-based educational policy and what's so good about it?', *Educational Research and Evaluation*, 25(1-2): 63-80.

Clark, A. and Moss, P. (2011) *Listening to Young Children: The Mosaic Approach*, 2nd edn, London: National Children's Bureau.

Clarke-Allan, S., Cooke, S., Edwards, E., Hotham, E., MacLauglin, P., Burnett, C., Merchant, G. and Guest, I. (2021) 'Doing data differently: Small slow data on literacy teaching', *English 4-11*, Autumn, 73: 10-13.

Cremin, T., Mottram, M., Collins, F. M., Powell, S. and Drury, R. (2015) *Researching Literacy Lives: Building Communities Between Home and School*, Abingdon, UK: Routledge.

Department of Education (DfE). (2019) *Initial Teacher Training (ITT): Core Content Framework*. Last updated 2024. Retrieved from: https://assets.publishing.service.gov.uk/media/6061eb9cd3bf7f5cde260984/ITT_core_content_framework_.pdf

Department for Education (DfE). (2022) *SEND Review: Right Support, Right Place, Right Time*. Retrieved from: www.gov.uk/government/consultations/send-review-right-support-right-place-right-time

Doak, L. (2018) 'Exploring the multimodal communication and agency of children in an autism classroom'. PhD, Sheffield Hallam University.

D'warte, J. (2020) 'Recognizing and leveraging the bilingual meaning-making potential of young people aged six to eight years old in one Australian classroom', *Journal of Early Childhood Literacy*, 20(2): 296-326.

ETI. (2009) *Chief Inspector's Report 2006-2008*, Bangor, NI: Education and Training Inspectorate. Retrieved from: www.etini.gov.uk/content/chief-inspectors-report-0 (accessed 7 November 2017).

Fives, A., Russell, D., Canavan, J., Lyons, R., Eaton, P., Devaney, C., Kearn, N. and O'Brien, A. (2015) 'The ethics of randomized controlled trials in social settings: Can social trials be scientifically promising and must there be equipoise?', *International Journal of Research and Method in Education*, 38(1): 56-71.

Galanouli, D. (2009) *School-based Professional Development: A Report for the General Teaching Council for Northern Ireland (GTCNI)*, Belfast, GTCNI. Retrieved from: www.gtcni.org.uk/publications/uploads/document/School-Based%20comp_V3.pdf (accessed 7 November 2017).

Guest, I. F. (2018) 'Exploring teachers' professional development with Twitter: A sociomaterial analysis'. PhD, Sheffield Hallam University.

Hall, K. (2003) *Listening to Stephen Read: Multiple Perspectives on Literacy*, Buckingham, UK: Open University Press.

Joyce, K. (2019) 'The key role of representativeness in evidence-based education', *Educational Research and Evaluation*, 25(1-2): 43-62.

Kellock, A. and Sexton, J. (2018) 'Whose space is it anyway? Learning about space to make space to learn', *Children's Geographies*, 16(2): 115-127.

Lankshear, C. and Knobel, M. (2004) *A Handbook for Teacher Research: From Design to Implementation*. Open University Press.

McGeown, S., Oxley, E., Practice Partners, L. to R., Ricketts, J. and Shapiro, L. (2023) 'Working at the intersection of research and practice: The Love to Read project', *International Journal of Educational Research*, 117: 102134.

Mertler, C. A. (ed.). (2019) *The Wiley Handbook of Action Research in Education*, Oxford: Wiley Blackwell.

Moll, L., Amanti, C., Neff, D. and Gonzalez, N. (1992) 'Funds of knowledge for teaching: Using a qualitative approach to connect homes and classroom', *Theory into Practice*, 31(2): 132-141.

OECD. (2023) *Who Really Cares about Using Education Research in Policy and Practice? Developing a Culture of Research Engagement*, Educational Research and Innovation, Paris: OECD Publishing. https://doi.org/10.1787/bc641427-en

Pluquailec, J., O'Connor, G. and Sadler, E. (2023) *Right to Review Project Report: Parent Responses to the SEND Review and Participation in the Public Consultation Process*. Available from the Sheffield Hallam University Research Archive (SHURA) at: http://shura.shu.ac.uk/31848

Rutten, L. (2021) 'Toward a theory of action for practitioner inquiry as professional development in preservice teacher education', *Teaching and Teacher Education*, 97: 103194.

Scholes, L., Spina, N. and Comber, B. (2021) 'Disrupting the "boys don't read" discourse: Primary school boys who love reading fiction', *British Educational Research Journal*, 47(1): 163-180.

Scottish Government. (2011) *Continuing to Build Excellence in Teaching: Scottish Government's Response to Teaching Scotland's Future*. Retrieved from: www.gov.scot/Resource/Doc/920/0114570.pdf (accessed 7 November 2017).

White, S., Down, B., Mills, M., Shore, S. and Woods, A. (2021) 'Strengthening a research-rich teaching profession: An Australian study', *Teaching Education*, 32(3): 338-352.

Zahawi, N. (2022) *Opportunity for All*, London: DfE. Retrieved from: www.gov.uk/government/publications/opportunity-for-all-strong-schools-with-great-teachers-for-your-child

INDEX

Page numbers in *italics* denote figures, **bold** a table

5Rights Foundation 502

'ability' groups, variability 118-119
Abouchaar, A. 529
accelerated learning 465
accountability, Ofsted 24
achievement gap, poverty and 378-380, 529-530
achievement, provision of evidence 336-343
action research 469, 589-590
adaptive teaching: attention, types and management 353, **354**; core learning processes 352-358, *352*; definitions and appliance 351-352; diverse classrooms and needs 350-351; memory, support strategies 354-355, **355**; motivations 349-350; in Northern Ireland 352; processing, support strategies 355-356, **356**; in Scotland 352; social and emotional learning (SEL) 357, **357-358**; in Wales 351
additional learning needs (ALN) (Wales) 363-364, 373
Additional Learning Needs and Education Tribunal (Wales) Act (2018) 373
Additional Learning Needs Co-ordinator (Wales) 368, 370
additional support needs (ASN) (Scotland) 365, 367, 369
Adey, P. 136
advice, seeking 117
affective domain 114-115
African American Policy Forum (AAPF) 383
age-in-cohort 58-59
'aims-based curricula' 211
Ajegbo Report (2007) 389, 391, 395, 396
Alagiah, G. 394-395
Alexander, R. 96, 97-98, 113
Allen, M. 278
analogies, science 280-282, *281-282*
Angelou, M. 246
Antoniazzi, T. 516-517, 523
Appiah, K.A. 389
Appleby, Y. 13
apprenticeship, models of learning 137, 143-144
approachability, teacher/parent 530-531

artificial intelligence (AI): arts curricula 293; educational issues 501; research sources 598
arts, curricula and practice: artificial intelligence use 293; central aims, multiple approaches 291-294; cross-curricular learning 288, 292; dance and drama strategies 292-293; diversity and cultural awareness 288; educational value 286; empathy and confidence building 287-288; future success, base for 288-289; ideas, expression/exploration 287; National Curriculum 289-290, *291*; in Northern Ireland 291; partnership collaborations 295-296; self-management 288; sketching and journaling 293, *293-294*; subject coverage 286; teacher's role 295; Teachers' Standards 290; in Wales 290; whole-child involvement 287, 292
ArtsMark 296
Askew, M. 102
Askew, S. 39
Asperger, H. 174
Asperger's Syndrome 174
Aspfors, J. 556
aspirational orientation 33, **33**
aspiration, outdoor learning 195
assessment: definition and purpose 334-335; high-stakes/low-stakes 335, 343; inclusive practice 119-120; reading skills 237-238; Reception Baseline Assessment (RBA) 77; statutory 216-217; summative approaches 335-345, **344**; Teachers' Standards **23**; see also standard assessment tests (SATs); testing
Assessment for Learning (AfL): children's work, recognition of 328-329; feedback 330; overview 319; peer and self-assessment 329; planning for 322-324; questioning 324-328, **326**; ten principles 320-322
Assessment Reform Group 319
Atkinson, C. 517
attachment, childhood 52, 60
attachment theory 168
Attention Deficit/Hyperactivity Disorder (AD/HD) 171-172
Attention Restoration Theory 194

attention, types and adaptive teaching 353, **354**
Aubin, G. 116
Aubrey, C. 70
Aussiker, A. 151
autism 174
autonomy 140-141, 249, 451

Babad, E. 150
Bächler, R. 91, 92
Back, J. 262
Baggini, J. 25-26
Bailey, E.G. 417
Baker, J. 572
Barfod, K. 195
bar model 262, 264, *264-265*
Barnes, J. 492
basic interpersonal communication skills (BICs) 412
Beard, M. 303
Beaton, M. 439
Beck, J. 102
Bedford, D. 521
behavioural methodologies 165, 172
behaviourism 85, 86
behaviour management *see* classroom behaviour management; professional behaviours
Beijaard, D. 572, *573*
beliefs and values 10, 18-19, 566
Bellchambers, E. 310
Bercow Report (2008) 362
Bergmann, J. 139
Berninger, V.W. 88
Berry, M. 506
Bethune, M.M. 88
'bicycle model' 489
Biesta, G. 96-97, 98, 304
bilingual learners *see* linguistic diversity
Bingham, S. 70
'biophilia hypothesis' 194
Birchall, J. 520, 521
Birth to 5 Matters 68
Bjorklund, P. 336
Black, P. 319
Blatchford, P. 370-371
Bloom's taxonomy of thinking skills 461-462, **462**
Boardman, K. 70
Bobbit-Nolan, S. 140
Boden, M.A. 101
Bondas, T. 556
Bosanquet, P. 518
'botheredness' 131
Bowlby, J. 168
Boylan, M. 13
'Brain Gym' 465
bridging 140

briefing, classroom routine 156
British Film Institute 503
British Psychological Society (BPS) 172
British values, fundamental **23**
Brock, A. 408
Bronfenbrenner, U. 56
Brown, R. 303
Bruner, J.: communication and language development 53, 56; knowledge and learning 97, 98, 136; reasoning 262; scaffolding 77, 85
'buddy system' 541
Bugental, J. 86
Bukor, E. 19
Bullock Report (1975) 245, 407
bullying 400-401
Burnett, C. 499, 508
Burningham, J. 246
Burn, K. 35
Burroughs, N.H. 88
Butler, J. 423

Cairns Vollans, E. 237
calculation methods 259-260, *259*, **260**, *261*
Cambridge Assessment International Education (CAIE) 406
Cambridge Oracy Skills Framework 183
Cambridge Primary Review: digital age, education in 499; diversity education 395; early reading ability 70; effective teaching 97-98; parents/carers, working with 534; pupil voice 438; special educational needs (SEN) 362, 372
Cantell, H. 489
Cantle, E. 391
case studies: linguistic diversity 410, 413; personal identities 394-395; school diversity 394, *394*; sustainability and climate change education 491, 492-493, 495; urban diversity 393; a vegetable garden 200-201
Catling, S. 308
Catney, G. 391
Catterall, J.S. 288-289
challenging pupils 159-160
Change4Life School Zone 51
Charlton, T. 530
Chartered College of Teaching (CCT) 118, 217, 219, 576
Chat GPT 501, 598
Child and Mental Health Service (CAMHS) 171
child development: age-in-cohort 58-59; communication and language 53-54; disrupted childhoods 60; family difficulties 59-60; foundational knowledge 49-54; holistic and situated 49-51; key theorists 54-57; physical 51-52; social and emotional 52; universal norms, critical appraisal 57-60

Index

Child Poverty Action Group (CPAG) 378
Child Protection Online Monitoring System (CPOMS) 548
Children and Families Act (2014) 364-365, 367, **543**
Children's Plan 437
Chin, C. 324
Chomsky, N. 53
Chowkase, A. 450
'Circle Time' 170
Claire, H. 395
Clark, A. 593
Clark, C. 249
Clarke-Allan, S. 592
Clark, L. 16-17
Clark, M. 59
class attention 155-156
classroom approaches 137-144, **145**, 146
classroom, entering 155
classroom layout 159
classroom behaviour management: (AD/HD) and 171-172; autism and 174; challenging pupils 159-160; classroom layout 159; difficult behaviours and 164-167, 173; first impressions 152-153; gendered behaviour and impacts 425-426; managing yourself 150-151; outdoor learning 201-202; rewards and sanctions **153-154**, 157, *158*, 159; rules and routines 154-157; strategies 151, **152**; teaching assistants' role 517-518, **518**; whole-school organisation 149
Classroom Management Plan (CMP) 149, 151-153
classroom organisation 118-119
classroom talk: dialogic teaching 180-181, **180**; exploratory **181**, 182-183, 186-187; group talk 180, 182; learning and talk 179-180, 184-186; listening 187-188; oracy skills 178, 183, 184-187; whole-class 179, 182-183
Claxton, G. 101, 452
Clemens, N.H. 357
Cline, T. 174, 366
coaching and CPD 580-581, *581*
Cochran-Smith, M. 380
Cockcroft, C. 517
codeswitching 412
cognitive academic language proficiency (CALP) 412
Cognitive Acceleration approach 136, 139-140
Cognitive Acceleration in Mathematics Education (CAME) 465
Cognitive Acceleration through Science Education (CASE) 465
cognitive challenge 462, 463
cognitive conflict 139-140
cognitive load theory 354
cognitive psychology 244
cognitivism 85

collaborative learning 463
Collis, S. 599
Comber, B. 595
Commission on Religious Education (CORE) 311
communication and language development 53-54, 197
communities of practice (CoP) 91
community links and networks 6, 237, 394, 400
computer science 506
computing curriculum 502, 506-507
concept map 468
concept/skill builder 99-100, 101
conceptual space 451
concrete preparation 139
constructivism 85, 86, 136, 139-140, 277
Conteh, J. 408
context of learning 89-92
continuing professional development (CPD): AFL principle 320-321; appraisal links 577; appraisal preparations 582-583; CCF expectations 21-22; coaching 580-581, *581*; courses and activities 576; enquiry, practice benefits 579-580; learning opportunities 574-575, *575*; mentors, working with 565-566, 574, 580-582, *581*; in Northern Ireland 577, 589, 600; parental engagement 528; personal accounts 6-9; professionalism implications 572-573, *573*; reflective practice 577-578; school provision, evaluation of 574, **574**; schools' responsibilities 576-577; in Scotland 571, 577, 579, 589, 591; in-service activities 575-576; Teachers' Standards 571; in Wales 577, 579
contrastive analysis 407
Cooper, A.J. 88
Cooper, K. 530
Cooper, V. 59-60
Coordinated Support Plan (CSP) (Scotland) 365
Copping, A. 101
Corsaro, W. 529
Cotson, W. 565
Council of Europe 501
Courtney, M. 231-232
Covid-19 pandemic, impacts: digital play research 503; learning development delays 18, 54, 436; online learning 137; physical development problems 51; school readiness 67; teaching assistant's duties 516; virtual parents' evenings 533; writing opportunities 249
Cox, B. 235
Crăciun, I.C. 545
Craik, F.I. 355
creative and inclusive learning communities 91-92
Creative Partnerships 446
'creative schools' 446
creative teaching 449-450

creativity and creative teaching: creative curricula 454-455; creative practice 446; definitions, forms and activities 446-447; environments of possibility 452-453; in Northern Ireland 449; pedagogical stance 450-452; planning 453-454; professional responsibilities 445; professional standards **15**; teacher's qualities 450; in Wales 448
creativity and knowledge 101-102
Cremin, T.: children's 'literacy lives' research 591; personal inspirations/development 4, 6-7, 8; reading aloud 231-232; sustainable and climate change education 492; writing, children's autonomy 249
'critical-evaluative' mode 447
critical stance 590
critical thinking 303, 309-310, 324
cross-linguistic transfer 407
Csikszentmihalyi, M. 447
cultural capital 529
cultural diversity: integration debate 391; school staff and pupils 390; in Scotland 393; in Wales 391-392; see also diversity; diversity education
culturalism 86
Cultural Learning Alliance (CLA) 286
Cunningham, L. 169
curriculum: diversity, celebration of 118, 398; enacted 216; international initiatives 218-219; in Ireland 213; irresistible 117-118; in Scotland 211, 212; teacher development 219; in Wales 212-213, 219. see also National Curriculum
curriculum deliverer 99
curriculum knowledge **23**, **255**
'curriculum overload' 210, 213
curriculum vitae (CV) 558, *559*
cyber-bullying 545

Dahl, R. 247
dance and drama strategies 292-293
Daniels, S. 59
datafication and children's rights 502
David, K. 530
DBS checks 534
Deci, E.L. 52
decisional capital 17
deficit thinking 521
deliberative approach (learning) 32-33, **33**, 39-40
deliberative judgements 41-42
Demkowicz, O. 79
Desforges, C. 529
destitution 378
developmental norms, critical appraisal 57-60
Devine, D. 102
Dewey, J. 85, 135, 288, 577
'dialogic' capacity 463

dialogic enquiry 142
dialogic pedagogy 113
dialogic teaching 180-181, **180**, 183, 467
differentiation 351
digital age, education in: artificial intelligence (AI) 501, 598; computing curriculum 506-507; datafication and children's rights 502; digital literacy, variations 500; digital texts and media literacy 502-503; e-safety, practices and guidance 504-505, 545; issues and responsibilities debate 499-500; in Northern Ireland 505, 506; research sources and collaborations 597-598; screen use 501-502; social media 504; in Wales 507
digital environment: CPD opportunities 576; enhanced interaction 139, 142; online learning 136, 137, 144; precautionary information 144
digital natives/immigrants 500
digital texts 502-503
direct interactive teaching 136, 138-139
'disadvantaged' children 350
disciplinary/procedural knowledge 306
discovery learning 85
discretionary judgements 17
dispositions, professional learning 32-33, **33**
disrupted childhoods 60
diversity: case studies 393-395, *394*; entitlement, obstacles to 396-397; ethnic populations, UK trends 389-391, *390*, 393; inclusion and 398, *399*
diversity awareness, value of 311, 397
diversity education: curriculum flexibility 398; dealing with controversial issues 401; entitlement 391, 395-396; school confidence in addressing 399-400; teacher attitudes 402
Doak, L. 595
Dodge, R. 475-476, *522*
Doing Data Differently project 592
Doyle, J. 237
dual-language picture books 414-415
Dumais, S.A. 288-289
Durmaz, D. 70
D'warte, J. 595
Dweck, C. 39, 88, 295

Early Career Framework (ECF) 97, 528, 563-564, 581
early career teacher (ECT): mentorship and ECF 563-564, *564*; mentors, working with 564-566; other UK nations' schemes 556, 564; professional identity consolidation 566-567; professional networks 567
Early Learning Goals 77
early professional development (EPD), Northern Ireland 564
early years: assessments and profile 77, *78*; foundations for 66-80; learning environment

70-74; in Northern Ireland 68, 74; policy 67-68; Reception Baseline Assessment (RBA) 77; role of adult in play 74-76, 76; school readiness 66, 67, 69-70; in Scotland 68; Teachers' Standards 67; transition, Foundation to KS1 78-79; in Wales 67, 75
Early Years Foundation Stage (EYFS): creativity, value of 445; Foundation Stage Profile 77, 78; history coverage 307; outdoor learning 191; principles and provision 51, 68-69; theoretical influence 56
Early Years Scotland 68
Eaude, T. 303
Education Act (1981) 363, 364
Education Act (1996) 364, 421
Education Act (2002) 437, 516
Education Act (2011) 527
Education (Additional Support for Learning) (Scotland) Act (2004), amended (2009), (2016) 365, 372-373
Education and Mental Health Practitioners (EMHPs) 479-481
Education Endowment Foundation (EEF): learning style, critique 88; research evidence for education 594; Teaching and Learning Toolkit 54; teaching assistants' role 517, 518
Education, Health and Care Plan (EHCP) 362, 368-369, 369
Education (Independent School Standards) Regulations (2014) 214
Education Inspection Framework (Ofsted) 305, 437, 445
Education Reform Act (1988) 212, 311, 408, 527
Education (Schools) Act (1992) 527
Education Scotland 577
Education (Scotland) Act (1980) 211
Edwards, A. 531
Edwards, V. 414
effective learning 320
Effective Provision of Pre-school Education (EPPE) 76
effective teaching: AFL principles 320-322; classroom management 155-157; concept/skill builder 99-100, 101; key aims and features 97-98, 102-103; knowledge combining 102; organisation of knowledge 98-99; pastoral role 540, 541; personal behaviour management 150-151; and planning 123-131, 125, 129, 132
efficiency, knowledge use 103
Elton-Chalcraft, S. 101
Elton Report (1989) 530
Emmer, E. 151
emotional development 52
'emotional intelligence' 461, 463
emotional issues in childhood 168
emotional labour 91-92
Emotional Literacy Support Assistant programme 522

empathy 115
Empathy Lab 237
enacted curriculum 216
Engel, G. 475
English as an additional language (EAL) 350, 400, 406
enquiry, practice benefits 579-580
environments of possibility, creativity and 452-453
equipment distribution, in class 156
equity 377
Erricker, C. 310
Estyn 577
Ethnic Minority Achievement Grant (1999) 408
European Film Literacy Advisory Group (FLAG) 503
Evans, J. 75, 78
Evered, R. 169
Every Child Matters 437, 516
expectations, high **23**
expert colleagues 21, 38-39; see also mentors, working with
exploratory talk **181**, 182-183, 186-187

Fahie, D. 102
family difficulties and development 59-60
feedback: Assessment for Learning (AfL) 330; disposition towards 33; expert colleagues 39-40; learner specific 120; professional conversations 41-42, 43
Feiler, A. 531
Feuerstein, R. 463
film-making 502-503
'finding a way through' 113, 116-117
Fingerson, L. 529
Fletcher-Wood, H. 102
'flexible purposing' 288
flipped classrooms 139
Flores, M.A. 560
Florian, L. 439
Flower, L. 244
Forest School Association 201
Forest School philosophy 195, *196*, 197
formative assessment 335; see also Assessment for Learning (AfL)
Foster, C. 258
Foundation Stage Profile 77, 78
frame of reference 32-33, **33**
Frederickson, N. 174, 366
Fredrickson, B.L. 91
Freeman, D. 89
Free School Meals (FSM) 378, 393
free schools, curriculum diversification 214, 215
Froebel, F. 85, 197
Fullan, M. 17, 436
futures literacy 494

Gager, A. 565
Galton, M. 454
Gascoigne Primary School, Barking 394, *394*
gender equity: childhood identity, supportive exploration 422-423, *424*; collective critical reflection 425, 429; heteronormativity issues 423-424; parents/carers' involvement 428; RSE, teaching approaches 427-428; in-between spaces and heteronormativity 426; stereotyping and classroom dynamics 425-426; teaching of, conflicting arguments 421-422, 427
General Teaching Council for Northern Ireland (GTCNI) **15**
generosity 115
GeoGebra 140
Geographical Association 308, 599
geography, teaching of 308-310, **309**
Ghaye, T. 534
Giangreco, M.F. 517
Gifford, S. 262
Gilead, T. 304
Gillborn, D. 382
Graham, S. 244, 248
grammar, writing and 246, 247
Greenberg, J. 57
Greene, M. 286
Greenfield, B. 483
Greenhalgh, P. 167, 168
Griffiths, R. 262
group talk 180, 182
group work 141-142
growth mindset 88
Gundarina, O. 416-417
Gypsy Roma Traveller (GRT) communities 382

Hacking, C. 228
Hadow Report (1931) 527
Hagger, H. 32-33, **33**
Hall, K. 591
Hall, S. 391, 516, 522
Hampden-Thompson, G. 288-289
Harding, J. 74
Hargreaves, A. 17, 91
Hargreaves, D.H. 571, 579
Harlen, W. 271
Harris, B. 231-232
Harris, D. 324
Harrison, A. 5, 7
Hart, B. 529
Hattie, J. 35
Hayes, J. 244
Headteacher, The 395
health, outdoor learning 194
Hedegaard, M. 57, 85

Helen Hamlyn Centre for Pedagogy 217, 219
Helix model 228, *229*
Hendry, H. 4-5, 7, 8-9
heteronormativity issues: classroom dynamics and stereotyping 425-426; lack of recognition 423-424; in-between space activities 426
heterosexual matrix 423-424
Hicks, D. 494
Higgins, A. 521
Higgins, S. 178
higher-order thinking 324-326, 327
Hills, R. 522
Hirst, P. 210
Historical Association 307
history, teaching and planning 306-308
Hodgen, J. 59
Holt, A. 520, 521
home language, promotion of 416-417
Hoodless, P. 300
hooks, b 91-92
Horvath, J. 98, 102-103
Hoult, E. 521
Hughes, D. 169
human capital 17
humanism 85-86
humanities: curriculum status and relevance 303-305; geography 308-310, **309**; history 306-308; learning contributions 300-301, *302*; metacognitive strategies 303; in Northern Ireland 304; Ofsted 304-305; planning sequence 312, *312*; religious education 310-312; in Scotland 301; subject coverage 300; in Wales 302
Hunt, E. 350
Huuki, T. 426

Icknield Primary School, Luton 492-493
ICT (information and communication technology) 502, 530
identity: dissonance experiences 18-19; personal 16, 394-395; professional 13, 16-19, *16*, 566-567
'imaginative-generative' mode 447
inclusion 362-373, 398
inclusive communities, building: affective domain 114-115; intellectual domain 112-114; *Learning without Limits*, principles 111-121; social domain 115-120
inclusivity 116
Independent Commission on Assessment in Primary Education (ICAPE) 217
individual development plans (IDPs) 373
inequality, countering 377, 380-381, 384
Initial Teacher Education (ITE) 20
insight, knowledge use 103
instruction, authentic 130
Instrumental Enrichment 463

'intellectual autonomy' 141
intellectual domain 112-114
interaction and learning 89-92
intersectionality 88, 399
'interthinking' 185
interviews, job 560-563
inventiveness 113-114
Ireland, national curricula 213
ITT Core Content Framework (CCF): adaptive teaching 351; evidence for education policy 594; expert colleagues 38, 39; key policy features 20, 349; 'learn that' and 'learn how' statements 20-21, 23; parental relationships 528; pedagogical principles 21, 408; professional behaviours 21-22; professional standards **15**

Jay, G. 303
Jerrim, J. 556
John Muir Award 492-493
Jones, L.S. 155
Jones, V.F. 155
Jordanova, L. 306
'judgementoring' 581

Kaufmann, E. 391
Keeping Children Safe in Education **544**, 545
Kellock, A. 593
Kellogg, R.T. 243
Kelly, J. 13
Kern, L. 357
Kersner, M. 53
Kim, L.E. 565
Knight, J. 414
knowledge: combining 102; and creativity 101-102; effective use 102-103; history, conceptual aspects 306; lesson planning skills 127-128; online sources and verification 303; organisation of 98-99; for the teacher 97-98, 255; theoretical approaches 86
'knowledge-based' curriculum 210-211
Kohli, R. 384
Kuiper, E. 101

Laluvein, J. 371
Lamb inquiry (2009) 362, 371
Lamb, J. 565
Language Acquisition Device (LAD) 53
Language Acquisition Support System (LASS) 53
language comprehension 228
language mats 415-416
language *see* classroom talk; linguistic diversity; reading, rich curriculum; writing
Lant, F. 249
Lave, J. 91, 137

league tables 343, 344
learner-oriented ethos 450-451
'learn how' statements 20-21, 23, 127
learning: accelerated 465; apprenticeship models 137, 143-144; constructivism 136, 139-140; and context 89-92; creative and inclusive communities 91-92; as an interactive process 89-90; levels of approach 86; organising 135-137; pedagogical approaches 89-91; social constructivism 136-137, 140, 140-142; talk and 179-180, 184-186; theorists and theories 84-88, *87*, 136-137
learning conversations 39-40
learning environment: creative opportunities 452-453; digital 136, 137, 139; early years 70-74; as enabler 117-118; linguistic diversity 416-417; in Scotland 72; Teachers' Standards **23**; in Wales 72; writing/reading space 249
'Learning Journeys' 77, *78*
learning objectives 130
learning style, critique 88
Learning without Limits, principles of 111-121
'learn that' statements 20-21, 23, 127
Lechner, V. 545
Le Cornu, A. 500
Leenders, H. 528
Leggett, E.L. 88
'lesson chat' 131, *132*
lesson evaluations: children's learning 35, **36**; future practice 37-38, **38**; placement focus 35; successes 35, **36**; your teaching 36, **37**; *see also* feedback
lesson plans 128, *129*, 130, 186-187, 320, 322-324
Let's Think programme 136
Levy, R. 237
Lewis, G. 516
Lewis, K. 529, 530
lexical sets 415-416
Lindorff, A. 350
linguistic diversity: bilingual learners, definition 406; case studies 410, 413; celebration and capitalisation 414-417; children's backgrounds, knowledge of 409-410; historical background 407-409; inclusive practice, bilingual approaches 413-417; in Northern Ireland 408, 413-414; positive contributions 406; in Scotland 408; second language learning 411-413; in Wales 408
linguistics 245, 246-247
Lipman, M. 461, 463, 465-466
listening 187-188
Listening to and Involving Children and Young People 437
Listening to Stephen Read 591
Literacy Hour 408
Liu, Y. 412, 414

Locke, J. 85
Lockhart, R.S. 355
Lodge, C. 39
looked-after children 541-542
López, I. F. H. 382
Lowndes, J. 310
Lucas, B. 447

Malik, K. 304
Mannion, G. 436
Mann, J. 194
Mantle of the Expert 381
Marsden, E. 417
Martin, J. 245
Maslow, A. 85
mathematical talk 260-262
mathematics, teaching of: belief influences 254-255; curriculum content, UK 256-257, **257**; fluency and conceptual understanding 257-260, *258-259*, **260**, *261*; knowledge types 255, **255**, *256*; mastery approach 267; mathematical reasoning 260-262, *263*, *264*, *265*; problem solving 264-267, **266**; social learning 140
Mazzei, L. 382
McGillicuddy, D. 102
McInnes, K. 76
McIntyre, D. 438
McLaughlin, H.J. 151
media literacy 502-503
Medwell, J. 102
memory, long-term 355
memory, working 244, 354
mental health: biopsychosocial model of health 475, *475*; children, identification and interventions 480, *481*, 548; curriculum coverage 480; definition 473; early career factors 482-483; Education and Mental Health Practitioners (EMHPs) 479-481; parental partnerships 480; peer mentoring 480-481; risk and protective factors 474-479; teacher related issues 481-482; teacher resilience 483-484, *483*; trainees, challenges and resources 475-477, *476*; trainees, support strategies 477; transitions, life and emotional 477-478; in Wales 479; whole-school approach 478-479, *479*; see *also* well-being
mentors, working with: continuing professional development (CPD) 580-582, *581*; dispositions towards learning 32-33, 43; early career teacher 563-566, *564*; expert colleagues 38-39; first teaching role, applying for 556
Merdon Junior School, Hampshire 491
Merrick, R. 439
metacognition 140, 194, 303, 463-464

metalinguistics 246-247
methods of enquiry, history 306
Miller, W.R. 530
'mindfulness' 170
mind mapping 468
Minecraft 507
models, science 278-282, *279-280*
Moll, L. 57, 591
Monaghan, F. 414
Montessori, M. 85
Moss, P. 593
motivation: assessment methods 321; outdoor learning 195; reading 228-229
motor development 51
movement play 52
multi-academy trusts (MATs) 25, 214, 215
multimodal teaching approaches 451
multiplication facts 257-259, *258*
Multiplication Tables Check 257, 343, **344**
Munby, H. 102
Murchan, D. 335
Myatt, M. 118-119, 235
Myers, V. 398
Mygind, E. 195
Myhill, T. 249

name-calling 400-401
NASUWT 577
National Advisory Committee on Creative and Cultural Education 248
National Child Measurement Programme 51
National College for Teaching and Learning (NCTL) 576
National Council for Curriculum and Assessment (NCCA) 213
National Curriculum: arts curricula 289-290, *291*; bilingual learners and 408; classroom talk 179-180; 'curriculum overload,' England 212, *213*; digital safety 504; establishment debates 210; geography 308; humanities, status of 303-305; implementation of 216; inclusion and 363; inspection and testing 216-217; international comparisons 209, *211*; locally planned curricula 217-218; multi-academy trusts, innovation concerns 214; outdoor learning 191; pastoral elements 540, 542; primary mathematics 256-257, **257**; primary science 270, 271-272; reading for pleasure (RfP) 230; spoken language 53; statutory requirements, current 214-216; summative assessments 343; sustainability and climate change education 491-492; teaching for thinking 466-467; UK and Ireland diversifications 209, 211-213; writing 249

Index

National Education Union (NEU) 379, 380, 384, 559, 577
National Literacy Strategy 408
National Literacy Trust (NLT) 225
National Professional Qualification (NPQ) for Headship 395
Nature Deficit Disorder 194
Neale, D. 73
Nelson, R. 576
Nemorin, S. 501
neuroscience 88, 101
Newham, London borough of 393
newly qualified teachers (NQTs), Wales 556
Newmann, F.M. 130
Newton, J. 590
Nias, J. 92
noise, class attention 155
Northern Ireland: adaptive teaching 352; arts curricula 291; creativity in 449; cultural diversity 397; early professional development (EPD) 564; early years in 68, 74, 75; humanities in 304; ICT and digital literacy 505, 506; linguistic diversity in 408, 413-414; mathematics in **257**; national curricula 212, 272; outdoor learning 191-192, 197, 201; professional learning 577, 589, 600; professional standards **15**; reading in 227; safeguarding 543; special educational needs (SEN) in 367, 373; sustainability and climate change education 490, 492; writing in 248
Northern Ireland Teacher Competences 577
North, M. 258-259
'Nurture groups' 170-171
Nurturing Creativity in Young People 446

O'Connor, G. 593
O'Connor, K. 92
Ofsted: accountability 24, 528; Covid-19 impacts 54; and CPD 577; cultural capital 529; curriculum and 217; diversity and 391, 395; Education Inspection Framework (EIF) 2019 305; history teaching 306; humanities allocations 304-305; learning and memory 355; mental health training 384; outdoor learning 191; positive teacher/pupil relationships 437; pupil premium reviews 379; science subject report 272; special educational needs or disability (SEND) 366, 529
O'Hara, M. 529
Oliver, L. 249
Olson, M. 530
open-ended play 75-76
open-ended questions 324
openness 112-113
oracy skills: direct teaching 183; 'interthinking' 185; learning intentions 184-187; listening 187-188

Organisation for Economic Co-operation and Development (OECD): curriculum content, UK 212, 213; Future of Education and Skills 2030 Project 218-219; professional development survey 575
Osborne, J. 324
O'Sullivan, K. 5
outdoor environment 72, 74
outdoor learning 191-204, 309
ownership of learning 448, 451-452

PACE (Playful, Accepting, Curious and Empathetic) 169
Papadopoulou, M. 52
parents/carers: communicating with 528-529, 530, 532-533; difficult situations, dealing with 531-533; expertise contributions 534; free schools meals, take-up issues 378, 379; gender equity issues 423, 428; inclusive collaboration 117, 395, 410; key stakeholders 527; mental health support 480; parents' evenings 533-534; pupil absence 529, 532, 545; reading and 231, 237; relationship development 17; secure relationships, benefits of 528-530; special educational needs (SEN) 371; teacher approachability 530-531
parents' evenings 533-534
Parent Teacher Associations (PTAs) 529, 530
Parry, J. 58
pastoral role, teacher's: attendance 545; classroom strategies 548; effective practice 540, 541; e-safety 545; family difficulties scenario, support approaches 546-547; looked-after children 541-542; in Northern Ireland 543; policy developments, UK 542; refugee child scenario, support approaches 547-548; safeguarding 543-545, **543-544**; transition support 541; in Wales 542, 544-545; whole-school strategies 548, **549**
Paul Hamlyn Foundation 291
pedagogical approaches: context of learning 89-91; lesson planning 130-131
pedagogical content knowledge **255**, 277
peer assessment 329
peer mentoring 480-481, 541
Percival, J. 565
Perkel, J. 545
Perry, Ruth 384
persistence 114
personal, social and health education (PSHE) 215, 480
Philosophy for Children 381, 461, 465-466
phonics 232-234
Phonics Screening Check 18, 58-59, 342, 343, **344**
physical development 51-52
Piaget, J. 54-55, 85, 136, 462, 465
Picton, I. 249
Pigeon, K. 171

Pilkington, R. 13
Pizmony-Levy, O. 336
placements: challenging feedback 41-42; dispositions towards learning 32-33, **33**, 42, 44; expert colleagues, working with 38-39; learning conversations 39-40, 41-42; lesson evaluations 35-38, **36-38**; 'practice shock' 32, 44; progression insights 42-43; reflective teaching 33-34, *34*; subject specialist support 40-41
planning: Assessment for Learning (AfL) 320, 322-324; building experience 130; collaborative support 131; for creativity 453-454; curriculum development 219; foundations of 124-127, *125*; history 307-308; humanities 312, *312*; importance 123, 132-133; knowledge, skills and understanding aspects 127-128; 'lesson chat' 131, *132*; long-term 216; medium-term 216; outdoor learning 198-199, *199*; pedagogical decisions 130-131; plan components and structure 128, *129*, 130; Teachers' Standards **23**; see also classroom behaviour management; lesson plans
play-based learning 70-76, *76*, 197
'Play Observatory' project 503
play therapy 171
Plowden Report (1967) 55, 527
Plumley, J. 303
Pluquailec, J. 593
Poet, H. 13
Porras, C. 91, 92
portfolios 339
positive behaviour: pedagogical approaches 169; reinforcement strategies 166-167; supportive conditions/actions 165-166
'post truth era' 303
poverty: definitions and causes 378; pedagogical, counter measures 380-381; school achievement, impacts on 378-380, 393
'practice shock' 32
practitioner enquiry 589-590
Prensky, M. 500
Prevent Duty, The **544**
Prevent strategy 394
Primary AGENDA 427, 429
Primary National Strategy 408
proactive approach (learning) 32-33, **33**, 39
problem solving, mathematics 264-267, **266**
'process' curricula 211
processing, sense-making 356
professional associations 598-599
professional behaviours 21-22
professional capital 17
professionalism: behaviours, CCF expectations 21-22; definitions and concepts 12-13; identity development 16-20, *16*, *19*, 26, 566-567, 572-573; identity dissonance 18-19, 70; institutional policies/practices 25-26; key policy documents 20-24; networking 567; overcoming challenges 8-9; performativity and accountability 572; personal qualities 6-7, 9-10, 13; teacher's role, focus changes 96-97; Teachers' Standards **23**; teaching standards, UK 13
professional relationships 21-22
Professional Standards and Professional Learning, Scotland 571
Programme for International Student Assessment (PISA) 209, 211, 527, 529
Programme for International Student Assessments (PISA) 335-336
Progress in International Reading Literacy Study (PIRLS) 209, 211
publications, critical reading 595-597
Public Health England 478-479
pupil absence 529, 532
pupil engagement 436-442
pupil participation 436
pupil premium 379
pupil progress and outcomes, good **23**
pupil voice: diversity education 395; facilitation strategies 439-441; listening/consultation, pupil benefits 438-439; listening/consultation, teacher benefits 439; listening, legislative/regulatory measures 436-437; school council 400; school policy, key principles 441; term meaning 435-436
puppets 156

Qualifications and Curriculum Authority (QCA) 401
qualified teacher status (QTS) 20, 23, 528
Qualter, A. 271
questioning 113, 303, 324-328, **326**, 468
questioning stance 451

race and racism: bilingual learners, underrated 408; bullying/name-calling 401; conflation issues 381-382; education inequalities, statistics of 383, 393; social constructs 382-383; systematic change needed 384; teaching assistants' challenges 521
racial micro-aggressions 383-384
Radford, J. 518
randomised controlled trials (RCTs) 594
Ravalier, J.M. 521
reactive approach (learning) 32-33, **33**, 39
reading, rich curriculum: assessment 237-238; being a reader 227; comprehension skills 234-236; early skills 232-234; interest decline issues 225; internal/external collaborations 237; motivation and enjoyment 228-229; in Northern Ireland 227; phonics 232-234; reading aloud 231; reading for pleasure (RfP) 230; in Scotland 228;

skills and knowledge 228, *229*; skills practice and engagement 225-226; texts and reading environment 230-231; in Wales 230
reading rope 228
Reception Baseline Assessment (RBA) 77, 343, **344**
Reception class 69-70, 77
Redfern, E. 59
reflective practice 21, 33-34, 534, 564, 577-578, 595
reflective teaching 33-34
reflexivity 34, 577, 578
relationships and sex education (RSE) 215, 421, 424, 427-428, 480
religious education (RE) 215, 310-312
Renold, E. 426
research and professional development: critical stance 590; evidence for education policy 593-594; interpretation, theoretical influences 591; investigation aims and processes 589-590; involvement opportunities 597; literacy teaching, practice analysis 592; online-based collaborations 597-598; professional associations 598-599; publications, critical reading 595-597; qualitative methods, insight benefits 594-595; school/home, participatory partnerships 591, 593
Researching the Arts in Primary School 291
responsibility and independence, outdoor learning 195, *196*, 197
restraining aggressive pupils 160
Rethinking Curriculum project 217, 219
rewards and sanctions, behaviour management **153-154**, 157, *158*, 159
Richards, C. 9
Rights Respecting Schools Award (RRSA) 395
risk assessment, outdoor learning 201-202, *202-203*
risk-taking, creative 452
Risley, T. 529
Riviere, H. 169
Rix, J. 58
Roberts, H. 131
Robertson, C. 371
Robinson, K. 452-453
Rogers, B. 166, 530
Rogers, C. 85-86
Rogers, S. 70, 74, 75, 78
Rogoff, B. 56, 57
role-play 74-76
Rollnick, S. 530
Rose, J. 70, 74
Rosenshine, B. 130
Rousseau, J-J. 85
routines 155-157
rubrics 339-341
Rudd, P. 13

Rudduck, J. 438
Ruggeri, A. 303
rules and routines 154-155
Russell, A. 371
Ryan, R.M. 52

Sachs, J. 42
Sadler, E. 593
safeguarding **23**, 540, 543-545, **543-544**, 546-547
safety, digital technology 504-505, 545
Salamanca Statement 366
Sams, A. 139
Save the Children 53
scaffolding 56, 77, 85
Scarborough, H.S. 228
Schaffer, H.R. 76-77
Scheithauer, H. 545
Scholes, L. 595
Schön, D.A. 577
school attendance 545
SchoolCloud 533
school context, attitude to 33, **33**
school council 400, 441
school diversity, case study 394, *394*
school readiness 66, 67, 69-70, 529-530
Schweisfurth, M. 145
science, teaching of: children's lived experiences, linking topics 274-276; misconceptions, identification/correction 277-278; models and analogies 278-282, *279-282*; National Curriculum 270, 271-272; in Northern Ireland 272; outdoor and off-site visits 276; pedagogical approaches 276-282; scientific enquiry skills 272, **273**, 274; scientific vocabulary 278; in Scotland 277; in Wales 271
Scotland: adaptive teaching 352; additional support needs (ASN) 365, 367, 369, 372-373; cultural diversity response 393; digital literacy 500; early years in 68; health and well-being 474; humanities in 301; learning environment in 72; linguistic diversity in 408; mathematics in **257**; national curricula 211, 212; outdoor learning 192, 198; professional learning 571, 577, 579, 589, 591; professional standards **15**; reading in 228; science curriculum 277; sustainability and climate change education 492, 496; Teacher Induction Scheme (TIS) 556; writing in 248
Scratch 507
second language learning 411-413
Segovia-Lagos, P. 91, 92
self-assessment 329
self-directed learning 322, 327
self-efficacy 151, 572

self-esteem 57, 60
Selwyn, N. 530
Sexton, J. 593
Sharp, J. 271
Shayer, M. 136
Shiel, G. 335
Shorrocks-Taylor, D. 59
short-term pupils 400
Shulman, L. 102, 255, 277
sibling relationships 50
silence, class attention 155-156
Simple View of Reading (SVR) 228
Simpson, J. 416-417
Sims Bishop, R. 230
Sims, S. 102
Singapore, mathematics and 262
Siraj-Blatchford, I 76-77, 89
Skarbek, D. 13
skills acquisition 136, 138-139
Skinner, B.F. 85, 165
slow pedagogy 72, 195
Smith, H. 178
Smith, R.L. 13
social and emotional learning (SEL) 357
social capital 17
social constructivism 85, 86, 136-137, 140, 277
social development 52
social domain 115-120
social, emotional and mental health (SEMH) difficulties: Attention Deficit/Hyperactivity Disorder (AD/HD) 171-172; autism 174; behaviour, rationalising challenges 167-168; definition 167; individual targeted therapies 171; positive relationships, key principles 169; pupil number rises 350; school/class, supportive strategies 168-171; trauma induced 168
socialisation 16-17
social issues in childhood 168
social justice 377-385
social learning 136-137, 140-142
social media 303, 504
Solórzano, D.G. 384
Sowerby, M. 436
Special Educational Needs and Disability Act (Northern Ireland) (2016) 371-372
Special Educational Needs Co-ordinator (SENCO) 368, 369, 370
special educational needs or disability (SEND): arts practice 287; *Code of Practice* 167, 350, 366-367, 368, **543**; identification comparisons *365*; Ofsted expectations 529; openness 113; participatory research 593; pupil number rises 350; teaching assistants' role 516; UK policy development 362

special educational needs (SEN): collaborative support 117; inclusion and 362-373; inclusion debate 365-366; inclusive practice 116, 117; legal definition 364-365; in Northern Ireland 367, 371, 373; policy and support 368-369, *369*, 516; in Scotland 365, 367, 369, 373; teachers, advice for 371-372; Teachers' Standards 370; teaching assistants 370-371; UK policies, development of 363-364; in Wales 373
speech, language and communication needs (SLCN) 53
Spence-Thomas, K. 576
Spielman, A. 303, 305
Spina, N. 595
'spiral curriculum' 85, 98
spiritual, moral, social and cultural development 391, 395
split-screen thinking 101
Sproson, B. 166
stability 115
standard assessment tests (SATs) 217, 343, **344**, 383
Standing Advisory Councils for Religious Education (SACREs) 311-312
Steadman, S. 23
Steer Report (2005) 530
Steinert, Y. 16-17, *16*
stereotyping 379-380, 384, 425
Sternberg, R. 98, 102-103, 450
'Stories for Thinking' 466
Strand, S. 350
Strategy for Sustainability and Climate Change (DfE) 488, 492
Street, B. 91
Styles, M. 4
subject knowledge 6, **23**
subject matter knowledge **255**
subject specialists, structured conversations 40-41
substantive knowledge 306
summative assessment: classroom tests 338-339; performance based 339; purposes of 335-336; reporting results 343-344, **344**; rubrics 339-341; standardised tests 341-343; teacher assessment 338-341, 344-345; validity, reliability and fairness 336-337
Supporting the Attainment of Disadvantaged Pupils **543**
support staff 22, 515-523, **518**, **519**, *522*; see also teaching assistants (TAs)
surprise achievement 120
sustainability and climate change education: cross curricula activities 492; curriculum content, UK nations 491-492; interconnected elements ('bicycle model') 489; international programmes 495; in

Northern Ireland 490, 492; positive pedagogies and engaged well-being 493-494; proposals and challenges 492; school awards 492-493; in Scotland 492, 496; Sustainable Development Goals (SDGs) 490-491; in Wales 489-490, 491-492; young people's focus 488
sustainable development, UN definition 489
sustained shared thinking 76-77
Sutton Trust 463
Swann Report (1985) 407
Swanson, H.L. 88
Swift, D. *302*

talk partners 326
TAME approach 292
Targeted Mental Health in Schools (TaMHS) 170
task manager 99, 101
Taylor, C. 576
teacher assessment 338-341, 344-345
Teacher Capability model 577
teacher expertise 97-100
Teacher Induction Scheme (TIS), Scotland 556
teacher knowledge 97-98, 102-103, 127-128
teacher resilience 483, *483*
teacher self-efficacy 151
Teachers' Standards: adaptive teaching 351; aims and expectations **14**, **23**; arts curricula 290; classroom management 164; and CPD 571, 578; early years 67; feedback 39; outdoor learning 193; overview 370; parental relationships 528; pastoral role 542; positive pupil relationships 437; reflective practice 33; teacher's role 349; teaching for thinking 466
teacher stress 149-150, 167
teaching: beliefs and values 10, 566; context of learning 89-92; emotional practices 91-92; 'hidden side' 89; mental health issues 481-482; nature of 9; personal behaviour management 150-151; personal inspirations and development 4-5, 6-10; professional networks 567; purpose of 6; qualities required 6; reflective 33-34, *34*; special educational needs (SEN) 371-372; teacher's role, focus changes 96-97; time management 8-9; unconscious bias 397; well-being strategies 482
teaching, applying for first role: application form guidance 558; curriculum vitae (CV) 558, *559*; first interview 560-563; key decisions 556-557; school visits 559-560, **560**
teaching assistants (TAs): collaborative activities 517-518, **518**; difficult behaviours, teacher support 520-521; effective communication 519-520; lesson planning 21, 131; positive contributions 515; reading curriculum 237; relationship developments 17; retention and enhancement 522-523, *522*; roles and responsibilities, changing 516-517; special educational needs (SEN) 370-371; teachers, professional relationship 119, 515, 517, 519-520, **519**; well-being, concerns and benefits 521-522, *522*
teaching methods, theoretical approaches 85-88
Tennent, W. 235
Terwel, J. 101
testing: standardised tests 341-343; statutory 216; summative assessment 338-339; see also assessment; standard assessment tests (SATs)
thinking skills: Bloom's taxonomy 461-462, **462**; competency benefits 462-463; curriculum integration 466-467; metacognition 463-464; questioning *328*; research insights 463; teaching approaches 465-466; teaching principles 463-464; teaching strategies 467-469; term, interpretated meanings 460-461
thinking time/wait time 325-326, 467
time management 8-9
Tochon, F. 102
Too Little, Too Late report (2020) 371
Tower Hamlets Oracy project 218
Transforming Children and Young People's Mental Health Provision 478
transient populations 400
transitional bilingualism 408
transitions: classroom movements 156; daily/periodic concerns 541; Foundation to KS1 78-79
translanguaging 412-413
trauma 60, 168
Trends in International Mathematics and Science Study (TIMSS) 209, 211
Trowsdale Art-Making Model for Education 292
Trussell Trust 378-379
Turner, J. 274
Tutt, R. 366
Twiselton, S. 99
Tyler, R. 210

unconscious bias 397
understanding lesson, check for 156
union membership 567
United Kingdom Literacy Association (UKLA) 598-599
United Nations (UN): Convention on the Rights of Persons with Disabilities 366; Convention on the Rights of the Child 366, 436, 437, 502; Sustainable Development Goals (SDGs) 490-491, 575
Universities' Council for the Education of Teachers (UCET) 20
University of Central Lancashire 495

VAK learning styles 465
values-practice gaps 578

Varley, N. 598-599
vegetable garden, case study 200-201
Verloop, N. 572, 573
Vermunt, J. 572, 573
virtual learning environments (VLEs) 530
vocabulary, scientific 278
Volman, M. 101
Vygotsky, L.: child development 55, 57; home language 416; interactive learning 195, 245; social learning 77, 136-137; thinking skills 462; zone of proximal development 55, 85

Wales: adaptive teaching 351; additional learning needs (ALN) 363-364, 373; arts curricula 290; creative contributors 448; cultural diversity response 391-392; early years in 67, 75; health and well-being 473-474, 479, 542; humanities in 302; ICT and digital literacy 507; learning environment in 72-73; linguistic diversity in 408; mathematics in **257**; national curricula 212-213, 219; newly qualified teachers (NQTs) 556; outdoor learning 192, 197-198, 200; pastoral role in 544-545; professional learning 577, 579; professional standards **15**; reading in 230; RSE, teaching approaches 427; safeguarding 545; sustainability and climate change education 489-490, 491-492; writing in 250
Waller, M. 504
Wall, K. 439-440
Walsh, J. 521
Warin, J. 531
Warnock, M. 363, 364, 366
Warnock Report (1978) 363
Webster, R. 119, 370-371, 516, 518, 522
Wehlage, G.G. 130
Wei, L. 412, 413
Weinstein, C. 151
well-being: categories 473; early career teachers 565, 566; in Scotland 474; strategies for teachers 482; teaching assistants (TAs) 521-523, *522*; trainees, support strategies 477; in Wales 473-474; wellbeing see-saw 475-476, *476*; *see also* mental health

well-being, children's: outdoor learning 194; physical health 51; transition challenges 477-478
Wenger, E. 91, 137
White, D. 500
Whitehead, D. 70
White, S. 590
whole-class talk 179, 182-183
Wigford, A. 521
William, D. 319
Williams, J. 324
Willy, T. 308
Wilson, E. 32, 42, 521
Winstanley, C. 516, 522
Wong, B. 276
word recognition 228
Working Together: Giving Children and Young People a Say 437
Working Together: Listening to the Voices of Children and Young People 437
Working Together to Safeguard Children 540, **544**
World Health Organisation (WHO) 473
Woyke, P.P. 73
Wren, A. 522
writing: autonomy and choice opportunities 249; cognitive theories 244; communication and technology 243; community of writers 247-248; complexity 243; creativity in 248; linguistic perspective 245; metalinguistic understanding 246-247; in Northern Ireland 248; in Scotland 248; socio-cultural perspectives 244-245; space and time for 249; in Wales 250
Wyse, D. 33, 34, *34*, 211, 213, 228

Xavier, A. *399*

Yates, C. 136
Young, M. 210

Zhang, L. 102
zone of proximal development (ZPD) 55, 57, 85

For Product Safety Concerns and Information,
please contact our EU representative GPSR@taylorandfrancis.com
Taylor & Francis Verlag GmbH, Kaufingerstraße 24,
80331 München, Germany

Printed by Integrated Books International,
United States of America